# Evangelical Calvinism

# Evangelical Calvinism

*Essays Resourcing the Continuing*
*Reformation of the Church*

*edited by*

MYK HABETS
*and* BOBBY GROW

PICKWICK *Publications* · Eugene, Oregon

EVANGELICAL CALVINISM
Essays Resourcing the Continuing Reformation of the Church

Copyright © 2012 Wipf and Stock Publishers. All rights reserved. Except for brief quotations in critical publications or reviews, no part of this book may be reproduced in any manner without prior written permission from the publisher. Write: Permissions, Wipf and Stock Publishers, 199 W. 8th Ave., Suite 3, Eugene, OR 97401.

Pickwick Publications
An Imprint of Wipf and Stock Publishers
199 W. 8th Ave., Suite 3
Eugene, OR 97401

www.wipfandstock.com

ISBN 13: 978-1-60899-857-9

*Cataloging-in-Publication data:*

Evangelical Calvinism : essays resourcing the continuing reformation of the church / edited by Myk Habets and Bobby Grow ; foreword by Alasdair Heron.

xxii + 494 p. ; 23 cm. — Includes bibliographical references and indexes.

ISBN 13: 978-1-60899-857-9

1. Evangelicalism. 2. Calvinisim. I. Title.

BR1640 E85 2012

Manufactured in the U.S.A.

The Prologue originally appeared in *Union in Christ: A Declaration for the Church. A Commentary with Questions for Study and Reflection*, xiii–xvii. Edited by Andrew Purves and Mark Achtemeier. Louisville: Witherspoon Press, 1999. © Witherspoon Press. Used by permission.

An earlier version of chapter 7 appeared as Myk Habets, "The Doctrine of Election in Evangelical Calvinism: T. F. Torrance as a Case Study," *Irish Theological Quarterly* 73.3–4 (2008) 334–54, © Sage Publications. Used by permission.

To my students at Carey Baptist College, Laidlaw-Carey Graduate School, Pathways College of Bible and Mission, and the South Asia Institute for Advanced Christian Studies, who have often asked for me to define and defend my Reformed faith to them and to which I have longed to place a volume such as this in their hands in response. Here it is! May the triune God of Grace bless you all.

Myk Habets

# Contents

# Contributors

**Dr. Julie Canlis**
Julie won the Templeton Award for Theological Promise in 2007 for her work on John Calvin, subsequently published as *Calvin's Ladder* (2010), which won a 2011 *Christianity Today* award of merit. Julie teaches Sunday School at Methlick Parish Church, Church of Scotland, where her husband is minister. She has four children.

**Rev. Dr. Jason Goroncy**
Lecturer and Dean of Studies at the Knox Centre for Ministry and Leadership in Dunedin, New Zealand. Jason teaches in the areas of theology, church history, and pastoral care. His book on the (mostly) unpublished sermons of P. T. Forsyth is forthcoming from Wipf and Stock.

**Bobby Grow**
Has an MA in Biblical Studies and Theology from Multnomah Biblical Seminary, Portland, Oregon. He has been accepted to a PhD program in Systematic Theology at South African Theological Seminary. He is a Theologian-at-large, runs several theological blogs, and lives with his wife and two kids in Vancouver, Washington.

**Rev. Dr. Myk Habets**
Head of Carey Graduate School and Lecturer in Systematic Theology, Carey Baptist College, Auckland, New Zealand. Myk is registered as a Minister of the Baptist Churches of New Zealand, is married and has two children. His publications include: *Theosis in the Theology of Thomas Torrance* (Ashgate, 2009), *The Anointed Son* (Pickwick, 2010), and has edited numerous works including *Trinitarian Theology After Barth*, with Phillip Tolliday (Pickwick, 2011).

### REV. DR. ALASDAIR HERON

Alasdair Heron is an ordained minister of the Church of Scotland and the Reformed Church in Bavaria. He previously taught in the Irish School of Ecumenics, Dublin and New College, Edinburgh. From 1981 to his retirement in 2007 he was Professor of Reformed Theology, University of Erlangen, Germany, and still lives in Erlangen. He and his wife have two daughters and four grandchildren. He is the author of *A Century of Protestant Theology, Table and Tradition* and *The Holy Spirit* as well as many articles and reviews in English, German, and French. He also served for over twenty years as editor of the *Scottish Journal of Theology* and has been visiting professor in several U. S. Presbyterian seminaries.

### DR. MARCUS JOHNSON

Assistant Professor of Theology at Moody Bible Institute, Chicago, Illinois. Marcus earned his PhD in Systematic Theology from the University of St. Michaels College (University of Toronto), and is the author of *Christ in You: The Hope of Glory: A Theology of Union with Christ* (forthcoming). Marcus is married and attends Holy Trinity Church in downtown Chicago.

### SCOTT KIRKLAND

A PhD candidate in Systematic Theology at the University of Newcastle, Australia. His research focuses on the intersection of Barth's theology of the cross and a political theology of judgment with reference to the Russian novelist Dostoyevsky and Kierkegaard. Scott is married and has been involved with Anglican, Presbyterian, and Baptist congregations.

### PROFESSOR JOHN McDOWELL

Since 2009 John has been the Professor of the Morpeth Chair of Theology and Religious Studies at the University of Newcastle, Australia, having moved from his post as the Meldrum Senior Lecturer in Systematic Theology at the University of Edinburgh. John has been involved in congregations in the Presbyterian Church in Ireland, the Church of Scotland, the Scottish Baptists, and the Church of England. He is married with five children. Among his publications are *Hope in Barth's Eschatology* (2000), *The Gospel According to Star Wars: Faith, Hope and the Force* (2007), and the co-edited *Conversing With Barth* (2004).

**Dr Gannon Murphy**

General Editor of *American Theological Inquiry* (www.atijournal.org), a biannual journal of theology, culture, and history. Gannon is married with three children, and is a member of Calvary Christian Reformed Church in Edina, Minnesota. His publications include: *Reasons for the Christian Hope* (2009), *Consuming Glory: A Classical Defense of Divine-Human Relationality Against Open Theism* (Wipf & Stock, 2006), *Voices of Reason in Christian History: The Great Apologists* (2005.), and numerous journal articles.

**Adam Nigh**

Adam has an MA in Theology from Fuller Theological Seminary, Northern California, and is currently a PhD candidate in Systematic Theology at the University of Aberdeen, writing a dissertation on the doctrine of Scripture and hermeneutics in T. F. Torrance under the supervision of John Webster. Adam is married with two children and is on the pastoral staff at Twin Lakes Church in Aptos, California.

**Rev. Dr. Charles Partee**

(Retired) P. C. Rossin Professor of Church History, Pittsburgh Theological Seminary, Pittsburgh, PA. Most of his scholarly writing concerns the Theology of John Calvin with works such as *Calvin and Classical Philosophy* (1977), and his recent work *The Theology of John Calvin* (2008). Partee has also written a book dealing with the pioneer missionary career of his father-in-law, a 1934 graduate of Pittsburgh Seminary, entitled *Adventure in Africa: The Story of Don McClure* (2000), and with Andrew Purves *Encountering God: Christian Faith in Turbulent Times* (2000).

**Rev. Dr. Andrew Purves**

Professor of Reformed Theology, Pittsburgh Theological Seminary, Pittsburgh, PA. Ordained to Ministry of Word and Sacraments, PCUSA. Andrew is married and has three children. His many books include *A Passion for the Gospel* (with P. Mark Achtemeier; 2000); *Encountering God: Christian Faith in Turbulent Times* (with Charles Partee; 2000); *Pastoral Theology in the Classical Tradition* (2001); *Reconstructing Pastoral Theology : A Christological Foundation* (2004); *The Crucifixion of Ministry* (2007); and *The Resurrection of Ministry* (2010).

# Foreword

ALASDAIR HERON

R ECENT YEARS HAVE SEEN more than one extensive collection of essays designed to represent the voices of contemporary Reformed
theology. The results have tended to be wide-ranging, in many ways
informative, but not notably thematically coherent. Given the complex
history and resultant diversity of what is now the world-wide family of
Reformed churches and Reformed theology, that is not perhaps surprising. For the Reformed churches—e.g., as now reflected in the recently
expanded and renamed World Communion of Reformed Churches—are
on the one hand the largest confessional grouping of Protestant churches
and the most widespread of the Reformation confessions beyond the
European heartlands of the Reformation, but at the same time they are
much more diverse than the Lutheran or Anglican families—diverse in
history, in patterns of church order, in liturgical forms and in the variety
of their theological traditions.

This collection of papers does not merely recognize or reflect this
diversity but seeks to establish a specific profile among the competing
traditions and patterns. It does not claim to represent all Reformed thinking but to point a way and propose a particular option from among the
choices to be found in the Reformed tradition. In view of sometimes
particularly radical conflicts within Reformed theology it aims to advocate the case for an Evangelical Calvinism as opposed to alternative
versions generally known by such names as "Federal," "Covenantal," or
"Predestinarian" Calvinism.

How is this "Evangelical Calvinism" to be understood? The authors
do not necessarily subscribe to a single definition, but the theological
constellation they have in view can be characterized most easily in terms
of its affinities in the Reformed tradition. It appeals to Calvin—though

not uncritically—and after him to a Calvinist tradition represented in Scotland in the sixteenth and seventeenth centuries by John Knox and the Scots Confession of 1560 and followed by other Scottish theologians, and distinguished both in style and substance from the more generally known Calvinism of the anti-Arminian Decrees of Dordt, the Westminster Assembly, and Federal Theology. This "alternative Calvinism" then resurfaced repeatedly in Scotland—in the eighteenth century with the Marrow–Men and in the nineteenth in thinkers such as Thomas Erskine, Edward Irving, and John McLeod Campbell. In the last century it was particularly advanced by the widely and internationally influential brothers Thomas and James Torrance from their chairs in Edinburgh and Aberdeen. In terms of the wider world-map of Reformed theology the affinities of this Evangelical Calvinism are with Karl Barth, though the widespread Anglo-Saxon "Barthianism," especially in America, has a distinctly different flavor from Barthianism on the European continent—a topic which is (perhaps not accidentally) rarely mentioned even in passing in this collection. Its focus is largely if not exclusively on Anglo–Saxon Calvinism. Nevertheless the collection does along the way supply a fair amount of information on the broad history of Calvinism to contextualize the variety being advanced here.

Within that spectrum the Evangelical Calvinist wing as understood here is not primarily evangelical in the well-known sense of being oriented towards religious experience and conversion. Its orientation is intended to be towards the Gospel, objective rather than subjective. Its implied antithesis is forensic legalism, of which the standard Calvinism which dominated the scene for centuries is seen as a prime example. It is, however, also well summed up by John McLeod Campbell's insistence, over against the dominant Calvinism of his own day, that in our relationship to God "the filial is prior to the judicial" rather than vice versa.

A further important differentiation is between "Evangelical" in this sense and "Liberal." Anglo–Saxon Liberal Theology as it emerged in the nineteenth century was also opposed to classical Calvinism, whose advocates therefore also may sometimes be tempted to refer to "Evangelical" Calvinists as Liberals. The Reformed antecedent of Liberal Theology was, however, Schleiermacher rather than Barth, and Evangelical Calvinism as represented here is in many manifestations and tendencies still "Conservative" rather than "Liberal," though it may be added that both terms are as slippery in theology as in politics. More extensive details are given in the following chapters and do not need to be anticipated here.

More significant perhaps as a pointer to the future is the fact that this collection includes writers from the Baptist churches, who do not always understand themselves as "Reformed," though they do often recognize and claim their theological descent from John Calvin. Contrary to what is often assumed, the most numerous and widespread Baptist churches of today do not derive from the Anabaptists of the Reformation era (though such churches do still exist) but from divisions opening up around 1600 in Western European, chiefly English Calvinism, on the issue of paedo-baptism.

If there are two themes which generally characterize the approach taken in this collection, in spite of all differences of emphasis and style, they must be "the vicarious humanity of Christ" and "union with Christ," themes particularly dear to Thomas and James Torrance as their writings—and generations of students—can testify. The first of these taken alone and by itself might seem to be only a topic of dogmatic theology, but taken together with the second it emerges as the foundation of Christian faith and life. As a result this collection does not remain locked in the realm of pure dogmatic or systematic theology but also—like Calvin's *Institute*—explores issues such as providence, preaching, piety, and prayer. It wishes to be what Reformed theology essentially always aimed for even if it did not always attain it: theology in and for the church, not simply for the academic book or lecture-room. Further, it does not wish to be confessionally Reformed in any narrowly denominational sense, but Reformed in the sense that its emphasis is essentially and profoundly Christian and ecumenical.

Readers will observe more than one theological posture maintained in the following pages and will not necessarily find all of them equally appealing. Some may find some of the positions maintained *too* conservative, e.g. in the use of biblical texts or in the selection of questions for discussion. Inevitably too, some will find some papers more interesting and challenging than others. But generally the attempt to profile this particular constellation of Calvinist Christian theology is one that I, as a former student and colleague of both Thomas and James Torrance, can gladly welcome.

Alasdair Heron
Erlangen, 2nd Sunday after Trinity, 2011

# Acknowledgments

MANY PEOPLE ARE TO be thanked for their welcome contribution to this volume. We thank Professor Heron for taking the time and interest to write the Foreword for this work, despite serious health concerns, we are honored. We also want to thank the contributors for being willing to offer pieces of constructive theology to the Christian community to the glory of God. Their devotion to God and exemplary lives are just as much an encouragement to us as their theological expertise. We especially thank those contributors with young families, as we know all too well the sacrifice and skill it takes to balance scholarship and family commitments in a way which brings honor to the triune God of grace. Special thanks for those who helped with the Introduction and to those who gave critical and much needed feedback on the final Theses.

Wipf and Stock continue to support the task of resourcing the Church and academy with works of theology that are at once orthodox and creative—thank you Chris, K.C., Diane, Christian, Robin, James, Raydeen, Patrick, and the many others who work behind the scenes to produce *our* books for you. Our thanks to Joseph Small of Witherspoon Press for permission to include "Union in Christ: A Declaration for the Church" as the Prologue. We are extremely grateful for Greg Liston, a research associate with the R. J. Thompson Centre for Theological Studies, for formatting and indexing the volume, and for Carey Baptist College for supporting theological scholarship in so many ways—thank you Charles and Laurie particularly.

No word of acknowledgment would be complete without mentioning the support and encouragement we receive from our family.

Odele—you are my greatest cheerleader and my dearest friend, thank you for the manifold ways you support me in ministry and contribute to our flourishing. You and the kids are a gift from God more precious than a thousand libraries and I love you dearly. (Myk)

Angela—you are my gift from the Lord, my most supportive and loving confidant. Without you this work would not be possible, thank you for being the sustaining force in all of our endeavors. Madeline and Jacob, you are both the light of my life. Your mom and I seek to show you Jesus more truly everyday, love you. (Bobby)

Myk Habets
*Doctor Serviens Ecclesiae*
Auckland, New Zealand

Bobby Grow
*soli Deo gloria*
Washington, America

# Prologue

## "Union in Christ: A Declaration for the Church"[1]

"He is before all things and in him all things hold together."
(Colossians 1:17)

With the witness of Scripture and the Church through the ages we declare:

I.

Jesus Christ is the gracious mission of God
>    to the world
>    and for the world.
He is Emmanuel and Savior,
One with the Father,
God incarnate as Mary's son,
Lord of all,
The truly human one.
His coming transforms everything.
His Lordship casts down every idolatrous claim to authority.
His incarnation discloses the only path to God.
His life shows what it means to be human.
His atoning death reveals the depth of God's love for sinners.
His bodily resurrection shatters the powers of sin and death.

II.

The Holy Spirit joins us to Jesus Christ by grace alone, uniting our life with his through the ministry of the Church.

---

1. *Union in Christ: A Declaration for the Church. A Commentary with Questions for Study and Reflection*, eds. Andrew Purves and Mark Achtemeier (Louisville: Witherspoon Press, 1999). Used by permission.

In the proclamation of the Word, the Spirit calls us to repentance, builds up and renews our life in Christ, strengthens our faith, empowers our service, gladdens our hearts, and transforms our lives more fully into the image of Christ.

> We turn away from forms of church life that ignore the need for repentance, that discount the transforming power of the Gospel, or that fail to pray, hope and strive for a life that is pleasing to God.

In Baptism and conversion the Spirit engrafts us into Christ, establishing the Church's unity and binding us to one another in him.

> We turn away from forms of church life that seek unity in theological pluralism, relativism or syncretism.

In the Lord's Supper the Spirit nurtures and nourishes our participation in Christ and our communion with one another in him.

> We turn away from forms of church life that allow human divisions of race, gender, nationality, or economic class to mar the Eucharistic fellowship, as though in Christ there were still walls of separation dividing the human family.

III.

Engrafted into Jesus Christ we participate through faith in his relationship with the Father.

> By our union with Christ we participate in his righteousness before God, even as he becomes the bearer of our sin.

> > We turn away from any claim to stand before God apart from Christ's own righteous obedience, manifest in his life and sacrifice for our sake on the cross.

> By our union with Christ we participate in his knowledge of the Father, given to us as the gift of faith through the unique and authoritative witness of the Old and New Testaments.

We turn away from forms of church life that discount the authority of Scripture or claim knowledge of God that is contrary to the full testimony of Scripture as interpreted by the Holy Spirit working in and through the community of faith across time.

By our union with Christ we participate in his love of the Father, manifest in his obedience "even unto death on the cross."

We turn away from any supposed love of God that is manifest apart from a continual longing for and striving after that loving obedience which Christ offers to God on our behalf.

## IV.

Though obscured by our sin, our union with Christ causes his life to shine forth in our lives. This transformation of our lives into the image of Christ is a work of the Holy Spirit begun in this life as a sign and promise of its completion in the life to come.

By our union with Christ our lives participate in the holiness of the One who fulfilled the Law of God on our behalf.

We turn away from forms of church life that ignore Christ's call to a life of holiness, or that seek to pit Law and Gospel against one another as if both were not expressions of the one Word of God.

By our union with Christ we participate in his obedience. In these times of moral and sexual confusion we affirm the consistent teaching of Scripture that calls us to chastity outside of marriage and faithfulness within the covenant of marriage between a man and a woman.

We turn away from forms of church life that fail to pray for and strive after a rightly ordered sexuality as the gracious gift of a loving God, offered to us in Christ by the power of the Holy Spirit. We also turn away from forms of church life that fail to forgive and restore those who repent of sexual and other sins.

V.

As the body of Christ the Church has her life in Christ.

> By our union with Christ the Church binds together believers in every time and place.
>
>> We turn away from forms of church life that identify the true Church only with particular styles of worship, polity, or institutional structure. We also turn away from forms of church life that ignore the witness of those who have gone before us.
>
> By our union with Christ the Church is called out into particular communities of worship and mission.
>
>> We turn away from forms of church life that see the work of the local congregation as sufficient unto itself, as if it were not a local representation of the one, holy, catholic and apostolic Church called together by the power of the Spirit in every age and time until our Lord returns.
>
> By our union with Christ our lives participate in God's mission to the world:
>
>> to uphold the value of every human life,
>>
>> to make disciples of all peoples,
>>
>> to establish Christ's justice and peace in all creation,
>>
>> and to secure that visible oneness in Christ that is the promised inheritance of every believer
>>
>> We turn away from forms of church life that fail to bear witness in word and deed to Christ's compassion and peace, and the Gospel of salvation.

By our union with Christ the Church participates in Christ's resurrected life and awaits in hope the future that God has prepared for her. Even so come quickly, Lord Jesus!

In the name of the Father, and of the Son, and of the Holy Spirit.

# 1

## Introduction

## *Theologia Reformata et Semper Reformanda*

### Towards an Evangelical Calvinism

MYK HABETS AND BOBBY GROW

## EVANGELICAL *CALVINISM*[1]

T HE QUINCENTENARY OF CALVIN'S birth in 2009 provided an opportunity for Calvinists around the world to celebrate his life, thought, and influence. The Calvin 500 Tribute Conference in Geneva, and the many other gatherings of Reformed thinkers around the globe, were occasions for joy and celebration as academic papers were read and expository sermons were preached, all under the banner of Calvinism.[2] In addition to a celebration of the past, the Quincentenary was also an occasion to reconsider the future of Reformed thought: what it may look like, where it may go, and who may lead such a future. As questions such as these were considered it quickly became evident that there were no easy or even obvious answers. Calvinism, in various guises, has a global

1.. The editors wish to thank a number of people for their critical interaction with the Introduction, especially John McDowell and Julie Canlis.

2. The two texts produced from the Calvin 500 Quincentenary are the expository sermons preached in St Pierre Cathedral, Geneva. Hall ed., *Preaching Like Calvin*; and the academic papers delivered in Calvin's Auditoire, Geneva: Hall ed., *Tributes to John Calvin: A Celebration of His Quincentenary.*

reach and influence. While there is geographical diversity there is also theological diversity. For the contributors to this book, this is not only to be expected but actually encouraged, for unity in diversity brings with it new perspectives, correctives, and opportunities for enrichment.

The contributors to this volume are Reformed theologians from various denominations who love their theological tradition and are committed to its truths, but understand that their tradition is a variegated one, with many tributaries and eddies. They represent a consistent feature of Reformed theology—the willingness and ability to enrich their tradition by mining its past and contributing to its future.[3] This is not, however, an expression of a "new-Calvinism" or even a "neo-Calvinism," if by those terms are meant a novel reading of the Reformed faith. We, along with the Reformed theologian Donald McKim, consider the Reformed faith an expansive tradition with many threads that make up the fabric of our tradition. McKim captures this well:

> The Reformed faith impels persons to confess their faith as part of the ecumenical church, the whole people of God. The movement here is first from what Christians believe to what Reformed Christians believe. Reformed churches are a portion of the full household of faith. As such, Reformed theology and Reformed faith are open to hearing, dialoguing with, and learning from other theological viewpoints and Christian communions. Though some Reformed bodies have tended to become more narrow and almost assume that their formulations are the only means of expressing God's truth, this impulse runs counter to the genuine heartbeat of Reformed faith. Reformed faith is open to God's Spirit, who may encounter us at any time in any place. Reformed Christians should see and listen to other voices since perhaps through them an essential theological insight will be given.[4]

Evangelical Calvinism is not a new movement, it does not to belong to any particular denomination, nor is it aligned with any particular seminary; there are no catch words that it sponsors, nor are there any high

3. According to Richard A. Muller, "John Calvin and Later Calvinism," 141: "the rise of scholastic orthodoxy is a single but variegated Reformed tradition, bounded by a series of fairly uniform confessional concerns but quite diverse in patterns of formulation—not two or more traditions, as is sometimes claimed." The identification of being Reformed with scholastic orthodoxy is debatable but the variegated nature of being Reformed is not.

4. McKim, *Introducing the Reformed Faith*, 7–8.

profile media stars that campaign on its behalf. Evangelical Calvinism as we suggest here, is more of a mood than a movement. The various contributors to the present volume are in their own ways taking steps toward articulating what that mood might look like, and their differences are part of a necessary element in that very mood of witness and argument. In attempting to outline features of an Evangelical Calvinism a number of the contributors compare and contrast this approach with that of Federal Calvinism. This latter form of Calvinism is currently dominant in North American Reformed theology and is considered, by many, to be the only orthodox Reformed theology acceptable; the present volume clearly challenges such assumptions.[5]

In the preface to one of his later works, *Scottish Theology from John Knox to John McLeod Campbell,* Thomas Torrance set out his understanding of the differences that exist between Classical and Evangelical Calvinism:[6]

> Following upon the teaching of the great Reformers there developed what is known as "federal theology," in which the place John Calvin gave to the biblical conception of the covenant was radically altered through being schematised to a framework of law and grace governed by a severely contractual notion of covenant, with a stress upon a primitive "covenant of works," resulting in a change in the Reformed understanding of "covenant of grace." This was what Protestant scholastics called "a two-winged," and not "a one-winged" covenant, which my brother James has called a bilateral and a unilateral conception of the Covenant. The former carries with it legal stipulations which have to be fulfilled in order for it to take effect, while the latter derives from the infinite love of God, and is freely proclaimed to all mankind in the grace of the Lord Jesus Christ. It was the imposition of a rigidly logicalised federal system of thought upon Reformed theology that

---

5. See Knight, *Orthodoxies in Massachusetts,* 4–5. She argues that the language of "orthodoxy" was originally used for rhetorical and sectarian purposes, rather than in service of symbolizing "right teaching;" in other words the language of "orthodoxy" has political overtones in its history of usage, and thus does not serve as "stable" of a term as those employing it today believe.

6. Torrance was speaking of "Scottish theology" rather than "Evangelical Calvinism," but the two refer to the same cluster of ideas. Cf. T. F. Torrance, *Scottish Theology,* 59–60, 65, 224. Torrance contrasts "Evangelical Clavnism" with "Federal Calvinism," "hyper-Calvinism," "Bezan Calvinism," "scholastic Calvinism," "Westminster Calvinism," and "Classic Calvinism." Throughout this volume we are taking these various titles as synonymous.

gave rise to many of the problems which have afflicted Scottish theology, and thereby made central doctrines of predestination, the limited or unlimited range of the atoning death of Christ, the problem of assurance, and the nature of what was called "the Gospel-offer" to sinners. This meant that relatively little attention after the middle of the seventeenth century was given to the doctrine of the Holy Trinity and to a trinitarian understanding of redemption and worship.[7]

Torrance highlights the development of a tradition of Calvinism that is particular to Scotland but is not unique to the Scots. Elements of what we are calling an Evangelical Calvinism may be found, to a greater or lesser extent, in the theology of such figures as John Calvin, John Knox, aspects of Scottish Reformed theology,[8] and Scottish divines specifically Henry Scougal, John Craig, Hugh Binning, The Marrow Men,[9] John McLeod Campbell, Thomas Torrance, and James Torrance. Evangelical Calvinism, though, is not limited to Scottish theology. One might naturally think of the English Particular Baptist John Gill who emphasized the *duplex gratia* as did Calvin,[10] or the Baptist pastor Charles Spurgeon, one of the few preachers in history able to preach adequately an evangelistic sermon based on the "Five Points of Calvinism"![11] In American history one may think of Augustus H. Strong, the Reformed Baptist theologian who came to reject Federal Theology and its account of imputation in favor of something her termed "ethical monism."[12] In

7. T. F. Torrance, *Scottish Theology,* x-xi.

8. See T. F. Torrance, *Scottish Theology.*

9. The Marrow Men were a dissenting group of twelve including Thomas Boston, Ralph Erskine, and Ebeneezer Erskine, in the early 1700s within the Scottish Kirk who emphasized the free grace of the Gospel against the then prevailing Neonomians of the Church of Scotland. The Marrow Controversy 1717–22 was occasioned by the republication with commentary by Thomas Boston of *The Marrow of Modern Divinity* by Edward Fisher. See Lachman, *The Marrow Controversy,* and McGowan, *The Federal Theology of Thomas Boston.*

10. See for instance Gill, *A Complete Body of Doctrinal and Practical Divinity.* While still a little too scholastic for the editor's tastes, this does approximate the approach of the present volume.

11. See Spurgeon, *A Defence of Calvinism*; taken from Chapter 13 of Spurgeon, *The Early Years.*

12. See Strong, *What Shall I Believe?* Strong argued there were three imputations in Scripture: 1) Adam's sin to the human race, 2) human sin to Christ, and 3) Christ's merits and righteousness to believers. Strong wrote that "My Federalism was succeeded by realistic Theology. Imputation is Grounded in Union, not union in imputation.

this briefest of surveys we should also mention such thinkers as what Janice Knight has called "The Spiritual Brethren,"[13] among many others, who could be considered its forebears. On the Continent it is, of course, Karl Barth who stands above all others in what we believe approximates an Evangelical Calvinist orientation.

This encapsulates something of the motivation for the present volume. The editors have picked up the baton passed on by Torrance and others in order to offer the family of Reformed theologies a theological and spiritual ethos. In terms of its confessional stance, Evangelical Calvinism follows the trajectory more in line with the *Scots Confession* (1560) than with the *Westminster Confession* (1647). It is not that the theology of the two is antithetical, despite there being substantial differences, but more in the tone of the two.[14] The inclusion of Matthew 24:14 on the title page of the first printing of the *Scots Confession* in 1561 already gives the reader reason to pause: "And this glaid tydings of the kingdom shalbe preached throught the hole world of a witness to all nations and then shall the end cum." As T. F. Torrance remarks, "This is quite startling, for, in contrast to every other confessional statement issued during the Reformation, it gives primary importance to the missionary calling of the Church."[15] Wright says of the confession "it illustrates the characteristically kerygmatic and pastoral tone that, through Knox, informed Scottish reformation theology."[16] In effect, then, Evangelical Calvinism stands in a heritage that provides theological ground to heed God's call to live out (and out of) the missional-life of Jesus. At its theological core, the approach of the present volume is bound to the Word of God as its compass; and motivated by the grace of the Lord Jesus Christ, the love of the Father, and the communion of

---

Because I am one with Christ, and Christ's life has become my life, God can attribute to me whatever Christ is, and whatever Christ has done. The relation is biological, rather than forensic" (ibid., 91). See Strong, *Christ in Creation and Ethical Monism.* Cf. Crisp, "Federalism vs Realism," 55–71.

13. Knight, *Orthodoxies in Massachusetts.*

14. See a sympathetic treatment to the same effect in Smith, *Letters to a Young Calvinist,* 55. Smith suggests, in line with our contention, that the Heidelberg Catechism provides a more "Trinitarian" and relational tone versus the tone given by the Westminster Confession of Faith.

15. T. F. Torrance cited in Wright, "The Scottish Reformation: Theology and Theologians," 175.

16. Ibid.

the Holy Spirit (2 Cor 13:14), to proclaim Christ to all of humanity for whom he gave his life.

The present volume seeks to model one of the tenets of the Reformed faith, namely, the need for *ecclesia reformata, semper reformanda*—"the church reformed and always reforming." While extremely popular within Reformed circles, the origin and context of this phrase are unknown. The phrase itself appears not to have been used prior to the middle of the seventeenth century, and thus it is not a catch cry of the Reformers, as so many mistakenly suggest.[17] As a more specific application of this term the related one, *theologia reformata semper reformanda est secundu Verbum Dei*—"Reformed theology having been reformed must be always reforming according to the Word of God," is utilized here.[18] In seeking to be faithful to texts such as Romans 12:2, "And do not be conformed to this world, but be transformed by the renewing of your mind, that you may prove what is that good and acceptable and perfect will of God," by this phrase is meant the continual humiliation of the Church and its doctors, under the Word of God written, in order to provide faithful service to the Church. It is not that a reformation like that of the fifteenth century is envisaged within Reformed theology today, nor that Reformed theology is inherently wrong and needs a great reformation. It is, rather, the contention that all human systems and articulations of theology are, outside of Jesus Christ himself, provisional and fallible. Karl Barth has rightly said:

---

17. The source of the phrase appears to have been derived either from Jodocus van Lodenstein or Jacobus Koelman. According to Michael Horton, the term first appeared in a 1674 devotional by Jodocus van Lodenstein, who was an important figure in Dutch Reformed pietism—a movement known as the Dutch Second Reformation. According to these writers, the Reformation reformed the doctrine of the church, but the lives and practices of God's people always need further reformation. Horton, "Semper Reformanda." The other contender for the origin of the term, Jacobus Koelman (published under the pseudonym Christophilius Eubulus), is found in his book *De pointen van nodige reformatie omtrent de kerk* (ET *Points where the Church needs Reforming*; VLissingen: 1678). For a useful online discussion see: http://firstword.us/2006/09/when-i-hear-semper-reformanda-i-reach-for-my-revolver/. Regardless of its exact origin, the point of the phrase appears relatively self-evident; even though there had been a reformation, the Church is always in danger of veering away from sound doctrine, and thus needs always to be called back to the Word of God. See Trueman, "Wrongheaded Reformations," 17.

18. This phrase is an adaptation of one used by Moltmann, "Theologia Reformata Et Semper Reformanda," 120.

> The Reformed confession points *beyond* itself. Its center of grav-
> ity, if not in fact its very content, is not in itself but rather *beyond*
> itself. *Faith* confesses. But it does not confess itself, but what is
> *written.* In the Reformed church, confession is in its entirety
> "testimony" [*testificatio*], a pointing toward. The object itself is
> and remains something other, a second thing, something en-
> countered outside oneself. This other issues a demand toward the
> person, which is a *power,* a power that is a *demand,* a humiliation
> that is a *knowing,* and a knowing that is a *humiliation.* One has
> called the Reformed church the church of the *formal* principle of
> the Reformation, the principle of Scripture . . .[19]

As such, our theology must always be attuned to the Word and Spirit of God in order to render ever-faithful witness to the God who speaks.

The present work is by and large one of constructive theology. While it establishes the context within which it works, and clears some of the epistemological and methodological ground early on; it is not content to settle only for deconstructive or apologetic engagement. Nor is it an argument to get "back to" John Calvin. One is reminded here of Barth's words, in quite a different context, when in the *Church Dogmatics* he wrote: "the slogan 'Back to Orthodoxy,' and even the slogan 'Back to the Reformers,' cannot promise us the help that we need to-day. 'Back to . . .' is never a good slogan."[20]

To be Reformed is not to follow any one rigid path (be it Calvin or Zwingli), confession (be it Westminster or Scots), or even denomination

---

19. Barth, *The Theology of the Reformed Confessions,* 38–9.

20. Barth, *CD* IV/1, 371–72. The full quote:

"It must be noted that the voice which we have heard is not that of 18th century rationalism but 17th century orthodoxy. This theology had not been taught by the Reformers themselves to learn from Jesus Christ as the substance and centre of Scripture what is the will and Law of God and therefore what the sin of man is. And the theology itself obviously had no power of itself to rectify the omission. For this reason it could and indeed had to think with a growing intensity and speak with an increasing clarity along the lines discussed. At this critical point in its exposition of revelation—hesitantly at first, but then more confidently—it could and had to go beyond the Scripture principle which it proclaimed so loudly to another principle, that of reason. The transition to the Enlightenment and all that that involved was not the terrible innovation that it has often been called. In many respects, and in this respect also, orthodoxy itself was engaged in a whole-hearted transition to the Enlightenment—a further proof that the slogan 'Back to Orthodoxy,' and even the slogan 'Back to the Reformers,' cannot promise us the help that we need today. 'Back to . . .' is never a good slogan."

(be it PC(USA), OPC, or PCA); that much is clear. Richard Muller has written that:

> Reformed orthodoxy, moreover, must be defined in terms of the limits set on theological speculation and development by the confessions of the Reformed churches and not, as some historians have done, in terms of particular preferred trajectories of thought, often defined entirely on the basis of their analysis of an individual founder of the faith, such as Calvin or Bullinger. This practice has led to a rather narrow view of Reformed orthodoxy as excluding, for example, the federal theology of Johannes Cocceius and his followers, the variant teachings of the seventeenth-century theologians at the Academy of Saumur, and the modified or even diluted Cartesianism of a fairly large number of mid– and late seventeenth-century Reformed theologians. Despite the intense debate over each of these seventeenth-century developments, none of them falls, strictly speaking, outside of the bounds of Reformed or Calvinist orthodoxy as defined by the confessional documents of the sixteenth and seventeenth centuries.[21]

While it does have its boundary markers it is, perhaps, better to think of being Calvinist as a centered-set than a bounded-set, to use a mathematical image.[22] At the center are those commitments of the Reformed faith that all subscribe to, the further from the centre the more diversity emerges, but not so that it threatens to destabilize the center. Away from the centre of the set exist many *theologoumena*, and at the extreme boundaries of such a set exist the theological *adiaphora*. Beyond the boundary, however this is measured, one moves into heterodoxy and beyond that, heresy. This is in line with Calvin's approach when he allows theological disagreement between theologians as long as they believe in common a few essential doctrines:

> For not all the articles of true doctrine are of the same sort. Some are so necessary to know that they should be certain and unquestioned by all men as the proper principles of religion. Such are: God is one; Christ is God and the Son of God; our salvation rests in God's mercy; and the like. Among the churches there are

21. Muller, "John Calvin and Later Calvinism," 141.

22. Christian missiologist Paul Hiebert discusses mathematical "set" concepts in Hiebert, *Anthropological Reflections on Missiological Issues*, Chapter 6. Since then the idea has had something of a life of its own.

other articles of doctrine disputed which still do not break the unity of faith.[23]

Numerous recent attempts at defining the Reformed or Calvinist tradition have been offered.[24] A number of these treatments have tended to present in objective fashion what is, ultimately, only a subjective judgment. Earlier popular works at definition, still in vogue among seminary and university students on campuses today, look to the five points of Dort—the so-called "doctrines of grace"—as the essence of what it means to be Reformed.[25] Dort, however, as with most if not all of the Reformed confessions, is a localized and contextual document. The *Canons of Dort* give a detailed and skilled reply to Arminianism; hence "TULIP" represents a response to the Arminian five-point *Remonstrance*. It was never intended as a sum of Reformed thought. The *Canons of Dort* are still to be consulted for a Reformed reply to Arminianism, but they should not be thought to represent the sum of our belief. As Muller has written:

> In other words, it would be a major error—both historically and doctrinally—if the five points of Calvinism were understood either as the sole or even as the absolutely primary basis for identifying someone as holding the Calvinistic or Reformed faith. In fact, the *Canons of Dort* contain five points *only* because the Arminian articles, the *Remonstrance* of 1610, to which they responded, had five points. The number five, far from being sacrosanct, is the result of a particular historical circumstance and was

---

23. Calvin, *Inst.,* 4.1.12.

24. Two recent works deserve mention. In the first, R. Michael Allen, *Reformed Theology,* presents a generous introduction to Reformed theology in its central tenets and throughout is generous in his dealings with those parts of the tradition he is not personally enamoured with. However, throughout the work a preference for conservative, confessional reformed Presbyterianism is presented, so much so, in fact, that Allen would be hard pressed to assert that Baptists, for instance, could genuinely be termed "Reformed." Compare that with a recent article by Teun van der Leer with the inflammatory title, "The True Calvinist is a Baptist." In the second work deserving mention, Scott Clark, *Recovering the Reformed Confession,* offers what he considers to be the essence of the Reformed faith and in the process seeks to show how much (most?) of contemporary Reformed thought and ecclesiology is, in fact, not Reformed at all. It is not surprising that for Clark the only valid form of Reformed thought is that of Westminster Calvinism. For a critique of Clark's reading of the Reformed tradition see Frame, http://www.frame-poythress.org/frame_articles/2010Clark.htm#_ftn1.

25. See for instance Steele et al., *The Five Points of Calvinism,* and Sproul, *What is Reformed Theology?*

determined *negatively* by the number of articles in the Arminian objection to confessional Calvinism.[26]

Others appeal to the teaching of the *Westminster Confession of Faith* and lift this up as the subordinate standard of doctrine to which the whole church must subscribe in detail. Now it is true that it is a subordinate standard of doctrine for Presbyterians in many countries, but it is not a universal document intended for all. Although this Confession is much broader it too is a historical document located within a specific context and, when shorn of this context, it too fails to represent Reformed faith in any comprehensive or definitive fashion. Westminster was largely the result of English Puritans and hardly represents the breadth and depth of the Reformed faith or theology at the time or since. A further attempt to define the Reformed faith is by means of the five *solas* of the Reformation-*sola scriptura, sola fide, sola gratia, solus Christus/solo Christo,* and *soli Deo gloria.*[27] This has more merit, given that the five *solas* are abiding marks of Reformed theology. These are, we suggest, as least integral to the *sine qua non* of Reformed doctrine.

Writing in the context of the earliest Reformed theologians, Richard Muller argues for a series of theological issues and conclusions that may be identified as essentially Reformed, notably, the priority of Scripture over tradition as the sole, absolute norm for theology, the unity of the message of Scripture and the covenant of God, sacramentology (specifically that there are two sacraments and both are viewed as signs and seals of grace), a Chalcedonian Christology which affirms the integrity of two natures in the one person of Christ, and an understanding of salvation by grace alone, with a corresponding emphasis upon God's gracious election to eternal salvation.[28] Evangelical Calvinism remains true to the *sine qua non* of the Reformed faith and then feels the freedom to explore the *adiaphora* within their traditional commitments.

## EVANGELICAL CALVINISM

The word "Evangelical" carries something of a three-fold significance. First, and most importantly, we believe the readings of the Reformed traditions offered in this book hope to remain consistent to the witness

26. Muller, "How Many Points?" 426.

27. Horton, "Reformation Essentials."

28. Muller, "John Calvin and Later Calvinism," 131–32.

of Holy Scripture—*the euangelion*—and thus it is evangelical primarily in this way. This is also what makes it thoroughly Reformed. Second, it is, we believe, a theology that is genuinely "good news." That all are created good by God, that all are included in Christ's salvific work, and that salvation is by grace alone and Christ alone is truly good news. And finally, it is Evangelical in that it does share a common boundary with that movement known as Evangelicalism.[29] Evangelicalism as used here denotes a movement that is biblical, that is reformational, that is, it affirms the formal and material principles of the Reformation: *sola scriptura* and of justification by faith alone. An Evangelicalism of this type is self-consciously post-fundamentalist in its commitment to the Word of God and the task of world evangelization within transdenominational fellowships. It is these common commitments which enable an Evangelical Calvinism to legitimately embrace more than one denominational tradition.[30]

Michael Horton offers an analogy for how the different theological traditions within Evangelicalism coexist—that of the village green. Horton writes:

> For all of this, I remain convinced that there is still a place for being "evangelical." Why? Quite simply, because we still have the

---

29. By the use of "Evangelical" in the title we do not intend by this a one-to-one identification with the Protestant movement known as Evangelicalism, arising in North America and England in the 1940s as a progressive development of the older conservative Fundamentalism. We are thus appealing to a set of broad theological convictions and not to a sociological reading of the history of Evangelicalism.

30. Many, but not all, of the contributors to the present volume would happily identify themselves as Evangelicals, if by this is meant the standard and basic four-point definition of it given by David Bebbington and repeated numerous times elsewhere, for example. David Bebbington, *Evangelicalism in Modern Britain: A History from the 1730s to the 1980s* (London: Unwin Hyman, 1989). Thus Evangelical Calvinism recommends itself as: 1) Bible based (following the formal principle of the Protestant Reformation), 2) Christocentric, advocating forms of, 3) conversionism, and, 4) activism. Those who object to this quadrilateral may raise such issues as: "Bible based" is not particularly descriptive, there are many different types of christocentrisms (e.g. Schleiermacher), the Reformed traditions called Presbyterianism have not particularly subscribed to "conversionism" in its more pietistic form (with the obvious exception of Jonathan Edwards), and "activism" is a naïve understanding of the relation of virtue / character / subjectivity to agency. Such criticisms are registered, and alternate definitions, more or less commensurate with Bebbington's quadrilateral, may be found in Larson and Treier eds., *The Cambridge Companion to Evangelical Theology*. Reformed contributors to the volume include Kevin Vanhoozer, John Webster, Leanne Van Dyk, and Stephen Holmes.

> evangel. In my view, evangelicalism, then, serves best as a "village green," like the common parks at the center of old New England towns, for everyone who affirms this evangel. It's a place where Christians from different churches meet to discuss what they share in common, as well as their differences. They help keep each other honest.[31]

It is in this "village green" sense of Evangelicalism that we use the term here, and it is upon this "commons" that we meet and fellowship with the broad spectrum of those who call themselves Christian.

The specific term "Evangelical Calvinism" as been used a number of times in history and so it is not unique to the editors or contributors of this volume. To generalize, this form of Calvinism can have an unintended consequence of not promoting a full-orbed Trinitarian theology, as can be discerned in Calvin himself. Due to historical and cultural factors, various aspects of Calvin's theology were diminished that Evangelical Calvinism seeks to redress. According to David Fergusson, the more "mainstream" forms of Calvinism tend "to subordinate grace to nature; it renders the justice of God essential but the love of God arbitrary; it yields a theory of limited atonement which is contrary to the plain sense of Scripture and which is divorced from the doctrine of the incarnation; and it fosters an introspective and legalist religion as the search for the signs of election is redirected away from Christ to the life of the individual believer."[32] It is the editors' belief that an Evangelical Calvinism can best represent the kind of Reformed theology Fergusson so rightly believes to be necessary.

Thomas Torrance typifies the Evangelical Calvinist's heart in this regard, and deserves to be heard at length:

> We preach and teach the Gospel evangelically, then, in such a ways as this: God loves you so utterly and completely that he has given himself for you in Jesus Christ his beloved Son, and has thereby pledged his very Being as God for your salvation. In Jesus Christ God has actualized his unconditional love for you in your human nature in such a once for all way, that he cannot go back upon it without undoing the Incarnation and the Cross and thereby denying himself. Jesus Christ died for you precisely because you are sinful and utterly unworthy of him, and has thereby already made you his own before and apart from your

31. Michael Horton, "Who Exactly Are the Evangelicals?".

32. Fergusson, "Predestination: A Scottish Perspective," 466.

ever believing in him. He has bound you to himself by his love in a way that he will never let you go, for even if you refuse him and damn yourself in hell his love will never cease. Therefore repent and believe in Jesus Christ as your Lord and Saviour. From beginning to end what Jesus Christ has done for you he has done not only as God but as man. He has acted in your place in the whole range of your human life and activity, including your personal decisions, and your responses to God's love, and even your acts of faith. He has believed for you, fulfilled your human response to God, even made your personal decision for you, so that he acknowledges you before God as one who has already responded to God in him, who has already believed in God through him, and whose personal decision is already implicated in Christ's self-offering to the Father, in all of which he has been fully and completely accepted by the Father, so that in Jesus Christ you are already accepted by him. Therefore, renounce yourself, take up your cross and follow Jesus as your Lord and Saviour.[33]

It is in this *ethos* that Evangelical Calvinism claims to be both *Evangelical* and *Calvinist*.

## EVANGELICAL CALVINISM

In what follows the contributors have been asked to contribute essays on a variety of topics which, together, reflect a theology and practice that is commensurate with what the editors are calling Evangelical Calvinism. Contributors were free to develop their essays in any way they wished and as will become evident, while the general contour of each essay is complementary to the whole, there is considerable disagreement at certain points. This is to be welcomed.

In Part One issues to do with theological prolegomena and historical theology are introduced. In chapter 2 Charles Partee reconsiders the history and development of Calvinism and offers a considered perspective on how contemporary Reformed theologies are to be understood. In the process he argues in his inimitable way for an understanding of the tradition, how to relate to Scripture, and how to be Reformed in a way which Calvin would condone. Chapter 3 offers a critical reflection by Adam Nigh upon Holy Scripture, through the lens of Thomas Torrance's "depth exegesis" and offers constructive proposals on the nature of Holy Scripture and the way it is to function in church and theology today.

33. T. F. Torrance, *The Mediation of Christ*, 103–4.

Bobby Grow reflects upon the analogy of faith and the analogy of being and argues that a Reformed theology should properly endorse the former if it is to reflect the contents of the Gospel itself. Finally, in chapter 5 Andrew Purves takes us on theological reading of the Scots Confession as interpreted by Karl Barth, and on the way exposes a number of key themes which, in his opinion, need reemphasizing in today's theological climate.

In Part Two various *loci* of systematic theology most germane to the ethos of an Evangelical Calvinism are presented, notably the themes of union with Christ and the place it occupies in a Reformed theology, the vicarious humanity of Christ, and the centrality of Christ for all of the theological task. This is worked out in one's Theology Proper, soteriology, atonement theology, and eschatology. Gannon Murphy reflects in chapter 6 upon the God who is and asks again how we should think, reflect upon, and worship such a God, as opposed to a god of our own imagination or creation. It is not the philosophers, and those influenced by them, who may provide appropriate reflection upon God, but God himself and those to whom he has been revealed. In chapter 7 Myk Habets follows a trajectory of thought found in a minor key throughout tradition but brought into acute focus by Karl Barth and then Thomas Torrance, namely the centrality of Christ to the doctrine of election. He challenges theologies of election which look to several covenants or to the divine decrees as the absolute basis for election and instead asks for us to follow Scripture and look to Christ—the object and subject of election. Chapter 8 sees Marcus Johnson present a thorough case for a "realistic" reading of Romans 5 and the Adam/Christ parallel. He rebuts those readings of the transmission of original sin that see it in purely legal category and argues for a personalist account whereby original sin is imputed to all, all participate personally in the transmitted sin nature, and argues that legal guilt and moral pollution are not causally related.

Union with Christ has been something of the overlooked child of contemporary theology and in chapter 9 Marcus Johnson seeks to restore this venerable doctrine to its rightful place at the start of the *via salutis*. at the center of God's saving action is a participation in the person of Jesus Christ, the One in whom salvation resides. Drawing especially on Calvin, the author explicates the nature of this union in terms of faith, Spirit, and intimacy. The chapter then draws out the consequences of union with Christ, particularly in terms of justification and sanctification, and argues that the benefits of Christ accrue to the believer only by way of a union with his very person. Finally, a succinct look at the implications of this participation in Christ towards a robust, Christological understanding of adoption, the church, and the Lord's Supper is provided. The vicarious humanity of Christ is addressed in chapter 10 by Jason Goroncy by means of a study of John McLeod Campbell and P. T. Forsyth. Emphasizing the ongoing ministry of Christ and his faith and faithfulness, Goroncy posits all of Christ—that is, all of grace—does not mean nothing of humanity, but precisely the opposite. To affirm otherwise is to either sever Christ's humanity from ours or to suggest that true humanity exists apart from that of the Incarnate Son. This means that no human being can repent or flourish apart from the Word made flesh. In Christ alone, and by the Spirit, are persons made fit, and led to share in Christ's confession and repentance, actions which commit persons to new life shared with the Father in the Spirit. Part 2 concludes with a constructive "solution" by Myk Habets in chapter 11 to the question of the fate of infants who die and that of the severely mentally disabled. Habets argues that only a consistent Reformed theology that adequately conceives of salvation as achieved fully in the election of Christ, by grace alone, through the vicarious faith and faithfulness of Christ alone, can positively affirm the salvation of all infants who die and of all the severely mentally disabled.

Part Three includes three essays that probe some of the more important ways in which the general theology already canvassed in the volume may be worked out and lived out in various Christian practices, namely, spiritual formation, prayer, and worship. In chapter 12 Julie Canlis provides a reading of Calvin's *Institutes* which highlights the pastoral and spiritual theology of his Reformed faith and seeks to mine this for contemporary reflection and application. Prayer is the theme of chapter 13 as John McDowell reflects on a cluster of issues arising from the work of John Calvin on providence, retrieving Calvin from some of the more deterministic readings of his account, and moves from there to make connections between theology and practice, the formation and transformation of judgment, and of persons in prayerful correspondence to the God of providential *concursus*. McDowell considers six key points from Calvin's theology of prayer, providence, and God, and draws these into an acute dialogue with contemporary concerns before offering a concluding definition of prayer. Scott Kirkland concludes this section in chapter 14 with an essay on worship in light of the Incarnation. We are to understand that existence itself has been refigured by the humanity of God in such a way that we are now given to be free for one another in worship. As we love, that is, as we obey the divine command, we exist in worship. This is what shapes human being in such a way that it comes to reflect something of the divine, that is we become *imago dei* as we live a doxological existence.

Finally, Part Four offers a prospect from the editors in which we have attempted to broadly define some of the key moments and aspects of what Evangelical Calvinists might be committed to. On saying that, however, the editors recognize that within this volume the very contributors themselves do not share all of the commitments specified. Fifteen theses are provided for further consideration, each of which seeks to outline the ways in which the editors believe an Evangelical Calvinism may proceed if it is to become a robust dialogue partner and contributor to the family of Reformed theologies.

In the spirit of Augustine we humbly invite the reader to *tolle lege*—"take up and read."

Myk Habets
*Doctor Serviens Ecclesiae*
Auckland, New Zealand

Bobby Grow
*Soli Deo Gloria*
Washington, America

# BIBLIOGRAPHY

Allen, R. Michael. *Reformed Theology*. London: T. & T. Clark, 2010.

Alston, Wallace M. and Welker, Michael, eds. *Reformed Theology: Identity and Ecumenicity*. Grand Rapids: Eerdmans, 2003.

Armstrong, Brian G. *Calvinism and the Amyraut Heresy: Protestant Scholasticism and Humanism in Seventeenth-Century France*. Madison, Milwaukee: The University of Wisconsin Press, 1969.

Barth, Karl. *Church Dogmatics*. 4 Vols. Edited by G. W. Bromiley and T. F. Torrance. Translated by G. W. Bromiley. Edinburgh: T. & T. Clark, 1961.

———. *The Theology of the Reformed Confessions*. Translated by Darrell L. Guder and Judith J. Guder. Louisville/London: Westminster John Knox, 2002.

Bagchi, David and Steinmetz, David C., eds. *The Cambridge Companion to Reformation Theology*. Cambridge: Cambridge University Press, 2004.

Bierma, Lyle D. *German Calvinism in the Confessional Age: The Covenant Theology of Caspar Olevianus*. Grand Rapids: Baker, 1996.

Bebbington, David. *Evangelicalism in Modern Britain: A History from the 1730s to the 1980s*. London: Unwin Hyman, 1989.

Bierma, Lyle D. *German Calvinism in the Confessional Age: The Covenant Theology of Caspar Olevianus*. Grand Rapids, Michigan: Baker, 1996.

Bozeman, Theodore Dwight. *The Precisianist Strain: Disciplinary Religion & Antinomian Backlash In Puritanism To 1638*. Chapel Hill/London: University of North Carolina Press, 2004.

Calvin, John. *Commentary on The Epistles of Paul the Apostle to the Corinthians*. Translated by John Pringle. Grand Rapids: Baker, 1979.

Calvin, John. *Institutes of the Christian Religion. Edited by* John T. McNeill. Translated by Ford Lewis Battles. Philadelphia: Westminster, 1977.

Clark, R. Scott. *Recovering the Reformed Confession: Our Theology, Piet and Practice*. Philipsburg: P & R, 2008.

Crisp, Oliver D. "Federalism vs Realism: Charles Hodge, Augustus Strong and William Shedd on the Imputation of Sin," *International Journal of Systematic Theology* 8 (2006) 55–71.

Cross, Richard. *The Metaphysics of the Incarnation: Thomas Aquinas to Duns Scotus*. Oxford: Oxford University Press, 2002.

Evans, William B. *Imputation and Impartation: Union with Christ in American Reformed Theology*. Studies in Christian Thought. Eugene: Wipf & Stock, 2008.

Fergusson, David A. S. "Predestination: A Scottish Perspective." *Scottish Journal of Theology* 46 (1993) 457–78.

Frame, John. http://www.framepoythress.org/frame_articles/2010Clark.htm#_ftn1.

Gill, John. *A Complete Body of Doctrinal and Practical Divinity*. Paris: Baptist Standard Bearer, 1984.

Hall, David W., editor. *Preaching Like Calvin: Sermons From the 500th Anniversary Celebration*. Phillipsburg: P & R, 2010.

———. *Tributes to John Calvin: A Celebration of His Quincentenary*. Phillipsburg: Presbyterian and Reformed, 2010.

Hesselink, I. John "Calvin's Theology." In *The Cambridge Companion to John Calvin*, edited by Donald K. McKim, 74–92. Cambridge: Cambridge University Press, 2004.

Hiebert, Paul. *Anthropological Reflections on Missiological Issues*. Grand Rapids: Baker, 1994.

Horton, Michael. *Introducing Covenant Theology*. Grand Rapids: Baker, 2009.

———. "Reformation Essentials—Five Pillars of the Reformation." *Modern Reformation* (March-April, 1994) no pages. Online: http://www.monergism.com/thethreshold/articles/onsite/essentials.html.

———. "Semper Reformanda," *Tabletalk Magazine* (October 1, 2009) no pages. Online: http://www.ligonier.org/learn/articles/semper-reformanda/.

———. "Who Exactly Are the Evangelicals?" No pages. 9Marks E-Journal. Online: http://www.9marks.org/ejournal/who-exactly-are-evangelicals.

———. *God of Promise: Introducing Covenant Theology*. Grand Rapids: Baker, 2006.

Kettler, Christian D. "The Vicarious Repentance of Christ in the Theology of John McLeod Campbell and R C Moberly." *Scottish Journal of Theology* 38 (1985) 529–43.

Knight, Janice. *Orthodoxies in Massachusetts: Rereading American Puritanism*. Cambridge, Massachusetts: Harvard University Press, 1997.

Lachman, David C. *The Marrow Controversy: An Historical and Theological Analysis*. Edinburgh: Rutherford House, 1988.

Lane, Anthony N. S. "Calvin's Doctrine of Assurance Revisited," in *Tributes to John Calvin: A Celebration of His Quincentenary*, 270–313. The Calvin 500 Series. Edited by David W. Hall. Phillipsburg: P & R, 2010.

Larsen, Timothy, and Daniel J. Treier, editors. *The Cambridge Companion to Evangelical Theology* Cambridge: Cambridge University Press, 2007.

Letham, Robert. *The Holy Trinity: In Scripture, History, Theology, and Worship*. Phillipsburg: P & R, 2004.

McCormack, Bruce L. "The Actuality of God: *Karl Barth in Conversation with Open Theism*." In *Engaging the Doctrine of God: Contemporary Protestant Perspectives*, edited by Bruce L. McCormack, 185–242. Grand Rapids: Baker/Edinburgh: Rutherford House, 2008.

McDonald, Suzanne. *Re-Imaging Election: Divine Election as Representing God to Others and Others to God*. Grand Rapids: Eerdmans, 2010.

McGowan, Andrew T. B. *The Federal Theology of Thomas Boston*. Rutherford Studies: Historical Theology Carlisle: Paternoster, 1997.

McKim, Donald K. *Introducing the Reformed Faith: Biblical Revelation Christian Tradition Contemporary Significance*. Louisville/London: Westminster John Knox, 2001.

———. ed. *The Cambridge Companion to John Calvin*. Cambridge: Cambridge University Press, 2004.

———. ed. *Major Themes in the Reformed Tradition*. Grand Rapids, Michigan: Eerdmans, 1992.

Moltmann, Jürgen. "Theologia Reformata Et Semper Reformanda." In *Toward the Future of Reformed Theology: Tasks, Topics, Traditions*, edited by David Willis and Michael Welker, 120–35. Grand Rapids: Eerdmans, 1999.

Muller, Richard A. *Christ And The Decree: Christology And Predestination In Reformed Theology From Calvin To Perkins*. Durham, NC: Labyrinth, 1986.

———. "How Many Points?" *Calvin Theological Journal* 28 (1993) 425–33.

———. "John Calvin and Later Calvinism: The Identity of the Reformed Tradition." In *The Cambridge Companion to Reformation Theology*, edited by David Bagchi and David C. Steinmetz, 130–49. Cambridge: Cambridge University Press, 2004.

Noll, Mark A. *The Rise of Evangelicalism: The Age of Edwards, Whitefield and the Wesleys*. Downers Grove, IL: InterVarsity, 2003.

Partee, Charles. *The Theology of John Calvin*. Louisville/London: Westminster John Knox, 2008.

Pinnock, Clark H. *Flame of Love: A Theology of the Holy Spirit.* Downers Grove, IL: InterVarsity, 1996.

Rohls, Jan. *Reformed Confessions: Theology from Zurich to Barmen.* Louisville: Westminster John Knox, 1998.

Smith, James K. A. *Letters to A Young Calvinist: An Invitation to the Reformed Tradition.* Grand Rapids: Brazos, 2010.

Sproul, R. C. *What is Reformed Theology? Understanding the Basics.* Grand Rapids: Baker, 2005.

Spurgeon, Charles H. *A Defence of Calvinism.* London: Banner of Truth, 2008.

———. *The Early Years.* London: Banner of Truth, 1962.

Steele, David N., and Thomas, Curtis C. *Five Points of Calvinism.* Phillipsburg: P & R, 1963.

Strong, Augustus H. *Christ in Creation and Ethical Monism.* Philadelphia: Roger Williams, 1899.

———. *Systematic Theology: A Compendium and Commonplace-Book*, 8th edition. 1886. Reprint. Philadelphia: Judson, 1946.

———. *What Shall I Believe? A Primer of Christian Theology.* Grand Rapids: Revell, 1922.

Torrance, James B. *Worship, Community and the Triune God of Grace.* Downers Grove, IL: InterVarsity, 1996.

Torrance, James B., and R. C. Walls, *John Duns Scotus: Doctor of the Church.* Edinburgh: Handsel, 1992.

Torrance, Thomas F. *Atonement: The Person and Work of Christ.* Edited by Robert T. Walker. Downers Grove, IL: InterVarsity Academic, 2009.

———. "Calvin's Doctrine of the Trinity." In *Trinitarian Perspectives: Toward Doctrinal Agreement,* 41–76. Edinburgh: T. & T. Clark, 1994.

———. *The Christian Doctrine of God: One Being Three Persons.* Edinburgh: T. & T. Clark, 1996.

———. *The Ground and Grammar of Theology: Consonacne Between Theolopgy and Science.* Edinburgh: T. & T. Clark, 2001.

———. *Incarnation: The Person and Life of Christ.* Edited by Robert T. Walker. Downers Grove, IL: InterVarsity Academic, 2008.

———. *The Mediation of Christ.* Grand Rapids: Eerdmans, 1983.

———. *Scottish Theology: From John Knox to John McLeod Campbell.* Edinburgh: T. & T. Clark, 1996.

———. *Theology in Reconstruction.* Grand Rapids: Eerdmans, 1965.

Trueman, Carl. "Wrongheaded Reformations." *The Monthly Record* (August 2008) 17.

van der Leer, Teun. "The True Calvinist is a Baptist." *Baptist Quarterly* 44 (2011) 21–35.

Warfield, Benjamin B. "Calvin's Doctrine of the Trinity." In *Calvin and Augustine,* edited by Samuel G. Crig, 187–284. Philadelphia: P & R, 1974.

Weinandy, Thomas G. *The Father's Spirit of Sonship: Reconceiving the Trinity.* Edinburgh: T. & T. Clark, 1995.

White, Thomas J., editor. *The Analogy of Being: Invention of the Antichrist or the Wisdom of God?* Grand Rapids: Eerdmans, 2011.

Wright, David F. "The Scottish Reformation: Theology and Theologians." In *The Cambridge Companion to Reformation Theology,* edited by David Bagchi and David C. Steinmetz, 174–93. Cambridge: Cambridge University Press, 2004.

# PART ONE

# Prolegomena—Historical Theology

# 2

# The Phylogeny of Calvin's Progeny

## *A Prolusion*

CHARLES PARTEE

## INTRODUCTION

PROFESSIONAL RESPONSIBILITY REQUIRES THAT ecclesiasticals heed the advice of Ecclesiasticus (44:1) to "praise famous men." This task requires relating properly to the most praiseworthy among them, and for those who choose to relate to the general designation "Calvinist," the result is specifically a serious appreciation of, and association with, his theology in sum or in significant part. However, this common destination is approached along widely different paths by theologians, who often stand uneasily together at the end of the road with elbows sharpened by numerous—and often complex and intense—disagreements along the way.

Given the endemic nominalism distantly derived from their kinsman, William of Occam; given the present megatrend of individualism, whether smooth or rugged; and given the genuine variety and reality of personal diversity, sorting theologians into species may be compared to herding catechumens. The older quest to identify subjects by an "unvarying essence" must be replaced by the more modest Wittgensteinian description of shifting "family resemblances." Some sweaty workers in Calvin's vineyard carry no union card and wear no pocket label, preferring to harvest the ripest fruit with no expression of fealty to the field boss. Additionally, selecting and enumerating similarities and differences is greatly complicated by one's own standpoint and one's point of standing is reciprocally affected personally and professionally by the community in which one is comfortable. This ancient struggle to draw the correct distinction between "we" and "they" occupies the Apostle Paul in Philippians 1:15–8. The psychological mysteries of theological friendships and the social processes that form theological communities, while not beyond the interest, are certainly beyond the competence of this writer. Moreover, some theologians are difficult to classify because, while not officers of the Calvin club, they seem to be honorary members by way of ethnicity, education, or friendship, albeit with varying degrees of commitment. Nevertheless, and therefore, an attempt to sketch a fair-minded analysis of the main theological issues that identify and then divide Calvinists should be useful in fostering further discussion. Hopefully, such a discussion can be generally helpful for types even without being actually precise for persons, who like Shakespeare's Antony claimed Cleopatra presented an "infinite variety" (II.3.241). Calvin observes a Christian's need "to communicate himself to those with whom he sees Christ in common."[1] The problem, of course, is the diversity of seeing Christ in common.

"Calvinism" as a descriptive label is applied in a bewildering variety of ways, especially its omnibus employment in literary contexts by such scriveners as Mark Twain, Herman Melville, William Faulkner, and John Updike.[2] Among theologies, and stroking broadly, there are four major Christian doctrinal traditions: Eastern Orthodoxy, Roman Catholicism, Lutheranism, and Calvinism. The latter two are sometimes counted together as different versions of one Protestant theology. Nowadays by some "Calvinism" is claimed to be more accurately described as Reformed theology because Calvin is regarded as only one and not the chief owner of that domain, but this view obfuscates the usual focus on Calvin and does not serve the purpose of this essay. These four rich traditions have provided the wider context for Christian reflections, and while every theologian hopes to be orthodox, catholic, and evangelical,

1. Calvin, *Institution of the Christian Religion*, 150. (*Calvini Opera Selecta*, I.147). Calvin's *Institutes of the Christian Religion* (1559) is cited in parentheses from the Library of Christian Classics edition by book, chapter, and paragraph. Calvin's Biblical commentaries are cited in the latest available English translation by book, chapter, and verse. CO indicates the *Calvini Opera*.

2. Cf. Shurr, *Rappacini's Children*.

the other traditions may be set aside for the present focus on Calvinism, until recently ordinarily divided between liberal and conservative.

The terms "liberal" and "conservative" are most often used politically, ethically, and sociologically. Applied to Calvinists theologically the dual (and duel) distinction between conservative and liberal is sufficiently commonplace to appear in popular novels. For example, the first major character in John Updike's *In the Beauty of the Lilies* is a minister educated by Warfield and the Hodges in the conservative "old Princeton theology." His manse, prominently displaying the forty-four volumes of Calvin's *Commentaries*, is located on the corner of Broad Way and Straight Street (Chapter One), adumbrating the conflict between straight and narrow, broad and wide which plunges this pastor into loss of faith. In a memorable confrontation, his judicatory superior (a graduate of Union Theological Seminary in New York) seeks to dissuade the resignation on the grounds that private loss of faith does not automatically compromise the public practice of ministry. However, the "conservative Princeton" conscience cannot accept this "liberal Union" casuistry and the Calvinist (or Presbyterian)-themed drama unfolds.[3]

For a long time the distinction between conservative and liberal Calvinists seemed adequate although there were always theologians in the robing room not appareled à la mode for either. In more recent days a third way is being identified by this book. In addition to sharp divergences from the two previously recognized options, now-named evangelical Calvinists in the English-speaking world have become aware of their convergences. The common terms conservative, liberal, and evangelical have wide ranging connotations with many volumes devoted to their explication. They are used in this essay to distinguish types of Calvinists. That is, this essay attempts to distinguish (1) The Conservative Calvinists from (2) The Liberal Calvinists from (3) The Evangelical Calvinists. Obviously Calvinists of all sorts (including those who are presently out-of-sorts) have in common that they are not Eastern Orthodox, Roman Catholic, Lutheran, or Pentecostal, meaning putatively they agree on many essential issues, but in fact vigorously disagree on some crucial components, including most notably the theological starting point.

According to the present heuristic analysis striving for simplicity and clarity, the Protestant Reformation put together three fa-

---

3. Updike explores loss of faith more directly in his novel, *Roger's Version*.

mous alones: Scripture alone, Faith alone, and Christ alone, which among Calvinists are commonly affirmed but differently interpreted.[4] (I) Conservative Calvinists, represented by Charles Hodge and his sympathizers, advance Scripture alone emphasizing its divinity before its humanity; (II) Liberal Calvinists, represented by Friedrich Schleiermacher and his sympathizers, advance faith alone emphasizing its subjectivity before its object; and (III) Evangelical Calvinists, represented by Karl Barth and his sympathizers, advance Christ alone emphasizing his person before his work. The doctrine of Scripture held by Conservative Calvinists is mostly rejected by Liberal and Evangelical Calvinists. The doctrine of Faith held by Liberal Calvinists is commonly disclaimed by Conservative and Evangelical Calvinists. The doctrine of Christ held by Evangelical Calvinists is generally not affirmed by Conservative and Liberal Calvinists. Since the centrality of Christ, the reality of faith, and the authority of Scripture are absolutely essential elements of every Christian witness, the defining differences among Calvinists are not with the doctrines as grasped but as held. In each case the doctrine selected for first focus by one group of Calvinists, and to receive a primary theological emphasis, is denied that place by others. In other words, the interplay of the context and content of the great doctrines that unite Calvinists also divide them. For conservatives the best way to Christ is through Scripture; for liberals the best way to Christ is through faith; for evangelicals the best way to Scripture and faith is through Christ. In matters of form a chief concern for conservatives appears to be understanding the faith with its concomitant passion for rational answers. For liberals a major concern is experiencing the faith with a passion for experiential certainty. For evangelicals a primary concern is confessing the faith with a passion for doxological encounter. Since each concern is a passion for all, the distinctions, being real, are not hard and fast but soft and loose. Thus a precise formula for differences and a precise identification for persons is not possible.

For all Christians worship and service are first-order, nonnegotiable activities. So, too, required of all is serious thinking about God (theo-logos), but not with the same range and depth that is expected of doctors of the church. Recognizing this reality, Calvin's *Draft*

---

4. As suggested by Nancy E. Lowmaster in personal correspondence, if Pentecostalism is considered a fifth major doctrinal tradition, then a first emphasis on grace (*charisma*) alone would be included.

*Ecclesiastical Orders* of 1541 specify, "four orders of office instituted by our Lord for the government of the Church." These orders consist of pastors, elders, deacons, and doctors, with the latter especially responsible for instruction in true doctrine that the purity of the Gospel might not be perverted by ignorance.[5]

The banishment of ignorance is not the sole goal of the Gospel but knowing "the only true God, and Jesus Christ whom thou has sent" (John 17:3) certainly includes it. Calvin believed that "None will ever be a good minister of the Word of God except that he be a first-rate scholar" (*CO* 26,406). Especially for the doctors, scholarship means understanding and accepting truth wherever it appears (*Inst.* 2.2.15). Calvin insists, "[I]t is superstitious to refuse to make any use of secular authors. For since all truth is of God, if any ungodly man has said anything true, we should not reject it, for it also has come from God" (*Com. Tit.* 1:12).

Perhaps in the rather near future theologians will be required to engage natural scientists as conversation partners, as recommended by Alister E. McGrath.[6] However, even if science and religion become a marriage of true minds to which we must not admit impediments, still theology cannot easily break away from its longtime romance with philosophy. If theology were ever the queen of sciences, then philosophy was ever her hand maid. At this level academic theological reflection is a second-order activity inevitably utilizing conceptual tools forged or sharpened in philosophical workshops. After all physicists, too, are designated doctors of philosophy. Certainly every professional theologian is connected to the broader intellectual tradition in which he was trained and within which her preferences and loyalties are expressed. These various contexts, choices, and commitments inevitably produce diversity.

Setting aside Hegel's influence on process theology and Kierkegaard's on existential theology, the believing heart encounters three major mind sets: the searching mind, represented by Plato; the answering mind, represented by Aristotle; and the critiquing mind, represented by Kant. To the extent these categories are useful, the Roman Catholics (as seen in Thomas Aquinas) and Reformed Scholastics (as exemplified in Jerome Zanchius and Peter Martyr Vermigli) evince a marked affinity for Aristotle's confidence in reason and therefore his logical writings.

5. Calvin, *Theological Treatises*, 58.

6. McGrath, *A Scientific Theology*.

Liberal theologians, turning to experience and away from reason, like their father Schleiermacher, seem to have Immanuel Kant sitting on their shoulder whispering in their ear about reason's limitations. Prior to the critical philosophy of Kant conceived in response to the skeptical philosophy of Hume, the counterweight to Aristotle was Plato, whose *Dialogues* of unrelenting search have an affinity for dialectical theologies like Karl Barth's. According to Barth, "Our viewing and conceiving of God and our speaking of Him will never be a completed work showing definitive results: and therefore we can never view what we do as something which has already 'succeeded.'"[7]

## THE CONSERVATIVE CALVINISTS

The largest and most obvious classification, by way of encomium or opprobrium, is variously called Orthodox Calvinism, Westminster Calvinism, Dutch Calvinism, Reformed Scholasticism, Federal Calvinism, hyper-Calvinism, or—by historical and terminological default—simply Calvinism. This category has occupied the longest historical time and produced the largest theological volume. The line is traced from John Calvin through Theodore Beza (1519–1605) to Francis Turretin (1632–87) to Francis Gomarus (1563–1641) (and other divines who are gathered in Heinrich Heppe's compendius *Reformed Dogmatics*). Along the way worthies like Jacob Arminius (1560–1609) and Moses Amyraut (1596–1664) were excluded from this form of Calvinism. Special public approval is applied to the Canons of Dort (1618–19) and The Westminster Confession (1648) with The Helvetic Consensus Formula (1675) hovering contentiously in the background. The American lineage includes Charles Hodge, Louis Berkhof, Richard A. Muller and their many learned and like-minded friends. They are designated as Conservative Calvinism here in recognition of their claim to conserve (by properly developing) the theology Calvin represents. The assumption behind the claim is the ability to identify and extend the essential features of Calvin's theology without substantial change (i.e., Calvin unaccommodated). Of course the issue is whether the result actually *defends*, as its proponents insist, or really *distorts* Calvin's theology, as its opponents believe.

---

7. Barth, *CD* II/1, 208. Barth's philosopher brother Heinrich caused Karl to be "faced once more with the wisdom of Plato," Busch, *Karl Barth: His Life from Letters and Autobiographical Texts*, 116.

Conservative Calvinism can be characterized as an answering theology. That is, its advocates have a genuine concern for answers and expend vast amounts of intellectual energy analyzing and explaining doctrines on the conviction that clear and distinct answers in theological reflection are not only desirable but achievable.[8] This presumption leads to a bold (even polemical) attitude toward those who question the proffered answers. This confidence is typified by the Westminster Confession, which, sweeping through the faith of the Church, appeals to "mystery" only once (concerning predestination). Presumably understanding how the omniscient and omnipotent God accepts petitions and grants prayers does not qualify as awe-full or mysterious, to say nothing of miraculous.[9]

The basis for confident answers is illustrated in the combination of revelation and reason. According to the *Westminster Confession*, "The whole counsel of God, is either expressly set down in Scripture, or by good and necessary consequences may be deduced from Scripture." (I.6). Revelation and reason are understood, if not defined, as one continuous rather than two separate concepts.[10] This view often entails an admiration of the "common sense philosophy" of Thomas Reid and denial of the critique of reason offered by the British Empiricists, especially David Hume.[11] Trust in reason among conservative Calvinists has an affinity

8. Bernstein, *Beyond Objectivism and Relativism*, 16–20, characterizes the need to find a clear and distinct idea on which to base knowledge the "Cartesian Anxiety," which he claims is one of the driving forces of Western civilization leading either to objectivism or relativism.

9. According to Mackintosh, *The Christian Apprehension of God*, 140, "Of our thoughts concerning the spiritual being of God it is supremely true that *omnia exeunt in mysterium*—unfathomableness is the end of all."

10. For a critical note on the theological confidence in reason expressed in the *Westminster Confession* see Partee, *The Theology of John Calvin*, 310–12.

11. According to Wolterstorff, *Thomas Reid and the Story of Epistemology*, Reid (1710–1796) ranks with Kant as the two great philosophers of the latter part of the eighteenth century. In his appeal to the piety of "common sense" Reid offers an alternative to Hume's skepticism by contemplating and trusting the mystery of what we cannot know by the "way of ideas." This defense of ungrounded trust makes Reid "the first great critic of what in recent years has come to be called 'classical foundationalism.'" Wolterstorff, "Hume and Reid," 406. Kant addresses Reid as an opponent of Hume with withering scorn. Reid "discovered a more convenient way to be obstinate and defiant without any insight, namely by appealing to *common sense*. [T]o appeal to common sense is one of the subtle inventions of recent times, by which the most vapid chucklehead (schalste Schwätzer) can confidently take up with the soundest thinker and hold his own with

with the high view of reason maintained by the classical philosophers, a dream of reason that has not disappeared with the dawn of the modern day but has faded considerably. Since the doctrine of reason is virtually coextensive with the history of philosophy, the use and ab-use of reason, perforce adjudicated by reason itself, is too complicated to analyze in detail as a distinction among Calvinists—all of whom seek to be reasonable, but in different and subtle ways.[12]

The greatest and most obvious disagreement among Calvinists concerns the view of Scripture. It can be argued that Calvin himself did not develop a doctrine of Scripture in the modern mode, but among conservative Calvinists the Bible is employed as the epistemological foundation for theological propositions. In defending this conviction conservatives (making common cause with fundamentalists) evince a strong sympathy for the divinity of the Bible with the concomitant claim of Biblical infallibility and/or inerrancy, which other Calvinists sharply reject.[13] Were the Bible not perfect, they reason, only imperfect conclu-

---

him. And seen in the light of day this is nothing but an appeal to the judgment of the crowd—applause at which the philosopher blushes but the common popinjay (populäre Witzling) struts and triumphs." Kant, *Prolegomena to Any Future Metaphysics*, 9. Of curious interest is the rejection by some Calvinists of philosophical foundationalism (reason) and the acceptance of Biblical foundationalism (revelation).

12. Unlike the rational confidence of Westminster is the equally Calvinistic conviction that God is both unfathomable and truly revealed. This means, according to Mackintosh (*The Christian Apprehension of God*, 73) that "the contradictories are held together firmly, that God is known and yet not known. In experience the difficulty does not vanish, but it becomes endurable because it is seen to be necessary[.] It is the same vital, not accidental, antinomy as we meet with in the familiar words: 'To know the love of Christ, which passeth knowledge'" (Eph 3:19). In short, Christian theology presents "internal difficulties [which] give us no rest" (147–48).

13. The identification of evangelicalism (called conservatism in this essay) with Biblical infallibility and inerrancy is presented by Lindsell, *The Battle for the Bible*, well summarized on page 210. Dockery lists six variations on inerrancy in Dockery, "Variations on Inerrancy," 10–11. Erickson, *Christian Theology*, 234, after a review of the issue adopts a position of "full inerrancy" which lies between "absolute inerrancy" and "limited inerrancy." Hodges, "Scripture," 210 writes "The word 'evangelical' today "refers to the branch of the Christian church that adheres firmly to several basic convictions, the principal one being that Scripture is the inspired Word of God that serves as the infallible guide for both knowledge of God and Christian living. [However], recently this strong tenet and its corollary of inerrancy have come under attack by thinkers who consider themselves evangelicals." Abraham, *The Divine Inspiration of Holy Scripture* offers both a defense and critique of inerrancy fearing that the fundamentalist wing of the evangelical tradition will repudiate those who do not hold the strict and traditional doctrine of inerrancy and appealing to the Wesleyan Quadrilateral. A trenchant at-

sions could be drawn from it. This position dodges the Roman objection that an infallible Book requires an infallible Church to interpret it.

The issues of infallibility and inerrancy can be separated or denied altogether, although if not shading into each other they seem to loom together in the near background. For instance, one could reject the applicability of the term inerrant and yet hold with Westminster that the Holy Scripture as the Word of God provides a "full persuasion and assurance of the infallible truth, and divine authority thereof" (I.5). Likewise, "[t]he infallible rule of interpretation of Scripture is the Scripture itself" (I.9). However, the term "infallible" is not applied to the text of the Bible here. In the first instance it modifies truth and in the second, the rule of interpretation. The erstwhile ministerial vow that the Bible is "the infallible rule of faith and practice" refers to the function of Scripture in the life of the Church. A doctrine of infallibility could be, and often is, maintained with regard to the general purpose of Scripture but abandoned as applied to specific Biblical texts. If so, the assertion of Scriptural infallibility becomes a doxological statement of personal faith rather than a purported description of the actual or original pages. Infallibility is now a confessional rather than an epistemological affirmation. The continuing problem is that any assertion of inability to error is being made by a fallible human being who presumably will fallibly judge infallibility. According to liberals and evangelicals, the Bible as a book (or collection of books) is more accurately considered perfectly reliable but not reliably perfect (as suggested by most theories of infallibility and required by all doctrines of inerrancy and verbal inspiration).[14]

Calvin and the other Reformers were convinced that the meaning of Scripture could be explained only by Scripture itself—not by Pope or Church. In opposition, *Sola Scriptura* was attacked as early as 1678 by the French priest Richard Simon who sought to reclaim ecclesiastical tradition by demonstrating the unreliability of the texts and thereby the incapacity of Scripture alone to support faith alone. With the Bible

---

tack on inerrancy is offered in chapter three by James Barr, *Fundamentalism*. A helpful survey of inerrancy, verbal inspiration and plenary inspiration is found in Beegle, *The Inspiration of Scripture*. Burtchall, *Catholic Theories of Biblical Inspiration Since 1810,* 164–229 devotes an interesting chapter to Roman Catholic views of inspiration without inerrancy.

14. The seriousness and range of defending *sola scriptura* with verbal inspiration is indicated by parallel developments in Lutheran orthodoxy. See Preus, *The Inspiration of Scripture.*

under critical attack as the sixteenth century ended, the newly emerging orthodoxy defended the epistemological authority of the Bible. Additionally, the distinction sharpened between "subjective" and "objective" with the Scripture claimed as the objective principle of authority. The Bible was regarded as the central epistemological base directly, inerrantly, and infallibly inspired by God, amenable to the logic of reason, susceptible to the discovery of principles, and the development of rational propositions.

This conservative or scholastic development is illustrated in the Article One location of Scripture in the *Westminster Confession* which, in identifying the infallible rule of interpretation, testifies to the sufficiency, necessity, extent, inspiration, and authority of Holy Scripture. The theory of the verbal inspiration of the Scriptures was advanced by Francis Turretin who insisted the Bible was inerrant. "The prophets did not fall into mistakes in those things which they wrote . . . not even in the smallest particulars; otherwise faith in the whole of Scripture would be rendered doubtful."[15] This view received confessional status in the Helvetic Consensus Formula, "a defense of the scholastic Calvinism of the Synod of Dort against the theology of Saumur."[16] The Swiss theologians, defending the literal integrity of the Masoretic text, claimed the divine inspiration of the Hebrew vowels against the emerging scholarly consensus that they were a separate work of later Jewish grammarians. They insisted "The Hebrew original of the Old Testament . . . is not only in its consonants, but in its vowels—either the vowel points themselves, or at least the power of the points—not only in its matter, but in its words, inspired of God."[17]

The transition to North American shores of Turretin's conviction of the Bible's inerrancy was fostered by Archibald Alexander (1772–1851) and his student, Charles Hodge (1797–1878) who repristinated Turretin even more fully than Alexander in defending the plenary verbal inspiration of the Bible as an infallible communication from God. In an 1857

15. Turretin, *Institutes of Elenctic Theology* (1679) 69. "[T]he Scriptures are inspired of God as the primary foundation of faith [being of] divine and infallible truth" (62). When the divinity of Scripture is proved, its infallibility necessarily follows (70) meaning that all "contradictions found in Scripture are apparent, not real" (72). For a brief account of the role of Turretin see Rogers and McKim, *The Authority and Interpretation of the Bible*, 172–84.

16. Schaff, *The Creeds of Christendom*, 478.

17. Leith, *Creeds of the Churches*, 310.

article on revelation and inspiration Hodge roundly contemns the new German theology as teaching that the Bible does not contain a revelation and therefore has no need for a doctrine of inspiration. To the contrary, "the simple end and object of inspiration was to render the sacred writers infallible" because "Faith in Christ involves faith in the Scriptures as the word of God, and faith in the Scriptures as the word of God is faith in their plenary inspiration." Hodge cautions that this faith is not founded on reason or feelings, but "rests in the demonstration of the Spirit." Nevertheless, appealing to reason, Hodge states, the Holy Spirit can "guide the mental operations of a man, so that he shall speak or write without error, and still be perfectly self-controlled and free." Hodge admits there are some difficulties in the text of the Bible but they are so "miraculously small" and so "wondrously few and trivial" that they can be safely ignored.

According to Hodge, the new Teutonic theology teaches that "Christianity does not consist in propositions, but is a life in the soul, the apostles did not go forth to teach a system of doctrine . . . but to awaken man's power of spiritual intuition." This doctrine, Hodge insists, destroys the authority of Scripture, and, in powerfully caustic images, Hodge suggests Christians in England and America "who strip themselves of their clothing that they may encounter *in puris naturalibus* the wintry blast of error" should dress more carefully. Attributing to the Bible only human authority "is lamentable when open infidels take this ground; but it is enough to make a man cover his face with his hands in shame, to see those who profess to be Christians, and who are set for the defense of the gospel, through treachery, vanity, or weakness, assuming the same position." Hodge concludes, "The contents of the Scriptures are not derived from the human mind . . . but are derived from the Holy Ghost, and consequently the authority of its teachings is not human but divine. The Bible is the Word of God, and not the word of man."[18] The younger Hodge and Warfield insist "that the Scriptures not only contain, but ARE The Word of God, and hence that all their elements and all their affirmations are absolutely errorless, and binding the faith and obedience of

18. Hodge and Warfield, "Inspiration," 690, 667, 661, 673, 682, 686, 691–92, 694, 695, 698. In his *Systematic Theology* Charles Hodge writes "The infallibility and divine authority of the Scriptures are due to the fact that they are the word of God; and they are the word of God because they were given by the inspiration of the Holy Ghost." See Hodge, *Systematic Theology*, vol. 1, 153.

men."[19] Most Calvinists affirm "the Bible is the Word of God" but many also insist the evidence requires the additional conclusion that the Bible is "the word of man."

During Hodge's long life the discipline of Biblical criticism continued to gather strength with its interest in applying to the Bible the same methods used with other books, such as questions of authorship, place, context, and intent. In opposition to the continuing development of critical studies and unnerved by developments in natural sciences, especially Darwin, Archibald Alexander Hodge (1823–86) re-presented his father's philosophical views but now in the sterner face of the developing historical and scientific revolutions. In dealing with admitted "difficulties" in the Biblical text, the elder Hodge had observed but dismissed "specks of sandstone" in the "marble of the Parthenon," but in the lifetime of his son these specks appeared too large to be overlooked. The result was the retreat of the location of inerrancy to an extremely problematic claim about non-existent manuscripts. According to A. A. Hodge only the original autographs of the Scripture were verbally inerrant. Since no discrepancy could ever be proved to reside on nonexistent pages, the doctrine of inspiration seemed perfectly secure. This assertion that the lost autographs of Scripture were inerrant and infallible has the inestimable advantage that no evidence exists capable of falsifying the claim. The disadvantage, of course, is that no evidence exists capable of verifying the claim either. In fact the affirmation of inerrancy is not based on evidence at all, but on a convictional deduction of logically necessary action derived from the concept of God's perfections. Writing in 1881, the younger Hodge defines the inspiration of Scripture as "the superintendence by God of the writers in the entire process of their writing, which accounts for nothing whatever but the absolute infallibility of the record in which the revelation, once generated, appears in the original autograph." Inspiration is taken to produce an infallible and absolutely errorless record of God's revelation applied to both facts and doctrines.

Hodge grants that the Bible may now contain "apparent affirmations presumably inconsistent with the present teachings of science, with facts of history, or with other statements of the sacred books themselves." Such results are only to be expected in imperfect copies of ancient writings. Still in the original autographs the Holy Spirit everywhere secured

19. Hodge and Warfield, "Inspiration," 237.

"the errorless expression in language of the thought designed by God." Interestingly, human agency is most emphatically asserted but within strict limits. "The Scriptures were generated through sixteen centuries of this divinely regulated concurrence of God and man, of the natural and supernatural, of reason and revelation, or providence and grace." For all these admissions Hodge concludes with a mighty "Nevertheless."

> Nevertheless, the historical faith of the Church has always been that all the affirmations of Scripture of all kinds, whether of spiritual doctrine or duty, or of physical or historical fact, or of psychological or philosophical principle, are without any error, when the *ipsissima verba* of the original autographs are ascertained and interpreted in their natural and intended sense.[20]

Continuing this interpretation and co-author with A. A. Hodge of the 1881 essay on inspiration, Benjamin Breckinridge Warfield (1851–1921) carried the fight for inerrancy and infallibility into the early twentieth century with decreasing success, but not without recent champions. In his chapter "God's Mighty Speech Acts: The Doctrine of Scripture Today" Kevin J. Vanhoozer defines and defends Warfield's as "the received view."[21] Warfield firmly believed he was following Calvin. "Nothing is more certain than that Calvin held both to 'verbal inspiration' and the 'inerrancy of Scripture[.]'"[22] According to Warfield, the Bible gives us truth without error. Moreover, since all the books of the Bible are equally inspired, all are alike infallible in what they teach.[23]

An entire volume (450 pages) of Warfield's collected articles is devoted to Revelation and Inspiration. Concerning inspiration, he complains, "Wherever five 'advanced thinkers' assemble, at least six theories as to inspiration are likely to be ventilated." These advanced thinkers reject "the church's constant and abiding conviction as to the divinity of the Scriptures." In opposition, Warfield writes that we need to "remind ourselves that this attitude of entire trust in every word of the Scriptures

---

20. Hodge and Warfield, "Inspiration," 237, 231, 230, 238.

21. In Vanhoozer, *God, Scripture, and Hermeneutics.*

22. Warfield, "Calvin's Doctrine of the Knowledge of God," 61 n. 36.

23. Nicole, "Induction and Deduction with Reference to Inspiration," 95–102, continues this interpretation declaring, "The doctrine of inerrancy appears in the first place as a corollary (or implicate) of the doctrine of the divine authorship of the Scripture," (98).

has been characteristic of the people of God from the very foundation of the Church."

On the divine origin of the Bible, Warfield proposes to lay down one after another "a series of propositions most baldly stated . . . which will, . . . it is hoped, be immediately partly evident from their simple statement." These propositions, Warfield declares, do not constitute an argument but only an inquiry. He claims the process, while not demonstrative, is inductive.[24] As a matter of fact, it is deductive. Warfield's approach is rationalistic or idealistic not analytical or empirical. The actual reality of the Biblical texts is more complicated than speculative and synthetic theories about the Biblical texts.

Among more recent proponents is G. Gresham Machen (1881–1937),[25] who believed that true Christianity is found only in Calvinistic faith as taught by Charles Hodge and Benjamin Breckinridge Warfield and others of the "Princeton school." On that conviction Machen conducted an unrelenting attack on modern naturalistic liberalism, insisting that in addition to an over emphasis on the humanity of Jesus as teacher to the neglect of his role as savior, liberalism emphasized human experience rather than the infallible and inerrant Scriptures as the source of

24. Warfield, *Revelation and Inspiration*, 51, 52, 53, 429–30. The hostility in which some "American fundamentalist-evangelicals" held "European neo-orthodoxy" is discussed by George Marsden, *Reforming Fundamentalism*, 94ff. Part of this hostility concerned inerrancy. According to Francis A. Schaeffer, "The Barthian will say that the Bible is infallible but he will not say that the Bible is inerrant" (111). Marsden points out that with the rise of higher criticism in America the assent to inerrancy was used "as a test for defining the community of true believers" (112). The General Assembly of the Presbyterian Church in the United States of America declared as late as 1910, 1916, and 1923 that Biblical inerrancy was an essential doctrine of the church (112). Cornelius Van Til in *The New Modernism* and *Christianity and Barthianism* contends that the theology of crisis cannot legitimately be called a Reformed Theology. According to Van Til not only is Barth's theology a denial of historic Protestantism but also a poor guide to the interpretation of Calvin. The judgment that the influence of Barth caused a drift away from "thoroughgoing Calvinists" like Charles Hodge and his conviction of inerrancy is repeated by Ligon Duncan in Duncan, "The Resurgence of Calvinism in America," 234. Gary North, *Crossed Fingers*, 999–1007, evaluates the role of Francis Schaeffer as an intellectual spokesman for American fundamentalism.

25. Warfield's resistance to higher critical study of the Bible led to polemical attacks on Henry Preserved Smith (1847–1927) and Charles Augustus Briggs (1841–1913) who were driven from the ministry of the Presbyterian Church only to have many of their higher critical positions adopted by Presbyterian seminaries later in the century. In 1935 Machen himself was suspended from the Presbyterian ministry—the conservative held in suspension with the liberals.

religious authority. For these and other reasons Machen concluded that Christianity and Liberalism were two mutually exclusive religions, not two varieties of the same faith.[26]

Some years later Edward J. Young admitted difficulties in understanding the Bible as inerrant, many of them presently irresolvable, but in a striking logomachy insisted these difficulties cannot be judged actual errors. Young continues, "In the nature of the case, then, inspiration extends only to the original manuscripts of Scripture. Since these manuscripts were inspired they were free from error."[27] However, these originals are lost and we only possess copies which are not free of errors. John H. Gerstner flatly declares, "Calvin believed in the inerrant inspiration of the New Testament as well as the Old Testament."[28] John Murray agrees that Calvin's view of the inspiration of Scripture is the same "high doctrine of plenary, verbal inspiration, espoused by the Reformed dogmaticians of the seventeenth century."[29] Even more recently Jelle Faber claims for Calvin, "Scripture is self-authenticated. The testimony of the Holy Spirit is not the ground of our faith in Scripture; the ground is Holy Scripture itself. But the witness of the Holy Spirit is the cause of our certainty with respect to Scripture."[30]

Among the curiosities of the claim that inerrancy/infallibility applies only to the autographs, is the stipulation that no presently existing manuscript exhibits such characteristics, meaning that all actual available evidence points to the contrary of the intellectual position occupied. It is true that recognizing the Bible as written by sinful men does not logically preclude its inerrancy. John Gerstner writes, "It does not follow that since God inspired men, he would be incapable of keeping them

---

26. All these themes are found in the chapter on the Bible in Machen, *Christianity and Liberalism*. North, *Crossed Fingers*, 942–46, reprints the acerbic obituary of Machen ("Dr. Fundamentalis") written by the old curmudgeon, H. L. Mencken.

27. Young, *Thy Word Is Truth: Some Thoughts on the Biblical Doctrine of Inspiration*, 61.

28. Gerstner, "The Church's Doctrine of Biblical Inspiration, 39.

29. Murray asserts that the doctrine of biblical inerrancy and infallibility is *not* based on meticulous precision in every detail but the Scripture remains "perfectly authentic." On the contrary, one would think the concept of inerrancy and infallibility required a conclusion of authentically perfect. Murray, *Calvin on Scripture and Divine Sovereignty*, 11, 30.

30. Faber, "The Saving Work of the Holy Spirit in Calvin," 2.

free of human error in writing."[31] However, granting to the autographs a divine preservation of the human writer from error raises the historical question why a divine preservation of the pages they wrote was not made actual since it, too, is possible. To this query Young responds, "Why God was not pleased to preserve the original copies of the Bible, we do not know."[32] Presumably all Christians are prepared to believe than an Almighty God *could* create an inerrant and infallible book, but the question remains, "Is the Bible actually inerrant and infallible?" Moreover, why are the theologians, who tell us we must believe the Bible was so created, unable to explain why it was not so preserved?[33] Additionally, if there is an oral tradition behind the written text, as Calvin avers (*Inst.* 1.8.3), was it remembered infallibly or corrected to be so in the process of writing the autographs.

Among some conservative Calvinists the inerrancy aspect of infallibility doctrine is pushed out the front door only to enter the living room through the back door. At least in his recent study of the Holy Scripture as the cognitive foundation of theology, Richard A. Muller claims to join Calvin in leaving "aside entirely all consideration of the modern debate over infallibility and 'inerrancy.'" Nevertheless, he considers that the infallibility of Scripture was taken for granted by Catholics, Reformers, and Orthodoxy. Moreover, "Calvin was certain that God . . . had given the Church an infallible rule of faith."[34] According to Muller's thesis, the intention of Reformed orthodoxy was to maintain the theological substance of the Reformers doctrine of Scripture while altering the form to meet historical exigencies, meaning that orthodoxy's doctrine of Scripture is neither a simple development nor a radical distortion of Calvin's theology.[35] Apart from what-appears-to-be a continuing emphasis on some kind of doctrine of Biblical infallibility, a "neither . . . nor" conclusion to the issue of development or distortion allows the "both . . . and" possibility that this "orthodox" alteration of form moves into a

31. Gerstner, "The Church's Doctrine of Biblical Inspiration," in *The Foundation of Biblical Authority*, 25.

32. Young, *Thy Word Is Truth*, 61.

33. Turretin, *Elenctic Theology*, 107, insists that the providence of God which willed the Scriptures to be written by inspiration would not allow them to be corrupted.

34. Muller, *Post-Reformation Reformed Dogmatics*, vol. 2, 301. In, *Calvin for Today*, 233, some of Muller's admirers think the resurgence of Calvinism in America today is due in part to the resurgence of the affirmation of the inerrancy of Scripture.

35. Muller, *Post-Reformation Reformed Dogmatics*, vol. 2, 96.

radical development of substance which produces a simple distortion. In any case, what is not questioned, but emphatically asserted, is that Holy Scripture functions as the cognitive foundation of theology requiring a strong affirmation of both the divinity and inspiration of Scripture. Its role is not as specific witness to Christ but as general epistemology, although Muller also notes the word of God is not restricted to Scripture, presumably indicating additional cognitive foundations for theology?[36]

The conception of theology based on good and necessary consequences derived from Scripture by reason transliterated from historical narrative into philosophical principles and eliciting the production of propositions to be faithfully affirmed is denied by Calvinists who are more modest in their confidence in human reason, and who consider the evidence provided by the Biblical text itself to preclude its sole function as cognitive foundation for theology and to exclude the concepts of infallibility and inerrancy applied directly to the text. Liberals and evangelicals insist that to the divinity of Scripture, its humanity must also be fully recognized.[37]

Additionally, while recognized, the role of the Holy Spirit is not emphasized among conservatives with the same fervor as among evangelicals. Muller correctly points out that presentations by orthodox theologians of "the objective authority and divinity of Scripture" should not be separated from "their frequent subjective assertions concerning the necessity of the *testimonium internum Spiritus Sancti*."[38] Nevertheless when Richard Gamble addresses the topic of Word and Spirit he concentrates on the "objective" aspect of Scripture while insisting that Word and Spirit cannot be separated. In claiming their elemental reciprocity he stipulates this distinction, "Calvin taught that there is an intrinsic

---

36. Ibid., 182.

37. Berkouwer, *Holy Scripture*, 22–23, writes, "I believe that I am judging no one unfairly when I say that fundamentalism, in its eagerness to maintain Holy Scripture's divinity, does not fully realize the significance [of its human character]." They suggest that [an]acceptance of Scripture's infallibility precludes all dangers." Interestingly Bloesch, *Essentials of Evangelical Theology*, xi, accepts "higher criticism," which Dockery characterizes as "qualified inerrancy," and which Bloesch admits would exclude him from the evangelical camp in the judgment of some. However, after defining the term "evangelical" and the sovereignty of God, he analyzes the primacy of Scripture, including reflection on its infallibility and inerrancy. In his chapter "Revisioning Biblical Authority," Stanley J. Grenz, *Revisioning Evangelical Theology* retreats to a weaker view of the inerrancy of the Bible and a stronger view of its humanity.

38. Muller, *Post-Reformation Reformed Dogmatics*, vol. 2, 78.

authority to the Scripture." Accordingly, the role of the Holy Spirit, while reciprocal, is not to establish the authority of the Bible but to persuade us of it.[39] Since the latter requires the former their roles appear separable. Among liberal and evangelical Calvinists the sequence of Word and Spirit is emphasized in reverse.

## THE LIBERAL CALVINISTS

In criticizing the labels "modernist" and "progressive" William Merrill recommends "liberal evangelical Christian" which he defines as an attempt to reconcile Christianity and modern culture based on scientific fact rather than dogmatic speculation. The liberal Christian "finds all his faith and hope realized in personality, pre-eminently in the supreme personality, Jesus Christ. And he cares supremely for present, vital spiritual experience." Reacting against *Christianity and Liberalism*, Merrill claims that Machen's book "can be saved from condemnation as false witness only by a plea of crass ignorance."[40]

The "liberal" label is here applied loosely to those seeking to free Calvin's theology from the cabined confines of orthodox Calvinism. As an articulated alternative this is likely the largest and also the smallest category. Liberals in general "try to retrieve, restate, rethink, and revise traditional theologies and beliefs in the face of contemporary knowledge and realities." At the same time, "[t]hey do so without acknowledging any single, central, and allegedly infallible institutional authority."[41] Of course the claim to progressive, up-to-the-minute thinking free from feckless fidelity to past authorities includes Calvin, with the inevitable result that the more liberal the commitment the less loyal to Calvinism. However, some appeal to thinkers of the past like Calvin, Kant, and Schleiermacher is allowed although they are usually cited to support rather than establish liberal views. The wider range includes those who admire Calvin's teaching on a number of doctrines but reject the shape

39. Gamble, "Word and Spirit in Calvin," 76–79. Berkouwer, *Holy Scripture*, deals with "The Testimony of the Spirit" in Chapter Two.

40. Merrill, *Liberal Christianity*, 10, 63, 12.

41. Ottati, *Theology for Liberal Presbyterians and Other Endangered Species*, viii. J. Harold DeWolf, *The Case for Theology in Liberal Perspective*, claims that the liberal perspective is "catholically human" and ecumenical which means answers are not sought exclusively or mainly in any tradition. On pages 201–2 DeWolf offers a list of books written from a liberal perspective.

of conservative Calvinism. Additionally, theologians belonging to the Reformed and Presbyterian tradition may be assumed to maintain some kind of commitment to Calvin's ecclesiology in the first place and presumed to show some kind of interest in its setting in the second place. This subdivision in opposition to scholastic Calvinism could be called "moderate Calvinism" or "progressive Calvinism." The former might describe Philip Schaff[42] and the latter Brian A. Gerrish, remembering that when "Calvinist" is not a self-description, it may be applied without being accepted.

In the seventeenth century, critical reading of the Bible, focused on the presumed Mosaic authorship of the Pentateuch, was pursued by philosophers Thomas Hobbes (1588–1679) and Baruch Spinoza (1632–1677). Not yet persuasive, these unsettling studies indicated that problematic passages in the Bible were not scattered and isolated but massive and pervasive. If conservative Calvinism was challenged by burgeoning textual difficulties, by the reassertion of tradition, and the development of the natural sciences, liberal and evangelical Calvinism was challenged by the philosophical revolt against reason and the revolutionary rise of historical understanding in the eighteenth and nineteenth centuries with its extension of historical-critical method to Bible study. John Calvin is recognized to be a pre-critical Biblical theologian but his spirit is claimed for both liberal and conservative Calvinism. The corps conservatives admire his affirmations concerning "dictation." For example, commenting on 2 Timothy 3:16 Calvin states, "Whoever wishes to profit in the Scripture, let him first agree to this, that the law and the prophets are not a doctrine delivered at the discretion of men, but are dictated by the Holy Spirit."[43] The liberal cohort praises his use of "critical method." In the comment on 2 Corinthians 4:6 Calvin says, "I see that it is possible to expound this passage in four different ways." Then after listing the four possibilities Calvin declares his preference for Chrysostom's understanding "although Ambrose's rendering is also quite suitable."

---

42. Schaff, and especially John Nevin, disagreed with Charles Hodge's version of Calvinism. See Sweeney, "Falling Away from the General Faith of the Reformation?"

43. Dowey, *The Knowledge of God in Calvin's Theology*, 90–105, devotes many pages to Calvin on dictation. According to Peter Stuhlmacher, the doctrine of dictation precludes "a free and critical scrutiny of the original biblical text." Protestant orthodoxy, he claims, developed a doctrine of inspiration that led the pioneering exegesis of the Reformation to become completely absorbed by dogmatics. Stuhlmacher, *Historical Criticism and Theological Interpretation of Scripture*, 36.

He generously suggests, "Everyone may use his own judgment." Again, Calvin notices that Matthew (27:27) describes Jesus' robe as scarlet while Mark (15:17) calls it purple. Calvin dryly concludes, "We need not sweat over this." Liberal and evangelical Calvinism differ from conservative Calvinism in the view of Scripture and also agree with modern philosophy on the limitations of reason. However liberal Calvinism emphasizes a subjective, phenomenological emphasis on faith as experience which conservative and evangelical Calvinists do not support.

Among Calvinists in the early nineteenth century one of the sharpest theological challenges to the conservative view of the Bible was delivered by Friedrich Schleiermacher (1768–1834), the so-called father of modern liberal theology, and himself a serious student of the New Testament. Responding to Kant's critique of pure reason and its restriction of experience to the phenomenal world, Schleiermacher against the conservatives eschewed dogmatic definitions derived from principles or propositions based on reason. According to Schleiermacher, the subject of dogmatics is Christian experience, i.e. the faith of Christians. Christian faith, he avers, did not originate either in knowing (metaphysics) or doing (ethics) but in personal and corporate piety (individual and social psychology) conceived as a modification of feeling or of immediate self-consciousness.[44]

Accepting the Kantian distinction between noumenal things-in-themselves and phenomenal things-as-they-appear-to-us, Schleiermacher applied this conviction to revelation and Scripture insisting that the Holy Scripture is not the foundation of faith in Christ, but rather the reverse. Faith cannot be based on the Bible without raising "the question how this authority itself is to be based." Schleiermacher concludes, "If we have no point of departure but ordinary reason, the divine authority of Scripture to begin with must admit on being proved on grounds of reason alone[.]" On the contrary, he thinks the real perception of Christ's spiritual power and the reality of the common faith does not rest on arguments or proofs. The Scripture does not so much interpret Christ as Christ interprets Scripture. Christian faith is initiated by Christ's preaching and continued by the preaching of the Apostles and many more.[45] Indeed faith pre-exists the reading of the Bible. Doctrines do not belong

44. Schleiermacher, *The Christian Faith*, 560.
45. Ibid., 591–92.

to Christianity because they are contained in Scripture, rather doctrines are contained in Scripture because they belong to Christianity.[46]

Schleiermacher's primary interest is in Christian faith as human awareness. Christ communicates through his teaching his own perfect God-consciousness to the original and subsequent disciples. The books of the New Testament are both inspired (therefore authentic) and collected (therefore canonical) under the guidance of the Holy Spirit.[47] However, denying the received theory of inspiration, Schleiermacher declares, the inspiration of the apostles does not belong exclusively to their writing the books of the New Testament. Only "an utterly dead scholasticism" could think so.[48] Their lives in general were guided by inspiration.[49] On that basis Schleiermacher suggests that Christians feel an inward impulse toward sanctification of which they are conscious "as the common Spirit of the new corporate life founded by Christ."[50]

Along with the continuing influence of the theology of Schleiermacher, the battle of the Bible was chiefly waged over the doctrine of inspiration between advocates and opponents of infallibility and inerrancy on the ground of historical recognition of fallible human involvement in the composition of Scripture. Earlier and grudging admissions by some conservatives of the diversity of the Bible within the conviction of its essential epistemic unity has reversed into the present search by many liberals and evangelicals for an essential unity within the impressive evidence of historical diversity.

The modern application of scientific (*wissenschaftlich*) historical principles to the examination of the Biblical text, now associated with such scholars as Julius Wellhausen (1844–1918) and Hermann Gunkel (1862–1932), raised an earlier firestorm in the English-speaking world

---

46. Ibid., 593.

47. Ibid., 597.

48. Ibid., 600.

49. Ibid., 599.

50. Ibid., 560. According to Schweitzer (*The Quest of the Historical Jesus*, 64, 62), Schleiermacher is a rationalist. His view of Christ is fanciful, rationalistic dialectic. "Schleiermacher is not in search of the historical Jesus, but of the Jesus Christ of his own system of theology; that is to say, of the historic figure which seems to him appropriate to the self-consciousness of the Redeemer as he represents it." Schweitzer declares that Schleiermacher's work on the life of Jesus "was rendered obsolete by the work of Strauss. For the questions raised by the latter's *Life of Jesus*, published in 1835, Schleiermacher had no answer, and for the wounds which it made, no healing."

lit by Anglicans with the 1859 publication of *Essays and Reviews*. The authors, all but one in holy orders, sought a reverent expression of honest thought but found instead violent currents of abuse. In "The Education of the World" Frederick Temple argues for progressive development in the world's education and therefore progressive revelation in the Scripture concluding, "The immediate work of our day is the study of the Bible." Benjamin Jowett immediately addressed the interpretation of Scripture in more than a hundred pages pointing to a great host of interpretative errors which must be folded into any theory of inspiration. Jowett suggested "There is no more reason why imperfect narratives should be excluded from Scripture than imperfect grammar; nor more ground for expecting that the New Testament would be logical or Aristotelian in form, than that it would be written in Attic Greek." He concludes that "the time has come when it is no longer possible to ignore the results of criticism." [51] The same historical critical advance was presented in *Lux Mundi* (1889) and William Sanday's 1893 Bampton Lectures. In the former the flash point for many readers focused on the subject of inspiration contained in the chapter on the Holy Spirit, which defends the mingled importance of Christian experience and Holy Scripture. That is, belief in the Scriptures requires belief in the work of the Holy Spirit, not vice versa. Addressing inspiration, Sanday distinguished two views. The traditional view held "that the Bible as a whole and in all its parts was the Word of God, and as such it was endowed with all the perfections of that Word." The Inductive or Critical view holds that inspiration "is present in different books and parts of books, in different degrees" with the possibility of error not exempted.[52]

Liberal and evangelical Calvinists agree with Gerhard Ebeling whose essay, "The Significance of the Critical Historical Method for Church and Theology in Protestantism," attacks "the fatal isolation of

---

51. In Hedge, *Essays and Reviews*, 54, 382, 412.

52. Gore, *Lux Mundi*, 244. Summing up, Gore, *The Doctrine of The Infallible Book* insists that devout believers can maintain critical conclusions. See especially the distinction between inspiration and infallibility. In his chapter H. R. Mackintosh declares, "Both Luther and Calvin were compelled by facts to break away from the rigid dogma of verbal inspiration which they had inherited" (p. 59). Sanday, *Inspiration*, 392, 400. Barr, *Holy Scripture*, 33, observes that in modern times biblical criticism has often been supposed to be essentially German. Barr claims, "it would be more true to say that it arose in the English-speaking lands, travelled from there to Germany, and eventually returned from Germany to both Britain and America."

the historical disciplines from systematic theology."[53] Ebeling claims the critical historical method has "attained increasing, and in the second half of the nineteenth century well nigh undisputed, dominance in theology."[54] Liberal Calvinists can support this historical judgment simply because it is a change from the past, but many evangelical Calvinists believe that acceptance of the critical historical method, because true to the text, is crucial to continuing Reformation theology. The objection that the doctrine of justification was presented by the Reformation and in early Protestant orthodoxy without knowledge of the critical historical method "merely betrays the basic error of a traditionalism that believes itself relieved by the Reformers' theology from responsible theological labor of its own."[55]

Moreover, according to Ebeling "in the [Roman Catholic] clerical church of the sacrament, theology, however vast may be the resources expended on it, is a peripheral matter. Whereas in the church of the Word, theology serves the preaching which is the source of faith."[56] On the proper relation between Scripture and theology, 'It was not sufficiently clearly realized that post-reformation theology must not be simply Reformed scholasticism, and that Reformed scholasticism in spite of its attempts at most loyal conservation is by no means identical with Reformation theology."[57] The significance of the critical historical method for Scripture and theology is not the dream of establishing a final, absolute doctrinal authority but the courage "to expose ourselves relentlessly to the vulnerability, the insecurity and the dangers . . . to go ahead with the critical examination of our foundations, to let everything burn that will burn and without reservations await what proves itself unburnable."[58]

Finely summarizing the contemporary scholarly consensus, John Webster objects to divinizing the text by applying divine attributes to the Bible. He insists,

53. Ebeling, *Word and Faith*, 58.

54. Ibid., 18.

55. Ibid., 57.

56. Ibid., 36.

57. Ibid., 40.

58. Ibid., 51. Issues resulting in the adoption of the historical-critical method are addressed in Braaten and Jenson, *Reclaiming the Bible for the Church*.

> Scripture's place in the economy of saving grace does not need
> to be secured by its divinization through the unambiguous as-
> cription of divine properties to the text[. Thus] it has to be as-
> serted that no divine nature or properties are to be predicated of
> Scripture.

Webster rejects the process by which "revelation and Scripture are strictly identified" so that "Christian theological talk about revelation migrates to the beginning of the dogmatic corpus, and has to take on the job of furnishing the epistemological warrants for Christian claims." This mislocation, he thinks, assigns Scripture the unwarranted role of "the formal principle from which . . . other doctrines are deduced." Moreover, to argue "that the church knows that what Scripture declares is a word of salvation because Scripture is inspired, is to allow the pressure of the need for epistemological reassurance to distort the whole." Put positively, and quoting Günther Dehn, Webster writes, "[Theology is promoted] by the belief in God's revelation as an event beyond all human history, to which Scripture bears witness[.]"[59] The point is Scripture is not co-extensive with God's revelation but is witness to it.

Evangelical Calvinists together with liberals are unwilling to treat the historical Bible as the epistemological source for the derivation of philosophical propositions. Moreover, the divine attribute inerrant applied to the autographs is not the controlling concept for modern Bible study. Additionally, for many the term infallible does not refer to the whole text of the Bible but to its function as a whole in the life of the church. In this sense George S. Hendry defends the theology of crisis in the acceptance of critical study of the Bible which does not mark an end but a new beginning.

> [T]he sifting of texts, the analysis of the documents, the tracing
> of the sources, and the illumination of the historical and cultural
> background" are all necessary work, but even more important is

---

59. John Webster, *Holy Scripture*, 28, 23, 12, 13, 32, 3. One of the most intriguing features of Webster's discussion of Scripture is his employment of the doctrine of sanctification with its dynamic and developing essence. Unlike justification which is accomplished once-for-all, sanctification has a continuing nature. According to Webster, Scripture is not a product which embodies but an activity which serves God's purpose (17ff.). Additionally, he claims, "Language about the Spirit extends talk of God into the creaturely realm." (37).

the attempt "to recover the theological interpretation of the Bible as the Word of God.[60]

Evangelicals strongly disagree with their liberal friends who, following Schleiermacher, think the subject of theology is Christian experience. According to Schleiermacher Christian doctrines are accounts of religious affections set forth in speech, which means religious experience is restricted to itself excluding contact to anything outside self-consciousness. In his *Invitation to Systematic Theology* Brian A. Gerrish (presumably accepting his wife's declaration that he is a Calvinist of a higher order)[61] defines the subject of dogmatics as Christian faith, that is, "one of the ways in which persons construe their experience religiously." The focus of faith is Christian consciousness considered as the gift of God in Christ. Piety is directed to the work of Christ rather than his person although the work of Christ is declared to be the gift of faith which is given through the word. This Kantian reserve is understood by Ernst Troeltsch, who is quoted with approval: "Here we take our stand with Schleiermacher: redemption is simply faith being made sure of God by the impression the image of Christ makes on us." [62] Unlike Schleiermachians, evangelical Calvinists expect believers to *encounter* the person of the risen Christ rather than to *emulate* his work of God-consciousness.

In addition to his influence on liberal theology generally and specifically the doctrine of Scripture already discussed, Schleiermacher is taken by some to be a helpful or superior interpreter of Calvin.[63] According to Gerrish, the two great modern interpreters of Calvin are Friedrich Schleiermacher and Karl Barth and the former, Gerrish thought, to be preferred to the latter.[64] Almost certainly evangelical Calvinists would choose to follow Barth (and against Melanchthon) that to know Christ's benefits (Work) cannot be separated from knowing Christ (his Person).

60. Hendry, "The Rediscovery of the Bible," 142, 143.

61. DeVries, *Jesus Christ in the Preaching of Calvin and Schleiermacher*, dedication page, vi.

62. Gerrish, *Saving and Secular Faith,* 68, 84.

63. See Moore, "Schleiermacher as a Calvinist" 167–83. Gerrish, "Theology within the Limits of Piety Alone." DeVries, *Jesus Christ in the Preaching of Calvin and Schleiermacher.*

64. In a lecture reported by my colleague, John P. Burgess. A recent trend proposes to treat Schleiermacher and Barth together rather than in opposition. See Duke and Streetman, *Barth and Schleiermacher.*

That is to say, theology is based not on the human experience of grace but on the reality of the divine and human Word of God (Barth) and the divine and human encounter with Truth (Emil Brunner). Mackintosh puts the point this way, "Unless Jesus Christ attests Himself to the soul in whom His Word has been made living and powerful by the Holy Spirit, the Christian religion cannot begin to live."[65] W. T. Jones denies that this position can be defended. Jones rejects an "encounter with a transcendent and ultimate reality," because "What is fundamental in religion is not theological descriptions of the religious experience, but that experience itself, and what it does here and now for men."[66]

Evangelical Calvinists insist that the subject of dogmatics is not a Christian's phenomenal experience but God's noumenal revelation in Jesus Christ. The problem with Kantian epistemology, liberally interpreted by Schleiermacher, is that it precludes direct encounter with God in favor of the feeling of absolute dependence on God. Evangelical Calvinists cannot acquiesce in the pervasive Kantian restriction of knowledge because they believe with Augustine, Calvin, and Barth among others that there is a divine and eternal realm above and beyond the realm of things for Christians perfectly revealed in Jesus Christ and imperfectly understood by us.[67] In other words theology is concerned with God's revelation of the Eternal Son, an event beyond human history, which entered human history in the Incarnate Son to which Scripture bears witness and the Church confesses in union with him.

## THE EVANGELICAL CALVINISTS

For a good part of its history the word "evangelical" denoted non-(Roman)-Catholic and was virtually synonymous with Protestant. More recently, the designation is used to distinguish between Protestants—liberal and conservative, the latter often veering into the position once called fundamentalism. John Stackhouse traces the term to the eighteenth-century revivals and regards its non-negotiable elements as (1) the importance of salvation in Christ, (2) the unique authority of the Bible, (3) the central role of conversion, (4) the mission of making

65. Mackintosh, *Types of Modern Theology*, 6.

66. Jones, *The Sciences and the Humanities*, 269, 261.

67. Karl Barth cites his brother, Heinrich, against Heidegger and Bultmann in referring to "something beyond itself" (*CD* I/1, 39), which appears to have intellectual affinities with Plato's theory of ideas.

disciples, and (5) its transdenominationalism.[68] As defined in this essay conservative and evangelical Calvinists can agree on all these points but divide on the emphasis placed on the divinity of the Bible with its concomitant concepts of textual inerrancy and infallibility. According to evangelical Calvinists the Bible should not be given an epistemological status apart from its witness to Jesus Christ. Additionally, among evangelical Calvinists the work of the Holy Spirit is not only considered in terms of the written word but also in relation to the spoken and living Word. Even more crucial is the focus on the person of Jesus Christ.

Chiefly recognizing that they are of a different spirit from Reformed Scholastics, now-named evangelical Calvinists until fairly recently were not conscious of a common identity. They thought they were classical Calvinists in the sense of reading Calvin honestly and fairly. However much of the dominant conservative Calvinism had been taught and imbibed, and however many of its positions and peoples might be admired, evangelical Calvinists saw themselves in a different light.[69] Equally, they had no credit with the small card-carrying Calvin sodality gathered around Schleiermacher's expression of *The Christian Faith*. From their different perspectives Conservatives (like Richard Muller) and Liberals (like Brian Gerrish) rejected the theology of Karl Barth in common and with considerable vigor while evangelicals like Thomas Torrance found much to admire.[70]

Unlike the conservatives, evangelical Calvinists distinguish between revelation and Scripture. This involves understanding the gift of faith as the principal work of the Holy Spirit (Inst. III.1.4) emphasizing the integral, rather than the reciprocal, work of the Spirit not only in relation to the written word but also to the spoken and living word. Most crucially, evangelical theology begins with the Lordship of Christ—not

---

68. Stackhouse, "Evangelical Theology Should Be Evangelical," 40–42. Abraham, *The Coming Great Revival*, 73, "So the term 'evangelical' embraces at least three constellations of thought: the Reformation led by Luther and Calvin, the evangelical revival of the eighteenth century as found, say, in Methodism, and modern conservative evangelicalism." The use of the term in this essay emphasizes the first connection. Bebbington, *Evangelicalism in Modern Britain*, 181–228, devotes a chapter to the distinction between conservative and liberal evangelicals in the early twentieth century.

69. For many fledgling Calvinistic theologians the basic introductory textbooks in systematic theology were Augustus Strong, Louis Berkhof, and Heinrich Heppe.

70. Torrance's view of natural theology and reason has, as it seems to me, some affinities with the scholastic view, but his christology and view of Scripture clearly sets his theology apart from theirs.

with the authority of Scripture nor with the analysis of faith. In addition to this content, the evangelical approach is more confessional than dogmatic. That is, theology is regarded as a human and doxological articulation of an ineffable and divine personal encounter.[71]

Since revelation is not co-extensive with Scripture, the latter is properly witness to the former. According to Otto Weber the concept of "revelation is primarily a concern of modern dogmatics," meaning that revelation as an epistemological warrant has replaced revelation as a confessional reality. The divine proclamation, "Thus saith the Lord" transmogrified into a human reflection on "How can I know for sure." Weber continues, "To put it succinctly: the concept of revelation has become the evidence for the fact that theology no longer derives its life from the reality of revelation."[72] Weber judges the uniqueness of theology, its "ontological" basis, to correctly consist in its proclamation of the truth revealed by God's Word personally self-disclosed in Jesus Christ. On that basis, Calvin writes, "God has ordained his Word as the instrument by which Jesus Christ, with all his benefits, is dispensed to us."[73] T. F. Torrance declares that evangelical fundamentalists substitute a static for a dynamic view of revelation."

> [The] Bible is treated as a self-contained corpus of divine truths in propositional form endowed with an infallibility of statement which provides the justification felt to be needed for the rigid framework of belief within which fundamentalism barricades itself. The practical and the epistemological effect of a fundamentalism of this kind is to give an infallible Bible and a set of rigid evangelical beliefs primacy over God's self-revelation which is mediated to us through the Bible.[74]

For evangelical Calvinists the Word of God is not in the first place referred to the objective Biblical text or to the subjective Christian consciousness. The Word is foremostly identified with Jesus Christ to whom Scripture is the pre-eminent witness made effective by the testimony of the Holy Spirit. The Bible laid out on pages is not the entirety of God's

---

71. For a longer reflection on this theme, see Partee, "Truth as Search and Encounter," 71–79.

72. Otto Weber, *Foundations of Dogmatics*, vol. 1, 172, 169.

73. "Short Treatise on the Holy Supper of our Lord and Only Savior Jesus Christ," in Calvin, *Theological Treatises*, 143.

74. Torrance, *Reality and Evangelical Theology*, 16, 17.

revelation but contains and remains the most central witness to the revelation in Christ. This latter point is illustrated by Weber where after two chapters of introduction and four on the history of dogmatics, he offers a detailed reflection on revelation and the knowledge of God, which includes a dialectical consideration of the Word of God (1) as event, (2) as witness, and (3) as proclamation.

The three-fold form of the Word of God is most prominent and familiar today in the work of Karl Barth, but the concept is not new, as he himself observes. Recognizing that numerous Christians encounter the Word first in its preached form, Barth expounds the meaning of the Word of God according to the ordinary way of knowing: 1. The Word proclaimed, 2. The Word written, 3. The Word revealed, rather than according to the way of being, which reverses the order. In either case the point is their interlocking relationship. Barth's final section emphasizes the three-fold unity by writing, "Revelation, Scripture, and proclamation have from the beginning stamped themselves upon Christian thought as the special forms of the Word of God." Barth praises the continuation of this theme in Luther[75], but does not mention in this place that the same dynamic concept is also powerfully present in Calvin and provides the context for his understanding of Scripture.[76]

Barth asserts that post-Reformation theologians undervalued preaching and overvalued reading. Protestant orthodoxy, he declares, lost the "dynamics of the mutual relationships between the three forms" first by essentially neglecting the form of proclamation and second by "freezing" the connection between Scripture and revelation into a doc-

75. Following Luther, Dietrich Bonhoeffer taught, "The form of the preached word is different from every other form of speech[.] The meaning of the proclaimed word . . . does not lie outside of itself; it is the thing itself." That is, it communicates the historical Jesus Christ. Bonhoeffer, *Worldly Preaching*, 123–30.

76. Wallace, *Calvin's Doctrine of the Word and Sacrament* devotes seven chapters to the revelation in Christ followed by a chapter on the preached word and then the written word as the Word of God. Each exposition testifies to the necessary work of the Holy Spirit. Recently Richard Lischer insists that faith comes by hearing because the Word of God broke into the silence of the world as a word of preaching. According to Martin Kähler "The real Christ is the preached Christ." The question, "Did preaching give rise to theology, or theology to preaching? [is pointless] for at their source they were one." "In preaching, theology recovers three elements it had at its origin: its kerygmatic impulse, its oral nature, and its character as worship" (Lischer, *A Theology of Preaching: The Dynamics of the Gospel*, 70, 74, 24, 23).

trine of inspiration.[77] Barth continues, "with all profound respect for the work achieved by orthodoxy," the present task is the recovery of Luther's thought (and Calvin's) especially taking proclamation with the seriousness it deserves. Barth famously declares, "The direct object of a present-day dogmatics must be just Church proclamation."[78]

While Calvin's view of the written word is dependent on the living Word, it is especially intimately related to the spoken word of God sounding in the ear (Com. Heb. 4:12). This relation is seen crucially in the debate with the Anabaptists who, Calvin says, receive the Holy Scripture, as we do.[79] Since the difference is not in the appeal to Scripture, it is in the correct understanding of Scripture which in turn depends on the "gift of interpretation" entrusted to preachers (Com. Dan 7:15).[80] According to Calvin, preaching is the instrument of faith (Com. Eph. 1:13). God could bring the faithful to himself by a secret impulse, but chooses the outward and human voice (Com. Is. 2:3). "Preaching is the mother who conceives and brings forth, and faith is the daughter who ought to be mindful of her origin" (Com. II Cor. 13:5). He continues, "[Christ] alone has been appointed our teacher by the Father, but he has put pastors and ministers in his place to speak as if out of his mouth" (Com. Acts 13:47). True ministers of the Word are messengers and ambassadors of God. "It is necessary to listen to them as to God."[81] The permanent life in God is communicated by the Word (Com. I Pet. 1:25). The task of proclamation is to "bring life-giving light to the blind, to transform men's hearts

77. Noll, *Between Faith and Criticism*, 6 makes the same point about the orthodox more gently (using the term "evangelical"). Conservatives, he writes, are willing to apply the Word to Christ, to proclamation, and to consider the human nature of the Bible but the emphasis is "where the Bible speaks, God speaks." "When examining the evangelical study of Scripture, everything hinges upon a recognition that the evangelical community considers the Bible the very Word of God . . . Whatever else one may say about the Word of God (and many evangelicals are willing to recognize the supremacy of Christ as Word or to organize community life around the Word of proclamation), the Word of God always involves the Bible. Although evangelicals typically give some attention to the human character of the Bible, they believe that Scripture itself teaches that where the Bible speaks, God speaks." When speaking of the supreme authority of the Word of God, Bloesch, *Essentials of Evangelical Theology*, vol. 2, 239 claims, "[Conservatism] appeals to the Bible above all other norms, but it is always the Bible as witness to the self-revelation of Jesus Christ."

78. Barth, *CD* I/1.4 (137, 139, 140).

79. Calvin, *Treatise against the Anabaptists*, 39.

80. See Balke, "Word and Spirit," 320–27.

81. *Calvin Theological Treatises*, 32.

into the righteousness of God, and to confirm the grace of salvation, which has been procured by the death of Christ" (Com. Acts 26:18). Again, "The Church maintains the truth, because in her preaching she proclaims and preserves it pure and complete and transmits it to posterity." Preaching is one of the marks of the true church which rescues "the truth from darkness and oblivion, falsehoods, errors, impostures, superstitions, and corruption of every kind" (*Com. I Tim.* 3:15).

In his chapter on Calvin and the doctrine of authority, R. A. Finlayson admits, "The question of authority did not arise in acute form in the early church," and he claims with some plausibility that the Reformers substituted the authority of Scripture for the authority of the Roman Church. However, he jumps too far in concluding "for them the objective authority lay indubitably in the Scriptures" and the Holy Spirit is understood as the subjective authority.[82] When Calvin uses the convenient distinction between inward and outward he does not apply outward teaching to the Bible but to the sermon, writing that God "by his Word and Spirit bends the hearts of men to obedience . . . inwardly by the influence of the Spirit and outwardly by the preaching of the Word" (*Com. Mic.* 4:3). Concerning the Spirit we are advised, "Learn, then, by your own experience, that it is no less unreasonable to boast of the Spirit without the Word, than it would be absurd to bring forward the Word itself without the Spirit."[83]

The Word of God proclaimed is made effectual by the hand of God, which means the secret inspiration (Com. Acts 11:21) or influence (Com. Mal. 4:6) of the Holy Spirit. Since Calvin insists the work of the Holy Spirit is essentially connected to preaching, both those who speak and those who hear should raise their expectations of the event of proclamation. God has two ways of teaching speaking to us outwardly by the mouth of men and inwardly by his Spirit (Com. Jn. 14:26). As summarized by T. H. L. Parker, Calvin uses "the most definite language to assert that the preaching of the Gospel is the Word of God."[84]

82. Finlayson, *The Story of Theology,* 48, 50.

83. Beveridge, *Selected Works of Calvin, Tracts,* 1:37. See the appendix in Milner, *Calvin's Doctrine of the Church,* 197–203, on "The Secret Impulse of the Spirit."

84. Parker, *John Calvin: A Biography,* 90. See also Parker, *The Oracles of God: An Introduction to the Preaching of John Calvin,* 50–56. Lischer, *Theories of Preaching* devotes an entire section to the Holy Spirit. See also Lischer, *A Theology of Preaching,* which analyzes the role of theology in preaching, especially chapter four "Preaching as the Word of God." Lischer's bibliography is helpful and his account of his first parish in Lischer, *Open Secrets,* is quite engaging.

Respecting the dynamics of the mutual relations among the three forms of the Word of God requires recognizing the Bible as a human book written in human time, language, and categories. As the living God was incarnate in human flesh and the spoken word of God is articulated by human vocal chords, so the written witness to divine action was set down by human hands. That God should be revealed in the relative and problematical literature of the Bible is comparable to the scandal and mystery of the Incarnation. Eschewing entirely the concepts of inerrancy and infallibility, Barth points to "the vulnerability of the Bible, i.e., its capacity for error, [which] also extends to its religious or theological content. [T]he biblical authors wrote with all the limitations imposed by their most varied possible historical and individual standpoints and outlooks."[85] For that reason historical analysis is appropriate. Still, for all its human and fallible character through the grace of God the Scripture is God's word of truth because of its witness to Jesus Christ. Barth insists, "The truth of Jesus Christ is not one truth among others; it is *the* truth, the universal truth that creates all truth as surely as it is the truth of God[.]"[86] The Reformation affirmation that "Holy Scripture alone has divine authority in the Church . . . was not ascribing a godlike value to the book as a book and the letter as a letter . . . it wanted Jesus Christ to be known and acknowledged as the Lord of the Church[.]"[87]

Evangelical Calvinists affirm that "Christ is the one and only foundation of the Church" (*Com. 1 Cor.* 3:11, cf. *Inst.*, 4.2.1), thus avoiding all other forms of foundationalism, including Holy Scripture as the cognitive foundation of theology. This position leads to the following penultimate, no-other-foundation, conclusions: that Jesus Christ is the Word of God cannot be deduced from any theological principle. That the Bible is the Word of God cannot be established by any quality of the text. That the sermon is the Word of God cannot be demonstrated by any rhetorical analysis. The ultimate, alpha-and-omega, conclusion is that the Word of God is a confession of faith engendered by the work of the Holy Spirit, leading to the double grace of justification and sanctification.

Emil Brunner of Zurich agrees with Barth, his prickly Basel colleague, in claiming a crucial opposition between the orthodox and re-

---

85. Barth, *CD* I/2.509. Emil Brunner, *Truth as Encounter*, dismisses the doctrine of the divine infallibility of the text of Scripture on one page, 176.

86. Barth, *Dogmatics in Outline*, 26.

87. Barth, *CD* I/2, 581.

formed doctrine of Scripture. In his dogmatics Brunner treats revelation as the Word of God in his prolegomena and the authority of Scripture as a final appendix. In the former Brunner insists that revelation is not a Word but a person. On that basis orthodoxy is criticized first for its equation of the Word of God with the Word of the Bible resulting in "the doctrine of Verbal Inspiration, with all its disastrous results." The second criticism of orthodoxy is its understanding of revelation as revealed doctrine.[88] Considering Scripture Brunner declares that "the content and real authority of Scripture is Christ." He continues, "We are not required to believe the Scriptures because they are the Scriptures; but because Christ . . . meets me in the Scriptures—therefore I believe." "For orthodoxy, the Bible as a book is the divinely revealed truth. It is thus a revealed thing or object. For unperverted Christian faith, however, Scripture is only revelation when conjoined with God's spirit in the present. The *testimonium spiritus sancti* and the clarity of God's word are one and the same thing."[89] Torrance concurs, we need to acknowledge "the transcendent Reality and Authority of the living Christ not only over the church and all its doctrinal formulations but over the Holy Scriptures themselves."[90]

For all Calvinists the conceptualization of God's revelation in relation to the Bible is formed with the tandem terms "Word and Spirit." However, in the centuries following Calvin many of his interpreters treated revelation as epistemology rather than pneumatology and asserted Scripture by virtually relegating the work of the Holy Spirit to the subjective function of inspiring the objective Bible rather than recognizing the inner testimony of the Spirit as the controlling concept in a great cluster of doctrines.[91] Benjamin Warfield admits the necessity of a final

88. Brunner, *The Christian Doctrine of God,* Dogmatics I, 28, 110. Brunner thinks Calvin's *exposition* of Scripture follows the new understanding but his *doctrine* of Scripture moves toward Verbal Inspiration (111). Muller, *Post-Reformation,* vol. 2, 98-103, 182-3, claims Brunner misunderstands orthodoxy.

89. Brunner, *The Philosophy of Religion from the Standpoint of Protestant Theology,* 151. See also Brunner, *Revelation and Reason.* Cobb, *Living Options in Protestant Theology,* considers the "theological positivism" of Brunner and Barth disagreeable but worthy of analysis. However, with astounding dismissiveness Cobb declares conservative and orthodox Protestant theology is not a living option. "[T]here are special assumptions and problems operative in orthodox Protestantism that render it not directly accessible to those who have been nurtured in the atmosphere of liberalism" (13).

90. Torrance, *Reality and Evangelical Theology,* 19.

91. Donald Macleod, "Calvin into Hippolytus?" 255, puts this point powerfully, "The Church is inalienably charismatic. It exists only in the Spirit, and its evangelists,

union between objective and subjective. Word and Spirit are conjoined, but he writes, "The Word supplies the objective factor; the Spirit the subjective factor."[92] Defending the objective authority of the Bible standing alone is to carve the owl of Minerva through the bone and not at the joint. According to Calvin, "God alone is a fit witness of himself in his word, so also the word will not find acceptance in men's hearts before it is sealed by the inward testimony of the Spirit" (Inst. I.7.4). In dealing with the Libertines on Scripture, Calvin affirms its authority through the confirming work of the Holy Spirit. "[W]e choke out the light of God's Spirit if we cut ourselves off from His Word. That is, provided it is [properly] preached to us. For preaching and Scripture are the true instruments of God's Spirit."[93]

If the difficult and subtle relation between Word and Spirit does not separate liberals from evangelicals, the even more subtle, difficult, and crucial relation between the person and work of Christ does. Evangelical Calvinists follow Calvin in confessing that "[A]ll thinking about God without Christ is a vast abyss which immediately swallows up all our thoughts" (*Com. 1 Pet.* 1:20) because God is fully "revealed to us in Christ, where we may behold [God] as in a mirror. For in Christ [God] shows us his righteousness, goodness, wisdom, power, in short, his entire self. We must, therefore, take care not to seek [God] elsewhere; for outside Christ everything that claims to represent God will be an idol" (*Com. Col.* 1:15). The confession of the personal Lordship of Christ includes the work of atonement and the resulting union with Christ, but

---

pastors, teachers, leaders, presbyters and bishops are all charismatic functionaries. This cannot mean less than that the ministers of the Church are totally dependent on the Spirit[.]"

92. Warfield, *Calvin and Calvinism*, 71, 82. In an understandable desire to impress the philosophers and to secure an epistemological base for grounding theological propositions the so-called "objective" authority of Scripture in Calvin has been so over-emphasized as to distort his actual teaching. The reality of the relation between Spirit and Word is too often dealt with only desultorily. Contrary to the view that the chief work of the Holy Spirit is the plenary inspiration of Holy Scripture, Reid, *The Authority of Scripture,* 53, declares that Calvin's doctrine of the Holy Spirit "makes it impossible to regard him as attaching inspiration exclusively to the written word." In opposition to the subjective-objective dichotomy Mackintosh, *The Christian Apprehension of God,* 72, declares, "[R]evelation is no revelation until it takes the shape of human thought."

93. Calvin, *Treatises Against the Anabaptists,* 224–25. See also the ecumenical and confessional analysis of Schepers, "The Interior Testimony of the Holy Spirit," 140–76, 295–321, 420–59.

union with Christ is not to be understood as some kind of functional relation to his Work. Rather, "The blessed and happy state of the church always had its foundation in the person (*persona*) of Christ." (*Inst.* 2.6.2). The source of our communion with each other is based on "the fact that we are united to Christ so that 'we are flesh of his flesh and bone of his bones.'" (*Com. I Cor.* 10:16). "Such is the union between us and Christ, that in a sense He pours Himself into us. For we are not bone of His bone, and flesh of His flesh, because, like ourselves, He is man, but because, by the power of His Spirit, He engrafts us into His Body, so that from Him we derive life" (*Com. Eph.* 5:31).

In its focus on the person of Jesus Christ Wilhelm Herrmann claims Luther's Christology was a step forward in the history of doctrine. "Wilt thou go surely and meet and grasp God rightly, so finding grace and help in him, be not persuaded to seek him elsewhere than in the Lord Christ."[94] Calvin makes the same point, "God is comprehended in Christ alone" (*Inst.* 2.6.4). Mackintosh follows Luther, Calvin, and his teacher, Herrmann, in asserting "The highest and purest faith in God can be attained in no way but one; it comes through a believing response to the person of Jesus Christ."[95] Likewise, Torrance follows his teacher, Mackintosh, by declaring, "In Jesus Christ we meet the very embodiment of the majestic Sovereignty of God breaking into the world to claim it for himself[.] He is the *Lord Jesus*, the divine Savior of mankind, [who is not] a kind of 'double' for God in his absence, but the incarnate presence of *Yahweh*, the Lord God himself[.]"[96]

According to Emil Brunner, liberal theology, pursuing "a mistaken autonomy," considers that Jesus is not the Christ but merely an outstanding religious personality. Orthodox theology, pursuing "a mistaken heteronomy," accepts Jesus as the Christ because the Bible says so. Against both, Brunner teaches "that the only true, concrete, valid ground for faith in Jesus Christ consists in what Jesus Christ Himself is."[97] That is to say, "In Jesus Christ we encounter the holy and merciful God *in persona*."[98] "The Christian Faith is simply (*nichts anderes als*) faith in Jesus Christ[.] Hence faith in Jesus Christ is not simply part of this faith, and Jesus

94. Mackintosh, *The Doctrine of the Person of Jesus Christ*, 230, 231.

95. Ibid., 346.

96. Thomas F. Torrance, *The Christian Doctrine of God*, 51.

97. Brunner, *The Christian Doctrine of Creation and Redemption*, 252.

98. Brunner, *The Scandal of Christianity*, 49.

Christ is not one 'subject' among other subjects in the Christian Creed." In other words, "Not only for the disciples, but also for us today, probably the first awareness of a superhuman mystery in the Person of Jesus is connected with the perception of His authority as Lord." His personal authority as Lord inheres in his person.[99]

Karl Barth recognizes "a paradox in the nature of God that we cannot unravel, because on the one hand we must necessarily understand God as the impersonal absolute, but at the same time (and in unavoidable logical contradiction to this) we must also understand Him as person." Therefore, accepting the problematic involved in the timelessness and historical remoteness of the abstract doctrine of "person" proceeding from the confessions of Nicaea, Constantinople, Ephesus, and Chalcedon, Barth insists "that Christ is the mystery of God, that all the treasures of wisdom and knowledge are hidden in Him and not elsewhere[.]" Thus "the insoluble mystery of the grace of God [is] enclosed in the name of Jesus Christ" which is the event of "God with us and we with God." According to Barth, "we have always to take in blind seriousness the basic Pauline perception of Colossians 3:3 which is that of all Scripture—that our life is our life hid with Christ in God." Barth thought his Christocentric theology could avoid "a single complete and self-contained chapter on Jesus Christ, the so-called 'Christology'," and thereby many of the problems associated with the traditional doctrine.

99. Brunner, *Christian Doctrine of Creation and Redemption*, 241, 239, 338. In his earlier work Brunner, *The Mediator*, 10, 407, 273, 268, 407–9 (which Mackintosh describes in his foreword as "Brunner's great book on the Person of Christ"), Brunner focuses directly on what he calls the "natural and logical" order of person and then work. He asserts, "while we lay so much stress on the fact that the Person of the Mediator is in itself the revelation, at the same time we do not wish to suggest . . . that we either ignore the 'work' of the Mediator or even relegate it to a subordinate position." With this caution in mind, Brunner declares, "God Himself reveals Himself personally in Jesus Christ." The term "'Person' means simply the divine personality who is recognized as God in the personal revelation." Brunner also warns about the danger of salvific egoism in Melanchthon's formula "*Hoc est Christum cognoscere, beneficia ejus cognoscere*," insisting that "the doctrine of the Person of the Mediator should not be subordinated to that of his Work." Nevertheless, while insisting person and work cannot be separated, in his later dogmatics Brunner expounds the work of Christ before his person, presumably reversing the cautions to apply in the other direction. Barth criticizes Melanchthon on this point at *CD* II/1, 259. Muller, *Post-Reformation Reformed Dogmatics*, vol. 2, 183, asserts that Brunner was led by his affirmation of Christ to relativize Scripture. Equally unhelpful would be Brunner's possible riposte that Muller is led by his affirmation of Scripture to relativize Christ.

According to Barth, "we have to do wholly with God and wholly with man, and with both in their complete and utter unity." Not pausing to worry about the Nestorian dimensions of the first eleven words or the Eutychian possibilities of the last eight, Barth claims, "As [Christ] is the meaning and basis of creation, so He is the bearer and substance of the redemption and consummation which closes the time of the creature, human time." Nevertheless, while claiming with a mighty focus to deal wholly with God and wholly with man, Barth declares that the middle between the reconciling God above and reconciled man below "is one person, Jesus Christ."[100]

## CONCLUSION

Among the many possible conclusions to be drawn from an analysis of the theological tensions existing among Calvinists, none is more interesting than the function of their identifying emphasis. The selected focus does not serve as an "essential tenet" to which other doctrines, also essential, could be added since every Calvinist already strongly affirms Scripture alone, Faith alone, Christ alone. Rather, the chosen avouchment operates as a "central dogma" setting the non-negotiable commitment from which all other doctrines may be discussed and maintained.

Competing central dogmas in theology resemble paradigms in science and root metaphors in philosophy[101] in that no rules for choice can be specified among various options. However, one's choice is susceptible to criteria of assessment, chiefly explanatory adequacy resulting in conviction. Once persuaded effectuating a change of one's central dogma becomes difficult, if not impossible. Additionally, the broad sweep of a central dogma resulting in a common first loyalty to Scripture alone, or faith alone, or Christ alone, while producing divisions among Calvinists, effects an admirable and amiable fellowship across denominational lines.

The commitment to a central dogma suggests the need for a renewed search for a grace-full dogmatics in which the role of sharp theological distinctions produced by different orienting standpoints can be seen to enrich the point of standing within the family of Calvin. Calvin himself did not articulate a "central dogma" although candidates like the

---

100. Barth, *CD* II/1, 287, I/1, 407–22; IV/1, 81, 83, 3–21; II/1, 149; IV/1, 122, 126, 117.

101. See Kuhn, *The Structure of Scientific Revolutions*. Pepper, "The Root Metaphor Theory of Metaphysics," 365–74.

sovereignty or glory of God have run for that office. On the other hand, Calvin does declare the importance of a central set of doctrines, but he is remarkably vague about which they are. The most famous illustration of "the proper principles of religion" asserts that "[1] God is one; [2] Christ is God and the Son of God; [3] our salvation rests in God's mercy; [4] and the like" (*Inst.* 4.1.12–13).[102] In a very general way these four proper principles summarize the four books of the 1559 *Institutes*: 1. God the Father Creator, 2. God the Son Redeemer, 3. Salvation as the gift of God, and 4. the charitable assumption that these three principles properly understood lead to the rest.

Among various Calvinists today their first focus serves as a summarizing, guiding, and identifying interpretive basis for theological reflection. However, when the lens widens something like Calvin's own four perspectives come into view. Undoubtedly a stronger experience of common worship and common service and a greater celebration of common tenets would permit central dogma differences to be recognized with respect and even admiration, if not emulation. Explicating predestination, once considered his central dogma, Calvin indicates the test for all doctrines, including first choices discussed in this essay. Each one [1] "builds up faith soundly, [2] trains us to humility, [3] elevates us to admiration of the immense goodness of God towards us, and [4] excites us to praise this goodness."[103]

Considering the second role, Calvin reminds his reader, "God has never so blessed his servants that they each possessed full and perfect knowledge of every part of their subject. It is clear that his purpose in so limiting our knowledge was first that we should be kept humble, and also that we should continue to have dealings with our fellows."[104] Accordingly of all real Calvinists, "The foundation of our philosophy is humility . . . so if you ask me concerning the precepts of the Christian religion, first, second, third, and always I would answer, 'Humility'" (*Inst.* 2.2.11).

To this end, excellent advice is offered to all by their mentor commenting on Psalm 133:1: "Behold how good and pleasant it is when brothers dwell in unity." According to Calvin, "[T]he Holy Spirit is to

---

102. See Partee, "Calvin's Polemic: Foundational Convictions in the Service of Truth," 97–122.

103. Calvin, *Concerning the Eternal Predestination of God*, 56.

104. "Dedication of Romans" (*CO* 10:405).

be viewed as commending in this passage that mutual harmony which should subsist among all God's children[.] As we are one in God the Father, and in Christ, the union must be ratified amongst us by reciprocal harmony, and fraternal love."

# BIBLIOGRAPHY

Abraham, William J. *The Coming Great Revival.* San Francisco: Harper and Row, 1984.
———. *The Divine Inspiration of Holy Scripture.* Oxford: Oxford University Press, 1981.
Balke, Willem. "Word and Spirit." In *Calvin and the Anabaptist Radicals,* 320–27. Translated by William Heyner. Grand Rapids: Eerdmans, 1981.
Barr, James. *Fundamentalism.* Philadelphia: Westminster, 1977.
Barth, Karl. *Church Dogmatics.* 4 vols. Edited by G. W. Bromiley and T. F. Torrance. Translated by G. W. Bromiley, et al. Edinburgh: T. & T. Clark, 1956–1975.
———. *Dogmatics in Outline.* Translated by G. T. Thomson. London: SCM, 1957.
Bebbington, David W. *Evangelicalism in Modern Britain: A History from the 1730s to the 1980s.* London: Unwin Hyman, 1989.
Beegle, Dewey M. *The Inspiration of Scripture.* Philadelphia: Westminster, 1963.
Beeke Joel R., editor. *Calvin for Today.* Grand Rapids: Reformation Heritage, 2009.
Berkouwer, G. C. *Holy Scripture.* Translated and edited by Jack B. Rogers. Grand Rapids: Eerdmans, 1975.
Bernstein, Richard J. *Beyond Objectivism and Relativism: Science, Hermeneutics, and Praxis.* Philadelphia: University of Pennsylvania Press, 1983.
Bloesch, Donald G. *Essentials of Evangelical Theology.* Vol. 1. San Francisco: Harper and Row, 1978.
Bonhoeffer, Dietrich. *Worldly Preaching.* Edited by Clyde E. Fant. Nashville: Thomas Nelson, 1975.
Braaten, Carl E., and Robert W. Jenson. *Reclaiming the Bible for the Church.* Grand Rapids: Eerdmans, 1995.
Brunner, Emil. *The Christian Doctrine of God.* Translated by Olive Wyon. 2 vols. Philadelphia: Westminster, 1960.
———. *The Christian Doctrine of Creation and Redemption.* Translated by Olive Wyon. Philadelphia: Westminster, 1952.
———. *The Mediator: A Study of the Central Doctrine of the Christian Faith.* Translated by Olive Wyon. New York: Macmillan, 1934.
———. *The Philosophy of Religion from the Standpoint of Protestant Theology.* Translated by A. J. D. Farrer and Bertram Lee Woolf. New York: Charles Scribner's Sons, 1937.
———. *Revelation and Reason.* Translated by Olive Wyon. Philadelphia: Westminster, 1946.
———. *The Scandal of Christianity.* Philadelphia: Westminster, 1950.
———. *Truth as Encounter.* Philadelphia: Westminster, 1964.
Burtchall, James T. *Catholic Theories of Biblical Inspiration Since 1810.* Cambridge: Cambridge University Press, 1969.
Busch, Eberhard. *Karl Barth: His Life from Letters and Autobiographical Texts.* Translated by John Bowden. Philadelphia: Fortress, 1976.
Calvin, John. *Calvin: Theological Treatises,* Translated by J. K. S. Reid. Philadelphia: Westminster, 1954.
———. *Concerning the Eternal Predestination of God.* Translated by J. K. S. Reid. London: James Clarke, 1961.
———. *Institutes of the Christian Religion* (1559). Edited by John T. McNeill. Translated by Ford Lewis Battles. 2 vols. Philadelphia: Westminster, 1960.
———. *Institution of the Christian Religion* (1536). Translated by Ford Lewis Battles. Atlanta: John Knox, 1975.

————. *Selected Works of Calvin, Tracts.* Edited and translated by Henry Beveridge. Grand Rapids: Baker, 1983.

————. *Treatises Against the Anabaptists and Against the Libertines.* Edited and Translated by Benjamin Wirt Farley. Grand Rapids: Baker, 1982.

Cobb, John B. Jr. *Living Options in Protestant Theology: A Survey of Methods.* Philadelphia: Westminster, 1962.

DeVries, Dawn. *Jesus Christ in the Preaching of Calvin and Schleiermacher.* Louisville: Westminster John Knox, 1996.

DeWolf, J. Harold, *The Case for Theology in Liberal Perspective.* Philadelphia: Westminster, 1959.

Dockery, David S. "Variations on Inerrancy." *SBC Today* (10 May 1986) 10–11.

Duke, James O. and Robert F. Streetman. eds. *Barth and Schleiermacher: Beyond the Impasse?* Philadelphia: Fortress, 1988.

Duncan, Ligon, "The Resurgence of Calvinism in America." In *Calvin for Today*, edited by Joel R. Beeke, 227–40. Grand Rapids: Reformation Heritage, 2009.

Ebeling, Gerhard. *Word and Faith.* Translated by James W. Leitch. Philadelphia: Fortress, 1963.

Erickson, Millard J. *Christian Theology.* 3 vols. Grand Rapids: Baker, 1983.

Faber, Jelle. "The Saving Work of the Holy Spirit in Calvin." In *Calvin and the Holy Spirit: Papers and Responses Presented at the Sixth Colloquium on Calvin & Calvin Studies*, edited by Peter deKlerk, 1–11. Grand Rapids: Calvin Studies Society, 1989.

Finlayson, R. A. *The Story of Theology.* London: Tyndale, 1963.

Gamble, Richard C. "Word and Spirit in Calvin." In *Calvin and the Holy Spirit: Papers and Responses Presented at the Sixth Colloquium on Calvin & Calvin Studies*, Edited by Peter DeKlerk, 75–92. Grand Rapids: Calvin Studies Society, 1989.

Gerrish, Brian A. *Saving and Secular Faith: An Invitation to Systematic Theology.* Minneapolis: Fortress, 1999.

————. "Theology within the Limits of Piety Alone: Schleiermacher and Calvin's Doctrine of God." In *The Old Protestantism and the New: Essays on the Reformation Heritage*, 196–207. Chicago: University of Chicago Press, 1982.

Gerstner, John H. "The Church's Doctrine of Biblical Inspiration." In *The Foundation of Biblical Authority*, edited by James Montgomery Boise, 23–58. Grand Rapids: Zondervan, 1978.

————. ed. *Lux Mundi: A Series of Studies in the Religion of the Incarnation.* London: John Murray, 1899.

Gore, Charles. *The Doctrine of The Infallible Book.* New York: George H. Doran, 1925.

Grenz, Stanley J. *Revisioning Evangelical Theology: A Fresh Agenda for the 21st Century.* Downers Grove, IL: InterVarsity, 1993.

Hedge, Frederic. ed. *Essays and Reviews.* Boston: Walker, Wise, 1860.

Hendry, George S. "The Rediscovery of the Bible." In *Reformation Old and New: A Tribute to Karl Barth*, edited by F. W. Camfield, 142–56. London: Lutterworth, 1947.

Hodge, A. A., and B. B. Warfield, "Inspiration." *The Presbyterian Review* 6 (1881) 225–60.

Hodge, Charles. "Inspiration." *The Biblical Repertory and Princeton Review* 29 (1857) 660–98.

————. *Systematic Theology.* 3 vols. New York: Scribner, Armstrong, 1877.

Hodges, Louis Igou. "Scripture." In *New Dimensions in Evangelical Thought: Essays in Honor of Millard J. Erickson*, edited by David S. Dockery, 209–34. Downers Grove, IL: InterVarsity, 1998.

Kant, Immanuel. *Prolegomena to Any Future Metaphysics.* Translated by Peter G. Lucas. Manchester: Manchester University Press, 1953.

Kuhn, Thomas. *The Structure of Scientific Revolutions.* Chicago: University of Chicago Press, 1962.

Jones W. T. *The Sciences and the Humanities: Conflict and Reconciliation.* Berkeley: University of California Press, 1965.

Leith, John H., editor. *Creeds of the Churches.* Atlanta: John Knox, 1963.

Lindsell, Harold. *The Battle for the Bible.* Grand Rapids: Zondervan, 1976.

Lischer, Richard. *Open Secrets: A Memoir of Faith and Discovery.* New York: Broadway, 2002.

———. *A Theology of Preaching: The Dynamics of the Gospel.* Nashville: Abingdon, 1981.

———. *Theories of Preaching: Selected Readings in the Homiletical Tradition.* Durham: Labyrinth, 1987.

McGrath, Alister E. *A Scientific Theology.* 3 vols. Grand Rapids: Eerdmans, 2001, 2002, 2003.

Machen, J. Gresham. *Christianity and Liberalism.* Grand Rapids: Eerdmans, 1923.

Mackintosh, H. R. *The Christian Apprehension of God.* 1929. Reprint, Eugene: Wipf & Stock, 2008.

———. *Types of Modern Theology: Schleiermacher to Barth.* London: Nisbet, 1956.

Macleod, Donald. "Calvin into Hippolytus?" In *To Glorify God: Essays on Modern Reformed Liturgy,* edited by Bryan Spinks and Iain Torrance, 255–67. Grand Rapids: Eerdmans, 1999.

Marsden, George. *Reforming Fundamentalism: Fuller Seminary and the New Evangelicalism.* Grand Rapids: Eerdmans, 1987.

Merrill, William Pierson. *Liberal Christianity.* New York: Macmillan, 1925.

Milner, Benjamin Charles Jr. *Calvin's Doctrine of the Church.* Leiden: Brill, 1970.

Moore, Walter L. "Schleiermacher as a Calvinist: A Comparison of Calvin and Schleiermacher on Providence and Predestination." *Scottish Journal of Theology* 24 (1971) 167–83.

Muller, Richard A. *Post-Reformation Reformed Dogmatics.* 4 vols. Grand Rapids: Baker Academic, 2003.

Murray, John. *Calvin on Scripture and Divine Sovereignty.* Grand Rapids: Baker, 1960.

Nicole, Roger, "Induction and Deduction with Reference to Inspiration." In *Soli Deo Gloria: Essays in Reformed Theology: Festschrift for John H. Gerstner,* edited by R. C. Sproul, 95–102. Phillipsburg: P & R, 1976.

Noll, Mark. *Between Faith and Criticism: Evangelicals, Scholarship and the Bible in America.* San Francisco: Harper and Row, 1986.

North, Gary. *Crossed Fingers: How the Liberals Captured the Presbyterian Church.* Tyler: Institute for Christian Economics, 1996.

Ottati, Douglas F. *Theology for Liberal Presbyterians and Other Endangered Species.* Louisville: Geneva, 2006.

Parker, H. L. *John Calvin: A Biography.* London: J. M. Dent & Sons, 1975.

———. *The Oracles of God: An Introduction to the Preaching of John Calvin* London: Lutterworth, 1947.

Partee, Charles. "Calvin's Polemic: Foundational Convictions in the Service of Truth." In *Calvinus Sincerioris Religionis Vindex,* edited by Wilhelm H. Neuser and Brian G. Armstrong, 97–122. Kirksville, MO: Sixteenth Century Journal, 1997.

———. *The Theology of John Calvin.* Louisville: Westminster John Knox, 2008.

———. "Truth as Search and Encounter." In *A Passion for the Gospel: Confessing Jesus Christ for the 21st Century,* edited by Mark Achtemeier and Andrew Purves, 71–79. Louisville: Geneva, 2000.

Pepper, Stephen C. "The Root Metaphor Theory of Metaphysics." *Journal of Philosophy* 32 (1935) 365–74.

Preus, Robert. *The Inspiration of Scripture: A Study of the Theology of the Seventeenth Century Lutheran Dogmaticians.* Edinburgh: Oliver & Boyd, 1955.

Reid, J. K. S. *The Authority of Scripture.* New York: Harper and Brothers, 1957.

Rogers, Jack B., and Donald K. McKim. *The Authority and Interpretation of the Bible.* New York: Harper and Row, 1979.

Sanday, W. *Inspiration.* London: Longmans, Green, 1914.

Schaff, Philip. *The Creeds of Christendom.* 1931. Reprint, Grand Rapids: Baker, 1983.

Schepers, Maurice B. "The Interior Testimony of the Holy Spirit: A Critique of Calvinist Doctrine." *The Thomist* 29 (1965) 140–76, 295–321, 420–59.

Schleiermacher, Friedrich. *The Christian Faith.* Edited by H. R. Mackintosh and J. S. Stewart. New York: Harper and Row, 1963.

Schweitzer, Albert. *The Quest of the Historical Jesus: A Critical Study of its Progress from Reimarus to Wrede.* Translated by W. Montgomery. London: A. & C. Black, 1936.

Shurr, William H. *Rappacini's Children: American Writers in a Calvinist World.* Lexington: University Press of Kentucky, 1981.

Stackhouse, John G. Jr., "Evangelical Theology Should Be Evangelical." In *Evangelical Futures: A Conversation on Theological Method,* edited by John G. Stackhouse, Jr., 39–58. Grand Rapids: Baker, 2000.

Sweeney, Douglas A. "'Falling Away from the General Faith of the Reformation'? The Contest over Calvinism in Nineteenth Century America." In *John Calvin's American Legacy,* edited by Thomas J. Davis, 111–46. Oxford: Oxford University Press, 2010.

Stuhlmacher, Peter. *Historical Criticism and Theological Interpretation of Scripture: Toward a Hermeneutics of Consent.* Translated by Roy A. Harrisville. Philadelphia: Fortress, 1977.

Thomas F. Torrance, *The Christian Doctrine of God: One Being Three Persons.* Edinburgh: T. & T. Clark, 1996.

———. *Reality and Evangelical Theology.* Philadelphia: Westminster, 1982.

Turretin, Francis. *Institutes of ElencticTheology.* Edited by James T. Dennison, Jr. Translated by George Musgrave Giger. 1979. Reprint, Phillipsburg: P & R, 1992.

Vanhoozer, Kevin. *God, Scripture, and Hermeneutics.* Downers Grove, IL: InterVarsity, 2002.

Van Til, Cornelius. *Christianity and Barthianism.* Grand Rapids: Baker, 1962.

———. *The New Modernism: An Appraisal of the Theology of Barth and Brunner.* Philadelphia: P & R, 1947.

Wallace, Ronald S. *Calvin's Doctrine of the Word and Sacrament.* Edinburgh: Oliver and Boyd, 1953.

Warfield, Benjamin Breckinridge. "Calvin's Doctrine of the Knowledge of God." In *Calvin and Calvinism,* 29–130. New York: Oxford University Press, 1931.

———. *Revelation and Inspiration.* New York: Oxford University Press, 1927.

Weber, Otto. *Foundations of Dogmatics.* Translated by Darrell L. Guder. Grand Rapids: Eerdmans, 1981.

Webster, John, *Holy Scripture: A Dogmatic Sketch.* Cambridge: Cambridge University Press, 2003.

————.*Thomas Reid and the Story of Epistemology.* Cambridge: Cambridge University Press, 2001.

Wolterstorff, Nicholas. "Hume and Reid." *The Monist* 70 (1987) 398–417.

Young, Edward J. *Thy Word Is Truth: Some Thoughts on the Biblical Doctrine of Inspiration.* Grand Rapids: Eerdmans, 1957.

# 3

## The Depth Dimension of Scripture

### A Prolegomenon to Evangelical Calvinism

ADAM NIGH

## INTRODUCTION

THE BIBLE IS THE foundation and criterion for Christian theology. Our presuppositions about what it is and how we are to interpret it will have decisive implications for our theology. What kind of presuppositions does an Evangelical Calvinist approach Scripture with and how are these related to the doctrinal convictions of Evangelical Calvinism? While the subsequent chapters will address the second part of this question, each focusing on a particular doctrinal locus, this chapter will address itself to the first part by examining the work of T. F. Torrance on the Bible's "dimension of depth" as a prolegomenon to such doctrinal development. Torrance's critical realist theological epistemology involves a view of Scripture that differentiates the divine Word and human words while yet refusing to divorce Scripture from the economy of God's self-revelation that has brought it into being and continues to make use of it in the life of his church. I will also draw, though to a lesser degree, on the work of Karl Barth, under whom Torrance studied, at points where Torrance's thought is largely indebted to Barth's and where interacting with Barth directly will help us see clearly what lies behind Torrance's insights. We will begin by considering Torrance's understanding of dualism as the chief obstacle to approaching Scripture in its full depth, moving then to an examination of concepts Torrance and Barth develop that are critical to the proper articulation of Scripture's ontology, and finally a consideration of several aspects of the kind of hermeneutic that naturally follows from perceiving Scripture in its depth dimension.

## DUALISM, ALLEGORY, AND FLAT EXEGESIS

Torrance frequently names varying problematic approaches to Scripture or its theological content as "dualistic." Dualism, as Torrance understands and criticizes it, is a pattern of thought the church inherited from ancient Hellenism as the preaching of the gospel expanded from Judea, and thus from a Hebraic conceptual context, into the broader Mediterranean world and began to be interpreted according to Greek philosophical categories of thought. This way of thinking understands reality according to a radical disjunction between those aspects of the world available to our sensory perceptions and those directly available to our minds apart from sensory stimuli, ascribing all sensible/material things to the realm of temporal and changing forms and ascribing all intelligible/spiritual things to the realm of eternal and immutable ideas.

> The Platonic separation (χωρισμός) between the sensible world (κόσμος αἰσθητός) and the intelligible world (κόσμος νοητός), hardened by Aristotle, governed the disjunction between action and reflection, event and idea, becoming and being, the material and the spiritual, the visible and the invisible, the temporal and the eternal, and was built by Ptolemy into a scientific cosmology that was to dominate European thought for more than a millennium. The combined effect of this all-pervading dualism was to shut God out of the world of empirical actuality in space and time.[1]

Dualism shuts God out of the observable world by identifying him in his nature as Spirit univocally with the spiritual, conceptual, intelligible side of its dichotomy, thus necessarily interpreting any statement or narrative of God's activity within the observable world in a mythological or allegorical way.[2]

The confusion created by dualist habits of thinking not only problematizes or disallows any notion of God performing particular historical acts within the visible world, but it also fails to make a radical enough

1. Torrance, *The Trinitarian Faith*, 47.
2. Torrance, *Theology in Reconstruction*, 34.

NIGH—*The Depth Dimension of Scripture*

distinction between God and creation by binding him to its intelligible aspects.[3] The dualist thinker fears that all intelligibility would be falsified if it were not eternal and is thus compelled to posit the eternality of either some or all of creation.[4] Thus dualism paradoxically banishes God from the historical and material sphere of creation and yet also binds God to creation on its spiritual, invisible, conceptual side, failing to understand his utter transcendence, sovereignty, and freedom over both the material and the spiritual.

When this form of thinking is present, biblical interpretation tends to follow two dominant strategies. The first is represented by the history of allegorical interpretation, which Torrance traces back to Philo of Alexandria in its application to the Old Testament through to the Gnostics in their varied allegorical interpretations of the Old and New Testament writings.[5] Since dualistic thinking is prohibited from interpreting biblical accounts of God's historical acts of redemption as actually historical, the Gnostics were forced either to cut all such accounts out of Scripture, as did Marcion, or to interpret them as signs taking the form of historical event whose real meaning is to be found entirely outside of the world of space and time, in the eternal and intelligible realm. This approach severs the literal meaning of the text, or what Philo called its "body" (σῶμα), from its inner meaning, or "soul" (ψύχη),[6] and thus "takes away all ground for positive control of man's thinking about God, and throws him back upon himself and the fancies of his own imagination."[7] With such a hermeneutic, the possible interpretations of a given passage are endless.

Torrance sees modern strategies of reading Scripture exemplified by Rudolph Bultmann's campaign of demythologization as manifesting the same revulsion to the notion of God's acts in space and time

---

3. Torrance traces the conflict of the Christian doctrine of creation *ex nihilo*, particularly its stress on the unity of matter and form as both are brought into being out of nothing, with the dualist Hellenistic forms of thinking it encountered, arguing that it was primarily the recognition that in Jesus Christ God himself acted within the observable historical world that forced the church to recognize the *ex nihilo* character of God's relationship to creation. This theme runs virtually throughout Torrance's study of Patristic hermeneutics. See Torrance, *Divine Meaning*, 44–45, 63, 93, 184–86, 344.

4. Ibid., 44–45.

5. Ibid., 22–34.

6. Ibid., 24.

7. Ibid., 34.

and thus extending the Gnostic error into modernity.[8] Though differing from ancient Gnosticism because of its focus on discovering the "historical Jesus," Bultmann's strategy nevertheless finds in the life of Jesus not the determinative historical event accomplishing God's revelation to and reconciliation with humanity but a symbol expressing humanity's basic self-consciousness before God. Thus humanity's shared existential experience replaces the Hellenistic emphasis on pure reason as offering access to truth in ancient Gnosticism, but both approaches to Scripture share the conviction that the text itself is basically dispensable, offering merely an occasion for ascending to truth through subjective re-interpretation.

The other dualistic strategy for reading Scripture we will call flat exegesis (biblicism[9] and fundamentalism[10] are Torrance's primary terms for it, though the latter expresses more than an approach to Scripture). Where allegorical and demythologizing readings of Scripture stretch the connection between the words of the text and the Word of God mediated through them to or beyond the breaking point, flat exegesis fails to make any differentiation at all between the human words and the divine Word. The Word of God is conflated with the intelligibility of the words of Scripture so that its verbal propositions are equated with the truth they propose.[11] Scripture is thus not a creaturely servant of the self-revealing God but functionally takes his place, possessing and dispensing his truth in its literary forms. John Webster notes that this typically takes place when the notion of biblical inspiration is focused more on the desire for an inerrant source of universal truth in the context of theological controversy rather than on the place of Scripture in the divine soteriological economy. "When this is allowed to happen, the scriptural word . . . becomes the Word, the Word made text, formalized, decontextualised and so dogmatically displaced."[12]

8. Torrance, *Karl Barth*, 206–7.

9. Torrance, "The Deposit of Faith," 23–24.

10. Torrance, *Reality and Evangelical Theology*, 17–19.

11. Such conflation is actually dualistic in that it assumes a total disjunction between the sensible/material and intelligible/spiritual, identifying the words of Scripture as "spiritual" and thus on the spiritual side of the disjunction. Since such dualism maps the distinction between divine and creaturely onto the distinction between spiritual and material, the dualist is constrained from conceiving of Scripture as both spiritual and creaturely.

12. Webster, *Holy Scripture*, 35–36.

These approaches, the allegorizing or demythologizing reading which detaches the truth of Scripture from its literary forms on the one hand and the biblicist reading which flatly equates the truth of Scripture with its literary forms on the other hand, are two opposite sides of the same dualist coin. Each approaches Scripture under a conceptual framework in which reality is divided into a realm where events are observed in their historical particularity, a realm of fact without truth, and a realm where universal truths are directly intelligible to the mind apart from external data, a realm of truth without fact. The first approach places Scripture on the side of facts, leaving the reader to ascend to truth by their own means through creative allegorical interpretation, while the second places Scripture on the side of truth, failing to understand that Scripture's truth is not intrinsic in its words and sentences but precisely in the extrinsic fact it bears witness to, God himself speaking and acting in history. God has acted in Jesus Christ to reveal himself to us and reconcile us to himself and continues to act by the Spirit of Christ through proclamation of the message of Christ on the basis of Scripture.

These dualist approaches to Scripture err because they are insufficiently theological, or more precisely, because they fail to understand what Scripture is according to its own theological content. They are unclear about the unbiblical presuppositions that drive their reading. What is needed is an understanding of Scripture's ontology and of what it means to read Scripture that arises from the content of Scripture itself. In this regard, the early church appealed to the "rule of faith", an understanding of the core content of the gospel message the apostles received from Christ and passed on to the church, often through concise confessions such as the Apostles' Creed or the Nicene Creed.[13] In other words,

---

13. In Torrance, "The Deposit of Faith," Torrance contrasts Tertullian's notion of the "rule of faith" (*regula fidei*), which Torrance sees as "a fixed formula of truth for belief" that is "rather legalist and anthropocentric", with Irenaeus' notion of the "canon of truth" (*kanōn tēs alētheias*), which "was in fact the *Truth* itself" in freedom from and Lordship over formal expression of it (15). However, elsewhere Torrance approvingly refers to the rule of faith as essentially indistinguishable with the deposit of faith and canon of truth. Cf. Torrance, *Atonement*, 397; and Torrance, *Divine Meaning*, 123–26, the latter in which he says that "the rule of faith is not just a formal summary of doctrine handed down in the ecclesiastical tradition, but that which is constantly imposed upon the Church by the truth itself and as such has objective and universal validity" (124). In Torrance, *The Trinitarian Faith*, 125–26, he allows the rule of faith to serve as a synonym for the canon of truth but distinguishes that synonymous use from Tertullian's more legalist conception of it in a footnote. I use the term "rule of faith" here

the rule serves as a brief summary of the central thrust of Scripture's message, allowing readers to keep an understanding of the whole in view as they navigate through particular passages.[14] Its intended function was to allow the objective reality of the Gospel message to continually re-form the minds of believers as they read Scripture by keeping its central content always in view and clearing away alien conceptual frameworks such as dualism. There has always been a temptation, however, parallel to the biblicist habit of flatly equating Scripture with the truth it mediates, to formalize the rule into a rigid set of doctrines and flatly equate those doctrines with the truth they articulate, a habit Torrance refers to as confessionalism, which is itself another manifestation of dualism.[15] Thus, both biblicism and confessionalism exhibit a dualist conflation of the truth that God reveals to us in Christ by the Spirit, that is, the truth in God himself, with expressions of that truth in intelligible human language, whether in the biblical text itself or in doctrinal formulations of its truth. The Truth of God and the truth of human words are flattened out and equated.

## SCRIPTURE'S DEPTH DIMENSION

What is needed is a theological understanding of Scripture, one aided by the rule of faith as expressed in the Apostle's Creed and Nicene Creed, which is yet able to distinguish between the words of Scripture and doctrinal confessions on the one hand and the Word that is God and became flesh in Jesus Christ on the other, but that nevertheless holds the words of Scripture and the Word of God together in their dimension of depth.[16] Four important concepts in Torrance's thought will be helpful to note here.

---

as Torrance allows it to be used as a more general synonym for Irenaeus' thought rather than in the sense he sees Tertullian giving it.

14. N. T. Wright speaks of doctrines and creeds as "portable stories", compressing aspects of the biblical narrative into short phrases in order to be made conveniently useful in teaching or argument. Wright, "Reading Paul, Thinking Scripture," 62–65.

15. Torrance, "The Deposit of Faith," 23–24.

16. Torrance, *Theological Science*, 129–30. Though the two must be distinguished, they must not be separated, for as Torrance has said, "in Christ Jesus event and message, fact and meaning, the Word and the word, the Truth and truths, are all intrinsically integrated and cannot be torn apart without serious dismemberment and distortion of the Faith." Torrance, "The Deposit of Faith," 4.

*Onto-relations*—Torrance defines an onto-relation as "the kind of relation subsisting between things which is an essential constituent of their being, and without which they would not be what they are. It is a being-constituting relation."[17] Relationality requires that a distinction subsist between two things which occasions their relation. Onto-relations, then, are the sort of relation in which the identity of a thing is not collapsed into that of something else but is nevertheless constituted by its relation to something else. Things are profoundly misunderstood when approached in atomized separation and related to one another only by external causality rather than through their being-constituting onto-relations.[18] Torrance observes that this approach to reality, which came about in the church's wrestling with the identity of Jesus Christ, has been confirmed in the last century and a half by the scientific developments of electromagnetic field theory by James Clerk Maxwell and relativity theory by Albert Einstein.[19] Thus the natural sciences are developing in a way which bears an important resemblance to Christian theology's Trinitarian methodology in which it seeks to know God not as an isolated monad nor through his external relations but through the incarnate Son's onto-relation with the Father in the Spirit.

In the case of Scripture, Torrance notes the need in hermeneutics for a "fully holistic approach in which the empirical and conceptual, or the historical and theological, ingredients of the New Testament are held together."[20] He goes on to lament the ways these ingredients have been severed in modern biblical scholarship. These problems in biblical interpretation are rooted in deeper problems in understanding the ontology of Scripture.

> The books of the New Testament are to be understood, therefore, not as just historical documents deriving from the primitive Church which give us information about God and his reconciling love and are to be interpreted in a merely phenomenalist fashion, but as the appointed means by which God continues through his

---

17. Torrance, *Reality and Evangelical Theology*, 42–43.

18. Ibid., 44–45.

19. Torrance, *The Mediation of Christ*, 47–50.

20. Torrance, *The Christian Doctrine of God*, 35. Though he speaks particularly of the New Testament here, his strong, though nuanced, understanding of the relation between the Old and New Testaments, or perhaps we could say their onto-relation, allows us to apply what he says here to all of Scripture. See Torrance, *Theology in Reconstruction*, 137–38.

Spirit to address his living Word to us and speak to us personally
and directly about himself in such a way that he is immediately
present to us in his Word.[21]

Torrance offers us here a description of Scripture in its onto-relation
to the self-revealing God. Scripture cannot be properly understood in
atomized isolation from the Gospel it serves, even through application
of the adjectives "holy," "inspired," "authoritative," or the like, but neither
can it be understood in flat identification between itself and God's revelation. Rather, it must be understood in its onto-relation to God's triune
economy of revelation and reconciliation as a specially called forth and
sanctified instrument of that economy.

*Objectivity*—The kind of theological thinking we engage in when reading Scripture takes place in a subject-object relation, God being the object of our thinking as subjects. In subject-object relations of knowing,
an obligation falls on the subject to allow the object to direct and form
his knowing, resisting the impulse to foist his own preconceptions in the
way of his knowledge of the object. This involves a difficult process of
removing preconceptions by continually returning to the object to have
one's subjective conceptions reformed in its light, requiring the formation of a personal detachment from one's preconceptions. This habit of
deference to the object is what we call "objectivity" in scientific thinking,
a concept that need not and should not imply a disinterested detachment from the object of inquiry: "It is sheer attachment to the object that
detaches us from our preconceptions, while we detach ourselves from
our preconceptions in order to be free for the object, and therefore free
for true knowledge of it."[22] Moreover, objectivity requires not only an attachment to and deference toward the object of inquiry, but also a mode
of inquiry derived from and appropriate to the object. In our reading
of Scripture, if our thinking about God is to be objective in this sense,
taking form under the pressure of its external object, we must think the
kinds of thought appropriate to God's being. That is, the manner of our
thinking and the questions we ask on our way toward knowledge of God
must not be wholly idiosyncratic lest they direct us only back to our own
biases, but must instead attend closely to the nature of our object, God,

21. Torrance, *The Christian Doctrine of God*, 36–37.
22. Torrance, *Theological Science*, 36.

and take their particular shape in correspondence to his nature.[23] Three aspects of that nature require treatment here.

First, God is personal. To understand and read Scripture rightly, we must recognize the personal nature of the knowledge of God it mediates. That is, since Scripture mediates knowledge of God and God is not a physical object or an idea but a personal being, our knowledge of him, though without precise parallel because it is not knowledge of a creature but of the Creator who is utterly free in relation to creation, must yet share more of an affinity with our knowledge of other creaturely persons than with our knowledge of impersonal objects or events.[24] In personal knowledge "we have to abandon the notion that the rational is accessible to logico-analytical processes in the conviction that here we have to do with intelligible order of a kind that is too interiorly rich and unitary for that rather simplistic and reductionist approach."[25] The truth of God is always a truth that approaches us in a personal way, calling for personal response, because the truth of God is the Truth, the Word, that he is. Therefore, the truth of the Word can never be reduced to mere words because it is the truth of a personal being, or in fact the "person-constituting Being"[26] or "personalizing person,"[27] and our approach to Scripture must always bear this in mind.[28]

Second, God is always Subject. In contrast to our subject-object relations with natural objects in which we exert a degree of control and mastery over the object of our knowledge, and in contrast even with our interpersonal relationships in which the subject-object relation is also a subject-subject relation of mutual knowledge and influence, knowledge of God involves what Torrance calls "an *epistemological inversion* in the order of our knowing" so that we actually know God in an object-subject relation, ourselves as the known objects and God as the knowing Subject.[29] That is, "we know only as we are known, and we conduct our

---

23. Torrance, *Theological Science*, 123–24.

24. To speak of such an affinity is not to ground our knowledge of God in our knowledge of human persons, but simply to draw an illustrative parallel, though an admittedly remote one.

25. Torrance, *Reality and Evangelical Theology*, 44.

26. Ibid., 43.

27. Torrance, *The Trinitarian Faith*, 230.

28. Of course, this need not imply that human words are excluded as a means of the Word's self-communication.

29. Torrance, *Theological Science*, 131.

research only as we are searched through and through by God."[30] This is because God is never passive object or even mutual subject but the sovereign Lord of all knowledge of himself. "Here our effort to subdue everything to our knowledge is halted and obstructed by God, for He is the one Object we cannot subdue. We can know Him only as we are subdued by Him, that is, as we obediently rely upon His Grace."[31] Our knowledge of God is a product of his work, not our own. This means that proficiency in exegetical skills alone cannot make us competent readers of Scripture; the inner work of the Holy Spirit is the primary criterion of proper biblical interpretation.

Third, God is self-objectifying.[32] That is, in his utterly free and gracious love for us he actively gives himself to us to be known where otherwise he would be entirely unknowable to us. Here Torrance appeals to Karl Barth's notion of God's twofold objectivity.[33] God's primary objectivity is the life he lives in himself in immediate knowledge of himself "for the Father is object to the Son, and the Son to the Father, without mediation."[34] God has this knowledge of himself, this objectivity, in his triune life "before creaturely objectivity and knowledge exist."[35] It is this primary objectivity of the knowledge God has of himself that is the precondition and basis of any knowledge of God that takes place in the realm of creaturely objectivity. But this primary objectivity is unavailable to us by itself, for God is he who "dwells in unapproachable light, whom no one has ever seen or can see"[36] and "no one comprehends what is truly God's except the Spirit of God." [37] That only God knows God in his primary objectivity is why he is always Subject in our knowing of him and never merely object—without his action toward us establishing our knowledge of him, such knowledge would be utterly impossible. In his grace, however, God takes to himself a secondary objectivity in which his primary objectivity is clothed by creaturely objectivities, that is, the objectivity of things other than God which we are able to directly

---

30. Ibid.
31. Torrance, *Theological Science*, 132.
32. Ibid., 37–38, 135–37.
33. Ibid., 136 n. 1.
34. Barth, *CD*, II/1, 16.
35. Ibid.
36. 1 Tim 6:16.
37. 1 Cor 2:11.

encounter in our creaturely sphere. "It is in, with and under the sign and veil of these other objects that we believe in God, and know Him and pray to Him."[38] Barth goes on:

> The objectivity of this other object *represents* the objectivity of God. In the objectivity of this other object [the human person] knows God, i.e., between himself and this other object the acts of distinguishing and uniting, uniting and distinguishing, take place. This other object he genuinely perceives, considers and conceives—but in and with this other object, the objectivity of God. This other object is thus the medium by which God gives Himself to be known and in which man knows God.[39]

Our knowledge of God is only in, because it is made possible by, this secondary objectivity. Said otherwise, our knowledge of God is always and only mediate and indirect, never immediate and direct. It is mediated by creaturely objectivity, yet not by creaturely objectivity in general but uniquely that having to do with the incarnation: "The basic reality and substance of the creatureliness which He has commissioned and empowered to speak of Him, the basic reality and substance of the sacramental reality of His revelation, is the existence of the human nature of Jesus Christ."[40] In the humanity of Christ we know his divinity and thus we know God. Thus, the meaning of faith is to be content to know God in Jesus Christ, to know God's primary objectivity only through this secondary objectivity he has taken to himself of our sakes.[41] Torrance sees Barth's understanding of faith as both giving Christian theology its scientific objectivity and giving Christian piety its humility:

> To try to get behind this creaturely objectivity, to go behind the back of the historical Jesus in whom God has forever given himself as the Object of our knowledge, and so to seek to deal directly with ultimate and bare divine objectivity, is not only scientifically false, but the *hybris* of man who seeks to establish himself by getting a footing in ultimate reality.[42]

As we have noted, knowledge of God means both distinguishing and uniting God's primary and secondary objectivities. Therefore, as we

---

38. Barth, *CD*, II/1, 16.

39. Ibid., 17. Emphasis mine.

40. Ibid., II.1, 53.

41. Ibid., II.1, 16–17.

42. Torrance, *Theological Science*, 137.

look exclusively to Christ for our knowledge of God, we must distinguish the divine objectivity in Christ, which was unseen in his earthly life, from his physical humanity, which was seen; but we must nevertheless understand their miraculous unity brought about in the incarnation so that we are truly able to know God in Christ, knowing Christ's unseen divine objectivity in his secondary creaturely objectivity. This distinguishing between God's primary and secondary objectivities in their onto-relational unity gives a depth perception to the Christian faith that proves particularly fruitful in interpreting Scripture, enabling an exegesis of the biblical text in its full "dimension of depth" [43] as testimony to the divine objectivity present in the creaturely objectivity of Christ and on that basis present in the testimony itself.

*Signification*—Some of the fruit an understanding of God's twofold objectivity yields has to do with the semiotics of Scripture. Darren Sarisky notes that for Torrance in his strategy of "depth exegesis," the Bible is "a *signum*, a text which certainly has literary and historical features, but which ultimately serves to reveal a transcendent *res*."[44] This transcendent *res* is of course God, but, as we have discussed, God is only to be known in his assumed creaturely objectivity, the humanity of Jesus Christ. Scripture thus serves as a creaturely sign of the transcendent reality of God made creaturely in Christ. This requires further analysis.

As we have seen, we must look nowhere but to Christ to know God because the humanity of Christ is the unique creaturely reality to which God has joined himself in the person of the Son. This union of God and humanity in Jesus Christ is utterly unique and cannot be construed as legitimizing a unification of God with creaturely reality in general or an extension of this union in Christ to any other creaturely reality outside his person. At the same time, says Barth, "because the revelation of God took place once and for all in Jesus Christ, we know the same revelation of God wherever it is attested in expectation and recollection."[45] In particular, Barth speaks of a sacramental continuity reaching back from Christ into Israel's expectation of him as their Messiah attested in the Old Testament and forward to the apostle's recollection of him attested

---

43. Torrance, *Karl Barth*, 186–87.

44. Sarisky, "T. F. Torrance on Biblical Interpretation," 333.

45. Barth, *CD*, II/1, 53–54.

in the New Testament.[46] The Old and New Testaments thus mediate knowledge of Christ by their respective expectation and recollection of him and through them we are given knowledge of him in the present as he mediates knowledge of himself through their authoritative testimony to him. As Torrance puts it, "It is still through these Holy Scriptures that we are given knowledge of God, for we may not know him except in accordance with the steps he has taken to make himself known or through the means he has provided for his continuing self-revelation."[47] The formation of the Scriptures is a part of these steps and means. Torrance has much to say about these steps: God's covenant with Israel and the history enacted with them from which the Old Testament Scriptures arose through the prophets,[48] Christ's appointing, training, authorizing and spiritual indwelling of the apostles, making their witness to him his own and thus giving their kerygmatic and didactic ministry enduring authority for the church founded upon them,[49] and the joining of the Old Testament Scriptures with the New Testament Scriptures through the ministry of the apostles "to form together, as the one apostolic-prophetic revelation of God in the language of our human flesh, the perpetual foundation of the Church as the Israel of God."[50] Thus the Bible is not a sign of Christ fashioned merely by the will and creativity of the prophets and apostles but called forth by the very God who revealed himself in Christ to signify that revelation.

To speak this way about Scripture as a divinely provided *signum* of the *res* of God in Christ entails some decisions about the ability of human language to speak of God. For "if human forms of thought and speech are to have a transcendental reference to what is really beyond them, it must be given them by God Himself."[51] For Torrance, such reference is only possible because of the hypostatic union of divine and human natures in the person of Christ.

---

46. Ibid., II/1, 54.

47. Torrance, *Reality and Evangelical Theology*, 121.

48. Ibid., 84–87.

49. Torrance, *Atonement*, 315–40. These pages comprise "Chapter Ten—The Biblical Witness to Jesus Christ: The Coming of the Spirit and the Creation of Apostolic Testimony and Gospel," which gives Torrance's most sustained and clear treatment of the doctrine of Scripture and its authority for the church.

50. Torrance, *Theology in Reconstruction*, 138.

51. Torrance, *Space, Time and Incarnation*, 19.

> It is only because Christ is himself personally God that his human speech and human actions, and his human forms of thought, are also divine revelation. The language of Jesus was creaturely language, and quite distinct from God's language, even his language about God, and creaturely language is only capable of speaking of creaturely things. If here God's language has become human and creaturely language, we would not hear God in Jesus' creaturely speech, unless there was a hypostatic relation between his creaturely language and God's own godly language. It is only in that union in which God's language condescends to take on creaturely form, and human language is joined to God's language, that there is real revelation.[52]

In Christ, God uses human language to speak of himself. In itself human language is inadequate to speak of God because it can only speak of creaturely reality, but God adapts it to speak of him by adapting himself to creaturely reality in Christ. However, this does not mean that human language is now invested with an inherent capacity to speak of God, anymore than it means that creaturely reality in general is made divine; rather, certain forms of human speech, particularly certain analogies or παραδείγματα,[53] are appropriated from among the vast range of human speech, and applied to God in his inner relations as they are revealed in Christ, namely, the analogical language of Father and Son such that the Son is the "image" or "form" of the Father.[54] We are thus enabled to speak of God as Father because the incarnate Son holds forth their relationship and speaks of it, speaks of the Father in heaven and of himself as the Son come to earth, as the image of God in creation. However, such human analogies are able to speak of God only in so far as they are rooted in and derive from the hypostatic union, the one true analogy between God and humanity.[55] Moreover, such an analogy is not to be thought of as "a simile of man's choosing or devising, but rather as an image taken from human things which divine Revelation has laid hold of and uses in a special way for its particular purpose."[56] Since it is only in Christ that hu-

---

52. Torrance, *Incarnation*, 193.

53. Παραδείγματα is a patristic term Torrance uses frequently which he translates as "pointer," disliking "model," "representation" and "archetype" as alternative translations. Torrance, *Space, Time, and Incarnation*, 16.

54. Torrance, *Divine Meaning*, 254–59.

55. Torrance, *Theology in Reconstruction*, 114.

56. Torrance, *Divine Meaning*, 255.

man words and analogies are enabled to reference God, Torrance speaks of the humanity of Christ as the "real text" of Scripture.[57]

This being the case, we must still carefully differentiate *signum* and *res*, sign and thing signified, referential language and its semantic referent. Scripture is not to be understood as revelation in and of itself, since revelation is not simply statements but God's personal *self*-revelation. Instead, Scripture is a sign directing our attention to the reality of that personal self-revelation in Christ which it is meant to signify. This is Scripture's onto-relation to Christ. It has no independent identity as a historical text, as possible as it may be to approach it as if it did.[58] Its words and sentences are meant to perform a transparent function, allowing the reality of Christ independent of them to "show through" them.[59] In reading Scripture, we must "allow the human expression to point us beyond itself, to what it is not in itself, but to what God marvellously makes it to be in the adoption of his grace."[60] Scripture can therefore be spoken of as itself revelation only in the sense in which it participates in God's self-revelation in this relation as *signum* to its *res* in Christ. There is thus a necessary process of differentiating and uniting in our approach to Scripture that is distinct from yet clearly parallel with that involved in understanding Christ in his dual natures or primary and secondary objectivities. This then leads us to see a double dimension of depth in Christian knowledge of God: Christ makes himself known to us through Scripture by the Spirit and God makes himself known to us through Christ by the Spirit. The hypostatic union of Christ's two natures is therefore where Scripture signifies God for us. The textual is thus differentiated from the personal, the secondary objectivity from the

---

57. Torrance, *The Mediation of Christ*, 78. Torrance speaks in this passage of Christ's humanity as the "real text" of the New Testament in particular. See n. 20 for justification for applying this to all of Scripture. See also Torrance, *Reality and Evangelical Theology*, 89 where Torrance speaks of Christ's humanity as the "real text" of God's self-revelation in general.

58. In this regard, Torrance levels the following criticism against modern biblical scholarship: "biblical scholars are too apt to treat the language of biblical documents in terms of its subjective reference or social matrix, that is, as primarily expressing the subjects of the authors or the mind of the community in which the documents arose" (Torrance, *Reality and Evangelical Theology*, 64).

59. Ibid., 65.

60. Torrance, *Theology in Reconstruction*, 139.

primary, and yet all are seen in their indivisible onto-relational unity in Christ as the self-revelation of God.

*Inadequacy and Fallenness*—We have already spoken of the inadequacy of human language to speak of God which God nevertheless adapts to speak of himself by adapting himself to humanity, taking on its verbal communication in the incarnation and applying certain analogies to himself. It is important for Torrance that even as such inadequate human language is adapted to and made adequate in divine use, it nevertheless retains its inadequacy. Acknowledged inadequacy is in fact a positive criterion for the adequacy of any human language or concepts to speak of God. Each creaturely sign retains a "measure of disparateness or discrepancy which is essential to its successful functioning as a sign. For a true statement to serve the truth of being, it must fall short of it, since it does not possess its truth in itself but in the reality it serves. Thus a dash of inadequacy is necessary for its precision."[61]

Going further, Torrance speaks not only of the inadequacy but even the fallenness of biblical language. This is rooted in his insistence that the humanity or "flesh" the Son took to himself in the incarnation was itself fallen. Torrance insists on this fallenness in Christ's flesh because in order for Christ to save us, his humanity must be our humanity under the curse of sin and at enmity with God.[62] Torrance often quotes Gregory Nazianzen's famous saying "the unassumed is the unredeemed" in this respect.[63] Though Christ committed no sin, he took our sinful flesh upon himself in order to put sin to death in his own body.[64] Taking our fallen humanity "he overcame its temptations, resisted its downward drag in alienation from God, and converted it back in himself to obedience toward God, thus sanctifying it."[65]

Since the flesh joined to the Word was fallen flesh, Torrance then reasons that the language of Scripture, which is the sign of Jesus' flesh, must be fallen as well.

---

61. Torrance, *Reality and Evangelical Theology*, 66.

62. Torrance, *Incarnation*, 62.

63. Cf. Torrance, *The Trinitarian Faith*, 164. The Gregory quotation can be found in Gregory, *Epistle 101*.

64. 1 Pet 2:24.

65. Torrance, *Incarnation*, 205.

> If the relation of the *Logos* to the *flesh* it assumed is the primary relation in theology, here in the doctrine of Holy Scripture we can only state the relation between the Word of God and the word of man in a way analogous to that primary and unique relation. If the flesh assumed by the *Logos* was flesh of our fallen humanity, sanctified in the very act of its assumption by the Word, then here we must say that the Word of God has assumed our fallen human speech into union with itself and sanctified it in that assumption so as to make it holy speech, holy scripture.[66]

Torrance draws a parallel here between the sanctification of fallen flesh in Christ and the sanctification of fallen speech in Scripture, but this must be understood according to the qualifications we have already made that human language can only speak appropriately of God at all because God has spoken our language as his own in Christ. Therefore, it is not the use of language in Scripture that sanctifies it but Christ's prior appropriation of it in the hypostatic union and its continued use in proclaiming him that does so. Nevertheless, as the biblical text participates in the attestation of Christ it is indeed sanctified so that Torrance can legitimately draw this parallel.

On the other hand we must carefully note the important difference between the sanctification of Christ's flesh in his sinless life and the sanctification of biblical language. Christ has already been raised as the first fruits of our redemption in him, but the rest of creation waits in eager expectation for its full inheritance of that redemption which is for now hidden with Christ in God.[67] Scripture, along with the church and all creation, thus bears an eschatological relation to Christ. In his ascension, Christ created an eschatological gap between himself and that which he redeemed so that the church stands in a tension between its participation in Christ as new creatures on the one hand and on the other its entanglement in the "contradictions and conflicts of history with another law in its members warring against the law of God."[68] Thus the participation of the apostles in Christ's perfect life does not immediately perfect them or their speech; it brings them into the eschatological gap, into the conflict Christ waged up to his death, calling them to take up their crosses and follow him.[69] For Torrance, though Scripture is au-

---

66. Torrance, *Atonement*, 336.

67. 1 Cor 15:20; Rom 8:19; Eph 1:14; Col 3:3

68. Torrance, *Atonement*, 405.

69. Ibid., 371–72.

thoritative over the church because its Lord speaks through it, Scripture nevertheless stands with the church on this side of the full manifestation of redemption, that is, as still fallen and under the judgment and mercy of God.[70]

> The Bible stands above the Church, speaking to the Church the very Word of God, but the Bible also belongs to history which comes under the judgment and the redemption of the Cross. That double place of Holy Scripture must always be fully acknowledged; else we confound the word of man with the Word of God, and substitute the Apostles in the place of Christ.[71]

It is precisely Scripture's solidarity with us in our present imperfection, in the inadequacy and fallenness of our language, which enables it to accomplish its paradigmatic purpose, pointing us to Christ in his redeemed and ascended humanity from this side of the eschatological divide.

This kind of treatment of Scripture certainly raises questions. Torrance seems to affirm utter contradiction and embrace irrationalism[72] when he makes this kind of statement: "Considered in itself it is imperfect and inadequate and its text may be faulty and errant, but it is precisely in its imperfection and inadequacy and faultiness and errancy that God's inerrant Holy Word has laid hold of it that it may serve his reconciling revelation and the inerrant communication of his Truth."[73] How can a faulty and errant text serve an inerrant communication of truth? When he speaks of the text or speech of Scripture as fallen, if by fallen he means sinful and/or under the curse of sin, how can text or words sin since they are not themselves moral agents? While this second question may linger, for the first it is helpful to note that Torrance's focus in speaking this way is to highlight that the revelatory power of Scripture lies in God himself and is never surrendered into our hands when we lay hold of the text. This emphasis is certainly helpful as long as

70. Ibid., 337.

71. Torrance, *Theology in Reconstruction*, 138.

72. See Torrance's written exchange with American philosopher Brand Blanchard over Blanchard's charge in his 1952 Gifford Lectures at the University of St. Andrews that Barth embraced exactly this kind of irrationalism in his doctrine of revelation. "A Skirmish in the Early Reception of Karl Barth in Scotland."

73. Torrance. *Divine Meaning*, 10. For a fuller treatment of this dialectical relation between the fallen creatureliness of the text and its holiness in divine use see Torrance, *Theology in Reconstruction*, 138–40.

the relationship between God's Word and the words of Scripture is not construed as arbitrary or accidental, which Torrance certainly does not. Moreover, we may see Torrance's use of such paradoxical expressions as his own faithfulness to his insistence on the use of open concepts in theological articulation, a topic we will discuss below. Torrance certainly does not indulge in simple irrationalism; his burden is to articulate the mysterious and miraculous rationality of God's self-revelation, a reality he is convinced cannot be put simply without cutting our minds loose from their object. Perhaps it is best to point to the recurring pattern in Scripture seen in the barren wombs, ill equipped warriors, alienated prophets, and other human weaknesses through which God chooses to demonstrate his power; Torrance sees Scripture itself as participating in this recurring pattern. The glorification of God in such a view certainly commends it.

To summarize up to this point, to understand Scripture aright we cannot approach it in isolation but only in its onto-relation to Jesus Christ, understood as God's own Word in himself or primary objectivity clothed in the secondary objectivity of our humanity, who is the reality of which Scripture is a sign. Scripture is only what it is in relation to the humanity of Christ who called it forth as proclamation of himself and thus serves as its true content external to it and to which it is meant to point transparently beyond itself. The intention in our explanation has been, having already laid aside dualistic allegorizing and demythologizing approaches to the text of Scripture as artificially detaching the meaning of the text from its concrete literary forms, to identify an ontology of Scripture in its full depth dimension in which the reality of God in Christ shows through its literary forms as he unites them with his own speech, as opposed to flattening approaches which conflate the text of Scripture with the Truth it is called to serve. A final word from Torrance will suffice before moving on: "Indeed it may be said that if the Scriptures are treated as having a light inherent in themselves, they are deprived of their true light which they have by reflecting the Light of Christ beyond themselves—and then the light that is in them is turned into a kind of darkness"[74]

---

74. Torrance, *Reality and Evangelical Theology*, 95.

## DEPTH EXEGESIS

In the remainder of this chapter, I will briefly make explicit what kind of hermeneutic this ontology of Scripture might be expected to give rise to. Torrance describes the exegetical task in this way: "our task in reading the outward text is to get at its inner meaning and basis, to read it at the deeper level of the solid truth on which the text rests. By a special act of the understanding that goes beyond mere reading, we penetrate into the objective *ratio* of the Word which enlightens and informs us."[75] This penetration involves several considerations.

First, as interpreters of Scripture, we must, as Torrance puts it, *indwell* the text "as a whole and in all its parts in such a way that we acquire a habit of looking *through* the various books and passages of the Scriptures and allowing their message to be interiorized in the depths of our mind."[76] Torrance goes on: "In this way a structural kinship becomes built up between our knowing and what we seek to know, which enables us intuitively to grasp the conjoint meaning latent in the biblical texts which we could not derive simply from the particularities and explicit features of the documents themselves."[77] Torrance is advocating an approach to Scripture that is both rigorous, involving a considerable commitment of time and energy working and reworking through the texts, and spiritual, devoted not simply to the accumulation of knowledge but the interiorizing of the truth of Christ. This kind of reading corresponds to the personal nature of the Bible's content, God revealing himself in Christ through the Spirit, which leads naturally to a second consideration.

Secondly, we must keep a constant eye to Christ as the personal *res* Scripture as a whole signifies. Or, as Torrance also frequently expresses it, we must read Scripture with an understanding of Christ as its scope (σκοπός), a term he appropriates from Athanasius meaning "the object on which the eye is fixed" or "the goal or end toward which attention is or ought to be directed."[78] This does not mean that we interpret every sentence of Scripture as being directly about Christ, but rather that we

75. Torrance, *Karl Barth*, 186.

76. Torrance, *The Christian Doctrine of God*, 37. Torrance's reference here is to the New Testament in particular, though his doctrine of Scripture certainly commends an expansion of his notion of indwelling to the whole biblical text.

77. Ibid.

78. Torrance, *Divine Meaning*, 235.

see Christ as what the Bible as a whole is about and, more importantly, that by the Spirit Christ speaks of himself throughout all of Scripture. J. Todd Billings has put it this way: "Apart from a special hermeneutic that sees the biblical canon as God's word fulfilled in Christ, there is no reason to think that the collection of writings in the Bible are truly one book—a book with diversity, but also with unity, in its witness to God in Christ."[79] Without an understanding of Christ as the scope of Scripture as a whole, we can only read it as a collection of ancient religious books plagued by historical inconsistencies and theological contradictions. However, read in faith it is unified as Christ's own self-testimony.

Thirdly, an understanding of Scripture's referential character will interrelate the semantic reference and the syntactic coherence in Scripture into an "interpretative framework of thought."[80] Torrance makes it clear that the denotative or semantic function of language, that accomplished by what he calls "existence-statements," is mutually dependent with its connotative or syntactic function, that accomplished by "coherence statements," for as he adapts a phrase from Kant, "coherence-statements without existence-statements are empty, existence-statements without coherence-statements are blind."[81] The semantic function has a basic priority since what we are concerned with is the reality of God in Christ external to the text whom we meet through it, but the inner coherence of God's presence and action in Christ is made known in the orderly syntactic internal relations of the Bible's semantic references.[82] In this way form and content are organically coordinated in Scripture. The interpreter's job is then to make this inner coherence explicit through "the construction of a consistent line of theological statements through which the 'inner logic' of the biblical message becomes disclosed."[83] This foundation must then be built upon in an ongoing progression of deepening engagement with Scripture in its full depth. Torrance sees this progressing through a stratification of conceptual levels in which "the lower levels are opened to the higher levels and the higher are controlled

79. Billings, *The Word of God for the People of God*, 33.

80. Torrance, *Reality and Evangelical Theology*, 113.

81. Torrance, *Theological Science*, 169.

82. Torrance, *Reality and Evangelical Theology*, 113–14.

83. Ibid., 118.

through coordination with the lower."[84] Ben Meyers offers more detail on this facet of Torrance's thought:

> According to this model, our conceptual knowledge arises from the ground level of our intuitive apprehension of reality; and, even as this knowledge becomes increasingly formalised, it remains closely coordinated with our basic intuitive experience of reality. Thus we advance towards ever more refined conceptuality not by moving away from concrete reality, but by penetrating more deeply into it. In this stratified process of knowing we are therefore progressively "grasping reality in its depth"—which is, for Torrance, the basic function of "scientific knowledge."[85]

This is how the rule of faith is meant to work and, in Torrance's estimation, the way it did work in the generation of the Nicene Creed as its authors broke themselves and their presuppositions on the objectivity of Christ in Scripture and reached a conceptual clarity in the *homoousion*, arising as it did not as an alien concept developed elsewhere and then foisted on Scripture but precisely as a condensed commentary on Scripture.[86]

But how do we avoid the kind of flat confessionalism Torrance worries about in this endeavor of crafting and building upon an interpretative framework through which we approach the text? How do we avoid setting up our creeds derived from this process of interpreting Scripture in its interrelation of form and content as an authority that takes Scripture's place? This brings us to our fourth consideration, the necessity that these conceptual interpretative frameworks use open rather than closed concepts, that is, "concepts that are relatively closed on our side of their reference through their connection with the space-time structures of our world, but which on God's side are wide open to the infinite objectivity and inexhaustible intelligibility of the divine Being."[87] Torrance often illustrates this point by referring to Byzantine icons of Christ in which he stands on a dais depicted with intentionally reversed perspective so that its front is narrower than its back; as its side lines are extended, rather than running parallel, they will converge toward the viewer but infinitely

---

84. Torrance, *Space, Time and Incarnation*, 20.

85. Meyers, "Stratification," 5–6.

86. Torrance, *The Trinitarian Faith*, 126–27.

87. Torrance, *Space, Time and Incarnation*, 21.

widen as they are extended beyond into the background.[88] Our conceptual frameworks through which we approach Christ through Scripture must similarly bear a general coherence in the foreground on the level of the creaturely analogies employed in them, but they must remain open in their reference the divine reality infinite beyond their semantic reach so that they are held as perpetually revisable in its light.[89] This approach is a natural outworking of differentiating between God's objectivity and the necessarily inadequate creaturely concepts and statements employed to point us to him.

Fifth, we must recognize the inherent integration of God's work of revelation and reconciliation. On the creaturely side, this means knowledge and holiness can only increase in equal stride. "To know God and to be holy, to know God and worship, to know God and to be cleansed in mind and soul from anything that may come between people and God, to know God and be committed to him in consecration, love and obedience, go inseparably together."[90] This, once again, means that critical and exegetical skill alone cannot guarantee an appropriate reading of Scripture. To know God through Scripture, not only is the objective externality of Christ and of the written text necessary, but so is the Holy Spirit as the "objective inwardness" of God within those in Christ.[91] The Holy Spirit is "the confrontation of human beings and their affairs with [God's] own Self in which he brings the impact of his divine power and holiness to bear directly and personally upon their lives in judgment and salvation alike."[92] God is Word and Spirit and cannot be known through the isolation of either from the other. The Spirit brings us knowledge of God by inwardly illuminating the message of Jesus Christ in our minds and simultaneously conforming our lives to his in resistance to the patterns of the world.[93] Knowledge of God cannot be gained apart from this simultaneity.

This stress on the work of the Holy Spirit of conforming us to the holiness of Christ leads naturally to our sixth and final consideration, the church of Christ as the proper context of biblical interpretation.

88. Torrance, *Theological Science*, 15.

89. Ibid., 10.

90. Torrance, *The Mediation of Christ*, 26.

91. Torrance, *Divine Meaning*, 198.

92. Torrance, *The Trinitarian Faith*, 192–93.

93. Torrance, *Atonement*, 435.

> It is there in the midst of the church, its fellowship of love, its med-
> itation upon God's self-revelation through the Holy Scriptures,
> its Eucharistic life, and its worship of the Father through the Son
> and in the Spirit, that we become inwardly so adapted to God's
> interaction with us that we learn, as Origen used to say, how to
> think *worthily* of God, that is, in a godly way appropriate to God.[94]

We can only properly understand Scripture's message and thus be joined
to God through his reconciling work if we follow that reconciling work
to the earthly community it has formed.[95] Torrance notes a danger in
this thought that we may confuse the church with God's revelation, giving the subjective pole of the knowing relation God establishes with us
primacy over the objective, which is why he says, following Barth, that
dogmatics must be a critical science, holding the church's ongoing tradition of doctrine and biblical interpretation up to the objectivity of the
Word in Scripture. The necessary point here, however, is that this critical
inquiry take place within the church as the "community of reciprocity"
God has established through his work of revelation and reconciliation in
Jesus Christ.[96] To connect this point with those above, it is in the church
that we engage Scripture and encounter the Word through the Holy
Spirit in a union of revelation and reconciliation, holding ourselves and
our conceptual presuppositions open before the objectivity of God in
Christ. In that engagement, we do not move past the text to Christ, following its semantic reference past its syntactic textuality, but rather we
collectively indwell Scripture in its entirety in communal worship and
study so that a conceptual kinship arises in our minds through which
the Spirit unites us to one another as he unites us to Christ.

## CONCLUSION

Torrance offers us a rich account of what Scripture is, giving consistent
attention to its location in the divine economy, and helpful suggestions
for how to interpret it according to its nature as testimony to Christ.
Through his approach, Scripture neither replaces Christ as the objective reality of divine revelation nor stands irrelevant to our knowledge
of God as a merely human expression of spiritual genius. Rather, it is

94. Torrance, *Reality and Evangelical Theology*, 48.

95. Ibid., 46.

96. Torrance, *The Mediation of Christ*, 12–14.

NIGH—*The Depth Dimension of Scripture*

human testimony called forth by the Spirit of God to testify to the incarnate Word and thus annexed by God to his own Word as he speaks
through it to us.

How does this construal of Scripture's ontology and the hermeneutic it engenders relate to the doctrinal concerns of Evangelical Calvinism?
The differentiation between the divine Word and the human words in
Scripture in their unity in God's redemptive economy along with a focus on the personal and transcendent nature of Scripture's content lies
squarely behind Evangelical Calvinism's focus on theo-logic over against
a purely deductive logic in the work of theology.[97] Evangelical Calvinism
does not begin with logical propositions read off the surface of the
biblical text and then work through deductive syllogism to systematic
statements about God. Such a theological method assumes a causal necessity at work in God's relations with his creation. Instead, Evangelical
Calvinism seeks to indwell the Scriptures and grasp the inner logic of
God's gracious self-revelation mediated in them, developing doctrinal
formulations that faithfully reflect both the coherence and the mystery
of the gospel. Therefore, for example, while Evangelical Calvinism discovers in Scripture that Christ died and accomplished atonement for all
humanity, it does not affirm universal salvation, though that might be
a legitimate conclusion operating on formal deductive logic, nor does
it back away from the universal reach of Christ's atonement by reading
the limited subjective appropriation of atonement on behalf of humanity
into the eternal will of God through a doctrine of limited atonement
precisely because such conclusions assume a causal necessity determining God's actions that is foreign to the testimony of Scripture and,
indeed, to God's being. Instead, Evangelical Calvinism recognizes that
while the atonement accomplished in Christ applies to all humanity, the
reality of sin that keeps so many from belief cannot be worked into a
logical continuity with God's grace but must be left unsystematized as an
utter irrationality over which, however, God will ultimately triumph and
against which he has struck the decisive blow in the person and work of
Jesus Christ.[98]

97. See theses eight through twelve in the final chapter of this volume for what
follows.

98. See the foreword to the second edition of Torrance's *The Mediation of Christ*,
xi–xiv.

Of greatest importance in matters of biblical interpretation and doctrinal formulation, the majesty of God as it is exposed to us by the Spirit in the person of Jesus Christ through Scripture's attestation of him must continually send the church into a posture of reverence and prayer before the God whose objectivity and intelligibility we can never exhaust but only enter into ever greater engagement with.

## BIBLIOGRAPHY

Barth, Karl. *Church Dogmatics*. 4 vols. Edited by G. W. Bromiley and T. F. Torrance. Translated by G. W. Bromiley, et al. Edinburgh: T. & T. Clark, 1956–1975.

Meyers, Benjamin. "Stratification of Knowledge in the Thought of T. F. Torrance." *Scottish Journal of Theology* 61 (2008) 1–15.

Sarisky, Darren "T. F. Torrance on Biblical Interpretation." *International Journal of Systematic Theology* 11 (2009) 332–46.

Torrance, Thomas F. *Atonement: The Person and Work of Christ*. Edited by Robert T. Walker. Downers Grove, IL: InterVarsity Academic, 2009.

———. *The Christian Doctrine of God: One Being Three Persons*. Edinburgh: T. & T. Clark, 1996.

———. "The Deposit of Faith," *Scottish Journal of Theology* 36 (1983) 1–28.

———. *Divine Meaning: Studies in Patristic Hermeneutics*. Edinburgh: T. & T. Clark, 1996.

———. *Incarnation: The Person and Life of Christ*. Edited by Robert T. Walker. Downers Grove, IL: InterVarsity Academic, 2008.

———. *Karl Barth: An Introduction to His Early Theology 1910–1931*. Edinburgh: T. & T. Clark, 1962.

———. *The Mediation of Christ*. 2nd Edition. Edinburgh: T. & T. Clark, 1992.

———. *Reality and Evangelical Theology*. 1982. Reprint, Downers Grove, IL: InterVarsity, 1999.

———. *Space, Time and Incarnation*. 1969. Reprint, Edinburgh: T. & T. Clark, 1997.

———. *Theological Science*. 1969. Reprint, Edinburgh: T. & T. Clark, 1996.

———. *Theology in Reconstruction*. 1965. Reprint, Eugene: Wipf & Stock, 1997.

———. *The Trinitarian Faith: The Evangelical Theology of the Ancient Catholic Church*. Edinburgh: T. & T. Clark, 1988.

Torrance, Thomas F., and Brand Blanshard. "A Skirmish in the Early Reception of Karl Barth in Scotland: The Exchange Between Thomas F. Torrance and Brand Balndshard." Edited by Iain and Morag Torrance. *Theology in Scotland* 16, Special Issue: *In Memoriam* The Very Rev. Professor Thomas F. Torrance (2009).

Webster, John. *Holy Scripture*. Cambridge: Cambridge University Press, 2003.

Wright, N. T. "Reading Paul, Thinking Scripture." In *Scripture's Doctrine and Theology's Bible*, edited by Markus Bockmuehl and Alan Torrance, 59–71. Grand Rapids: Baker Academic, 2008.

# 4

## *Analogia Fidei or Analogia Entis?*

### Either through Christ or through Nature

BOBBY GROW

## INTRODUCTION

IF THE CHRISTIAN GOD is triune in nature; then would it not make sense to begin thinking about him from within the contours of who he has revealed himself to be versus modes that are foreign to who he is, and then try to construe his life as God through those media? This is exactly the dichotomy that has obtained in the history of Christian ideas. Either God is approached through the categories provided by his self-revelation in Christ; or he is approached *via* abstract philosophical reflection that methodologically starts in creation and makes analogical inferences from there.

This chapter will elaborate upon the general differences provided by this either/or approach to knowing God. It will argue that the best approach to knowing God is the one that starts with God as he has revealed himself to be as Father and Son by the Holy Spirit; and that the alternative approach leads to a flawed understanding of who God is, because it primarily thinks of him as a brute creator; and thus fails to adequately provide a trajectory for knowing God that best captures the uniquely Christian specification of God as Triune and relational.

As a result, the prolegomenon for an Evangelical Calvinist understanding of God will be laid bare. Furthermore, the confessional nature

94

of Evangelical Calvinism will be highlighted by correlating certain Reformed confessions and a catechism with the prolegomenon that is coordinate with an Evangelical Calvinist approach. This latter move will be made in order to underscore Evangelical Calvinism's place within the boundaries of confessional and thus "Reformed" Christianity.

## PROLEGOMENON AND TWO MODES FOR KNOWING GOD

The *conditio sine qua non* of an Evangelical Calvinist understanding of God begins where God begins, with his Son. As Thomas Torrance makes clear, starting with God as revealed by the Son allows God's triune nature to determine the way that we, as Christians, come to know him. That is, this is the proper way to think about the Christian God, trinitarianly; and we believe that this must lead to and from the conviction that God, as Athanasius held, has always already been Father and Son by the Holy Spirit before he ever becomes Creator.[1] This becomes important, as Colin Gunton has explained in regards to the Nicene Council's thinking; because ". . . By insisting . . . that God is eternally Son as well as Father, the Nicene theologians introduced a note of relationality into the being of God: God's being is defined as being in relation. Such is the impact of the doctrine of the incarnation on conceptions of what it is to be."[2] The problem that arises if we fail to engage God on his (these) terms, if we start with God as creator before Father; is that the Son can come to be thought of as part of God's creation, instead of the creator himself[3] resulting in a project that simply looks at Jesus as another one of "God's" works whereby we come to know God (as demiurge). Torrance makes this point vividly clear:

> [I]n such an approach we can do no more than attempt to speak of God from his works which have come into being at his will through his Word, that is, from what is externally related to God, and which as such do not really tell us anything about who God is or what he is like in his own nature. That line of approach, as both Athanasius and Hilary insisted, is entirely lacking in accuracy or precision. . . . They differentiated themselves here sharply from the thesis of Basileides, the Gnostic of Alexandria, who taught, with reference to Plato's statement that God is beyond all being,

1. See Torrance, *The Trinitarian Faith,* 49; Molnar, *Torrance,* 73.
2. Gunton, *The Promise of Trinitarian Theology,* 8.
3. Molnar, *Torrance,* 74–76.

that we cannot say anything about what God is, but can only say something about what he is not. It was pointed out by Gregory Nazianzen, however, that if we cannot say anything positive about what God is, we really cannot say anything accurate about what he is not.[4]

The other approach, the one that stands in contrast to the Evangelical Calvinist "way," has been called *Natural Theology*, or more technically the *analogia entis*. The *analogia entis* is often captured by the language of *Classical Theism*,[5] which follows a procedure for establishing a doctrine of God by way of viewing him through "his works" or *per accidens*, analogically reasoning from the effects and predicates to their ultimate cause and subject, as we just noted with Torrance's account. This method of theological construction is given its most salient Christian exposition by Thomas Aquinas. Aquinas writes,

> the proposition that "God exists" is self evident in itself, for, as we shall see later, its subject and predicate are identical, since God is his own existence. But, because what it is to be God is not evident to us, the proposition is not self-evident to us, and needs to be made evident. This is done by means of things which, though less evident in themselves, are nevertheless more evident to us, by means, namely, of God's effects.[6]

4. Torrance, *The Trinitarian Faith*, 50.

5. Bruce McCormack says, "Classical theism presupposes a very robust Creator-creature distinction. God's being is understood to be complete in itself with or without the world, which means that the being of God is "wholly other" than the being of the world. Moreover, God's being is characterized by what we might think of as a "static" or unchanging perfection. *All* that God is, he is changelessly. Nothing that happens in the world can affect God on the level of his being. He is what he is regardless of what takes place—and necessarily so, since any change in a perfect being could be only in the direction of imperfection. *Affectivity* in God, if it is affirmed at all, is restricted to dispositional states which have no ontological significance." McCormack, ed., *Engaging the Doctrine of God*, 186–87. There is debate whether or not the approach of Thomas F. Torrance—and thus Evangelical Calvinism—fits within the definition of Classical Theism provided by McCormack. See McCormack, "Election and the Trinity," 203–24, for example. The issue revolves around, as McCormack presents it, the concern of presenting any "metaphysical" understanding of God (the traditional approach) versus the "post-metaphysical" approach that McCormack argues for through his constructive work with Karl Barth. Evangelical Calvinism works within the parameters provided by the *analogia fidei* albeit not as strictly defined by Karl Barth or Bruce McCormack.

6. Aquinas, *Summa Theologiae*, 7.

Thinking from God's effects to his person, necessarily delimits the possibility for thinking of God as he is *in se;* since this discursive route must start with creation, and created effects, versus God as personal, loving Father of the Son. According to *The Oxford Dictionary of the Christian Church,*

> The role of analogy in theology was much discussed by medieval writers, esp. St Thomas Aquinas; his treatment of the subject, together with that of Thomas de Vio Cajetan, proved very influential. In modern times the concept has again come into prominence: the RC philosopher Erich Przywara (1899–1972) made the analogy of being (*analogia entis*) central to his thought, whereas K. Barth rejected the notion as an attempt to subjugate the Divine to human categories and propounded as an alternative the notion of *analogia fidei* (analogy of faith).[7]

Karl Barth rejects the possibility of being able to engage in this kind of theologizing as a Reformed theologian. Here he is reflecting on a calling he had received to deliver the Gifford Lectures at the University of Aberdeen in 1937 and 1938:

> As a Reformed theologian I am subject to an ordinance which would keep me away from "Natural Theology," even if my personal opinions inclined me to it. I am of course aware that both in the past and in recent times there have been Reformed theologians also, to whom "Natural Theology," at least in a rather weakened and obscure sense of the term, appeared to be no impossible pursuit. I feel, however, that precisely the strong and clear understood the term—and he was perfectly correct in understanding it in this way—there does exist a knowledge of God and His connection with the world and men, apart from any special and supernatural revelation. This is a knowledge which perhaps requires and is capable of development and cultivation, but is none the less a knowledge which man as man is master of, just as he is of chemical and astronomical knowledge. . . .[8]

Barth elucidates, in response to Lord Gifford, what he finds problematic with trying to approach the knowledge of God in this format; for him the problem is that this only gives us "a knowledge which man as man is master of." Similarly this rubs the wrong way for Evangelical Calvinist's engagement of knowing God; like Barth we must not bend our *Theology*

7. Cross and Livingstone, eds., *The Oxford Dictionary of the Christian Church,* 56.

8. Barth, *The Knowledge of God,* 3–4.

*Proper* to the will of Lord Gifford or natural theology (as understood in its *classical* form). Our course to knowing God is to submissively bow our thinking to God's self-revelation for making himself known to us. That is, that knowledge of God is properly provided traction through a robustly oriented christological endeavor; as Thomas Torrance writes,

> Our task in Christology is to yield to the obedience of our mind to what is given, which is God's self-revelation in its objective reality, Jesus Christ. A primary and basic fact which we discover here is this: that the object of our knowledge gives *itself* to us to be apprehended. It does that within our mundane existence, within our worldly history and all its contingency, but it does that also beyond the limits of previous experience and ordinary thought, beyond the range of what is regarded by human standards as empirically possible. Thus when we encounter God in Jesus Christ, the truth comes to us in its own authority and self-sufficiency. It comes into our experience and into the midst of our knowledge as a *novum,* a new reality which we cannot incorporate into the series of other objects, or simply assimilate to what we already know.[9]

As we do this, we are able to better appreciate God as *Father of the Son by the Holy Spirit;* versus conceiving of god as a brute creator who simply creates, and does not intimately relate with his creation.

As we move forward it will become more apparent how it is that Evangelical Calvinism offers a *way* that grounds its starting point for theological engagement in its doctrine of God as Father, Son, and Holy Spirit. All of this is undertaken with the continuing caveat that Evangelical Calvinism works from a prolegomenon that is incommensurate with the classical theist tradition.[10] The Father and Son distinction, in relation to knowing who the God of the Bible is really cannot be overstated relative to the pivotal point that it plays in providing Evangelical Calvinism with a shape for her theology that emphasizes her evangelical nature.[11]

9. Torrance, *Incarnation,* 1.

10. Classic Calvinism is a subset of Classical Theism. This point will be further developed as we discuss the disparate approaches in the Reformed Confessions considered later.

11. As Thomas F. Torrance has made clear in regards to the primary importance of thinking of God as Father; he writes, "Hilary of Poitiers argued that it was the primary purpose of the Son to enable us to know the one true God as *Father.* This was the theme to which he gave considerable theological reflection in view of the Nicene *homoousion* and what it implied for our two-fold belief in God the Father Almighty and in God the

Foci developed prior to this juncture, involve issues that revolve around articulating a genuinely Christian prolegomenon; encompassing dogmatic points of interest that flow from the primary idea of God's relationality. That is to say, Evangelical Calvinism is committed to principles of communicating theology that are self-consciously, trinitarian in orientation. It is this kind of prolegomenon, or theological method that gives rise to the type of theology that can be uniquely identified as Christian. John Webster says,

> prolegomena to systematic theology are an extension and application of the content of Christian dogmatics (Trinity, creation, fall, reconciliation, regeneration, and the rest), not a "pre-dogmatic" inquiry into its possibility. "[D]ogmatics does not wait for an introduction." The fact that in its prolegomena systematic theology invokes doctrine means that this preliminary stage of the argument does not bear responsibility for establishing the possibility of true human speech about God, or for demonstrating how infinite divine truth can take finite form in human knowing. Prolegomena are, rather, the contemplative exercise of tracing what is the case, and explicating how and why it is so.[12]

In this vein, we are not providing an *apologetic* for Evangelical Calvinism's doctrine of God, or any of the other subsequent doctrines that follow this pivotal doctrine. We are not even giving argument for how we have come to our conclusions about God (only to describe), and thus all of our dogmatic expression. Instead we are introducing an Evangelical Calvinist explication of God as Father of the Son by the Holy Spirit which is constitutive for its entire theological program and as such is genuinely a prolegomena for the whole dogmatic enterprise.

---

Son of the Father. 'All who have God for their Father through faith have him for Father through the same faith whereby we confess that Jesus Christ is the Son of God.' Again: 'The very centre of saving faith is the belief no merely in God but in God as Father; nor merely in Christ, but in Christ as the Son of God; in him, not as a creature, but as God the Creator born of God.' 'The work which the Lord came to do was not to enable you to know him as the Father of the Son who addresses you . . . The end and aim of this revelation of the Son is that you should know the Father . . . Remember that the revelation is not of the Father manifested as God, but of God manifested as the Father." Torrance, *The Christian Doctrine of God*, 139.

12. Webster, "Principles of Systematic Theology," 57.

## THE RELATIONAL GOD OF EVANGELICAL CALVINISM

Evangelical Calvinism's doctrine of God, like that of John Calvin's,[13] is broadly *Scotist* in orientation. That is not to say that Evangelical Calvinism reflects a full blown Scotism, but that John Duns Scotus' thought on what constitutes God's ontological nature; and it is this which becomes central to how God's being and act are understood. This means that God's identity is shaped primarily by *who* he is and not, as per Classical Theism and Classical Calvinism, with *what* God is. This assertion is grounded upon God's self-revelation through his self-interpreting Word to us in Jesus Christ. A corollary of this is that Jesus externalizes God's antecedent life, *in se,* through his personal incarnate activity, *ad extra* (cf. John 1:18). As we come to know God the triune God as he is revealed in Christ, we quickly realize that God is love. Bruce McCormack provides some important nuance on what "God is love" entails when read from a Barthian (and, we may add, Evangelical Calvinist) perspective:

> It follows . . . that we can know what is meant by the statement "God is love" only when we have before us the divine "person" and not human persons. "God is love" does not mean simply that God is well disposed toward us, that God has strong feelings of affection for us, and so forth. It is not merely a question of dispositional states, though this is certainly included. Rather, fundamentally, "God is love" is a statement which describes the nature and meaning of the act in which God gives himself his own being. The act in which God gives to himself his own being is an act of love. . . .[14]

Consonant with this, an Evangelical Calvinism understands that God's gracious movement in Christ toward us is based upon his self-determined freedom to be *pro nobis* out of his ontological life.[15] Myk Habets clarifies this when he states,

13. See Muller, *Christ and the Decree,* 37.

14. See McCormack, ed., *Engaging the Doctrine of God,* 216. It should be borne in mind that the way McCormack further explicates this, in relation to Karl Barth's theology, is not without controversy. For further reference to the controversy that ensues, in-house, see Webster, ed., *The Cambridge Companion to Karl Barth,* 92–110; where McCormack presents a view of God that is at odds with another Princeton Theological Seminary Karl Barth scholar, George Hunsinger's interpretation of Karl Barth; this controversy has been dubbed "The Companion Controversy."

15. This thought appeals to the doctrine of God's *aseity.* According to John Webster: "God is *a se* in the eternal fullness of the loving relations of Father, Son, and Spirit. From

The Scotistic thesis on the primacy of Christ essentially comes down to one word—love. The predestination of Christ is a completely gratuitous act of God. The corollary is that the incarnation is not conditioned by any creaturely factor such as sin. This utter independence from a creaturely factor is true in the case of all the elect. Therefore, *a fortiori*, it must be true of the predestination of Christ who, as head of the elect, was predestined to the greatest glory. The basic reason given by the Scotists for the works of God *ad extra* is the supreme love of God.[16]

In other words, we hold that God's life is completely free and self-determined. He acts out of who he is in himself from himself (*a se*); as John Webster so poignantly develops:

> The movement of God's triune life has its perfection in and of itself and is utterly sufficient to itself, but this perfect movement is not self-enclosed or self-revolving. In its perfection, it is also a movement of self-gift in which the complete love of the Father, Son, and Spirit communicates itself *ad extra*, creating and sustaining a further object of love. Of himself, God is *gracious*. . . . [17]

Hence, because God *is* love in his intra-Trinitarian, coinhering, onto-relations;[18] he moves graciously in accord with this in his acts of salvation and redemptive purpose. In the words of Thomas F. Torrance we may conclude that "Our knowledge of the economic Trinity in the *ordo cognoscendi,* and our knowledge of the ontological Trinity, in the *ordo essendi,* may not be separated from one another, for they arise together, interpenetrate each other and regulate each other."[19]

---

himself God has life in himself. But God is from himself not only in his inner life but also in the external works which correspond to his inner life. With this we can complete the material description of God's aseity by expanding the second statement that "from himself God gives himself." See McCormack ed., *Engaging the Doctrine of God,* 119.

16. Habets, "On Getting First Things First," 347.

17. Webster, "Life in and of Himself," in McCormack ed., *Engaging the Doctrine of God.*

18. Thomas F. Torrance articulates what onto-relations mean amongst the persons who are the God-head: ". . . Thus the Father *is* Father precisely in his indivisible ontic relation to the Son and the Spirit, and the Son and the Spirit *are* what they are as Son and Spirit precisely in their indivisible ontic relations to the Father and to One another. That is to say, the relations between the divine Persons belong to what they are as Persons—they are constitutive onto—relations. 'Person' is an onto-relational concept." Torrance, *The Christian Doctrine of God,* 157.

19. Ibid., 136.

One obvious conclusion to be drawn from such a methodology is that the attempt to approach God in "negative ways" (*via negativa*) is a dead end[20] (or the *analogia entis*). Rather, we must think "scientifically" about God, meaning that our knowledge of who is God must necessarily be tied to his own revealed being as God. Thomas Torrance is instructive on this as he reflects upon what this kind of construal meant for Karl Barth:

> Barth found his theology thrust back more and more upon its proper object, and so he set himself to think through the whole of theological knowledge in such a way that it might be consistently faithful to the concrete act of God in Jesus Christ from which it actually takes its rise in the Church, and, further, in the course of that inquiry to ask about the presuppositions and conditions on the basis of which it comes about that God is known, in order to develop from within the actual content of theology its own interior logic and its own inner criticism which will help to set theology free from every form of ideological corruption.[21]

It is this methodology that is being endorsed when appeal is made to a "scientific" theology.

Christian prolegomena must not create an *a priori* construct of who we think god is prior to meeting him in Christ; instead the method is rooted in *a posteriori* reflection upon the God who has revealed himself through the identity and mission of Jesus Christ, and as we participate with Christ through being brought into union with his vicarious humanity by the Holy Spirit. Thus, Evangelical Calvinism eschews any system of theology that tries to develop a theology proper through preconceptions of god that are tied to methods like the *analogia entis* which infer a concept of godness from creation; or which seek to pursue methods of god-reflection that fail to recognize God's *aseity* (or His unique reality, *sui generis*). Simply put, Evangelical Calvinism's approach is positive and grounded in revelation—not philosophy or metaphysics. Thomas F. Torrance muses on this front:

> It is the Gospel of God's revealing and saving acts in Jesus Christ that provides us with this perspective for a formulation of the Christian doctrine of God. It belongs to the essence of the Gospel that God has come among us and become one with us in such

20. See Torrance, *The Trinitarian Faith*, 50.

21. Torrance, *Theological Science*, 7.

a reconciling and miraculous way as to demolish the barriers of our creaturely distance and estrangement from him, and has spoken to us directly and intimately about himself in Jesus Christ his beloved Son. In him he has made himself known to us as God the Father Almighty, the Creator of heaven and earth and of all things visible and invisible, the one Lord and Saviour of mankind. Only God can know and explain himself, so that he may be apprehended by us his human creatures only through his incarnate condescension to be one with us and through his Spirit to make us participate in the knowledge which God has of himself. . . .[22]

Knowledge of God as Father is uniquely related to the knowledge that the Son has of the Father, relative to his eternal relationship to the Father; and it is only through our pnuematologically shaped personal union with the Son, through grace, that knowledge of God becomes possible. This kind of knowledge is *sui generis,* and reserved only for those who have an intimate and penetrating knowledge of God by faith (*analogia fidei*). Andrew Purves and Mark Achtemeier concur with this sentiment when they write,

> The center of the New Testament is the relationship between Jesus Christ and the One he addresses as Father. The communion between Jesus and his heavenly Fatherly is an utterly unique relationship, of which we can know nothing apart from Jesus' own testimony. . . . God is thus Father not by comparison to human fathers, but *only* in the Trinitarian relation, as Father of the Son. Whenever *Father* is used of God it means "the One whom Jesus called Father." The paradigm text is John 1:18: "No one has ever seen God. It is God the only Son, who is close to the Father's heart, who has made him known." In Greek, the word for "made him known" is *exegesato.* Jesus "exegetes" or "interprets" the Father. The term does not denote a generic title for God outside of the Father and Son relationship. *Father* thus functions in Trinitarian language not as a descriptive metaphor but as a proper name, whose home is the relationship that exists from all eternity between the first and second Persons of the Trinity. . . .[23]

Evangelical Calvinists do not believe that "Father" language is simply *metaphorical* or of *epistemological* import alone; instead we see this as an antecedent, and ontological reality which the eternal Logos reveals

22. Torrance, *The Christian Doctrine of God,* 16.

23. Purves and Achtemeier, *Union In Christ,* 34–36.

to us and for us in the incarnation. While this is an *a priori* reality about God, *in se*, we only realize this *a posteriori* through his *ad extra* self revelation, "in Christ."

The *Traditional* approach (i.e., Classical Theism and Classical Calvinism) does not emphasize this reality as constitutive of God's being; that is to say, it does not start with God as Father and Son as revealed by the Christ through the Holy Spirit. Instead it follows that mode of theological discourse that speaks of God through abstract essentialist categories that, at the least, misconstrues who god is by speaking of him as a composite reality defined by an addition of his equal parts or energies, attributes, or accidents. Purves and Achtemeier write,

> The traditional naming of the Trinitarian God as Father, Son, and Holy Spirit is sometimes replaced today by the functional titles of Creator, Redeemer, and Sustainer. This works as an occasional use, describing God's acts, but not as a substitute for the Trinitarian Name. The Fatherhood of God is tied utterly to Jesus' naming of his own relationship to God, into which relationship we, by the Spirit, participate. . . . It was St. Athanasius who noted that the only reason we have for calling God "Father" is that God is so named by Jesus in the Bible. This points to the historical shape that the Gospels took: Christian faith is a biblical faith and a Jesus-based faith. God's Fatherhood was understood relationally in and through Jesus Christ as self-giving love, and not as a human image or concept projected onto God. . . .[24]

Purves and Achtemeier are operating out of the Barthian tradition of an *analogia fidei as opposed to the* classical approach, best articulated by Thomas Aquinas and the *analogia entis*. As alluded to earlier, the analogy of faith grounds its approach in revealed theology; so that the epistemic ground is fastened to the ontological ground provided by God's self revelation in the humanity of Christ.[25] This contrasts, in

---

24. Ibid., 34–36

25. See Myers, "The Stratification of knowledge in the thought of T. F. Torrance," 1–15, where he explains how Thomas Torrance construes the inter-relation between God's ontological reality being communicated to humanity, epistemologically, through the humanity of Christ for us: "Thomas F. Torrance's model of the stratification of knowledge is one of his most striking and original contributions to theological method. Torrance's model offers an account of the way formal theological knowledge emerges from our intuitive and pre-conceptual grasp of God's reality as it is manifest in Jesus Christ. It presents a vision of theological progression, in which our knowledge moves towards an ever more refined and more unified conceptualisation of the reality of God,

general, with the analogy of being that finds its epistemic starting point in humanity's self-mediated reflection upon nature and the effects of nature in relation to God.

The God we come to know in Jesus Christ is his Father. We do not first know him as Creator before we *know* him as Father; that is, our knowledge of God is contingent upon our knowledge of the Father as revealed in Jesus Christ. According to the Apostle John: "No one has seen God at any time; the only begotten God who is in the bosom of the Father, He has explained Him" (John 1:18 NRSV). Therefore, to be consistent with the theo-logic that John argues from; we must likewise assume—along with Molnar, Torrance, Barth, Webster, Gunton, *et alia*— that God is the Father of the Son by the Holy Spirit. Colin Gunton says,

> In worship, Christians are brought into relationship with the Father through Jesus Christ in the Holy Spirit. To be true to the logic of such experience, we are bound to say that if God is truly God, he must be eternally what he shows himself to be in time. The threeness of the trinitarian understanding of the Godhead is the outworking of the implications of the threeeness of his movement into time.[26]

## CONFESSIONAL SHAPE

Instead of discussing what the distinctions are, in particular, between the so called *analogia fidei* and *analogia entis* we shall focus on how these two disparate approaches play out theologically; and for our purposes, *confessionally*. What happens if a particular theologian, or school of theologians, follows Aquinas' approach to articulating God, theologically; versus a more Evangelical Calvinist approach?

A brief comparative analysis of three Reformed Confessions—The Westminster Confession of Faith, The Belgic Confession of the Faith, The Scots Confession of Faith—and one Catechism—The Heidelberg

---

while remaining closely coordinated with the concrete level of personal and experiential knowledge of Jesus Christ. According to this model, our thought rises to higher levels of theological conceptualisation only as we penetrate more deeply into the reality of Jesus Christ. From the ground level of personal experience to the highest level of theological reflection, Jesus Christ thus remains central. Through a sustained concentration on him and on his homoousial union with God, we are able to achieve a formal account of the underlying trinitarian relations immanent in God's own eternal being, which constitute the ultimate grammar of all theological discourse."

26. Gunton, *The Promise of a Trinitarian Theology*, 20.

Catechism—may be sufficient to illustrate how theological prolegomena can impact the tone and emphases that present themselves in the historic confession and catechism making of the Reformed church. What emerges through this analysis is the reality that while each confession has its own particular style[27]; there can also be a shared dogmatic thread that coordinates common themes of approach per the disparate confessions and catechisms—i.e., like with a doctrine of God.

## THE CONFESSIONS AND CATECHISM

After the opening chapter on Holy Scripture, the Westminster Confession of Faith begins Chapter 2 with a discussion on God and the Holy Trinity as follows:

> 1. There is but one only, living, and true God, who is infinite in being and perfection, a most pure spirit, invisible, without body, parts, or passions; immutable, immense, eternal, incomprehensible, almighty, most wise, most holy, most free, most absolute; working all things according to the counsel of his own immutable and most righteous will, for his own glory; most loving, gracious, merciful, long-suffering, abundant in goodness and truth, forgiving iniquity, transgression, and sin; the rewarder of them that diligently seek him; and withal, most just, and terrible in his judgments, hating all sin, and who will by no means clear the guilty.[28]

The *Belgic Confession of Faith, 1561 begins Theology Proper*:

*Art. I: There Is One Only God*

> We all believe with the heart, and confess with the mouth, that there is one only simple and spiritual Being, which we call God; and that he is eternal, incomprehensible, invisible, immutable, infinite, almighty, perfectly wise, just, good, and the overflowing fountain of all good.[29]

---

27. Barth reminds us that, ". . . Each Reformed confession is really a *singular work*, one next to many others. Its confessors had little or no actual drive, whether out of a sense of duty or even ambition, to compose a confession for *all* the Reformed churches . . ." (Barth, *The Theology of the Reformed Confession*, 12).

28. Williamson, *The Westminster Confession of Faith*, 23.

29. See Cochrane, *Reformed Confessions of the Sixteenth Century*, 189.

Art. VIII: God Is One in Essence, yet Distinguished in Three Persons

According to this truth and this Word of God, we believe in one only God, who is one single essence, in which are three persons, really, truly, and eternally distinct, according to their incommunicable properties; namely, the Father, and the Son, and the Holy Ghost. The Father is the cause, origin, and beginning of all things, visible and invisible; the Son is the Word, Wisdom, and Image of the Father; the Holy Ghost is the eternal Power and Might, proceeding from the Father and the Son. . . .[30]

Contrast the above with The Heidelberg Catechism, "Of God The Father—Lord's Day 9":

Q. 26. What do you believe when you say: "I believe in God the Father Almighty, Maker of heaven and earth"?

A. That the eternal Father of our Lord Jesus Christ, who out of nothing created heaven and earth with all that is in them, who also upholds and governs them by his eternal counsel and providence, is for the sake of Christ his Son my God and my Father. I trust in him so completely that I have no doubt that he will provide me with all things necessary for body and soul. Moreover, whatever evil he sends upon me in this troubled life he will turn to my good, for he is able to do it, being almighty God, and is determined to do it, being a faithful Father.[31]

Finally we can consider The Scots Confession of Faith, 1560, "Chapter 1—God":

We confess and acknowledge one God alone, to whom alone we must cleave, whom alone we must serve, whom alone we must worship, and in whom alone we must put our trust. Who is eternal, infinite, immeasurable, incomprehensible, omnipotent, invisible; one in substance and yet distinct in three persons, the Father, the Son, and the Holy Ghost. By whom we confess and believe all things in heaven and earth, visible and invisible to have been created, to be retained in their being, and to be ruled and guided by his inscrutable providence for such end as his

---

30. Ibid, 192–93. See ibid., 185–88 for historical background to *The Belgic Confession of Faith, 1561.* See also Beeke and Ferguson, *Reformed Confessions Harmonized,* ix.

31. Heidelberg Catechism quoted in Cochrane, *Reformed Confessions of the Sixteenth Century,* 309.

> eternal wisdom, goodness, and justice have appointed, and to the manifestation of his own glory.[32]

At first blush there might not be much apparent difference between The Westminster Confession of Faith (WCF), The Belgic Confession of the Faith (BC), The Heidelberg Catechism (HC) and The Scott's Confession 1560 (SC); but this requires further reflection. The "Westminster" tradition starts talking about God by highlighting his "attributes," these are characteristics that are contrasted with what humans are not (*analogia entis*). We finally make it to God as "Father, Son, Holy Spirit," but not before we have qualified him through "our" categories using humanity and nature (*analogia entis*) as our mode of thinking about "godness." This is true for both the WCF and the BC. Jan Rohls provides a helpful insight on this when he speaks to the nature of the composition of many of the Reformed Confessions (including both the WCF and the BC):

> It is characteristic of most of the confessional writings that they begin with a general doctrine of God's essence and properties, and only then proceed to the doctrine of the Trinity. The two pieces "On the One God" (*De deo uno*) and "On the Triune God" (*De deo trino*) are thus separated from each other . . . .[33]

Nevertheless, this is not the case for all Reformed confessions and/ or catechisms. We should consider the possibility of learning to read some confessions and catechisms together, relative to shared theological emphases.[34]

---

32. Henderson, ed., *Scots Confession 1560*, 166. See ibid., 159–62 for historical introduction to the Scots Confession of Faith, 1560.

33. Rohls, *Reformed Confessions*, 48.

34. Reading confessions and catechisms together is not a foreign practice in the Reformed churches, for example the Dutch Reformed church has, historically, read The Belgic Confession of the Faith, The Heidelberg Catechism, and The Canons of the Synod Dort together as an ecclesiological basis for "unity" among the Reformed churches—known as "The Three Forms of Unity." Jonathan Neil Gerstner writes,

> The Three Forms of Unity, the Belgic Confession, Heidelberg Catechism, and the Canons of the Synod of Dort, form the confessional basis of the Dutch Reformed Church. They also demonstrate how much the Dutch Reformed church was influenced by the broader Reformed community. The Canons of Dort were the only one of the three Dutch Reformed confessions composed in the Netherlands, and it included delegates from every Reformed church in Europe which were permitted to attend. The earlier two creeds reflect the two major

The Heidelberg Catechism *and* The Scots Confession both emphasize the Triune nature of God as Father; in other words, as Rohls notes above, these two statements do not separate God's personal relations from his works or attributes—as does both The Belgic Confession of the Faith and The Westminster Confession of Faith. The emphasis of these documents is thus on the *economic* revelation of God in Christ as the "eternal Son of God" who exegetes God's inner-life as loving Father of, Son, by the Holy Spirit as the shape of his being. James K. A. Smith picks up on this same reality as he comments on The Heidelberg Catechism:

> But I have to confess that when I discovered the Heidelberg Catechism, it was like discovering a nourishing oasis compared to the arid desert of Westminster's cool scholasticism. The God of the Heidelberg Catechism is not just a Sovereign Lord of the Universe, nor merely the impartial Judge at the trial of justification; the God of the Heidelberg Catechism keeps showing up as a *Father*. For example, when expounding the first article of the Apostles' Creed ("I believe in God, the Father almighty, creator of heaven and earth"), the Heidelberg Catechism discusses all the ways that God upholds the universe by his hand, but also affirms that this sovereign Creator attends to me, a speck in that universe. And it concludes the answer to question 26 by summarizing: "He is able to do this because he is almighty God; he desires to do this because he is a faithful Father."[35]

This illustrates the reason why, out of the Reformed *Confessions and Catechisms, these* reflect themes which are central to Evangelical Calvinism. It is the all important Doctrine of God embedded within these statements that Evangelical Calvinism believes is so important. In Smith's words, it is the language of Father that should be emphasized; the Father of the Son by the Holy Spirit—or the Trinitarian nature of God.

---

strands of the Reformed tradition which merged in the Netherlands, the French and the German. (Gerstner, *The Thousand Generation Covenant*, 11)

For more discussion on various usages of the Reformed confessions and catechisms see Rohls, *Reformed Confessions*, 265–302. Given the subordinate nature of the Reformed confessions to Scripture, there is a flexibility that inheres with their relative usage. Just as the Dutch Reform church adopted three particular Reformed statements within the confessional framework; likewise, Evangelical Calvinists operate with the same liberty in appropriating The Heidelberg Catechism and The Scots Confession of Faith for theological purposes.

35. *Smith, Letters to a Young Calvinist*, 55.

To repeat for sake of emphasis: according to Evangelical Calvinism, God is Father of the Son by the Holy Spirit—constituently—before he ever becomes or is known as Creator (Law-giver, etc.). God becomes Creator by a free act of gracious love for the other, and out of this free un-restrained act he graciously creates *because* he is a lover first; which shapes his creating (and saving and re-creating) activity in grace.

Thomas Torrance quite clearly understood how important this emphasis is to our understanding of God, especially as this is expressed in our confessional documents. He is worth quoting in full:

> [I]n the *Scots Confession* as in John Knox's *Genevan Liturgy*, the doctrine of the Trinity is not added on to a prior conception of God—there is no other content but the Father, the Son, and the Holy Spirit. There was no separation here between the doctrine of the One God *(De Deo Uno)*, and the doctrine of the triune God *(De Deo Trino)*, which had become Roman orthodoxy through the definitive formalisation of Thomas Aquinas. This trinitarian approach was in line with *The Little Catechism* which Knox brought back from Geneva for the instruction of children in the Kirk. "I believe in God the Father, and in Jesus Christ his Son and in the Holy Spirit, and look for salvation by no other means." Within this trinitarian frame the centre of focus in the Confession and Catechism alike is upon Jesus Christ himself, for it is only through him and the Gospel he proclaimed that God's triune reality is made known, but attention is also given to the Holy Spirit. Here once again we have a different starting point from other Reformation Confessions. Whereas they have a believing anthropocentric starting point, such as in the *Heidelberg Catechism*, this is quite strongly theocentric and trinitarian. Even in Calvin's *Institute*, which follows the fourfold pattern in Peter Lombard's *Sentences*, the doctrine of the Trinity is given in the thirteenth chapter within the section on the doctrine of God the Creator. Calvin's *Genevan Catechism*, however, understandably followed the order of the *Apostles' Creed*. The trinitarian teaching in the *Scots Confession* was by no means limited to the first article for it is found throughout woven into the doctrinal content of subsequent articles.[36]

This delineates how Evangelical Calvinism substantially moves away from the Thomist doctrine of God presented by Classical Theism and Classical Calvinism. Torrance's point on a wedge between the "single

---

36. Torrance, *Scottish Theology*, 3–4.

substance" of God versus the "thrice personages" of the Trinity within "'Classical' Theologies" is significant. In other words, as Torrance highlights, we should not start with a notion of "god," and then add on the *hypostasis* of the Trinity to that concept; instead Evangelical Calvinists believe, along with Torrance, that the *ousia* of God (*de Deo uno*) finds its shape in the coinhering inter-relations of the Father, the Son, and the Holy Spirit (*de Deo trino*).[37]

## CONCLUSION

The contention of this chapter has been to provide insight into the inner workings of an Evangelical Calvinist prolegomenon. The procedure has been to introduce the specific way that Evangelical Calvinism understands the triune nature of God as Father of the Son by the Holy Spirit. All such thinking is diametrically opposed to the Thomistic way of construing God; namely, by use of the *analogia entis*. These two ways were then illustrated by means of several of the significant Reformed Confessions and a Catechism.

Evangelical Calvinism is committed to the tradition of dogmatic reflection known as the *analogia fidei;* that is, our grounding in the "analogy of faith" means that our epistemic root is centered in our union with Christ, and that out of this fertile ground we have a knowledge of God that necessarily understands him in terms of being eternally Father of the Son by the Holy Spirit; and then finally, we see ourselves standing within the confessional shape of the Reformed tradition as evinced by our resonance with both The Scots Confession of Faith, 1560, and The Heidelberg Catechism.

---

37. It is important to keep in mind that all "Protestant Reformed Confessions" intend on presenting a way to think about God that accurately captures who he has revealed himself to be. The point of contention then is not over an issue of intention, but instead whether or not the chosen philosophical apparatus actually allows some of these Confessions to present a doctrine of God that should be emphasized if in fact we are being sensitive to the Revelation of God in Jesus Christ; and all of the categories and emphases that are attendant with "that" *Revelation.*

# BIBLIOGRAPHY

Aquinas, Thomas. *Summa Theologiae: Existence and Nature of God.* Translated by Timothy McDermott O. P. New York: McGraw-Hill, 1964.

Barth, Karl. *The Knowledge of God and The Service of God According to the Teaching of the Reformation.* Translated by J. L. M. Haire and Ian Henderson. London: Hodder and Stoughton, 1961.

———. *The Theology of the Reformed Confessions.* Translated by Darrell L. Guder and Judith J. Guder. Louisville: Westminster John Knox, 2002.

Beeke, Joel R., and Sinclair B. Ferguson, editors. *Reformed Confessions Harmonized: With an Annotated Bibliography of Reformed Doctrinal Works.* Grand Rapids: Baker, 1999.

Cochrane, Arthur C., editor. *Reformed Confessions of the Sixteenth Century.* Louisville: Westminster John Knox, 2003.

Cross, F. L., and E. A. Livingstone, editors. *The Oxford Dictionary of the Christian Church.* New York: Oxford University Press, 1997.

Gerstner, Jonathan Neil. *The Thousand Generation Covenant: Dutch Reformed Covenant Theology and Group Identity in Colonial South Africa, 1652-1814.* Leiden: Brill, 1991.

Gunton, Colin E. *The Promise of Trinitarian Theology.* Edinburgh: T. & T. Clark, 1991.

Habets, Myk. "On Getting First Things First: Assessing Claims for the Primacy of Christ." *New Blackfriars* 90 (2009) 343-64.

McCormack, Bruce L. "Election and the Trinity: Theses in Response to George Hunsinger." *Scottish Journal of Theology* 63 (2010) 203-24.

———, editor. *Engaging the Doctrine of God: Contemporary Protestant Perspectives.* Grand Rapids: Baker Academic, 2008.

Molnar, Paul D. *Thomas F. Torrance: Theologian of the Trinity.* Surrey: Ashgate, 2009.

Muller, Richard A. *Christ and the Decree: Christology and Predestination in Reformed Theology from Calvin to Perkins.* Durham, NC: Labyrinth, 1986.

Myers, Benjamin. "The Stratification of Knowledge in the Thought of T. F. Torrance." *Scottish Journal of Theology* 61 (2008) 1-15.

Purves, Andrew, and Mark Achtemeier. *Union in Christ: A Declaration for the Church.* Louisville: Witherspoon, 1999.

Rohls, Jan. *Reformed Confessions: Theology from Zurich to Barmen.* Louisville: Westminster John Knox, 1998.

Smith, James K. A. *Letters to a Young Calvinist: An Invitation to the Reformed Tradition.* Grand Rapids: Brazos, 2010.

Torrance, Thomas F. *The Christian Doctrine Of God: One Being Three Persons.* Edinburgh: T. & T. Clark, 1996.

———. *Incarnation: The Person and Life of Christ.* Edited by Robert T. Walker. Downers Grove, IL: InterVarsity Academic, 2008.

———. *Scottish Theology: From John Knox to John McLeod Campbell.* Edinburgh: T. & T. Clark, 1996.

———. *Theological Science.* London: Oxford University Press, 1969.

———. *The Trinitarian Faith.* Edinburgh: T. & T. Clark, 1993.

Webster, John. "Principles of Systematic Theology." *International Journal of Systematic Theology* 11 (2009) 56-71.

———, editor. *The Cambridge Companion to Karl Barth.* Cambridge: Cambridge University Press, 2000.

Williamson, G. I. *The Westminster Confession Of Faith: For Study Classes.* Philadelphia: Presbyterian and Reformed, 1964.

# 5

# The Christology of Vicarious Agency in the Scots Confession According to Karl Barth

ANDREW PURVES

E VANGELICAL CALVINISM IS UNDOUBTEDLY a complex notion. Who worthily carries the mantle of John Calvin? Who is to decide? Calvin's texts are nowhere a subordinate standard for any church. Yet as a principal reformer he remains the genitor of a multi-textured tradition—the Reformed tradition—rather than someone who gave his name to an ecclesiastical entity. Calvinism flows forward somewhat like a great river, while now and then rivulets cut away to irrigate newly found dry ground, in fact, so much so, that one is left wondering if the once great river exists anymore apart from these. Calvinism is not one theological perspective, but many, each of which will claim, more or less, allegiance to Calvin, and to the designation "Reformed."

*Evangelical* Calvinism is also undoubtedly a complex notion when the adjective is heavily weighted with political and theological content. In its historical setting the Scots Confession, as a theological confession, was also a political manifesto. Today a perspective labeled "evangelical" carries ideological and political associations (at least in North America) rather than, as formerly, theologically political implications, as in support of a Protestant and not a Roman Catholic monarch. Some care must be given to clarity with respect to the meaning of "evangelical" in present use. The descriptor will be discussed here in terms of its own claim drawn from the Scots Confession, 1560, referenced in its theme scripture verse and in the first paragraph of the Preface (both of which are unaccountably missing from the Presbyterian Church (USA)'s *Book of Confessions*). Thus, respectively: "And this glad tiding of the Kingdom shall be preached through the whole world for a witness to all the nations; and then shall the end come" (Matt 24:14); "The Estates of Scotland, with the inhabitants of Scotland who profess the holy Evangel of Jesus Christ, to their fellow countrymen and to all other nations who confess the Lord Jesus with them, wish grace, mercy, and peace from God the Father of our Lord Jesus Christ, with the Spirit of righteous judgment, for salvation."[1]

We use the word "evangelical" of the Scots Confession and in present discussion in two regards. First, the central focus of the Confession is Jesus Christ. Second, the Scots Confession is a theology in the service of evangelism and preaching,[2] addressed not only to the Scots but also to all peoples. Thomas F. Torrance comments that "in contrast to every other confessional statement issued during the Reformation, (the Scots Confession) gives primary importance to the missionary calling of the Church."[3]

In this essay I propose that *Evangelical Calvinism* as a theological designation, with respect to the Scots Confession, was brought to dogmatic expression in a remarkable way by Karl Barth in his 1937–38 Gifford Lectures, given in the University of Aberdeen.[4] That the Confession is a document indebted to Calvin is without dispute, though I will presently recount briefly the ambiguity of its "Calvinist" identity. I will argue that Barth read the Confession *at nearly every turn* in terms of the Christology of vicarious agency, and that, precisely that, entails that here we have evangelical Calvinism.[5] What follows is a reading of Barth's reading of the Scots Confession, not an historical analysis of a document of the Reformation. In this respect I follow Barth's intention "of a theological paraphrase and elucidation of the document as it speaks today."[6]

1. All citations of the Scots Confession are from Henderson, *The Scots Confession 1560*, 56 and 58.

2. Torrance, *Scottish Theology*, 3.

3. Ibid., 1.

4. Barth, *The Knowledge of God*.

5. Torrance, in his chapter on Knox in Torrance, *Scottish Theology*, 42–43, closes with a vigorous reconstruction of Knox's Eucharistic doctrine precisely on the point of reclaiming the vicarious humanity of Christ.

6. Barth, *The Knowledge of God*, 10. Barth may be slightly misleading when he tells us that what follows is not his personal opinion. It remains a question for another day

## THAT THE SCOTS CONFESSION IS NOT "PURE CALVINISM" IN A CALEDONIAN ACCENT[7]

The Confession needs to be situated. While the Scots Confession is its own document, it stands within a family identity. It reflects its peculiar provenance, while rightly being "Reformed." On August 17th, 1560, the Scottish Parliament adopted a document that was four days in its writing as "doctrine founded upon the infallible Word of God." Nevertheless, there is no easy path from Calvin, through John Knox and his co-writers, to a Scottish statement of "Calvinism." The Confession is a setting forth of the faith of the Scottish Reformers. But, as noted in the Preface, this Confession is open to amendment and correction should it be found to be contrary to God's Word. As is common within Reformed traditions, confessions are subordinate or provisional standards, never to be confused with authoritative declarations of the church.[8] In keeping with the notes by which the true church is determined, the confession of Christ Jesus rather than the confession of the Scots Confession is avowed, and this in local congregations rather than in some abstraction called the universal church (Article 18). Further, given its setting in mid-sixteenth century Scotland, the tone is militant. Barth refers to its "decidedly masculine, not to say warlike, spirit"[9] The Confession is a call to action[10] in a local context, albeit is also addressed "to all other nations" (Preface), written by men who have suffered greatly for their faith and have a battle for the faithfulness of the church on their hands.

The authors claim to be guided everywhere by Scripture, but there is an architecture that gives coherence to the whole. It corresponds to the structure of the Apostles' Creed: from theology to anthropology, to Christology, to pneumatology, to ecclesiology, and to eschatology.[11] Throughout Christology is to the fore; there is a soteriological focus.

---

whether Barth's thorough-going Christology of vicarious agency was read out off the Confession or imposed upon it. Whatever the judgment, it is Barth's conversation with the Confession that is of interest here.

7. Hazlett, "The Scots Confession 1560," 287. Much of what follows in the brief section is taken from Hazlett's article.

8. Hazlett notes that "among the Reformed churches, it may be recalled, local theological self-expression tended to be the norm" (ibid., 295).

9. Barth, *The Knowledge of God*, 131.

10. Hazlett, "The Scots Confession 1560," 295.

11. Ibid., 298.

Further, there is an antiphonal modulation between what is confessed and what is condemned.

The Confession confesses a biblical theology. But undoubtedly Calvin is chief among the secondary influences.[12] Hazlett gives three examples of Calvin's approach to theological themes found in the Confession: 1. the continuity between the Old and New Testaments; 2. the Old Testament Law is adjudged to be normative for the Christian life in the sense of Calvin's "third use;" 3. Calvin's notion of the "double grace" of justification and regeneration and his concept of a "double justification" of the sinner and the justified are found in the Confession, though perhaps developed somewhat differently.[13] There are also characteristics in the Confession which strike an independent tone, whether from Calvin himself or from later developed Calvinism. Hazlett discusses five such instances.[14]

First, the Confession's (lengthy) presentation on the Lord's Supper has a strongly anti-Zwinglian note: "if anyone slanders us by saying that we affirm or believe the sacraments to be symbols and nothing more, they are libelous and speak against the plain facts" (Article 21). The Confession in some ways satisfies Lutheran concerns: the sacraments are gifts that convey the content of God's promises; believers participate in the substance of the body of Christ; the corporeal aspect of the Lord's Supper is emphasized. Second, the Confession inserts ecclesiastical discipline as a third mark of the church. This is a departure from Calvin's teaching. Third, the word 'predestination' nowhere occurs, while election is developed in strictly Christological terms. This is largely in keeping with other Reformation confessions. It was not until Dordrecht and Westminster in the next century that the "double decree" was advanced as confessional orthodoxy.[15] Fourth, unlike other confessions of the period, the Confession, using the familiar notions of testament and promise, seems to have in mind covenants between God and humankind (Articles 4 and 5 with regard to promise, Article 6 with regard to fulfillment). Hazlett wonders if this is an embryonic source of Federal theology.[16] Finally, with reference to civil authority, the Confession al-

---

12. Ibid., 300.

13. Ibid.

14. Ibid., 307–8.

15. Ibid., 313.

16. Ibid., 314.

lows for active resistance. Article 14 instructs the repression of tyranny as a divine command. This goes beyond Calvin's teaching.

Summarily: "Those who look for the clear-cut principles of impeccable Calvinism in the Scots Confession will do so in vain. There is no double predestination, there is no limited atonement . . . and no irresistible grace; the perseverance of the saints is only cursorily mentioned . . . 'total depravity' assumes a less intimidating form."[17] Further, "while Calvin seems to be the major inspiration for the Confession, his theology undergoes a considerable degree of refraction in it. This ought to be borne in mind when the purity of the Confession's Calvinism is asserted."[18]

## THE KNOWLEDGE OF GOD IN THE TEACHING OF THE SCOTS CONFESSION ACCORDING TO KARL BARTH

### *The Discussion of Articles 1, 2a and 2b: God and Creation*[19]

What is the theology of the Scots Confession? Barth's identification of the Christology of vicarious agency in the Confession, it will be argued, is the answer to the question.

Barth, in the beginning, notes that Reformation teaching lives by its positive content (and not as a response to natural theology),[20] and that content is given precisely as the Christology of vicarious agency. Barth asks: "What if the Son of God has taken our place that we might come to stand in His place?"[21] And the answer: "He keeps faith with us by becoming *man* and taking *our place*. But that means that He makes all our incapacity *His own*."[22] (The emphases throughout are from Barth.) The Christology of vicarious agency is the positive teaching that in his person, through word and act, Jesus Christ, the Word of God, offers himself to the Father in our place, doing for us thereby what we cannot do for ourselves. The positive content is both incarnational and soteriological.

17. Ibid., 319.

18. Ibid., 301. Hazlett's article gave much more detail in support than is useful to give account here.

19. Barth divides up his discussion of the Confession according to his own scheme, mostly, but not entirely, following the movement of the Confession.

20. Barth, *The Knowledge of God*, 9.

21. Ibid., 74.

22. Ibid., 76.

This positive content that Barth identifies is found immediately in Article 1. The Confession confesses and acknowledges one God only, who, says Barth, "proves Himself to be such by His being both the Author of His own Being and the source of all knowledge of Himself."[23] God makes himself known, not through revelation of some sort or another, but through his self-revelation.[24] Who is this one God? He is, says Barth, *majesty* ("eternal, infinite, immeasurable, incomprehensible, omnipotent, invisible"). Immediately this God is revealed as a *person*, "since in His simple majestic essence He is the Father, the Son, and the Holy Spirit."[25] Certainly the notion of person here is to be theologically construed. As this person God is Lord, and thereby personal in an incomprehensible way insofar as this divine person surpasses all views of personality.[26] The knowledge *that* God is and *who* God is, is the knowledge of faith, knowledge through revelation, and therefore positive knowledge which is unconditionally bound to its object: the revelation of God in Jesus Christ. Thus, Barth points out (in reference to a remarkable second sentence in Article 1), the Confession links together faith in the God who is hidden in his eternity, infinity, etc., and the confession of faith in the same God as he is known as Father, Son and Holy Spirit. Made known to us as the Triune God, "He meets us as the One who is hidden, the One about Whom we must admit that we do not know what we are saying when we try to say who He is."[27] The astonishing claim is that as God in his incomprehensible majesty, God meets us as an "I" who calls us "Thou," and whom we can call "Thou" in return.[28] To this one God only we must cleave, serve, worship, and put our trust.

In the revelation of God in Jesus Christ, God and humankind meet and therefore are really together.[29] It is a caricature of Reformed theology to say that God is to be so emphasized as God as to imply that the human is correspondingly worthless. God is God, but God is not alone. There exists a glory which belongs to the world and to human beings.[30]

23. Ibid., 19.
24. Ibid., 21.
25. Ibid., 25.
26. Ibid., 31.
27. Ibid., 27.
28. Ibid., 33.
29. Ibid., 36.
30. Ibid., 35.

Human beings in their glory exist under a definite ordinance: glory is received from God that the glory of God might be the greater thereby. The human is addressed as God's *vis-à-vis*, as God's partner. The gospel of Jesus Christ, in which the Word becomes human without ceasing to be God, and in which Jesus returns to the Father without ceasing to be human, means God will not be God without this partner.

Barth's language is sparse and his argument elusive as he moves from his discussion of Article 1 to the discussion of the first part of Article 2. His theme is the meeting of God and humankind in Jesus Christ, given already in the discussion of majesty and person as the summation of Article 1. This meeting is an act of grace, putting creation under a debt of gratitude to God.[31] Why is this grace and why is there a debt of gratitude? Here is the point: God meets with humankind in Jesus Christ, and not apart from him. All people, in which case, are partnered by God in Jesus Christ. In Jesus Christ the human is no longer alone. That is why it is grace. And because it is grace the response of gratitude is solicited. Thus Barth reaches a gentle first conclusion with regard to the Christology of vicarious agency. It is slipped in unobtrusively: "Let us return once more to God's revelation in Jesus Christ. It is man who meets God here and it is man whom God is with here."[32] We can add by way of commentary that humankind meets God and God is with humankind *vicariously* in Jesus Christ.

Because in Jesus Christ God and humankind have met, the Confession begins Article 2 with an unexpected, delightful and intuitively astute note of familiarity that is picked up by Barth. Says Barth: "By God's taking thought for man in Jesus Christ, now as in the past, He has provided us with knowledge about the creating, sustaining and governing of the world and man and about His glory and ours... It was no mere chance that the *Confessio Scotica* in its exposition of the Creation of man and his special appointment to be God's image, did not use the word God abstractly but said concretely *Our* God, Immanuel."[33]

31. Ibid., 38.
32. Ibid., 40.
33. Ibid., 44.

## *The Discussion of Articles 2c and 3: The Fall and Original Sin*

The Confession's teaching on the Fall and sin of humankind derives from the christology of vicarious agency. "The history of man and his sin can only be presented in the way in which we see it presented in the history of the man Jesus Christ."[34] That is to say, we know ourselves before God only in Christ's knowing of us and in the infinite agony which it cost God to take our place in the man Jesus Christ.

The Confession did not follow the standard confessional form by developing an independent doctrine of human sin.[35] The Confession's words concerning Adam's Fall are cast in terms of human destiny appointed by "our God;"original sin is cast as an introduction to the doctrine of saving faith in Jesus Christ.

> The Scottish Confession indicates in the strongest of terms the horror of the fact that man became and is a sinner, by setting it clearly in a connection in which it is both preceded and followed by the grace of God, the Creator and Reconciler of men . . . The authors of our confession manifestly wished to avoid considering even for a moment this fact of sin separately and as such. That man is *against* God is true and important and has to be taken seriously. But what is even truer, more important and to be taken more seriously is the other fact that God in Jesus Christ is *for man*. And it is only from the standpoint of the latter fact that it can be seen how true and important the former is, and how seriously it must be taken.[36]

The truth of the human situation can only be known from the greater truth of God's way with us in Jesus Christ. It is Jesus Christ who reveals the dire situation. This means, says Barth, that "this connection of sin and grace forbids us ever to speak of sin as if it were the first or last word."[37] And then this stunning sentence: "How could man know that he had sinned against God and that he is against God, unless he knew that *God is for him*?"[38] It is the knowledge of faith alone—knowledge of God for us in Jesus Christ in which he takes our place, our judgment and the suffering that ensues, in order that we are no longer judged—that

34. Ibid., 48.
35. Ibid., 45.
36. Ibid., 46.
37. Ibid., 51.
38. Ibid., 52.

reveals our sin, debt and punishment. It is Christ's humiliation and exal-tation *for us* that reveals our situation.

Barth develops what is explicit in the Confession. He does not im-pose an alien construal. In Article 3 the Confession conjoins original sin and the grace of redemption, allowing the former no independent platform. We know sin in the light of grace. What is implicit, on the other hand, is the "inner logic" of this conjunction which Barth brings out. God's knowledge of us in Jesus Christ—not what we lack but who we are, that we conspire "against the sovereign majesty of God," (Article 2), that we are sinners—means Christ's knowledge of us and our situ-ation stand over and against and displace our knowledge of ourselves referenced solely to ourselves. Christ knows us in our stead, and lives the consequence. Christ knows us for us, that is, vicariously, and acts accordingly achieving our redemption. This Barth saw clearly.

### The Discussion of Articles 4, 5, and 6: The Promise and the Fulfillment

The three Articles under review here mark a turn toward the Gospel of redemption in an explicitly christological direction. The Christology of vicarious agency becomes progressively more pointed as Barth works his way through the Articles.

The hermeneutical presupposition of the Confession, according to Barth, is that "God reveals Himself to man in Jesus Christ."[39] Following the Confession itself, Barth interprets Articles 4 and 5 on the promise in christological terms. Obviously Article 6, "The Incarnation of Jesus Christ," speaks for itself. Thus Barth refers to two histories concerning Jesus Christ in which God proves his faithfulness in the midst of human unfaithfulness, the history of promise and the history of fulfillment.[40] The history of Israel is the history of the church under the sign of prom-ise; the history of Jesus Christ is the history of God's becoming one with humankind.[41]

The Old Testament speaks of the sin of Israel, who nevertheless lives under a divine promise. The promise is that someone will come from within the midst of this people, "a representative who bears the sins of others . . . who cries from the depths to God and is justified by

39. Ibid., 57.

40. Ibid., 58.

41. For an introductory discussion of Barth's theological interpretation of scripture see Treier, *Introducing Theological Interpretation of Scripture.*

God on high . . . It is in Him and through Him that Israel will live."[42] While Israel rejects the promise, the promise is that Israel shall be good in and through the person of her coming prophet, priest and king. Says Barth: "If Israel does not abide by the promise, yet the promise abides by Israel."[43] At this point Barth admonishes the Confession for its omission of reference to a remnant who remained faithful and obedient within Israel, who, though they share still in Israel's guilt, know and hold fast in the hope of the promise. "It is in them therefore," Barth argues, "that Israel continues to exist despite all her unfaithfulness and despite the wrath of God which pursues it."[44] This vicarious remnant prefigures the vicarious Savior as the hope of Israel "til the Messiah came according to the promise." (Article 5) Because the covenant that bears the promise cannot fail on God's side, the basis and object of faith is "He who truly comes to make amends for the evil men do . . . (T)he promise does not abandon them (the remnant), but remains with them despite the unfaithfulness of the whole to which they belong and despite their own unfaithfulness."[45]

Thus Barth interprets the Confession's teaching on the Kirk under the sign of the promise given to Israel in terms of a people who receive help from another, first the remnant who keep the hope on behalf of the whole, and second in terms of the Messiah himself who makes amends for their guilt. "The Old Testament is a witness to Christ in so far as it makes the existence of the church of Jesus Christ manifest."[46]

The prospect of what now lies ahead is given in one summary sentence from the Confession that declares the evangelical intent: "When the fullness of time came, God sent his Son, his eternal wisdom, the substance of his own glory, into the world, who took the nature of humanity" (Article 6). Doing so, says Barth, God "submitted Himself to being in Jesus Christ what we are . . . Israel and the church live by the truth of the promise that a member of this people, and therefore One who is Himself a *man*, will make amends for all, for what all the others fail to

---

42. Barth, *The Knowledge of God*, 61.
43. Ibid., 63.
44. Ibid.
45. Ibid., 64.
46. Ibid.

make amends for."[47] In which case, the vicarious humanity of Christ is the core of the gospel.

### The Discussion of Articles 7 and 8: God's Decision and Our Election

The die of the "eternal and immutable decree of God" (Article 7), from which our salvation proceeds and on which it depends, has an undoubted christological character. Barth characterizes the teaching of the Confession (in a cautious statement, the reasons for which we will note presently) as a "noteworthy innovation . . . By this arrangement (the) authors have made it known unambiguously that they wish the whole body of material which is called the *doctrine of Predestination* to be explained through *christology* and conversely *christology* to be explained through the *doctrine of Predestination*."[48] The eternal God is revealed as the *God* who deals with humankind. In time, the just and merciful God deals with sinful humankind, deciding in our favor in order to have fellowship with us. According to Barth's interpretation, this is a course of action at once eternal and in time *which is identical with the existence of Jesus Christ.* "The existence of Jesus Christ is God's decision and man's election."[49] Here supremely we see the depth of God's goodness which can be described only haltingly by the word "grace."[50]

God himself as the man Jesus has taken our place, whereby God finds himself again in us, finding in Christ's human life and death, the fullness of active obedience.[51] The content of the eternal and immutable decree is that God will look at humankind in no other way than in Jesus Christ. "What if the Son of God has taken our place that we might come to stand in His place? What if we might be permitted to become by grace what He is by nature? . . . God sees us in His beloved Son—that is the joy of the good news."[52]

To know Jesus Christ is to know of the election of humankind. To know Jesus Christ is to know the elect human being. This comes to us as free mercy and as miracle because God chooses to make it so. The vicarious thrust is brought out by Barth: "By the power of God's action

47. Ibid., 65.
48. Ibid., 69–70.
49. Ibid., 70–71.
50. Ibid., 72.
51. Ibid., 73.
52. Ibid., 74.

(in election) man *becomes* what he *cannot* be by his own strength . . . (*Jesus Christ*) is the miracle of Grace, in whom what is impossible for any man, is possible for man, i.e., in Him it is possible for man to have not merely a part in God but to include the fullness of Godhead in himself and be the son of God."[53] In this way, God keeps faith with us "by becoming *man* and taking *our place* . . . He makes all our incapacity *His own* . . . Our burden, the fact that we cannot live with Him, but must perish without Him, becomes *His* burden. He Himself becomes the One Who cannot choose salvation, but can choose only the curse."[54] Election is not an opportunity; the vicarious thrust in Barth's discussion is heightened in intensity by his insistence on the actuality of election. "Because that has happened we *are* already those whose place has been taken by Jesus Christ, who has made our rejection His own, and therefore we are already the elect of God."[55]

Has Barth gone too far in reading a christology of vicarious actualism into the Confession's teaching on election? He admits as much, suggesting that the authors made a promising start, and at first sight appeared to be on the right track, but later lost their way somewhat. *Cur Deus homo?* The Confession states that it was by grace alone that God chose us in Jesus Christ before the world was laid (Article 8). The supralapsarian christological emphasis in the doctrine of election in the Confession at the beginning of Article 8 serves to heighten the sense of the miracle and wonder at God's will to have fellowship with us, and is congruent with the earlier discussion on sin, which was also placed within christological framing. The Confession leaves no doubt regarding the vicarious nature of this: "It behooved the Messiah and Redeemer to be true God and true man, because he was able to undergo the punishment of our transgressions and to present himself in the presence of his Father's judgment *as in our stead.*" (Article 8, emphasis added). But Barth, while affirming the position the Confession takes interpreting in close connection the doctrine of predestination and the divine-human nature of Christ, argues that the connection must be considered even closer than the authors thought it to be. There is, for Barth, still too much in the Confession that might indicate Calvin's influence whereby

53. Ibid., 75.

54. Ibid., 76.

55. Ibid., 77. Barth's use of italics in these citations serves to magnify his insistence on the point he is making.

the doctrine of predestination is still somewhat expressed in terms "other than what has taken place in Jesus Christ,"[56] that is, in terms of a lurking natural theology in which the freedom of God is based on one philosophical system or another, and in which the sending of Jesus Christ was an act of divine determination which took place in some sort of eternity before and without Jesus Christ.

Undoubtedly the vicarious actualism that Barth's discussion develops belongs more to Barth than to the authors of the Confession. This notwithstanding, Barth salutes the doctrine of election in the Confession, demurring only at what he calls "certain delimitations"[57] in his brief and hurried critique at the close of the lecture.

### Discussion of Articles 9 through 12: Christ's Death, Resurrection, Ascension, and the Work of the Holy Spirit

With the discussion of these Articles Barth brings the lectures on the knowledge of God in the Confession to a close. The final four lectures of year one are here linked together because they build to a common end: our becoming new persons in Christ. We become new persons in Christ because of God's vicarious agency in Christ.

The way of God's vicarious agency in Christ, God's work, is the way God accomplishes the salvation of humankind. The Confession is clear that we must speak entirely of the work of God. With characteristic intensity, Barth drives to the heart of the matter : salvation (though Article 9 does not use the word). This work of God is the incarnation of God's Son, and the death and resurrection of Jesus Christ which are the epitome and consummation of that incarnation.[58] Barth notes that the guiding conception by which the Confession develops its view of the death of Jesus is that of sacrifice. Jesus Christ "takes the place of sinful man and undergoes the punishment which man was bound to undergo, in order that man may be free and his sins forgiven."[59] As *a man* Jesus is able to offer himself as a sacrifice, and does so; as *God* Jesus is able to make the sacrifice profitable and beneficial, and does so. This way of God's vicarious agency in Christ is, then, the way of the humiliation of

---

56. Ibid., 78.

57. Ibid., 77.

58. Ibid., 82.

59. Ibid., 83.

God in which Jesus Christ takes upon himself everything which human rebellion against God has made inevitable—suffering and death, perdition and hell, punishment in time and in eternity.[60] Barth asks pointedly: "Where does God remain and what still remains His, as God, when God's Son has been slain on Calvary?"[61] In answer Barth drives hard into the "inner logic" of soteriology. On Calvary God does not cease to be God, and as such accepts the sacrifice made by himself, letting his own humiliation operate as satisfaction, acknowledging Christ's bearing of human sin, guilt and punishment as an atonement.[62] There is something here, perhaps, of Luther's notion of the crucified God.[63]

Barth is right to note that Article 10 on the resurrection of Christ is less complete than the Article on the death of Christ.[64] Barth, however, discovers an obverse symmetry with the movement of atoning sacrifice discussed above. Previously Barth moved from Jesus as a man to Jesus as God; with respect to the resurrection he moves from the resurrection of Jesus as God to the resurrection of Jesus as a man. Because Jesus is God, death cannot hold him. It is not within the power of Jesus' humanity that he can rise from the dead. Thus, corresponding to the humiliation of the Son of God in his death we have the exaltation of the Son of man through his power as the Son of God.[65] As true human, Jesus has risen from the dead due entirely to his divinity.[66] Jesus is thus both the resurrected God and the resurrected man: "this dead man, as such, has appeared in a new life to His own people and as man is God for ever and ever."[67] As such, Jesus Christ is the exaltation of humankind now in righteousness, innocence and blessedness. Jesus Christ, Barth asserts boldly, is eternal life both for God and humankind.[68]

---

60. Ibid., 83.

61. Ibid., 84.

62. Ibid. Barth is faithful to the Scottish text of the Confession in speaking of the humiliation of God in Christ as a satisfaction. The contemporary rendering puts the original "the everlasting purgatioun and satisfactioun" as "everlasting atonement."

63. Luther, WA I, 614, 17, cited by Moltmann, *The Crucified God*, 47.

64. Barth, *The Knowledge of God*, 85.

65. Ibid., 86.

66. Ibid., 88.

67. Ibid., 87.

68. Ibid., 89.

Again, Barth's account seems to be more Barth than the Confession. That notwithstanding, it is curious that neither the Confession nor Barth discusses the resurrection in Trinitarian terms. The Father in particular is oddly absent. In both accounts, divinity is referred to in a manner intrinsic to Jesus Christ. The Confession states that "our Lord Jesus crucified, dead, and buried, who descended into hell, did rise again" (Article 10). Barth, however, as we now expect, brings out the vicarious dimension of Christ's resurrection very clearly with his insistence that in his resurrection Christ did not cease to be truly human, and that in him we, insofar as he has taken us and our whole nature upon himself, including our death, are partakers of his human life. This is something positive: righteousness and the freedom to be God's children, not only freedom from guilt and punishment; immortal life victorious over death, not only the reduction of death to relative unimportance and comfort thereby.[69]

The discussion of Christ's Ascension in the Confession (Article 11) is longer than the Articles on Christ's death and resurrection together. One can surmise the reason in part is the elevation of the victory and rule of Jesus Christ (which is important for setting the ground for the second half of the Confession on the service of God). This is congruent with the centrality of Christology throughout the Confession. Salvation in Christ through his ruling session is not only a past, completed event, but also a continuing and an anticipated reality. As an historical speculation, perhaps this was important for confidence in the future of the Kirk in turbulent mid-sixteenth century Scotland.

The theme of vicarious agency is expressed in what may be the most-cited sentence from the Confession. "We do not doubt but that the selfsame body which was born of the virgin, was crucified, dead, and buried, and which did rise again, did ascend into the heavens, for the accomplishment of all things, where *in our name and for our comfort* he has received all power in heaven and earth, where he sits at the right hand of the Father, having received his kingdom, the only advocate and mediator for us" (Article 11, emphasis added).

Barth focuses on the theme of the kingdom of God, which translates as Christ's sovereignty and authority over all things. Barth picks up the mention of the ascension of the "selfsame body," interpreting this to mean the man Jesus Christ of whom the Confession has spoken all

---

69. Ibid.

along.[70] This "Jesus Christ is *Kurios* . . . He is *the* great *change* in man's life"[71]—this only makes sense as a statement of Christ's vicarious agency. Albeit is a hidden change, nevertheless Christ is the great change for us. All that has gone before—God's decision and our election, the death of Jesus and his resurrection—is irrevocable because it is God who has acted. Our future is given in Christ's rule. He is our "tomorrow" in the change accomplished by him. Says Barth: "I do not know who or what I will be tomorrow. *He* has to decide about that."[72] Faith in Christ, in which case, looks toward him as the Lord of our future. The Confession here refers pointedly to the judgment of Jesus Christ: this judgment is "the time of refreshing and restitution" for those who belong to Christ. On the other hand there those who are rejected by Jesus Christ, whose first characteristic, interestingly, is that they are stubborn. What is at issue here? Barth notes that the Confession emphasizes what Jesus Christ has done for us, not what we should do to prepare for this judgment.[73] Already it has been decided, of course, that we are all sinners, and that in Christ we are all righteous. The issue here is whether we face the judgment of Christ, looking for him who asks of us that we acknowledge our sin only as already forgiven and our condemnation only as already borne by him.[74] That is what will be decided at the judgment.

Barth's discussion on the Article on the Ascension is oddly lacking in intensity. The framers clearly evinced the Lordship and reign of Christ as a huge issue. Barth, on the other hand, seems to lose steam. It is not clear why this should be other than to suppose that the interpretive brilliance of his advocacy of the Christology of vicarious agency hitherto has left him with little that remains to be said.

Coming to the end of the first part of the Confession with the discussion on faith in the Holy Spirit (Article 12), Barth rightly notes that we have reached the center, the transition from consideration of knowledge of God to the consideration of the service of God.[75] Knowledge of God according to the teaching of the Confession has been knowledge of the God who deals with us in his revelation in Jesus Christ. Throughout

70. Ibid., 94.
71. Ibid.
72. Ibid., 96.
73. Ibid., 98.
74. Ibid., 99.
75. Ibid., 103.

Barth has interpreted this in terms of vicarious agency: Christ for us is Christ in our place. To know this is to become a new person, a person whose knowledge of God consists in having faith.[76] Such a person lives faced by Jesus Christ.

The Confession acknowledges that faith is not a human possibility. It is entirely the inspiration of the Holy Ghost (Article 12). Barth (could he not resist?) sharply contrasts this Spirit-given faith with the human capacity for religion. We have as little share in our rebirth as we have in being created, or as we have in what Christ has done for us.[77] Or, in the words of the Confession: "For by nature we are so dead, blind, and perverse, that neither can we feel when we are pricked, see the light when it shines, nor assent to the will of God when it is revealed, unless the spirit of the Lord Jesus quicken that which is dead, remove the darkness from our minds, and bow our stubborn hearts to the obedience of his blessed will" (Article 12). It is not unbelief but faith that speaks in this way.[78]

Who then has faith? The positive answer according to the Confession, as Barth highlights, is that we have faith when we receive the salvation through Jesus Christ. "By receiving what he was permitted to receive from Jesus Christ, he confessed and acknowledged that *the fact that* he did receive (instead of refusing to receive) was itself the receiving of a divine gift—God's faithfulness reaching over and grasping him, and in this he, who found in himself nothing but unfaithfulness, could only see an undeserved act of kindness and an incomprehensible miracle."[79] The person of faith acted, but this too was the work of the Holy Spirit. Says Barth: "The possibility of faith becomes manifest in its actuality, but it is in its actuality that it becomes manifest as a *divine* possibility."[80] Perhaps it would not be stretching the theology of the Confession or the theology of Barth's paraphrase of it to say that faith is the receiving (by the work of the Holy Spirit) of the faith of Jesus Christ which he has for us. We have knowledge of God through God's revelation in Jesus Christ, in which at all points he stands in for us, doing all things for us, who "became for us wisdom from God, and righteousness and sanctification

---

76. Ibid., 104.
77. Ibid., 107.
78. Ibid.
79. Ibid., 108.
80. Ibid., 109.

and redemption, in order that, as it is written, 'Let the one who boasts, boast in the Lord'" (1 Cor 1:30).

## THE SERVICE OF GOD IN THE TEACHING OF THE SCOTS CONFESSION ACCORDING TO KARL BARTH

*Discussion of Article 13: The Cause of Good Works—The Christian Life*

The Confession turns now to consider the practice of faith. The danger is that the theology will be left behind, or be turned into ethical guidelines, under pressure to make pragmatic responses to presented situational needs. The practice of faith becomes practice without theology where the burden of performance is cast upon us. On the face of it, the christology of vicarious agency is expected in discussion of soteriological concerns; it is likely not so clear that it is equally expected in discussion of the practice of faith. Both the Confession and Barth in his interpretation, however, are at pains to make clear that the christology of the knowledge of God continues into the theology of the service of God.

One further introductory observation: just over half of the wording of the Confession is given to the theology of the service of God. Why was so much attention given to this? One can surmise that it was due to the nature of practically-minded Scots to be down-to-earth. Beyond such stereotyping, a better answer might be found in the Christology of the ascended Lord, which the Confession expounded at length. For there we find reference to Christ's continuing ministry which is now no less for us and in our place than his ministry was while he was among us in the flesh.

Article 13 begins with a two-fold delimitation. The first is the assumption that the believer is free and able to live the Christian life. The second is the error that we can have faith without good works. The Confession understands sanctification by the Holy Spirit as a radical change in the nature of the objects towards which we direct love and hate—Barth calls it a sober realistic discussion.[81] We live under a dual determination, as it were. We live in the real world, with all its pressures and temptations, and the person of faith sometimes acts no better than those who do not believe. But, in the light of the knowledge of God, we begin to love what was hated, and to hate what was loved. We no longer own allegiance to our sin but are free to own allegiance to the forgiving

81. Ibid., 117.

grace of God.[82] As a corollary, knowing that God has given himself in love for us, we begin to hate what before we loved. The reversal of the objects of affection and dislike is the consequence of the vicarious divine agency, though the old loves and the old hatreds are still in action. There is no doctrine of going on to perfection here; and though the change in the objects of affection is small and weak, it is nevertheless a radical change.[83]

Barth suddenly hits his stride with a vigorous affirmation of vicarious agency. "In the conflict with ourselves we shall as little look for help or salvation to the struggle which we are putting up, whether it be good or bad, victorious or unsuccessful, serious or half-hearted. On the contrary, when we have faith, we shall have the right to see in this change and in the conflict bound up with it only a sign—the sign of a crisis divine and not human, which has overtaken our existence."[84] For what saves us in this battle is not our effort, "but the battle which Jesus Christ has fought and in which He has already been victorious."[85] In other words, Jesus Christ is our sanctification. Guilty of sin, we are assured of the grace of God. Jesus Christ has borne the wrath of God for us and revealed God's love. The meaning and content of our daily struggle, says Barth, is involvement in the real struggle of the Spirit against the flesh, i.e. against ourselves, in our piety as well as our godlessness.[86] That is to say, in faith we find ourselves involved in the struggle of God *on our behalf.* "That we are the scene and the witness of this struggle is what constitutes the real Christian life, which is a life in which God intervenes on man's behalf."[87]

The Confession discusses repentance at the end of the Article on sanctification. Repentance is our turning back to God our only helper; it is turning away from ourselves to Jesus Christ. And, says Barth, "it is just as legitimate to put *thankfulness* before repentance, because we thereby make clear what true repentance is."[88] We turn to God because in Christ

82. Ibid., 118.
83. Ibid., 120.
84. Ibid.
85. Ibid., 121.
86. Ibid.
87. Ibid., 122.
88. Ibid.

God has already, daily, turned to us through the Holy Spirit. The practice of the Christian life begins and ends with thankfulness.

Barth, following the lead of the Confession, has cast the die for the ensuing discussion of the service of God. The christology of vicarious agency continues to dominate throughout, and the concern with which this discussion of Article 13 began, namely, a turn away from theology towards an ethically driven pragmatism, is avoided right at the start.

*Discussion of Articles 14 and 15: The Christian Life and the Law of God*

Articles 14 and 15 belong together, for they treat two common themes in the Christian life, although Barth gives each a separate lecture: the Christian life is an ordered life of a quite specific character, and is possible for us insofar as Jesus Christ has taken our place. Arguably, Barth's Christology of vicarious agency is more to the front in his discussion of these Articles than we found in the last discussion.

Barth begins his discussion on the Divine Law with this programmatic statement: "The true ordinance governing the Christian life is *Jesus Christ*, and it is therefore superior to both the church and the individual in the church. The authority and freedom which are valid in the Christian life are the authority and freedom by which Jesus Christ makes His Word heard and obeyed among men—and His Word means Himself."[89] The two tables of the Law bear witness to Jesus Christ by claiming us for God and for each other. There is no appeal to natural law or rights in the Confession, nor to church tradition, nor to individual conscience. The appeal is to the revealed will of God, Jesus Christ.

Says Barth: "The Divine Law regulates the Christian life in the relationship of man to *God*."[90] In faith, with regard to God, some things are enjoined upon us, others are forbidden. The Confession is explicit in laying this out. Barth repeats his central point: "This renewing of man and consequently the Christian life consists in Jesus Christ, as true God, having taken our place." Everything "rests entirely on the perfection of the eternal God, who has made Himself in Jesus Christ our Representative, Counsel and Advocate. If we *stand firm*, we do so by means of God's decision which has already taken place, and by means of God's work which has already taken place in Jesus Christ and is real to-day and for ever.

89. Ibid., 127.
90. Ibid., 128.

We could only *fall headlong* into the bottomless pit, if this decision has not been made and this work not taken place."[91] Jesus Christ has taken our place. For this reason we are bound to God in accordance with the commandments of the first table. This requires from us that we should be what we are, people elected and saved by God in Jesus Christ, and not be what we are not, people lost without God and forsaken by God.[92] This is not to do something special, but to stand in that place where we can breathe and have life.

The second table of the Law regulates the Christian life with regard to relations with others. Barth notes that "we see with particular clearness at this point the decidedly masculine, not to say warlike, spirit of the document."[93] His reference is to the discussion of the 6th commandment, where the Confession bids us "to repress tyranny." (We will return to this in the discussion on the final Article.) Barth again makes his general point in an unambiguous way:

> It should be clearly noted that here, in the Christology of the Scottish Confession, we find the source without which it is impossible to understand, let alone to adopt, its doctrine of the divine commandment . . . (O)ur renewing consists in Jesus Christ as true man taking precisely our place. Our election and salvation and so once again our whole existence is absolutely dependent on the fact that the Son of God came down to us, and became like us and became therefore *a man*: a poor, weak, mortal and dying man, such as we. At the very place where we would have to stand, God stands as the bearer of the burden which we could not bear, in order that His glory might remain for us. We owe it to His human nature that there is election for *man* on the basis of God's decision, and that there is salvation for *man* through the action of God.[94]

In Christ we are bound to one another as those who have been elected and saved in the poor man Jesus. Our relation to one another is the sign of our relation to God. Seen in this way, Barth suggests, Christianity is not collapsed into morality. Rather, in Christ we are doing what is, in a sense, now natural for those chosen and saved in Jesus Christ. In the freedom of Jesus Christ we are bound to God and to one

91. Ibid., 129.
92. Ibid., 130.
93. Ibid., 131.
94. Ibid., 132–33.

another. "For by faith in Him it is true for us and it becomes true for our life, that Jesus Christ as true God and true man stands in our place."[95] The Christology of vicarious agency could hardly be put more clearly.

Barth's discussion of Article 15 takes us farther into the relation of the Christology of vicarious agency and the Christian life. Once again the Confession would have us take our imperfections with utter seriousness. How then is the Christian life possible? Is there a genuine thankfulness and repentance? Is there a fulfillment of the Law of God? Barth reflects that the Confession allows no third, middle course of approximated obedience. Human imperfection means disobedience and unrighteousness, no caveat allowed.[96] We remain Law-breakers; we live in untruth. Whatever the Christian life is, it cannot be discovered in our lives. Barth calls this living on a razor's edge.[97] Either we recognize there is no Christian life for us, no obedience, but only death, leading to lives of frivolity and despair, or we bury our heads in the sand, ostrich-like, and pretend our predicament is not so bad after all.

Barth is quick to shoot down these options. "The Scottish Confession presupposes that *Jesus Christ* is our life . . . This is the same as to say *faith* in Jesus Christ is our life. We live precisely in so far as we believe and allow God in Jesus Christ to be our Lord . . . (We) live precisely in so far as God lives in Jesus Christ and is our Lord and permits and commands us to live in Him. Not before Him or behind Him, below Him or beside Him, but *in* Him."[98] We are in Him and therefore in Him is our *life*. Barth has deepened the Christology of vicarious agency to include now the doctrine of our union with Christ. Christ fulfils the Law for us, and his life is our life. Because he has fulfilled the Law for us, we, in Him, have done what he has done! Surely this is the meaning of "evangelical Calvinism." In Christ we do live the Christian life. In him our thankful, penitent, love for God and one another is true.

The response to this good news is now addressed by the Confession: given all this, "(we) do not mean that we are so set at liberty that we owe no obedience to the Law . . . but we affirm that no man on earth, with the sole exception of Christ Jesus, has given, gives, or shall give in action that obedience to the Law which the Law requires" (Article 15). If Christ

95. Ibid., 135.

96. Ibid., 138.

97. Ibid., 139.

98. Ibid., 140–41.

is our life, why should we bother? The answer to this foolish question is that in Christ we are for the first time really and completely subjected to the Law.

Barth's discussion now is elusive, but radical as he follows the Confession closely. He wants to hold together that Christ is our life, that he stands in for us and we are bound to his obedience, on the one hand, yet action is required of us, on the other. But what is not required is our fulfilling the Law with this life of ours. "Our true action is the action of Jesus Christ, but it is required of us as our action."[99] In other words, faith in Christ, that he is the fulfillment of the Law for us, sets us in motion, moves us to gratitude and repentance, and to love of God and one another. Says Barth: "Provision for our sanctification here in time is made by our justification before God having taken place once and for all in Jesus Christ, and by our having the right to believe in it."[100] The Confession asserts there can be no Christian sphere in human life, in worship and culture, customs or ethics, in which we could in some degree serve God and God's cause well, even aided by God's grace. In fact, Christianity distinct from the sole righteousness of Christ is explicitly called "damnable idolatry." Our new life in Christ, which sets us in motion in him, means the end of all self-righteousness, for our entire confidence is in Jesus Christ alone. When called to obedience, trusting alone in Christ, in his election, grace and forgiveness, God's judgment is, says Barth, unmerited judgment. The grace of our Lord Jesus Christ is the first and last word about what is true concerning the Christian life.[101]

A brief comment on intelligibility is in order. Unless we catch how utterly thorough-going the christology of vicarious agency is, how it is complete and adequate at every turn, and that nothing in the Christian life can stand outside of it, we will miss the point of the discussion. The christology continues through the remaining discussions, but here it has come to special fruition. The christology soars to the heavens and plummets to the deepest, darkest places on earth. That is why it is gospel; that is why it is evangelical. It might be argued that Barth, following the Confession, has dismissed any place for human agency. In one sense that is true. There is no place left for human autonomy, human aspiration, or even, maybe especially, human piety, religion and ethics. On the other

99. Ibid., 144.

100. Ibid., 145.

101. Ibid., 147.

hand, everything is placed upon the human agency of Jesus Christ, and on our life in that agency lived, died, and ascended to rule on our behalf. The argument may be that the christology of vicarious agency is too big, too engulfing, too imperial. Barth and the authors of the Confession might well reply that this is what the Lordship of Jesus Christ means. Faith is the gift of God to trust our lives at every point to this Lordship.

### *Discussion of Articles 16, 17, and 25a: The Mystery of the Church, and Article 18: The Human Form of the Church*

The Confession is emphatic in its sense of the Trinitarian and christo-logical constitution of the church. It professes the true Kirk to be made up of people "who have communion and society with God the Father, and with his Son, Christ Jesus, through the sanctification of his Holy Spirit" (Article 16). The church is a mystery insofar as it is those people who are united with Christ in faith, so that his life becomes their life, and their life his. Thus constituted the church has a vertical and a horizontal view. We consider now Barth's fourteenth and fifteenth lectures together as he reflects on "the area within which Jesus Christ lives His divine life in human form."[102]

This divine establishment and foundation of the church is hidden; but as a human assembly it is manifest.[103] In either case it is the church of Jesus Christ. As hidden, the divine establishment and foundation lies in Christ our mediator, advocate and high priest, who lives in measureless exaltation over the church as her heavenly and invisible head. On the other hand, Jesus Christ, whose life is the Christian life, is not without his people. Says Barth: "He lives for us on earth and in time nowhere else than in the midst of his people, as the meaning and content of (*the church's*) history, the ground and truth of the promise made to *it* and the object of *its* faith. Jesus Christ lives by the tidings about Him being proclaimed and heard. This is His life on earth."[104] Christ's life as the head of the church is not to be separated from the life of the body, for the body has no life without its head as the one who lives his life in our stead and for us. The church, then, is the form in which Christian faith exists because it is the community which has faith in Jesus Christ who is its life.

---

102. Ibid., 151.

103. Ibid., 152.

104. Ibid., 153.

Thus one cannot hold the Christian faith or live the Christian life outside the church: "Out of this Kirk there is neither life nor eternal felicity" for "there is neither life nor salvation without Christ Jesus" (Article 16).

The hidden establishment and foundation of the church means also that the Christian life, and the unity and holiness of the church, are nowhere visible or public. "It is in Jesus Christ that she possesses her true nature, unity and holiness—not in what the men gathered together in her, as men, even the greatest and most serious of them, are, say and do, but in what Jesus Christ is for them, has said to them and done for them. She possesses her true nature, unity and holiness in the hidden work of the Holy Spirit, in His electing, calling, directing and comforting."[105] Insofar as the mystery of the church is nowhere visible, but lies in Jesus Christ who lives his life in our stead, the church is the manifestation of Christ's life for the world. The life of Jesus Christ is the life of this people, for he does not live his life for his own sake. "Having life in Himself, He pours it forth on those who through the Holy Spirit have their life in Him by faith."[106] In this way the church is vicariously constituted in Christ, subsisting entirely on his life for her. This is the mystery of the church.

The mystery of the church has a human form; as a human assembly it is manifest. Considering the notes of the true church the Confession clearly has actual congregations in mind: "Such Kirks, we the inhabitants of the realm of Scotland confessing Christ Jesus, do claim to have in our cities, towns, and reformed districts because of the doctrine taught in our Kirks" (Article 18). The one church of Jesus Christ exists only in such individuality and plurality.[107] The church is not an ideal to which congregations attach themselves for their identity. Yet as a congregation the congregation is the whole church in this or that place.

Further, as the mystery of the church in human form, the congregation is always becoming the church again and again, and is nowhere exempt from the danger of losing her identity. The Confession seems to be very anxious about this loss of identity, and determines to be clear about the marks of the true church. Says Barth: "the *church* is *always* threatened by the question whether or not she is the true or the false church . . . This fact brings a necessary unrest into the life of the church

105. Ibid., 157.
106. Ibid., 150.
107. Ibid., 162.

. . . Both the true and false church exist."[108] Such entities are as fire and water. The true church lives on and in the truth, and truth will not admit of fusion with its contrary.[109] The true church lives in a struggle over the question of her true nature, facing up to temptation to give up her true nature and become the false church.[110]

Everything depends on the resistance against untruth being the right resistance. Barth returns to his central thesis (of which he never tires) by reminding us of the nature of faith. He insists once again that faith consists in thankfulness and penitence, fulfils the law of God by loving God and one's neighbor, in all of which we are comforted by the fact that "the Son of God has intervened on our behalf."[111] The true church exists where this faith (as defined) takes place, which is the working of the Holy Spirit. Following the teaching of the Confession, the question of true identity is not settled by the antiquity of the church, nor by its apostolic succession, nor by its numbers, or by the beauty of its worship or the felicity of its theology. "The true church is distinguished from the false only by the fact that in her Jesus Christ is *present in power*."[112] This is a spiritual determination, and only as such can it become manifest. It is a distinction made by God, and for us only to be recognized. The Confession, then, specifies three points at which this determination made by God can be seen. It is worth citing the Confession in full at this point.

> The notes of the true Kirk, therefore, we believe, confess and avow to be: first, the true preaching of the Word of God, in which God has revealed himself to us, as the writings of the prophets and apostles declare; secondly, the right administration of the sacraments of Christ Jesus, with which must be associated the Word and promise of God to seal and confirm men in our hearts; and lastly, ecclesiastical discipline uprightly ministered, as God's Word prescribes, whereby vice is repressed and virtue nourished. Then wherever these notes are seen and continue for any time, be the number complete or not, there, beyond any doubt, is the true Kirk of Christ, who, according to his promise, is in its midst. (Article 18)

108. Ibid., 166.
109. Ibid., 167.
110. Ibid., 169.
111. Ibid.
112. Ibid., 171.

We will allow Barth to supply the commentary. "What the Reformed Confession means by specifying these three points is that, when we enquire about the true church and consider preaching, the sacraments and the ordinance of the church, it is Jesus Christ Himself as the Word of God, who has to be the subject of our enquiry."[113] Thus Barth drives us back again to the christology of vicarious agency, for Jesus Christ present in power through preaching, sacraments and church ordinance is always the Son of God who has acted *on our behalf and in our stead.*

### Discussion of Articles 18b, 19, and 20: Ecclesiastical Order

The Confession now discusses the nature of authority in the church manifest. In doing so, and under the rubric that the church is in no account called to govern herself, the Confession rejects two opposing forms of authority in the church. First, the Confession rejects the Roman system, which consists in government by ecclesiastical order. Barth calls this order "aristocratic and monarchial."[114] This rejection implies a second rejection, namely, of the modern democratic idea which looks upon the majority of believers as the source of authority in the church. "But the government of the church does not take place through men in either the monarchical or democratic way. It takes place through the *Word of God.*"[115]

Thus Barth expounds a profound connection that is made by the Confession itself between authority in the church and the Holy Scriptures. Barth insists that the Scriptures "are the concrete form of Jesus Christ,"[116] the one testimony to Jesus Christ in which God has spoken about himself. The church only takes an interest in God and in God's voice through the human testimony of the Bible. This book alone bears that testimony to God. Following the lead of the Confession, the question now rightly arises: Who expounds the Scriptures? The Confession is to the point: "The interpretation of Scripture, we confess, does not belong to any private or public person, nor yet to any Kirk for pre-eminence or precedent, personal or local, which it has above others, but pertains to the Spirit of God by whom the Scriptures were written"

---

113. Ibid., 172.

114. Ibid., 177.

115. Ibid.

116. Ibid.

(Article 18). Only God can expound the scriptures. As such, Jesus Christ is Lord of Scripture.

Considering the debates, past and present, over the so-called authority of scripture and the modernist fascination with hermeneutics, Barth really does not have much to say. Abstract, even metaphysical, questions carry no interest. The issue, after all, is Jesus Christ, and Barth has mostly already said his piece. Even questions of church government, which would much fuss the Scots for centuries, are discussed by him in a speedy, almost dismissive, fashion, recognizing this and that, but concluding that neither Episcopal nor Presbyterian forms of church government is the issue, for this concern is not one in which the true nature of the church is at stake.[117]

### *Discussion of Article 21: The Sacraments as the Church Service—*
### *Divine Action*

Notably, the Confession grounds service of God in worship—not abstractly, but in the worship of the congregation, and not generically, but from the perspectives of the sacraments, and not with equal exposition, but in the main in terms of the Lord's Supper. Undoubtedly there is an historical context for this focus. The Reformers were concerned to overcome a Roman sacramental heritage they believed to have gone much astray from the Word of God. However, in making enquiry about the sacraments, a Godly heritage was forged that remains neglected today in the Reformed churches. The Confession held the Supper in very high regard; the whole service of God could be seen and ordered from this vantage point. Barth approves: "In fact it may well be the case that it is not possible to tackle the problem of the church service in any better way than from this aspect, namely, that of the sacraments."[118]

Barth interprets the teaching of the Confession thus: "a sacrament is an action in which God acts and man serves, his service taking the form of the execution of a divine precept. In accordance with this precept and by means of definite concrete media witness is borne to God's grace and through this men's faith is awakened, purified and advanced."[119] The church service is divine action. This is the subject of Article 21. The

117. Ibid., 187.
118. Ibid., 191.
119. Ibid., 191–92.

church service considered as human action is the subject of Articles 22–23. The "very God" is, says Barth, first and conditions what is to be said about "very man."[120] The action of the church is derivative and secondary to the divine action. God wills the divine action. God provides the media for it. God bears witness through them of his grace, awakening, purifying and advancing faith.

Barth discusses both the divine and human actions in terms of ground, content and form. First of all, ground: "The primary ground for church service lies outside ourselves. It lies in the presence and the action of Jesus Christ."[121] With respect to the Lord's Supper, for example, it is not the church that mediates Christ; it is Christ who gives himself according to his own appointment. The church in her actions only serves this prior appointment.

Second, the content of church service corresponds to the ground. The work of the Spirit is to bring about what the Lord of the church wills and commands: this the church must do. We can understand why the Confession refers only to baptism and the Lord's Supper. The authors think that in doing so they have said enough. "By Baptism we are engrafted into Christ Jesus, to be made partakers of his righteousness, by which our sins are covered and remitted" (Article 21). "Thus we confess and believe without doubt that the faithful, in the right use of the Lord's Table, do so eat the body and drink the blood of the Lord Jesus that he remains in them and they in him" (Article 21). Comments Barth: "So we see that what we are concerned with in *Baptism* is the church's *existence*. But the church is undergoing reformation. And thus all the emphasis falls now in the *Lord's Supper*. For what we are concerned with in the Lord's Supper is the church's *continuance*. Hence the Divine command embraces, regulates and delimitates the whole church service by Baptism and the Lord's Supper."[122] Everything in the church has its origin in baptism: Jesus Christ has once for all died and risen for us, we are his, and we have no other destiny than to be justified and glorified through him. Everything in the church has its end in the Lord's Supper: the continuance of the church, that he gives us to share in his life as life with God and that therefore we constantly fulfill our destiny.[123] Through

120. Ibid., 192.
121. Ibid., 193.
122. Ibid., 195.
123. Ibid.

baptism the church is mindful of whence she comes, of creation through the Word of God; through the Lord's Supper the church is mindful of wither she goes, of preservation through the Word of God.[124] As such, the church is characterized by thanksgiving, receiving what God has given.

Further considering the content of the sacraments, Barth, following the Confession, notes that it matters little what we experience. What matters is the work of the Holy Spirit. "In point of fact it is just in connection with the church service that we cannot sufficiently reflect on the fact that faith is something which defies our own lack of faith and disobedience and which must hold fast to God's gracious and Almighty Lordship and care in Jesus Christ and to that alone . . . [T]he church service is the most important, momentous and majestic thing which can possible take place on earth, because its primary content is not the work of man, but the work of the Holy Spirit and consequently the work of faith."[125]

Third, the primary form of the church service corresponds to its content. Testimony is borne to revelation and faith in concrete acts – the gathering of the community, water, bread and wine, speech and action. Yet, says Barth, even the form of the church service belongs first of all to the action of God. These things that we do, and the media that are used, are because of God's choice and appointment.[126] And here the Confession draws its lines against false teaching and practice. First, against Catholicism and Lutheranism it drew attention to the fact that form is form and not content. The elements render a service but they are not themselves the end for which they serve.[127] Second, against fanatics and spiritualists, it drew attention to the fact that the form of the church service is instituted by God, and not thereby separated from its content. The forms are appointed by God, and so cannot be despised or neglected. As the Confession famously attests, they are not mere symbols. The content and form are related, the latter subordinate to the former. "God has not bound *Himself*," says Barth, "but He has bound *us*."[128]

124. Ibid., 195–96.
125. Ibid., 198.
126. Ibid., 199.
127. Ibid.
128. Ibid., 201.

The ground of the service of God is Jesus Christ, his will and purpose, his command and act, for us. In the sacraments we act in obedience to receive Christ's vicarious life for us. So receiving we confess the "Amen" of faith to his sacrifice for us, for he is our life and faith. The form of the church's service is vicariously given, and what we offer is our sharing in the worship, piety and faith of Jesus Christ.

### Discussion of Articles 22 and 23: The Sacraments as the Church Service—Human Action

We turn to what is expected of us, and, as Barth notes, the Confession is clearly bound to its context and the fight against the Roman church.[129] The right administration of the sacraments is the point of contact between the sacraments and the people. For this reason, Article 22 is a long discourse on sacramental practice. Again Barth follows the typology of ground, content and form in his discussion. There is much detail in the Articles that Barth does not mention. He is trying to see through the mass of detail to discover the essential content of what is presented.

The human action in the church service is the secondary action, being subordinate to the primary, divine action. The ground of human action consists in obedience, not, Barth stresses, in meeting our religious needs and capacities.[130] Religion and the service of God are two quite different things, the one invention, the other obedience. In view is not solemnity, beauty, drama, education, psychology, even mystery. Rather, the issue is to enquire how the human service of God corresponds to the primary ground, Jesus Christ, and in obedience to him. Neither ostensible human need nor consideration for the world is in view. "What the church does owe the world is not her own cleverness or adaptability or the attempt made in all lands at all times to suit the people's wishes, but the gospel of Jesus Christ."[131]

The human content of the church service corresponds to the divine content in revelation and faith, and in a manner proper to it, "and does not consist in a busy waste of time (!)"[132] For the church to act in obedience is for the church to hear the Word of God, and to do this with

129. Ibid., 205.
130. Ibid., 206.
131. Ibid., 208.
132. Ibid., 210.

loyalty and power. "It is because the church hears the Word of God and must hear it again that she preaches, baptises, observes the Lord's Supper and offers thanks . . . It is by listening to God that she serves Him . . . It is by hearing God that the church is built up, lives, grows, works and glorifies God's name in her own midst and in the world. She is the true church in proportion as she is the listening church."[133] Hearing the Word of God is our work,[134] and hearing the Word of God includes receiving the sacraments of the church's beginning and continuance. While in the church service some speak and other listen, this does not mean that a fundamental breach is made in the church; both those who speak and those who listen do so as those who hear the Word of God. The division is technical and not one of principle.[135]

The form of the church service is definite, not arbitrary, given not invented. The waters of baptism, the bread and wine of the Supper, and the scriptures are to be received as water, nourishment and words which bear a testimony. On the human side obedience is enquiry after the institution of the church established by Jesus Christ—an enquiry that must be continuous, scrutinizing and discriminating.[136] That is, the hearing of the Word of God in the church service, with faith and thanksgiving, the work of obedience, must be done with sincerity and humility, open to God's truth and ready to bow before it. Such hearing is our task.[137]

Here the Confession has words of counsel for both preachers and congregants (and a mass of detail). While everything depends upon the efficacy of the Holy Spirit, that is not without corresponding effort on our side. At its core the work of criticism, scrutiny, and discrimination is the work of theology. "It enquires if our hearing of God's Word is being duly qualified and it enquires about the adequacy of our proclamation and perception in relation to the institution of the church as established by Jesus Christ. It asks the church about her sincerity and humility. To this extent theology, too, belongs to the church service and is itself a

---

133. Ibid.

134. Barth at this point has a digression in which he criticizes the Roman church for having sacramental services without preaching, and the Protestant church for having preaching without sacraments. A service without both is incomplete. John Knox surely would have agreed.

135. Ibid., 213.

136. Ibid., 214.

137. Ibid., 215.

leaven for the church's liturgy. And to this extent it must be admitted, too, that the church service is necessarily a theological act."[138]

Given the contextual importance of Articles 22 and 23, Barth seems to have missed something of the urgency involved in proper understanding and practice of the church service in its human aspect. In the discussions of the Articles thus far, consistently, though sometimes more to the fore than other times, the christology of vicarious agency was evident as indicated. It is odd that it appears to be missing in the discussion of these Articles. Why this is the case can only be the subject of conjecture. But perhaps an opportunity was missed. It would have been appropriate for Barth to have reflected on the practice of human agency in terms of Christ's receiving, hearing and obeying the Word of God on our behalf.[139]

### Discussion of Articles 24 and 25b: The State's Service of God and the Comfort and Hope of the Gospel

The Article on "The Civil Magistrate" is a curiosity in the context of increasing secularism and separation of church and state today. Undoubtedly it reflects an historical situation far different from our own. Yet Barth is immediately quick to note that Reformed doctrine has always found a place for the service of God rendered by the state.[140] The theological affirmation that the state is not arbitrary, but exists to the glory of God and the well-being of society, is a reminder that the world in its claim to be merely the world and to be its own law-giver is not to be taken seriously.[141]

The Church and Christians live in the world, even a world which largely does not listen to the Word of God. This world is always the object of the church's mission. The church is appointed to speak the Word of God to the world. Even in its refusal to hear the Word of God, however, the world is under Christ's Lordship, albeit is hidden and secret. Thus Barth makes the clear observation: "Jesus Christ is Lord not only of the church but also of the world."[142] Thus faith claims the political order

138. Ibid., 216.

139. See, for example, Athanasius, *"Four Discourses"* 1.45 and 4.6–7; and Torrance, *Theological Science*, 143.

140. Barth, *The Knowledge of God*, 218.

141. Ibid., 220.

142. Ibid., 221.

for the service of God, even though this service is only a sign pointing to life in Jesus Christ.

Barth again makes his characteristic move. After a review of the basic theme of the whole, namely, that Jesus is the answer to the question of true service of God and the true nature of the church and the Christian life,[143] the question is put to the state: does the political order do what it is its business to do? The Confession asserts that the state must protect, and if necessary, undertake the reform of the church. For Barth this is to claim too much for the state. The task of the state is to provide for freedom for the church.

Barth briefly returns to something discussed under Article 14, active resistance to political power, which can mean opposing force with force. No doubt with the European situation in 1938 in mind, Barth follows the Confession.[144]

The significance of the christology of vicarious agency in church and world, in the church's service of God and in the state's service of God, in which the true and the false are present together, is stated in this way: "that this world is the world of sinful man, whose reconciliation is indeed *already accomplished* in Jesus Christ but is *still hidden*."[145] What was done for us on Calvary and what our lives are in the mystery of God's eternity is one thing, what we experience and do here and now is another. The gulf between the two, in both church and state, is only bridged by the Word of God and faith, as they have been discussed previously, that is, by Jesus Christ. For this reason, and in spite of the enigmatic and riddle-filled experience of life, faith knows the gift of the comfort of forgiven sins and the hope of resurrection and eternal life.[146] With respect to sin forgiven: "what comforts the church is that our present position is seen in the light of that place (Calvary) and our times are utterly in the hands of Him who revealed Himself at that time as the Lord. There and then the gulf was already closed for today. There the judgment has already taken place in so far as His verdict on us has already been given and He has already decided there in our favor with justice and mercy."[147] With respect to resurrection hope: "His resurrection and eternal life *are*

143. Ibid., 222.

144. Ibid., 231.

145. Ibid., 236.

146. Ibid., 239.

147. Ibid., 240.

our future also, because He is our Lord, the Lord of Creation and of our whole existence, both our souls and bodies, and because we belong to Him and not to ourselves . . . In Him the verdict on us has not only been given but put into effect."[148] In the doctrines of comfort and hope the christology of vicarious agency comes to eschatological expression.

The Confession ends with a prayer for God's own action. In this the Confession places its trust in God, in the comfort and hope whose name is Jesus Christ, and in the power of the name of God the Father, the Son and the Holy Spirit. Jesus Christ in our stead: this is the christology of the Scots Confession according to Karl Barth.

148. Ibid., 242.

# BIBLIOGRAPHY

Athanasius, "Four Discourses Against the Arians." In *The Nicene and Post-Nicene Fathers*, 307–447. Edited by Philip Schaff and Henry Wace. 2nd series. Edinburgh: T. & T. Clark.

Barth, Karl. *The Knowledge of God and the Service of God according to the Teaching of the Reformation: Recalling the Scottish Confession of 1560*. Translated by J. L. M. Haire and Ian Henderson. Eugene: Wipf & Stock, 2005.

Hazlett, W. Ian P. "The Scots Confession 1560: Context, Complexion and Critique." *Archive for Reformation History* 78 (1987) 287–320.

Henderson, G. D. *The Scots Confession 1560*. Rendered into modern English by the Reverend James Bulloch. Edinburgh: Saint Andrew, 1960.

Moltmann, Jürgen. *The Crucified God*. New York: Harper & Row, 1974.

Treier, Daniel J. *Introducing Theological Interpretation of Scripture: Recovering a Christian Practice*. Grand Rapids: Baker Academic, 2008.

Torrance, Thomas F. *Scottish Theology from John Knox to John McLeod Campbell*. Edinburgh: T. & T. Clark, 1996.

———. *Theological Science*. London: Oxford University Press, 1969.

# PART TWO

# Systematic Theology

# 6

## Pietas, Religio, and the God Who Is

GANNON MURPHY

IF IT IS GOD who makes thinking possible, how may he be thunk? A distinctive trajectory of Calvinist theology in general has always been that theology proper is intimately bound up with religious epistemology, but not just any religious epistemology. The latter term itself tends to be detached from truly *knowing* God, and occupies itself, rather, with the "God talk" of the philosophers who arrogate their pursuits to the fated enterprise of penetrating the Divine essence. Such knowledge is not only idle but unlawful. The Christian religion (*qua religare*) at its core, reveals *who* God is *to and for us*. Evangelical Calvinism celebrates and preserves this trajectory. Having an understanding of the God *who is*, is coextensive with understanding how we may truly come to possess such an understanding and ultimately finds its locus in our union with him. Knowledge, doctrine, and existential union with the Father, through Christ, by the work of the Holy Spirit does—of necessity and by design—form a seamless garment. It is no surprise, then, that in the first two books of the *Institutes*, Calvin occupied himself exclusively with knowledge of God the Creator and knowledge of God the Redeemer. An understanding of such knowledge sets the course for our understanding of God. This chapter, then, considers knowledge of God and a fecund doctrine of God to be mutual.

A central concern of Evangelical Calvinism is that much of modern and contemporary Reformed theologies have been dominated by both federalism and forensicism and, hence, have not done enough to

153

unpack, much less emphasize, Divine-human relationality particularly as concerns the *unio mystica* ("mystical union"). Reformed theology, as currently received, has excelled in its explication of forensic theology, the relationship between law and gospel, covenant(s), and many of the Divine attributes considered within theology proper, but it has been lacking in its articulation of the nature of the reciprocality between God and created humanity. Of the roughly 48 major theologians since the Reformation who specifically composed a systematic theology (or that which closely resembles one), only nine of them include an explicit treatment of union with God.[1] This deficiency should be a clarion call to Reformed theologians to move into a phase of theological investigation concerned with better understanding our dynamic—not merely forensic—relationship with God. This is a theological enormity which T. F. Torrance had already detected and direly warned against. Torrance puts things in no uncertain terms:

> When . . . the Protestant doctrine of justification is formulated only in terms of forensic imputation of righteousness or the non-imputation of sins in such a way as to avoid saying that to justify is to make righteous, it is the resurrection that is being by-passed. If we think of justification only in the light of the crucifixion as non-imputation of sins because of what Christ has borne for our sakes, then we have mutilated it severely. No doubt we can fill it out with more positive content by relating it to the incarnate life of Christ and to his active obedience—and that would be right, for then justification becomes not only the non-imputation of sins but the clothing of the sinner with the righteousness of Christ. Nevertheless, that would still be empty and unreal, merely a judicial transaction, unless the doctrine of justification bears in its heart a relation of real union with Christ. Apart from such a union with him through the power of his Spirit, as Calvin puts it, Christ would remain, as it were, inert or idle...this is a point which must be taken much more seriously today. If justification is only a forensic or judicial act of imputation or non-imputation, then the resurrection is correspondingly an 'event' of the same kind. But if the resurrection is an actual event in the raising of

1. I deal with possible reasons for this in Murphy, *Consuming Glory*, 201ff. These figures are based, in part, on Wayne Grudem's cataloguing of systematic theologies in Appendix 4 of his Systematic Theology. (See Grudem, *Systematic Theology*, 1224–230.) The nine exceptions include Louis Berkhof, Robert Dabney, Millard Erickson, Wayne Grudem, Edward Arthur Litton, Edgar Young Mullins, Robert Reymond, Augustus Strong, and Henry Clarence Thiessen.

Jesus Christ in the fullness of his humanity from corruption and
death, then justification must correspondingly be a creative, regenerating event. A proper doctrine of justification and a proper
doctrine of the resurrection hang together—when one is muti-
lated the other becomes attenuated.[2]

Now, in asking the question of how knowledge of God may be attained and a doctrine of God profitably formed, the philosophers[3] have
not, and *cannot*, supply an answer. Only the dogmatician, to the extent
that he has bent the knee before Christ and has submitted to his Word,
can. There are two reasons for this. First is the philosopher's perennial
assumption of the universal autonomy of man, especially with regard to
his innate powers of reason. Second is that the philosopher, when considering God, does not begin with a *who*, but a *what*. In Calvinist theology, to the extent that it has striven to be Scripturally-based has been
a continual resourcement to the Fathers (particularly Augustine), this
trajectory is utterly reversed. The question to be asked is not "What is
God" (*quid sit Deus*), but "What is God like?" (*qualis sit Deus*) and what
is appropriate to ask about His nature?[4] Indeed, for Calvin, "If God is
truly like He is portrayed in Scripture, that is, the God who cares actively
for his creation and who therefore deserves man's *pietas* and *religio*, then
such a question as 'What *is* God' betrays a complete lack of knowledge
of God, apart from being unlawful curiosity about God's essence and
majesty."[5]

God is not an object to be studied, but a Father to be honored and
adored—the Creator made approachable and relationally known to us
by the mediatory work of the Son. Veridical knowledge of God is itself
a *relation* rather than an *object*. The unmediated reason of man can at
best proffer the brute existence of a metaphysical principle, a Platonic
demiurge, an Aristotelian *prima causa*, a Force, or some such "thing"
that cares not a fig for fruitful relation with man. This is precisely why
Calvinistic theology proper is wholly intertwined with what we might

2. Torrance, *Space, Time and Resurrection*, 63–64.

3. By "philosophers" I have principally in mind Pascal's notion of the "independent"
mind. The philosophers have thrown themselves into a thousand different sects, but
unite in the assumption "Retire within yourselves" (Pascal, *Pensées*, 464). Nevertheless,
to be more specific, I'll mention here the schools of rationalism, empiricism, idealism,
existentialism, and their contemporary derivatives.

4. Parker, *Calvin: An Introduction to His Thought*, 16.

5. Ibid.

call "knowledge proper," or better, what Edward Dowey has termed "existential knowledge."[6] Pascal, a century or so after Calvin, noted that "knowledge of God is very far from the love of Him" and that God will "only be perceived by those who seek Him with all their heart."[7] What a pity, as history would have it, that Pascal had such a low opinion of Calvin but such a high one of Jansen![8]

Such an understanding or approach, not surprisingly, led Calvin (as it had with Luther) to generally look upon "philosophers" with disdain, describing them variously as "profane," suffering from "stupidity," and "silliness," even "madness." They are those who "wander and stumble."[9] Scholastic theology, which (as the Reformers in general saw it) had come to dominate the teachings of the church of Rome and, as far as contemplating the nature of God was concerned, had blurred the perspicuity of Scripture and even that of the church's own storied tradition, particularly as embodied in the patristical literature. Calvin consistently appealed to the Fathers and recoiled at the charge that Reformed theology was a cor-

6. Dowey, *The Knowledge of God in Calvin's Theology*, 24.

7. Pascal, *Pensées*, 280, 194, 46, 31.

8. To wit, "In 1646, though not yet fully converted to the Christian faith, Pascal began to follow the teachings of the Jansenists, a Catholic sect led by Cornelius Jansen. It fell into disfavor with the Roman Church hierarchy due to its emphasis on predestination and its opposition to the moral lapses of the Jesuits . . . After [his seminal conversion experience], Pascal became somewhat of a recluse. [Though he had set it aside for a time] he took up Jansenism once again, practiced it diligently and even wrote a defense of it called the *Lettres Provinciales* under the pseudonym Louis de Montalte (to avoid repercussions by the Roman Church). The writing also strongly denounced the moral laxity of the Society of Jesus and called Christians to a higher standard and a stronger focus on God's grace." Murphy, *Voices of Reason in Christian History*, 149, 151. Jansenist theology was, more or less, a micro-Augustinian revival which maintained, nevertheless, its amenability within the Roman ecclesial fold. This all changed, of course, when it was declared heretical by Pope Innocent X in 1655. Jansenism centered around five key doctrines: original sin, human depravity, predestination, the necessity of divine grace, and justification by faith—all constituent elements of Calvinist theology. The primary difference between Jansenism and Calvinism was that the former rejected the doctrine of perseverance. Nevertheless, the similarities between Calvinism and Jansenism are plainly obvious, and the difference(s) between them pale in comparison with their similarities. And yet, Pascal considered the Calvinists to be both "deceived" and a cause of disillusionment (Pascal, *Pensées*, 862). It is perhaps unwise to fiddle about in the realm of counterfactuals, or worse to play the role of a psychologist with special mind-reading powers; but I cannot help conjecture that had the times been different, that is, had they not been quite so socio-politically charged, that Pascal might have given Calvin a second, more sympathetic, read.

9. Calvin, *Inst.*, 1.5.11.

ruption of the tradition represented therein: "It is a calumny to represent us as opposed to the Fathers (I mean the ancient writers of a purer age)... Were the contest to be decided by such authority (to speak in the most moderate terms), the better part of the victory would be ours."[10]

Calvin, nevertheless, is not to be taken to the extreme of a Tertullian-esque, utterly anti-philosophical disposition. For Calvin (and, I would contend, for Evangelical Calvinists today) it is a matter of one's starting point. To begin with the autonomous reason of man and the philosophy it manufactures, we may agree with Calvin that therein is that "immense flood of error with which the whole world is overflowed."[11] If we have imbibed of worldly philosophy (at least to the extent that it is divorced from revelation), we have come to know very well its unending viscidities and have understood the ultimate outcome of its collective output. We must have arrived, in the very least, at this: that philosophy confronts us with the reality of our own unspeakable limitedness. We find, as Pascal did, that we are unable to circumscribe the very "circle" of which we are a part.[12] Even as our sphere of knowledge increases, which no doubt it has exponentially, so too, then, has our surface contact with mystery. The more knowledge, the more mystery. No matter how much we might militate against it, we're veritable morons and, in the absence of humble reverence before the Lord, and in not having taken recourse to the Divine Word, we enter only into rooms with no exit.

Theology proper is a systematic "thinking through" or reflection about God with an eye toward doctrinal development or retrospective ratification. And yet, *finitum non capax infiniti* ("the finite cannot contain the infinite"). How, then, are we to engage in a proper thinking through of God? From what or where do we derive a fecund conceptual framework? These twin questions are foundational. As Bobby Grow has written, "Everything we do in theology starts with *how we conceive of God* . . . depending on this defining point, one will end up on one trajectory or the other . . ."[13]

10. Ibid., Prefatory, 4.

11. Calvin, *Inst.,* 1.5.12

12. Pascal, *Pensées,* 72.

13. Bobby Grow, "The Themes of Evangelical Calvinism", n.p. [cited November 20, 2010]. Online: http://evangelicalcalvinist.com/the-themes-of-evangelical-calvinism/, emphasis added.

Evangelical Calvinism preserves the Scripturally-undergirded intuition that God is understood only insofar as he has condescended to reveal himself to us and, even then: 1) in a manner befitting our created nature and its constitutive faculties (intellectual, spiritual, moral, physical); and 2) to the extent that God reveals to us his plans and purpose as it relates to us. God does not supply us with a "definition" of himself. To do so would not only be pointless, but impossible. Calvin, then, naturally begins the *Institutes* with a direct consideration of our *knowledge* of God—where it comes from, how it is imparted and gleaned, precisely what sort of knowledge it is, and its God-ordained limits. This is a crucial departure from other approaches, most notably that of scholasticism and, more recently, philosophical theologies such as processianism and panentheism,[14] the first relying primarily on analogical predication, the latter two assuming a crass sort of univocal predication wherein human reason can furnish not only autonomous predications of God, but can penetrate the Divine essence (in some cases, with or without the help of Scripture).

Evangelical Calvinism seeks to know its limits, not so that knowledge may be prematurely or preemptively curtailed, but in order that rightful knowledge may be celebrated and God glorified. Such knowledge is found where God intends it to be found and wherein he creates a suitable nexus. Asking *what* God is certainly is an area in which "loquacious tongues must be dumb."[15] But seeking *who* God is, what he is like, and what his revealed purpose is for our lives *in relation to him* is not only rightful, but enjoins a benediction: "they who seek the Lord shall not be in want of any good thing" (Ps 34:10b).

## THREE STRANDS OF UNDERSTANDING

There are at least three immediately discernable strands that form the rope of Calvin's doctrine of the knowledge of God, which then gives natural rise to the proper formation of a fecund doctrine of God: *religio* and *pietas* (religion and piety), the *sensus Divinitatis* (the natural "sense of the Divine"), and *accommodation*. It is the first of these, however, *pietas* and *religio*, that is of chief importance and which forms a plumb-line

---

14. Concerning these latter two, their historical development, contemporary manifestations, and relationship to Reformed theology, see Cooper, *Panentheism*, 2006.

15. Calvin, *Inst.*, 3.23.7.

which passes through the other two. Calvin, and Evangelical Calvinism today, has relied implicitly on Scripture in the development of this religious epistemology. Such principles are not setup as a framework prior to Scripture but, rather, are derived from it.

### Religio and Pietas

The very beginning of the *Institutes* commences in a statement concerning that which constitutes true wisdom, to wit, that wisdom "consists almost entirely of two parts: the knowledge of God and of ourselves."[16] Some theologians have argued that this first statement is actually the *entire* point of the *Institutes*, a contestable, but not entirely meritless, claim.[17]

It is perhaps customary in our technological age to think of *knowledge* as a purely apprehensive or propositional enterprise—we have knowledge of this *object*, or that *thing*, or such-and-such a set of *data*. The key to preserving Calvin's doctrine of knowledge (*cognitione*), however, is to see it as something much fuller and more "holistic." In sum, *to truly know God is to love him.* Theological knowledge is not merely propositional in nature or a matter of mere intellectual assent (*assensus*). Rather, it must also be experiential, stemming from love that also manifests itself in adoration, trust, fear, and obedience to God. Edward Dowey, for example, refers to Calvin's concept of knowledge, as "existential knowledge."[18] The idea of coming to God merely in *mind* is an utterly foreign concept throughout the Calvinian corpus. Further, Calvin (like Luther) alludes to the nonsensical nature of conceiving of God as a mere *object* of knowledge.

Calvin uses the terms *religio* and *pietas*[19] which, unfortunately, do not translate well into our English words, *religion* and *piety*, both of which tend to connote merely a system of ecclesiology or perfunctory, external religious observance. Both words in the Latin, however, denote something much deeper. *Re-ligio* derives from *re*, "again" and *ligere*, "to bind." Our contemporary words "ligament" or "ligature" come from this root. *Religare* literally means "to bind fast." The cognate term, *religiens*,

---

16. Ibid., 1.1.1.

17. See, for example, Parker, *Calvin: An Introduction to His Thought*, 13.

18. Dowey, *The Knowledge of God in Calvin's Theology*, 24.

19. Calvin, *Inst.*, 1.2.1.

literally means "careful," the opposite of *negligens*. *Religio*, then, means something more along the lines of "careful attention to" and to be "rebound." *Pietas*, while often suggesting merely "dutifulness," is better understood as "dutiful kindness," stemming from the Latin root *pius* (literally, "kind"). Thus, *pietas* is friendly obedience toward the things of God. It is the perfect opposite of animosity toward godly things—to find oneself welcoming of, and delighting in, his or her Creator.

Calvin, characteristically never wanting to be misunderstood but always desiring clarity for his readers, defines *religio* as, "confidence in God coupled with serious fear—fear, which both includes in it willing reverence, and brings along with it such legitimate worship as is prescribed by the law."[20] On the other hand, *pietas* is "that *union* of reverence and love to God which the knowledge of his benefits inspires."[21] Expounded here is something rather far removed from trajectories that find natural theology as their starting point—the idea of an irrefragable knowledge of God garnered apart from reverence and revelation, that is, a special and specific Word from God. Rather, Calvin speaks of the first step of *pietas* being, "to acknowledge that God is a Father, to defend, govern, and cherish us, until he brings us to the eternal inheritance of his kingdom."[22]

That true knowledge of God cannot be torn asunder from *pietas* and *religio* means, then, that overly-philosophical speculation about the *essence* or *substance* of God is necessarily ruled out. Calvin derides such pursuits as "Epicurean," as "frigid speculations," and admonishes us rather to seek out "what things are agreeable to his nature."[23]

### The Sensus Divinitatis

There is no *saving* knowledge of God apart from *religio* and *pietas*. Nevertheless, Calvin insists that "there exists in the human mind and indeed by natural instinct, some sense of Deity [which is] beyond dispute, since God himself, to prevent any man from pretending ignorance, has endued all men with some idea of his Godhead, the memory of which he constantly renews and occasionally enlarges, that all to a man being

20. Ibid., 1.2.2.
21. Ibid., 1.2.1, emphasis added.
22. Ibid., 2.6.4.
23. Ibid., 1.2.2.

aware that there is a God, and that he is their Maker, may be condemned by their own conscience when they neither worship him nor consecrate their lives to his service."[24] Fittingly, Calvin titles the third chapter in Book I, "The Knowledge Of God Naturally Implanted In The Human Mind." This natural sense of God we call the *sensus Divinitatis.*

But if God has imbued all humans with such a natural knowledge of him, why then are there atheists and unbelievers? Calvin's answer is that, while many people may live as though there is no God, nevertheless, "the worm of conscience, keener than burning steel, is gnawing them within."[25] In short, created humans deny God because they ignore Him through their hardness of heart. And this hardness of heart is born of *sin.* Even so, a natural sense of God's reality cannot be completely extinguished in any person:

> For the world labours as much as it can to shake off all knowledge of God, and corrupts his worship in innumerable ways. I only say, that, when the stupid hardness of heart, which the wicked eagerly court as a means of despising God, becomes enfeebled, the sense of Deity, which of all things they wished most to be extinguished, is still in vigour, and now and then breaks forth. Whence we infer, that this is not a doctrine which is first learned at school, but one as to which every man is, from the womb, his own master; one which nature herself allows no individual to forget, though many, with all their might, strive to do so.[26]

Humanity's innate knowledge of God is corrupted by sin such that it fails to acknowledge its own natural state. Indeed, Calvin suggests earlier in the *Institutes* that unhappiness—coming to recognize one's own misery and spiritual poverty—is the initial key to the breaking forth of the Spirit's activity in one's life. This is ultimately the *sine qua non* of true knowledge of God, leading to salvation.[27]

Calvin's appeal to the *sensus Divinitatis* is not, however, an appeal to a natural *saving* knowledge of God. This, as we shall see shortly, comes only from the internal witness of the Holy Spirit, coupled with the external revelation of the Biblical message. Romans 1:18–32 figures heavily in Calvin's treatment of the *sensus Divinitatis* throughout chapters

24. Ibid., 1.3.1.
25. Ibid., 1.3.3.
26. Ibid., 1.3.3.
27. Ibid., 1.1.1.

3–9 of Book 1. He appeals to St. Paul's assertion that, ". . . that which is known about God is evident within them; for God made it evident to them. For since the creation of the world His invisible attributes, His eternal power and divine nature, have been clearly seen, being understood through what has been made, so that they are without excuse" (Rom 1:19–20). This is more a vindication of God's justice in punishing those who do not worship and adore him since, what knowledge of God they do possess, is thought to be sufficient for *judgment* to the extent that, morally-speaking, humans prefer atheism or idolatry to a Holy God. Calvin labours the point that humanity is without excuse. Though God has made himself plain to all people, and regularly instils new awareness of his Being into us, we have instead chosen a different, deeply-unnatural path.

Calvin's *sensus Divinitatis*, then, is more a convicting animal than a saving grace. It is precisely because humans have this sense that they are justly and condignly judged for not honouring their Creator. Its positive side, however, is that the misery this constant state engenders can, and often is, used of the Spirit of God to spurn one on toward seeking the truth of Biblical revelation. To recognize one's own misery is a sign of the transformative in-breaking of the Spirit.

### Accommodation(ism)

In the centuries preceding Calvin, it was common—especially among the Scholastics—to affirm the doctrine of *analogy* in reference to human knowledge of God. Analogical predication was defended chiefly by Thomas Aquinas in the first book of his *Summa Theologica*.[28] Aquinas reasoned that, while perfect (*univocal*) knowledge of the infinite God by finite humans is manifestly impossible, it would also be absurd to posit a muddled, confused, or flatly erroneous knowledge (*equivocal*). Thus, knowledge of God was thought to be somewhere in between these extremes, to wit, *analogical*. Perhaps the easiest way to think of the doctrine of analogy is simply in terms of similarity and dissimilarity, that is, two analogates are partly the same and partly different. Analogates share a common "perfection," but exemplify that perfection differently depending on what they are (i.e., their ontology).

---

28. Thomas Aquinas, *Summa Theologica*, 1.13.5.

Though Calvin warned against "the subtlety of Thomas"[29] with regard to other matters, he never spoke explicitly *against* the Thomistic doctrine of analogy. He did, however, proffer a conception of the knowledge of God which does, it seems to me, to be closer to the heart of Christian faith. Calvin refused to philosophize too deeply about such matters, staying as close as he could to Scripture. His theory, then, is much less complex than that of Aquinas, and is often referred to as the *accommodation theory* or *accommodationism*.

Accommodation refers to "the process by which God reduces or adjusts to human capacities what he wishes to reveal of the infinite mysteries of his being."[30] Calvin's well known description of the nature of revelatory language likens the Divine discourse with humanity to a kind of "baby talk". Indeed, "God, in so speaking, lisps with us as nurses are wont to do with little children . . . Such modes of expression, therefore, do not so much express what kind of a being God is, as accommodate the knowledge of him to our feebleness."[31] For Calvin, created humans—in terms of their creatureliness itself—simply *cannot* know God "as he is in himself" but only as he is "in *relation* to us."[32] This is to say that God discloses himself to humanity in accord with his causal-relationality with them and to the limited capacity of the human mind to give us a picture of who he is as our Creator. This is in keeping with Calvin's frequent insistence that we know God only as he reveals himself to us, that is, in the context of the Divine-human relationship, not as God is *in himself.*

God communicates with us by accommodating himself to our finitude. Calvin was well aware that the Bible uses many different sorts of analogies and metaphors in describing God which some might erroneously construe to be either univocal or equivocal. But, for Calvin, the analogies employed in Scripture are not just *any* analogies. They are divinely *chosen* and, conversely, humans are *designed* to be the recipients of them so that—even though limited—true knowledge is nevertheless transferred. Brian Gerrish observes that, for Calvin, "God does not merely condescend to human frailty by revealing himself in the prophetic and apostolic word and by causing the Word to be written down in sacred

---

29. Calvin, *Inst.*, 3.22.9.

30. Dowey, *The Knowledge of God in Calvin's Theology*, 3.

31. Calvin, *Inst.*, 1.13.1.

32. Ibid., 1.10.2.

books: he also makes his witness employ accommodated expressions."[33] These "expressions" are the very vehicles by which God imparts knowledge to us. Insisting upon perfect knowledge of God's infinite being (univocal predication) would not only be to demand something which we cannot—by our very nature—have, but would also be to derogate the inestimable value of that which the Creator *has* imparted to us.

The use of anthropomorphism and metaphor in Scripture also plays a key role in Calvin's understanding of accommodation. He criticized the "Anthropomorphites" who "dreamed of a corporeal God, because mouth, ears, eyes, hands, and feet, are often ascribed to him . . ."[34] This was a hyper-literal reading of Scripture (still often found among many today!). To Calvin, the folly of such a position is plain and the evidence of accommodation to our limited understanding is clearly evident. The Scriptures, for example, plainly teach that God is *spirit* (John 4:24) which by nature precludes such a literal rendering of anthropomorphism. Human beings, however, cannot possibly understand all that it means to be an eternal, self-existent, *personal* Spirit. God, however, gives us a mode for *apprehending* His being even though we cannot fully *comprehend* it. Though, *finitum non capax infiniti*, nevertheless, *finitum posse apprehensio infiniti* ("the finite can apprehend the infinite").

Calvin's approach in which language is Divinely accommodated permits a multifaceted understanding of God's self-disclosure in which we understand it to be constituted of "sign-posts" along the way to the person of God, but ones which never exhaust his being or provide a total understanding. As Calvin says, "all the signs he ever employed were in apt accordance with the scheme of doctrine, and, at the same time, gave plain *intimation* of his incomprehensible essence."[35] Scripture, in this manner, can be unified in contrast to those conceptions of Divine "speech" which leads either to hyper-literalism, or unfettered relativism. Calvin's accommodationism affirms that we have a word from God, but reminds us that God is using a chosen means to describe himself in the context of his relationship to us as Creator. God "stoops far below his proper height,"[36] condescending to speak to us in the human words we

33. Gerrish, *The Old Protestantism and the New*, 175.

34. Calvin, *Inst.*, 1.13.1.

35. Ibid., 1.11.3, emphasis added.

36. Ibid., 1.13.1.

were created to employ, in order that God may become *relationally* near to us.

## SCRIPTURE

As we've seen, the *sensus Divinitatis* imparts a certain "natural" knowledge of God. But, for Calvin, this knowledge is at once obscured, incomplete, and most importantly, *insufficient*. Indeed, such knowledge only serves to make humans inexcusable before God. That is, natural knowledge is inherently condemnatory and non-salvific. Therefore, Calvin contends that the only saving knowledge of God is to be found in the particular, special revelation of God through Scripture. In this regard, Calvin deploys his famous "spectacles metaphor" in which Scripture interprets nature and existence for us, while revealing the true God: "Just as old or bleary-eyed men and those with weak vision, if you thrust before them a most beautiful volume, even if they recognize it to be some sort of writing, yet can scarcely construe two words, but with the aid of spectacles will begin to read distinctly; so Scripture, gathering up the otherwise confused knowledge of God in our minds, having dispersed our dullness, clearly shows us the true God."[37]

The sole manner in which human beings may come to a right view of God and religion is to "put on" the spectacles of Scripture. Once the Biblical spectacles are adorned, the broader picture comes into focus. Again, Scripture supplies what general revelation cannot: "It is therefore clear that God has provided the assistance of the Word for the sake of all those to whom he has been pleased to give useful instruction because he foresaw that his likeness imprinted upon the most beautiful form of the universe would be insufficiently effective."[38]

Calvin's doctrine of Scripture includes the notion of Divine inspiration, built upon the Bible's apostolic authority which enjoins "with unmistakable marks and tokens the one true God."[39] The apostles did not write "except from the Lord, that is, with Christ's Spirit as precursor in a certain measure dictating their words [*verba quodammodo dictante Christi Spiritu*]."[40] The McNeill-Battles translation of the *Institutes* notes

37. Ibid., 1.6.1.
38. Ibid., 1.6.3.
39. Ibid., 1.6.2.
40. Ibid., 4.8.8.

that the adverb *quodammodo* (meaning, "in a certain way," "in a manner," or, more colloquially, "so to speak"), is a deliberate modifier of
*dictante* ("to dictate") which would preclude a construal—from Calvin's
use of the word "dictating"—any theory of mechanical dictation, or even
technical, *verbal inerrancy*. Rather, the context is wholly didactic, that is,
the Scripture bears the apostolic authority to teach the Divine subject.[41]

Calvin adds that the apostles "were sure and genuine scribes of
the Holy Spirit [*certi et authentici Spiritus sancti amanuenses*], and their
writings are therefore to be considered oracles of God; but the sole office
of others is to teach what is provided and sealed in the Holy Scriptures."[42]
Again, the McNeill-Battles translation notes that *amanuenses* (literally
"by hand," but typically used to describe something akin to secretarial
work), is also not indicative of plenary, verbal inspiration, but of didactic authority.[43] Nowhere does Calvin explicitly defend a theory of mechanical dictation. Rather, his point is simply that the Scripture alone
is imbued with the authority to teach about the things of God and right
religion.

Calvin frequently asserts humans to be the spectators of the theatre
of God's glory (*theatrum gloriae Dei*)[44], but must heed the Scriptures to
really behold it: "Therefore, however fitting it may be for man seriously
to turn his eyes to contemplate God's works, since he has been placed
in this most glorious theatre to be a spectator of them, it is fitting that
he prick up his ears to the Word, the better to profit."[45] Believers must
attend to the Divine Word in order to clearly see the fuller revelation of
the Creator.

Lastly, Calvin argues that the knowledge of God which comes
through the authority of Scripture, is a knowledge shared *only by believers*
when they regard the Scriptures to have "sprung from heaven, as if there
the living words of God were heard."[46] Here, Calvin is arguing against
the notion that the Bible gleans its authority through any pronounce-
ment of the institutional church. In accord with the Reformational principle of *sola Scriptura*, Calvin guards against the idea that the Bible has

41. Calvin, *Institutes* (ed. John McNeill), 1155, n. 7.

42. Ibid 4.8.9.

43. Ibid, 1157, n. 9.

44. Calvin, *Inst.*, 1.6.2.

45. Ibid., 1.6.2.

46. Ibid., 1.7.1.

authority outside of itself. Rather, it is self-authenticating (*autopiston*): "Let this point therefore stand: that those whom the Holy Spirit has inwardly taught truly rest upon Scripture, and that Scripture indeed is self-authenticated."[47] This statement shores up the notion of both regenerating faith which engenders *pietas* and *religio* and, in turn, opens up the knowledge of God through Scripture to the believing community.

## TRANSCENDENCE "VERSUS" IMMANENCE

Much of the history of the doctrine of God has been a tussle between immanentist and transcendental schools, as though these categories present a mutually-annihilating set of concerns. Stanley Grenz and Roger Olson went to the extent of calling the chronic undulation between these two poles "the *central* theological concern" dominating Western theology for much of its history and certainly for the last one hundred years.[48] This is a "tension," however, that Evangelical Calvinism rejects outright.

The recent "openness theology" movement provides an excellent contemporary window into how corrosive such faulty tensions can become. The movement, for the most part, took its cues from process theology, adorned it with familiar Evangelical language, and functioned as a reaction to the dominant Reformed theologies that had set the course for Evangelical theology throughout much of the 20th century. Such Reformed theologies were decidedly forensic in character and, left to the wayside, was much of any consideration of the genuineness of Divine-human relationality as situated in an understanding of *Christus in nobis* ("Christ in us"). I have written about this at length elsewhere—coupled with the Eastern notion of *theosis*—and will not rehash it here.[49]

Rather, the point to be made is that much of Evangelicalism has now shifted toward more immanentistic theologies in an attempt to recover that which was never really lost, but rather eclipsed by other concerns (e.g., forensicism, federalism, biblical inerrancy, etc.). A false tension was thereby erected by ignoring that which had earlier held the two emphases not in opposition, but in distinction. It came to be thought contradictory that a timeless being could "enter in to" time and interact with temporal beings and that it is existentially ineffectual to

47. Ibid., 1.7.5.

48. Stanley Grenz and Roger Olson, *20th Century Theology,* 10.

49. Gannon Murphy, "Reformed *Theosis*?" 194–235.

try and *relate* to a timeless being. Similarly, so it goes, it is rationally antithetical to maintain God's meticulous providence of world events and also hold to human freedom; and it is existentially repugnant to disaffirm the human intuition of autonomous freewill (a seemingly unquestioned presupposition be it the man in the street or the tenured academician). The classical understanding of the so-called *incommunicable* attributes of God has got to be wrong if theologians are to salvage any of the so-called *communicable* attributes, the rubric under which the logical opposite of the items in the second set would fall (that is, relatedness, reciprocity, concern, passion, affection, mobility, and so on as "opposed" to eternality, omnipotence, omniscience, omnipresence, etc.). The recently departed open theist, Clark Pinnock, wrote,

> Two models of God in particular are the most influential that people commonly carry around in their minds. We may think of God primarily as an aloof monarch, removed from the contingencies of the world, unchangeable in every aspect of being, as an all-determining and irresistible power, aware of everything that will ever happen and never taking risks. Or we may understand God as a caring parent with qualities of love and responsiveness, generosity and sensitivity, openness and vulnerability, a person (rather than a metaphysical principle) who experiences the world, responds to what happens, relates to us and interacts dynamically with humans.[50]

The language here is strong and pits the classical incommunicable attributes against the communicable ones. But is this really the only choice? Hardly. The immanence and transcendence of God are not competing notions, vying for theological dominance or even emphasis. Rather, transcendence *supplies* immanence. God is not an "aloof monarch" at all, but is present in every detail of redemptive history, complete with its human machinations. As Fr Thomas Weinandy, though certainly not an Evangelical Calvinist, rightly observes, "For the early Fathers the act of creation which manifests and establishes the complete otherness of God, and thus his eternal, all-powerful and unchanging nature, is the very same act which relates him to the created order and so founds his loving and salvific relation to it."[51] Evangelical Calvinism, though it has its work set out for it, seeks to expose the canard of the endless "tran-

50. Pinnock, *The Openness of God,* 103.
51. Weinandy, *Does God Suffer?* 113.

scendence versus immanence" imbroglio by bringing (back) to the fore, the Biblical revelation that the transcendent "I AM" is the very one in whom we abide and he in us (John 15:4–5), and is able to do so precisely because He is "I AM."

## WHO GOD IS—THE REDEEMER

Our understanding of God comes ultimately through the revelation of the Son. In terms of situating this theology historically, Calvin neither departed from nor added to the traditional Chalcedonian Christology of the fifth century holding, as it were, that Christ enjoins two natures, fully Divine and human. Nothing in Calvin's writings ever questions the more "metaphysical" formulations of early, historic Christology. Where Calvin makes a more important and unique contribution is with regard to his giving greater form to the designation of Christ according to the three-fold office (*triplex munus Christi*) of prophet, priest, and king.[52] Though this is not a totally new development with Calvin (Luther also gave it expression), he gave it a more classic, systematic form which also serves as a central feature of his overall doctrine of Christ. The designation is more concerned (as all the Reformers tended to be) with the existential matter of salvation, rather than the more "speculative" modes of other theologies, especially that of the schoolmen—a trajectory also upheld by Evangelical Calvinism.

Calvin describes Christ's activity as Mediator to involve each of these offices. As he has already shown redemption to be necessary in Book 1, Book 2 of the *Institutes* focuses upon the Old Testament first revealing to us our futile plight for salvation based on autonomous merit, whereas the New Testament has revealed to us the atoning work of Christ which provides for us the redemption we cannot attain for ourselves.

Christ fulfils the three central offices seen in different individuals throughout the Old Testament and sums them up in himself. As *prophet*, Christ announces that the kingdom of God has come upon all humanity in his own person. As *priest*, he makes final atonement for human sins. As *king*, Christ reigns supreme over the redeemed, calling them into communion with himself as one people, constituted nevertheless of Jew and gentile, male and female (i.e., "all tribes, tongues, and nations").

---

52. Calvin, *Inst.*, 2.15.

Calvin further stresses here, that the work of Christ involved a ministry of *active obedience*. When it is asked how Christ has abolished sin and bridged the chasm between God and humanity, Calvin answers that Christ "has achieved this for us by the whole course of his obedience."[53] So, when the proper time had come under God's superintendent wisdom, Christ the Son was sent to humankind and made to be "under the law," to be in total obedience to it, and to redeem those who are also under the law, but in disobedience to it. From the moment of his birth, through to his baptism, ministry, and ultimate death, Christ was actively redeeming humankind.[54] Nevertheless, Calvin places special emphasis on the efficacy of the cross, in which humans are "acquitted" in virtue of "the guilt which made us liable to punishment [and] transferred to the head of the Son of God."[55] This forensic aspect of Calvin's theology, however, is not the end of the story, but the beginning of a deeper reality in God's relation to humans.

## UNION WITH GOD—THE CREATOR

A central question for Calvin had always been how humanity—as universally under the curse of law and sin—is to be reconciled to God. The answer is found in Christ the Redeemer. Calvin elaborates on this reconciliation, summing the doctrine up in terms of the believer's union with God. As with Calvin himself, this is a central, catalyzing emphasis with Evangelical Calvinism today. More recently, Myk Habets has written, "Calvin insists on the forensic nature of justification but is equally adamant that we are justified as a result of our union with Christ."[56]

Though Calvin designates the *unio mystica* with Christ as categorically "incomprehensible by nature,"[57] he nevertheless writes that "to that union of the head and members, the residence of Christ in our hearts, in fine, the mystical union, *we assign the highest rank*, Christ when he becomes ours making us partners with him in the gifts with which he was endued. Hence we do not view him as at a distance and without us, but as we have put him on, and been ingrafted into his body, he deigns

53. Ibid., 2.16.5.
54. Ibid.
55. Ibid.
56. Habets, *Theosis in the Theology of Thomas Torrance*, 98.
57. Calvin, *Inst.*, 4.17.1.

to make us one with himself, and, therefore, we glory in having a fellowship of righteousness with him."[58] Calvin further draws upon this "oneness" language saying, "Christ does not so much come to us as become encumbered with our nature to make us one with him."[59] Further, this union is not merely a matter of "forensic" justification, but is an *indwelling*: "The phrase *in ipso* (in him) I have preferred to retain, rather than render it *per ipsum* (by him) because it has in my opinion more expressiveness and force. For we are enriched in Christ, inasmuch as we are members of his body, and are engrafted into him: nay more, being made one with him, he makes us share with him in every thing that he has received from the Father."[60]

Calvin's doctrine of God hinges upon the Lord who saves fallen sinners who stand in need of redemption. Christ himself is God and is the sole Mediator who sums up in himself the threefold office of prophet, priest, and king. He atones for human sin and reconciles humanity back to the Godhead. This work of grace through Christ, and the benefits it confers on those who receive it, is summed up in terms of union with God.

## CONCLUSION

How do we bring all of this together in our understanding of God and who he is in relation to us? We must first stop making the demands upon theology proper that empirical science makes upon its finite subjects. As I asserted at the start, God is not an object to be studied, but a Father to be honored and adored. We must also take pains to remind ourselves, as we live and as we theologize, that now we see through a glass, darkly—knowing only in part (1 Cor 13:12). We are caught between two worlds: the world of man marked with the stamp of unceasing estrangement, and the world of the Lord which is our true home. But this is not a state to be lamented. Rather, it is celebrated as, firstly, we are assured that Christ abides in us even now and that we *do* know God and possess understanding. Our unitive bond with Christ transforms our world of disconnected aloneness into one in which *the Lord is our world*. This unspeakable bond is incomplete in this life, though progressively increased

58. Ibid., 3.11.10, emphasis added.
59. John Calvin, *Commentaries*, 598.
60. John Calvin, *Commentary on Corinthians*, 1999.

through sanctifying grace as we turn our face to the Lord. Secondly, the Christian hope is also that we shall see God "face-to-face," knowing then all that God intends for us to know, even as we are also known by him.

## BIBLIOGRAPHY

Aquinas, Thomas. *Summa Theologica*. Translated by the Fathers of the English Dominican Province. Grand Rapids: Christian Classics Ethereal Library, 1999.

Calvin, John. *Commentaries*. Edited and Translated by J. Haroutunian. Philadelphia: Westminster, 1958.

———. *Commentary on Corinthians*, Translated by John Pringle. Grand Rapids: Christian Classics Ethereal Library, 1999.

———. *Institutes of the Christian Religion*. Translated by Henry Beveridge. Grand Rapids: Eerdmans, 1989.

———. *Institutes of Christian Religion*. Edited by John McNeill. Translated by Ford Lewis Battles. 2 vols. Louisville: Westminster John Knox, 1960.

Cooper, John W. *Panentheism: The Other God of the Philosophers—From Plato to the Present*. Grand Rapids: Baker Academic, 2006.

Dowey, Edward. *The Knowledge of God in Calvin's Theology*, 3rd edn. Grand Rapids: Eerdmans, 1994.

Grow, Bobby. "The Themes of Evangelical Calvinism." Np. Cited November 20, 2010. Online: http://evangelicalcalvinist.com/the-themes-of-evangelical-calvinism/.

Gerrish, B. A. *The Old Protestantism and the New: Essays of the Reformation Heritage*. Chicago: University of Chicago Press, 1982.

Grenz, Stanley, and Roger Olson. *20th Century Theology: God & the World in a Transitional Age*. Downers Grove: InterVarsity, 1992.

Grudem, Wayne. *Systematic Theology: An Introduction to Biblical Doctrine*. Grand Rapids: Zondervan, 1994.

Habets, Myk. *Theosis in the Theology of Thomas Torrance*. Surrey: Ashgate, 2009.

Murphy, Gannon. *Consuming Glory: A Classical Defense of Divine-Human Relationality Against Open Theism*. Eugene: Wipf & Stock, 2006.

———. "Reformed *Theosis*?" *Theology Today* 65 (2008) 191–212.

———. *Voices of Reason in Christian History*. Camp Hill: Christian Publications, 2005.

Parker, T. H. L. *Calvin: An Introduction to His Thought*. Louisville: Westminster John Knox, 1995.

Pascal, Blaise. *Pensées*. Translated by W. F. Trotter. Grand Rapids: Christian Classics Ethereal Library, 2002.

Pinnock, Clark. *The Openness of God: A Biblical Challenge to the Traditional Understand of God*. Downers Grove: InterVarsity, 1994.

Torrance, Thomas F. *Space, Time and Resurrection*. Edinburgh: T. & T. Clark, 1976.

Weinandy, Thomas. *Does God Suffer?* Notre Dame: University of Notre Dame Press, 2000.

# 7

# "There is no God behind the back of Jesus Christ"

## Christologically Conditioned Election

MYK HABETS

## TOWARDS A TRULY EVANGELICAL SOTERIOLOGY

THE DOCTRINE OF ELECTION is often considered the central dogma of Reformed theology.[1] While this estimation is of course inaccurate, the doctrine of election is important in a Reformed soteriology. Numerous elucidations of election have been offered by Reformed theologians many of which fall into the category of determinism and sometimes fatalism. This is especially the case in some scholastic Federal Calvinist presentations of the doctrine. Reacting to this determinacy many believers have adopted a form of Arminianism to explain those passages of Scripture which speak of God's electing will. For many, an Arminian explanation of election is more compatible with modern sensibilities and with the existential requirements of contemporary people. Calvinism has fallen on hard times in recent years as a result. Instead of defending a classical federal view of election, in which the divine decrees hold pride of place and every other aspect of God's redemptive plan is drawn from there, what is required is a doctrine which adheres much closer to the presentation of election as it is found in Scripture, and also one which avoids the hard determinacy of the Classic Calvinists.

1. This chapter is a revised and adapted version of an earlier paper published as Habets, "The Doctrine of Election in Evangelical Calvinism," used with permission.

173

In short, what is required is an *evangelical* Calvinism. Such a position is formulated by Thomas Forsyth Torrance and with critical modifications it recommends itself as a viable model of election today.

While election is examined in various places throughout Torrance's publications, characteristically he does not treat this doctrine in any final or systematic way.[2] He lays the blame for the doctrine of election occupying pride of place in much Reformed theology at the foot of Protestant scholasticism which, unlike Calvin, raised the decree of predestination to a separate article of Christian theology and came very near to becoming an independent principle, a *Denknotwendigkeit*.[3] According to Torrance "predestination is not to be understood in terms of some timeless decree in God, but as the electing activity of God providentially and savingly at work in what Calvin called the 'history of redemption.'"[4] Torrance's objection against Westminster theology in particular, his appreciation of a version of universal atonement, coupled with his acceptance of much of Barth's theology requires a thorough examination and at times critique.

## THE *PROTHESIS* OF THE FATHER

Torrance adopts the language of *prothesis* to refer to divine election whereby the Father purposed or "set-forth" the union of God and humanity in Jesus Christ. Divine election is a free sovereign decision and utterly contingent act of God's love; as such it is neither arbitrary nor strictly necessary.[5] Torrance holds to the Reformed doctrine of unconditional election,[6] one which represents a strictly theonomous way of thinking, from a centre in God and not in ourselves.[7] "Predestination"

2. The doctrine of election is dealt with specifically in one of Torrance's first published essays, T. F. Torrance, "Predestination in Christ." Also see: T. F. Torrance, "Introduction," xi–cxxvi; *Conflict and Agreement in the Church*, 83–88; *Christian Theology and Scientific Culture*, 127–37; and *Scottish Theology from John Knox to John McLeod Campbell*.

3. Torrance, "Predestination in Christ," 108. See further the comments in T. F. Torrance, "The Distinctive Character of the Reformed Tradition," 4–5.

4. T. F. Torrance, "The Distinctive Character of the Reformed Tradition," 4.

5. That is, it must not be constructed in the fashion of Protestant scholasticism or of process theology. T. F. Torrance, *Christian Theology and Scientific Culture*, 131.

6. It is based on unconditional election "for it flows freely from an ultimate reason or purpose in the invariant Love of God and is entirely unconditioned by any necessity, whether of being or knowledge or will, in God and entirely unconstrained and unmotivated by anything whatsoever beyond himself," ibid., 131.

7. See ibid.,131–32.

simply emphasises the truth that God has chosen us in Christ *before* the
foundation of the world (Eph 1:4), which Torrance links with the teaching that Christ as Lamb of God was slain before the foundation of the
world. The eternal decrees of the Father are not to be thought of in exclusion of the Son, for the eternal purposes of God do not take place apart
from Christ or "behind his back" as it were. As such "predestination was
understood simply as the *decretum Dei speciale*, a particular part of the
*decretum Dei generale* . . ."[8] This allows Torrance to distinguish between
predestination and election in the following way: *predestination* refers
"everything back to the eternal purpose of God's love for humanity,"
while the cognate term *election* refers "more to the fulfilment of that
purpose in space and time, patiently worked out by God in the history
of Israel and brought to its consummation in Jesus Christ."[9] In one of his
earlier works he writes, "Election is not therefore some dead predestination in the past or some still point in a timeless eternity, but a living act
that enters time and confronts us face to face in Jesus Christ the living
Word of God."[10]

One of the distinctive features of a Reformed doctrine of election
is the recurring instance that election "is *christologically conditioned*."[11]
Following Calvin, Torrance claims that Christ is the "cause" of election
in all four traditional senses of "cause": the efficient and the material, the
formal and the final. "He is at once the *Agent* and the *Content* of election,
its *Beginning* and its *End*."[12] Election proceeds from the eternal decree of
God but this eternal decree of election assumes in time once and for all
the form of the wondrous conjunction of God and humanity in Christ.[13]
The hypostatic union is the heart of any understanding of election as
Torrance makes clear when he writes, "How are we to relate God's action to our faith? The secret of that is seen only in the God-manhood
of Christ, for that is the very heart of election, and the pattern of *our*

8. T. F. Torrance, "Predestination in Christ," 108.

9. T. F. Torrance, "The Distinctive Character of the Reformed Tradition," 4.

10. T. F. Torrance, "Universalism or Election?" 315.

11. T. F. Torrance, *Scottish Theology*, 14 (emphasis his). For an overview see
Sonderegger, "Election," in *The Oxford Handbook of Systematic Theology*, 105-120,
especially 112–17. Earlier Sonderegger examines election when placed within the doctrine of God (ibid., 107–12) and supports Torrance's criticisms, and those of the current
book, of Classical Calvinism in this regard, see especially 109–11.

12. T. F. Torrance, "The Distinctive Character of the Reformed Tradition," 4.

13. T. F. Torrance, *Scottish Theology*, 14.

election, and is visible only there since it is election in Christ."[14] Here Torrance clearly follows the essential trajectory initiated by Barth's own work on election.[15]

Torrance is adamant that election and predestination must be expounded in terms of christology for it has to do with the activity of God in Christ.[16] As a direct consequence it is to Christ and the salvation he purchased that one must look for the ground of election, not to some secret decree of God "behind the back of Christ."[17] Torrance even subjects Calvin to criticism at this point for not holding strongly enough to the fact that Jesus Christ is the *ground* of election, not only the instrument and author of election.[18] When Christ is seen as the object and subject of election then more deterministic conceptions of election are done away with. "These then are the two sides of the Christian doctrine of predestination: that the salvation of the believer goes back to an eternal decree of God, and yet that the act of election is in and through Christ."[19] It is Christ's election which forms the basis of a correct understanding of his person and work, something Torrance affirms is reflected supremely in the *Scots Confession*. In general agreement with Torrance is David Fergusson who, when referring to the *Scots Confession*, considers it to root election in the person and work of Christ so that it "produces a strikingly evangelical exposition of election."[20]

14. Ibid.

15. For a through examination of a christologically conditioned doctrine of election, and with critical modifications, see McDonald, *Re-Imaging God*. McDonald's work focuses on the doctrines of election put forth by John Owen and Karl Barth and proceeds to interrogate each of them from the vantage point of pneumatology. It is a creative and stimulating work which has much in common with what we are calling Evangelical Calvinism.

16. T. F. Torrance, *Scottish Theology*, 172.

17. Ibid. Torrance considers the one covenant of grace to be completely fulfilled in Christ so that the covenant idea is completely subordinated to Christ. See T. F. Torrance, "Introduction," lv–lvi, and "Predestination in Christ," 111.

18. On Torrance's reading, Calvin attributed the ultimate ground of election to the inscrutable will of the Divine decree. He cites Calvin, *Inst.,,* 3.22.1, which asserts that election precedes grace. A similar criticism of Calvin is given by Barth, *CD* II/2, 111.

19. T. F. Torrance, "Predestination in Christ," 109.

20. Fergusson, "Predestination: A Scottish Perspective," 462. He also notes that "Barth claimed [it] was without parallel in the other Reformed confessions," 462, referring to Barth, *The Knowledge of God and the Service of God*, 68–79, and *Church Dogmatics*, II/2, 308. And yet, Fergusson does admit that even the *Scots Confession* does not entirely escape the "errors of double predestination," ibid.

Because election is bound up with Christ it must not be thought of in any impersonal or absolutely deterministic sense.[21] The encounter between God and humanity in Christ is the exact antithesis of determinism; it is the "acute personalisation" of all relations with God in spite of sin. Interestingly, because Christ is the ground of election there can be no thought of indeterminism in relation to the encounter between God and humanity either![22] Due to the adoption into Protestant scholasticism of deterministic thinking, something Torrance attributes to an artificial importation of Greek determinism, election is often thought of in terms of cause or force, and so forth.[23] But this is to transpose onto God our thought and in the process distort the doctrine of election. It is here Torrance becomes most animated: "Thus, for example, in the doctrine of "absolute particular predestination" the tendency is to think of God as a "force majeure" bearing down upon particular individuals. That is to operate with a view of omnipotence that has little more significance than an empty mathematical symbol."[24] Evident in this statement is Torrance's methodological commitment to work from an *a posteriori* basis rather than an *a priori* one, and so reject a natural theology.[25] Omnipotence, for instance, is what God *does*, not what God is thought to be able to do because of some hypothetical metaphysical *can*. What God does is seen in Christ.

What then does the "pre" stand for in "predestination"? asks Torrance. Originally it made the point that the grace by which we are saved is grounded in the inner life of the Trinity.[26] "That is to say, the *pre*

21. See Fergusson, "Predestination: A Scottish Perspective," 457–78, who argues that "In the early centuries of the Church, theology was marked by an emphasis upon the compatibility of divine foreknowledge and human freedom, largely to combat Stoic determinism and astrological fatalism," 457.

22. Fergusson sees this as one of the weaknesses of Augustine's doctrine of predestination, that due to God's foreknowledge God passes over the reprobate and this is an explanation why some believe and some do not. Ibid., 457–59. Cf. Barth, *CD*, II/2, 16, 307.

23. It was not simply Calvinistic scholasticism that made this determinist move but also Lutheranism. See for instance Luther and Erasmus, *Free Will and Salvation*.

24. T. F. Torrance, "Predestination in Christ," 114.

25. Torrance comments that ". . . there is no doctrine where natural theology causes more damage than in the doctrine of predestination," T. F. Torrance, "Predestination in Christ," 114.

26. Torrance, *Christian Theology and Scientific Culture*, 134.

in predestination emphasises the sheer objectivity of God's Grace."[27] It was this view of the priority of divine grace which fell away in scholastic Calvinism so that predestination could be spoken of as "preceding grace" and election came to be regarded as a causal antecedent to our salvation in time. The result of this shift was a strong determinist slant.[28]

## UNION WITH CHRIST

Utilising the language of the Scottish divine John Craig, Torrance distinguishes between Christ's "carnal union" with humanity from his "spiritual union." Our carnal union with Christ refers to the union between Christ and humanity through his incarnation.[29] He was made man for us that he might die for us and so there is a carnal union established between Christ and all of humanity. Our spiritual union with Christ refers to the fact that the Holy Spirit unites the believer with Christ so that the benefits of Christ may be ours. It is important that the carnal union and the spiritual union are not separate but rather, spiritual union is a sharing in the one and only union between God and humanity wrought out in Jesus Christ.[30] If the spiritual union were another union, then our salvation would depend upon something additional to the finished work of Christ. Torrance argues that one of the problems with Westminster theology is that it separates these two unions and in the process thrusts justification by (*our*) faith into supreme prominence rather than union with Christ *by grace alone.* "If there has to be a priority in our understanding," writes Torrance, "then we must say with Calvin and Craig ... that it is through participating in Christ that we partake of His benefits ..."[31] Accordingly, the forensic element in the atoning work of Christ rests upon the basis of Christ's incarnation, upon his person and life

27. Ibid.

28. A weakness of Torrance's argument is his refusal to acknowledge this determinist element within Calvin's own theology and not simply that of his followers. It seems clear that Calvin presents a doctrine of double predestination, albeit not as strictly as many of his followers do. See Calvin, *Inst.,* 3.21–24 (especially 3.23.1), and Calvin, *Concerning the Eternal Predestination of God.* An account of Calvin's doctrine of the double decree can be found in Klooster, *Calvin's Doctrine of Predestination,* 55–86. Someone who shares Torrance's basic convictions on election but does not share his views on Calvin is Fergusson, "Predestination: A Scottish Perspective," 460–62.

29. See Rankin, "Carnal Union with Christ in the Theology of T. F. Torrance."

30. Torrance, "Introduction," cvi–cvii.

31. Ibid., cx.

"and therefore that the forensic element in justification reposes for its substance and meaning upon our union with Christ."[32]

Having established a definition of carnal union and its relation to spiritual union, Torrance then asks about the range of the carnal union: does it refer to all people or just the elect? The question behind this is whether or not Christ entered into a generic relation with humanity by becoming a particular man, or also entered into an ontological relation with all humanity in the assumption of our human flesh. The first position is rejected outright on two grounds: first, it would separate the carnal union from the spiritual union and as a result diminish the sufficiency of Christ's work, and second, the Church could then only be construed in terms of an extension of the Incarnation. In line with Torrance's commitment to a version of a universal atonement, the carnal union establishes an ontological relation between Christ and all humanity. As a consequence Torrance asserts "that human beings have no being apart from Christ."[33] Without the Incarnation the estrangement between God and humanity would have continued to grow to such an extent that the alienation caused by sin would be complete so that humanity would disappear (along with the rest of creation) into nothingness. The Incarnation means that God refused to hold back his love for humanity and entered our alienated human existence to lay hold of it, bind it in union with himself, and heal it for all humanity. As a direct consequence all humanity is laid hold of by God and kept in existence by God. Humans "can no more escape from [God's] love and sink into non-being than they can constitute themselves [persons] for whom Christ has not died".[34] God has not given up on creation but has poured his love on all humanity and in this expression of love humanity exists because God has not given up on his creation. "God does not say Yes, and No, for all that He has done is Yes and Amen in Christ. That applies to every man, whether he will or no [*sic*]. He owes his very being to Christ and belongs to Christ, and in that he belongs to Christ he has his being only from Him and in relation to Him."[35] So far Torrance has asserted the fact that because of the Son's incarnation human persons are loved and kept in existence by this love.

32. Ibid., cx.

33. Ibid., cxiii.

34. Ibid., cxiv.

35. Ibid., cxiv.

The conclusion must not be drawn from this that because Torrance is committed to a view of universal atonement and an ontological communion created through our carnal union with Christ, that all humanity will be saved. Torrance is no universalist. While the carnal and spiritual unions are not separate, the former is universal while the latter is particular. While we shall have more to say on the possibility and state of the reprobate shortly we note Torrance's acknowledgement of an objective and subjective element in election. Objectively election is consummated in the "wondrous conjunction between God and man in Christ" as revealed through the incarnation. Hypostatic union and atoning union are held together as the obverse of one another, thus the person and work of Christ are rigorously held together. Subjectively our election is consummated when this "most holy fraternity" between God and humanity is restored to us, a unique work of the Holy Spirit.[36] The role of the Holy Spirit thus plays a crucial role in the doctrine of election and enables Torrance to maintain a commitment to a universal atonement but not a universal salvation (universalism).[37]

In light of Barth's famous doctrine of election in Jesus Christ as God's "Yes" and "No,"[38] and Torrance's comment above that "God does not say Yes and No," are we right to assume that Torrance is at odds with Barth here? In a word, no.[39] According to Torrance's christologically conditioned doctrine of election Christ took on the entire human condition for the entire world and judged sin in his flesh and on the cross ("No"). On the basis of that finished work Christ has forgiven sinful humanity and offers salvation as a free gift of grace ("Yes"). As such "we are in fact all elected and damned in Him,"[40] Torrance opines. Does

36. T. F. Torrance, *Scottish Theology*, 15.

37. It is disappointing that in her work on election from a pneumatological perspective Suzanne McDonald did not draw upon or interact with the pneumatology of election developed by Thomas Torrance. I believe in Torrance she would have found additional resources to aid her in her task of re-imaging election. See McDonald, *Re-Imaging Election*, especially 153 n. 15, and 154 n. 16, where she does make mention of the work of James B. Torrance in this regard.

38. See Barth, *CD*, II/2, 3–34; IV/1, 350, 591–92.

39. It is Torrance's conviction that one of Barth's primary contributions to Reformed theology is precisely in his doctrine of election, a doctrine Torrance considers himself to be advancing. See Torrance, "The Distinctive Character of the Reformed Tradition," 5.

40. Torrance, "Predestination in Christ," 119.

this imply universalism? Once again, in a word, no.[41] In a discussion of free-will Torrance defends Luther's basic position that sinful humanity possesses *voluntas* (will) which is applied in respect of "lower things." However, sinful humanity does not possess an innate *arbitrium* (choice) which is neutral and so free to accept or reject divine grace. According to this reading, strictly speaking, only God has free-will, and therefore humans have no *arbitrium* at all.[42] The point Torrance wishes to make is that "man has no *arbitrium* over his sin and salvation just because it is objective as well as subjective, positive as well as negative; just because it means something to God as well as man."[43] What then happens in salvation? When confronted with God, humans for the first time become free to decide for God. "The personal encounter of Christ with forgiveness on His lips, singles out a man . . . and gives him freedom to say "yes" or "no" . . . freedom is only possible face to face with Jesus Christ."[44] If there is a universal atonement, as we shall consider shortly, then surely it is a corollary that all who are confronted with God's forgiveness, and as a consequence are free, will repent and receive salvation. Torrance disagrees. While freedom is possible face to face with Jesus Christ "the mystery is—and this we shall never fathom—that such a man may commit the sin of Adam all over again."[45] This is the absurdity of sin which we shall examine below.

In order to further understand how Jesus can be both God's "Yes" and "No" Torrance turns to the cross where Christ died for us. In the cross Christ is the propitiation for the sins of all humanity where God

41. Many argue that Barth did not espouse universalism either. For a defense of this position see Colwell, *Actuality and Provisionality*, 249–52, 264–74. Colwell argues that for the charge of universalism to hold true one must posit it as a theological necessity. In his view, Barth does not make universalism a necessity but simply holds out the hope that God's salvation will be more extensive than we may currently imagine. See Barth, *CD*, II/2, 417–19; IV/3, 461–77; and Barth, *The Humanity of God* (London: Fontana, 1967) 59–60. Where Barth and Torrance diverge on this point is in Torrance's explicit and repeated affirmations of the reality and population of Hell, construed along traditional lines of theological thought, something an Evangelical Calvinism also supports, although individual adherents would hold differing views on the nature of eternal separation from God. What does seem to be ruled out *tout court* is any version of annihilationism or conditional immortality.

42. T. F. Torrance, "Predestination in Christ," 120, 121.

43. Ibid., 123.

44. Ibid.

45. Ibid.

has judged sin, and judged us all in Christ. The cross results in election and damnation, mercy and judgement. "But the important thing to note here is that it is not election *or* damnation in the first place. In Christ we are all judged—and in so far as Christ died for all, then all are dead—but in Him we are all chosen by God's Grace."[46] How does this work out in practice? Torrance replies,

> When we are brought face to face with decision in this encounter, and answer No or disobey—and God does not allow us to be neutral—then we choose damnation in the second place, that is the Cross of Christ is our judgment only and not our salvation. When we answer Yes or obey, then we learn that Christ has already answered for us! We are chosen already in Christ—man cannot damn himself any more than he can elect himself. We must say that both election and damnation are in Christ . . .[47]

Torrance provides one further insight into how he conceives the precise relation between the divine and human decision, or between the subjective and the objective—"it is the Holy Spirit in fact Who constitutes the relation between the Divine decision and the human decision."[48] To further elaborate Torrance uses an analogy, the only one available to us, "if Grace means the personal presence of God to men, then that means concretely, Jesus Christ. Therefore it is in the relation of the deity to the humanity in Jesus Christ that we are to look for our final answer to this question."[49] Just as in the Incarnation Christ is *vere homo vere Deus*, so in the divine encounter we have a real human decision and a real divine decision. The human decision, like Christ's humanity, is *anhypostatic*, it has no independent existence apart from the divine, but it is concrete and personal, and so *enhypostatic*.[50] There can be no separation between the divine and human decisions but neither can there be any (con)fusion.[51] "In the end therefore," writes Torrance, "these errors re-

46. Ibid., 125.

47. Ibid., 126.

48. Ibid., 127.

49. Ibid.

50. Torrance develops the analogy of Christ's incarnation in ibid.,128–29, although he does not use the terms *an/enhypostatic*. He also develops the analogy of Christ's virgin conception in ibid., 130–31.

51. Behind both misconceptions Torrance sees the same dangers inherent in faulty christologies, "Separation or fusion inevitably result in Pelagianism or determinism, which correspond respectively with a Docetic and an Ebionite Christology, on the one

duce themselves to two main types in which the extremes are a doctrine of irresistible grace and independent free-will."[52] In place of either what actually happens is that a sort of hypostatic union between grace and faith, through the Holy Spirit occurs. In relation to the human decision to reject God's offer of salvation in Christ, Torrance can only say it is the mystery of evil which cannot be explained in rational categories.

What Torrance's position explicitly rules out, at least, is a Westminsterian construal of divine and human relations. In certain articulations of classical Calvinism the divine decision swamps that of the human so that it is hard to maintain any genuine human decision whatsoever. While all genuinely Reformed thinking posits a *concursus* theory of divine and human agency, not all such theories are equal. What Torrance has argued for has affinities with what Kathryn Tanner has rightly argued is a non-competitive relation between God and creatures such that "the creature does not decrease so that God may increase."[53] Torrance echoes this theme with his own oft-repeated adage on "the logic of grace," namely: "'All of grace does' not mean nothing of man . . . *all of grace means all of man*."[54] Torrance's linking of such *concursus* activity to the Incarnation, and specifically to the an-/enhypostatic couplet offers a considerable advance on the tradition.

## FORENSIC CAPTIVITY

This understanding of Christ and election affects the way a theory of the atonement is constructed. While Torrance does not reject a doctrine of penal substitution outright he challenges the hegemony it has on Western theology. Without denying the juridical elements evident in Paul's atonement theology, these are not the central features of the atonement. If juridical elements are allowed to occupy centre stage, as they have in Federal Calvinism, then the atoning sacrifice of Christ is fulfilled only as a human, and it is this which draws Torrance's charge of Nestorianism against this stream within the Reformed tradition.[55]

---

hand, or in a doctrine of mystic infused grace . . . or a doctrine of synergism, which correspond respectively to a Eutychian and a Nestorian Christology, on the other hand," ibid., 129.

52. Ibid., 129–30. I think it is more true to say that this rules out *a certain construal* of irresistible grace and any notion of a *libertarian* free-will.

53. Tanner, *Jesus, Humanity and the Trinity*, 2.

54. T. F. Torrance, *The Mediation of Christ,* xii, emphasis in original.

55. Torrance, *Scottish Theology,* 18–19.

Christ must be viewed as the one Mediator between God and humanity; who is himself God and human in one person. Under this reformulated construction Jesus Christ does not placate God the Father but rather atonement is a propitiatory sacrifice in which God *himself* through the death of his Son draws near to humanity and draws humanity near to himself. This is precisely why John affirms that "*God* so loved the world that *he* gave his only Son, that whoever believes in him shall not perish, but have eternal life" (Jn 3:16). If the Nestorian tendencies apparent within Westminster Calvinist notions of atonement hold sway then the inevitable result is an overly forensic understanding in which atonement is thought of as a transaction external to God, rather than as the ultimate expression of the love of God for all.

It is well known that the Torrance brothers, Thomas and James, are outspoken against Calvinism after Calvin,[56] what Torrance variously describes as "federal Calvinism," "hyper-Calvinism," "Bezan Calvinism," "scholastic Calvinism," and "Westminster Calvinism." All such Calvinisms as Torrance styles them present a federal scheme of salvation, a moralising of the Christian life, the intellectualising of faith, a logicalising of theology, and an overly forensic notion of election and justification in which faith and assurance tend to be torn apart from each other.[57] Torrance considers his own position to be an "evangelical Calvinism."[58]

Federal theology, in Torrance's estimation, works on the premise of a contract or bargain made between the Father and the Son in eternity

56. See: J. B. Torrance, "The Concept of Federal Theology," 15–40; "Strengths and Weaknesses of the Westminster Theology," 40–53; "The Covenant Concept in Scottish Theology and Politics and Its Legacy," 225–43; and "Covenant or Contract," 51–76.

57. T. F. Torrance, *Scottish Theology*, 59; and *Christian Theology and Scientific Culture*, 133–34. The root cause of Protestant scholasticism, according to Torrance, is the acceptance of a determinate yet dualist framework of the Augustinian-Aristotelian thought which developed soon after the Reformation and then of the Augustinian-Newtonian thought which succeeded it. According to another Scotsman, this form of Calvinism "tends to subordinate grace to nature; it renders the justice of God essential but the love of God arbitrary; it yields a theory of limited atonement which is contrary to the plains sense of Scripture and which is divorced from the doctrine of the incarnation; and it fosters an introspective and legalist religion as the search for the signs of election is redirected away from Christ to the life of the individual believer" (Fergusson, "Predestination: A Scottish Perspective," 466).

58. Torrance, *Scottish Theology*, 59–60, 65, 224. Torrance sees himself in line with J. Calvin, J. Knox, and many of the early Scottish theologians, as opposed to Calvinists such as T. Beza, W. Perkins, J. Owen, and J. Edwards.

past, and interpreted in necessary, causal, and forensic terms, rather than grounding election in the incarnate person of Christ, as it was with Calvin and Knox. Torrance rejects a strictly causative relation between God's eternal decrees and their end because they eclipse any real meaning to such passages as John 3:16 on the one hand, and as a result, on the other hand, they tended to restrict the proclamation of the Gospel to the "heathen" due to a "forensically predetermined covenant-structure."[59]

Torrance attributes the ascendancy of penal substitution in Scottish Reformed theology to the acceptance of the Synod of Dort and the *Westminster Confession of Faith*. The Synod of Dort promulgated the absolute decrees of predestination and reprobation, and advocated a strict form of limited atonement. "With the scholastic brand of Calvinism that arose in this way the Anselmic concept of satisfaction of the infinite gravity of sin was allied to a doctrine of divine punishment conceived in terms of contractual and governmental law, and synodal authority was given to this concept of atonement in the strict terms of penal substitution."[60] It was this form of Calvinism which was accepted by the Kirk of Scotland under the influence of the Puritan Calvinism of the *Westminster Confession of Faith* in 1647.[61] It is Torrance's contention that this brand of theology brought with it a more legalistic Calvinism to the more evangelical Calvinism of the older Scottish tradition deriving from the *Scots Confession*.[62] Along with Torrance, we wish to retrieve the positive insights of this evangelical Calvinism in our doctrine of election.

## UNIVERSALISM?

Because Jesus is the God-man his Mediatorial work represents all humanity, not simply some smaller category of the elect. If Christ died only for some then he would not be the Saviour of the world but rather an instrument in the hands of the Father for the salvation of a chosen few. "In other words, a notion of limited atonement implies a Nestorian heresy in which Jesus Christ is not really God and man united in one Person."[63]

59. Ibid., 107.

60. Ibid., 96.

61. Fergusson, "Predestination: A Scottish Perspective," 457–78.

62. T. F. Torrance, *Scottish Theology*, 127. Torrance does concede that the Westminster Confession of Faith is an outstanding work of great theological substance and power, but it lacks a spiritual freshness and freedom about it.

63. Ibid., 19.

Torrance, in line with many Scottish divines,[64] holds to a position of universal atonement, however, this is not to imply a notion of universal redemption.[65] Christ gave himself freely in atoning sacrifice or "ransom for all" (1 Tim 2:6). In his articulation of universal atonement Torrance, along with Calvin, rejects the notion, often stated, that Christ died *sufficiently* for all but *efficiently* for the elect.[66] What Torrance does assert is that Christ did die, as Hebrews 2:2 clearly states, for all people—he tasted death for all. The fact that Christ died, even for reprobates, means that the minister of the Gospel is free to offer salvation to all. In the event of their rejection of Christ, his death constitutes the ground of their judgment. Hence universal atonement does not imply universal salvation. "The doctrine of unconditional grace and universal pardon cannot be twisted into universal salvation without evacuating the Cross of its profound nature and ultimate meaning, and distorting the self-revelation of God as Holy Love,"[67] Torrance argues.

This is a deliberate rejection of the scholastic way of thinking of atonement in terms of logico-causal relations, by which if Christ dies for all then all must be saved. As Torrance understands it, Christ assumes a real humanity, assuming a fallen human nature, and joins humanity to God by means of the hypostatic union. Through his sinless life and his sacrificial death he makes atonement for all people without reserve. Anything short of universal atonement, according to Torrance, is an assertion of God's limited love for humanity as it would imply a circumscribed incarnation. The reprobate do not simply reject God's judgement, they reject God's pardon, his loving provision of salvation. Sin is so irrational, such an "accident," that it is a rejection of God's love revealed in universal pardon. It is this theology which Torrance sees working in John McLeod Campbell and Edward Irving no less than in Barth.[68]

---

64. Notably Robert Boyd (1578–1627) and John McLeod Campbell (1800–1872); see ibid., 70.

65. Torrance makes this clear in distancing his own point of view from that of Thomas Erskine, ibid., 275.

66. Ibid., 196. See Calvin's rejection of this in Calvin, *Concerning the Eternal Predestination of God*, IX, 5, 148 (cited by Torrance).

67. Ibid., 277.

68. Other Scottish theologians who basically follow a Barthian doctrine of election include Reid, "The Office of Christ in Predestination," 5–18, 166–83, and Reid, "Introduction," 9–44; Hendry, *The Westminster Confession in the Church Today*, 49–58;

What this conception of election also does is repudiate any theology of double predestination whereby the elect are predestined and reprobates are damned *simpliciter*.[69] So what is Torrance rejecting and what is he accepting when he makes these comments? Torrance is rejecting on the one hand the idea common in much Reformed thinking that there is an election to life and an election to death and this is worked out in a causal and deterministic sense. On the other hand he is rejecting the Arminian position that humans are in a neutral position and respond to the Gospel from free-will and so accept and are saved (elect), or reject the gospel, also by free-will, and are damned (reprobate). What is the alternative? Torrance contends the word "predestination" emphasises the sovereign freedom of grace "and so the "pre" in predestination refers neither to a temporal nor to a logical *prius*, but simply to God Himself, the Eternal."[70] To fully comprehend this statement involves an understanding of Torrance's thinking about time, something we don"t wish to elaborate on in any detail here. What may be noted is that Torrance sees time not merely as a series of sequential events but as relative to the subject and object of time. So for God, election was not an event of the past as much as it is an action *a se*. Because Christ is the ground of election, and Christ came in space-time, election took on a temporal component. The "pre" in predestination thus refers to the will of God to save humanity *in Christ*.[71]

Election is another word for God's freedom of choice or his decision. God does not act arbitrarily nor by necessity but by personal decision. Election is God's personal decision. A doctrine of election that involves necessity at the human end cannot escape the element of necessity at the divine end. If election were determinism "God would not be God but blind fate, sheer necessity."[72] God is love and election is a concrete

---

and Fergusson, "Predestination: A Scottish Perspective," 457–78, to which I am indebted for these references. Fergusson also includes T. F. Torrance in his list.

69. Torrance calls this the "Jones-Smith theory of predestination, in which one is damned and the other elected simpliciter," T. F. Torrance, "Predestination in Christ," 115. Cf. ibid., 124 n. 32.

70. T. F. Torrance, "Predestination in Christ," 116.

71. Barth also made the concept of time ("eternity") essential to his doctrine of election, and it is from this foundation that Torrance constructs his own views. For more on Barth's doctrine of eternity see the discussion in Colwell, "The Contemporaneity of the Divine Decision," especially 150–53; and his *Actuality and Provisionality*.

72. T. F. Torrance, "Predestination in Christ," 117.

expression of that love. Torrance expresses the relation between God's love and election as follows: "Election means God has chosen us because He loves us, and that He loves us because He loves us. The reason why God loves us is love."[73] Any other reason for election such as some divine *prius* that precedes grace would deny love. Because election is God's personal decision acted from within his freedom by love, humans can only acknowledge it in obedience or deny it in disobedience. "No matter what he does or thinks man cannot constitute himself a being under grace, he cannot constitute himself a man loved by God, he is that already. It is without the scope of human *arbitrium* altogether. [*sic*] and to bring in the concept of free-will is simply beside the mark."[74] In what Torrance intends to be a self-evident statement he concludes that, "It might be said that when everything is boiled down the doctrine of predestination or election comes to this: I am saved by God, by the eternal God. But if I am saved by Eternity, I am saved from all eternity unto all eternity."[75]

Colwell raises several critical questions in his examination and critique of Barth's doctrine of election which can be equally applied to Torrance. According to Colwell a central objection to Barth's doctrine of election is the assumption that because humanity is now defined ontologically in Jesus Christ, then all people must be ontologically related to Christ and thus saved, that is, universalism.[76] However, in defence of Barth, Colwell argues that he "clearly prohibits too simplistic a relationship between the ontological definition of man as elect in Jesus Christ and the actual election of individual men."[77] Ontological definition is apparently different from ontic participation and noetic affirmation. Colwell continues, ". . . the ontic inclusion of any man in the election of Jesus Christ cannot be considered as an *a priori* necessary consequence of the actuality of the ontological definition of man as elect in Jesus Christ . . ."[78] According to Barth, God is dynamic and so his eternality includes the past, the present, and the future in all his being and acts. The ontological definition of humans in Jesus Christ includes the actual participation of "humanity" in that election. "The participation of man

73. Ibid.

74. Ibid., 117–18.

75. Ibid., 118.

76. Colwell, *Actuality and Provisionality*, 273–74.

77. Ibid., 274.

78. Ibid., 274–75.

in the election of Jesus Christ is an event of God's Triunity: it occurs in the primal decision of the Father, it occurs in the actualization of that decision in the Son, and it occurs in the realization of that decision in the Holy Spirit."[79] Pneumatology thus comes to the fore and is the foundation from which to apprehend the way in which Jesus Christ establishes an ontological bond with all humanity and yet two individual persons may or may not be actually saved or participate personally in a saving way with Jesus Christ through the Holy Spirit. Colwell concludes:

> Only when the doctrine of election is understood in dynamic and not static terms, only when the primal decision of God is understood as an event of His eternity which includes human history and not as a timeless abstraction, only when election is understood as a trinitarian event and not as a unitarian or binitarian event that excludes its subjective realization in the Holy Spirit and thereby invalidates the authentic futurity of God's eternity, only then can universalism be avoided without logical contradiction.[80]

While key differences emerge between Barth and Torrance, their respective constructions of election have often been "lumped" together and critiqued along a "guilt-by-association" tactic. Be that as it may, Torrance's doctrine of election is sophisticated but ultimately logical and consistent, not to mention compelling. However, if the role of the Holy Spirit is misplaced or worse still, overlooked, then his doctrine of election, like Barth's, can only be seen as contradictory in that it affirms an ontological absoluteness regarding the humanity of Jesus Christ and yet continues to assert the reality of ultimate judgment and hell. Both the reprobate and the elect are ontologically related to Jesus Christ because of his incarnation. The difference between the two is that reprobates do not know of this ontological relation nor do they participate in the Son by the Holy Spirit.[81] The elect, by contrast, are not only objectively

79. Ibid., 282.

80. Ibid., 283 (slightly adapted). Colwell proceeds to unravel Barth's doctrine of the application of salvation by the Holy Spirit and provide insights into the nature of time and eternity in his theology.

81. Barth has been consistently criticized for presenting salvation in "purely noetic" terms, as for instance by Rosato, *The Spirit as Lord,* 161. Colwell refutes this position vigorously in Colwell, *Actuality and Provisionality,* 295–301. Despite his best attempt Barth's theology does tend to give the impression that epistemology is of supreme importance and in fact may even define what it means to be saved. Torrance's theology

related to Christ ontologically but also subjectively participate in the triune communion through the Son by the Spirit. While it is correct to say a believer has faith while a reprobate does not, it must be maintained that faith itself is a gift of the sovereign Spirit and so free-will is never the ultimate cause of salvation.

## *ACCIDENTAL* REPROBATION

Torrance parts company with Knox when he takes up Calvin's explicit teaching that people's rejection of God's grace and their reprobation by God can be understood only as something rationally inexplicable: "Reprobation is to be regarded, then, as happening *per accidens*, or *accidentaliter*, as Calvin said."[82] Torrance often appeals to the category of irrationality in relation to the reprobate—it is simply something inexplicable to reason. Of the possibility of refusing God's love and grace Torrance can only say "that is a bottomless mystery of evil before which we can only stand aghast, the surd which we cannot rationalise, the enigma of Judas. But it happens."[83]

Behind this inexplicability lies the assertion on Torrance's part that there is only one will of God not two, and yet his will is secret and hidden from us, reserved in his eternal wisdom, to be revealed at his glorious return.[84] When applied to election this means that strictly syllogistic logical equations are not appropriate, as for instance, in an argument which would have "horrified Calvin," that "If Christ died for all, so that they may perchance suffer for their sins in hell, God shall be unjust in punishing Christ for their sins and in punishing those same sinners in hell."[85] Torrance also sees such a view of double election results in a position

---

suffers from a similar, though not as comprehensive, tendency. For Torrance, "knowing" is a participatory knowledge in which one indwells the subject, hence for Torrance "knowing" moves well beyond the merely noetic, something Barth moved towards but never fuller developed. See Barth, *CD*, IV/3, 510; IV/1, 538.

82. T. F. Torrance, *Scottish Theology*, 16, 109, 277. See T.F. Torrance, "Introduction," lxxviii; and *Kingdom and Church*, 106–7.

83. T. F. Torrance, "Introduction," cxiv–cxv.

84. T. F. Torrance, "The Distinctive Character of the Reformed Tradition," 4.

85. T. F. Torrance, *Scottish Theology*, 109. Torrance is citing an argument from Samuel Rutherford (1600–1661). Rutherford was one of the Scottish commissioners to the Westminster Assembly and one it's most ardent supporters in Scotland, committed to supralapsarianism, absolute divine decrees, and double predestination. See Bell, *Calvin and Scottish Theology*, 70–91.

in which infants who die outside of baptism are thought to be damned. According to Torrance, "We cannot, therefore, think of election and reprobation in any kind of equilibrium." He explains, "In election we lay all the weight upon 'the hidden cause,' the grace of God, and not upon 'the manifest cause,' the faith of man; but in reprobation we lay all the weight upon 'the manifest cause,' man's rebellion or unbelief, and not upon 'the hidden cause,' the action of God."[86] It is this lack of equilibrium which requires Torrance to repeatedly assert that we must not think out the doctrine of election and reprobation in terms of logical propositions for, in his opinion that cannot be done without falsification.[87]

There is only one true Gospel and that is that Christ has died for all. When the Gospel is preached some believe and some reject it but it is the same Gospel which is being proclaimed (2 Cor 2:14–15). "In that light it may be said that while the preaching of the Gospel of Christ crucified for all mankind is meant for their salvation, it can also have the unintended effect of blinding and damning people—it becomes a 'savour of death unto death.'"[88] Thus the Gospel has what Calvin called a "two-fold efficacy" in which it acts one way on the elect and another on the reprobate.[89] Accordingly, while Christ dies for all his death affects those who believe and those who do not believe in different ways.[90]

---

86. Torrance, "Introduction," lxxviii. In a later work, "The Distinctive Character of the Reformed Tradition," 4, Torrance undermines his earlier position to a degree when he writes, "If predestination is to be traced back not just to faith as its 'manifest cause' but to the *yes* of God's grace as its 'hidden cause,' so reprobation is to be traced back not just to unbelief as its 'manifest cause' but to the *yes* of God's grace as its 'hidden cause' as well . . ." The reason this is not an actual contradiction is found in the continuation of the quotation, ". . . and not to some alleged 'no' of God. There are not two wills in God, but only the one eternal will of his electing love. It is by the constancy of that love that all who reject God are judged." While stress should be put on the "manifest cause" in reprobation, even when it is pressed further into the "hidden cause" what one finds is still the constant love of God, not an eternal decree of damnation deterministically worked out in time-space.

87. See Torrance, "Introduction," lxxix. In a similar way Barth contends that the "Yes" and "No" of God in election are not to be thought of symmetrically. The "Yes" and the "No" of God are not equal and opposing forces. Rather, the "Yes" of God overwhelms the "No," in Christ Jesus. Barth, *CD*, II/2, 13; IV/1, 591–92. Because Barth also contends that in God there is one will not two, God determines to save all people, rejection of this salvation is only made possible by God's "non-willing," see ibid., II/2, 458.

88. Torrance, *Scottish Theology*, 200.

89. See ibid., 201.

90. Torrance cites Scripture (Lk 2:34; 2 Cor 2:16; 1 Pet 2:8; Jn 10:39) and Calvin in support, see ibid., 283–84.

With John Cameron (1579–1625), Torrance can say that Christ died absolutely for the elect, and conditionally for all.[91] How different this position is from the earlier one he rejected, that Christ died *efficiently* for all but *sufficiently* for some, is debateable.

According to Torrance's evangelical Calvinism, the reprobate are actually rejecting God's offer of salvation, his love and grace and mercy, not simply some hollow shell or fictitious offer. In this Torrance is echoing the thought of Barth when he writes:

> A "rejected" man is one who isolates himself from God by resisting his election as it has taken place in Jesus Christ. God is for him; but he is against God. God is gracious to him; but he is ungrateful to God. God receives him; but he withdraws himself from God. God forgives him his sins; but he repeats them as though they were not forgiven. God releases him from guilt and punishment of his defection; but he goes on living as Satan's prisoner. God determines him for blessedness, and His service; but he chooses the joylessness of an existence that accords with his own pride and aims at his own honour.[92]

In speaking of the reprobate, Torrance concedes that it is an "abysmal irrationality of evil, which cannot be resolved away by rational means—that would mean that God need not have taken the way of the Cross in order to save us."[93] Amidst discussing John Howe's theology Torrance reveals his own position that "while there is no divine decree of reprobation, God allows his will for the salvation of all for whom Christ died, to be frustrated, so that in view of the tears of the Redeemer for the lost, it may be said that God wills the salvation of those that perish."[94] This does not mean, however, that the reprobate will one day cease to exist or be annihilated. According to Torrance this is an ontological impossibility for the incarnation and death of Christ cannot be undone. Because of the carnal union the sinner cannot undo the fact that Christ has gathered him into a relation of being that exists for eternity. "His being in hell is not the result of God's decision to damn him, but the result of his own decision to choose himself against the love of God and therefore of the negative decision of God's love to oppose his refusal of

---

91. Ibid., 65.
92. Barth, *CD*, II/2, 449–50.
93. Torrance, *Scottish Theology*, 277.
94. Ibid., 283.

God's love just by being Love. This negative decision of God's love is the wrath of the Lamb . . ."[95] Torrance envisions Hell as the place in which the sinner is "for ever imprisoned in his own refusal of being loved and indeed that is the hell of it."[96]

## SOLA GRATIA

Torrance is critical of Roman Catholics, certain evangelicals, and liberals alike who, in direct antitheses to a Reformed doctrine of election,[97] rest salvation upon our own personal or existential decision.[98] The Arminian error is not in subscribing to universal atonement but in subscribing to universal redemption based upon an erroneous reading of 2 Cor 2:15.[99] Free-will is nothing other than self-will and it is the self which is enslaved to sin, therefore no human truly has free-will; therefore, salvation must be by grace alone. A vivid picture of this is provided when Torrance turns to the story of Zacchaeus found in Lk 19:1–10. Interested in Christ but wanting to retain his freedom to stay aloof from him, Zacchaeus, short in stature, hides in a tree to observe Jesus from a safe distance. But Jesus invades his space and announces his decision to lodge in Zacchaeus" house and tells him to make haste and come down. "Then the astonishing thing happened," Torrance notes, "This man who did not have it in him to change his heart, who was not free to rid himself of his own selfish will, found himself free to make a decision for Christ, because Christ has already made a decision on his behalf."[100] This is what Torrance sees as the heart of the Gospel—that the Son of God has come into the far country to men and women enchained in their self-will and crushed by sin, in order to take that burden wholly upon himself and to give an account of it to God.

---

95. T. F. Torrance, "Introduction," cxv.

96. Ibid., cxvi.

97. By a "Reformed doctrine of election" Torrance has in mind simply the stress on the priority of God's action in salvation over and against that of human free will. He is not, at least in this context, endorsing Barth's doctrine of election over that of earlier Reformed positions such as John Owen, Jonathan Edwards, or even John Calvin. See ibid., lxxviii–lxxix.

98. T. F. Torrance, "Justification: Its Radical Nature and Place in Reformed Doctrine and Life," 162.

99. Torrance, *Scottish Theology*, 200.

100. T. F. Torrance, *Conflict and Agreement in the Church*, 130.

This view is contrasted to that of the Arminian who, in Torrance's opinion, throws people back upon themselves for their ultimate salvation, something he considers "unevangelical." The Gospel is preached in this unevangelical way when it is announced that Christ died and rose again for sinners *if* they would accept this for themselves. Torrance considers this a repetition of the subtle legalist twist to the Gospel which worried St Paul so much in the Epistle to the Galatians. "To preach the Gospel in that conditional or legalist way has the effect of telling poor sinners that in the last resort the responsibility for their salvation is taken off the shoulders of the Lamb of God and placed upon them—but in that case they feel they will never be saved."[101] In contrast Torrance proposes the following as an example of how the Gospel is preached in an evangelical way:

> God loves you so utterly and completely that he has given himself for you in Jesus Christ his beloved Son, and has thereby pledged his very being as God for your salvation. In Jesus Christ God has actualised his unconditional love for you in your human nature in such a once for all way, that he cannot go back upon it without undoing the Incarnation and the Cross and thereby denying himself. Jesus Christ died for you precisely because you are sinful and utterly unworthy of him, and has thereby already made you his own before and apart from your ever believing in him. He has bound you to himself by his love in a way that he will never let you go, for even if you refuse him and damn yourself in hell his love will never cease. Therefore, repent and believe in Jesus Christ as your Lord and Saviour.[102]

Torrance's presentation of the Gospel in such a way is instructive. The love of God is not in question, not even for the reprobate. All are elect in Christ as Christ died for all, thus universal pardon is announced in the free and gracious offer of salvation. And yet, two other things are equally clear; first, not all are saved. The sinner has the right and the ability to refuse the love of God and to damn themselves, no matter how impossible this may seem. While this will forever remain a mystery it is nonetheless a reality. Second, the sinner does have to do something, namely, repent and believe. While faith is a gift it must be responsive.

---

101. Torrance, *The Mediation of Christ*, 93.

102. Ibid., 94.

This is why Torrance asserts, as mentioned earlier, one of his catch cries, "all of grace does not mean nothing of man, but the reverse."[103]

One final issue deserves mention and that is the issue of synergism or the cooperation of the believer with the grace of God. In his soteriology Torrance, standing squarely in the Reformed tradition, allows no place for synergism conceived in either an Eastern Orthodox or an Arminian way, if the use of synergism is meant to imply that human freedom co-operates with divine grace in effecting salvation.[104] A rejection of synergism thus defined does not rule out a conception of human co-operation with grace in a non-meritorious sense, hence a non-synergistic co-operation is entirely possible and is indeed something Torrance, and the Reformed tradition generally, affirm.[105] The elect co-operate with grace and in that co-operation make salvation a reality in the present tense. This co-operation, however, is the response of the believer to the grace of God; it is not a meritorious or efficacious act. According to Torrance's logic, and here he is thoroughly Reformed, in salvation the believer is united with the whole Christ so that all his saving benefits become theirs. This is salvation in the perfect tense. However, this perfect salvation must be realised in the present and so salvation does not take place completely without the response or co-operation of the believer at some point in space-time. Clearly such a conception of co-operation is not Pelagian or semi-Pelagian for this human response does not effect salvation: forgiveness and eternal life come by grace alone (*sola gratia*) through faith alone (*sola fidei*) (Eph 2.8).

While highly sophisticated, Torrance's doctrine of election is not unique. It is compatible with a particular strand of Scottish Calvinism and with Barth's theology. David Fergusson outlines a similar view when he argues that "the triumph of divine love when considered eschatologically can be cast in three possible ways, and that, because the first two are

103. Ibid., 95. The virgin birth of Jesus is used as a model to illustrate this.

104. For a brief history of synergism see Peterson, "Synergistic Controversy," in *The Oxford Encyclopedia of the Reformation,* 4:133–35, and for a definition see Erickson, *The Concise Dictionary of Christian Theology,* 194.

105. See for instance Barth, *CD*, IV/2, 557. This is one of the areas Fergusson calls for more rigorous thinking in Reformed theology when he concludes, "If predestination is to remain a credible theological notion in Scotland outside the shrinking citadels of Federal Calvinism, it will need to affirm with greater vigour that human freedom and love are made universally possible by God's grace," Fergusson, "Predestination: A Scottish Perspective," 478, cf. 475–78.

unacceptable, some version of the third requires development."[106] The first view is a limiting of the scope of God's love and an Augustinian disjunction of divine love and justice, as seen in much of Reformed theology. The second view is a universalising of divine love along the lines of Barth's doctrine of universal predestination in Christ. Fergusson considers both to be unacceptable and moves to present a third view, one in which "the freedom finally to rebel against God can avoid the determinism of either double predestination or universalism."[107] Fergusson believes that for true freedom to exist the creature must really have a freedom to believe or to reject Christ. However, what separates his view from that of synergistic semi-Pelagianism, or Arminianism is his employment of something Torrance also utilises, the recognition that "there is no symmetry between acceptance and rejection, and no sense in which the trust we show is of equal weight to God's mercy."[108] This leads Fergusson to admit that "this libertarian notion of freedom must find a place in one's theological system, but perhaps only as an addendum to explain the possibility of one's rejecting God."[109] Like Torrance, Fergusson believes human freedom is not to be invoked as an explanation for our redemption, "the love of God in Christ and the influence of the Holy Spirit are all-sufficient."[110] But human freedom, made possible by the love of God in universal atonement, is what finally allows for the incredibly absurd possibility of rejecting God. "Without some such appeal to deliberate human rejection of God, we can explain the possibility of unbelief only in terms of ignorance or a divine decree. Neither alternative can be consistent with the love of God declared in Scripture,"[111] Fergusson determines.[112]

---

106. Fergusson, "Will the Love of God Finally Triumph?" 188.

107. Ibid., 196. According to Fergusson, universalism is just as deterministic as double predestination as it does not allow any human being the freedom to finally say "No." See ibid., 199.

108. Ibid., 200.

109. Ibid.

110. Ibid., 200–201.

111. Ibid., 201.

112. Fergusson has developed his ideas on human freedom further in Fergusson, "Divine Providence and Action," 153–65. Fergusson's view shares some affinities with Alvin Plantinga's free-will defence theodicy in Plantinga, *God, Freedom, and Evil.*

## ELECTION AND THE *EUANGELION*

Torrance's doctrine of election, the contours of which we have critically surveyed, is clear on the centrality of Christ, the trinitarian nature of theology; and election in particular, and the condition of those who refuse God's love and grace. However, questions remain, especially that of how the work of the Holy Spirit takes place in effecting salvation subjectively in the believer, and of the exact relationship between election in Christ and a full explication of Divine providence. Questions not withstanding, a doctrine of election according to Evangelical Calvinism offers the church significant resources to both understand and witness to the Good News of God's love and reconciliation of the world in Christ Jesus, our blessed Lord and Saviour.

# BIBLIOGRAPHY

Barth, Karl. *Church Dogmatics*. 4 vols. Edited by G. W. Bromiley and T. F. Torrance. Translated by G.W. Bromiley, *et al*. Edinburgh: T. & T. Clark, 1956–1975.

———. *The Humanity of God*. London: Fontana, 1967.

———. *Knowledge of God and the Service of God according to the Teaching of the Reformation: Recalling the Scottish Confession of 1560*. Translated by J. L. M. Haire and Ian Henderson. London: Hodder & Stoughton, 1938.

Bell, Charles M. *Calvin and Scottish Theology: The Doctrine of Assurance*. Edinburgh: Handsel, 1986.

Calvin, John. *Concerning the Eternal Predestination of God*. Translated by J. K. S. Reid. London: James Clarke, 1961.

———. *The Institutes of the Christian Religion*. Edited by J. T. McNeill. Translated by F. L. Battles. Philadelphia: Westminster, 1960.

Colwell, John *Actuality and Provisionality: Eternity and Election in the Theology of Karl Barth*. Edinburgh: Rutherford House, 1989.

———. "The Contemporaneity of the Divine Decision: Reflections on Barth's Denial of 'Universalism'," 139-160. In *Universalism and the Doctrine of Hell. Papers Presented at the Fourth Edinburgh Conference on Christian Dogmatics*. Edited by N. M. de S. Cameron. Carlisle: Paternoster, 1992.

Erickson, Millard J. *The Concise Dictionary of Christian Theology*, 2nd edition. Wheaton: Crossway, 2002.

Fergusson, David. "Divine Providence and Action." In *God's Life in Trinity*, 153–65. Edited by M. Volf and M. Welker. Minneapolis: Fortress, 2006.

———. "Predestination: A Scottish Perspective." *Scottish Journal of Theology* 46 (1993) 457–78.

———. "Will the Love of God Finally Triumph?" In *Nothing Greater, Nothing Better: Theological Essays on the Love of God*, 186–202. Edited by K. J. Vanhoozer. Grand Rapids: Eerdmans, 2001.

Habets, Myk. "The Doctrine of Election in Evangelical Calvinism: T. F. Torrance as a Case Study." *Irish Theological Quarterly* 73 (2008) 334–54.

Hendry, George. *The Westminster Confession in the Church Today*. London: SCM, 1960.

Hillerbrand, H. J. *The Oxford Encyclopedia of the Reformation*. 4 vols. New York: Oxford University Press, 1996.

Klooster Fred H. *Calvin's Doctrine of Predestination*. 2nd ed. Grand Rapids: Baker, 1977.

Luther, Martin and Erasmus. *Free Will and Salvation*. London: Library of Christian Classics, 1969.

McDonald, Suzanne. *Re-Imaging God: Divine Election as Representing God to Others and Others to God*. Grand Rapids: Eerdmans, 2010.

Plantinga, Alvin. *God, Freedom, and Evil*. Grand Rapids: Eerdmans, 1974.

Rankin, William D. "Carnal Union with Christ in the Theology of T. F. Torrance." Unpublished PhD Thesis. University of Edinburgh, 1997.

Reid, John K. S. "Introduction." In *Concerning the Eternal Predestination of God*, 9–44. John Calvin. London: James Clarke, 1961.

———. "The Office of Christ in Predestination." *Scottish Journal of theology* 1 (1948) 5–18, 166–83.

Rosato, Philip J. *The Spirit as Lord: The Pneumatology of Karl Barth*. Edinburgh: T. & T. Clark, 1981.

Tanner, Kathryn. *Jesus, Humanity and the Trinity: A Brief Systematic Theology.* Minneapolis: Fortress, 2001.

Torrance, James B. "The Concept of Federal Theology—Was Calvin a Federal Theologian?" In *Calvinus Sacrae Scripturae Professor*, 15–40. Edited by W. H. Neuser. Grand Rapids: Eerdmans, 1994.

———. "The Covenant Concept in Scottish Theology and Politics and Its Legacy," *Scottish Journal of Theology* 34 (1981) 225–43.

———. "Covenant or Contract: A Study of the Theological Background of Worship in Seventeenth-Century Scotland." *Scottish Journal of Theology* 23 (1970) 51–76.

———. "Strengths and Weaknesses of the Westminster Theology." In *The Westminster Confession in the Church Today: Papers Presented for the Church of Scotland Panel on Doctrine*, 40–53. Edited by A. I. Heron. Edinburgh: St Andrew Press, 1982.

Torrance, Thomas F. *Christian Theology and Scientific Culture.* New York: Oxford University Press, 1981.

———. *Conflict and Agreement in the Church:* vol. 2 *of The Ministry and the Sacraments of the Gospel.* London: Lutterworth, 1960.

———. "The Distinctive Character of the Reformed Tradition." In *Incarnational Ministry: The Presence of Christ in Church, Society, and Family. Essays in Honor of Ray S. Anderson.* Edited by C. D. Kettler and T. H. Speidell, 2–15. Colorado Springs: Helmers & Howard, 1990.

———. "Introduction." In *The School of Faith: The Catechisms of the Reformed Church.* Translated and edited by T. F. Torrance, xi–cxxvi. London: James Clarke, 1959.

———. "Justification: Its Radical Nature and Place in Reformed Doctrine and Life." In *Theology in Reconstruction*, 150–68. Grand Rapids: Eerdmans, 1965.

———. *Kingdom and Church: A Study in the Theology of the Reformation.* Edinburgh: Oliver & Boyd, 1956.

———. *The Mediation of Christ.* 2nd ed. Edinburgh: T. & T. Clark, 1992.

———. "Predestination in Christ," *Evangelical Quarterly* 13 (1941) 108–41.

———. *Scottish Theology from John Knox to John McLeod Campbell.* Edinburgh: T. & T. Clark, 1996.

———. "Universalism or Election?" *Scottish Journal of Theology* 2 (1949) 310–18.

Webster, John, Kathryn Tanner, and Iain Torrance, editors. *The Oxford Handbook of Systematic Theology.* Oxford: Oxford University Press, 2007.

# 8

## A Way Forward on the Question
## of the Transmission of Original Sin

MARCUS JOHNSON

T HE TRANSMISSION OF ADAM'S sin to his posterity remains a complex
and thorny issue in Christian theology. Among Reformed theologians, where conversation on this issue has been most lively, there is
still no general consensus on the central question involved: how exactly
have Adam's guilt and corruption been transmitted to his descendants?
The fact that humanity has sinned in Adam, and that the guilt and corruption of his sin has been transmitted to us, has not historically been
in dispute; nor is the deeply mysterious nature of the question denied.
Romans 5:12–19, the *crux interpretum*, is both the source of the doctrine
and the source of the mystery; Paul affirms the fallen estate of humanity
in and through Adam, but does not specifically explain the nature of
the relationship. The doctrine of the transmission of original sin in the
Reformed tradition seeks to describe the results of Adam's sin for his
posterity and typically includes two aspects: original guilt and original
pollution. Original guilt refers to the state of condemnation incurred on
account of Adam's transgression of God's commandment and is legal in
nature. Original pollution refers to the corruption of human nature inherited from Adam which produces actual sin, and is a moral concept.[1]

---

1. Cf. Hoekema, *Created in God's Image*, 148; Berkhof, *Systematic Theology*, 245–47.
Berkhof nicely summarizes the distinctions theologians have made within each aspect:
original guilt (*reatus culpae* and *reatus poenae*); original pollution (privation of original
righteousness and depraved moral nature).

Given these categories, any view that seeks to explain the transmission of original sin must grapple with at least three interrelated questions: (i) How do Adam's progeny become guilty of his sin?; (ii) How do Adam's progeny inherit his polluted nature?; (iii) What is the relationship between the declaration of guilt and the corruption of nature? Heretofore, two viewpoints have dominated Reformed hamartiology: federalism and realism.[2] In the pages that follow, I will briefly expound both views and note their attendant strengths and weaknesses. A third position, which I will call "Pauline realism," is then advanced which—without jettisoning the truths of the other views—develops and seeks to correct them by drawing heavily on the rich and pervasive Pauline theme of union with Christ; a theme implied already in Romans 5 and developed elsewhere in the Pauline corpus. This position is a systematic-theological move in keeping with a suggestion made in a recent article by Oliver Crisp,[3] but that has yet to be developed. The argument herein draws upon the implied parallel in Romans 5 between the condition humanity inherits "in Adam" and that which the redeemed enjoy "in Christ"—only the latter of which does Paul elaborate upon in a substantive way so as to give us true, though limited, insight into the mystery. Pauline realism represents a step forward in answering the three interrelated questions involved in the problem of original sin, and draws on tenets broadly associated with what this volume refers to as evangelical Calvinism.

## FEDERALISM

As to the first question involved in the transmission of original sin—How do we become guilty of Adam's sin?—the federalist position holds

2. The federalist view is variously known as the "representative" or "immediate imputation" view, the latter of which has specific reference to the imputation of Adam's *guilt* and as such is too conceptually narrow for the present purposes. Realism is often referred to as Augustinian realism, recognizing its debt to its most famous advocate, but is also too narrow given the consequent development of realism in Reformed theology. Theologians in the Reformed tradition recognize other views on the transmission of original sin, such as those associated with Pelagius (humanity is born essentially unaffected by Adam's sin) and Placeus (mediate imputation) but rightly find them biblically and therefore theologically untenable. Cf. Hoekema, *Created in God's Image*, 154–57; Berkhof, *Systematic Theology*, 240–43; Johnson, "Romans 5:12," 306–13.

3. Crisp, "Federalism vs Realism," 71. Crisp is seeking to fortify the metaphysical weaknesses in realism, but he also suggests that a chastened realism may open up new ways of thinking about the imputation of Christ's righteousness. It is in the direction of the latter suggestion that this article moves.

that Adam was divinely constituted as federal head of humankind, representing his posterity in his action. Adam thus stood in the place of humanity when he sinned, and the guilt and condemnation of his transgression is accounted to all his descendants. The relationship between Adam and subsequent humanity, on this view, is typically framed in forensic terms such that humanity is declared guilty on account of Adam's sin by virtue of his legal headship.[4] The guilt and condemnation that follow upon Adam's sin is said to be immediately imputed (or, perhaps better, "directly imputed"[5]), insofar as the declaration of guilt is unmediated by any intervening factor (such as our moral corruption). Because Adam acted as our federal representative, his transgression of God's commandment serves as the judicial ground of the condemnation of those united to him.

As to the second question—How have we inherited Adam's polluted nature?—federalists maintain that, in distinction from the direct imputation of guilt, humanity also inherits a corrupt nature by reason of its solidarity with Adam. This transmission of a corrupted condition is typically thought to be biological in nature as opposed to legal. Adam's depraved condition is propagated rather than directly imputed. And it precisely on this point that many federalists stress that they do not reject in total the realist position, which position may account best for the transmission of Adam's corrupt nature.[6] Thus, while the guilt of Adam's sin has relation to his federal headship, the transmission of his corruption is related to his natural or "seminal" headship. It should be said, however, that federalists are not of one accord here regarding the transmission of corruption, and some of their conceptions remain discordant.

As to the third question—What is the relationship between the declaration of guilt and the transmission of corruption?—again, federalists do not appear to have reached a consensus. Some, like Murray, appeal to two kinds of union with Adam to relate the two aspects of

4. C.f. Berkhof, *Systematic Theology*, 242–46; Johnson, "Romans 5:12," 312.

5. Hoekema, *Created in God's Image*, 161.

6. Johnson, "Romans 5:12," 308–9; Murray, "The Imputation of Adam's Sin," 40, writes: "With reference to misrepresentation or at least misconception on the part of opponents, it may not be unnecessary to repeat that the representative view does not deny but rather affirms the natural headship of Adam and posterity, that all derive from Adam by natural generation a corrupt nature, and that therefore original sin is passed on by propagation."

original sin: the guilt/condemnation of Adam's primal sin is imputed by virtue of his representative headship, and the corruption of Adam's nature is transmitted by virtue of his natural or seminal headship. Others, curiously, hold that innate corruption is the consequence of, the result of, the direct imputation of Adam's guilt. Corruption is viewed as part of the penalty of legal involvement in Adam's guilt.[7] In still others, as in Hoekema, there is a conflation of the two positions: corruption is viewed as linked both to the direct imputation of Adam's guilt and to a mediated transmission through propagation.[8]

Despite the valuable contributions of federalism, this brief account reveals some important weaknesses. The first weakness is the problem of the *peccatum alienum* and the justice of God: How is it just that God imputes the sin of Adam to those who did not personally commit his sin? The federalist position posits what Crisp calls a "rather peculiar state of affairs wherein God ordains that one person represents everybody else, and commits a sin that everybody has to suffer for."[9] The difficulty, as even some federalists recognize, lies in the fact that Adam's descendants are accounted guilty for a sin they are not personally present for, or volitionally involved in—thus, the imputation of an "alien sin."[10] On this view, Adam's posterity are quite some distance removed from actual participation in Adam's sin, except by way of divine, legal fiat. Typically, advocates appeal to the imputation of Christ's righteousness in justification as a plausible solution: just as Christ acts as representative head of those "in him" in such a way that his righteousness is imputed to those not themselves actually righteous, so Adam's guilt is imputed to those who did not themselves commit his trespass.[11] This solution may not be as convincing as it first appears, perhaps running the danger of justifying one "legal fiction" by appeal to another. The question of injus-

---

7. Berkhof, *Systematic Theology*, 242: "In His righteous judgment God imputes the guilt of the first sin, committed by the head of the covenant, to all those that are federally related to him. And as a result they are born in a depraved and sinful condition as well . . ." See also Reymond, *A New Systematic Theology*, 439, 449. Henri Blocher refers to this federalist account as a "rather provocative thesis," in Blocher, *Original Sin*, 73.

8. Hoekema, *Created in God's Image*, 161–62.

9. Crisp, "Federalism vs Realism," 67.

10. See Berkouwer, *Sin*, 449–61. Johnson candidly admits, "We do not for one moment belittle the problem of the *peccatum alienum*, acknowledging that it tends to weaken the case for immediate imputation." Johnson, "Romans 5:12," 315.

11. Murray, "Imputation," 42–44.

tice is not necessarily rectified by appeal to a merely extrinsic notion of imputation, whether of Adam's guilt or Christ's righteousness; unless of course this imputation is grounded in a logically antecedent and realistic union with the First or Second Adam (there is more on this to follow).

The second weakness pertains to the federalist position that the direct imputation of guilt leads to, or has as its consequence, the corruption of our nature.[12] Those who hold this position have not made clear, in my view, why a forensic declaration of guilt/condemnation necessarily or (theo-) logically entails a corruption of nature, unless by divine ordination (which is difficult to sustain biblically). Guilt and corruption may both be real consequences of original sin, but it is not at all obvious that they are related by way of cause and effect. The legal declaration of guilt associated with Adam's sin is a judicial reckoning and it does violence to the forensic metaphor to contend that a legal declaration has as its consequence an actual transformation of nature. It is not even transparent in Adam's case that his depraved nature came about as a consequence of his first sin; does his primal sinning not imply that he was already spiritually compromised?[13] In defense of the view that the imputation of guilt leads to sinful corruption, federalists are prone to appeal again to the parallel with the imputation of Christ's righteousness: the imputation of the righteousness of Christ has as its consequence the moral transformation of the sinner; in other words, as justification leads to sanctification "in Christ," so guilt leads to corruption "in Adam."[14] This construal shall be challenged below.

## REALISM

Realism constitutes the other main Reformed option for addressing the question of the transmission of original sin. With regard to the imputation of Adam's guilt, A. H. Strong writes, "(Realism) holds that God imputes the sin of Adam to all his posterity, in virtue of that organic unity of mankind by which the whole race at the time of Adam's transgression existed, not individually, but seminally, in him as its head. The total life of humanity was then in Adam; the race as yet had its being

12. Johnson, "Romans 5:12," 311: "Human sinfulness in the sense of hereditary depravity stands in relation to Adam's first sin as an effect stands to a cause."

13. For a nuanced account of Jonathan Edwards on this point, see Crisp, "The Theological Pedigree of Jonathan Edwards's Doctrine of Imputation," 308–27, esp. 322.

14. Reymond, *Systematic Theology*, 438–39.

only in him."[15] This view postulates that the progeny of Adam were "realistically" present in him as he sinned. Realists have construed this "real presence" in various ways,[16] but the uniformly integral insight provided here is that the imputation of Adam's sin is predicated upon a real, rather than merely representational, participation in his sin. Whereas in federalism Adam's sin is imputed and so becomes mine, in realism the sin is imputed precisely because it *is* mine.[17] Realism avoids the charge of injustice, then, insofar as God is said to declare people guilty who actually are guilty. We may say that the sin that is imputed is at one and the same time *peccatum alienum* and *peccatum proprium*—it is the sin of Adam but also my sin by virtue of a realistic union with Adam.[18]

By positing a realist union between Adam and progeny, realists are able to seamlessly account for the second aspect of the transmission of original sin: pollution. All who are really united to Adam in his first sin—and the guilt and condemnation that follow—are also participants, by propagation, of his corrupt condition. As we have seen, some federalists have appealed to a "natural" or "seminal" union with Adam as the explanation for the transmission of pollution. Thus, on the question of the relation between the transmission of guilt and pollution realists differ markedly from federalists. Federalists either posit two headships—a federal headship with respect to the imputation of Adam's guilt/condemnation, and a natural headship with respect to the transmission of pollution—or they postulate that innate pollution is a *consequence* of

15. Strong, *Systematic Theology*, 619.

16. See esp. Crisp, "Federalism vs Realism," for the nuanced accounts of William G. T. Shedd and Augustus Hopkins Strong.

17. Crisp, "Federalism vs Realism," 60. The term *impute* is thus used by realists in the sense of "to reckon or to regard Adam's sin as mine." Federalists use the term in a more causal and remote way, as in the sense of "to cause Adam's sin to become mine." Both are legitimate uses of the term *impute*, but they may convey different realities, as in the case of the doctrine of the *imputation* of Christ's righteousness.

18. Berkouwer, *Sin*, 459: "On the one hand, federalism has pointed to a real guilt and to sin as *peccatum proprium*; on the other hand, it speaks of a declaration of guilt on the basis of God's ordinance. Thus we are left with a different doctrine of *imputation* from when man is held responsible for an act which he himself commits. No matter how the federalists try to combine the *peccatum proprium* and *peccatum alienum*, the relativizing that is implicit in the words "in a certain sense" compels them to understand "imputation" as a forensic judgment of God. Therefore the federalists have been challenged to show how *such* an imputation is in harmony with Scripture. How can we speak of an 'imputation' when we do not mean *an active and personal sinning* in the fullest sense of those words?"

the guilt established through the legal representation of Adam. Realism, on the other hand, accounts for both the imputation of guilt and the transmission of pollution by appealing to a realistic, natural union with Adam. In other words, this union has both legal and transformative implications. The realist thus avoids the apparent incongruity of making innate corruption the consequence of a forensic declaration of guilt, or of positing two distinct headships.[19]

Opponents of realism have pointed to several weaknesses in the position, which have been ably catalogued elsewhere.[20] Two criticisms are of special importance and deserve careful attention. The first, which all federalist stress in varying degrees, is the admittedly difficult task before the realist of attempting to define the *nature* of a realistic union with Adam that is metaphysically/ontologically coherent. What does it mean to say that humanity as a generic whole really existed in Adam? Whether one speaks of the classical Augustinian seminal version, the *common human nature version* propounded by William G. T. Shedd, or the *unindividualized whole of humanity version* maintained by A. H. Strong, each version of realism remains either conceptually and/or metaphysically obscure or even implausible.[21] Further, even if realism appears to best account for the question of the justice of God in the imputation of Adam's sin, opponents still wonder if God's justice is truly vindicated by attributing Adam's sin to those who did not *personally* and *individually* sin.[22] Attempts by realists to be (overly-?) specific about the nature of a union which is at bottom inscrutable have been basically unsuccessful in clarifying the issue at hand.

---

19. There is a sense for the realist in which pollution does in fact follow upon guilt/condemnation, specifically in the case of Adam's primal sin. It is safe to say that, in one sense, Adam's corrupt nature followed upon the breaking of God's commandment. Part of the effect of this transgression of God's commandment was therefore depravity (although it might be equally valid to suggest that Adam must have been spiritually compromised in order to break the command in the first place!). The corruption of Adam's nature does not appear to "wait" for the divine declaration of guilt in order to take effect. Rather, Adam is corrupted in and through his breaking of God's gracious command. See Strong, *Systematic Theology*, 620, for comments to this effect.

20. Cf. Johnson, "Romans 5:12," 309–10; Berkhof, *Systematic Theology*, 241; Murray, "Imputation," 35–39.

21. These helpful delineations are borrowed from Crisp, "Federalism vs Realism," who nicely brings out the nuances and potential weaknesses in Shedd and Strong.

22. Cf. Johnson, "Romans 5:12," 309; Blocher, *Original Sin*, 115–16.

Another weakness federalists see in realism is the failure to render congruent the analogy drawn in Romans 5 between Adam and Christ. Federalists assert, rightly, that Christ acts as representative head for the redeemed, and that his righteousness is directly imputed rather than inherently possessed. Similarly, therefore, humanity must be condemned in Adam for an unrighteousness not personally their own.[23] The realistic account has shredded the analogy, it is thought, dissolving the parallel between Christ and Adam as representative heads of humanity by positing a "realistic" account of Adamic union that does not exist with respect to Christ and his people. Surely there is no "common human nature" or "unindividualized whole of humanity" that exists in seminal form or otherwise in Christ through which people are justified. As John Murray noted, the natural union (advanced by realists) that exists between Adam and posterity "provides no analogy to the union that exists between Christ and his people." He goes on to write,

> We conclude, therefore, that more than natural headship is necessary, that natural headship does not carry with it the notion of "specific unity" in Adam, that the *plus* required to explain the imputation of Adam's *first* sin and no other is not shown by Scripture to be the kind of union which realism postulates, and that when we seek to discover the specific character of the union which will ground the imputation of Adam's first sin we find it to be the *same kind of union as is analogous to the union that exists between Christ and his people and on the basis of which his righteousness is theirs unto justification and eternal life.*[24]

Thus, one of the more forceful objections leveled against realism is its incongruity on the Adam-Christ analogy of Romans 5, an analogy that seems conspicuous enough in Scripture to warrant an attempt at symmetry. If the relationship that obtains between Christ and his people—particularly with the respect to the imputation of righteousness—is that of a representative headship, then this must certainly bear forcibly on one's interpretation of the Adam-progeny relationship; it must also be essentially representative in order to preserve the symmetry.

---

23. Ibid., 310.

24. Murray, "Imputation," 43–44 (emphasis added). It should be noted that Murray does not deny the natural/seminal headship of Adam, he simply finds it unable to account for the imputation of Adam's sin.

This symmetry rests, of course, on the assumption that the relationship between Christ and his people in justification is primarily or exclusively a federal-representational headship, an assumption shared by most federalists who tend to view justification as the primary soteriological paradigm. But this assumption only seems to beg the question. What if the relationship between Christ and his people is *not* primarily or exclusively federal-representational, and what if Paul had in mind a rather mysterious but certainly "realistic" union with Christ? And, further, what if this "realistic" union Paul envisages allows him to speak both in *forensic* terms regarding the imputation of righteousness and *transformative* terms regarding the transmission of holiness? If this can be established, then it seems by analogy we would have an instructive Pauline paradigm for understanding the transmission of original sin which is able to encompass the truths of both federalism and realism without succumbing to the inherent weaknesses of either. Admittedly, Paul does not elaborate a sophisticated metaphysical argument. He is content, it seems, with a degree of mystery. Nevertheless, his account of the nature of union with Christ and its implications may prove highly instructive for understanding our union with Adam.[25]

## PAULINE REALISM

Federalism offers a number of important insights into the nature and implications of our dreadful condition "in Adam." Its salutary emphasis on the forensic aspects of our relationship with Adam has proved exceptionally influential, but it is weakened by its over-stress on the representational character of that relationship. Realism is an advance on federalism in this respect, but it is itself weakened by the obscurity or implausibility of its metaphysical construals which tax biblical, theological and philosophical credulity.

In this section I advance what I am tentatively referring to as "Pauline realism,"[26] which may be viewed as a chastened, evangelical

25. "How does life 'in Adam' help us to understand how we are 'in Christ?' Paul looks at everything from his vantage point in Christ; this was true of the law, and it is true of Adam. When he says that we are 'in Christ' as we are 'in Adam,' he brings in the parallel because he first sees man as in Christ." Smedes, *Union with Christ*, 82. See also Berkouwer, *Sin*, 509–10.

26. Every term or phrase is bound to have both its strengths and liabilities. For instance "Pauline realism" is helpful in that it attempts to convey the extreme intimacy of Paul's thought on this matter. However, it is not meant to suggest that Federalism is somehow less than "real."

Calvinist version of classical realism. It is "chastened" because it does not attempt a technically sophisticated metaphysical construal of the union of which Paul writes, opting instead to affirm the mystery element in Paul's thought. However, it is still "realistic" or "actual" in the sense that the union between Christ and believer, which has its analogy in Adam and posterity, transcends the merely representational or virtual. In an attempt to offer some conceptual clarity, I will describe this union with Christ as vital, organic, and personal.[27] The crux of this proposal rests on the pervasive theme of union with Christ in Pauline theology.[28] If it can be shown that Paul's notion of union with Christ can indeed qualify as "realistic," even if not in any metaphysically or ontologically sophisticated sense, then it seems appropriate by way of analogy to apply this Pauline realism to our understanding of union with Adam, along with the implications that follow for the transmission of original sin.

The theme of union with Christ, or participation in Christ, is ubiquitous in the Pauline corpus, and has consequently occupied a formally prominent place in Reformed soteriology.[29] It is indeed central to his understanding of the redemptive relationship between Christ and his people.[30] His use of the various terms and phrases to denote the believer's incorporation into Christ numbers well into the hundreds.[31]

27. By using these terms, I am intending to convey that the union is life-giving, consists of us being made limbs/organs (members) of Christ's body, and involves our persons and the person of Christ (as opposed to a union thought of as merely between souls, minds or wills). These terms are exactly those used by Berkhof in his description of the mystical union with Christ. Berkhof, *Systematic Theology,* 450. While Berkhof, a federalist, is willing to speak of union with Christ in these intimate ways, that is because he has essentially reduced this union to sanctification alone, reserving for justification a prior, legal union. Evans writes that for Berkhof, ". . . union with Christ has, for all intents and purposes, ceased to function as an umbrella category unifying all of salvation . . . the term "mystical union" applies only to sanctification, and not at all to justification." Evans, *Imputation and Impartation,* 236–37.

28. Of course union with Christ is an extensive theme in the Johannine corpus as well, but our focus will remain on Paul given that he clearly posits an Adam-Christ analogy.

29. Evans, *Imputation and Impartation*; Billings, "John Calvin's Soteriology," 428–47; Gaffin Jr., "Union with Christ," 271–88; Johnson, "Luther and Calvin on Union with Christ."

30. Cf. Dunn, *The Theology of Paul the Apostle,* 390ff.

31. Demarest, *The Cross and Salvation,* 313, counts two hundred sixteen such occurrences in Paul. Dunn, *The Theology of Paul the Apostle,* 396, details Paul's "participation in Christ" language and notes that the phrase "*en Christo*" alone occurs 83 times

Many of these uses indicate that Paul understands union with Christ in "realistic" ways (vital, organic, personal). A few examples will suffice. Ephesians 5:29–32 is a remarkably intimate depiction of the union between Christ and his members, weaving together vital, organic and physical/sexual imagery. Although Paul describes this union as a "profound mystery", he does not thereby minimize the reality or intimacy, nor does his conception seem reducible to federal headship.[32] Consider also Paul's use of the phrase "members of the body of Christ" (e.g., 1 Cor 6:15; 12:27). Although Pauline "member" language has in modern evangelical thought often suffered from a kind of reductionistic metaphoricalizing—as if the equivalent were being the "member" of a health club—there is sufficiently good reason to think that Paul has in mind a real, living, organic union with the very body of Christ.[33]

A passage like Galatians 2:20 ("It is no longer I who live, but Christ who lives in me") may be subject to two interpretive errors. The first would be to read pagan notions of mystical absorption into the divine into Paul's thought, but the other would be to deny that Paul speaks of the reality of personal communion with Jesus Christ.[34] Further, we might contemplate Paul's notion of participation in the death and resurrection of Jesus Christ (Rom 6; Col 2; 1 Cor 15). This notion, while it most certainly carries with it a vicarious meaning, cannot be reduced to mere substitution. The death and resurrection of Christ have *operative effects* on those with whom he is in union, suggesting that the believer who is incorporated into Christ actually experiences the effectual power of that death and resurrection in her life.[35] In sum, while Paul's understanding of union with Christ includes within it the idea that Christ is our vicarious representative, so too does his understanding extend beyond it. It eclipses mere imaginative or sympathetic participation in

---

in the Pauline corpus. See also, Reid, *Our Life in Christ*, 12. Reid refers to the important work of Adolf Deismann, *Die Neutestamntliche Formel "in ChristoJesu"*, who counts at least 164 occurrences of such language in Paul.

32. Calvin, *Calvin's Commentaries*, Eph 5:30–32.

33. Cf. Robinson, *The Body*, esp. 45–83; Gary Badcock, "The Church as "Sacrament," 194–200; Thiselton, *The Hermeneutics of Doctrine*, 481. Calvin interpreted passages such as these in highly realistic terms: Calvin, *Calvin's Commentaries*, 1 Cor 6:15; 12:27. Many, unfortunately, see passages like these as related specifically to ecclesiology rather than soteriology, a dichotomy that is foreign to Paul.

34. Longnecker, *Galatians*, 93.

35. Cf. Dunn, *Romans*, 330; Moo, *The Epistle to the Romans*, 367; Calvin, *Calvin's Commentaries*, Col 2:12; Rom 6:3–5.

the actions of another, and certainly exceeds mere moral exemplarism. And Paul gives no indication that he is thinking of multiple unions, as if there were a "federal" kind of union through which we received legal benefits in Christ, and a "mystical" union with Christ though which we receive transformative benefits. Indeed, the argument advanced in the pages that follow rests on the assumption that when Paul writes of our salvation "in Christ" he is thinking of no other union than one that is vital, organic, and personal (and which is also representative). If we receive any benefit from being "in Christ" it is because we have really been united to the very person of Christ himself.[36]

We are now in a position to extend Paul's realistic understanding of union with Christ and demonstrate its relevance for understanding the Christ-Adam analogy. Doing so necessitates a return to the three questions with which we began regarding the transmission of original sin and, all the while keeping in mind John Murray's words regarding the respective headships of Adam and of Christ:

> All who die die in Adam; all who are made alive are made alive in Christ. In view of this comprehensive philosophy of human history and destiny and in view of the pivotal and determinative roles of the first and last Adam, we must posit constitutive ordination on God's part to these unique relationships. And since the analogy instituted between Adam and Christ is so conspicuous, it is surely necessary to assume that the kind of relationship which Adam sustains to men is after the pattern of the relationship which Christ sustains to men.[37]

(i) *How do we become guilty of Adam's sin?* Drawing on Paul's analogy in Romans 5:18, we may say that we are condemned in Adam in a way that corresponds to our justification in Christ. Justification is a declaration by God that we are "in the right," that is, not subject to the condemna-

36. Smedes, *Union with Christ*, 133: "There is, it is safe to say, no hint that when Paul says "Christ lives in me," he has anyone or anything else in mind than the very person of Jesus Christ. He means Jesus who died and rose again and is coming to establish his kingdom. He means the Jesus who is nothing if not an authentic and concrete person." The assertion that a real union with Christ (logically) precedes and is the source of redemptive benefits like justification and sanctification is clearly found in Calvin (e.g., Calvin, *Institutes*, 3.1.1), and has been enshrined in the Reformed Standards. The Westminster Larger Catechism refers to the elect as "spiritually, mystically, really, inseparably" united to Christ and has this union preceding all other graces of Christ (Q's 66 & 69). See also the Second Helvetic Confession (Chapter XXI).

37. Murray, *Imputation*, 42.

tion we deserve as Adamic sinners. Justification is a crucial redemptive category in Paul that does not exhaust union with Christ and cannot be properly understood apart from being "in Christ." "If we speak of justification or of imputation . . . *apart* from a grasp of this incorporation into Christ, we will constantly be in danger of contemplating some sort of transfer *apart* from being included in Christ, *apart* from union with Christ."[38] There are a host of passages that bear out this observation. For example, "Therefore, there is now no condemnation for those who are in Christ Jesus" (Rom 8:1). Just as through/in Adam we inherit his trespass, are declared guilty, and are sentenced to death, so through/in Christ we inherit his righteousness, are declared not guilty, and receive eternal life. Through the disobedience of Adam we are "made sinners," and through the obedience of Christ we are "made righteous" (Rom 5:19).

It is at this point that we come face to face with the federalist insistence that in justification Christ's righteousness is directly imputed to us insofar as he acts as our representative and legal head. The righteousness that is imputed is an *aliena iustitia*; we do not realistically participate in Christ's righteousness any more than we realistically participate in Adam's trespass. We recall that this was at the center of the federalist objection to realism with respect to the imputation of Adam's sin. Realism insists that Adam's primal sin is imputed to us on account of the fact that Adam's sin really is ours. This is an apparent incongruency for the federalist because Christ's relationship with his people—with respect to justification—is construed along merely representational lines. The imputation of Christ's righteousness is a forensic mechanism that is based on a legal solidarity. However, if we follow Paul must we sacrifice his "realism" in order to accommodate his "federalism"? I think not. Paul's understanding of intimate union with Christ *includes within it* the forensic notion of imputation. It is "in Christ" that we "become the righteousness of God" (2 Cor 5:21). Or as he writes elsewhere, "I consider [all things] rubbish, *that I may gain Christ and be found in him*, not having a righteousness of my own that comes from the law, but that which comes through faith in Christ—the righteousness that comes from God and is by faith" (Phil 3:8–9). In other words, the fact

---

38. Carson, "The Vindication of Imputation," 72. Thiselton, *The Hermeneutics of Doctrine*, 349: "Being in Christ is the horizon of understanding within which the various problems associated with justification by grace through faith alone become simply questions that receive intelligible answers."

that we are reckoned/regarded as righteous takes place because we have been included in Christ. "It is because of (God) that you are *in Christ Jesus* who has become for us wisdom from God—that is, our righteousness, holiness and redemption" (1 Cor 1:30). To put it another way, intimate union with Christ includes along with it a forensic aspect: we are declared righteous because Christ's righteousness has become ours and therefore it is imputed as such. Only as we participate in Christ the Righteous One do we share in a righteousness not inherently our own: we are justified. "In the final analysis, the imputation of Christ's righteousness is best understood as that aspect of union with Christ that supplies the judicial ground of justification."[39] On this reading, a "real" union with Christ does not preclude the crucial legal aspect but is not reduced to mere legal representation either. The ready advantage here is that the charge of legal fiction evaporates: God is declaring sinners righteous precisely because they *are* righteous, but only "in Christ." The benefits of this Pauline notion become obvious when applied to Adamic solidarity. If we assume that our union with Adam is analogous to our union with Christ we are in a position to assert that our participation in Adam's sin is "real" because our participation in Adam is real. God, therefore, imputes the sin of Adam to us in very much the same way that he imputes the righteousness of Christ to us: he regards it as ours *because we really share in it*. The *alienum peccatum* is at the same time *proprium peccatum*. Just as there is a real union with Christ that includes within it a forensic aspect (justification), so there is a real union with Adam that includes within it a forensic aspect (condemnation). And just as union with Christ protects justification from the charge of legal fiction, so does union with Adam protect the imputation of his sin from being capricious or unjust. Thus, the federalists are right to insist that the imputation of Adam's primal sin is a forensic affair (and so corresponds with the imputation of Christ's righteousness), but they are mistaken in their insistence that this imputation is best conceived apart from a real union with Adam. The realists, on the other hand, are right to insist on the reality of the Adamic union, but their attempts to be articulate this nature of this union metaphysically have been less than convincing.

---

39. Tipton, "Union with Christ and Justification," 38. See also Gaffin, "Union with Christ," 286.

(ii) *How has the pollution of Adam's nature become ours?* This question is less debated among federalist and realists, but Paul's conception of union with Christ may again lend some conceptual clarity to the remaining ambiguities. For Paul our intimate union with Christ has both legal and transformative benefits. We are both justified and sanctified "in Christ Jesus," in a way that answers both our guilt and pollution in Adam.[40] Our nature has been corrupted in Adam, and is being restored in Christ. Just as we are born spiritually dead in Adam, we are reborn spiritually in Christ. And so the doctrine of justification which answers the question of our guilt/condemnation is paralleled by the doctrine of sanctification which answers the question of our inborn depravity. Paul writes of this newness of life and holiness in myriad ways and typically grounds his teaching in our participation in Christ. For instance, when we participate in Christ, he is our holiness (1 Cor 1:30), we have newness of life (Rom 6), we are a new creation (2 Cor 5:17), we are transformed into his image (2 Cor 3:18; 1 Cor 15:49), we are created to do good works (Eph 2:10), and we have life in our mortal bodies (Rom 8:10–11). This list could easily be extended, but it suffices to show that in union with Christ we receive more than legal benefits which absolve us of guilt and condemnation. Christ is also the One through whom we are being made new and transformed in order to overcome our spiritual deadness and depravity. In other words, our being-in-Christ is a thorough overcoming of our being-in-Adam.

The vast majority of Reformed theologians, be they federalist or realist on the question of original sin, agree that the union by which we receive newness of life in Christ must be described in something more than merely external or representational terms. That is, something more than federal headship is required to account for our being new creatures that are transformed into the likeness of Christ. Our union with Christ is, with respect to the transformation of our persons, a vital, intimate, organic, personal union through which believers are empowered by Christ to overcome Adamic depravity.[41] We have noted that some feder-

40. For the sake of conceptual simplicity, I am using sanctification in its broadest sense as inclusive of both its definitive and progressive aspects. In the former sense, sanctification is related to the doctrine of regeneration: newness of life in Christ. On this point, see Hoekema, *Saved by Grace*, 107.

41. E.g., Berkhof, *Systematic Theology*, 449–51, refers to this union with Christ as mystical, organic, vital, personal, spiritual and transforming. However, as we have noted, he distinguishes this "mystical" union from "legal unity" with Christ, which is the basis of justification.

alists posit two unions with Adam, representative and natural/seminal, in order to account for the dual problem of original sin.[42] But the Adam/ Christ analogy seems to suffer on this point unless one is willing to affirm two unions with *Christ*, as Berkhof does—one legal and one vital. The federalist position certainly points in this direction,[43] and yet this hardly seems to do justice to Paul's theology. The union believers have with Christ appears to be *singular and comprehensive*, encompassing both legal and transformative benefits (1 Cor 1:30). The problem is that federalists are willing to affirm a vital, personal, organic, real union with both Adam and Christ, but unwilling—in many cases—to extend the implications of this union to either the imputation of Adam's guilt or Christ's righteousness. To put it another way, many have been willing to adopt a kind of realism, but only willing to apply this realism to either the transmission of corruption or to newness of life. And, historically, realism (for federalists and others) has appeared to be a metaphysically implausible solution to Adamic guilt. Is there a way forward in relating the guilt and pollution transmitted from Adam while simultaneously maintaining the analogy between Christ and his people?

(iii) *What is the relationship between the declaration of guilt and the corruption of our nature?* The Apostle Paul's conception of the relationship between justification and sanctification "in Christ," and the analogy it provides for the relation between guilt and pollution "in Adam," proves extremely helpful on this question. As we have noted, Paul conceives of our dilemma in Adam as answered by the multiple consequences of our union with Christ: justification and sanctification.[44] To put it clearly:

---

42. Hoekema, *Created in God's Image*, 161–62, writes regarding federalism ("immediate imputation") that Adam's guilt is thought to be directly imputed, while Adam's corruption is thought to be mediately transmitted from parents to children. This implies two kinds of union, one legal and one natural.

43. Although this direction is not always pursued. Reymond, *A New Systematic Theology*, argues for a "realistic" view of union with Christ as the fountainhead through which justification and every other blessing flows, and yet simultaneously argues for a federal (immediate imputation) view of the transmission of Adam's sin. Reymond is especially difficult to understand insofar as he claims both that "the representative principle" is alone that which governs the relationship between Christ and his people (437), and later that the relationship between Christ and his people is "as real as though there were in fact a literal umbilical cord uniting them" (738).

44. We may, of course, speak of union with Christ as the source of many more benefits besides: e.g. adoption (Gal 3:26), resurrection (1 Cor 15:23), glorification (2 Cor 3:18), election (Eph 1:3–5) and the church (Eph 5:32).

by virtue of a vital, organic, intimate, personal union with Christ one receives justification (forgiveness of sins, imputation of righteousness) and sanctification (newness and holiness of life). If this reading of Paul is correct, we may say that he distinguishes these benefits without confusing or separating them. They are concurrent, inseparable benefits that issue forth from our participation in the righteous, holy, life-giving Christ.[45] Paul does not posit multiple unions to account for the multiple benefits, nor does he make one benefit the cause or consequence of the other. The singular, realistic union with Christ is the cause of all blessings. If we take this understanding of the implications of being in Christ and apply it to the implications of being in Adam we derive the following assertion: by virtue of our singular, realistic union with Adam we experience both the guilt and condemnation of his primal trespass as well as the corrupt condition into which he fell. We need not, on this understanding, posit multiple unions (federal and natural) to account for the multiple dilemmas, nor do we need to make one dilemma the cause or effect of the other. Guilt and pollution are distinguishable but inseparable dilemmas that issue forth from our union with Adam.

As we have noted, some federalists relate guilt and pollution in terms of cause and effect.[46] On this view, the guilt imputed to Adam's descendants by reason of his federal headship has as its consequence the corruption of their nature as well. Again, it is not immediately clear why the imputation of Adam's legal guilt should *cause* one to become corrupt. After all, imputation is a forensic notion while corruption is a moral one. Imputation is by definition not intended to describe the change in one's moral condition, it is the reckoning of one's legal status. The analogy with Christ is especially instructive here. We do not say that in the imputation of Christ's righteousness one's moral condition is changed, we say rather that one is forensically *declared* in the right—justified *in Christ*.

45. See Gaffin, *Resurrection and Redemption*, esp. 129–43.

46. See n.7. Many Reformed theologians mirror this thinking in their soteriology, referring to justification as the cause or basis of sanctification, or of sanctification as the consequence of justification. See Berkhof, *Systematic Theology*, 418, 536; Reymond, *A New Systematic Theology*, 438–39; Horton, *Covenant and Salvation*, chp. 7, esp. 129–30, 139, 143. The realist W. G. T. Shedd put it as bluntly as any federalist: "Sanctification does not justify, but justification sanctifies." Shedd, *Dogmatic Theology*, 2:559. Lane Tipton, *Union with Christ and Justification,* has argued that a soteriological paradigm in which justification stands in a causal relationship to sanctification is more typically Lutheran. Tipton, *Union with Christ and Justification,* 41–45. For a stimulating historical account, see Lillback, "Calvin's Development of the Doctrine of Forensic Justification," 51–80.

The change in moral condition is brought about not by justification, but by transformation into the likeness of Christ—sanctification *in Christ*. Justification and sanctification address different aspects of the transmission of original sin and both benefits come about through union with the Last Adam. The fruit of this understanding, when applied to the First Adam, allows us to avoid the problem of relating the problems of guilt and pollution in terms of cause and effect, as well as the awkwardness of positing two distinct unions.

Illustratively, we may point to the problems that surface in Murray's treatment of original sin and recall that he proposes both a federal headship in order to account for the imputation of Adam's guilt and a natural/seminal headship in order to account for the transmission of his corruption.[47] Murray then writes, apparently without noticing the ostensible inconsistency, that in our union with Christ there are both legal and transformative effects: justification and renewal.[48] It is not altogether clear whether Murray intends us to (i) think of a federal and natural union with Christ (or legal and mystical, as Berkhof) that is consistent with his Adamic construal, or (ii) of a single union with Christ with dual implications. If the former, we have the difficulty of finding such an idea in Paul's theology. If the latter, then we are suggesting that Murray (et al.) apply in full the Adam/Christ analogy as they have rightly insisted we ought. If there is a single union with Christ with multiple implications, why not say the same of union with Adam?

## CONCLUSION

In an important essay, S. Lewis Johnson voiced the concern of many who sympathize with federalism when he criticized realism on the following point:

> . . . (R)ealism has difficulty in handling the analogy drawn in the passage (Rom 5) between Adam and Christ. Just as men are justified for a righteousness which is not personally their own, so they were condemned for a sin which was not personally their own. Of course, it must be recognized that this analogy is not a complete one. But it does seem essential to Paul's point to maintain that the *nature of the union* between the principals and their people is parallel.[49]

47. See n.6.
48. Murray, "Imputation," 19.
49. Johnson, "Romans 5:12," 310.

This present essay has been an attempt to maintain Paul's point that the "nature of the union between the two principals and their people is parallel." Johnson's criticism is only decisive, of course, if the nature of the union Paul conceptualizes between Christ and his people is essentially representational (federal). This thesis has been challenged in the foregoing pages with the assertion that Paul in fact understands the nature of this union in "realistic" ways (vital, organic, personal), even as it includes a representational aspect. To maintain the Christ/Adam parallel I have argued that the union between Adam and his progeny be viewed in similarly realistic categories.

Paul's realistic account of the nature of union with Christ is at bottom inscrutable—it is a mystery exceeding rational bounds—and so does not solve the metaphysical/ontological ambiguities present in classic realism.[50] However, Paul's conception of the union is so intimate and personal that it is surely exceeds mere representationalism. By extending Paul's "in Christ realism" to the Adamic union, the important insights of federalism and realism are maintained, the weaknesses avoided, and the inevitable inscrutability is honored. Three principal conclusions result from this study. First, the legal guilt of Adam's primal sin is imputed to his posterity because all have really sinned in Adam by virtue of a real participation in him. Because we truly participate in him and so truly participate in his sin, Adam's guilt is also regarded as ours (forensically imputed). Adam's sin is both *aliena peccatum* and *proprium* peccatum—the sin of Adam and our sin—and so it is reckoned to us. This parallels the imputation of Christ's righteousness where by virtue of our union with him we *participate* in an *aliena iustitia* and so are regarded as righteous (forensic imputation)—we are justified "in Christ."[51] The weakness in federalism—the problem of legal fiction and of God's jus-

50. Attempts to fortify classic realist accounts may go some way in strengthening the case I have presented here, from a metaphysical point of view. For an introductory account of how this might look see Crisp, "Scholastic Theology," 17–28 , and his forthcoming book, *An Essay on Original Sin.*

51. Or, as Calvin famously put it in (Calvin, *Institutes*, 3.11.10: "Therefore, that joining together of Head and members, that indwelling of Christ in our hearts—in short, that mystical union—are accorded by us the highest degree of importance, so that Christ, having been made ours, makes us sharers with him in the gifts with which he has been endowed. We do not, therefore, contemplate him outside ourselves from afar in order that his righteousness may be imputed to us but because we put on Christ and are engrafted into his body—in short, because he deigns to make us one with him. For this reason, we glory that we have fellowship of righteousness with him."

tice—is handled because God is perfectly just in imputing sin to those who *really* share in it. Meanwhile, the representational element in federalism is maintained with this view: we are in union with Adam our representative head. Secondly, Adam's sinful, polluted nature is transmitted to his posterity because all are vitally, organically, personally, inscrutably united to him. This is a different aspect of the same union by which we are declared legally guilty in Adam. This parallels that aspect of union with Christ by which his people are morally renewed unto newness and holiness of life. This aspect of union with Christ is not to be thought of as a discrete, "mystical" union, but rather an *aspect* of the singular, comprehensive union with Christ. This understanding avoids the artificiality of positing multiple unions—federal and natural—to account for the legal and moral implications of original sin. Finally, this understanding bypasses the confusing construction among federalists who maintain that legal guilt and moral pollution are causally related. A forensic imputation of guilt can no more cause moral degradation than a forensic imputation of righteousness can cause moral renovation. Just as justification and sanctification are two distinct but inseparable consequences of union with Christ (the righteous *and* holy One), so guilt and pollution are similarly distinct but inseparable consequences of union with Adam (the unrighteous *and* depraved one).

Our relation to both Christ and Adam remains at bottom a mystery, and as such this proposal is subject to the inevitable complexities and ambiguities included in any attempt to unfold this mystery. The conclusions reached here, which incorporate many of the emphases of evangelical Calvinism, rest on the supposition that Paul's understanding of the nature of our union with Christ is closer to realism than federalism without being reduced to either, and that the benefits of this understanding when applied to the transmission of original sin provide a way to unify the insights of both positions without rashly or unnecessarily succumbing to either legal extrinsicism or metaphysical abstrusity.

# BIBLIOGRAPHY

Badcock, Gary. "The Church as 'Sacrament.'" In *The Community of the Word: Toward an Evangelical Ecclesiology*, 188–200. Edited by Mark Husbands and Daniel J. Treier. Downers Grove, IL: InterVarsity, 2005.

Berkhof, L. *Systematic Theology.* Grand Rapids: Eerdmans, 1996.

Berkouwer, Gerritt C. *Sin*, Studies in Dogmatics Series. Grand Rapids: Eerdmans, 1971.

Billings, J. Todd. "John Calvin's Soteriology: On the Multifaceted "Sum" of the Gospel." *International Journal of Systematic Theology* 11 (2009) 428–47.

Blocher, Henri. *Original Sin: Illuminating the Riddle.* Downers Grove, IL: InterVarsity, 1997.

Calvin, John. *Calvin's Commentaries.* 22 Vols. Calvin Translation Society (Edinburgh, 1844–56) Grand Rapids: Baker, 2003.

Calvin, John. *Institutes of the Christian Religion*, 2 vols. Library of Christian Classics 20–21. Edited by John T. McNeil. Translated by Ford Lewis Battles. Philadelphia: Westminster, 1960.

Carson, D. A. "The Vindication of Imputation: On Fields of Discourse and Semantic Fields." In *Justification: What's at Stake in the Current Debates*, 446–78. Edited by Mark Husbands and Daniel J. Treier. Downers Grove, IL: InterVarsity, 2004.

Crisp, Oliver. *An Essay on Original Sin.* Oxford: Oxford University Press, 2011.

———. "Federalism vs Realism: Charles Hodge, Augustus Strong and William Shedd on the Imputation of Sin." *International Journal of Systematic Theology* 8 (2006) 55–71.

———. "Original Sin and Atonement." In *Oxford Handbook of Philosophical Theology*, 430–51. Edited by T. P. Flint and M. C. Rea. Oxford: Oxford University Press, 2009.

———. "Scholastic Theology, Augustinian Realism and Original Guilt." *European Journal of Theology* 13 (2004) 17–28.

———. "The Theological Pedigree of Jonathan Edwards's Doctrine of Imputation." *Scottish Journal of Theology* 56 (2003) 308–27.

Demarest, Bruce. *The Cross and Salvation.* Wheaton, Crossway, 1997.

Dunn, James D. G. *Romans.* Word Biblical Commentary. Vol. 38a. Dallas: Word Books, 1988.

———. *The Theology of Paul the Apostle.* Grand Rapids: Eerdmans, 1998.

Evans, William B. *Imputation and Impartation: Union with Christ in American Reformed Theology.* Eugene, OR: Wipf & Stock, 2009.

Gaffin, Jr., Richard B. *Resurrection and Redemption: A Study in Paul's Soteriology.* Philipsburg: P. & R., 1987.

———. "Union with Christ: Some Biblical and Theological Reflections," in *Always Reforming: Explorations in Systematic Theology*, 271–88. Edited by A. T. B. McGowan. Downers Grove, IL: InterVarsity, 2006.

Horton, Michael S. *Covenant and Salvation: Union with Christ.* Louisville: Westminster John Knox, 2007.

Garcia, Mark. *Life in Christ: Union with Christ and Twofold Grace in Calvin's Theology.* Eugene, OR: Wipf & Stock, 2008.

Hoekema, Anthony. *Created in God's Image.* Grand Rapids: Eerdmans, 1986.

Johnson, Marcus. "Luther and Calvin on Union with Christ." *Fides et Historia* 39 (2007) 59–77.

Johnson, S. Lewis "Romans 5:12—An Exercise in Exegesis and Theology." In *New Dimensions in New Testament Study*, 298–316.Grand Rapids: Zondervan, 1974.

Lillback, Peter A. "Calvin's Development of the Doctrine of Forensic Justification: Calvin and the Early Lutherans on the Relationship of Justification and Renewal." In *Justified in Christ: God's Plan for us in Justification*, 51–80. Edited by Scott K. Oliphint. Great Britain: Mentor, 2007.

Longnecker, Richard. *Galatians*. Word Biblical Commentary. Vol. 41. Dallas: Word Books, 1990.

Moo, Douglas J. *The Epistle to the Romans*. NICNT Grand Rapids: Eerdmans, 1996.

Murray, John. "The Imputation of Adam's Sin." *Westminster Theological Journal* 19 (1956) 146–62.

Reid, J. K. S. *Our Life in Christ*. Philadelphia: Westminster Press, 1963.

Reymond, Robert. *A New Systematic Theology of the Christian Faith*. Nashville: Thomas Nelson, 1998.

Robinson, John A. T. *The Body; A Study in Pauline Theology*. Philadelphia: Westminster, 1952.

Shedd W. G. T. *Dogmatic Theology*. 3 vols. Nashville: Thomas Nelson, 1980.

Smedes, Lewis. *Union with Christ: A Biblical View of the New Life in Jesus Christ*. Grand Rapids: Eerdmans, 1983.

Strong, Augustus H. *Systematic Theology*. Valley Forge: Judson Press, 1976.

Thiselton, Anthony. *The Hermeneutics of Doctrine*. Grand Rapids: Eerdmans, 2007.

Tipton, Lane. "Union with Christ and Justification." In *Justified in Christ: God's Plan for us in Justification*, 23–50. Edited by Scott K. Oliphint. Great Britain: Mentor, 2007.

# 9

# "The Highest Degree of Importance"

## Union with Christ and Soteriology

MARCUS JOHNSON

First, we must understand that as long as Christ remains outside
of us, and we are separated from him, all that he has suffered and
done for the salvation of the human race remains useless and of
no value to us. Therefore, to share in what he has received from
the Father, he had to become ours and to dwell within us . . . for,
as I have said, all that he possesses is nothing to us until we grow
into one body with him.

—Calvin, *Institutes*.[1]

Through union with Jesus Christ the church shares in his life
and in all that he has done for mankind. Through his birth its
members have a new birth and are made members of the new
humanity. Through his obedient life and death their sins are forgiven and they are clothed with a new righteousness. Through
his resurrection and triumph over the powers of darkness they
are freed from the dominion of evil and are made one body with
him . . . Thus the church finds its life and being not in itself but in
Jesus Christ alone, for not only is he the head of the church but
he includes the church within his own fullness

—T. F. Torrance, *Atonement*.[2]

1. Calvin, *Institutes*, Book 3, chapter 1, paragraph 1 (hereafter Calvin, *Inst.*, 3.1.1).
2. Torrance, *Atonement*, 361.

THE AIM OF THIS chapter is a biblically-faithful soteriology rooted in the Evangelical and Reformed/Calvinian tradition. To use theological jargon, this chapter is about applied soteriology or, as Calvin had it phrased more eloquently, "The way in which we receive the grace of Christ: what benefits come to us from it, and what effects follow." This phrase is from the title of Book 3 of his *Institutes*, the subject of which we have come to refer to as the application of salvation, or the application of the redemptive person and work of Christ. Calvin insists at this pivotal point in the *Institutes* that we cannot benefit from the redemptive work of Christ (the subject of Book 2) unless we are "engrafted into him," or "grow into one body with him," that is, unless we are united to Jesus Christ. By virtue of this union, which is appropriated through Spirit-wrought faith, Christ himself and all his benefits accrue to the Church, his body.

The recognition that union with Christ does indeed exist at the core of Calvin's applied soteriology has been fortified by a number of recent publications, chief among them in terms of influence may be Charles Partee's *The Theology of John Calvin*, in which union with Christ provides the organizing outline.[3] Due in large measure to Calvin's influence, union with Christ has played a central role in Reformed soteriology for centuries after him, ostensibly at least. W.B. Evans has ably demonstrated not only the ubiquity and significance of the theme in Reformed soteriology, but also the ambiguity in speaking of the 'centrality' of union with Christ in the Reformed tradition. Given the changes in both emphasis and formulation that the theme of union with Christ underwent after Calvin, to speak of the centrality of union with Christ ". . . is at best a formal statement. There is no single Reformed doctrine of union with Christ."[4] The changes that Evans documents—in particular what he calls the "bipolar soteriology" that came to fruition in nineteenth and twentieth century Calvinism—essentially eclipsed the theme of union with Christ, at least as Calvin had formulated it.[5] Richard Gaffin, Jr. maintains that Post-Reformation theology, despite its laudable theologi-

3. Partee, *The Theology of John Calvin*. For other recent publications, see Billings, "John Calvin's Soteriology"; Garcia, *Life in Christ*; Garcia, "Imputation as Attribution"; Gaffin, "Union with Christ"; Johnson, "New or Nuanced Perspective on Calvin?"; Johnson, "Luther and Calvin on Union with Christ"; and Evans, *Imputation*.

4. Evans, *Imputation*, 259.

5. Ibid., 260.

cal advances, represents a shading of Calvin's soteriology that has been overly preoccupied with the benefits of Christ at the expense of his person. "In concentrating on the various benefits of Christ's work or on one particular benefit, like justification, he, in his person and work, recedes into the background."[6] At the turn of the twentieth century, Augustus H. Strong was lamenting the dearth of the theme of union with Christ: "The majority of printed systems of doctrine, however, contain no chapter or section on Union with Christ, and the majority of Christians much more frequently think of Christ as a Savior outside of them, than as a Savior who dwells within."[7]

In the course of articulating an evangelical, Calvinian soteriology with the theme of union with Christ at the center, Calvin will prove to be an invaluable guide. His engagement with the theme is rich, vibrant and expansive. There is an important, if sometimes overlooked, reason for this: Calvin was faithfully expounding a central theme in the Scriptures, particularly in the writings of Paul and John. The fact that we find union with Christ pervading Calvin's writings is simply an indication of the prevalence of the theme in the Bible itself. For instance, Paul's use of union/incorporation language—by some estimates, over two hundred occurrences[8]—may have prompted the assertion from James S. Stewart, "The heart of Paul's religion is union with Christ. This, more than any other conception . . . is the key which unlocks the secrets of his soul."[9] This is to say nothing of the participation and incorporation language so regnant in the Johannine corpus.[10] Thus, to say that Calvin had a rich and pervasive understanding of union with Christ that lies at the heart of his soteriology may be saying nothing more than that the New Testament was the material from which Calvin drew. Despite some who caution otherwise, it seems safe to insist that Calvin did indeed have a "doctrine of union with Christ," and that it was central to his soteriology,

6. Gaffin, "Union with Christ," 280.

7. Strong, Systematic Theology, 795.

8. Demarest, The Cross and Salvation, 313, counts two hundred sixteen such occurrences in Paul, another twenty-six in John. Dunn, The Theology of Paul the Apostle, 390–92, details Paul's "participation in Christ" language. See also, Reid, Our Life in Christ, 12. Reid refers to the important work of Adolf Deismann, Die Neutestamntliche Formel "in ChristoJesu," who counts at least 164 occurrences of such language in Paul alone.

9. Stewart, Man in Christ, 147.

10. See Thiselton, The Hermeneutics of Doctrine, 354.

just as it was for many of those who shaped his thought.[11] Besides the Apostolic writings, Calvin was surely influenced by the Church Fathers on this point,[12] and his writing echoes a theme that resounded from the pulpit and pen of his predecessor in the Reformation, Martin Luther.[13] Calvin's extensive presence in this chapter owes itself both to his authoritative position in the Reformed and evangelical tradition and to his particularly insightful articulation of the biblical theme for which this chapter is titled. It is hoped that a retrieval of his insights will prove significant for contemporary soteriological expression.

The contention of this essay—integral to Evangelical Calvinism—is that union with Christ is indeed central and determinative for understanding salvation and its application. One might even say that union with Christ "unites" salvation in such a way as to allow the work and person of Christ to cohere; extolling the benefits of Christ's work without ever losing sight of the one in whom those benefits inhere. Union with the person of Jesus Christ is necessary *in order* to benefit from the work of Christ in salvation. Christ does not merely *perform* the atonement, "Christ Jesus IS the atonement."[14] The assertion that there is no participation in the benefits of Christ unless one participates in the person of Christ himself is a safeguard against what may be called the "objectification" of salvation. There is a danger in turning the saving gifts of Christ, such as justification and sanctification (and many besides!) into lovely abstractions that exist independently of, and so can be received independently of, the Gift-Giver. This all-too-common soteriological construal runs the risk of de-personalizing the gospel, neglecting the necessary union with the One who is himself "our righteousness and sanctification and redemption" (1 Cor 1:30). The offer of the gospel, the

11. As Richard Muller writes, "The point is, simply, that there are both useful and fundamentally misleading ways in which to examine Calvin's doctrine . . ."Muller, *The Unaccommodated Calvin*, 5. I take it that recognizing the centrality of union with Christ is useful and is by no means a "dogmatic accommodation" of Calvin, nor is it meant to suggest a central dogma approach.

12. Billings, "Calvin's Soteriology," 436–37. "[F]or a second-generation theologian like Calvin, the question was not whether to have a broadly Augustinian theology of 'union with Christ,' but what *kind* of theology of union with Christ" (ibid., 431). Donald Fairbairn's *Life in the Trinity* makes a good case, albeit unintentionally, that Calvin was indeed a student of the Church Fathers on this point. Also see Lane, *John Calvin: Student of the Church Fathers*.

13. Johnson, "Union with Christ in Luther and Calvin."

14. Torrance, *Atonement*, 94.

sheer mystery and wonder of it, is surely not less than "Christ in you, the hope of glory" (Col 1:27).

> *For this is the design of the gospel, that Christ may become ours, and that we may be ingrafted into his body.* Now when the Father gives him to us in possession, he also communicates himself to us in him; and hence arises participation in every benefit.[15]

Does any benefit of salvation—eternal life, forgiveness, holiness, resurrection, divine familial status, the church—exist apart from Jesus Christ and therefore apart from union with him? The aim of this chapter is to explore why the answer to the question is *no*, and why that answer is important, beautiful and compelling. The first section is an exploration of the nature of our union with Christ suggesting that our conception of that union is significant for our resulting conception of Christ's saving benefits. Two sections follow which treat the *duplex gratia* which flows from Christ, namely justification and sanctification: the forensic and transformative benefits of Christ. Each is set in the context of union with Christ and the significance of this is demonstrated. A final section with some brief concluding theological implications regarding adoption, the Lord's Supper, and the body of Christ conclude the chapter.

## THE NATURE OF OUR UNION WITH CHRIST

> ". . . For we are members of his body. 'For this reason a man will leave his mother and father and be united to his wife, and the two will become one flesh.' This is a profound mystery—but I am talking about Christ and the church." (Eph 5:30–32)

The *mysterion* of the one-flesh union between Christ and his body, the church, was a subject of great soteriological import for Calvin. The attempt to plumb the depths of this mystery was for him nothing less than explicating the gospel, precisely because the essence of the gospel offer is Christ himself, into whom we are ingrafted[16] through faith. Thus a pas-

---

15. Calvin, *Calvin's Commentaries*, 1 Cor 1:9. Hereafter, Calvin, *Comm*. Calvin might well have endorsed Melanchthon's famous dictum "To know Christ is to know his benefits." Melanchthon, *Loci Communes Theologici*, 21. However, the context of Melanchthon's phrase suggests he is speaking of proper cognitive knowledge of the gospel, whereas Calvin's point in this passage and countless others is "To be really *united* to Christ is to enjoy his benefits."

16. The terms "ingrafting" and "engrafting" are to be understood as synonymous when Calvin is being quoted (reflecting the English translations). Otherwise, "ingrafting" will be the preferred usage.

sage like Ephesians 5:30–32, quoted above, was for Calvin a substantive depiction of salvation. This did not mean, however, that the nature of this soteriological union was self-evident.[17] The fact that Paul refers to the union between Christ and his body as a "profound mystery" sets a divine limit on its ultimate explicability, but this did not mean for Calvin that the Apostolic witnesses left no room to articulate aspects of the saving mystery. He did this by defining union with Christ as (i) occurring through the instrument of divinely-wrought faith; (ii) being made efficacious through the presence and power of the Holy Spirit; (iii) an actual and true participation in the very person of Jesus Christ himself.

i) *United to Christ through Faith.* Protestant theology is often marked by its allegiance to the *solas* of the Reformation, of which *sola fide* is perhaps especially prominent. The Reformers and their progeny have insisted that salvation is received "by faith alone" in Christ, rejecting the spurious introduction of good works, holiness or even love alongside faith as the means to salvation. In classic Protestant doctrine, faith—confident trust in the mercy of God in Christ Jesus—is considered saving (or justifying), and is not to be confused with personal merit or holiness. To use Heiko Oberman's phrasing, Luther had replaced the medieval formulation *fides charitata formata* with *fides Christo formata*,[18] demonstrating that one is declared righteous by faith alone on account of Christ, not on account of the (love-infused) quality of one's faith. *Sola fide* has ever since strongly characterized Protestant soteriology. There are, however, important and neglected questions that attend this hallmark of Protestant doctrine. For instance: What is it *about* faith that makes it saving? What lies underneath the assertion of the sufficiency of *sola fide* for salvation? After all, could not even the Protestant conception of faith be construed as a virtuous exercise in religiosity that meets the condition of salvation? Could faith itself not be considered a good work?

17. I use the phrase "soteriological union" in part to distinguish this from what may be called the "incarnational" union, or the union Christ has with all humanity by virtue of his taking on flesh. T. F. Torrance used the phrases "carnal" and "Spiritual" to refer to these distinguishable, yet not independent, unions. See Myk Habets, "The Doctrine of Election in Evangelical Calvinism," 338–39. For a very interesting exchange between Calvin and Peter Martyr Vermigli on this issue, see Gorham, *Gleanings of a Few Scattered Ears,* 340–44. Also see Johnson, "Eating by Believing: Union with Christ in the Soteriology of John Calvin," 31ff., 197–99. I refer the reader to Jason Goroncy's chapter in this volume for a fuller discussion.

18. Oberman, "'Iustitia Christi' and 'Iustitia Dei,'" 20.

Faith, Luther and Calvin maintained, is called "saving" not because of some intrinsic power or merit, but because of the object to which faith is directed: Jesus Christ. Thus it is not, properly speaking, *faith* which saves, but rather *Christ* who saves, and he through faith. The power of faith lies in its object. Faith, as Luther had it, was as the unadorned ring which encloses Christ the gem.[19] For Calvin, faith was as an empty pot, filled by the treasure who is Christ.[20] For neither was this way of speaking mere affectionate feeling or religious sentimentality. Faith is saving precisely because through the instrumentality of faith one is united to the Christ who is believed. Luther, for instance, wrote of the way that faith "grasps" and "possesses" Christ and makes him present. In his justly famous treatise, *The Freedom of a Christian*, he wrote of the way that faith unites the soul to Christ as bride to bridegroom, so that all that is Christ's becomes ours.[21] Faith must be more than an historical acknowledgment or a mere principle of holiness; it must really accomplish intimacy with the Savior.

> But faith must be taught correctly, namely, that by it you are so cemented to Christ that He and you are as one person, which cannot be separated but remains attached to Him forever and declares: "I am as Christ." And Christ, in turn, says: "I am as the sinner who is attached to me and I to him. For by faith we are joined together into one flesh and bone." Thus Eph. 5:30 says: "We are members of the body of Christ, of his flesh and bones," in such a way that faith couples Christ and me more intimately than a husband is coupled to his wife.[22]

Calvin echoes Luther on this point in his commentary on Ephesians 3:17.

> What a remarkable commendation is here bestowed on faith, that, by means of it, the Son of God becomes our own, and "makes his abode with us!" By faith we not only acknowledge that Christ suffered and rose from the dead on our account, but, accepting the offers which makes of himself, we possess and enjoy him as our Saviour.

---

19. Luther, *Luther's Works*, 26:89–90, 132, 134. Hereafter, Luther, *LW*.
20. Calvin, *Inst.*, 3.11.7.
21. Luther, *LW* 31:351. See also Luther, *LW* 26:88–90, 132, 172, 177.
22. Luther, *LW*, 26:168.

Faith certainly includes knowledge of, consent to, and trust in, God's mercy *pro nobis* in Christ, and in the efficacy of his death and resurrection. Yet, faith is not saving *because* it believes, but because of what this faith *receives*:

> Where (Christ) has shone, we possess him by faith, and, therefore, we also enter into the possession of life; and this is the reason why the knowledge of him is truly and justly called saving, or bringing salvation.[23]

Especially enlightening on this point is a disagreement Calvin had with the Zurich Reformer Ulrich Zwingli's interpretation of the "bread of life" discourse in John 6, a passage which has indeed proved exceptionally "hard teaching" in Jesus' time and beyond. Calvin contended that Zwingli's interpretation of these passages suffered from dangerous reductionism which led to an obscuring of the gospel. On Zwingli's interpretation, Jesus' words "whoever feeds on my flesh and drinks my blood has eternal life," are best explained by simply *identifying or equating* eating and drinking with faith; thus, Jesus meant *no more* than to invite people to believe. For Calvin, this passage was not about faith *per se*, but about the result of faith.

> Those who infer from this passage that to eat Christ is faith, and nothing else, reason inconclusively. I readily acknowledge that there is no other way in which we eat Christ than by believing; *but the eating is the effect and fruit of faith rather than faith itself.* For faith does not look at Christ only as at a distance, but embraces him, that he may become ours and may dwell in us. It causes us to be incorporated with him, to have life in common with him, and, in short, to become one with him. It is therefore true that by faith alone we eat Christ, provided we also understand in what manner faith unites us to him.[24]

Calvin sensed the danger that the gospel may be obscured in any attempt to reduce "eating and drinking" terminology to mere allusions

23. Calvin, *Comm.*, John 17:3. "Now, what is our purpose in discussing faith? Is it not that we may grasp the way of salvation? But how can there be saving faith except in so far as it engrafts us into the body of Christ?" Calvin, *Inst.*, 3.2.30. See also Calvin, *Comm.*, Luke 8:11; John 6:29; 3:16; 1:12: Hebrews 5:1; Galatians 2:20, and Calvin, *Inst.*, 3.2.6, 13, 16, 24, 35; 4.17.5.

24. Calvin, *Comm.*, John 6:35 (emphasis added). That Calvin is referring to Zwingli here is made clear in Calvin, *Inst.*, 4.17.5. See Zwingli, *Commentary on True and False Religion*.

or invitations to human faith. If Christ meant nothing more in these words than a veiled reference to one's faith activity, if Jesus Christ is not truly present in his saving person though faith, then whence salvation? Saving intimacy with Christ is not the same thing as faith; our saving union with him is the *result of faith*.[25] The genuine insight here, of Johannine and Pauline pedigree,[26] is that while faith is surely saving, faith is not salvation; Christ is salvation. Faith should never be separated from salvation in Christ, but faith surely needs to be distinguished from the Christ whom faith receives. The pastoral significance of this notion is enormous given that assurance of salvation is not focused on the quality of one's faith, but the quality of the One given to faith. Believers may be encouraged that their true faith, however weak and imperfect, is not the measure of their salvation; Jesus Christ is. Thus, the logic of the Reformation *sola fide* is preserved not by "saved by faith alone," but "saved in Christ through faith alone."

ii) *United to Christ by the Spirit*. The stalwart Princeton theologian B. B. Warfield famously dubbed Calvin "the theologian of the Holy Spirit" in honor of his robust pneumatology.[27] The truth of this moniker is evident in Calvin's doctrine of union with Christ. Having noted above that this union occurs through faith, we must expound the role of the Holy Spirit who looms large both in the scriptural accounts and in Calvin's. In numerous biblical passages there is a close identification of the presence of the Spirit and the presence of Christ (e.g., Rom 8; John 14, 16; 1 Cor 6; Gal 4; 1 John), and this did not escape Calvin's attention. In the first chapter of Book III of the *Institutes*, he refers to the Spirit as "the bond by which Christ effectually unites us to himself." The Spirit is that bond both in the sense that through the grace and power of the Spirit that we are made Christ's members, and because this is accomplished through Spirit-wrought faith. Faith "is the principal work of the Holy Spirit," through whom the promise in Christ is "revealed to our minds and sealed upon our hearts."[28] Through faith, as we have seen, Christ becomes ours.

25. Calvin, *Comm*, Ephesians 3:17.

26. Cf., Gal 2:20, 3:26–27; Eph 1:13; 2 Cor 13:5; Col 2:12; John 1:12; 6:32ff., 17:21, 26. Ridderbos, *Paul: An Outline of His Theology*, 232–33.

27. Warfield, *Calvin and Augustine*, 484–85; See Hesselink, *Calvin's First Catechism*, 177–87.

28. Calvin, *Inst.*, 3.1.3, 4; 3.2.7.

François Wendel, Calvin's eminent biographer, claimed that Calvin's understanding of this union was a "purely spiritual one," a phrase which is unfortunate because misleading.[29] To say that Calvin thought of the believer's union with Christ as "spiritual" is accurate only with appropriate qualifications. If the term "spiritual" is taken to mean that the union between believer and Christ lacks a specific, essential reality, and can be reduced to ethereal and mystical notions wholly beyond intelligibility, then the term is not helpful.[30] Calvin certainly thought of the union as a mystery beyond our ultimate powers of explanation, but this did not preclude him from pursuing serious theological reflection on the matter. Further, if by the term "spiritual" it is meant that the union in view is solely that between the believer and the third person of the Trinity, abstracted from Jesus Christ, then the term is again unhelpful. The purpose of Christ in sending the Spirit is not so that we may have a surrogate for an absent Christ, but that we may have the actual presence of Christ (through the Spirit). The Spirit is thus the *manner* or *mode* of Christ's dwelling in us. "When Christ says, I will come to you, he shows *in what manner* he dwells in his people, and *in what manner* he fills all things. It is by the power of his Spirit."[31]

In his characteristic insistence on the inseparability between Word and Spirit, Calvin wished to avoid two equally intolerable views: the first is the view that the Spirit comes to erect a new kingdom—*extra Christum*; the second is that the Spirit functions as the successor to Christ's kingship. The office of the Spirit is to glorify and communicate Christ. The Spirit is always accompanied by the Word (Jesus Christ) and the Spirit conveys nothing less, or other than, Jesus Christ and his benefits.

> Nothing, therefore, is bestowed on us by the Spirit apart from Christ, but he takes it from Christ, that he may communicate it to us . . . for he does not enlighten us to draw us away in the smallest degree from Christ . . . In a word, the Spirit enriches us

29. Wendel, *Calvin,* 238. See Partee, *The Theology of John Calvin,* 200–208.

30. Calvin only employs the phrase *unio mystica* twice in the *Institutes*. He preferred by far more concrete terms such as "en/ingrafting (*insitio*)," "communion (*communio*)," and "participation (*participes*)." See the helpful appendix of terms Calvin employed in Tamburello, *Union with Christ,* 111–13. "Although Calvin calls it so, it is not, in the technical sense of the term, a mystical union," Wendel, *Calvin,* 237.

31. *Comm., John* 14:18 (emphasis added). See Calvin, *Comm., Rom* 8:10.

with no other than the riches of Christ, that he may display his glory in all things.[32]

As Calvin even writes elsewhere, it is *Christ* who unites us to himself and he does this by the power of the Spirit.[33] For Christ is the fountain of salvific blessings for us, and it is to him that we must be joined. Union with Christ is *Spiritual* in the sense that believers are united to the Savior through the power of the Spirit and Spirit-wrought faith.

> Christ, then, is the source of all blessings to us; from him we obtain all things; but Christ himself, with all his blessings, is communicated to us by the Spirit. For it is by faith that we receive Christ, and have the graces applied to us. The Author of faith is the Spirit.[34]

iii) *True and actual participation in Christ himself.* What does it mean to say that believers are truly and actually united to Christ? To answer this we must move beyond what may be called the "instrumentality" (faith) and "efficacy/agency" (Spirit) of union with Christ and on to the *essentia* of the union. Here we must face the more difficult and mysterious question, What is the reality or substance of this communication—in what *sense* do we commune with Christ? This point needs to be pursued due to its significance for what follows in this chapter; the *essence/reality* of this union bears considerably on how one construes the *benefits* of the union (e.g., justification and sanctification).

Calvin believed that the constitutive nature of the gospel was the offer of Christ himself.[35] If faith did not engraft us into Christ it would be nothing more than a meaningless religious abstraction. And if the Spirit did not engraft us into Christ then the Spirit's soteriological function would evaporate. The purpose and aim of faith, the Spirit, and the gospel, is to communicate Jesus Christ. Calvin even thought that the language used to convey this truth was important. For example, he faulted Erasmus at least twice for failing in his New Testament translation to capture the essence of Paul's thought on this matter. Erasmus had

32. *Comm.*, John 16:14.

33. See Calvin, *Inst.*, 3.1.1-4; Calvin, *Comm.*, Rom 8:4.

34. Calvin, *Comm.*, 1 Cor 6:11.

35. "For this is the design of the gospel, that Christ may become ours, and that we may be ingrafted into his body," Calvin, *Comm.*, 1 Cor 1:9. Cf., *Inst.*, 3.1.4; 3.2.6; 3.5.5; 3.11.1; Calvin, *Comm.*, John 3:16.

translated Romans 6:11 with the phrase "through Christ Jesus" rather than "in Christ Jesus." This translation failed, Calvin protested, to express the force of our grafting into Christ by which we become one.[36] To say that salvation is "through" or "by" or "because of" Christ may convey a truth that is rather imprecise. If the intended meaning of these terms is that Christ accomplished salvation on our behalf then the terms can be useful (e.g., one can be saved from drowning "by" the work a lifeguard does). If, however, the terms end up conveying the message that salvation is something Christ secures for our enjoyment outside of participation in his very person, then the terms are misleading (e.g., one can be saved from drowning "by" a lifeguard without being "ingrafted" into the lifeguard).

Similarly, neither is the gospel to be thought of as merely the offer of the benefits of Christ's redemptive accomplishments apart from the Redeemer. There is no enjoyment of the fruits of salvation apart from a union with the fruit-bearer. We only experience forgiveness, resurrection, adoption, holiness and every other blessing in so far as we are made members of Christ's body. After all, how do we know we have redemption unless we know we have Christ himself?

> For the promises offer him, not for us to halt in the appearance and bare knowledge alone, but to enjoy true participation in him. And indeed, I do not see how anyone can trust that he has redemption and righteousness in the cross of Christ, and life in his death, unless he relies chiefly upon a true participation in Christ himself. *For those benefits would not come to us unless Christ first made himself ours.*[37]

This best explains Calvin's characteristic phrasing, "Christ with all his benefits," "Christ clothed with his gospel," etc. Christ is not a distant Savior who transmits or imputes redemptive benefits from a distance. "For we await salvation from him not because he appears to us afar off, but because he makes us, ingrafted into his body, participants not only in all his benefits but also in himself."[38] Perhaps a way of stating this truth is that however much we may, and should, adore the accomplished work of Christ in history (e.g., his obedient life, his suffering on our

---

36. Calvin, *Comm.*, Romans 6:11; Cf., Calvin, *Comm.*, 1 Cor 1:5, 9.

37. Calvin, *Inst.*, 4.17.11 (emphasis added). Cf., Calvin, *Comm.*, Rom 3:24.

38. Calvin, *Inst.*, 3.2.24. Cf., ibid, 3.1.1; 3.3.19.

behalf, his resurrection, his ascension), our salvation and assurance lie in the very present reality of the indwelling Jesus Christ.

Calvin went to some length to clarify that the union believers have with Christ is much more than "virtual."[39] While the union includes the experience of faith, the indwelling of the Spirit, and the benefits of Christ, it cannot be reduced to any or all of these. The language Calvin used to describe the intimacy of the union simply does not allow for such a soteriologically minimalistic reading. He was adamant that participation in Christ meant a true partaking of the vital flesh and blood of the incarnate, risen Christ. In the incarnation, the eternal life-giving Word of the Father took on human flesh and endowed it with life-giving power and all the heavenly gifts of the Father so that we may participate in the "inexhaustible fountain" of his flesh.[40] Calvin's comments on John 6 and Ephesians 5 are sufficient to demonstrate this point. We have already noted Calvin's aversion to the under-interpretation of Jesus' enigmatic words in John 6 ("unless you eat the flesh of the Son of man, and drink his blood"), eschewing the overly-simplistic notion that these words could be reduced to the mere act of faith. He also refused to circumscribe these words as a reference to Eucharistic reception of Christ: "For this discourse does not relate to the Lord's Supper, but to the uninterrupted communication *of the flesh of Christ*, which we obtain *apart* from the use of the Lord's Supper"; "It is certain, then, that (Jesus) now speaks of the *perpetual and ordinary* manner of eating the flesh of Christ, which is done by faith only."[41] To participate in the life-giving Christ requires that we partake of his flesh and blood, and this eating and drinking is done "ordinarily" *outside* of the Supper, and is represented *by* the Supper. A similar sentiment occurs in his comments on Ephesians 5:31.

> As Eve was formed out of the substance of her husband, and thus was part of himself; so, if we are true members of Christ, we share his substance, and by this intercourse unite into one body. In short, Paul describes our union with Christ, a symbol and pledge of which is given to us in the ordinance of the supper . . . All depends on this, that the wife was formed of the flesh and bones of her husband. Such is the union between us and Christ, who in some sort makes us partakers of his substance. 'We are

---

39. I am indebted to Evans, *Imputation*, for this helpful term.

40. Calvin, *Inst.*, 4.17.8, 9; Calvin, *Comm.*, John 6:51.

41. Calvin, *Comm.*, John 6: 53, 54 (emphasis added).

bone of his bone, and flesh of his flesh," (Gen: 2:23); not because like ourselves he has a human nature, but because by the power of the Spirit, he makes us part of his body, so that from him we derive our life.

Notice again that the union by which we are partakers of Christ's "substance," united into one body with Christ "flesh and bone," is not first accomplished in the Supper but though the Spirit and extra-Eucharistically. Notice also that Calvin differentiates between the nature we share with Christ by virtue of his taking on flesh (common humanity), and the intercourse we have with him and his flesh by the Spirit (saving union). Calvin goes on to write that he is "overwhelmed by the depth of this mystery," satisfied to affirm the reality of the mystery even if he cannot fully comprehend it.

A further note is in order regarding Calvin's use of "substance" language in describing the intimacy of participation in Christ. Wendel asserts that Calvin grew cautious about the use of this term after his debate with Osiander,[42] but this is not accurate. He continued to use the term in Eucharistic and non-Eucharistic contexts throughout the length of his career, no doubt aware of the provocative import of the language given the state of the Eucharistic debates. Calvin felt at liberty to use the word once certain "absurdities" were put aside, in order to express the fact that the true flesh and blood of Christ are the reality in salvation and therefore Supper.[43] W. B. Evans has convincingly argued that while it is true that Calvin firmly denied a substantial communion with Christ in the sense of a divine-human mixture of essences (e.g., versus Osiander), he is equally firm that participation in Christ is substantial in the sense that it includes the "very life of Christ." Thus, while he is not employing the term in a modern, philosophically critical fashion, it is still accurate to say that Calvin is indeed making an "ontological" statement. Evans rightly concludes that Calvin's doctrine of union with Christ "affirms nothing less than the reception by the believer of the substance, of the very being, of the incarnate Christ. This union is the *impartation* of the

---

42. Wendel, *Calvin*, 236–37.

43. Calvin, *Inst.*, 4.17.19. On Calvin's use of *substantia*, see Johnson, "Eating as Believing," 93–110, in which section I refer to Calvin's debate with Heshusius and Calvin's defense of the term in *The Clear Explanation of Sound Doctrine Concerning the True Partaking of the Flesh and Blood of Christ in the Holy Supper, to Dissipate the Mists of Tilemann Heshusius*, in Calvin, *Theological Treatises*.

risen Christ to the believer, albeit in a manner which does not diminish the personal individuality of both Christ and the individual believer."[44]

A final historical occurrence deserves mention here in order to bring out the significance of this present section for what follows. In 1846 John Williamson Nevin, the noted Reformed theologian and co-founder (with Philip Schaff) of the Mercersburg Theology, formulated an articulate defense of Calvin's applied soteriology centered on the theme of union with Christ. In *The Mystical Presence: A Vindication of the Reformed or Calvinistic Doctrine of the Holy Eucharist*, Nevin sought to show that nineteenth century American Protestantism had departed from the Reformed Eucharistic doctrine of the sixteenth century and moved toward Zwingli's symbolic memorialism. Central to Nevin's thesis is that this departure assailed the heart of Reformed soteriology (Calvin's view in particular): a real, substantial, essential union with Christ. In this, Nevin had understood Calvin well and had also understood clearly the implications for Reformed soteriology.

> Any theory of the Eucharist will be found to accord closely with the view that is taken, at the same time of the nature of the union generally between Christ and his people. Whatever the life of the believer may be as a whole in this relation, it must determine the form of his communion with the Saviour in the sacrament of the Supper, as the central representation of its significance and power.[45]

In a scathing 1848 review of Nevin's book, the eminent Princeton theologian Charles Hodge offered a rebuttal in which, most importantly, Hodge dismissed *Calvin's* Eucharistic views as an "uncongenial foreign element" in Reformed doctrine. Hodge went on to accuse Nevin of abandoning Reformed soteriology and of jeopardizing the doctrine of justification with his understanding of union with Christ.[46] Apparently, Hodge was unaware that in rejecting Calvin's view of the Eucharistic presence of Christ, he was at the same time rejecting Calvin's view of union with Christ more generally. Nevertheless Hodge, and other Reformed theo-

---

44. Evans, *Imputation*, 28–29. Cf., Willis, "Calvin's Use of *Substantia*," 289–301. On the possibility of a Reformed notion of Theosis, see Habets, "Theosis, Yes; Deification, No," 124–49.

45. Nevin, *The Mystical Presence*, 54.

46. Hodge, "Doctrine of the Reformed Church on the Lord's Supper," 251, 273. For a helpful overview, see Mathison, *Given for You*, 136–56.

logians who rejected Calvin's Eucharistic views,[47] seemed to notice no inconsistency here, given their professed allegiance to Reformation soteriology. The inconsistency arises in the realization that Calvin's understanding of union with Christ is simply integral to his understanding of justification.

## THE BENEFITS OF OUR UNION WITH CHRIST: JUSTIFICATION

> "It is because of (God) that you are in Christ Jesus, who has become for us wisdom from God—that is, our righteousness, holiness and redemption." (1 Cor 1:30)

> "Therefore, there is now no condemnation for those who are in Christ Jesus . . ."(Rom 8:1)

For many scholars of Reformation theology Calvin's assertion that the doctrine of justification is "the main hinge on which religion turns" goes side by side with Luther's "article by which the church stands or falls" as an indication of the programmatic and theological significance of the article of justification for the Protestant movement. One may even say, with good reason, that justification, as it was articulated and defended by Luther and Calvin (*et al.*) was the *sine qua non* of Evangelical, Protestant theology. J. I. Packer goes as far as to say of the *Institutes* that "justification by faith is central . . . both theologically and spatially," and that justification is the "framing notion" of the great work.[48] Without going as far as Packer, it is still essential to affirm with him that justification was critically important for Calvin and, indeed, ought to remain so for contemporary Reformed and Evangelical theological expression. Our hesitation at Packer's statement has to do not with his pointing out the significance of the doctrine in Calvin but rather with the claim of theological centrality. The previous pages, I trust, have been an ample demonstration of Calvin's belief that none of the benefits of Christ become ours outside of our being incorporated into him. One of these benefits—perhaps the chief benefit—is justification. Justification, as with every other benefit of salvation, only becomes ours as we are ingrafted

47. Evans, *Imputation*, 225, cites the Presbyterian theologian Robert L. Dabney and the Scottish federalist William Cunningham as two distinguished theologians in the Reformed tradition who abandoned Calvin's views on the Supper.

48. Packer, "Foreword," xii.

into Christ by faith; which certainly qualifies as a kind of soteriological priority in Calvin's thinking. The following pages seek to describe the relation between justification and union with Christ and to "flesh out" (pun intended!) the implications for justification more generally, thus "avoiding the enormous error of explaining Calvin's doctrine of justification by forensic imputation alone and apart from union with Christ."[49]

Calvin's doctrine of justification, like Luther's before him, functioned within a theology of union with Christ inherited from a broadly Augustinian tradition. As Billings points out, the question for Calvin was not whether he should have a theology of union with Christ or of justification, but rather what *kind* of theology of both.[50] Perhaps even more clearly than Luther, Calvin rooted justification in the believer's participation in Christ.[51] Justification was by no means, for Calvin, a merely extrinsic affair or transaction involving an abstraction referred to as "the righteousness of Christ." The righteousness of Christ inheres the person of Christ; it is *his* righteousness and has no independent existence outside of him, as if it could alone be the subject of justification. To be justified means to be justified *in Christ*, that is, to be ingrafted into the person of Christ and only then to share in his righteousness.

> Therefore, that joining together of Head and members, that indwelling of Christ in our hearts—in short, that mystical union— are accorded by us the highest degree of importance, so that Christ, having been made ours, makes us sharers with him in the gifts with which he has been endowed. We do not, therefore, contemplate him outside ourselves from afar in order that his righteousness may be imputed to us but because we put on Christ and are engrafted into his body—in short, because he deigns to make us one with him. For this reason, we glory that we have fellowship of righteousness with him.[52]

Calvin refers to union with Christ as having the "highest degree of importance"—perhaps the secure foundation on which the hinge rests?—if justification is to be properly understood. If we seek to be justified, it will do us no good if we are detached from the One who is righteous. To "share" in Christ's righteousness, to have "fellowship

49. Partee, *The Theology of John Calvin*, 223.

50. Billings, "John Calvin's Soteriology," 431.

51. See Johnson, "Luther and Calvin on Union with Christ," 59–77.

52. Calvin, *Inst.*, 3.11.10.

of righteousness" with him, requires that we are ingrafted into him; an ingrafting of the most intimate sort. There are dozens of passages in Calvin's writings which should suffice to demonstrate that justification is a grace of salvation that happens *by virtue of* being united to Christ through faith.[53] In fact even the phrase "justifying faith" may be misleading if it is taken to mean that faith is worthy of justification. "For in what way does true faith justify save when it binds us to Christ so that, made one with him, we may enjoy participation in his righteousness?"[54] *Sola fide* needs to be qualified by *sola Christi* (in this case, "in Christ alone"). Calvin's language here may strike some as puzzling or problematic given the way the doctrine of justification is sometimes described: the forensic imputation to the believer of the alien righteousness of Christ *extra nos*. Calvin's understanding of justification is most certainly forensic and imputative,[55] but this hardly means for him a merely extrinsic affair. The declaration that the believer is in the right is based on the righteousness of Christ imputed to the believer—and the "precondition" of this declaration/imputation is union with Christ. Justification is therefore first and foremost forensic, and it stems from a participation in Christ's person. Calvin maintains here what many heirs of the Reformation have sometimes found more difficult to maintain: the grounding of the forensic in the participatory. A forensic justification, it is assumed, cannot be made to depend upon a prior relation obtaining between Christ and believer. To use terminology that crystallized after Calvin's time, justification must be "immediate" as to its mode, taking into account no prior condition or state of the believer. But, as Calvin had it, justification is a forensic declaration involving the *imputation* of the righteousness of Christ, *mediated* through a personal and intimate union with Christ.[56] The insistence, shared by Luther and Calvin, that the righteousness by which we are justified is *extra nos* and *aliena* (it is *in Christ*) was never intended to mean that Christ himself is "alien" to us or that justifica-

53. Cf., Calvin, *Inst.*, 3.11.21, 23; 3.13.5; 3.15.6; 3.16.1; 3.17.8; Calvin, *Comm.*, Rom 5:17; 2 Cor 5:21.

54. Calvin, *Inst.*, 3.11.23. Cf., ibid, 3.11.7; Calvin, *Comm.*, Rom 3:22.

55. Calvin, *Inst.*, 3.11.2: "Therefore, we explain justification simply as the acceptance with which God receives us into his favor as righteous men. And we say that it consists in the remission of sins and the imputation of Christ's righteousness."

56. As Evans shows, Calvin's view of the soteriological imputation of the righteousness of Christ conforms to neither of the views which came to be characterized as "mediate" and "immediate." Evans, *Imputation*, 32–37.

tion occurs "outside" of a participation in him. The forensic, imputative character of justification is meant to highlight the crucial point that the justifying verdict is not based on any quality of righteousness intrinsic to the believer. The righteousness is properly Christ's, and it is the only basis for imputation. At the same time, believers come to "share" in this righteousness and have "fellowship of righteousness" in union with him. As Gaffin puts it, "The basic *unio-duplex gratia* structure of Calvin's applied soteriology is such that the participatory (union) has both forensic (justifying) and non-forensic (sanctifying, renovative) dimensions or aspects, without any confusion or interpenetration of these two aspects."[57]

Importantly, Calvin's construal of justification preserved the forensic character of justification while it simultaneously effectively refuted the accusation emerging from Rome that the Reformation doctrine amounted to little more than a "legal fiction": God declaring sinners righteous when in point of fact they are not. On Calvin's construal, however, the sinner enters by faith into an actual union with Christ and so truly participates or shares in the righteousness of another. The righteousness of Christ, intrinsic to his person by reason of his fleshly active and passive obedience, is now shared with those truly united to him. In this nuanced and qualified sense, God declares of the believer what is in fact true by virtue of the real unity between Christ and believer. Imputation, on this view, is not a transfer of an abstract quality of Christ to a disassociated sinner. Imputation is the accounting (reckoning, regarding) of the sinner as righteous precisely because she is in union with Christ and is thus a participant in *his* righteousness. Imputation preserves the forensic character of justification, ensuring that the declaration has to do with a righteousness that "resides solely in Christ." Gaffin is worth quoting on this point.

> This Spirit-worked union or bond, however, does not exclude imputation or make it somehow redundant. Rather, on its forensic side, union is a "fellowship of righteousness," and it is that by imputation. "We do not, therefore, contemplate him outside ourselves from afar in order that his righteousness may be imputed to us." Here Christ's righteousness imputed is alien or other in the sense that it is his doing, his obedience, not ours. But in another sense, in union with him, it is not alien at all. Union

---

57. Gaffin, "Justification and Union with Christ," 262.

brings justification as a forensic fellowship, a sharing in Christ's righteousness, and it does so by imputation.[58]

Some of Calvin's Reformed heirs have found his interplay of the forensic and participatory puzzling and even contradictory and have treaded divergent paths. Bruce McCormack finds Calvin's doctrine of justification incompatible with his teaching on union with Christ. On McCormack's reading, Calvin has made regeneration (which McCormack equates with union) the root of justification and so has blurred what is forensic about justification. Remarkably, McCormack's complaint about Calvin mirrors Calvin's complaint about his opponent Osiander: the grounding of justification in the transformation of the sinner.[59] On a different reading of Calvin, Michael Horton claims that Calvin bases union with Christ upon justification. "Forensic justification through faith alone is the fountain of union with Christ in all of its renewing aspects."[60] Both authors seem to adopt a more typically Lutheran position, making justification the basis for sanctification, possibly because they have equated union with Christ with one or the other benefit. This Calvin did not do. Union with Christ *includes* justification and *includes* sanctification, but it is not equated with either. This soteriological union is the causal priority of both the forensic and transformative; that is, the incarnate Christ is the source of both justification and sanctification. Or, as Calvin wrote in his opening paragraph on justification in the *Institutes*:

---

58. Ibid., 265.

59. McCormack, "What's at Stake in Current Debates over Justification?" 101–2. It appears that McCormack conceives of union with Christ as largely an ethical relation, perhaps equated with regeneration. In this way, he has collapsed union with Christ into sanctification. McCormack's correction of Calvin is to render imputation itself transformative, a construal which seems to compromise the purely forensic character of justification, and ironically align McCormack closer to Osiander than to Calvin.

60. Horton, *Covenant and Salvation: Union with Christ*, 143. Elsewhere, Horton refers to justification as the "forensic basis" of union with Christ and as "the Word which creates a "living union" between Christ and believer (138–39). I find Horton baffling on this point. At points he clearly quotes Calvin to the effect that union with Christ is the basis for justification and sanctification, and at others he refers to justification as the basis of union. The two possibilities I see are that Horton has equated union with sanctification/regeneration (as McCormack), or that he is positing two unions, a forensic and a transformative. Horton's follows the same line in his recent *The Christian Faith*, 588–99, 610–11, 649, 676.

Christ was given to us by God's generosity, to be grasped and possessed by us in faith. *By partaking of him,* we principally receive a double grace: namely, that being reconciled to God through Christ's blamelessness, we may have in heaven instead of a Judge a gracious Father; and, secondly, that sanctified by Christ's spirit we may cultivate blamelessness and purity of life.[61]

## THE BENEFITS OF UNION WITH CHRIST: SANCTIFICATION

"Do you not know that all of us who have been baptized into Christ Jesus were baptized into his death? We were buried therefore with him by baptism into death, in order that, just as Christ was raised from the dead by the glory of the Father, we too might walk in newness of life." (Rom 6: 3–4)

"We always carry around in our body the death of Jesus, so that the life of Jesus may also be revealed in our body." (2 Cor 4:10)

Union with Christ is not just another way of talking about sanctification, or vice versa; sanctification is an *effect* of being united to Christ, the sanctified One. Just as justification is not in ourselves but in Christ, so sanctification is also in Christ and is no merely human possibility. It is just as much of an "enormous error" to attempt to explain Calvin's doctrine of sanctification apart from union with Christ as it is his doctrine of justification. Calvin defined repentance (sanctification) as a genuine turning of our life to God in earnest fear of Him that consists of two parts: mortification and vivification.[62] Mortification is the destruction of the evil inclinations of the fallen flesh, and vivification the newness of life that inclines one toward true righteousness. Calvin's remark about these components of sanctification is crucial:

Both things [mortification and vivification] happen to us by participation in Christ. For if we truly partake in his death, "our old man is crucified by his power, and the body of sin perishes" (Rom. 6:6), that the corruption of the original nature may no longer thrive. If we share in his resurrection, through it we are

61. Calvin, *Inst.,* 3.11.1 (emphasis added).
62. Calvin, *Inst.,* 3.3.5.

raised up into newness of life to correspond with the righteousness of God.[63]

Notice that Calvin wrote of sanctification as taking place through
partaking in "his death" and "his resurrection," indicating that the death
and life *of Christ* are the fulcrum of the sanctified life. The mortification
and vivification that constitute sanctification are first of all accomplished
in Christ's death and resurrection. It is *his* death and resurrection that are
realized in the Christian life. Christ's death is the power of the Christian's
mortification, and Christ's resurrection is the power of her vivification.
Sanctification is thus a product of being untied to Christ in his death
and resurrection. Calvin will have nothing to do with reducing Paul's
language in Romans 6 to moral exhortation to imitate Christ. Christ's
death and resurrection are more than merely morally exemplary; they
are *themselves* efficacious in sanctifying those joined to Christ (again,
much more than a "virtual" union). Indeed, baptism, as Paul shows, is a
clear sign that we have been ingrafted into Christ's death and resurrection that we might feel their "efficacy" in sanctifying us.[64]

A Christian's participation in Christ's death and resurrection extends beyond bondage and freedom from sin, however. It also includes
conformity to the image of Christ in the bearing of one's cross. Dying
with Christ means a fellowship of suffering, and rising with Christ
means fellowship in blessedness. "We must all therefore be prepared
for this—that our whole life shall represent nothing else than the image of death, until it produce death itself, as the life of Christ is nothing
other than a prelude of death. We enjoy, however, in the meantime, this
consolation—that the end is everlasting blessedness. For the death of
Christ is connected with the resurrection."[65] Here, Calvin was expressly
concerned with the tribulations, trials, and miseries that, because they
characterized the life of Christ, also characterize the lives of those who
participate in him. Just as Christ endured the misery of the cross and

---

63. Calvin, *Inst.*, 3.3.9.

64. Calvin, *Inst.*, 4.15.5. Cf. Calvin, *Inst.*, 2.16.7, 13; Calvin, *Comms.* Rom 6:3–6;
1 Pet 2:24; 4:1; Gal 5:24; John 16:14. I suggest that the "crucicentrism" that so rightly
characterizes evangelicalism should be extended beyond justification and in the direction also of sanctification, in the interests of avoiding the circumscription of Christ's
death. Biblically, the efficacy of Christ's death is not limited to justification. The effects of this soteriological extension might also serve to curb both extremes latent in
Reformed and evangelical thought: moralism and antinomianism.

65. Calvin, *Comm.*, Phil 3:10. Cf. Calvin, *Comm.*, 2 Cor 4:10.

death so that he might be resurrected, those ingrafted into him endure affliction and death that they may have newness of life. This mortification of the "outward" man is what Calvin often called the "bearing of the cross," or fellowship with the suffering of Christ. "As, therefore, Christ has suffered once in his own person, so he suffers daily in his members, and in this way, there are filled up those sufferings which the Father hath appointed for his body by his decree."[66] In sum, union with Christ includes an ingrafting into his death and resurrection through which the believer, by the power of the Spirit, experiences the efficacy of Christ in sanctification: (i) death to the sinful nature, (ii) newness of life, and (iii) conformity to Christ through suffering unto resurrection.

How does Calvin then relate sanctification to justification? Calvin makes it abundantly clear that all those who are united to him through faith receive the *duplex gratia* of Christ Jesus. The two-fold grace is both sanctification and justification, which he possesses in himself.

> Although we may distinguish between them [justification and sanctification], Christ contains both of them *inseparably in himself*. Do you wish, then, to attain righteousness in Christ? You must first possess Christ; but you cannot possess him without being made partaker in his sanctification, because *he cannot be divided into pieces* . . . Since, therefore, it is *solely by expending himself* that the Lord gives us these benefits to enjoy, he bestows both of them at the same time, the one never without the other. Thus it is clear how we are justified not without works yet not through works, since in our sharing in Christ, which justifies us, sanctification is just as much included as righteousness.[67]

As Evans rightly argues, Calvin is not asserting that these benefits are inseparable because they are concomitant in the economy of salvation, but because they are both communicated through union with the mediatorial person of Christ himself (by the power of the Spirit).[68] Christ himself is the "everlasting and indissoluble tie" who unites free justification and holiness of life.[69] So adamant is Calvin on this point that he refers to any attempt to sever these benefits from each other as

66. Calvin, *Comm.*, Col 1:24. Cf. Calvin, *Comm.*, Rom 8: 29–20; *Inst.*, 3.5.4; 3.8.1. For an excellent article on this point see Zachman, "Deny Yourself and Take up Your Cross," 466–82.

67. Calvin, *Inst.*, 3.16.1 (emphasis and parentheses added).

68. Evans, *Imputation*, 34.

69. Calvin, *Comm.*, 1 Cor 1:30.

"tearing Christ into pieces," an especially graphic way of insisting that Christ does not bestow either benefit without first bestowing himself.[70] Thus, while these benefits need to be distinguished—to confuse them obscures the utter liberality of grace—they must never be separated, for that would be to impair the integrity of the gospel.[71] In Partee's memorable phrase, "Refusing to separate these fraternal, but not identical, twins is crucial for understanding Calvin."[72] Justification and sanctification are received simultaneously because one is united to the *whole* Christ. Justification does not precede or cause sanctification, nor does sanctification precede or cause justification; the indwelling Christ is himself the cause and source of both.

The fact that Calvin placed his primary locus on sanctification before that of justification in the *Institutes* has caused consternation among many of his interpreters. Was this move not a transgression of the material principle of Reformation doctrine? Interestingly, Calvin made perfectly clear that he might very well have begun with either justification or sanctification—after all, they are simultaneous consequences of possessing Christ in faith[73]—and thus his decision cannot be explained away as a mere concession to Rome, as if Calvin would have sacrificed soteriological coherence in order to prove a point. Calvin began with sanctification for partly polemical reasons to be sure, but his soteriology made this move perfectly coherent.[74] To borrow Calvin's own illustration: the sun (Son) is the source of both heat (sanctification) and light (justification), and one could begin describing the sun with either of its benefits. Most of Calvin's Reformed and evangelical heirs have not followed his lead, privileging light over heat in theological formulation (as most systematic theology texts demonstrate). This divergence is relatively unproblematic as long as justification is located in Christ and does not overshadow its radiant counterpart.[75] The change is transparently

70. Ibid.; cf. Calvin, *Comm.*, Rom 8:9, 13; Calvin, *Inst.*, 3.16.1.

71. Calvin, *Comm.*, Isaiah 59:20; Acts 5:31; Col 1:22; Rom 8:2; Calvin, *Inst.*, 3.11.6; 3.11.11.

72. Partee, *Theology of John Calvin*, 209.

73. Calvin, *Inst.*, 3.3.1.

74. Partee, *Theology of Calvin*, 211, makes the wise assertion that these categories may be better understood as confessional as opposed to logical if we are to understand Calvin.

75. Gaffin rightly notes that because sanctification is a life-long process it may be said to "follow" justification in a sense. "But this is not the same thing as saying, what

problematic, however, when justification is construed as the source or
cause of sanctification thus rendering justification (or imputation) itself
transformative.[76] This type of construal appears to jeopardize the fundamental insight of the Reformation regarding justification: "to be justified
means something different from being made new creatures." Calvin had
censured Osiander on this very point, accusing him of confusing the
light of the Son with his heat, transferring the "peculiar qualities of the
one to the other."[77] Justification is, by Protestant definition, a forensic
declaration of the sinner's status and is not to be confused with the sinner's growing purity of life. Put straightforwardly, justification does not
*make* anyone righteous, and a doctrine of justification characterized
as such runs the danger of collapsing justification into sanctification,
rendering the centuries-long disagreement with Rome on this question
inexplicable.[78] I wonder if Alister McGrath's comment is instructive
here: "The (Western) church has chosen to subsume its discussion of
the reconciliation of man to God under the aegis of justification, thereby
giving the concept an emphasis quite absent from the New Testament."[79]
Is it possible that Protestant doctrine has placed too much weight to
bear on justification because it has not attended carefully enough to the
New Testament emphasis on the source of that justification (and every

---

Calvin does *not* say, that justification is the source of sanctification or causes sanctification." Gaffin, "Justification and Union with Christ," 256. Billings suggests a kind of
priority in the sense that sanctification in terms of gratitude is "profoundly dependent
upon the forensic declaration of justification," Billings, "John Calvin's Soteriology," 446.
I think Billings is right in this very specific sense (although I still do not know whether
this demands "logical" priority). Unfortunately, many believers see sanctification as
nothing more than a response of gratitude for justification, a position which obviously
does not reflect Calvin's view.

76. McCormack, "What's at Stake," 107-110; Horton, *Covenant and Salvation*,
136–52. One important difference is that McCormack attempts to correct Calvin's view
while Horton reads Calvin as supporting his own view that justification is the basis
for union with Christ and thus sanctification. On this, Horton appears to be following Louis Berkhof. Evans has argued persuasively that Berkhof is the culmination of a
trajectory in the Reformed tradition which had "bifurcated" the theme of union with
Christ as it was found in Calvin, resulting in "bipolar soteriology" that effectively rendered union with Christ superfluous. Evans, *Imputation*, passim but esp. 230–60.

77. Calvin, *Inst.*, 3.11.6.

78. See Garcia, "Imputation as Attribution," 422–23, who argues for a difference
between Reformed and Lutheran *theologies* of justification at exactly this point, despite
confessional consensus. See also Tipton, "Union with Christ and Justification," 34.

79. McGrath, *Iustitia Dei*, 2.

benefit besides)—our incorporation into Christ? An indication of this might be a striving to relate benefits to each other in terms of cause and effect (mechanically) rather than in terms of their location in the person of Christ (personally). "To be in Christ is to be in the one who has become for believers the crucified and resurrected embodiment of all saving benefits. Therefore, there are no benefits of the gospel apart from union with Christ."[80]

## CONCLUDING THEOLOGICAL REFLECTIONS

There are some further theological implications that can be derived from a soteriology in which union with Christ is the fundamental reality. The following are very brief reflections on three of these implications.[81]

(i) *Adoption*—"*But to all who did receive him, who believed in his name, he gave the right to become the children of God*" (John 1:12). In Protestant soteriology adoption has been the victim of under-emphasis and/or misinterpretation. Often it has suffered the same fate as sanctification; being subsumed under, or explained by, justification.[82] However, adoption seems to flow rather seamlessly not from justification but from union with Christ as yet another benefit of being united to Christ, who is of course the very Son of God and in whose Sonship we participate.[83] "Having been ingrafted into Christ by faith, we obtain the right of adoption, so as to be the sons of God. And, indeed, as he is the only-begotten Son of God, it is only in so far as we are members of him that this honor at all belongs to us."[84]

(ii) *The Church*—"*Now you are the body of Christ and individually members of it*" (1 Cor 12:27). A return to the theme of union with Christ as it is presented in the New Testament and in the Church Fathers and Reformers would certainly provide a rich ecclesiology lacking in much

---

80. Tipton. "Union with Christ and Justification," 34.

81. Baptism, incarnation, resurrection, glorification, the imputation of Adam's sin, and a theology of marriage seem to me as naturally derived from, or illuminated by, union with Christ.

82. Consider that Hoekema (*Saved by Grace*) and Demarest (*The Cross and Salvation*) both render adoption as a benefit of justification. See Burke, *Adopted into God's Family*, 23–29.

83. See Garner, "The First and Last Son," 276–79.

84. Calvin, *Comm.*, John 1:12.

modern western Christianity, mainstream evangelicalism in particular.[85] Incorporation into Christ is a pervasive biblical theme that harmonizes interpenetrating doctrines—Christology, soteriology and ecclesiology—that are often atomized in theological discussion. The tendency to privatize the faith experience (privileging the justification of the individual sinner) and to reduce the biblical "body of Christ" imagery to mere metaphor are among the factors that have led to a polarization of soteriology and ecclesiology, leaving little room to jointly confess with the historic Christian church—including the Reformers—*extra ecclesiam non salus*. The union with Christ motif allows us to heartily affirm the *solas* of the Reformation without reducing the church to an "accidental appendage" of the gospel;[86] indeed, we are saved precisely *by* inclusion into the body of Christ.

> That the church is the body of Christ means that it participates in him, draws it life and nature from him, sharing in all he has done for it and sharing in his very life as the incarnate Son of the Father . . . It is only through participating and sharing in Christ that the church is to be regarded as his body, as his image and likeness among humankind . . .[87]

iii) *The Lord's Supper—"The cup of blessing that we bless, is it not a participation in the blood of Christ? The bread which we break, is it not a participation in the body of Christ?"* (1 Cor 10:16). A robust, realistic theology of union with Christ would serve to clarify again—for a contemporary church increasingly unaware—the relationship between soteriology and sacramentology.[88] As we have seen, Calvin (and many before and after him) did not conceive of the Lord's Supper as abstracted from salvation; the sacred mystery of the Supper is knowledge of the sacred mystery of the gospel itself: union with Christ and his benefits. Eucharistic union

---

85. The rather thin ecclesiology of evangelicalism is being acknowledged and addressed in at least two recent works: Husbands and Treier, *The Community of the Word*; Harper and Metzger, *Exploring Ecclesiology*.

86. Badcock, "The Church as 'Sacrament,'" 199.

87. Torrance, *Atonement*, 363.

88. Nevin's quote above (n. 45) is worth recalling here. One's theology of the Eucharist is reflected in one's soteriology, and vice versa. The contemporary Evangelical church has largely abandoned the centrality of union with Christ for its soteriology, and has become dominated by a Zwinglian emphasis in its theory of the Eucharist. Probably these phenomena are mutually influential.

with Christ is the sign and seal of the soteriological union because it provides utter clarity about the nature of the gospel—the Supper *explains* the essence of salvation.[89] This elemental principle in Calvin's soteriology makes Charles Hodge's rejection of Calvin's Eucharistic views all the more perplexing. After all, for Calvin the Eucharistic union in which we truly partake of Christ's flesh and blood (through faith, by the Spirit) is of precisely the same nature as the saving union through which we are justified.

It is hoped that the foregoing account of soteriology—an approach central to Evangelical Calvinism—that is rooted in the expansive biblical theme of union with Christ, attested historically in the Church Fathers, and explicated here by way of the Reformation, will prove compelling and fruitful to the contemporary Reformed and Evangelical church rooted in these very sources.

89. See Davis, *The Clearest Promises of God*, 202: "How does Calvin explain this great mystery of union with Christ? By explaining the sacrament of the Eucharist. Thus, knowledge about the sacrament, which it is Calvin's purpose to disclose, leads to the sacrament serving its function as source of knowledge about union with Christ."

# BIBLIOGRAPHY

Badcock, Gary. "The Church as 'Sacrament.'" In *The Community of the Word: Toward an Evangelical Ecclesiology*, 188–200. Edited by Mark Husbands and Daniel J. Treier. Downers Grove, IL: InterVarsity, 2005.

Billings, Todd. "John Calvin's Soteriology: On the Multifaceted 'Sum' of the Gospel." *International Journal of Systematic Theology* 11 (2009) 428–47.

Burke, Trevor. *Adopted into God's Family*. Downers Grove, IL: InterVarsity, 2006.

Calvin, John. *Institutes of the Christian Religion*, 2 vols. Library of Christian Classics 20–21. Edited by John T. McNeil. Translated by Ford Lewis Battles. Philadelphia: Westminster, 1960.

———. *Calvin's Commentaries* (1844–56). Reprinted in 22 vols. Grand Rapids: Baker, 2003.

———. *Calvin: Theological Treatises*. Translated by J. K. S. Reid. Philadelphia: Westminster, 1954.

Davis, Thomas. *The Clearest Promises of God: The Development of Calvin's Eucharistic Teaching*. New York, AMS Press, 1995.

Demarest, Bruce. *The Cross and Salvation*. Wheaton, Crossway, 1997.

Dunn, James D. G. *The Theology of Paul the Apostle*. Grand Rapids: Eerdmans, 1998.

Evans, William B. *Imputation and Impartation: Union with Christ in American Reformed Theology*. Eugene, OR, Wipf & Stock, 2009.

Fairbairn, Donald. *Life in the Trinity: An Introduction to Theology with the Help of the Church Fathers*. Downers Grove, IL: InterVarsity, 2009.

Gaffin, Richard B. Jr. "Union with Christ: Some Biblical and Theological Reflections." In *Always Reforming: Explorations in Systematic Theology*, 271–88. Edited by A. T. B. McGowan. Downers Grove, IL: InterVarsity, 2006.

Garcia, Mark. *Life in Christ: Union with Christ and Twofold Grace in Calvin's Theology*. Milton Keynes: Paternoster, 2008.

———. "Imputation as Attribution: Union with Christ, Reification and Justification as Declarative Word." *International Journal of Systematic Theology* 11 (2009) 415–26.

Garner, David. "The First and Last Son: Christology and Sonship in Pauline Soteriology." In *Resurrection and Eschatology*, 255–79. Edited by Lane G. Tipton and Jeffrey C. Waddington. Philipsburg: P. & R., 2008.

Gorham, G. C. *Gleanings of a Few Scattered Ears*. London: Bell & Daldy, 1857.

Habets, Myk. "The Doctrine of Election in Evangelical Calvinism: T. F. Torrance as a Case Study." *Irish Theological Quarterly*, 73 (2008) 334–54.

———. "Theosis, Yes; Deification, No." In *The Spirit of Truth: Reading Scripture and Constructing Theology with the Holy Spirit*, 124–49. Edited by Myk Habets. Eugene, OR: Pickwick, 2010.

Hall, David W., and Peter A. Lillback, editors. *A Theological Guide to Calvin's Institutes*. Philipsburg: P. & R., 2008.

Harper, Brad, and Paul Metzger, editors. *Exploring Ecclesiology: An Evangelical and Ecumenical Introduction*. Grand Rapids: Brazos, 2009.

Hesselink, I. John. *Calvin's First Catechism: A Commentary*. Philadelphia: Westminster John Knox Press, 1997.

Hodge, Charles. "Doctrine of the Reformed Church on the Lord's Supper." *Biblical Repertory and Princeton Review* 20 (1848) 277–78.

Horton, Michael S. *The Christian Faith: A Systematic Theology for Pilgrims on the Way*. Grand Rapids: Zondervan, 2011.

———. *Covenant and Salvation: Union with Christ.* Louisville: Westminster John Knox, 2007.

Husbands, Mark, and Daniel J. Treier, editors. *The Community of the Word: Toward an Evangelical Ecclesiology.* Downers Grove, IL: InterVarsity, 2005.

Johnson, Marcus. "Eating by Believing: Union with Christ in the Soteriology of John Calvin." PhD diss., University of Toronto: St. Michaels, 2007.

———. "Luther and Calvin on Union with Christ." *Fides et Historia* 39 (2007) 59–77.

———. "New or Nuanced Perspective on Calvin?: A Reply to Thomas Wenger." *Journal of the Evangelical Theological Society* 51 (2008) 543–58.

Lane, Anthony N. S. *John Calvin: Student of the Church Fathers.* Grand Rapids: Baker, 1999.

Luther, Martin. *Luther's Works,* 55 vols. Edited by Jaroslav Pelikan. St. Louis: Concordia Publishing House, 1955–1975.

Mathison, Keith. *Given for You; Reclaiming Calvin's Doctrine of the Lord's Supper.* Philipsburg: P. & R., 2002.

McCormack, Bruce. "What's at Stake in Current Debates over Justification? The Crisis of Protestantism in the West." In *Justification: What's at Stake in the Current Debates,* 81–117. Edited by Mark Husbands and Daniel J. Treier. Downers Grove, IL: InterVarsity, 2004.

McGrath, Alister. *Iustitia Dei: A History of the Christian Doctrine of Justification.* Cambridge: Cambridge University Press, 2002.

Melanchthon, Philip. *Loci Communes Theologici* in *Melanchthon and Bucer.* Library of Christian Classics 19. Edited by Wilhelm Pauck. Philadelphia: Westminster Press, 1969.

Muller, Richard. *The Unaccommodated Calvin.* Oxford: Oxford University Press, 2009.

Nevin, John Williamson. *The Mystical Presence: A Vindication of the Reformed or Calvinistic Doctrine of the Holy Eucharist.* Vol. 20 of *American Religious Thought of the 18th and 19th Centuries.* New York: Garland, 1987.

Oberman, Heiko. "'Iustitia Christi' and Iustitia Dei': Luther and the Scholastic Doctrines of Justification," *Harvard Theological Review* 59 (1966) 1–26.

Packer, J.I. "Foreword." *A Theological Guide to Calvin's Institutes,* ix–xiv. Edited by David W. Hall and Peter A. Lillback. Philipsburg: P. & R., 2008.

Partee, Charles. *The Theology of John Calvin.* Louisville, Westminster John Knox, 2008.

Reid, J. K. S. *Our Life in Christ.* Philadelphia: Westminster Press, 1963.

Ridderbos, Herman. *Paul: An Outline of His Theology.* Grand Rapids: Eerdmans, 1975.

Stewart, James S. *Man in Christ.* Vancouver: Regent College, 2002.

Strong, Augustus Hopkins. *Systematic Theology.* Valley Forge: Judson Press, 1907.

Tamburello, Dennis. *Union with Christ: John Calvin and the Mysticism of St. Bernard.* Louisville, KY: Westminster John Knox, 1994.

Thiselton, Anthony. *The Hermeneutics of Doctrine.* Grand Rapids: Eerdmans, 2007.

Tipton, Lane. G. "Union with Christ and Justification." In *Justified in Christ: God's Plan for Us in Justification,* 23–49. Edited by K. Scott Oliphant. Fearn: Christian Focus Publishing, 2007.

Torrance, Thomas F. *Atonement: The Person and Work of Christ.* Edited by Robert T. Walker Downers Grove, IL: InterVarsity, 2009.

Warfield, Benjamin B. *Calvin and Augustine.* Philipsburg: Presbyterian and Reformed, 1980.

Wendel, François. *Calvin: Origins and Development of His Religious Thought.* Reprint, Grand Rapids: Baker, 2002.

Willis, David. "Calvin's Use of Substantia." In *Calvinus Ecclesiae Genevensis Custos,* 289–301. Edited by Wilhelm H. Neuser. New York: Peter Lang, 1984.

Zachman, Randall. "'Deny Yourself and Take up Your Cross': John Calvin on the Christian Life." *International Journal of Systematic Theology* 11 (2009) 466–82.

Zwingli, Ulrich. *Commentary on True and False Religion.* Durham, NC: Labyrinth Press, 1981.

# 10

## "*Tha mi a' toirt fainear dur gearan*"[1]

## J. McLeod Campbell and P. T. Forsyth on the Extent of Christ's Vicarious Ministry

JASON GORONCY

THE NOTION THAT IN the gracious act of election God enters into the very conflict that has erupted between God's own covenant faithfulness and the unfaithfulness of humanity as God's covenant partner (and there in full solidarity with humanity—standing with and among sinners—has borne human infidelity and recalcitrance to its deathly end in order to heal and restore humanity to participation through the *koinonia* of the Spirit in the eternal and triune life and love) lies at the very heart of the recovery of that stream of Reformed thought identified as "Evangelical Calvinism," and which has been most clearly articulated in recent decades in the work of T. F. and J. B. Torrance. With seemingly tireless energy, these two brothers (and many of their students) maintained the view that a bifurcation of streams emerged early on in Reformed thought, one which ran from John Calvin through John Knox, James Fraser of Brae, Robert Leighton, and the Marrow men, and found fresh articulation in the nineteenth century in a parish minister of the Kirk in Row on the Gareloch in Dunbartonshire; namely, John McLeod Campbell. This stream, in Torrance parlance, represents "Evangelical Calvinism." The other stream, associated with names such as Theodore Beza, William Perkins, John Owen, Thomas Watson, George and Patrick

1. Gaelic: "I note your objection."

253

Gillespie, and Samuel Rutherford, among others, represents, in Torrance parlance, "Federal Calvinism."

At the heart of so-called "Evangelical Calvinism" lies belief in the vicarious nature of Jesus Christ's ministry, i.e., that "Christ was anointed by the Spirit in our humanity to fulfil his ministry for us," or "on our behalf."[2] Among those who wish to highlight the ministry secured in and by Christ's vicarious humanity, however, there remains some debate over the extent to which Jesus' work "on our behalf" reaches, and the implications of such for human participation in that work by the Spirit. This essay shall attend to this debate, and will do so by bringing John McLeod Campbell into conversation with a compatriot of his—albeit of a later generation—the Aberdeenshire-born Congregationalist minister, Peter Taylor Forsyth.

## JOHN MCLEOD CAMPBELL (1800–1872) ON CHRIST'S VICARIOUS CONFESSION AND REPENTANCE

John McLeod Campbell's 1856 *magnum opus*, *The Nature of the Atonement*, is fundamentally an exploration of a notion introduced, but not followed up, by Jonathan Edwards. In his miscellaneous remarks on *Satisfaction for Sin*, Edwards, a theologian who writes "with the profundity and inventive élan that belong to only the very greatest thinkers,"[3] notes,

> [It] is requisite that God should punish all sin with infinite punishment; because all sin, as it is against God, is infinitely heinous, and has infinite demerit, is justly infinitely hateful to him, and so stirs up infinite abhorrence and indignation in him. Therefore, by what was before granted, it is requisite that God should punish it, *unless there be something in some measure to balance this desert; either some answerable repentance and sorrow for it, or some other compensation.*[4]

Campbell departs from the bulk of the tradition (and Edwards) and follows Edwards' second possibility (what Oliver Crisp coins "Edwardsian non-penal substitution"[5]) of an "answerable repentance

---

2. J. B. Torrance, "The Vicarious Humanity of Christ," 145.

3. Jenson, *America's Theologian*, 3.

4. Edwards, *Works*, 565. Italics mine.

5. Crisp, "Non-Penal Substitution," 415–33.

and sorrow," rather than punishment, in the atonement.[6] Theoretically, Edwards suggests, this equivalent sorrow and repentance would equally satisfy the demands of justice. Campbell transforms what for Edwards is hypothetical into the very voice of the gospel itself: "There would be more atoning worth," he writes, "in one tear of true and perfect sorrow which the memory of the past would awaken . . . than in endless ages of penal woe."[7] A. B. Bruce summarizes Campbell's position: "It is not necessary, in order to pardon, that the penalty of sin be endured, adequate confession of sin being an alternative method of satisfying the claims of divine holiness."[8]

While Western orthodoxy has mostly stressed the Godward side of the atonement, Campbell laid the weight on the creaturely side, following Anselm: "None therefore but God can make this reparation . . . Yet, none should make it save a man, otherwise man does not make amends."[9] Campbell recognized that an adequate repentance by those disabled by sin, while required, was morally impossible, and therefore if such were to be offered it would have to be by God, albeit from our side—that is, by God in fallen flesh.[10] This is because, Campbell argued, genuine repentance involves seeing the sin (and sinners) "with God's eyes,"[11] viewing broken humanity from within, feeling the deep sorrow

6. The notion was anticipated in the work of Westminster theologian Samuel Rutherford (1600–1661). See T. F. Torrance, *Scottish Theology*, 100, 305. It seems that Robert Paul's assessment was right: "By the middle of the nineteenth century the time was ripe for a complete revision of the doctrine [of atonement]" (Paul, *The Atonement and the Sacraments*, 140).

7. Campbell, *The Nature of the Atonement*, 124. Contrary to Stott's assessment, Campbell does not reject penal substitution, or all forensic elements in the atonement. Stott, *The Cross of Christ*, 142. While he recognises the reality of legal elements at work in the atonement, Campbell is critical of "penal sufferings," especially in those crude articulations which suggest that the Father was in any way punishing the Son. Such notions, he believes, distort the doctrine of God and drive a wedge between the unity of the Father and the Son in the atonement. See Thimell, "Christ in Our Place," 197–8; T. F. Torrance, *Scottish Theology*, 308–9. This debate finds fresh, and even less satisfactory, expression in Sölle's critique of Moltmann's doctrine of God. See Sölle, "Gott und das Leiden," 111–17.

8. Bruce, *The Humiliation of Christ*, 351.

9. Anselm, *Cur Deus Homo?* 66–67. Hart convincingly argues that the long-thought divergence between Anselm and Campbell is unjustified. Hart, "Anselm," 311–33.

10. Campbell, *The Nature of the Atonement*, 120.

11. Ibid., 107. Hart suggests that things which may seem trivial to us might be an unbearable burden and pain to one who has eyes to see and ears to hear. Hart, "Anselm," 329.

that sin creates and confessing the righteousness of God's judgment upon it. As R. C. Moberly recalls, sin "has blunted the self's capacity for entire hatred of sin, and has blunted it once for all."[12] Only one, therefore, who could see things *as they really are* could make an adequate confession both of God's righteousness and of human sin. Such confession is not made in order to avoid sin's consequences but precisely that sin's consequences may be embraced in all their dreadfulness, "meeting the cry of these sins for judgment, and the wrath due to them, absorbing and exhausting that divine wrath in that adequate confession and perfect response on the part of man."[13]

Genuine repentance and confession for "the sin of His brethren" would have to come from one who, as it were, stood on God's side in the human dock.[14] What was impossible for sinners was possible for this man who in the fullness of the hypostatic union penetrated into the depths of our humanity to see sin as God sees it, and to condemn sin as God condemns it, and yet do so from our side and as our head. That is, in "the High Priest of redeemed humanity"[15] such confession and condemnation of sin happened not only with "great sorrow" but *from the side of sin.* So Campbell: "This confession as to its nature, must have been *a perfect Amen in humanity to the judgment of God on the side of man.* Such an Amen was due in the truth of things. He who was the Truth could not be in humanity and not utter it—and it was necessarily a first step in dealing with the Father on our behalf. He who would intercede for us must begin with confessing our sins."[16]

Christ's "perfect Amen in humanity to the judgment of God" has value *for humanity* insofar as Christ, "spiritually speaking . . . *is* the hu-

---

12. Moberly, *Atonement*, 42. See Moberly, *Atonement*, 26–47; Tuttle, *So Rich a Soil*, 105–7.

13. Campbell, *Atonement*, 124. See also Campbell, *Sermons and Lectures* vol. 1, 70.

14. Campbell, *Atonement*, 118; cf. Forsyth, *The Cruciality of the Cross*, 213.

15. Campbell, *Fragments of Truth*, 15:176; cf. Redding, *Prayer*, 197–98; J. B. Torrance, *Worship, Community, and the Triune God of Grace*, 47–48.

16. Campbell, *Atonement*, 118. Inherent in this confession was the confession of God's holiness; Christ's suffering forming a "condition and form of holiness and love under the pressure of our sin and its consequent misery." Ibid., 107; cf. Lidgett, *The Spiritual Principle of the Atonement*, 172–73; Forsyth, *Work*, 150, 189; Karl Barth, *Church Dogmatics* IV/1, 258–59; Macquarrie, "John McLeod Campbell 1800–72," 266; Goroncy, "The Elusiveness, Loss, and Cruciality of Recovered Holiness," 195–209; Goroncy, "The Final Sanity is Complete Sanctity," 249–79.

man race, made sin for the race, and acting for it in a way so inclusively total, that all mortal confessions, repentances, sorrows, are fitly acted by him in our behalf. His divine Sonship in our humanity is charged in the offering thus to God of all which the guilty world itself should offer," as Horace Bushnell notes.[17] In offering that perfect response from the depths of humanity Christ "absorbs" the full realization of God's judgment against sin. Standing as God, Christ knows "a perfect sorrow" regarding sin. And, standing with no "personal consciousness of sin" but fully clad in fallen flesh,[18] Christ is able to offer "a perfect repentance" that is required from humanity's side offering that perfect "Amen" to God's mind concerning sin.[19] With this response—even in the midst of Calvary's darkness—God re-speaks those words first heard over Jordan's waters: "This is my beloved Son, in whom I am well pleased" (Matt 3:17).[20] And in response, humanity cries out "Our Father, hallowed be thy name" (Matt 6:9).[21]

But to conclude at this point is to misrepresent Campbell's position. His notion of Christ's representative repentance must also be conceived as that to be exercised with the full weight of the prospective goal of Christ's atonement—that those for whom Christ died might be enabled by the Spirit to participate in the confession and repentance of their elder brother, his repentance being "reproduced" in them.[22]

---

17. Bushnell, *Forgiveness and Law*, 30. Bushnell proceeds to criticise Campbell's view.

18. Campbell, *Atonement*, 118; cf. Stevenson, *God in Our Nature*, 153–91; Weinandy, *In the Likeness of Sinful Flesh*, 17–18; Schaff, ed., *Hilary of Poitiers, John of Damascus*, 44: "For He took upon Him the flesh in which we have sinned that by wearing our flesh He might forgive sins; a flesh which He shares with us by wearing it, not by sinning in it" (St. Hilary).

19. Campbell, *Atonement*, 118; cf. Van Dyk, *The Desire of Divine Love*, 55. It seems that Campbell may have gleaned this notion from his two close friends, Edward Irving and Thomas Erskine. The idea also finds some voice in Gregory of Nazianzus, John Calvin, John Owen, Jonathan Edwards, Karl Barth, Hans Urs von Balthasar, and Thomas Weinandy. See Erskine, *The Brazen Serpent*, 38; Hanna, ed., *Letters of Thomas Erskine*, 547–48; Irving, *The Collected Writings of Edward Irving*, vol. 5; Horrocks, *Laws of the Spiritual Order*, 187–92; Stevenson, *Campbell*, 187–89; Weinandy, *Does God Suffer?* 212.

20. See Tuttle, *Campbell*, 93–96.

21. See T. F. Torrance, *The Mediation of Christ*, 79; T. F. Torrance, *God and Rationality*, 143. I have argued elsewhere that such hallowing is a key motif for understanding Forsyth's entire corpus. See Goroncy, *Hallowed Be Thy Name*.

22. Campbell, *Atonement*, 142. See Calvin, *Institutes*, 3.1.1, 3.1.4. In Campbell's defense, retorts that suggest Campbell replaces a legal fiction with a moral one do

Motivated in no small part by what Campbell observes as the fruits of a high Calvinist commitment to the doctrine of limited atonement, of a doctrine of God in which justice (for all) is necessary while love and mercy (for the elect alone) are "arbitrary,"[23] and its attendant undermining of assurance,[24] Campbell was in no doubt that the notion of Christ's vicarious confession and repentance provided a more satisfactory witness to the divine atonement than did merely juridical views. Identified with a preaching tradition that conserved the priority of law before gospel, and made repentance logically prior to forgiveness, "deep in [the high Calvinist's] thinking was a doctrine of conditional grace."[25]

## P. T. FORSYTH'S (1848-1921) APPRECIATION OF CAMPBELL

Before proceeding to identify and discuss Forsyth's "one criticism" of Campbell, it behooves us to pause and highlight five areas where Forsyth is deeply indebted to Campbell, whom Alfred Cave named "That chaste, patient, and loving Spirit."[26]

1. Like Campbell, Forsyth rejects any logic or speculation about the atonement that would imply any wedge between the persons of the Trinity.

2. There is no sense in the atonement that God is punishing Jesus.

3. God's love is neither subservient to, nor dependent on, nor divorced from, God's righteousness (justice). Both provide the ground for human assurance, and both find clearest expression in the atonement where God acts lovingly to put things right. The atonement, therefore, does not change God's disposition towards humanity but rather reveals it and secures it in history.[27]

---

little justice to the subtlety of Campbell's thought. See Taylor, "The Best Books on the Atonement," 267; cf. Van Dyk, *Desire*, 113.

23. Campbell, *Atonement*, 73–76.

24. See Campbell, *Reminiscences and Reflections*, 24, 132.

25. J. B. Torrance, "Introduction," 3.

26. Cave, *The Scriptural Doctrine of Sacrifice*, 350. Forsyth's relationship to Campbell is a vexed one. While Forsyth's close friend and pupil, Sydney Cave, promotes the essential congruity of their staurology, Anglican clergyman John Kenneth Mozley seeks to distance the two thinkers. It may be, however, that Mozley is reading Campbell through Moberly.

27. As *Lux Mundi* stresses. See Lyttelton, "The Atonement," 275–312.

4. Both Forsyth and Campbell reject the doctrine of limited atonement. It was humanity that was united to Christ in the incarnation; it was neither a select group nor "an event in the individual's religious experience."[28]

5. While Forsyth lays more weight on the legal aspects of the atonement than does Campbell, both reject those staurologies which construe God's action in the cross as a legalistic (and mechanistic) outworking of the divine decrees in history. The primacy of the filial relation that Campbell champions does not need to be at the cost of the royal relationship, as Forsyth models. Like Campbell, Forsyth sought to not deny the judicial aspects of the atonement but to, in James Orr's words, "remove from it the hard legal aspect it is apt to assume when treated as a purely external fact, without regard to its inner spiritual content."[29] Neither Campbell nor Forsyth deny the atonement's reference to the vindication of divine Torah. Their concern, however, is to include alongside this vindication the atonement's prospective elements—that is, filiality. In so doing they posit divine justice as serving God's broader soteriological purposes, discarding any presumed antithesis between divine justice and love.

In 1909, Forsyth gave a series of talks at a ministers' study conference during which he declared "I hope you have read McLeod Campbell on the Atonement. Every minister ought to know that book, and know it well." Forsyth shares with Campbell's "great, fine, holy book"[30] the notion that the atonement includes a confessional, or penitential, element. Indeed, the cross is "the Great Confessional."[31] There are not a few pas-

28. Jinkins, *A Comparative Study*, 7.

29. Orr, *The Christian View of God and the World*, 341.

30. Forsyth, *The Work of Christ*, 148. Forsyth's work proceeds on the assumption that most of Campbell's work on the atonement is beyond debate. Certainly most of the points made by Forsyth in his essay on the atonement were made previously in one way or another by Campbell. The fact that many of Campbell's previously debated ideas were widely accepted by the turn of the century is evident in a series of articles on the atonement published in *The Christian World* during the winter of 1899–1900, later published as Godet, *et al.*, *The Atonement in Modern Religious Thought*, wherein Campbell's name is relied upon for support more often than any other.

31. Justyn Terry misconstrues when he writes: "It is unfortunate that Forsyth entitles one of his chapters in *The Work of Christ*, 'The Great Confessional' . . . with all its connotations of the confession of sin rather than the confession of holiness." Terry, *The Justifying Judgement of God*, 96; cf. Smail, *Once and For All*, 11–12.

sages in which Forsyth appears to offer unqualified agreement with Campbell. One example will suffice:

> The faith which [Christ] alone has power to wake is already of-
> fered to God in the offering of all His powers and of His finished
> work. That obedience of ours which Christ alone is able to create,
> is already set out in Him before God, implicit in that mighty and
> subduing holiness of His in which God is always well-pleased.
> All His obedience and holiness is not only fair and beloved of
> God, but it is also great with the penitent holiness of the race
> He sanctifies. Our faith is already present in His oblation. Our
> sanctification is already presented in our justification. Our re-
> pentance is already acting in His confession.[32]

## FORSYTH'S ONE OBJECTION

While Campbell's "positive doctrines found a broad measure of acceptance,"[33] and his approach "more 'objective' and coherent than his critics have allowed,"[34] identifying his "serious shortcomings" continued well beyond his lifetime.[35] The most serious concern concerned Campbell's notion of Christ's vicarious ministry. Forsyth's "one criticism," too, concerns Campbell's sponsoring the notion of Christ becoming humanity's "great confessor" before God.[36] With John Scott Lidgett and Horace Bushnell, Forsyth asks, "How could Christ in any real sense confess a sin, even a racial sin, with whose guilt He had nothing

32. Forsyth, *Work*, 193–94.

33. Tuttle, *Campbell*, 112. Tuttle identifies James Orr, R.W. Dale, John S. Lidgett, P. T. Forsyth, and James Denney as among the not-uncritical-but-largely-sympathetic readers of Campbell's work. See Tuttle, *Campbell*, 114–16). Orr and Dale are particularly uncomfortable with Campbell's notion of vicarious repentance. See Tuttle, *Campbell*, 127. Also Lidgett, *Spiritual Principle*, 171; Bushnell, *Forgiveness and Law*, 28–29. More recent interest is largely due to the work of the Torrances, and their students. See Torrance, *Rationality*, 145; Elmer M. Colyer, *How to Read T. F. Torrance*, 97–123.

34. Stevenson, *Campbell*, 272.

35. Lidgett, *Spiritual Principle*, 175. See Stevenson, *Campbell*, 8–15. Charles Gore, B. B. Warfield, John Stott, Vincent Taylor, R. S. Paul, and George Carey all accuse Campbell of evacuating any Anselm-like objective content from the atonement. See Hart, "Anselm," 314–15; Stott, *Cross*, 141–42; Paul, *Atonement*, 140–49; Carey, *The Gate of Glory*, 125–30. Others have considered Campbell a successor to Abelard, Socinus, and Schleiermacher. Bewkes, "John McLeod Campbell," 252; and Bewkes, *Legacy of a Christian Mind*, 220.

36. Campbell, *Sermons 2*, 28.238; cf. Stevenson, *Campbell*, 145–47.

in common?"[37] Campbell agrees that there is "this difference between Christ and us, that Christ, being perfectly holy had not personal sin to confess,"[38] but he does not share Forsyth's view that therefore Christ had "nothing in common" with humanity's guilt—so complete is God's identification with humanity in the incarnation.[39]

Forsyth maintains that Christ could not bear the guilt that only a sinner could bear. While we can, Forsyth says, speak of Christ's vicarious *obedience*, it is senseless to speak of vicarious *repentance*, for Christ had no personal guilt to confess: Christ bore the curse of guilt, rather than guilt itself. Forsyth argues that while our union with Christ is the source of our repentance, Christ could not repent for us. While guilt's sting was never Christ's (he could not know what it means to confess his own sin), he alone could enter and feel to its full force the awful atmosphere of guilt, effect its death and evoke and enable our repentance. "He saw sin as it appeared before God. Only one who sees it so can understand it."[40] While Christ alone could offer due recognition to wounded Torah, he could never know in his person the sense of affliction that attends the wounders. While the penalty and judgment could never be ours to bear, the repentance, Forsyth avers, is ours alone.[41]

It could be argued that the difference here between Forsyth and Campbell is one of emphasis rather than of substance, of accent rather than of theology itself. Where they do part company, however, is in the

37. Forsyth, *Work*, 148. "Here McLeod Campbell and Moberly seem to me to come short. They do not get their eye sufficiently away from the confession of sin." Forsyth, *Cruciality*, 206; Forsyth, *Work*, 149.

38. Campbell, *Sermons 2*, 28:238; cf. Lidgett, *Spiritual Principle*, 177–78; Bushnell, *Forgiveness and Law*, 28–32. Alfred Cave argues that as attractive as the doctrine of vicarious confession is, it remains foreign to Scripture. Cave, *Sacrifice*, 358–62.

39. The argument is hampered by a lack of precision or definition in Campbell's employment of the grammar of "vicarious repentance;" a phrase that he does not in fact employ at all. See Stevenson, *Campbell*, 55. It seems that what Campbell mostly has in mind is "confession" more than "repentance," the latter being subsumed under the former. See Campbell, *Atonement*, 119–20.

40. Forsyth, "The Paradox of Christ," 129.

41. Forsyth, "The Atonement in Modern Religious Thought," 76; cf. Seifrid, *Christ, Our Righteousness*, 178: "Faith in the Son is the one "work" which God demands of the human being." The complaint that the notion of a sinless Christ offering "repentance" vicariously is meaningless fails to appreciate that far from being a disqualification, it is precisely Christ's sinlessness that enables him to confess human sin and submit fully to its consequent judgement. It is worth noting here that Forsyth makes no reference in this context to the representative and substitutionary ministry of Israel's high priest.

contribution that *sinners* make to the confession of sin. While Campbell contends that Christ has fulfilled "whatever is necessary to consummate the perfect condemnation of sin,"[42] Forsyth maintains that if we are to take seriously the moral dignity and responsibility of creation, then genuine human response to God—what Tom Smail terms our "authentic" response[43]—*cannot be offered vicariously.* At this point, Forsyth also has an ally in Emil Brunner: "If responsibility be eliminated, the whole meaning of human existence disappears."[44]

Forsyth is concerned that something not be done that belittles human responsibility, leaving us "too little committed."[45] He conceives of the new humanity as the company of those who answer and seal Christ's act with their own faith.[46] This is why the notion of substitution, when pushed too far, is distortive, finally excluding us from any real unity with Christ whose work includes us and commits us to new life.[47] Forsyth acknowledges that there can be no experience of assurance or filiality except by faith in "an objective something, done over our heads, and complete without any reference to our response or our despite."[48] But while the greatest thing ever done in the world was "done for us behind our backs"[49]—submerged and largely hidden like an iceberg—it does not stay behind our backs but creates a turning from darkness to the new

42. Moberly, *Atonement*, 129; cf. Moberly, *Atonement*, 110. Forsyth is a little selective in his reading of Moberly, setting up a caricature that does not entirely reflect Moberly's position, a position which, to be fair, includes a place for the human penitential response to Christ's penitence. See, for example, Moberly, *Atonement*, 118, 121, 129.

43. Smail, *The Giving Gift*, 110.

44. Brunner, *Man in Revolt*, 258.

45. Forsyth, *Work*, 225.

46. Ibid., 227.

47. It is questionable that Campbell would have entertained the use of the notion of vicarious repentance if it seemed to bear the substitutionary ideas which had been affixed to the word "vicarious." Thus Lidgett noted that the notion of a repentant Christ is "The faulty expression of a great truth" (Lidgett, *Spiritual Principle*, 177). And Denney referred to it as "an objectionable name for the indubitable and essential facts" (Denney, *The Christian Doctrine of Reconciliation*, 260). Even if the grammar is problematic and without "even a faint allusion" in the New Testament (so Mackintosh, *Some Aspects of Christian Belief*, 79), however, Campbell clearly believed that the idea is correct, and called for by the New Testament's wider witness to the Gospel itself.

48. Ibid., 187; cf. Tymms, *The Christian Idea of Atonement*, 259; Warfield, "Atonement," vol. 9, 266, 272; Moberly, *Atonement*, 352.

49. Forsyth, *God the Holy Father*, 19.

reality. While the seventeenth and eighteenth-century Calvinists were right to concentrate on the atonement's action *on God*, they treated that work, Forsyth believes, "in a way far too objective."[50] In his own day, however, the accent had shifted to an equally-distortive subjectivism. Forsyth calls for a "balance of aspects," a thinking together "the various aspects of the Cross . . . [making] them enrich and not exclude one another."[51] The atonement puts creation on a new footing, but remains incomplete until it reach us, claim us, affect us, and involve us.[52] Forsyth urged, the work finished "*for us* was the first condition of doing anything *with us;*"[53] the *with us* being an integral aspect of the *for us*. Thus the new humanity is not a *fait accompli* in the cross. If it were, creation would be shut down to a natural system, and moral action rendered meaningless. Without the unfinished world of "ought" and its tension with "is," there is no moral possibility, for action is meaningless in an absolutely comprehended world. To account for the moral agent whom we know, the redemptive act must be final, but only proleptically. Its finality lies in the new relation between God and humanity, in the faithfulness of God to God's own self, and in an ongoing series of "acts of choice, in which the personality asserts itself against the processes that would but hurry it, as a thing, down a stream."[54]

With Campbell (and probably Moberly) in his sights, Forsyth hones in on the question of personal guilt. A sinless Christ could never vicariously confess guilt, nor "bear the penalty of remorse."[55] There is no ledger transfer of guilt from the guilty to the guiltless as if God was involved in some game of "divine finance" in which God lifted our load onto another's back.[56] There is something about guilt, Forsyth insists, "which can only be confessed by the guilty. 'I did it.' That kind of confession Christ could never make." Sin is so deeply graven into our humanity

50. Forsyth, *Work*, 220.

51. Ibid., 221.

52. Ibid., 172. Behind this assertion is Forsyth's conviction that reality is both personal and moral, the whole of history being constituted by choice and act. Personality and act complement one another as the content of the moral structure of reality. See Forsyth, *The Justification of God*, 49; McKay, "The Moral Structure of Reality"; also Moberly, *Atonement*, 136–53; Jüngel, *God as the Mystery of the World*, 308–9.

53. Forsyth, *Father*, 19.

54. Forsyth, *Justification*, 49.

55. Forsyth, *Work*, 157; cf. Moberly, *Atonement*, 117–18, 131.

56. Forsyth, *Cruciality*, 79.

that it cannot be transferred by legal fiat or any other means from one to another. Therefore, in order "to be of final value," Forsyth insists, "the atoning judgment must be also within the conscience of the guilty."[57] To be sure, Forsyth avers that this confession cannot be effectively made "until we are in union with Christ and His great lone work of perfectly and practically confessing the holiness of God. There is a racial confession that can only be made by the holy; and there is a personal confession that can only be made by the guilty."[58] Forsyth maintains that it is impossible for sinners to confess the holiness of God because their very being *as sinners* undermines their confession. So, with Campbell and with almost the unanimous weight of the tradition behind him, Forsyth reiterates that God did for humanity what humanity was unable, and unwilling, to do. *But,* and with one exception, Christ could not confess in our stead the guilt that only the guilty can confess: "We alone, the guilty, can make that confession."[59] Forsyth proceeds to argue that although this is part of the confession the guilty must make, it is not done unaided, for the confession of the guilty cannot be made effectively apart from the great confessional of the cross which is "the source of the truest confession of our sin that we can make."[60]

## VICARIOUS REPENTANCE

Forsyth vies that the notion of vicarious repentance is meaningless. Even if we only refer (as Moberly does) to the 'supreme" or "perfect" nature of Christ's penitence instead of ours, but undergirding ours,[61] Forsyth

57. Forsyth, *Work*, 191; cf. Brunner, *The Mediator*, 534: "If we could repent as we should no atonement would be needed, for then repentance would be atonement. Then the righteousness of God would have been satisfied. But this is precisely what we cannot do."

58. Forsyth, *Work*, 151; see Forsyth, *Work*, 189.

59. Forsyth, *Work*, 151.

60. Forsyth, *Work*, 151–52.

61. Moberly, *Atonement*, 129–30. Newman pushes the notion further in his description of Christ's passion: "He cries to His Father, as if He were the criminal, not the victim; His agony takes the form of guilt and compunction. He is doing penance, He is making confession; He is exercising contrition with a reality and a virtue infinitely greater than that of all Saints and penitents together; for He is the One Victim for us all, the sole Satisfaction, the real Penitent, all but the real sinner." Newman, *Discourses Addressed to Mixed Congregations*, 253. See also Newman, *The Dream of Gerontius*, 62: "Jesu! by that mount of sins which crippled Thee; Jesu! by that sense of guilt which stifled Thee."

is adamant that there is no sense in which Christ could repent for us: "There is an atoning substitution and a penal; but a penitential there is not."[62] He insists that Christ could not directly offer a repentance "wide enough to cover the sin of a guilty world" precisely because he could not feel the pathos of guilt.[63] Smail agrees: "The notion of vicarious repentance carries an inherent contradiction between the adjective and the noun. Only the one who has committed the sin is in a position to repent of it. Like punishment and confession, repentance is something that is inalienably personal to the sinner and cannot justly be transferred from him to one who like Christ has not sinned at all."[64]

Forsyth also avers that "rivers of water from our eyes will not wash out the guilt of the past; nor will they undo the evil we have set afloat in souls far gone beyond our reach or control,"[65] but the penalty Christ has borne works itself out in the represented through *their metanoia*.[66] Forsyth's concern is that an over-objectification of the atonement means that a "finished religion would then be set up without the main thing—the acknowledgment by the guilty. That acknowledgment, that repentance, would then be outside the complete act, and would be at best but a sequel of it." In order to give reconciliation its "full and final value, i.e., its value to God" we ought to "include in some way the effect in the cause."[67] Therefore, Christ's confession elicits a response of penitence in human beings that God accepts as adequate satisfaction for sin. God's holy love goes to work in the human conscience deepening

---

62. Forsyth, "Atonement," 84.

63. Forsyth, *Work*, 189; see also Forsyth, *Work*, 191–92.

64. Smail, "Can One Man Die," 86. Also ibid., 90; Smail, *Once*, 161–62. Smail accuses Torrance of blurring the boundary here between Christology and Pneumatology. Kettler argues that Smail has misread Torrance at this point. Kettler, *The Vicarious Humanity of Christ*, 139–42. Both Moberly and Holmes offer a defence of vicarious "punishment" where Christ is the "corporate personality" or "public person." Moberly, *Atonement*, 118–19, 130; Holmes, "Can Punishment Bring Peace?" 120–21. At this point, Forsyth and Moberly are in agreement. See Forsyth, *Work*, 150, 159, 172, 184; Forsyth, *The Person and Place of Jesus Christ*, 352–53; Forsyth, *Positive Preaching and Modern Mind*, 364; Forsyth, *The Principle of Authority in Relation to Certainty, Sanctity and Society*, 190; Forsyth, *Revelation Old and New*, 34.

65. Forsyth, *Work*, 203.

66. Warfield, "Modern Theories of the Atonement," vol 9. 292. Warfield articulates that Forsyth's position is that human redemption rests ultimately on Christ's work, but proximately on our own repentance.

67. Forsyth, *Work*, 187–88; cf. Forsyth, *Work*, 191.

error into sin, sin into guilt, and guilt into repentance. Anything short of this, Forsyth contends, "would be but an anodyne and not a grace, a self-Battering unction to the soul and not the peace of God."[68] Still, human faith and repentance constitute part of Christ's one complete act of new creation and are not mere sequels to it. The creation of obedience in human persons is therefore also the work of the obedient Christ who reproduces in humanity the same "kind of holiness which alone can please God after all that has come and gone."[69] In Christ, God authors his own satisfaction.[70] The "Yes" of the cross from humanity's side really is a "Yes." But it is a "Yes" that does not reach its satisfactory end until it finds voice from the lips and lives of those that the Crucified One is not ashamed to call his sisters and brothers. God receives Christ's confession not only because it is the perfect offering, but also because laden in it is the anticipation of humanity's confession.[71]

Christ's practical and adequate recognition of the broken law is an end in itself—it satisfies God. But because reconciliation involves two parties, Christ's work also creates space in which the Last Adam's vicarious and loving sacrifice is effected in the new humanity through repentance which was, in Forsyth's words, "the one thing that God's gracious love required for restored communion and complete forgiveness." God could now deal with us as God had felt about us from before the foundation of the world, thus satisfying "the claim and harmony of His holy nature" and "the redemptive passion of His gracious heart."[72] Expressed otherwise, Christ's going to the cross involved "bringing His sheaves with Him. In presenting Himself He offers implicitly and proleptically the new Humanity His holy work creates."[73]

## ASSESSING FORSYTH'S OBJECTION

Forsyth accepts the claim that Christ's obedience was in some sense vicarious, and he entertains no illusions that a human being might come to God unaided. This would, he asserts, "destroy grace" and suggest that

68. Ibid., 181.
69. Ibid., 203.
70. See ibid., *Work*, 203–6.
71. Ibid., 209.
72. Forsyth, "Atonement," 86.
73. Forsyth, *Work*, 192.

one could satisfy God if only God would but give one "time to collect the wherewithal."[74] The capacity of positive response to God is not "natural," as it were, but has to be created – God creating *in* us what God promises *for* us. This, Forsyth urges, is "the Creator's self-assurance of His own regenerative power."[75]

But I want to press Forsyth further here and ask whether his critique of Campbell is not undermined by some of his own rhetoric. Forsyth maintains both (i) that confession and repentance must come from sin's side, and yet (ii) no sinful human could duly repent.[76] Does not Campbell's notion, therefore, provide a most satisfying basis for constructing a theology of confession, repentance and Christian discipleship? Forsyth may reply that this grants logic too big a hand and fails to account for the paradoxical nature of faith. But, with T. F. Torrance, I suggest that in a profound and proper sense we must speak of Jesus as "constituting in himself the very substance of our conversion," repentance and personal decision, apart from which "all so-called repentance and conversion are empty" and vain.[77] Yes *we* do repent, and, as it must if it is to come home, it is really *our* repentance (as Campbell was also keen to stress, especially in his sermons). But it is a repentance that finds its authorship, reception, and finishing in another. Our repentance, like the rest of our salvation, is given to us *as gift*, made possible because of the vicarious repentance of the firstborn from the dead and by the grace of the Spirit. If Calvin is correct to assert that "our whole salvation and *all* its parts are comprehended in Christ"[78] and that salvation involves human repentance, then however difficult the mechanics might be to explain, Christ performed precisely such an act. As in prayer, we can pray because Christ is praying. Similarly, our repentance is made possible and its reception certain because of the perfect repentance of Christ. The important thing here is that, as Forsyth avers, "what Christ presented to God for His complete joy and satisfaction was a perfect racial obedience . . . God's holiness found itself again in the humbled holiness of Christ's

---

74. Ibid., 212.

75. Ibid., 212; cf. Lidgett, *Spiritual Principle*, 407–8.

76. Forsyth, *Work*, 212.

77. Torrance, *Mediation*, 86.

78. Calvin, *Inst.*, 2.16.19, italics added.

'public person.'"[79] It is this notion of Christ as "public person" which will occupy the remainder of this essay.

## CHRIST AS REPRESENTATIVE HEAD

Given Forsyth's acceptance of the notion of vicarious confession (a confession which Campbell maintains "must have been present"[80] in Christ's intercessory ministry) it is difficult to understand his objection to Campbell's framing of Christ's "penitent substitution." Surely both form part of Christ's high-priestly and royal ministry in which Christ mediates God to humanity and humanity to God, fully re-presenting *fallen* Adam where Adam is incapable of doing so itself.[81] Moreover, God has so constituted humanity that what happens to our Head happens for all. Just as elders of some "nations" decide whether the community will embrace the Christian narrative or not, and just as Israel's High Priest represented the nation before God (or David represented Israel in his battle with the Philistines' own representative, the "champion from Gath" (1 Sam 17:23), the fate of both nations being decided vicariously), in humanity's Representative and Head, humanity's destiny is gathered and decided.[82] To posit otherwise is to break up the human community. Here, more than anywhere, individualism is disabled. We might recall here Paul Ricœur's contention that "the selfhood of oneself implies otherness to such an intimate degree that one cannot be thought

79. Forsyth, *Work*, 129; cf. Forsyth, *Work*, 228.

80. Campbell, *Atonement*, 131; cf. Campbell, *Atonement*, 141; Barth, *Church Dogmatics* I/2, 40.

81. Here, Lidgett's Abelardian word concerning Christ's death as "The perfect expression of the spiritual intention of those who, through repentance, abandon the false" betrays the very Achilles of which Campbell was so aware (Lidgett, *Spiritual Principle*, 178). The notion of priesthood is most fully worked out by Forsyth in his ecclesiology and teaching on pastoral ministry. See Forsyth, *Authority*, 283; Forsyth, *The Charter of the Church*, 56–59; Forsyth, *Congregationalism and Reunion*, 57, 73–78; Forsyth, *Father*, 95; Forsyth, *Faith, Freedom and the Future*, 174; Forsyth, *Person*, 12; Forsyth, *Revelation*, 97–99, 132–33, 140; Forsyth, *Rome, Reform and Reaction*, 40, 47, 59, 178–96, 204, 206, 209, 212–14, 223, 229; Forsyth, *The Church and the Sacraments*, 145–46, 184–85.

82. See, for example, Donovan, *Christianity Rediscovered*, 88–94; Moberly, *Atonement*, 352. The notion also presents itself in the decision of a head of state to go to war, a decision that has direct implications for potentially millions of people, whether they approve of the decision or not. We also use the idea to describe our mood when *our* sports team wins, or looses, a match: "We won!" "We lost!" A further example might be when, on February 13, 2008, the Australian Prime Minister, Kevin Rudd, offered a long-awaited apology to the stolen generations on behalf of all Australians.

of without the other, that instead one passes into the other."[83] Only in community can one possibly exist as an individual. Who *I* am cannot be realized apart from the race. So when preaching on our dying and rising in Christ, the young minister of Row expressed it thus: "When Christ gave his flesh to death, willingly and freely, he did not as an individual, but as our head and representative . . . Christ did not suffer as a private person, but as a head and representative, so also, all rose when Christ rose: he rose not as a private person, but as a Head."[84]

Both McLeod Campbell and Forsyth concur that in the sacrifice of this one man is the concentration of all. It is, in Colin Gunton's words, "The kind of offering that, so to speak, longs to offer not only itself, but all flesh."[85] The vicarious response made on humanity's behalf is not made apart from us, but includes us precisely because Jesus is one *with* us and one *of* us, born not only of the Spirit but also of Mary. That is why understanding Christ's work as *only* representative is inadequate.[86] As Forsyth saw, the notion of Christ as "Representative" (taken in isolation) suggests too much of the idea of him as a "spiritual protagonist" who draws his power and authority democratically from those he represents.[87] Instead, Christ's "relation to us is royal." As humanity's "federal person," Christ is "head of the human race by *his voluntary self-identification*," "all humanity is in him and in His act"[88]—a decision that does neither await nor require our approval!

83. Ricœur, *Oneself as Another*, 3. One implication here is that "To do evil is to make another person suffer." Ricœur, "Evil," 259; cf. Sartre, *Being and Nothingness*, 346–51. Buber and Marcel also argue that "I" is never a self-contained, self-comprehending and self-sufficient referent but can exist only in the direction of a "Thou" and a "We" lest it become a hell for itself. Marcel, "Structure de l'Espérance," 80. See also Bonhoeffer, *Sanctorum Communio*, 51, 54–57.

84. Campbell, *Sermons 2*, 23.95–96; cf. Barth, *CD* IV/1, 236, 295; Erskine, *Brazen Serpent*, 44.

85. Gunton, *Father, Son, and Holy Spirit*, 193.

86. While Forsyth (with Pope and Lidgett) preferred the word "Representative" to "substitution," the fact is that he was not enamoured of either. His preference was for the word "surety." See Forsyth, "Atonement," 83–84; Forsyth, *Authority*, 81–82; Forsyth, *Cruciality*, 85, 141, 157–58; Forsyth, *The Preaching of Jesus*, 35; Forsyth, *Work*, 116, 126, 129, 153, 158–61, 172, 182, 191–94, 206, 210–15, 227–28; Forsyth, *Father*, 93; cf. Pope, *The Person of Christ*, 51; Denney, *Atonement*, 97–99.

87. Forsyth, *Work*, 210. Denney expresses similar concern, though contends that we retain the grammar and emphasise that this Representative was "not produced by us, but given to us." Denney, *Atonement*, 99, 102; cf. Smail, *Once*, 149.

88. Forsyth, *Work*, 210, 172, 159.

## CHRIST AS SUBSTITUTE

Jesus Christ is "the man in our place as he was in Barabbas,"[89] doing something for us which we *could not* do for ourselves. Forsyth's rejection of Campbell's notion of vicarious repentance is fundamentally over the question of how deep this "could not do for ourselves" reaches. Could it be that the doctrine of total depravity finds deeper resonance in Campbell's Presbyterianism than it does in Forsyth's Congregationalism? Campbell quotes with approval George Whitefield: "our repentance needeth to be repented of, and our very tears to be washed in the blood of Christ."[90] While Forsyth certainly accepts that "Christ had to save us from what we were too far gone to feel,"[91] humanity's depravity, for Forsyth, is not total in fact, only in principle: "There was still greatness and goodness among men, even among some who failed to see [Christ's]."[92]

If, in the incarnation, Christ became not only "found among sinners" but, as Luther argued, "the one transgressor," "the greatest thief, murderer, adulterer, robber, desecrator, blasphemer, etc., there has ever been anywhere in the world,"[93] and human repentance is as called for as confession, then Forsyth's objection is mute. If in Christ is one whose "flesh differed not in one particle from mine"[94] and so is fully able to "sympathize" with fallen, weak and distressed humanity,[95] does Forsyth's portrait open the door to a docetic, or at least pseudo-Socinian, Christology, a Socinianism that he fought so long and hard against?[96]

89. See Barth, *CD* IV/1, 230, 253.

90. Campbell, *Atonement*, 123.

91. Forsyth, *Work*, 18.

92. Forsyth, *Father*, 56; cf. Forsyth, *Authority*, 404; Forsyth, *Christian Aspects of Evolution*, 22; Forsyth, *Father*, 100; Forsyth, *Freedom*, 94, 109; Forsyth, *Justification*, 143.

93. Luther, *Luther's Works*, vol. 26:277. Cf. Campbell, *Atonement*, 124. This theme was already present in Campbell's Row sermons. See Campbell, *Sermons* 1:238; cf. McLean, *The Cursed Christ*, 144.

94. Campbell, *Notes of Sermons*, 1.8.7. Cited in Stevenson, *Campbell*, 84.

95. Rom 8:3; Heb 4:15. See Anderson, *The Soul of Ministry*, 75; Bloesch, *Essentials of Evangelical Theology*, vol 1. 130; Colyer, *Torrance*, 85, 88, 93, 109–15; König, *Here Am I*, 88; Mackintosh, *The Person of Jesus Christ*, 400–404; Ellingworth, "For our sake God Made him Share our Sin?" 237–41.

96. What I have in mind here is Socinianism's denial of *substitutionary* atonement and forensic imputation. Until the close of the nineteenth century, Socinianism was almost synonymous with Unitarianism, and both—alongside Arianism—came under Forsyth's sustained criticism. See Forsyth, *Person*, 76–78; 246, 328; Forsyth, "Revelation and the Person of Christ," 133; Forsyth, *Work*, 218–19. On Unitarianism see Forsyth,

While it would certainly be over-reaching to offer an unqualified "Yes" here, by rejecting the full measure of Christ's vicarious work Forsyth's Christology appears—at this point—more Socinian and less Athanasian than he would like. Such a move threatens to undermine the very basis of assurance that Campbell and Forsyth seek to bear witness to in the Incarnation *alone*, and re-open the door to a works-righteousness, a move which neither theologian wishes to sponsor. There is no question for Forsyth that in Christ, *God* entered the world, announced himself, gave himself. Jesus really stood in *God's* place. The question I am directing at Forsyth is whether or not he can say that Christ equally stood in *humanity's* place. In Forsyth's defense, his polemic targets an over-humanized Christ gaining popularity in his day. Still, if the sinless Christ can identify with humanity enough to confess human sin, then it is a small leap—if any at all—to say that he also offers vicarious repentance.

It is at this point that my criticisms of Forsyth's Christology converge somewhat with Gerhard Forde's: that Forsyth's Jesus dies "too much like a good Kantian. There are still too many roses on the cross."[97] If Forde's concern here can be sustained, then this may assist us to see why Forsyth shies away from fully identifying Christ with fallen humanity, thus making any vicarious confession meaningless, even impossible. If, on the other hand, the confession of the cross was made by one who has truly entered "the deep stream of pollution in our flesh"[98] whilst retaining, in the Spirit, uncompromised fellowship with God, then his action necessarily involves humanity and God, affecting both parties in such a way that the grammar of vicarious confession and repentance is not only appropriate but necessary if we are both to understand God's humanity and ours, and bear witness to the good news that incarnation means grace from first to last.

## CHRIST AS HIGH PRIEST

One thing I have tried to articulate in this essay is that Forsyth's criticism of Campbell is inconsistent with his own theological matrix. In Forsyth's own words, "The chief function of Christ's love was to repre-

---

*Authority*, 224; Forsyth, *Cruciality*, 74; Forsyth, *Missions in State and Church*, 33–34; Forsyth, "Revelation," 115. Stott falsely assesses Campbell as standing "in the same general tradition" as Socinus (Stott, *Cross*, 141).

97. Forde, "The Work of Christ," 34–35; cf. Terry, *Judgement*, 79, 97.

98. Campbell, *Fragments of Expositions of Scripture*, 18.275.

sent man in a solidary way, a priestly way."[99] If humanity's High Priest can confess God's holiness and work out a real reconciliation "from the flesh"[100]—that is, in "entire identification," "perfect sympathy" and "moral solidarity" with fallen humanity[101]—then certainly he also, as High Priest, confesses the sin and guilt on behalf of those for whom he has undertaken responsibility. Surely this is what a High Priest is ordained to do. As Forsyth himself observes: "What God sought was nothing so pagan as a mere victim outside our conscience and over our heads. It was a Confessor, a Priest, one taken from among men . . . His offering of a holy obedience to God's judgment is therefore valuable to God for us just because of that moral solidarity with us which also makes Him such a moral power upon us and in us."[102]

Few have put this more forcefully than James Torrance who, citing Calvin, and commenting on the Yom Kippur liturgy, observes that when the high priest entered into the holy presence of Yahweh in the sanctuary, "all Israel entered *in his person* . . . Conversely, when he vicariously confessed their sins, and interceded for them before God, God accepted them as his forgiven people *in the person of their high priest.*"[103] Certainly every theory of the atonement reveals not only the paradox of the cross but also its scandalous mystery, a mystery captured in the Yom Kippur liturgy. For Campbell, "The central mystery is the absorption of God's wrath in Christ's own perfect response to God's just judgment *and [Christ's] realization of sin in his own spirit.* In this, somehow, is salvation. In this, somehow, God's justice is satisfied and human need is met."[104]

Forsyth maintains that Christ could not offer vicarious repentance because he had no sense, pathos or personal experience of guilt, and then proceeds to distinguish between *actual* guilt and the *sense* of guilt. What Christ confessed, Forsyth insists, was the former without the latter. But then Forsyth also wants to demand that it is precisely this *actual* guilt that must be confessed and that this "essence of repentance . . . only a sinless Christ could really do."[105] He outlines the dilemma: "How shall

99. Forsyth, *Preaching*, 250.

100. Campbell, *Fragments of Truth*, 258.

101. Forsyth, *Preaching*, 250; cf. Mackintosh, *Person*, 400.

102. Forsyth, *Work*, 190.

103. Torrance, "Vicarious Humanity," 139.

104. Van Dyk, *Desire*, 114, italics added.

105. Forsyth, *Work*, 189.

I know how much repentance is deep enough? Where find a repentance wide enough to cover the sin of a guilty world? Could Christ offer that?" Campbell says "Yes," this is precisely what Christ offers. And Forsyth: "No; directly, He could not. He could not offer it as a pathos, a personal experience, for He had no guilt."[106] While properly avoiding the temptation to second guess Jesus' psychology, Forsyth's objection to Campbell's notion of vicarious repentance makes greater sense if the repentance that Christ offers is on behalf of an individual, or even a select group of individuals (though the latter may be more easily defended). The objection, however, becomes more difficult to sustain if that vicarious repentance is offered by and as one who is the head of a corporate body for whom one has taken responsibility.[107] Thus Luther's reminder that "we should not imagine Christ as an innocent and private person."[108] Rather in his sinless humanity, Christ enters the matrix of besmirched human community—"a despairing and broken world trapped in lostness"[109]—into "all the responsibilities that sin has created for us"[110] and completely assumes—as the new Head of that community—"the human condition of estrangement from God,"[111] converting a "Lancelot race"[112] into "a chosen race, a royal priesthood, a holy nation, God's own people" (1 Pet 2:9).

106. Ibid., 189.

107. See Crisp, "Non-Penal Substitution," 429–30. Crisp follows Forsyth in addressing the notion of where the representative of a group is said to offer an apology for the past misdeeds of the group (or some of the group) of which s/he is a representative, citing as an example the regret expressed by the Japanese government for their part in wartime atrocities. "But," he writes, "we cannot take such actions with metaphysical seriousness. They have to do with the observation of diplomatic convention, or perhaps of international etiquette, or courtesy. Real regret is surely offered in many such cases; I am not denying that. But the representative of any group or nation cannot literally offer an apology for sinful actions committed by some members of the community he or she represents, if by apology is meant a real act of contrition and repentance for past sin." One wonders, therefore, how Crisp understands what might be going on when Israel's high priest literally clothes himself with the full symbolic weight of the community he represents before God in the holy of holies. Surely he does not want to suggest that what is going on here is merely an example of "diplomatic convention," "etiquette," or "courtesy."

108. Luther, *Works 26*, 287.

109. Kruger, *The Parable of the Dancing God*, 28.

110. Denney, *Atonement*, 93; cf. Hunter, *Forsyth*, 63.

111. Rossé, *The Cry of Jesus on the Cross*, 67.

112. Forsyth, *The Church, the Gospel and Society*, 102.

This does not make human confession or repentance accidental or redundant. On the contrary, it creates the necessity of such creaturely response, and also the assurance that such confession might be received by God. Forsyth *and Campbell* are equally concerned that the fact of personal confession be not undermined. It is precisely because sin is personal that it cannot be forgiven by divine fiat but only by a personal act. And it is precisely because one from the sin-gnarled stock of Adam has already offered to God the perfect repentance that we can offer our repentance. This we do not out of our own "moral awareness, inner strength and spiritual resolve"[113] but in the Great Repenter himself, and as we are led by the Spirit to confess our "Amen" to the "Amen" already offered to the Father on our behalf. The pastoral power of such a theology is given voice in James Torrance's stirring hymn, "I know not how to pray, O Lord," written during a visit to Australia in 1996:

> I know not how to pray, O Lord,
> So weak and frail am I.
> Lord Jesus to Your outstretched arms
> In love I daily fly,
> For You have prayed for me.
>
> I know not how to pray, O Lord,
> O"erwhelmed by grief am I,
> Lord Jesus in Your wondrous love
> You hear my anxious cry
> And ever pray for me.
>
> I know not how to pray, O Lord,
> For full of tears and pain
> I groan, yet in my soul, I know
> My cry is not in vain.
> O teach me how to pray!
>
> Although I know not how to pray,
> Your Spirit intercedes,
> Convincing me of pardoned sin;
> For me in love He pleads
> And teaches me to pray.
>
> O take my wordless sighs and fears

---

113. Redding, *Prayer*, 199.

And make my prayers Your own.
O put Your prayer within my lips
And lead me to God's throne
That I may love like You.

O draw me to Your Father's heart,
Lord Jesus, when I pray,
And whisper in my troubled ear,
"Your sins are washed away.
Come home with Me today!"

At home within our Father's house,
Your Father, Lord, and mine,
I"m lifted up by Your embrace
To share in love divine
Which floods my heart with joy.

Transfigured by Your glory, Lord,
Renewed in heart and mind,
I'll sing angelic song of praise
With joy which all can find
In You alone, O Lord.

I'll love You, O my Father God,
Through Jesus Christ, Your Son.
I'll love You in the Spirit, Lord,
In whom we all are one,
Made holy by Your love.[114]

The Gospel commands us to repent, to believe, to take up the cross, and to follow Christ. That, as T. F. Torrance has shown, is "something that each of us must do, for no other human being can substitute for us in that ultimate act of man in answer to God—no other, that is, except Jesus."[115] Reluctance to recognize that Jesus Christ substitutes for us at this point threatens to make his atoning substitution for us something that is partial and not total, a move which would finally empty it of all soteriological puissance. T. F. Torrance continues:

> What Jesus did was to make himself one with us in our estranged
> humanity when it was running away into the far country, farther

114. J. B. Torrance, "I know not how to pray, O Lord."
115. Torrance, *Mediation*, 84.

and farther away from the Father, but through his union with
it he changed it in himself, reversed its direction and converted
it back in obedience and faith and love to God the Father. The
Gospel tells us that at his Baptism Jesus was baptised "into repentance" (*eis metanoian*), for as the Lamb of God come to bear
our sins he fulfilled that mission not in some merely superficially
forensic way, though of course profound forensic elements were
involved, but in a way in which he bore our sin and guilt upon
his very soul which he made an offering for sin. That is to say,
the Baptism with which he was baptised was a Baptism of vicarious repentance for us which he brought to its completion on the
Cross where he was stricken and smitten of God for our sakes, by
whose stripes we are healed. He had laid hold of us even in the
depths of our human soul and mind where we are alienated from
God and are at enmity with him, and altered them from within
and from below in radical and complete *metanoia*, a repentant
restructuring of our carnal mind, as St Paul called it, and a converting of it into a spiritual mind. As fallen human beings, we
are quite unable through our own free-will to escape from our
self-will for our free-will is our self-will. Likewise sin has been
so ingrained into our minds that we are unable to repent and
have to repent even of the kind of repentance we bring before
God. But Jesus Christ laid hold of us even there in our sinful
repentance and turned everything round through his holy vicarious repentance, when he bore not just upon his body but upon
his human mind and soul the righteous judgments of God and
resurrected our human nature in the integrity of his body, mind
and soul from the grave.[116]

What took place in Christ was the "vicarious sanctification of our
human nature."[117] In the incarnate unity of his person, Jesus of Nazareth
is the divine-human Word "spoken to [humanity] from the highest and
heard by [humanity] in the depths, and spoken to God out of the depths
and heard by [God] in the highest."[118] The gospel, therefore, is not to
be understood only as the Word of God drawing near to us, inviting
our response, but also as including "the all-significant middle term, the
divinely provided response in the vicarious humanity of Jesus Christ."[119]

116. Ibid., 84–85.

117. T. F. Torrance, *Incarnation: The Person and Life of Christ*, 205. See also T. F.
Torrance, *Incarnation*, 124–25, 204.

118. T. F. Torrance, *God and Rationality*, 138.

119. Ibid., 145.

## HUMANITY'S PARTICIPATION IN CHRIST'S "AMEN" BY THE SPIRIT

Forsyth and Campbell are obdurate that God's atoning work remains incomplete apart from its subjective appropriation. So too Gunton: "Substitution is *grace*. [Christ] goes, as man, where we cannot go, under the judgment, and so comes perfected into the presence of God. But it is grace because he does so as God and as our representative, *so that he enables us to go there after him.*"[120] As Forsyth has it, Christ's confession of God's holiness is the ground of ours.[121] This calls for faith that accepts the relation as atoned, and which is, in Campbell's words, the glad "Amen of our individual spirits to that deep, multiform, all-embracing, harmonious Amen of humanity, in the person of the Son of God, to the mind and heart of the Father in relation to [humanity]."[122] The new humanity created in the cross confesses the holiness of God by accepting and praising the very cross which brought an end to its old existence and created it anew. And as we draw near to God the only offering in our hands is that which was made for us and in our stead. As one has it: "We put out empty hands and bread and wine are put into them which we eat and drink . . . for we have no other offering with which to draw near to God but that one offering which is identical with Jesus Christ himself, through whom, with whom and in whom we glorify the Father."[123]

Forsyth believes that "the race could duly confess its sin and repent only if there arose in it One who by a perfect and impenitent holiness in Himself, and by His organic unity with us, could create such holiness in the sinful as should make the new life one long repentance transcended by faith and thankful joy. This was and is Christ's work."[124] Christ's "holy soul," he contends, was both the "cause and creator of the race's confession, both of holiness and of sin, in a Church of the reborn."[125] Genuine human response is possible only in union with Christ. Forsyth proceeds to name Christ "the author of our sanctification and repentance," averring that human repentance and sanctity are of saving value before God "only as produced by the creative holiness of Christ. Christ creates our

---

120. Gunton, *The Actuality of Atonement,* 166.

121. Forsyth, *Work,* 191.

122. Campbell, *Atonement,* 171.

123. Torrance, *Mediation,* 92.

124. Forsyth, *Work,* 213.

125. Ibid., 213.

holiness because of His own sanctification of Himself—John 17:19—and His complete victory over the evil power in a life-experience of moral conflict."[126]

Forsyth is concerned that Campbell's notion of vicarious ministry shortchanges grace's end work in humanity. As I have suggested, Forsyth (among others[127]) has misread Campbell here, and that perhaps because he seems unfamiliar with Campbell's sermons wherein the human response of repentance and confession in the Spirit is made more explicit. By concentrating exclusively on Campbell's *Atonement* essay and ignoring his sermons—which constitute the bulk of Campbell's published material—Forsyth falls into the same trap as most of Campbell's critics. While in one sense it is an understandable neglect given how quickly the Row sermons went out of print, one cannot help thinking that Forsyth's concern may have been alleviated had he attended to Campbell's sermons as well as his later opus, and read the latter in light of, or alongside, the former, and so gleaned a less distorted picture of Campbell's Christology. Campbell, on the other hand, could have done more in his *Atonement* essay to recount some of his earlier teaching, assisting his readers (and especially his critics) to better appreciate his position.

Forsyth's reservation regarding Campbell's position is echoed in Tom Smail's concern for that of T. F. Torrance, a Christology which is at this point Campbellian and recalls an anxiety which at least the instinct of is, I think, understandable.[128] Forsyth does not, however, respond as Smail does, in stressing the ministry of the Holy Spirit who re-creates in the human subject Christ's perfect and vicarious response. Serving as "the natural bridge between the retrospective and the prospective,"[129] the Spirit's work is "simply to bring over to us from Christ what he has done for us, so that it can be done in us as well."[130] The Spirit, Smail argues, gives to our humanity all that is in Christ's, but "Christ's response on my behalf has to become my own response to Christ before it can take

126. Ibid.

127. Van Dyk suggests that the Spirit plays only a 'shadowy role" in *The Nature of the Atonement*, and Paul believes that "This omission in Campbell means that for all the apparent objectivity of Christ's vicarious work, the effective appropriation of grace depends upon our own effort." Paul, *Atonement*, 149.

128. See Torrance's response in Torrance, *Mediation*, xii; cf. ibid., 94.

129. Van Dyk, *Desire*, 170.

130. Smail, *Giving Gift*, 108.

effect in me . . . I must answer for myself . . . My 'Yes' is not just an echo of [Christ's]."[131] The Christian life, Smail avers, is that in which the Spirit brings human beings "into a wholly new order of responsivness to God," enabling us to do "for ourselves" what we could never do "by ourselves."[132] Smail writes:

> The "Yes" that we say to God in Christ is our own "Yes;" yet it is ours not as an achievement that has its source in us, but as a gift of which the Giver is the Life-giving Spirit. The paradox . . . summed up in the phrase *"for* ourselves but not *by* ourselves" is the mystery of his relationship with us.[133]

While one may certainly sympathize here with Smail's concern, one might also find it difficult to see how it does not—even with all the necessary qualifiers concerning the unity between the Son and the Spirit in their work—threaten to re-open the Pelagian door. (Perhaps this is a risk inherent always in the telling of the good news, an action latent with all number of paradoxes to be sure.) Whatever else our faith is, it is a participation in a response already fully made, and which is continually being made, for us in Christ—who is both God's text to humanity and humanity's text to God. With the Spirit, the new humanity participates in the incarnate Son's life, worship and communion with the Father, and in God's mission to the world. In Jesus Christ, our humanity, and our human response, is "taken up, purified and sanctified, and addressed to God the Father for us as our very own—and that is the word of man with which God is well pleased."[134] We can take up our cross and follow Jesus because Jesus has already acted in our place, authored all our decisions and responses to God's love, even our acts of faith. This was, in Barth's words, "the making possible of that which seemed to be contrary to every possibility."[135]

In his *Ethics*, Dietrich Bonhoeffer draws attention to the fact that Christ is not only the fulfillment of history but also its norm. True moral action, otherwise named ethics, has its "origin," "essence," and "goal"[136]

131. Ibid., 109, 110.
132. Ibid., 172.
133. Ibid., 174.
134. Torrance, *Mediation*, 79.
135. Barth, *CD* IV/1, 223.
136. Bonhoeffer, *Ethics*, ed. Bethge, 191.

in the divine economy rather than in some deontological ethic or subjectivism. The concrete form of this economy is "the all-embracing life which is Jesus Christ," the person who was "willing to become guilty."[137] Bonhoeffer continues: "All human responsibility is rooted in the real vicarious representative action of Jesus Christ on behalf of all human beings. Responsible action is vicarious representative action."[138] That Jesus Christ really is our life means that when we are called to account (by others or by God) faith can "answer only through the witness of Jesus Christ."[139] Faith can only answer for itself in confessing Jesus Christ. And to confess Jesus Christ is to say "Yes"—and to hear God's "Yes"—to our own humanity and to the authentic human response offered on our behalf.

What I am positing here is that all of Christ—that is, all of grace—does not mean nothing of humanity, but precisely the opposite. To affirm otherwise is to either sever Christ's humanity from ours or to suggest that true humanity exists apart from that of the Incarnate Son (whom even Kant recognizes as "the prototype of a humanity well-pleasing to God."[140]) We receive our humanity as gift from God mediated through Christ. The relation between divine and human agency is "not something that can be understood logically"[141] or causally, a trajectory that has created a competition between divine and human agency in the *ordo salutis*. We are speaking here of an event of such a unique, *sui generis*, character that it remains beyond the simplistic causalist categories. While it may be simpler to employ either *monergistic* (all of God, nothing of humanity) or *synergistic* (partly God, partly humanity) concepts, both are woefully inadequate descriptions of what is happening in the centre and *telos* of the Gospel. "All of Christ" means "all of humanity" is gathered up in Spirit-led action, entering into the "event between God and God,"[142] and called to participate by the same Spirit in the worshipful life of the Son. This means that no human being can repent or flourish apart from the Word made flesh. In Christ alone, and by the Spirit, are persons made

137. See Bonhoeffer, *Ethics*, ed. Green 228–29 n. 44.
138. Ibid., 232.
139. Bonhoeffer, *Ethics*, ed. Bethge, 192.
140. Kant, *Religion Within the Boundaries of Mere Reason*, 125.
141. Torrance, *Mediation*, xii.
142. Rossé, *Cry of Jesus*, 138.

fit, and led to share in Christ's confession and repentance, actions which commit persons to new life shared with the Father in the Spirit.

A final note: one thing that the divergence of accent discussed in this essay illustrates is that even within the family of those who advance "Evangelical Calvinism" there is a vigorous and ongoing conversation regarding interpretation and faithful witness. Such exchanges betray a tradition that is healthy, mature, and robust, and looking for fresh ways to faithfully tell the old, old story of one anointed by the Spirit in our humanity to fulfill ministry on our behalf. Good News indeed.

# BIBLIOGRAPHY

Anderson, Ray S. *The Soul of Ministry: Forming Leaders for God's People.* Louisville: Westminster John Knox, 1997.

Anselm. *Cur Deus Homo?* Edinburgh: John Grant, 1909.

Barth, Karl. *Church Dogmatics I.2.* Edited by G.W. Bromiley and T.F. Torrance. Translated by G.T. Thompson and T.F. Torrance. Edinburgh: T&T Clark, 2000.

———. *Church Dogmatics IV.1.* Edited by G.W. Bromiley and T.F. Torrance. Translated by G.W. Bromiley. Edinburgh: T&T Clark, 1961.

Bewkes, Eugene G. "John McLeod Campbell—Theologian. His Theological Development and Trial, and a New Interpretation of His Theory of Atonement." PhD, University of Edinburgh, 1924.

———. *Legacy of a Christian Mind; John M'Leod Campbell, Eminent Contributor to Theological Thought.* Philadelphia: Judson, 1937.

Bloesch, Donald G. *Essentials of Evangelical Theology.* 2 vols. New York: Harper & Row, 1982.

Bonhoeffer, Dietrich. *Ethics.* Edited by Eberhard Bethge. Translated by Neville Horton Smith. New York: Macmillan, 1955.

———. *Ethics.* Edited by Clifford J. Green. Translated by Reinhard Krauss, Charles C. West, and Douglas W. Scott. Vol. 6, Dietrich Bonhoeffer Works. Minneapolis: Fortress, 2005.

———. *Sanctorum Communio: A Theological Study of the Sociology of the Church.* Edited by Clifford Green. Translated by Reinhard Krauss and Nancy Lukens. Minneapolis: Fortress Press, 1998.

Bruce, Alexander B. *The Humiliation of Christ in its Physical, Ethical and Official Aspects.* Edinburgh: T. & T. Clark, 1895.

Brunner, Emil. *Man in Revolt: A Christian Anthropology.* Translated by Olive Wyon. Cambridge: Lutterworth, 1957.

———. *The Mediator: A Study of the Central Doctrine of the Christian Faith.* Translated by Olive Wyon. London: Lutterworth, 1934.

Bushnell, Horace. *Forgiveness and Law, Grounded in Principles Interpreted by Human Analogies.* New York: Scribner, Armstrong, 1874.

Calvin, John. *Institutes of the Christian Religion.* 2 vols. Edited by John T. McNeill. Translated by Ford Lewis Battles. Philadelphia: Westminster, 1977.

Campbell, John McLeod. *Fragments of Expositions of Scripture.* London: J. Wright, 1843.

———. *Fragments of Truth: Being the Exposition of Several Passages of Scripture chiefly from the Teaching of John McLeod Campbell, D.D.* Edinburgh: David Douglas, 1898.

———. *The Nature of the Atonement.* Grand Rapids: Eerdmans, 1996.

———. *Notes of Sermons by the Rev. J. McL. Campbell.* Paisley: J. Vallance, 1831, 1832.

———. *Reminiscences and Reflections: Referring to His Early Ministry in the Parish of Row, 1825–31.* London: Macmillan, 1873.

———. *Sermons and Lectures.* 3rd ed. 2 vols. Vol. 1. Greenock: R. B. Lusk, 1832.

Carey, George. *The Gate of Glory.* London: Hodder and Stoughton, 1986.

Cave, Alfred. *The Scriptural Doctrine of Sacrifice.* Edinburgh: T. & T. Clark, 1877.

Colyer, Elmer M. *How to Read T.F. Torrance: Understanding His Trinitarian & Scientific Theology.* Downers Grove, IL: InterVarsity, 2001.

Crisp, Oliver. "Non-Penal Substitution," *International Journal of Systematic Theology* 9 (2007) 415–33.

Denney, James. *The Christian Doctrine of Reconciliation.* London: James Clarke, 1959.

Donovan, Vincent J. *Christianity Rediscovered: An Epistle from the Masai.* London: SCM, 1982.

Edwards, Jonathan. *The Works of Jonathan Edwards.* Vol. 2 of 2. Edinburgh: Banner of Truth Trust, 1998.

Ellingworth, Paul. "For our sake God Made him Share our Sin? (2 Corinthians 5:21, GNB)." *The Bible Translator* 38 (1987) 237–41.

Erskine, Thomas. *The Brazen Serpent; or, Life Coming Through Death.* Edinburgh: David Douglas, 1879.

Forde, Gerhard O. "The Work of Christ." In *Christian Dogmatics*, vol. 2 of 2, edited by Carl E. Braaten and Robert W. Jenson, 2:5–99. Philadelphia: Fortress, 1984.

Forsyth, P. T. "The Atonement in Modern Religious Thought." In *The Atonement in Modern Religious Thought: A Theological Symposium*, edited by F. Godet et al., 61–88. New York: Thomas Whittaker, 1901.

———. *The Charter of the Church: Six Lectures on the Spiritual Principle of Nonconformity.* London: Alexander & Shepherd, 1896.

———. *Christian Aspects of Evolution.* London: Epworth, 1950.

———. *The Church and the Sacraments.* London: Independent, 1947.

———. *The Church, the Gospel and Society.* London: Independent, 1962.

———. *Congregationalism and Reunion: Two Lectures.* London: Independent, 1952.

———. *The Cruciality of the Cross.* London: Hodder & Stoughton, 1910.

———. *Faith, Freedom and the Future.* London: Hodder & Stoughton, 1912.

———. *God the Holy Father.* Blackwood: New Creation, 1987.

———. *The Justification of God: Lectures for War-Time on a Christian Theodicy.* London: Independent, 1957.

———. *Missions in State and Church: Sermons and Addresses.* London: Hodder & Stoughton, 1908.

———. "The Paradox of Christ." *London Quarterly Review* 102 (1904) 111–38.

———. *The Person and Place of Jesus Christ: The Congregational Union Lecture for 1909.* London: Congregational Union of England and Wales/Hodder & Stoughton, 1910.

———. *Positive Preaching and Modern Mind: The Lyman Beecher Lecture on Preaching, Yale University, 1907.* London: Hodder & Stoughton, 1907.

———. *The Preaching of Jesus and the Gospel of Christ.* Blackwood: New Creation, 1987.

———. *The Principle of Authority in Relation to Certainty, Sanctity and Society: An Essay in the Philosophy of Experimental Religion.* London: Independent, 1952.

———. "Revelation and the Person of Christ." In *Faith and Criticism: Essays by Congregationalists*, 95–144. London: Simpson Low Marston, 1893.

———. *Revelation Old and New: Sermons and Addresses.* Edited by John Huxtable. London: Independent, 1962.

———. *Rome, Reform and Reaction: Four Lectures on the Religious Situation.* London: Hodder & Stoughton, 1899.

———. *The Work of Christ.* London: Hodder & Stoughton, 1910.

Goroncy, Jason A. "The Elusiveness, Loss, and Cruciality of Recovered Holiness: Some Biblical and Theological Observations." *International Journal of Systematic Theology* 10 (2008) 195–209.

———. "The Final Sanity is Complete Sanctity: Universal Holiness in the Soteriology of P. T. Forsyth (1848–1921)." In *"All Shall Be Well": Explorations in Universalism and Christian Theology, from Origen to Moltmann*, edited by Gregory MacDonald, 249–79. Eugene: Cascade, 2010.

———. *Hallowed Be Thy Name: The Sanctification of All in the Soteriology of Peter Taylor Forsyth.* T. & T. Clark Studies in Systematic Theology. London/New York: T. & T. Clark, forthcoming.

Gunton, Colin E. *The Actuality of Atonement: A Study of Metaphor, Rationality and the Christian Tradition.* Edinburgh: T. & T. Clark, 1988.

———. *Father, Son, and Holy Spirit: Essays Toward a Fully Trinitarian Theology.* London: T. & T. Clark, 2003.

Hanna, William. ed. *Letters of Thomas Erskine of Linlathen.* Edinburgh: David Douglas, 1884.

Hart, Trevor A. "Anselm of Canterbury and John McLeod Campbell: Where Opposites Meet?" *Evangelical Quarterly* 62 (1990) 311–33.

Horrocks, Don. *Laws of the Spiritual Order: Innovation and Reconstruction in the Soteriology of Thomas Erskine of Linlathen.* Studies in Evangelical History and Thought. Carlisle: Paternoster, 2004.

Hunter, Archibald M. *P. T. Forsyth: Per Crucem ad Lucem.* London: SCM, 1974.

Irving, Edward. *The Collected Writings of Edward Irving,* vol. 5 of 5. London: Strahan, 1865.

Jenson, Robert W. *America's Theologian: A Recommendation of Jonathan Edwards.* New York: Oxford University Press, 1988.

Jinkins, Michael. *A Comparative Study in the Theology of Atonement in Jonathan Edwards and John McLeod Campbell: Atonement and the Character of God.* San Francisco: Mellen Research University Press, 1993.

Jüngel, Eberhard. *God as the Mystery of the World: On the Foundation of the Theology of the Crucified One in the Dispute between Theism and Atheism.* Translated by Darrell L. Guder. Edinburgh: T. & T. Clark, 1983.

Kant, Immanuel. *Religion Within the Boundaries of Mere Reason and Other Writings.* Translated by Allen W. Wood and George di Giovanni. Cambridge: Cambridge University Press, 1998.

Kettler, Christian D. *The Vicarious Humanity of Christ and the Reality of Salvation.* Lanham: University of America Press, 1986.

König, Adrio. *Here Am I: A Believer's Reflection on God.* Grand Rapids: Eerdmans, 1982.

Kruger, C. Baxter. *The Parable of the Dancing God.* Jackson: Perichoresis, 1994.

Lidgett, John S. *The Spiritual Principle of the Atonement: As a Satisfaction Made to God for the Sins of the World: Being The Twenty-Seventh Fernley Lecture delivered in Leeds, July, 1897.* London: Chas. H. Kelly, 1907.

Luther, Martin. *Luther's Works,* vol. 26, *Lectures on Galatians, 1535,* chapters 1–4. Edited by J. J. Pelikan, H.C. Oswald and H. T. Lehmann. Translated by J. J. Pelikan. Saint Louis: Concordia Publishing House, 1999.

Lyttelton, Arthur. "The Atonement." In *Lux Mundi: A Series of Studies in the Religion of the Incarnation,* 275–312. Edited by Charles Gore. London: J. Murray, 1890.

Mackintosh, Hugh Ross. *Some Aspects of Christian Belief.* London: Hodder & Stoughton, 1923.

———. *The Person of Jesus Christ.* Edinburgh: T. & T. Clark, 1912.

Marcel, Gabriel. "Structure de l'Espérance." *Dieu vivante. Perspectives religieuses et philosophiques* 19 (1951) 73–80.

McKay, Clifford A. "The Moral Structure of Reality in the Theology of Peter Taylor Forsyth." PhD diss., Vanderbilt University, 1970.

McLean, B. Hudson. *The Cursed Christ: Mediterranean Expulsion Rituals and Pauline Soteriology.* JSNTSup 126. Sheffield: Sheffield Academic, 1996.

Moberly, Robert C. *Atonement and Personality.* London: John Murray, 1901.

Newman, John Henry. *Discourses Addressed to Mixed Congregations.* Boston: Patrick Donahoe, 1853.

———. *The Dream of Gerontius.* New York: Cosimo, 2007.

Orr, James. *The Christian View of God and the World, as Centring in the Incarnation: Being the Kerr Lectures for 1890–1891.* New York: Anson D. F. Randolph, 1893.

Paul, Robert Sydney. *The Atonement and the Sacraments: The Relation of the Atonement to the Sacraments of Baptism and the Lord's Supper.* London: Hodder & Stoughton, 1961.

Pope, William Burt. *The Person of Christ: Dogmatic, Scriptural, Historical. The Fernley Lecture of 1871, with two additional essays on the Biblical and Ecclesiastical development of the doctrine, and illustrative notes.* London: Wesleyan Conference Office, 1875.

Redding, Graham. *Prayer and the Priesthood of Christ in the Reformed Tradition.* London: T. & T. Clark, 2003.

Ricœur, Paul. "Evil: a Challenge to Philosophy and Theology." In *Figuring the Sacred: Religion, Narrative, and Imagination,* edited by Mark I. Wallace, translated by David Pellauer, 249–61. Minneapolis: Fortress, 1995.

———. *Oneself as Another.* Translated by Kathleen Blamey. Chicago: University of Chicago Press, 1992.

Rossé, Gérard. *The Cry of Jesus on the Cross: A Biblical and Theological Study.* New York: Paulist, 1987.

Sartre, Jean-Paul. *Being and Nothingness: An Essay on Phenomenological Ontology.* Translated by Hazel E. Barnes. London: Methuen, 1957.

Schaff Philip. ed. *Hilary of Poitiers, John of Damascus.* Edinburgh: T. & T. Clark, 1898.

Seifrid, Mark A. *Christ, Our Righteousness: Paul's Theology of Justification.* New Studies in Biblical Theology. Leicester/Downers Grove: Apollos/IVP, 2000.

Smail, Thomas A. "Can One Man Die for the People?" In *Atonement Today: A Symposium at St John's College, Nottingham,* edited by John Goldingay, 73–92. London: SPCK, 1995.

———. *The Giving Gift: The Holy Spirit in Person.* London: Hodder & Stoughton, 1988.

———. *Once and For All: A Confession of the Cross.* Eugene OR: Wipf and Stock, 2005.

Sölle, Dorothee. "Gott und das Leiden." In *Diskussion über Jürgen Moltmanns Buch "Der gekreuzigte Gott,"* edited by Michael Welker. 111–17. Munich: Chr. Kaiser Verlag, 1979.

Stevenson, Peter K. *God in Our Nature: The Incarnational Theology of John McLeod Campbell.* Carlisle: Paternoster, 2004.

Stott, John R.W. *The Cross of Christ.* Leicester: InterVarsity, 1986.

Taylor, Vincent. "The Best Books on the Atonement." *Expository Times* 48 (1937) 267–73.

Terry, Justyn. *The Justifying Judgement of God: A Reassessment of the Place of Judgement in the Saving Work of Christ.* Milton Keynes: Paternoster, 2007.

Thimell, Daniel P. "Christ in Our Place in the Theology of John McLeod Campbell." In *Christ in Our Place, The Humanity of God in Christ for The Reconciliation of the World: Essays Presented to Professor James Torrance,* edited by Trevor A. Hart and Daniel P. Thimell, 182–286. Eugene, OR: Pickwick, 1989.

Torrance, James B. "Introduction." In J. McLeod Campbell, *The Nature of the Atonement*, 1–34. The Stables/Grand Rapids: Handsel/Eerdmans, 1996.

———. "The Vicarious Humanity of Christ." In *The Incarnation: Ecumenical Studies in the Nicene-Constantinopolitan Creed,* 127–47. Edited by T. F. Torrance. Edinburgh: Handsel, 1981.

———. "I know not how to pray, O Lord." Hymn 347 in *New Creation Hymn Book.* Blackwood: New Creation, 1996.

———. *Worship, Community, and the Triune God of Grace.* Carlisle: Paternoster, 1996.

Torrance, Thomas F. *God and Rationality.* London: Oxford University Press, 1971.

———. *Incarnation: The Person and Life of Christ.* Edited by Robert T. Walker. Downers Grove, IL: InterVarsity, 2008.

———. *The Mediation of Christ.* Colorado Springs: Helmers & Howard, 1992.

———. *Scottish Theology: From John Knox to John McLeod Campbell.* Edinburgh: T. & T. Clark, 1996.

Tuttle, George M. *So Rich a Soil: John McLeod Campbell on Christian Atonement.* Edinburgh: Handsel, 1986.

Tymms, Thomas Vincent. *The Christian Idea of Atonement: Lectures Delivered at Regent's Park College, London, in 1903.* London: Macmillan, 1904.

Van Dyk, Leanne. *The Desire of Divine Love: John McLeod Campbell's Doctrine of the Atonement.* New York: Peter Lang, 1995.

Warfield, Benjamin B. "Atonement," in *Studies in Theology,* vol. 9 of 10. In *The Works of Benjamin B. Warfield,* 259–80. Grand Rapids: Baker, 2003.

———. "Modern Theories of the Atonement." In *The Works of Benjamin B. Warfield,* 9:281–97. Grand Rapids: Baker, 2003.

Weinandy, Thomas. *Does God Suffer?* Edinburgh: T. & T. Clark, 2000.

———. *In the Likeness of Sinful Flesh: An Essay on the Humanity of Christ.* Edinburgh: T. & T. Clark, 1993.

# 11

## "Suffer the little children to come to me, for theirs is the kingdom of heaven."

*Infant Salvation and the Destiny of the Severely Mentally Disabled*

MYK HABETS

## INTRODUCTION[1]

As of April 20, 2007 the Roman Catholic Church no longer holds to a view of Limbo, a state which includes the souls of infants who die subject to original sin and without baptism, and who, therefore, neither merit the beatific vision, nor yet are subjected to any punishment, because they are not guilty of any personal sin.[2] This reassessment was occasioned by a number of factors of which two seem uppermost. The first factor is based upon pragmatic-pastoral motives, namely; the increased number of infants today who are born to parents who are not

1. I am grateful to Amos Yong, Bobby Grow, Charles Hewlett, Marcus Johnson, and others for providing critical feedback on a draft of this article and to those who interacted with its contents when it was read at the annual conference of the Systematic Theology Association of Aotearoa Zealand, Auckland, 20 November, 2009.

2. The official position of the Roman Catholic Church was made public by the International Theological Commission in a forty-one page report published as, "The Hope of Salvation for Infants Who Die Without Being Baptized." The thirty-member International Theological Commission acts as an advisory panel to the Vatican, in particular to the Congregation for the Doctrine of the Faith. See Roman Catholic Church, "Hope of Salvation."

practicing Catholics and the many others who are the unborn victims of abortion who die without baptism.[3] The second factor is due to semi-theological motives, namely; the principle that grace has priority over sin, and a greater theological awareness today that God is merciful and "wants all human beings to be saved." God's love and mercy is considered incompatible with the idea that infants who die do not enter God's saving presence. In short, the official Report states:

> [P]eople find it increasingly difficult to accept that God is just and merciful if he excludes infants, who have no personal sins, from eternal happiness, whether they are Christian or non-Christian. From a theological point of view, the development of a theology of hope and an ecclesiology of communion, together with a recognition of the greatness of divine mercy, challenge an unduly restrictive view of salvation. In fact, the universal salvific will of God and the correspondingly universal mediation of Christ mean that all theological notions that ultimately call into question the very omnipotence of God, and his mercy in particular, are inadequate.[4]

The Report makes it clear that belief in Limbo has never been a dogmatic definition of the Magisterium of the Roman Catholic Church, and at least since the 1992 *Catechism of the Catholic Church* (*CCC*) the doctrine has not been taught. In the relevant section of *CCC* we read:

> As regards children who have died without Baptism, the Church can only entrust them to the mercy of God, as she does in her funeral rites for them. Indeed, the great mercy of God who desires that all men should be saved, and Jesus' tenderness toward children which caused him to say: "Let the children come to me, do not hinder them," (Mark 10:14, cf. 1 Tim 2:4), allow us to hope that there is a way of salvation for children who have died

---

3. In addition to this are the sheer numbers of infant deaths we now know of due to advances in medical science. Up to twenty-five percent of all human conceptions do not complete the twentieth week of pregnancy. One out of four conceived human embryos die. Seventy-five percent of fatal deaths occur in the first twelve weeks. Neonatal death (that is, death in the womb), Paranatal death (that is, death at the time of birth) occur in massive numbers. According to one conservative study an estimated 4,350,000 babies (foetuses, embryos, infants) died in 1999 alone. See the United Nations website for infant mortality rates and other information at http://data.un.org/Data.aspx?d=PopDi v&f=variableID%3A77.

4. Roman Catholic Church, "The Hope of Salvation for Infants Who Die Without Being Baptized," para. 2.

without Baptism. All the more urgent is the Church's call not to prevent little children coming to Christ through the gift of holy Baptism.[5]

Belief in infant salvation is thus raised to the level of hope not dogma. The Report makes this clear when it concludes:

> [T]hat the many factors that we have considered above give serious theological and liturgical grounds for hope that unbaptised infants who die will be saved and enjoy the Beatific Vision. We emphasise that these are reasons for prayerful hope, rather than grounds for sure knowledge. There is much that simply has not been revealed to us (cf. Jn 16:12). We live by faith and hope in the God of mercy and love who has been revealed to us in Christ, and the Spirit moves us to pray in constant thankfulness and joy (cf. 1 Thess 5:18).[6]

Equally clear within the Report are the many theological issues which have to be considered in making such a decision, most notably in a Roman Catholic context the principle of the "hierarchy of truths",[7] the universal salvific will of God, the unicity and insuperability of the mediation of Christ, the sacramentality of the Church in the order of salvation, and the reality of original sin.[8] What the Roman Catholic revision of Limbo highlights is both the theological and pastoral issues bound up with the question of the fate of infants who die. Central to such issues are the universality of sin, the doctrine of original sin, the universality of the work of Christ, and the nature of God, amongst others. Each of these issues requires careful examination before a conclusion over the issue of infant salvation can be reached, tentative as it must be, given the sparse biblical testimony.

While this is not an exegetical essay it is incumbent upon us to at least outline the representative texts upon which any discussion of the fate of infants who die is based upon. While there are no biblical texts which directly answer the question before us there are a cluster of texts

5. Roman Catholic Church, *Catechism*, Part Two, Section Two, Chapter One, Article One, VI The Necessity of Baptism, para. 1261.

6. Roman Catholic Church, "The Hope of Salvation for Infants Who Die Without Being Baptized," para.102.

7. That is, the primacy of Christ and his grace, which has priority over Adam and sin. Ibid., para. 7.

8. Ibid., para. 1.

which shed light on the issue, if one is attuned to them. Among these we may at least mention the following:

1. Deuteronomy 1:39. The children of the rebellious Israelites were not penalised on account of their parents' sin. They were too young to have knowledge of good and evil and, unlike their parents, would be permitted to enter the Promised Land. The Promised Land which the children would inherit was typical of God's eternal kingdom (see Hebrews 11:13–16). This is argued convincingly by Mohler, Jr. and Akin, "The Salvation of the 'Little Ones.'"[9]

2. 2 Samuel 12:23. Since David believed in the reality of the heavenly afterlife, his words would make no sense if the dead child was not safe in heaven. Compare this with David's despairing cry over his rebellious son Absalom's death in 2 Samuel 18:33. The Cushite's report of Absalom's death offers no hope for the dead rebel (see v.32).

3. 2 Kings 4:26. Concerning the dead child of the Shunammite woman, the mother affirmed—in answer to Gehazi's question, "Is it well with the child?"—that "it is well." The inference is obvious. In its dead condition, there was nothing to fear in respect of the child's eternal welfare. Interestingly, no mention is made of the child's circumcision, the sign of its Israelite status and gracious acceptance by God.

4. Ezekiel 16:21. During Israel's wicked and idolatrous apostasy, children were sacrificed by fire to the ancient pagan Canaanite deity Moloch. God calls the sacrificed little ones "my children." They were evidently safe with God despite the sins of the parents.

5. Jonah 4:11. God showed particular compassion towards the infants of wicked Nineveh (assuming that those who don't know their right hand from their left include infants). Significantly, God was "gracious and merciful...slow to anger and abundant in loving-kindness" (v.2) towards Gentile children. Being outside of the covenant community was no barrier to their salvation.

6. Jeremiah 31:15–17 and Matthew 2:18. There is every reason to believe that the children killed by Herod's men were as eternally

9. Mohler and Akin, "The Salvation of Little Ones."

safe as those sacrificed to Moloch (see no. 4 above). We may say of such victims that "the children shall come back," (see Jer 31:17). Notwithstanding the parents' grief, their children's position was not hopeless however horrific their death was.

7.  Mark 10:13–16, Matthew 18:1–6, and 21:15–16. The loving view of little children expressed by Jesus Christ is consistent with the Old Testament—they are eternally safe.

8.  If God's kindness extends to animals and birds, we dare not imagine infants are less kindly regarded (see Matthew 10:29–31).

9.  Matthew 19:14 expressly states that the kingdom belongs to little children.

10.  The basis of their salvation is the same for adults, i.e. by God's free, unmerited grace and favour alone (see Ephesians 2:8).

11.  Their salvation is not based on their supposed absolute innocence (since all fell in Adam, see Romans 5:12ff.).

12.  God is able to act directly on those incapable of responding to God's saving truth. In short, regeneration can occur in the womb. Clearly, Jeremiah and John the Baptist are examples of this (see Jer 1:5 and Luke 1:44).

13.  The Baptist C. H. Spurgeon and the Presbyterian Charles Hodge believed that since the saved are a "great multitude which no one could number" (Rev 7–9), this must include infants many of whom have died throughout human history. On the analogy that the prison population is much smaller than the general population, it is argued that more are saved than lost. This must also include children dying in infancy.[10]

## VOICES FROM THE PAST

The destiny of children who die before baptism has been of perennial interest in the Christian tradition. One of the first to explicitly and directly consider the idea was Gregory Nyssen who wrote a work specifically on the destiny of infants who die entitled *De infantibus praemature abreptis libellum*.[11] Gregory is clear that infants have the stain of original sin and

---

10. For some of these texts I am indebted to Clifford, "Infant Salvation: Are All Those Who Die in Infancy Saved?"

11. Gregory of Nyssa, *On Infants Early Deaths*, 35–41.

yet they have no personal guilt. They have not done any deeds and thus they cannot be recompensed or rewarded. Furthermore, they certainly have committed no wrong deeds and so they cannot be punished. They are, in a sense, in a neutral position, not good enough for heaven and not bad enough for hell. As such, Gregory cannot say that unbaptised infants attain the same state as the baptised. Gregory thus retains a typically Eastern apophatic reticence on the issue and fails to finally explain what the state of unbaptised infants is or where they go.

This rather neutral position was roundly dismissed by Augustine of Hippo in a rather typical, Western-Latin, imperialist tone.[12] Augustine insisted instead that baptism was necessary for salvation and that due to the stain and guilt of original sin even babies would be consigned to hell if they were not baptised.[13] He did, however, concede that once in hell their torment would be the mildest of all its residents. Little comfort to grieving parents I am sure. Augustine addressed the question because Pelagius was teaching that infants could be saved without baptism. In countering Pelagius, Augustine affirmed the necessity of baptism as he applied the logic of his doctrine of original sin to the issue.[14] Nothing could be clearer for Augustine, than that without baptism one cannot inherit eternal life.

The Council of Carthage in AD 418 formally rejected the teaching of Pelagius and enshrined Augustine's position as authoritative. It condemned the opinion that infants "do not contract from Adam any trace of original sin, which must be expiated by the bath of regeneration that leads to eternal life." Positively, this council taught that "even children who of themselves cannot have yet committed any sin are truly baptised for the remission of sins, so that by regeneration they may be cleansed from what they contracted through generation." It was also added that there is no "intermediate or other happy dwell-

---

12. See Augustine, *De verbis apostoli sermo* xiv, coll. 1738.

13. Augustine earned the unenviable title *durus infantum pater* for his part in the controversy with Pelagius over the destiny of infants. In Warfield's opinion this is "a designation doubly unjust," and that "he was even preparing its destruction by the doctrines of grace, of which he was more truly the father," Warfield, "The Development of the Doctrine of Infant Salvation," 412–13. In Warfield's opinion Fulgentius, Alcimus, and Gregory the Great gave far stronger expression to the woe of unbaptised infants than Augustine ever did. See ibid., 413.

14. For a history of the debate and an exposition of Augustine's position see Warfield, "Introductory Essay on Augustin and the Pelagian Controversy," 12–109.

ing place for children who have left this life without Baptism, without which they cannot enter the kingdom of heaven, that is, eternal life."[15] This teaching was adopted by the Council of Trent in its fifth session, thus becoming part of Canon law.[16]

Augustine's strict view held sway throughout much of the middle Ages. Anselm of Canterbury and Hugh of St Victor are typical advocates here as is Dante's description in one of his poems. Dante pictures

> "young children innocent, whom Death's sharp teeth have ere yet they were freed from the sin with which our birth is bent," as imprisoned within the brink of hell, "where the first circle girds the abyss of dread," in a pale where "there is no sharp agony," but "dark shadows only," and whence "no other plaint rises than that of sighs; which from the sorrow without pain arise."[17]

It was not until Peter Abelard and Peter Lombard that this view was softened. From this point on a milder version of Augustine's position predominated and paved the way for Aquinas's formal revision. According to this softer version infants who die without being baptised are denied the beatific vision due to original sin but they are not subjected to any punishment due to a lack of mortal sin. In effect, as per the earlier position, they exist neither in a state of heaven nor hell. From the turn of the 12–13th centuries the concept of Limbo was a common belief of the Roman Catholic Church that espoused such thinking.

## PERENNIAL ISSUES: GRACE, SIN, AND SALVATION

Placing this question squarely in the middle of a Protestant context the issue of baptism is substituted for that of personal faith. Given the Reformation *solas* (*gratia, fide, scriptura, Christus,* and *Deo gloria*), and a rejection of a Roman Catholic sacramentalism, the issue revolves around the lack of personal faith in Jesus Christ by an infant. For this reason the same issues pertain to the fate of the severely mentally disabled.

In order to account for such situations various Protestant traditions devised their own responses to the issue. For my purposes I will limit

---

15. See *Enchiridion Symbolorum,* 223.

16. The Council of Trent, Fifth Session, Decree on Original Sin, see ibid., 1514; and *The Christian Faith in the Doctrinal Documents of the Catholic Church,* 511.

17. Cited in Warfield, "The Development of the Doctrine of Infant Salvation," 414–15.

myself to two such Protestant traditions, the Reformed and the Baptist, and I do so for various reasons. In the first place, I am a Reformed theologian and so I am seeking to resource my own tradition as much as any other. Second, Reformed theology stands self-consciously in the stream of the Augustinian tradition, thus the themes of original sin, the centrality of Christ, and its constituent sacramental dynamics are present. Third, the Reformed tradition has given divergent answers to this dilemma and thus a fresh study of the theme may be of use today. Finally, as Warfield once remarked, "It is the confessional doctrine of the Reformed churches and of the Reformed churches alone, that all believers' infants, dying in infancy, are saved."[18] It would seem Warfield's bold claim is not as universally held as he thought. In addition to thinking through these issues within the context of Reformed theology I will bring this perspective into dialogue with certain Baptist thinkers, and again I will do so for various reasons. In the first place I am a Baptist (Baptist Union of New Zealand). In the second place I lecture at a Baptist college and thus the Baptistic world is the one in which I am most typically immersed. Thirdly, Baptists have also considered these issues in some depth and have attempted to come to their own conclusions and thus it will be worthwhile bringing these two traditions into critical dialogue for the mutual benefit of each. Finally, being personally Reformed and Baptist I believe that these traditions are best suited to represent an Evangelical Calvinist answer to the fate of infants who die and that of the severely mentally disabled.[19]

In 1891 the Princeton Presbyterian Benjamin B. Warfield outlined various proposals to account for the destiny of infants who die.[20] In his

18. Ibid., 436.

19. Perspectives on this issue from outside Reformed and Baptistic ones are, of course, available. One thinks, for instance, of Lusk, *Paedofaith*, 67–72. Written from the perspective of the Federal Vision it seems to argue that all children of Christian parents have "faith" and are thus saved, as faith is not cognitive assent but covenant inclusion. This typically Federal Vision perspective is not conducive at all to an Evangelical Calvinism. Wesleyan, Eastern Orthodox, and others views are not part of the discussion in this chapter.

20. Warfield, "The Development of the Doctrine of Infant Salvation," 411–44. For an analysis of Warfield's position see Clark, "Warfield, Infant Salvation, and the Logic of Calvinism," 459–64. Clark criticises Warfield's arguments and concludes that "Contrary to Warfield's thesis, then, it seems most reasonable—given the inner logic of his Calvinist system—to resolve the trilemma by affirming that only some of the infants who die are elected by God and will be saved," ibid., 464. It is unclear if this is Clark's

view there were three general positions: the "ecclesiastical," the "humanitarian," and the "gracious." The ecclesiastical view asserts that salvation comes through membership in the visible church, of which baptism is the vehicle of entry. Thus baptised infants will be saved, all others will not. This was quickly recognized as the Roman Catholic view.[21] The humanitarian view asserts that the individual must cooperate with God in salvation in using their free will to accept salvation. Infants cannot exercise this free will (neither can the severely mentally disabled), thus an "age of accountability" is introduced. Those under this age are not held responsible for the guilt of Adam and are saved. Many Baptists and Arminians were included in this view.[22] Finally, the gracious view asserts that salvation is by grace alone therefore the elect are saved, the numbers and identity of such are known only to God. Thus infants who are elected by God will be saved. Warfield identifies this with the Reformed position and accepts it as his own.[23]

As useful as his taxonomy is, Warfield has yet failed to give a clear answer as to the destiny of those who die in infancy. His position, however, accords most clearly with those of Loraine Boettner when he wrote:

> Most Calvinistic theologians have held that those who die in infancy are saved. The Scriptures seem to teach plainly enough that the children of believers are saved; but they are silent or practically so in regard to those of the heathens. The Westminster Confession does not pass judgment on the children of heathens

---

personal position or simply the logic he sees in Warfield's arguments. This issue will be taken up later in the essay.

21. It is also identified with the Lutheran and Anglican views. Martin Luther is perhaps the strongest advocate of such a position when in response to the Anabaptists, he argued forcefully for the salvation of baptised infants only, or of those who intended to get baptised but died before being able to do so. See Luther, *The Holy and Blessed Sacrament of Baptism*, 35:27, 37; *Concerning Rebaptism*, 40:251; *Comfort for Women Who Have Had a Miscarriage*, 43:245; and for an overview of his theology at this point, see Zietlow, "Martin Luther's Arguments for Infant Baptism," 150. Luther's strong stance was adopted in the original 1530 *Augsburg Confession*, but under Melanchthon's guidance this was mitigated in the subsequent 1540 revision. See Schaff, *The Evangelical Protestant Creeds*, 3–73, especially 13.

22. A representative Baptist text here is Erickson, *Christian Theology*, 654–56. Erickson's view is predicated on the idea of an age of accountability or responsibility coupled with the idea of a "conditional imputation of guilt" from Adam to the infant until the age of moral accountability.

23. He goes on to outline five distinct Reformed interpretations of this position, however, in Warfield, "The Development of the Doctrine of Infant Salvation," 431–34.

who die before coming to years of accountability. Where the Scriptures are silent, the Confession, too, preserves silence. Our outstanding theologians, however, mindful of the fact that God's "tender mercies are over all His works," and depending on His mercy widened as broadly as possible, have entertained a charitable hope that since these infants have never committed any actual sin themselves, their inherited sin would be pardoned and they would be saved on wholly evangelical principles.[24]

He goes on to include Charles Hodge, W. G. T. Shedd, and B. B. Warfield as holding to such a view. But is an appeal to and hope in God's "mercy" sufficient here?

There are, however, contrary voices in the Reformed tradition. G. C. Berkouwer believes that "the practice of infant baptism rests upon a definite confession,"[25] and thus guarantees the security of believer's children. Thus baptism is the means by which infants may be assured of salvation. This is the Reformed doctrine of covenant succession. This is illustrated well in the old Dutch Reformed "Form for the Baptism of Infants." This Form states that believing parents acknowledge their children are sinful objects of wrath from conception and are therefore subject to all manner of misery, even eternal condemnation; yet as recipients of the divine promise of grace, they are "sanctified in Christ" and so as "members of his church ought to be baptised."[26] Here baptism and salvation are linked so as to affirm that the *baptised* infants of believers, if they should die, are saved, while those of unbelievers, and thus the unbaptised, are not. The theological rationale for such practice is that of covenantal succession by means of baptism.[27]

A defense of this possession, despite not using the technical vocabulary, was given recently by Mark Beach.[28] Beach critiques a number

---

24. Boettner, *The Reformed Doctrine of Predestination*, 143.

25. Berkouwer, *The Sacraments*, 161.

26. *Psalter Hymnal*, 125.

27. Perhaps the strongest current advocate of such a position today is Engelsma, *The Covenant of God and the Children of Believers*, 13–16. For a discussion of this point see Mouw, "Baptism and the Salvific Status of Children," 238–54. For a possible Reformed defence of the position that un-baptised infants who die go to hell, see Sproul Jr., "Conform Ye My People," 26. It is a "possible" defence as Sproul says that all who die without receiving Christ as saviour go to hell, while also equivocating over the exact destiny of children who die.

28. Beach, "Original Sin, Infant Salvation, and the Baptism of Infants," 47–79. Beach appeals to the following texts to prove his point: Gen 7:21–23; Exod 6:12; Lev 19:23;

of contemporary Baptist theologians charging their theology as "hopelessly inconsistent."[29] According to his reading, Stanley Grenz, Millard Erickson, Gordon Lewis, and Bruce Demarest all present, in the final analysis, an argument for the salvation of all infants who die on the basis that they are not guilty of original sin, judgment is according to works which they cannot commit, and they cannot exercise saving faith. Thus God graciously saves them by a direct act of grace. Beach correctly shows how this view evades a doctrine of original sin, and posits two kinds of salvation for two different kinds of people—infants and adults. In the former, faith is not a requirement while for the latter it is. Beach then perceptively asks why infants who die need the cross of Christ to be saved. He answers that according to Baptist logic they don't, despite assertions from such Baptists to the contrary. If infants are not guilty of original sin then the cross of Christ has no impact upon them. Infants are thus saved apart from Christ's work on the cross. This, argues Beach, is patently unbiblical.

Instead, Beach resorts to a standard Reformed interpretation of original sin and imputed guilt, and then appeals to the cross of Christ as the only means of salvation for the elect, young or old. He then adds the concept of covenant succession by asserting the necessity of baptism for salvation as infants, like adults, require faith to be saved. In the case of infants, faith is supplied by the believing parents such that the infants are children of promise and are thus covered by the blood of Christ. In the final analysis, according to Beach, *baptised* infants who die are saved while the rest are not. Warfield's fears over baptismal regeneration are thus realized in Beach's argument.

As tightly argued as Beach's argument is, it is not compelling nor is it, in the final analysis, consistent with confessional Reformed theology, as the next section highlights.[30]

---

26:41; Deut 10:16; 30:6; Jer 4:4; 6:10; 9:25; Exod 11:4–7; 12:12, 29–30; Num 21:21–35; Deut 2:34; 3:6; 7:2; and 1 Cor 7:14, ibid., 76–77.

29. Ibid., 72.

30. Other significant discussions on infant salvation from a Reformed perspective include: Webb, *The Theology of Infant Salvation*; Shedd, "Infant Salvation as Related to Original Sin"; Schenck, *The Presbyterian Doctrine of Children in the Covenant*; and Strawbridge, ed. *The Case for Covenantal Infant Baptism.*

## CONFESSIONAL THEOLOGY

Beach's conclusions go against much of the standard Reformed arguments that assert that no Reformed confession states either that *all* infants who die are saved or that infants of unbelievers are *not* saved. All that can be found within the Reformed confessions is a positive assertion that infants of believers who die are saved.[31] We see this illustrated in a sophisticated way in the Synod of Dort, Article I/17, which teaches the salvation of believer's children, but importantly, remains silent on the fate of unbelievers.[32] It reads:

> Since we must make judgments about God's will from his Word, which testifies that the children of believers are holy, not by nature but by virtue of the gracious covenant in which they together with their parents are included, godly parents ought not to doubt the election and salvation of their children whom God calls out of this life in infancy.

In the words of Cornelis Venema, ". . . Article I/17 offers a ringing, unqualified affirmation of the confidence believers may have in the election and salvation of their children whom God calls to himself in infancy."[33] This, it can be argued, should be the universal position of Reformed theology.

The reason for the inclusion of Article I/17 in the Canons of Dort was the insistence of the Arminian Remonstrant's that according to Calvinistic logic, God incomprehensibly (arbitrarily) elects some people to salvation and others to reprobation. This applies to infants as equally as it does to adults, thus some children of believers who die in infancy will be reprobates. The Synod of Dort inserted Article I/17 to categorically refute such a position. In studying the background material to the Synod of Dort, and to the writing of Article I/17 in particular, it is interesting to note the diversity of views amongst the delegates on the issue of infant salvation. Venema's study has shown that the various delegations at the Synod were asked to draft responses to the Remonstrant articles and amongst them the responses varied.

---

31. For a comprehensive overview of infant salvation in the various creeds and confessions of the Reformed churches see Webb, *The Theology of Infant Salvation*, 298-330.

32. For a brief background study of Article I/17 see Gootjes, "Can Parents Be Sure?"; and Godfrey, "Election and Covenant."

33. Venema, "The Election and Salvation of the Children of Believers Who Die in Infancy," 57–100.

On the basis of texts such as Rev 20:1; 21:17; and Luke 18:16, the English delegates to the Synod of Dort argue for the elect status of all infants who die.[34] The Swiss delegates argued that the children of believers who die are elect as they are part of the covenant of grace, they have not reached "the years of discretion" and thus are saved, and their ministering angels will be sent out for their sake.[35] The Bremen delegates likewise affirm the elect status of infants of believers who die and add "they also, with a view to the covenant, are holy. In order to confirm this, they are initiated by holy baptism and put on Christ."[36]

It was the three Dutch professors—Polyander, Thysius, and Walleus—invited to present formal papers at the Synod, that most clearly present an argument against the Arminian charge and argue, in forthright language, that the infants of believers alone are saved, all others are "unclean, alienated from Christ and from the covenant of grace."[37] Apart from exclusion from the covenant of grace by not being baptised, the professors appealed to a common Reformed practice that argued that infants of believers were incapable of breaking the conditions of the covenant given they had not reached an "age of discretion" and thus would not be judged by God on this account.[38] This general line of argument was followed by Sybrandus Lubbertus and Franciscus Gomarus, theologians who were also invited to make a response.[39] The Drench delegates follow the same line of argument and importantly, also include in their discussion "adults who have been insane from the beginning of their life,"[40] that is, those we now classify as severely mentally disabled.

34. Ibid., 66–67.

35. Ibid., 67–68.

36. Ibid., 69.

37. Ibid., 69–71.

38. Ibid., 70 n.18, points to various Reformed theologians who support such an idea of an "age of discretion," before which infants cannot break the covenant and thus will not be judged on this basis. Venema includes in this list Ulrich Zwingli and Heinrich Bullinger.

39. Ibid., 71–72.

40. Ibid., 74–75. Vos, *The Covenant of Grace*, 23, applies this principle with vigour when he writes: "It is true that some of the children of believing parents are not of the elect, and turn out to be covenant-breakers. But an infant that dies before reaching the years of discretion cannot be a covenant-breaker; it cannot despise and violate the obligation of the Covenant of Grace. Therefore we have the best of reasons for believing that all children of believing parents dying in infancy are not only within the Covenant of Grace, but also of the number of the elect and shall certainly be saved."

Still another group, the delegates from the Particular Synod of South Holland, presented something of a mediating theology between the Reformed responses we have so far considered. While offering hope for all believing parents whose infants have died, they still affirm the possibility of the reprobation of some children of believers. In the final analysis they leave it to the judgment of God.[41]

As it stands, Article I/17 is a clear statement that believing parents of infants who die may have an assurance that their child is with the Lord, and an equally clear statement that all children of believers who die in infancy or are severely mentally disabled are elect and saved. In the subsequent history of Reformed theology there have been no formal arguments over Article I/17, thus we must take this to mean this is the prevalent Reformed confessional view.[42] What is not clear, however, is the role that baptism plays. Is baptism required for infants of believing parents for them to be considered part of the covenant community or not? As we have seen, various delegations to the Synod of Dort held differing views on the issue of covenantal succession. These differing views have continued within Reformed theology.

The other major confessional treatment of the destiny of infants who die is found in the Westminster Confession of Faith. It will be instructive to compare the Canons of Dort to the WCF in order to build a clearer picture of formal Reformed stances on this topic.[43]

41. Venema, "The Election and Salvation of the children of Believers Who Die in Infancy," 72–73.

42. This is not to imply there have not been a variety of views on the Article. Venema clearly canvasses two broad reactions to the Article which he calls, the objective view and the subjective view. The objective, stronger, or positive view insists Article I/17 is a positive affirmation of the salvation of all children of believing parents who die in infancy. The subjective, or weaker view argues that Article I/17 only speaks of the attitude or hope that believing parents should have with respect to their infant children, ibid., 81–92. Examples of the first position include Vos, *The Covenant of Grace*; and Bavinck, *Reformed Dogmatics: vol. 4*, 724–27; and Bavinck, *Saved by Grace*, 69. Examples of the second position include Hoeksema, *Believers and their Seed*, 149–58; and Beeke, "Children Dying in Infancy," 22–23.

43. Also relevant are the writings of the Westminster divines on infant salvation outside of the WCF. Davis (http://www.the-highway.com/infant-salvation_Davis .html) lists the following: Baillie, *Anabaptisme*; Burgess, *Baptismall Regeneration of Elect Infants*; Carter, *The Covenant of God with Abraham, opened*; Cawdrey, *The Inconsistencie of Independent way with Scripture and it self*; Cawdrey, *A Sober Answer to a Serious Question propounded by Mr. G. Firmin*; Dury, *A true relation of the conversion and baptism of Isuf*; Marshal, *A Defence of Infant-Baptism*; Marshal, *A Sermon of the Baptizing of Infants*; and Wallis, *A Defense of Infant-Baptism*.

The Westminster Confession of Faith follows in the same vein as that of Dort. In WCF 10.3 we read:

> Elect infants, dying in infancy, are regenerated, and saved by
> Christ, through the Spirit, who works when, and where, and how
> He pleases: so also are all other elect persons who are incapable
> of being outwardly called by the ministry of the Word.[44]

Immediately we can see the continuity between WCF 10.3 and Article 1/17 of the Canons of Dort. Both refer specifically to the doctrine of election as the means by which infants may be saved, both make reference to the severely mentally disabled as being included in the same category of infants who die, and both unequivocally provide an assurance of salvation for the parents of such individuals. The Canons of Dort and the WCF also make it clear that a Reformed doctrine of infant salvation (and that of the severely mentally disabled) does not rest on their supposed innocence (Roman Catholicism), is not based on anything intrinsic within the individuals, such as implicit faith or some such (Arminians),[45] nor is it based on a sentimental appeal to the mercy and grace of God (many Baptists).[46]

As with the Canons of Dort, however, WCF 10.3 does have a variety of interpretations attached to it. Some interpretations have asserted that there are non-elect infants who die and are thus damned. This is, however, a mistaken interpretation and one that a close study of the Confession rules out immediately. In order to guard against this misinterpretation the PCUSA added a Declaratory Statement to the WCF in 1903 which reads:

> . . . with reference to Chapter 10, Section 3, of the Confession
> of Faith, that it is not to be regarded as teaching that any who
> die in infancy are lost. We believe that all dying in infancy are

---

44. It is noteworthy that the *Second London Baptist Confession* follows the exact wording here in chapter 10, article 3. See *The Baptist Confession of Faith and The Baptist Catechism*, 25.

45. See Wesley's letter to John Mason dated 21 November 1776, in Wesley, *Works,* vol. 12, 453. Cf. Rishell, "Wesley and Other Methodist Fathers on Childhood Religion," 778–784; and Willhauck, "John Wesley's View of Children." I am grateful to Peter Benzies, a former student of mine, for pointing me to these Wesleyan sources.

46. This last position is clearly modelled by the Reformed theologian Smedes, "Can God Reach the Mentally Disabled?" 94, but is found in many popular tracts on infant salvation amongst Baptists, Reformed, and the many who make up those called the Evangelicals.

included in the election of grace, and are regenerated and saved
by Christ through the Spirit, who works when and where and
how he pleases.[47]

Thus all infants who die are elect and thus saved. This view is clearly
presented by Vos in his contention that WCF 10.3 does not support the
assertion that there is a class of "non-elect infants dying in infancy."[48]
Article 10 of the WCF describes the effectual calling of the elect and
clarifies that this normally takes place through the "ordinary means of
grace." The inclusion of 10.3 speaks to how infants may be saved without
such "ordinary means" and thus presents their salvation in terms of an
extraordinary manner. When we note the inclusion of the infants of unbelievers and also include the severely mentally disabled, this addition is
a significant clarification of the issue and addresses Warfield's fears over
baptismal regeneration.

One final Reformed confession is worth mentioning, the Confession of the Cumberland Presbyterian Church (1829), Tennessee,
USA. Written as a corrective to certain aspects of the WCF, chapter 10,
article 3 of the Confession reads:

> All infants dying in infancy are regenerated and saved by Christ
> through the Spirit [Luke 18:15,16; Acts 2:38, 39], who worketh
> when, and where, and how he pleaseth [John 3:8]; so also are
> others who have never had the exercise of reason, and who are
> incapable of being outwardly called by the ministry of the Word.[49]

According to this confessional Reformed view, infant death and severe
mental disability is indicative of divine election.[50] It would appear this is
the final Reformed position (though not confession) on the topic.

47. For the background to and commentary of these changes see Hart and Muether,
"Turning Points in American Presbyterian History."

48. Vos, *The Covenant of Grace*, 24.

49. *The Creeds of Christendom*, 3:773. Formed in 1810, the Cumberland Presbyterian
Church is a small Reformed and Presbyterian denomination with its headquarters in
Memphis, Tennessee. It has its own Confession which is a revision of the Westminster
Confession of Faith, specifically in regards to predestination, the eternal decrees, and
infant salvation. It's official website http://www.cumberland.org/center/believe.htm
describes itself as a moderate form of Calvinism and evangelical, and to this extent it
approaches an Evangelical Calvinism.

50. A 1908 article in the *New York Times* reported that the issue of infant salvation
was a dead one and that a proposed paper for Calvin Day at the next Assembly entitled
"Calvin and Infant Salvation" be deleted from the programme as it was "hurting the

## BAPTIST RESPONSES

This latter view is shared by many theologically Reformed figures, past and present, including many Baptists. There is a modest body of literature in Baptist circles on infant salvation given the generally held assumption that all infants who die go to heaven.[51] The following surveys several Reformed and Baptist thinkers on the topic.[52] The famous Baptist pastor, Charles Spurgeon believed that all infants who die go to heaven and that there is no other Calvinist view. He then characteristically went on to use this as an occasion for an evangelistic sermon![53] Spurgeon argues his point on the basis of the goodness of God, the character of Christ, the ways of grace, the fact that the number of saved souls will be a great multitude, and selected biblical texts. He then asks parents to make sure they are saved so they may see their dead infants again. So certain is Spurgeon that he wrote, "I rejoice to know that the souls of all infants, as soon as they die, speed their way to paradise. Think what a multitude there is of them!"[54]

John MacArthur recently argued for the salvation of all infants who die on similar grounds to Spurgeon.[55] MacArthur's arguments are

Church to keep up discussion as to infant salvation and infant damnation, and that it was a dead issue." The motion was lost 86 to 55, however "Most of the speakers expressed the opinion that the Presbyterian Church of today does not teach nor believe in infant damnation," see "Presbyterians on Calvin."

51. See the typically brief discussion by Lemke, "A Biblical and Theological Critique of Irresistible Grace," 109–62.

52. While modest, Baptist thinking on infant salvation does exist. In addition to what follows, Richard Fuller's (1804–1876) short tract on the topic has been highly influential on Baptist thinking; Fuller, *Infant Salvation, Baptism and Dedication*; as evidenced in part by its regular citation and that it is reprinted as "Infant Salvation, Dedication, and Baptism," in Haynes, *The Baptist Denomination*, 185–93; and "Infant Salvation," in Cathcart, *The Baptist Encyclopaedia*, 2:581. Perhaps the earlier statement on infant salvation from the Anabaptist tradition goes to Hübmaier, *On the Christian Baptism of Believers*, 93.

53. Spurgeon, "Infant Salvation."

54. Spurgeon, *Spurgeon at His Best*, 95. The fact that Spurgeon thought there may be more infants in heaven than adults is also found in the thought of John Newton, who once said the number of infants in heaven "so greatly exceeds the aggregate of adult believers that, comparatively speaking, the kingdom may be said to consist of little children." Newton, *The Works of John Newton*, 4:552.

55. Although MacArthur is a Dispensationalist, by aligning himself with a version of Reformed theology in recent years he has adopted a pseudo-Reformed-Dispensational theology. MacArthur, *Safe in the Arms of God*. For MacArthur's MP3 sermons on the

generally based on four premises: first, all children are conceived and born as sinners;[56] second, the salvation of every person is a matter of God's grace, not human works; third, salvation is based upon the sacrificial work of Jesus Christ on the cross; fourth, salvation is by grace, damnation is based on works. This last point is crucial for MacArthur's argument: infants and young children are incapable of sins which cause damnation, especially the sin of unbelief; children are incapable of believing; therefore they are incapable of unbelief; thus infants are saved. In arguing on this basis MacArthur appears to rely on the same theological foundation as the 2007 Roman Catholic statement on Limbo when it argued that "Grace is totally free, because it is always a pure gift of God. Damnation, however, is deserved, because it is the consequence of free human choice."[57]

John Piper holds a slightly different and idiosyncratic view. According to him infants become believers in heaven and thus they grow up there and exercise saving faith. He writes,

> God in his justice will find a way to absolve infants who die of their depravity. It will surely be through Christ. But beyond that we would be guessing. It seems to me that the most natural guess would be that babies will grow up in the kingdom (either immediately, or over time) and will by God's grace come to faith so that their justification is by faith alone just like ours.[58]

---

topic see: MacArthur, "The Salvation of Babies Who Die," Part 1: and Part 2. Another Dispensational perspective by a Baptist is offered by Zuck, *Precious in His Sight*, 217–41, especially 218–26; and included in Radmacher, another Baptist, in *Salvation*, 229–236. Dispensationalists have long discussed this topic, in addition to those already cited see for instance: Chafer, *Systematic Theology*, 7:196–99, who argues that the salvation of infants is "on other terms than those imposed upon the adult portion of humanity," ibid., 196; Baker, *A Dispensational Theology*, 460–466; and Geisler (also Baptist), *Baker Encyclopedia of Christian Apologetics*, 360–66.

56. This is a crucial point and one that is made clearly by a number of Baptists including Zuck, *Precious in His Sight*, 221; and Lightner, *Heaven for Those Who Can't Believe*, 7–8; as well as by non-Baptists, for instance, Downs, "Child Evangelization," 5–13.

57. Roman Catholic Church, "The Hope of Salvation for Infants Who Die Without Being Baptized," Introduction, para. 7. The fact that this argument, in itself, is incompatible with Reformed theology seems to be lost on MacArthur. This is most probably due to his lack of familiarity with confessional Reformed theology and his commitments to Dispensational theology.

58. See Piper, "What Happens to Infants Who Die?" Based largely upon John 9:41, Piper contends that "if a person lacks the natural capacity to see the revelation of God's

Albert Mohler and Daniel Akin, however, correctly point out that this is actually an argument for a post-mortem salvation, something first suggested by Gregory of Nyssa.[59] In their opinion, "The problem with this position is that Scripture teaches no such post-mortem opportunity. It is a figment of a theologian's imagination, and must be rejected."[60] In this they are surely correct. What Piper upholds is a view of salvation by faith alone which takes priority over a theology of salvation by grace alone.[61]

The final Baptist theologian we shall consider, Ronald Nash, argues for infant salvation in his little work *Answers to Grieving Parents*, but he is clear that it is not based on any of the following four faulty arguments: infants are innocent,[62] universalism, post-mortem salvation, or baptismal regeneration.[63] Infant salvation is based upon the fact that infants are incapable of moral good or evil, yet divine judgment is administered based on sins committed in the body (1 Cor 5:10). This view, argues Nash,

---

will or God's glory then that person's sin would not remain. God would not bring the person into final judgment for not believing what he had no natural capacity to see." Appealing to Romans 1:20, Piper makes clear that this principle does not apply to the unevangelized given their access to general revelation. See the useful distinction between those who die in infancy and the unevangelized in Nash, *When a Baby Dies*, 98-99. Buswell, *Systematic Theology*, 2:162, offers an alternative (and untenable) position, that all infants about to die are given the full consciousness of an adult that enables them to make the decision to accept God's gift of salvation.

59. See the view of Roman Catholic theologian Dyer, "The Unbaptized Infant in Eternity," 10–22.

60. Mohler and Akin, "The Salvation of the "Little Ones." Mohler is a Reformed Southern Baptist. Universalism is also rejected, as is the argument based on election. According to Mohler and Akin, to argue for infant salvation based on the doctrine of election is to "avoid answering the question." No further explanation is given as to why this may be the case. Oddly enough, however, they go on to ague for the salvation of all infants who die on the basis of their election! Perhaps Mohler and Akin are arguing against the charge of arbitrariness in God only electing some not all infants to salvation? It is hard to tell.

61. This unusual view is shared by Geisler, *Baker Encyclopedia of Christian Apologetics*, 360–66.

62. This is a commonly held to view amongst Baptists. See for instance the Southern Baptist theologian, Ingle, who writes that infants do not inherit "lostness" from Adam but choose it when they become a "morally responsible person." See "Children and Conversion," 9, and "Moving in the Right Direction," 153–54. This view is shared by Inchley, *Kids and the Kingdom*, 14, 33; and Jeschke, *Believers Baptism for Children of the Church*, 104.

63. Nash, *When a Baby Dies*.

is consistent with that established by Charles Hodge, B. B. Warfield, and others. Nash also makes the explicit link between infants who die and the mentally handicapped when he writes, "I will argue that all children who die in infancy and all mentally handicapped persons whose intellectual and moral judgment cannot exceed that of children are saved."[64] How is this Reformed and not an Arminian theology? "For Arminians, active repentance and faith are necessary conditions of salvation . . ." According to Reformed theology, however, "if Christ died specifically for those whom God chose or elected, then infant salvation [and that of the severely mentally disabled] becomes possible."[65] It is Reformed, then, because it is grounded in God's gracious election.[66] Nash, in arguing this way, is being consistent with the Reformed confessions, as we have seen, and is also modeling a pastoral approach which is theologically robust.

By way of summary, Reformed theology, while sponsoring a degree of interpretations on the matter, is confessionally clear that the children of believers who die in infancy may, with assurance, be considered elect, and as such, are saved. It also teaches that this also applies to the severely mentally disabled and, with less certainty, it is implied that all infants who die are, in fact, elect and saved. The arguments for such a position rest on the testimony of Scripture which points in this direction, a theology of God's gracious election, the reality of original sin and guilt applied to all, and the saving work of Christ for the elect. An appeal to some form of covenant succession is sometimes combined with the necessity of baptism, but as we have seen, this is a minority view and cannot be held to be the confessional Reformed position. Warfield summarizes this well:

> [A]ll who die in infancy are children of God and enter at once into His glory—not because original sin is not deserving of eternal punishment (for all are children of wrath), nor because they are less guilty than others . . . nor because they die in infancy (for that they die in infancy is not the cause but the effect of God's mercy toward them), but simply because God in His infinite love has chosen them in Christ, before the foundation of the world, by a loving foreordination of them unto adoption as sons in Jesus

64. Ibid., 59–60.

65. Ibid., 82.

66. Unlike MacArthur, Nash does not place the emphasis for his view upon the inability of infants to damn themselves, but uses this as a subordinate argument to unconditional election. Ibid.

Christ. Thus, as they hold, the Reformed theology has followed the light of the Word until its brightness has illuminated all its corners, and the darkness has fled away.[67]

Warfield's summary should not be taken to imply that the current Reformed position is without its problems. It is not. There remain darkened corners into which the light of the Word has yet to shine. In a critique of Warfield's view, which is really the same as the standard Reformed position on election, David Clark questions the arbitrary nature of affirming the election of *all* infants but only of *some* adults, and in so doing he resuscitates the Remonstrant complaint made at the Synod of Dort. We read, "The position that all infants who die are saved and only some adults are saved can be held, given the gracious view, only by conceding that God's decisions are based on arbitrary grounds. Is the salvation of all infants who die held for sentimental reasons?"[68] Here we come full circle back to the argument based on sentiment. Clark concludes, "Someone taking Warfield's gracious view, however, cannot hold that God acts reasonably in saving all infants who die and only some adults."[69] To this we could add the salvation of the severely mentally disabled and thus intensify Clark's complaint of arbitrariness.

I believe Clark is correct to challenge Warfield's Classic Calvinist arguments in this way. However, such criticisms are misplaced when they do not consider the wider theological commitments that instruct such a view. Here I am specifically thinking of Warfield's and older Reformed views of original sin, imputed guilt, and double election in the line of the scholastic-Westminster theology. Under such a logico-casual scheme as is offered by Reformed scholasticism, the charge of arbitrariness does indeed seem warranted. In addition, the doctrines of original sin and limited atonement, with which such scholastic theology works, are insufficiently coordinated so as to give the impression that the work of Christ for the salvation of infants who die and the severely mentally disabled is merely a general prevenient grace applied to those without

---

67. Warfield, "The Development of the Doctrine of Infant Salvation," 438.

68. Clark, "Warfield, Infant Salvation, and the Logic of Calvinism," 462. A defence against the charge of arbitrariness in God's election is offered by Berkouwer, *Divine Election*, 53–101. It may also be noted that Article I/17 of the Canons of Dort was devised precisely to answer this charge of arbitrariness raised by the Remonstrant Arminians of the day, specifically for the children of believers. See Venema, "The Election and Salvation of the children of Believers Who Die in Infancy," 60–64.

69. Clark, "Warfield, Infant Salvation, and the Logic of Calvinism," 462.

recourse to the ordinary means of grace. This would be a consistently Arminian doctrine of salvation! A reconsideration of a Reformed doctrine of original sin from the perspective of an Evangelical Calvinism is thus in order to more robustly address the destiny of infants who die and the severely mentally disabled.

## REFORMING THE DOCTRINE OF ORIGINAL SIN

No doctrine of salvation can ignore the doctrine of original sin. This is especially true within the context of Reformed theology which adheres to a broadly Augustinian view of sin and the generally held view of imputed guilt. The primary aspect of sin in Genesis is its entrance into the world. Genesis 3 presupposes certain things. First, the primitive perfection of humanity is assumed. This perfection enabled Adam and Eve to fulfill the purpose for which God had made them. Humanity was not originally sinful. The biblical account does not leave open the possibility for us that sinfulness is a necessary predicate of humanness. A good God cannot create a bad human. Scripture teaches that the world was a good place, with good people in it. Sin was alien, intrusive, and foreign.

Second, Genesis 3 presupposes the fall of Satan into sin. The story of humanity's fall is precipitated by sin already in the Devil, who comes personally to Eve and addresses her. Whether the speaking serpent is literal or figurative, for our purposes we must agree that sin did not originate with humanity, although it originated in humankind through a man and a woman.

Third, Genesis 3 presupposes a specific probationary command given by God to Adam. Adam and Eve were placed in the Garden of Eden with a specific prohibition addressed to them by God, namely the command forbidding them to eat of the tree of the knowledge of good and evil (Gen 2:17). Whether one accepts the covenant scheme (the covenant of works) or not it is clear that the probationary period involved Adam and Eve in a choice between good and evil, sin and holiness, right and wrong. However, there is more at stake than merely a personal choice. It is clear from the terms of the curse meted out (Gen 3:17–19) that the choice Adam made had profound consequences for himself and *all* humanity after him. Similarly, the curse on Eve in Gen 3:16 had respect to every child-bearing woman after her. Adam and Eve's actions had private and public, personal and community (covenantal) consequences. But what was the nature of this Edenic probation? John Murray answers:

> The Adamic administration is . . . an administration in which God, by a special act of Providence, established for man the provision whereby he might pass from the status of contingency to one of confirmed and indefectible holiness and blessedness, that is, from *posse peccare* and *posse non peccare* to *non posse peccare*.[70]

Against this backdrop the fall had drastic results. The divine response to Adam and Eve's sin is manifold, and corresponds to the seriousness of the crime of each of the characters. All of Adam's relationships are affected—with himself, with Eve, and with God. There is now enmity between God and his creatures. In addition the woman will have pain in child-bearing, and Adam in his work, and finally, the primitive couple are driven by God away from the garden, and are subject to laws of death and corruption. In its simplest form we may summarize the effect of this original sin by adopting these words from Gary Wills:

> . . . we are hostages to each other in a deadly interrelatedness. There is no "clean slate" of nature unscribbled on by all one's forebears . . . At one time a woman of unsavoury enough experience was delicately but cruelly referred to as "having a past." The doctrine of original sin states that humankind, in exactly that sense, "has a past."[71]

Original sin has two aspects, first; spiritual perversion, pollution, and disintegration, and second; guilt. The first aspect is universally agreed upon; the second is contested in much recent theology.[72] While it is clear that Adam and Eve were guilty before the Lord and had to accept the consequences of their actions, what about their descendants? What lies behind these questions is the specific question of imputation or impartation: Adam, as the first human being, represents every human being morally and legally. This appears to be the simple and uncontested fact from Scripture. Adam's sin may justly and legally implicate all

70. Murray, *Collected Writings of John Murray*, 2:49.

71. Wills, *Reagan's America: Innocents at Home*, 384, cited in Plantinga, *Not the Way It's Supposed to Be*, 198.

72. Whilst a bit dated the following is still a useful survey, McDermott, "Current Theology: The Theology of Original Sin: Recent Developments," 478–512. Cf. Henry, "Original Sin: A Flawed Inheritance," 3–12; and Fitzpatrick, "Original Sin or Original Sinfulness?" 701–17.

Adam's human descendants as a consequence of God's solemn promise to him that if he even touched the tree in the middle of the garden he would die (Gen 3:3). Although the text does not specifically call this a "covenant", it does exhibit the elements of a solemn promise or legal agreement made by God with Adam.

In Paul's theology Adam's sin implicated his descendants. Adam has a relationship to the fallen race parallel to Christ's relation to the redeemed in Rom 5:12–18. Adam's one sin brought condemnation to all generated in the fallen human family (vv. 16, 18). Christ's one sacrifice brings justification to all who have been regenerated in his moral and spiritual family. Adam's representation of all humans is not an arbitrary legal fiction. His legal representation is justified by the fact that each descendant has an Adamic nature not only as human but also as depraved or fallen (John 3:6).

In light of the importance of Rom 5:12–21 for a doctrine of original sin it will pay us to consider it in a little more detail. A reading of Rom 5:12–21 clearly shows two things: first, there is *continuity* between Adam and Christ, and second, there is a very real *discontinuity* between them; thus the relationship between the two is asymmetrical. In light of this we should not expect from this text a perfect symmetry between the two parallel stories.[73]

As we begin to look at this text we may immediately dismiss a few erroneous views from the start. Whatever one may think about the literalness or otherwise of Adam one must take Paul here at face value and on his own terms. For *him* Gen 3 is definitely literal. He is interested in the distinction of epochs. "We may be certain," writes Henry Blocher, "that Paul, in Romans 5, attributed a major role to an individual Adam and to his transgression in the beginning; this is what he meant, regardless of whether it appeals to our sensitivities."[74] The interpreter is tempted to do one of two things: first, loosen the link between Adam and Christ (Pelagianism), or second, tighten it (strict Augustinianism).[75] According

73. See Grenz, *Theology for the Community of God*, 258–75, especially 258–66. Many of Grenz's conclusions are conducive to those of Henry Blocher's and my own which follow.

74. Blocher, *Original Sin*, 64. I am indebted to Blocher's work on original sin as the following will indicate. Blocher has developed his views in the following: Blocher, "The Theology of the Fall and The Origins of Evil," 149–72.

75. C. E. B. Cranfield and James D. G. Dunn are examples of the first move; Augustine, William Shedd, and John Murray of the second. See further in ibid., 65–76.

to the first view all sin because they have *inherited* a bent towards sinning from Adam. They inherit from Adam a *propensity* to sin but are guilty because of their *personal* sins. This may be referred to as *original death* over *original sin*. In reply, Paul's emphasis in Rom 5.18ff. on the one act of disobedience, which constituted all human beings sinners, is so insistent that the idea of Adam simply as the remote cause of sin's introduction fails to match the force of Paul's language.

According to the second view, by virtue of Christ's headship, and of our being "in him," his righteousness, which is alien to us, is reckoned (*imputed*) to our account. Similarly, by virtue of Adam's headship, and of our being "in him," his sin and guilt, which are alien to us, are reckoned (*imputed*) to our account. This position argues that *immediate imputation* of sin and guilt is the possession of every human being. This position requires "death" in Rom 5 to be primarily *spiritual*—death as inflicted before birth, before conception even, in a logical sense at least. However, natural death seems prominent in Paul's mind in vv. 13, 14, not spiritual death (1 Cor 15 would seem to confirm this). This classical Calvinist account fails to adequately account for v.14 that "they did not sin after the likeness of Adam's transgression", and the emphasis in Reformed thought that all sinned in Adam.

Both interpretations above appear to share a disjunctive presupposition: *either* we are condemned for our own sins (and Adam's role is reduced to that of a remote fountainhead, losing much of its significance), *or* we are condemned for Adam's sin (and the equity of that transfer is hard to see). Now, what if this "either/or" were misleading? What if there was a third possibility intended by Paul? French Reformed theologian Henry Blocher presents an alternative hypothesis. In short it is as follows: The role of Adam and of his sin in Rom 5 is to make possible the imputation, the judicial treatment, of human sins. His role thus brings about the condemnation of all, and its sequel, death. Why? Because if there is no law and sin is left undefined, then it cannot be made the object of judgment. But God sees each individual in Adam and through Adam, in the framework of creation. Therefore God sees all sins as committed against the Genesis 2 command, as grafted on to Adam's sin in Eden. How did the punishment—death—reach all persons on the basis of their actual sinning? It reached them in the same way that death entered Adam's person: since all were in Adam, the head, sin could be reckoned to them according to the terms of the Adamic covenant, as offshoots of his sin.

In other words, Adam represents all humanity as its federal or legal head. But all humanity is not simply condemned due to Adam's *personal* sin. Rather, Adam, representing humanity, sinned and thus made it lawful for God to punish all human sin according to a violation of the covenant he made with Adam (humanity). We are punished for our own sinful actions but we are punished on the basis of the covenant which Adam, on behalf of us all, entered into. Adam is thus our covenant representative, not our substitute in the garden in committing a personal sin. In this regard Mohler and Akin argue that:

> [T]he Bible teaches that we are to be judged on the basis of our deeds committed "in the body." [2 Corinthians 5:10] That is, we will face the judgment seat of Christ and be judged, not on the basis of original sin, but for our sins committed during our own lifetimes. Each will answer "according to what he has done," [2 Corinthians 5:10] and not for the sin of Adam. The imputation of Adam's sin and guilt explains our inability to respond to God without regeneration, but the Bible does not teach that we will answer for Adam's sin. We will answer for our own. But what about infants? Have those who die in infancy committed such sins in the body? We believe not.[76]

What is important for Paul in Rom 5:12–21 is not the power of Adam's headship but the more pervasive power of Christ's work in redemption! A "refrain" is evident throughout this text holding it all together: "how much more" vv. 9, 10, 15, 17; and "overabundance" in v. 20, to say that Christ is a more powerful head than Adam ever was. Since justification has been established in chapters 3 and 4 of Romans (hence Rom 5:1, "Being therefore, justified . . ."), the issue is now that of *assurance*, of the fullness of the life to come as a sure inheritance. And the grand parallel with Adam serves as the grounding of that assurance: if Adam's role was so dramatically efficacious in securing the condemnation of all people in him, and therefore the reign of death, *how much more* is Christ's work efficacious for those in him, leading to eternal life!

The hypothesis Blocher proposes easily accounts for the imperfect symmetry between the two "heads" of humanity. Adam's role is more firmly cast than in the "looser" reading of Romans 5; at the same time,

---

76. Mohler and Akin, "The Salvation of the 'Little Ones.'" The fact that the guilt of Adam is imputed to all people is still an inherent problem in this position, however, making it ultimately unacceptable.

the unattested and difficult thesis of the imputation of an *alien* (another's) personal sin is avoided—without downplaying the tragic realism of the Augustinian-defined human predicament.[77] For Blocher, and I agree, Paul is not really talking about "inherited" sin. A better reading, truer to the text, would be to recognize that "the notion of inherited sin is not really in view here. Paul is talking about the universal nature of sin in that it affects all peoples."

If a federal headship is adopted then many of the objections raised so far do not apply. The doctrine preserves individual distinction. If God appointed Adam as the head of the human race, his acts rightfully counted as those of the entire community. That all members should stand under the obligation to pay the legal debt agrees with legal principle and practice, biblical and otherwise. The problem with the federal view is that the imputation of alien *guilt* strains the sense of justice in most readers.

I find the forensic or federal view of Adam's headship to be the most acceptable in the face of the biblical testimony. However, I do not find classical Calvinist statements of this position entirely satisfactory. It appears obvious to me that there is something different about Adam and me—the first temptation came *to* Adam. But our plight is different. Because sin lies at the core of our being, temptation already has a foothold *within* us (cf. James 1:14). According to Ephesians 2:1 we, unlike Adam, are born "dead in our trespasses and sins." Adam's sin has tainted us and permanently tainted the world. It has altered us and our world. But we are also told that we sin when we commit evil actions. So how do we rethink the problem of original sin within the confessional boundaries of Reformed theology?

A first observation has to be that we must not succumb to the rigid separation of the biological versus the spiritual, seeing them as mutually exclusive. After all, we are a synthesis of biology and Spirit: we are spiritual down to our toes, or to our instincts; we are living bodies right up to our mental activities, our longings, our loves.[78] If original sin involves both, it is human indeed. Contemporary studies in both theology and biology show convincingly that while there is a distinction there is no separation between bodily processes and personal freedom. This

---

77. Blocher, *Original Sin*, 80.

78. Humans are, in fact, bodies of their souls and souls of their bodies. The language comes from Karl Barth and Thomas Torrance. See Habets, *Theosis in the Theology of Thomas Forsyth Torrance*, 37–39.

brings us back to the issue of original sin: while we have a sinful nature does that mean we are automatically guilty before God *for the sin Adam personally committed*? In sympathy with Blocher I agree:

> With all due respect to the Reformed theology to which I am indebted, I have been led to question the doctrine of alien guilt transferred—that is, the doctrine of the imputation of all of Adam's own trespass, his act of transgression. If Scripture definitely taught such a doctrine, however offensive to modern taste, I should readily bow to its authority. But where does Scripture require it?[79]

This position is entirely consistent with Calvin's when he argued in the *Institutes* that depravity is passed along from Adam to his progeny, while guilt is not. What is passed along "is the inherited corruption, which the church fathers termed 'original sin,' meaning by the word 'sin' the depravation of a nature previously good and pure."[80] Calvin continues:

> . . . Adam, by sinning, not only took upon himself misfortune and ruin but also plunged our nature into like destruction. This was not due to the guilt of himself alone, which would not pertain to us at all, but was because he infected all his posterity with that corruption into which he had fallen.[81]

As has been pointed out before, such a mediated notion of inherited sin reads Romans 5 differently.[82] Being born sinners is not a penalty, or strictly speaking the result of transference, but simply an existential, spiritual fact for human beings since Adam. As a result of what Adam did humanity is no longer innocent but rather, born in sin and thus find themselves hostile to an all holy God. How is this fair? It is fair because of the covenant structure found within the narrative of Genesis 1–3. When God enters into covenant relationship with a people it is at his prerogative and initiative—and it is so for both the original covenant partner and their descendants. This is the right the Creator has over the creation. Calling upon Genesis 5:3 for support, the mandate and blessing of Genesis 1:28 is that the male and female should multiply, thus fathers

---

79. Blocher, *Original Sin*, 128.

80. Calvin, *Inst.*, 2.1.5.

81. Ibid., 2.1.6.

82. See the discussion by Allen, *Reformed Theology*, 97–98.

beget children in their own image and likeness. Since procreation is not merely biological, but is also human, it is no wonder that the determinant of the father's condition should be reproduced in the child's. Fallen Adam multiplies as fallen, and "what is born of the flesh is flesh." It is a fact that generates tragic consequences, but a rightful fact nevertheless.

Adam's headship involves a deeper privilege than ordinary fatherhood. It includes the dignity of defining what it means to be human. Being human *after the fall* is equivalent to bearing Adam's image (1 Cor 15:49)—this is how we come to be, and to be what we are. We are created "in Adam"; hence the impossibility of the blessing of divine fellowship remaining on Adam's descendents after he had rebelled. Grace is now, as always, necessary for the *visio Dei*.

How is this view different from the standard Reformed "federal" view? In reply we may note: it sees no necessity for the idea that alien guilt was transferred (that is, Adam's *particular* act was reckoned to the account of all). It emphasizes loss or deprivation in a relational framework (which immediately entails guilty depravity), since the rightness of the consequences "from Adam to his seed" is more easily perceived from that angle. Adam's legal capacity as the representative of the race is buttressed by a wider conception of his headship (biological and spiritual).

## THE VICARIOUS HUMANITY OF CHRIST

As we have had occasion to see, common to classic Arminianism, classic Calvinism, and much Baptist thought, explicit, conscious faith is required for one to be saved. In the case of the Arminian and Baptist, a supposed innocence of all infants is proffered, or for classic Calvinists, the faith of the believing parents is substituted for that of the infant through baptism. But both positions are incorrect biblically and theologically. What is required is a middle position in which faith is required but not the faith of the individual as an independent work. A *vicarious* faith is necessary—but who's? Parents' or a sponsor's faith for Baptism is not sufficient any more than it is with an adult or believer, if it were then it would be a work and thus Pelagian. Only the faith of Christ is sufficient, for adult/believer and infants and the severely mentally disabled. Thus the vicarious humanity and faith of Christ is necessary. According to Christian Kettler:

> Let me carefully define what "vicarious" means in terms of the vicarious humanity of Christ. Unfortunately, it can often mean to some people, "pseudo" or "false," as in the father getting a "vicarious" thrill from his son's accomplishments as an athlete . . . In that way it is "false," not real . . . . [But] the vicarious humanity of Christ does not mean that Christ's humanity is unreal. Quite the contrary! It does mean that the vicarious humanity of Christ speaks of the deep interaction between Christ's humanity and our humanity at the level of our being, the ontological level. So the atoning work of Christ is neither simply a means by which we are declared righteous by God, nor simply a demonstration of God's love. It is both, but much more, in the sense of God desiring to recreate our humanity at the deepest levels, addressing our needs and fears, our doubts from within our very being.[83]

Pressing the issue further, we can at least suggest that if regeneration precedes conversion, as all forms of Reformed theology assert, and one is saved by the faith of Christ as Galatians 2:20 and many other such texts witness to, and election is Christologically conditioned, then infants who die are saved on the same basis as adults and thus they do not require baptism to be saved (baptismal regeneration), nor to be included in the covenant community, the vicarious humanity and faith of Christ is sufficient for the salvation for all the elect—for infants who die, the severely mentally disabled, and adults. Contrary to Dispensational theology and certain articulations of Covenant theology, the basis of salvation is always the same for all people at all times.

It was Thomas Torrance who, throughout his lengthy career, sought to bring the doctrine of the vicarious humanity of Christ back to its central place in Reformed thought, when, for instance, he wrote:

> However, it is still this emphasis upon the vicarious humanity of Christ which we lack. If the emphasis is upon the fact that God has acted for us in Christ, then our human response is by way of cooperation, because an act on the part of man is required in addition to and complementary to the act of God. Hence Protestantism often teaches, or tends to teach, that we are all co-workers and "co-redeemers" with Christ and God! But for Calvin and Knox that error is obviated in their teaching about the vicarious and priestly nature of the human Jesus. It was in the Eucharist that their stress upon that came out most strongly. It was through union with Christ in his vicarious humanity nourished in sacra-

83. Kettler, *The God Who Believes*, 6.

mental communion that the concern of the Reformed Kirk with human and social care in the lives of people was grounded.[84]

In a previous work I have argued that it is not only for theological reasons but also pastoral that we need to bring back the doctrine of the vicarious humanity of Christ.

> According to Torrance the vicarious humanity of Christ means that only Christ's response is ultimately valid. All other responses to God are excluded because Christ is the ground and the norm of our response to God. Torrance makes this clear throughout his essay "The Word of God and the Response of Man" where we read, "In the Gospels we do not have to do simply with the Word of God and the response of man, but with the all-significant middle term, the divinely provided response in the vicarious humanity of Jesus Christ." The humanity of Christ occupies a unique place in which he is the exclusive representative and substitute in all our relations with God, "including every aspect of human response to Him; such as trusting and obeying, understanding and knowing, loving and worshipping" . . . Because the incarnate Son of God is fully human (*enhypostasis*), his response personalises ours. In all of his soteriological activity: "Jesus Christ is engaged in personalising and humanising (never depersonalising and dehumanising) activity, so that in all our relations with him we are made more truly and fully human in our personal response of faith than ever before."[85]

According to Evangelical Calvinism, the vicarious humanity of Christ means that only Christ's response is ultimately valid. All other responses to God are excluded because Christ is the ground and the norm of our response to God. The humanity of Christ occupies a unique place in which he is the exclusive representative and substitute in all our relations with God, "including every aspect of human response to Him; such as trusting and obeying, understanding and knowing, loving and worshipping."[86] Christ is the exclusive response of God to humanity and the exclusive response of humanity to God. Torrance can write: "therefore when we are justified by faith, this does not mean that it is our faith that justifies us, far from it—it is the faith of Christ alone that justifies us

---

84. Torrance, *Scottish Theology*, 45.

85. Habets, *Theosis in the Theology of Thomas Torrance*, 76. Citing Torrance *God and Rationality*, 145; and *The Mediation of Christ*, 64–66.

86. Torrance, *God and Rationality*, 145.

. . ."[87] The incarnate Son of God is the only proper response of humanity to God and God to humanity. In short, "We have no speech or language with which to address God but the speech and language called Jesus Christ."[88] Only through a participation in his person and work can men and women achieve union and communion with God.[89] For infants who die and for the severely mentally handicapped, this means that salvation is certain on the same grounds as for the rest of the elect.

Thus only an Evangelical Calvinism has the necessary resources to adequately address such a theologically rich and pastorally pressing issue such as the one before us.

## WHAT OF THE SEVERELY MENTALLY DISABLED?

So far we have been examining the case of the eternal destiny of infants who die and I have tentatively concluded that they go to be with the Lord in blessedness. Now we turn our attention to a class of peoples which, I believe, conform to the same theological conditions as infants who die—the severely mentally disabled. Severe mental disability may be defined as cognitive disability, those with severely diminished mental capacity, the mentally defective, or the older nomenclature, the mentally retarded. By such terms is meant those human persons who's IQ may be measured as 25/20 and below.[90] When we take into consideration social as well as medical factors we may further define the severely mentally disabled with recourse to the category of the "moral imbecile." The moral imbecile is one who lacks the kind of abstract thinking that can make connections, follow out consequences of their actions, or learn from past mistakes. Thus the severely mentally disabled persons of which this essay speaks of are unable to make rational decisions, and are unable to account for moral right and wrong. They live in a world of their own

---

87. Torrance, *Theology in Reconstruction*, 159–160.

88. Torrance, *The Mediation of Christ*, 78–79.

89. Torrance, *God and Rationality*, 145; 153–64; and *Reality and Evangelical Theology*, 88–89.

90. Standard IQ tests are divided into various sections: 140+ genius; 120–140 very superior; 110–100 superior; 91–100 normal/average; 80–90 dull/feebleminded; 50–70 moron; 20/25–50 imbecile; below 20/25 idiot. It is the last category of "idiot" alone that I am calling the severely mentally disabled. On the emergence of the IQ test and its various adaptations see Yong, *Theology and Down Syndrome*, 57–60.

seemingly affected only by external physical stimuli, and often not even that.[91]

To further define the severely mentally disabled we may appeal to the definition of such given by the World Health Organization's 1985 report *Mental Retardation: Meeting the Challenge.*[92] According to this report mental retardation involves four levels—mild, moderate, severe, and profound. Furthermore, the definition includes two essential components: intellectual functioning and adaptive behavior. Of these four levels only 1.5 to 5 percent of all individuals classed as "retarded"[93] are found in the category of the profoundly mentally retarded.[94] It is these individuals I refer to as the severely mentally disabled.[95]

Scripture is largely silent on the presence or destiny of the mentally disabled. "In fact, researchers who set out looking for a biblical theology of disability will be quickly disappointed because our contemporary notions of disability are for the most part foreign to the worldview of the biblical authors,"[96] writes Amos Yong. He continues to add that "the Bible does not say anything about what we today call intellectual disability."[97] That is not to say Scripture is of no use to us in formulating a theological account of and response to disability. Scripture does speak of people with physical deformities and disabilities, notably it speaks of

91. This definition approximately corresponds to the definition of "idiot" given by Alfred Binet and Theodore Simon, authors of the modern (Binet-Simon) IQ test. Henry H. Goddard further refined this test which became the standard in the field of mental retardation: "idiots" were those with a mental age of fewer than two years; "imbeciles" ranged from two to seven years; "proximates"/"morons" were ages eight to twelve. See Scheeringberger, *A History of Mental Retardation*, 144.

92. World Health Organization and Joint Commission on International Aspects of Mental Retardation, *Mental Retardation: Meeting the Challenge*.

93. Ibid., 9. The profoundly mentally retarded according to WHO are those with IQ scores less than 20 and thus correspond to the earlier category of "idiot" according to the Binet-Simon test.

94. Webb, *The Theology of Infant Salvation*, 4, offered a definition of the severely mentally disabled as "an instance of arrested mental development . . . [who thus] lingers in the region of intellectual childhood." This suits our definition here very well.

95. In addition to biological, cognitive, and genetic factors, I am aware of the social, cultural, economic, and political constructions of human disability. These do not concern us in this essay, however.

96. Yong, *Theology and Down Syndrome*, 20.

97. Ibid., 21. For a survey of Scripture and disability see further in ibid., 21–27; and in a more comprehensive treatment in a forthcoming volume by Yong provisionally entitled *The Bible, Disability, and the Church: A New Vision of the People of God*.

the deaf, the blind, the lame, and the dumb/mute. While a biblical theology of disability is not my goal here we may simply say that in Scripture human disability is abnormal, even though those with disabilities come from the Creator God (Ex 4:11). Such severe disability is often portrayed as a result of the fall and corruption of the world. In the Old Testament it is linked to uncleanness (although even here see the later reversal of the eunuch in Isa 56:3–5), or being unfit to serve in priestly service and other activities to do with the religious cult (Lev 21:16–23).

Given these restrictions, however, Scripture does make it clear that all people, even those with disabilities, are equal image bearers of God and thus deserve respect and dignity, care and inclusion (Lev 19:14; Job 29:12–17; Jer 31:8; Zeph 3:19). The fact that disabilities are not God's final intension for people is implicit in the healing narratives of the New Testament. This is evident in Jesus' healing of the blind, the lame, and the deaf (cf. Luke 5:17–26; 9:37–43; 13:10–13; 18:35–43).[98] In a world in which God has, for whatever reason, allowed disabilities to exist, however, lessons of hospitality, service, grace, love, acceptance, and friendship are embodied in faith communities which are made of people from the "centre" and those of the "margins."

After defining the severely mentally disabled and briefly noting the biblical texts which speak to it, I think it a fair conclusion that the same issues that have to do with the destiny of infants who die are bound up with the destiny of the severely mentally disabled. Both categories of persons are in the same position, it would seem to me. Thus the theological principles which apply to the one group, infants, apply also to the other group, the severely mentally disabled. We need not say more about the salvation of the severely mentally disabled here, then, given there is nothing more to add.

## CONCLUSION: ECCLESIAL INCLUSION AND SACRAMENTS

There is one substantial difference between infants who die and the severely mentally disabled, however, and it is the obvious fact that the severely mentally disabled are not dead; they are with us and are part of our lives, our families, and our communities of faith. A fundamental

---

98. In his helpful survey of Scripture, Yong concludes, "Clearly, then, 'disability' in the New Testament functions rhetorically to call attention to negative realities such as sin, evil spirits, spiritual degeneration, and moral reprobation" (*Theology and Down Syndrome*, 27).

issue thus arises, if we are to consider the severely mentally disabled as "saved" by the gracious election of God then what status should we accord them within the church? More specifically, should the severely mentally disabled be baptised and take communion? This question has not been asked before in the literature, at least not to my knowledge. Amos Yong has addressed these issues in relation to the mentally disabled in general, but not to the severely mentally disabled. Thus he approvingly cites Joseph Bernardin who seeks to find signs that would indicate the readiness of a developmentally delayed person to receive the sacraments. Included in his helpful list are desire, relationships, and a sense of the sacred; however that may be made manifest.[99] In short, cues are taken from the disabled person of an interrelation, interpersonal, and intersubjective kind.

Such indicative signs as are noted above are all well and good in general but do not apply to the *severely* mentally disabled as we have defined them here for such persons exhibit no such signs of the sacred or of any outward response to God. At this point I can accept the position of Beach, who, in a recent essay argued that,

> Any doctrine of infant salvation which bypasses the necessity and fullness of Christ's redemptive work is contrary to Scripture and must be rejected. I also argue that all humans—whether young or old, mentally handicapped or of sound mind—reach eternal blessedness only through Christ's full redemptive work on the cross and the Spirit's renewing operation.

He then provides what is most important at this point in my own argument: "From that perspective, I also argue that the sign of salvation may not be separated from the thing signified, which is to say, if one participates in the reality of salvation he or she must receive the sign of that salvation—the mark of baptism."[100] And later we read:

> This means, then, that if any class of children are recipients of the divine promise of salvation, such that they are saveable and in fact saved only by the saving operation of Christ and his Spirit, then they are likewise the proper subjects of the sign and seal of that salvation, baptism.[101]

99. Bernardin, *Access to the Sacraments of Initiation and Reconciliation for Developmentally Disabled Persons*, 9, cited in Yong, *Theology and Down Syndrome*, 210.

100. Beach, "Original Sin, Infant Salvation, and the Baptism of Infants," 51.

101. Ibid., 76.

In the ecclesial contexts of Roman Catholicism, Eastern Orthodoxy, and Presbyterianism, the issue of baptising the severely mentally disabled is a mute one, given their commitment to paedobaptism. But in Free Church and especially Baptist ecclesial contexts, of which I am involved, where believer's baptism is the norm, the issue of baptising the severely mentally disabled is as acute as is the issue common to all ecclesial traditions of whether or not to administer the Eucharist to the severely mentally disabled.

If the arguments proffered in this essay so far are accepted, then Beach is correct to insist on the baptism of all those considered part of the family of faith—young and old, men and women, and the severely mentally disabled. This is obviously not an argument for paedobaptism as only infants who die are considered elect of God and saved. Thus, before their death their elect status is uncertain. Baptismal regeneration has never been acceptable to Reformed or Baptist theology and thus it is not valid to appeal to this in the case of infants or adults who may be severely mentally disabled. The only legitimate consequence of the theology developed so far is to baptise, if their parents or guardians are willing (normally believing parents), the severely mentally disabled and, also if their parents or guardians allow it, to allow them to receive the Eucharist. As means of grace Baptism and the Eucharist feed and nourish the recipient and these acts, speak powerfully to the inclusion of all God's children in the covenant of grace by grace through faith, not of works (Eph 2:8, 9).

Reformed and Baptist communities are thus on solid theological ground to offer Baptism and Communion to the severely mentally disabled, thus showing their inclusion in the family of God, the Body of Christ, and the fellowship of the Saints. Such acts of inclusion, grace, and fellowship would provide a powerful sign of the reality of the Kingdom of God, breaking into the structures of fallen reality, pointing powerfully to the salvific work of the triune God of grace. To exclude such persons from our central ecclesial acts is, I suggest, a violation of the very meaning of what it means to be the Church–Baptist, Presbyterian, or otherwise.

Bold infidelity turn pale and die;
  Beneath this stone four sleeping infants lie.
Say, are they lost or saved?
  If death's by sin, they sinned
For they are here.
  If heaven's by works in heaven they can't appear.
Ah, Reason, how depraved.
  Revere the Bible's sacred page.
The knot's untied:
  They died; for Adam sinned.
They live; for Jesus died.[102]

102. This epitaph was found on a grave in St Andrews' Churchyard in Edinburgh, Scotland. Cited in Baker, *A Dispensational Theology*, 465.

# BIBLIOGRAPHY

Allen, R. Michael. *Reformed Theology*. London: T. & T. Clark, 2010.

Augustine, *De verbis apostoli sermo* xiv, Sermo ccxciv in *Opera*, Paris, tom. v. pars. Ii, 1838, coll. 1738.

Baillie, Robert. *Anabaptisme, the true Fountaine of Independency, Brownisme, Antinomy, Familisme, and most of the other errours which for the time doe trouble the Church of England, unsealed. Also the questions of paedobaptisme and dipping handled from Scripture: In a second part of The Dissuasive from the errors of the time*. 4 to. pp. 179. M. F. for Samuel Gellibrand: London, 1647.

Baker, Charles F. *A Dispensational Theology*. Grand Rapids: Grace Bible College Publications, 1971.

*The Baptist Confession of Faith and The Baptist Catechism*. Carlisle, PA: Reformed Baptist, 2010.

Bavinck, Herman. *Saved by Grace: The Holy Spirit's Work in Calling and Regeneration*. Translated by N. D. Kloosterman. Grand Rapids: Reformation Heritage, 2008.

———. *Reformed Dogmatics: vol. 4. Holy Spirit, Church, and New Creation*. Translated by J. Vriend. Grand Rapids: Baker, 2008.

Beach, J. Mark. "Original Sin, Infant Salvation, and the Baptism of Infants." *Mid-America Journal of Theology* 12 (2001) 47–79.

Beeke, Joel. "Children Dying in Infancy: Young People Ask. . . ." *The Banner of Truth* (January, 1988) 22–23.

Berkouwer, Gerrit C. *Divine Election*. Grand Rapids: Eerdmans, 1960.

———. *The Sacraments*. Translated by H. Beker. Grand Rapids: Eerdmans, 1969.

Bernardin, Joseph. *Access to the Sacraments of Initiation and Reconciliation for Developmentally Disabled Persons: Pastoral Guidelines for the Archdiocese of Chicago*. Chicago: Liturgy Training, 1985.

Blocher, Henry *Original Sin: Illuminating the Riddle*. Downers Grove, IL: InterVarsity, 1997.

———. "The Theology of the Fall and The Origins of Evil." In *Darwin, Creation and the Fall: Theological Challenges*, edited by R. J. Berry and T. A. Noble, 149–72. Nottingham: Apollos, 2009.

Boettner, Loraine. *The Reformed Doctrine of Predestination*. Philadelphia: Presbyterian and Reformed, 1963.

Burgess, Cornelius. *Baptismall Regeneration of Elect Infants, professed by the Church of England, according to Scriptures, the Primitiue Church, the present Reformed Churches, and many particular divines apart*. Oxford: I. L. Henry Curteyn, 1629.

Buswell, J. Oliver. *Systematic Theology*. Vol. 2. Grand Rapids: Zondervan, 1962.

Carter, William. *The Covenant of God with Abraham, opened. Wherein 1. The Duty of Infant-Baptism is cleared. 2. Something added concerning the Sabbath, and the nature and increase of the Kingdom of Christ. Together with a short discourse concerning the manifestations of God unto his people in the last dayes, etc*. London: T. C. for John Rothwell, 1654.

Cawdrey, Daniel. *A Sober Answer to a Serious Question propounded by Mr. G. Firmin . . . viz. Whether the Ministers of England are bound by the Word of God to baptise the children of all such parents which say they believe in Jesus Christ; but are grossly ignorant, scandalous in their conversation, scoffers at godliness, and refuse to submit to church-discipline . . . Which may serve also as an appendix to the diatribe with*

*Mr. Hooker, lately published, concerning the baptisme of infants, etc.* London: Christopher Meredith, 1652.

———. *The Inconsistencie of Independent way with Scripture and it self; manifested in a threefold discourse: 1, Vindiciae Vindiciarum with M. Cotton; 2, a review of M. Hookers Survey of Church-discipline: the first part; 3, a diatribe with the same M. Hooker, concerning baptism of infants, etc.* London: A. Miller, C. Meredith, 1651.

Cathcart, William. ed. *The Baptist Encyclopaedia.* 3 vols. Reprint. Arkansas: Baptist Standard Bearer, 2001.

Chafer, Lewis S. *Systematic Theology.* 8 vols. Dallas: Dallas Theological Seminary Press, 1948.

Clark, David K. "Warfield, Infant Salvation, and the Logic of Calvinism." *Journal of the Evangelical Theological Society* 27 (1984) 459–64.

Clifford, Alan C. "Infant Salvation: Are All Those Who Die in Infancy Saved?" No pages. Online: www.nrchurch.co.nr.

Davis, Robert E. "Infant Salvation." No pages. Online: http://www.the-highway.com/infant-salvation_Davis.html.

Denzinger, Heinrich, and Adolf Schönmetzer, eds. *Enchiridion symbolorum definitionum et declarationum de rebus fidei et morum.* Freiburg: Herder, 1997.

Downs, Perry G. "Child Evangelization." *Journal of Christian Education* 3 (1983) 5-13.

Dury, John. *A true relation of the conversion and baptism of Isuf, etc.* Substance of a sermon on Acts x. 47. R. Christophilus. 8 vols. 1658.

Dyer, Fr George J. "The Unbaptized Infant in Eternity." *Chicago Studies* 2 (1963). Reprinted in *Chicago Studies* 48 (2009) 10–22.

Engelsma, D. J. *The Covenant of God and the Children of Believers: Grace in the Covenant.* Grandville: Reformed Free Publishing Association, 2005.

Erickson, Millard J. *Christian Theology.* 2nd ed. Grand Rapids: Baker, 1998.

Fitzpatrick, Joseph. "Original Sin or Original Sinfulness?" *New Blackfriars* 90 (2009) 701–17.

Fuller, Richard. "Infant Salvation, Dedication, and Baptism." In *The Baptist Denomination: Its History, Doctrines, and Ordinances,* edited by D. C. Haynes, 185–93. New York: Sheldon, Blakeman, 1856.

———. *Infant Salvation, Baptism and Dedication.* American Baptist Publication Society, n.d.

Gataker, Thomas. *De baptismatis infantilis vi et efficacia disceptatio, privatim habita inter . . . S. Wardum . . . et T. Gatakerum.* 8 vols. 1653.

———. *Stricturae ad Epistolam J. Daven, de Baptismo Infantum.* 1654.

Geisler Norman L. *Baker Encyclopedia of Christian Apologetics.* Grand Rapids: Baker, 1999.

Godfrey, Robert. "Election and Covenant: The Synod of Dort and Children Who Die in Infancy." No pages. Online: http://www.meetthepuritans.com/tag/godfrey.

Gootjes, N. H. "Can Parents Be Sure? Background and Meaning of Canons of Dort I, 17." *Clarion* 44 (1995), np. Online: http://www.spindleworks.com/library/gootjes/cd_17.htm.

Gregory of Nyssa. *On Infants Early Deaths.* Translated by William Moore and Henry Austin Wilson. In *NPNF,* 2nd Series, edited by Philip Schaff and Henry Wace, 5:35-41. Buffalo, NY: Christian Literature, 1893.

Grenz, Stanley J. *Theology for the Community of God.* Carlisle: Paternoster, 1994.

Habets, Myk. *Theosis in the Theology of Thomas Torrance.* Surrey: Ashgate, 2009.

Hart, Darryl G. and John R. Muether, "Turning Points in American Presbyterian History; Part 8: Confessional Revision in 1903." *New Horizons* (August/September 2005) no pages. Online: http://opc.org/nh.html?article_id=56.

Henry, Martin. "Original Sin: A Flawed Inheritance." *Irish theological Quarterly* 65 (2000) 3-12.

Hoeksema, Herman. *Believers and their Seed: Children in the Covenant.* Grand Rapids: Reformed Free Publishing Association, 1971.

Hübmaier, Balthasar. "On the Christian Baptism of Believers." In *Anabaptist Beginnings (1523-1533): A Source Book,* edited by William R. Estep, 65-98. Nieuwkoop: D De Graaf, 1976.

Inchley, John. *Kids and the Kingdom: How They Come to God.* Wheaton: Tyndale, 1976.

Ingle, Clifford. "Children and Conversion." *Sunday School Builder* (March 1989) 9.

———. "Moving in the Right Direction." In *Children and Conversion*, 153–54. Edited by Clifford Ingle. Nashville: Broadman, 1970.

Jeschke, Marlin. *Believers Baptism for Children of the Church.* Scottdale: Herald, 1983.

Kettler, Christian D. *The God Who Believes: Faith, Doubt, and the Vicarious Humanity of Christ.* Eugene, OR: Cascade, 2005.

Lemke, Steve W. "A Biblical and Theological Critique of Irresistible Grace." In *Whosever Will: A Biblical-Theological Critique of Five Point Calvinism*, edited by David L. Allen and Steve W. Lemke, 109–62. Nashville: Broadman & Holman, 2010.

Lightner, Robert. P. *Heaven for Those Who Can't Believe.* Schaumburg: Regular Baptist Press, 1977.

Lusk, Rich. *Paedofaith: A Primer on the Mystery of Infant Salvation and a Handbook for Covenant Parents.* Monroe: Athanasius, 2005.

Luther, Martin. *The Holy and Blessed Sacrament of Baptism, 1519.* In *Luther's Works,* 23–44. Vol. 35. Philadelphia: Fortress, 1958.

———. *Concerning Rebaptism, 1528.* In *Luther's Works,* 225–62. Vol. 40. Philadelphia: Fortress, 1958.

Luther, Martin. *Comfort for Women Who Have Had a Miscarriage, 1542.* In *Luther's Works,* 243–50. Vol. 43. Philadelphia: Fortress, 1958.

MacArthur, John. *Safe in the Arms of God: Truth from Heaven about the Death of a Child.* Nashville: Thomas Nelson, 2003.

———. "The Salvation of Babies Who Die." Part 1. No pages. Online: http://www.gty .org/Resources/Sermons/80-242; and Part 2. Online: http://www.gty.org/Resources/ Sermons/80-243.

McDermott, S. J. Brian O. "Current Theology: The Theology of Original Sin: Recent Developments." *Theological Studies* 38 (1977) 478–512.

Marshal, Stephen. *A Sermon of the Baptizing of Infants,* preached from 1 Pet. iii. 21, in Abbey-church at Westminster, at the Morning Lecture, appointed by the Hon. House of Commons. London, 1644.

———. *A Defence of Infant-Baptism: In Answer to two Treatises, . . . concerning it; lately published by Mr John Tombes. Wherein that controversie is fully discussed.* London, 1646.

Mohler, R. Albert, and Daniel L. Akin, "The Salvation of the 'Little Ones': Do Infants Who Die Go To Heaven?" *The Covenant News* (January 17, 2005). No pages. Online: http://covenant news.com/mohler050117.htm.

Mouw, Richard J. "Baptism and the Salvific Status of Children: An Examination of Some Intra-Reformed Debates." *Calvin Theological Journal* 41 (2006) 238–54.

Murray, John. *Collected Writings of John Murray.* Vol. 2. *Lectures in Systematic Theology.* Edinburgh: Banner of Truth, 1978.

Nash, Ronald. *When a Baby Dies: Answers to Comfort Grieving Parents.* Grand Rapids: Zondervan, 1999.

Neuner, J., and J. Dupuis, editors. *The Christian Faith in the Doctrinal Documents of the Catholic Church.* Bangalore: Theological Publications in India, 2004.

Newton, John. *The Works of John Newton.* 6 vols. 1820. Reprint. Edinburgh: Banner of truth Trust, 1985.

Piper, John. "What Happens to Infants Who Die?" (January 23, 2006) No pages. Online: http://www.desiringgod.org/library/theological_qa/infant_salv/infants.html.

Plantinga, Cornelius. *Not the Way It's Supposed to Be: A Breviary of Sin.* Grand Rapids: Eerdmans, 1995.

"Presbyterians on Calvin." *The New York Times* (May 26, 1908). No pages. Online: http://query.nytimes.com/mem/archive-free/pdf?res=9906E0D8143EE233A25755C2A9639C946997D6CF.

*Psalter Hymnal.* Grand Rapids: Board of Publications of the Christian Reformed Church, 1976.

Radmacher, Earl D. *Salvation.* Swindoll Leadership Library. Nashville: Word, 2000.

Rishell, Charles W. "Wesley and Other Methodist Fathers on Childhood Religion." *Methodist Review* 84 (1902) 778–84.

Roman Catholic Church. *Catechism of the Catholic Church.* Cited 20 August, 2009. Online: http://www.vatican.va/archive/ENG0015/__P3M.HTM.

———."The Hope of Salvation for Infants Who Die Without Being Baptized." *Origins* 36 no. 45 (April 20, 2007). Online: http://www.vatican.va/roman_curia/congregations/cfaith/cti_documents/rc_con_cfaith_doc_20070419_un-baptised-infants_en.html.

Schaff, P. *The Creeds of Christendom.* Vol. 3. *The Evangelical Protestant Creeds,* 6th edition. Edited by P. Schaff. Revised by D. S. Schaff. 1931. Reprint, Grand Rapids: Baker, 1990.

Scheeringberger, R. C. *A History of Mental Retardation.* Baltimore: Paul H. Brookes, 1983.

Schenck, Lewis B. *The Presbyterian Doctrine of Children in the Covenant.* New Haven: Yale University Press, 1940. Reprint, Philipsburg, NJ: Presbyterian and Reformed, 2003.

Shedd, William G. T. "Infant Salvation as Related to Original Sin." In *Calvinism: Pure and Mixed,* edited W. G. T. Shedd, 112–20. Edinburgh: Banner of Truth, 1986.

Spurgeon, Charles H. "Infant Salvation." A Sermon (No. 411), Delivered on Sunday Morning, September 29th, 1861, at the Metropolitan Tabernacle, Newington. Online: http://www.spurgeon.org/sermons/0411.htm.

———. *Spurgeon at His Best.* Grand Rapids: Baker, 1988.

Smedes, Lewis B. "Can God Reach the Mentally Disabled?" *Christianity Today* 45 (March 1, 2001). Online: http://www.christianitytoday.com/ct/2001/march5/31.94.html.

Sproul Jr., R. C. "Conform Ye My People-Justification By Youth Alone: When does Comfort Become Confusion?" World 10 no. 7 (May 6, 1995) 26. Online: http://highlandsstudycenter.org/article/comfortYeMyPeople.php.

Strawbridge, Gregg, editor. *The Case for Covenantal Infant Baptism.* Philipsburg, NJ: Presbyterian and Reformed, 2003.

Torrance, Thomas F. *Theology in Reconstruction.* Grand Rapids: Eerdmans, 1965.

————. *God and Rationality*. London: Oxford University Press, 1971.

————. *The Mediation of Christ*, new edition. Edinburgh: T. & T. Clark, 1992.

————. *Scottish Theology from John Knox to John McLeod Campbell*. Edinburgh: T. & T. Clark, 1996.

Venema, Cornelis P. "The Election and Salvation of the Children of Believers Who Die in Infancy: A Study of Article 1/17 of the Canons of Dort." *Mid-America Journal of Theology* 17 (2006) 57–100.

Vos, Geerhardus. *The Covenant of Grace*. Pittsburgh: Crown and Covenant Publications, no date.

Wallis, John. *A Defense of Infant-Baptism. In answer to a letter, here recited, from an Anti-Paedo Baptist*. L. Lichfield: Oxford, 1697.

Warfield, Benjamin B. "Introductory Essay on Augustin and the Pelagian Controversy." In *NPNF*, 1st Series, vol. 5, *Augustin: Anti-Pelagian Writings*, edited by Phillip Schaff, 12-109. Albany, OR: Ages Software, 1996.

Webb, Robert A. *The Theology of Infant Salvation*. Richmond: Presbyterian Committee of Publication, 1907. Reprint, Harrisonburg: Sprinkle, 2003.

Wesley, John. *The Works of John Wesley*, vol. 12, *Letters*, 3rd ed. 1872. Reprint, Grand Rapids: Baker, 2007.

Willhauck, Susan. "John Wesley's View of Children: Foundations for Contemporary Christian Education." PhD diss., Catholic University of America, 1992.

Wills, Garry. *Reagan's America: Innocents at Home*. Garden City: Doubleday, 1987.

World Health Organization and Joint Commission on International Aspects of Mental Retardation, *Mental Retardation: Meeting the Challenge*. Geneva: WHO, 1985.

Yong, Amos. *Theology and Down Syndrome: Reimagining Disability in Late Modernity*. Waco: Baylor University Press, 2007.

————. *The Bible, Disability, and the Church: A New Vision of the People of God*. Grand Rapids: Eerdmans, 2011.

Zietlow, Paul. "Martin Luther's Arguments for Infant Baptism." *Concordia Journal* 20 (April 1994) 147–71.

Zuck, Roy B. *Precious in His Sight: Childhood and Children in the Bible*. Grand Rapids: Baker, 1996.

# PART THREE

# Applied Theology

# 12

## Living as God's Children

### *Calvin's* Institutes *as Primer for Spiritual Formation*

JULIE CANLIS

The gospel is a doctrine not of the tongue but of life. It is ... received only when it possesses the whole soul, and finds a seat and resting place in the inmost affection of the heart. (Calvin, *Institutes*, 3.6.4)[1]

WHEN IT CAME TO life on earth, Calvin was a realist. In fact, he was something of a pessimist.[2] His mother had died when he was three. His undemonstrative father died little more than a decade later, excommunicated from the church. His teenage years brought on chronic headaches, indigestion, and asthma that never left him. His experience of life was as one "lost in a labyrinth,"[3] with fear so palpable that he writes, "I wanted to die to be rid of those fears."[4] But this cloud

1. Calvin, *Institutes,* Book 3, chapter 6, paragraph 4 (hereafter Calvin, *Inst.,* 3.6.4).

2. See the delightful chapter, Selderhuis, "Pilgrim," in which he gleans this sense of uncertainty from Calvin's letters. For example, Calvin's reflection that our life "hangs as if from a silk thread" or his exposé on the dangers of "modern" living: "If you step onto a ship, you are only one step away from death. If you climb onto a horse, your foot only needs to slip and your life is in danger. Just walk through the city streets one time, and there are as many dangers as there are roof tiles on the houses. If you or your friend are carrying a weapon, injury lies in wait" (36).

3. See Bouwsma, *John Calvin,* for a penetrating analysis.

4. Selderhuis, "Pilgrim," 33.

of fragility and loneliness was not without its silver lining. Calvin, intellectual genius that he was, understood from early on that religion was not only for the mind but also for the heart. For Calvin, the gift of the gospel was not in correct doctrine but in its ability to penetrate to the heart and emotions—indeed, even to transform them.

Modest about his conversion,[5] we know little of how the self-disciplined, introverted young man was converted—but, one thing we do know is that he was converted *to Christ*. Not to reform-minded thinking. Not to humanist methods of biblical scholarship. Not to more "authentic" eucharistic practices. But to Jesus Christ himself. And this, for Calvin, was everything. This was the centre from which Calvin worked, and it is the centre for all of his theological projects. And this, not incidentally, is the only place where Calvin believed the transformation of our hearts and lives could occur—in an ongoing encounter with Jesus the Christ.

An encounter with Jesus was not something one could label and date (as Calvin himself refused to label and date his own conversion), then to be put on display in one's spiritual archives.[6] From Calvin's perspective, it was a new way of living and being, and its shape was *sonship*. "Adoption . . . is not the cause merely of a partial salvation, but bestows salvation entire."[7] Calvin's theology, for all its clarity and polemic usefulness, loses its centre when it is pulled away from sonship—both the Sonship of Jesus and, consequently, our own adoptive sonship.[8] If we are going to read Calvin's theology as it was intended, for spiritual formation,[9] then it must begin here, with Calvin's grasp of the transformative impact of sonship.

5. The scant statements we have are from the "Preface" to his *Commentary the Psalms*, in which he relates that it was "unexpected" (*subita*).

6. In Calvin's writings, there is tremendous movement "upward" toward deeper and deeper communion with God. One's reference point is not backward to a point in time (such as conversion), but forward into the intimacy of obedience and love, as enacted by the Son.

7. Calvin, "True Method of Obtaining Concord," 275.

8. I am unwilling to drop the gendered term "sonship," as our "sonship" is founded upon Christ's own Sonship. For those who find the term suspect, I do think it can be interchanged with all sorts of terms like "becoming children of God" or "being adopted," but these lose the christological clarity that Calvin intended.

9. A better term, though more inaccessible to our modern ears, is Calvin's own use of the word "piety." For Calvin, this was not a holier-than-thou term, but a holistic, life-affirming one that spoke of unity among our life, beliefs, and emotions. For Calvin,

## CALVIN'S INSTITUTES:
## PRIMER FOR SPIRITUAL FORMATION

Calvin's *Institutes of the Christian Religion* is not where many would turn for his understanding of spiritual formation. Its later polemical and dogmatic additions belie its origins as a small catechetical handbook (following exactly the program of Luther's *Lesser Catechism*), intent on shaping persecuted Christians for right belief and living. Yet over all the years that it grew (from six chapters to eighty) and that it matured (from 1536 to 1559), Calvin's original purpose never wavered. His desire was that it give believers not only a right understanding of the gospel, but that it "pass into daily living, and so transform us."[10] The "systematic" Calvin who was later to be admired is more of an anachronism, for he viewed doctrine not as the communication of beliefs about God but as a personal experience of the gospel. It must not be forgotten that Calvin was first and foremost a pastor who was intent on forming a people for and by union with Christ.

The *Institutes* gives forth wonderful gems when subjected to intense analysis; but, like the Scriptures, there are elusive diamonds that can only be found when an entire book is read in one sitting. I'll never forget the experience of reading the book of Revelation straight through, when I saw the forest for the first time, rather than the trees. There are themes and nuances in Calvin's *Institutes* which may be hindered by intense analysis and scrutiny, where one does not breathe in the book as a whole, but only in fits and spurts. And perhaps for this reason the *Institutes* is rarely consulted for spiritual formation. Although it is obvious that I have never read the *Institutes* in a day, let alone a week (and not just because I have young children!), I would encourage its broad perusal for the nurturing of our interior lives. Calvin, at least, would approve.

---

piety is one's reverential life-response in the face of knowing God's true character. Since Calvin says that the first step toward true piety is "to know that God is a father to us" (Calvin, *Inst.*, 2.6.4). I am taking the liberty to use the more contemporary term "spiritual formation" (with all its baggage), as I argue that the first step of spiritual formation (according to Calvin's theology) is knowing God as Father.

10. Calvin, *Inst.*, 3.6.4.

## SPIRITUAL FORMATION: THE TRINITARIAN CONTEXT

What a detailed analysis of the *Institutes* often overlooks is the structure of the work—a structure that gives crucial clues for Calvin's vision of the spiritual life. He toyed with how to configure the *Institutes* for over two decades, until at last, he arranged it into four books, loosely conceived as the Father, the Son, the Spirit, and the church. Of this final structure, he writes, "although I did not regret the labor spent, I was never satisfied until the work had been arranged in the order now set forth."[11] Scripture does not reveal God's nature but instead reveals God's disposition—his "benevolence" toward us, as Calvin would say. All through the Old Testament we have the story of God's benevolent pursuit of humanity, a pursuit culminating in Christ and his cross. So even as Calvin uses the Trinity as a structuring tool, it is not an abstract framework but God triunely relating *to us*.[12] The Trinity is not an organizing principle for spectators. It is profoundly personal, making a claim on the reader's life. In the gospel, Calvin says, we have the "heart of Christ opened"[13] to us, which is the revelation of the heart of the Triune God.

Demonstrated even by the way he organizes the *Institutes*, Calvin declares: *all must begin with the Trinity*. Before we even enter into the words on the first page, the Trinity gives shape to Calvin's understanding of where we have come from and where we are going. The *Institutes* shimmers with this unstated presence of a trinitarian, personal God who is above, before, ahead of, behind, and all around us—loving us, calling us, breathing life into our beings. The *Institutes* follows the steady pursuit of (Book I) God the *Father*, who creates us for love and fellowship, and who incarnates the Word as (Book II) Jesus the true *Son*, who has come to redeem us from sin and show us what this fellowship is really like. The *Spirit* (Book III) continues this wooing, building the life of Jesus the Son into our broken lives so that we can truly be God's children who, as the *church* (Book IV), live a familial life responding to this

11. Ibid., "Preface to the Reader."

12. For this reason, Calvin does not use the titles "Father," "Son," "Spirit," and "Church" but instead speaks of "I: The Knowledge of God the Creator," "II: The Knowledge of God the Redeemer in Christ," "III: The Way in Which We Receive the Benefits of Christ," and finally "IV: The External Means . . . by Which God Invites Us into the Society of Christ and Holds Us Therein." Note the emphasis on how the triune God works *in Christ* to bring humans to salvation and communion.

13. Calvin, *Comm.*, John 15:15.

Triune God of grace. Here we begin to see that for Calvin, the Trinity is not merely a test of orthodoxy, or a mathematical conundrum that we must believe by faith. Instead, the Trinity is to be *entered into*. It is the lived experience of the Christian life. The Trinity is our clue and access to spiritual formation as both its means and end.

The Trinity provided more than just a handy organizational pattern for Calvin's theological primer; it ensured its *personal* nature. Thus far, Luther had pioneered the catechism as a way for people to "own" their faith, to lure theology out of the cathedral and into their daily living and practice. (For example, the 1549 Catechism of the Church of England begins with the question, "*what is your name?*" suggesting that catechisms have very much to do with the personalization of the faith).[14] Yet, over the years that he laboured over the *Institutes*, Calvin began to move away from Luther's catechetical structure to a trinitarian structure.[15] Though we do not know all the reasons why, I'd like to suggest that in doing so, Calvin provided a more sure foundation for making one's faith personal. For catechisms (and other helpful spiritual practices) do not secure the personal nature of our faith. God does.

The doctrine of the Trinity is a way of reminding us that everything God does is personal, because God is *three persons*, who can only be received in a personal way. It is not we who make the gospel personal; rather, it is God who is eternally personal—who is himself a communion of love—who offers his gospel to us. I don't want to risk misunderstanding here: we can attend to the gospel's eternally personal nature through our own devotional life. We *must* attend to it. But unless we rest in God's personalizing of us, we will try and "personalize" our faith through our own intensity and emotions. Often, the "personalness" of the gospel is secured through second-rate means, such as gratitude for salvation, or an individual sense of God's presence, or a missional call. These are wonderful things, but they are false securities. On the contrary, the only thing that can guarantee the personal nature of our faith is God's own

14. This is from the catechism found in the first edition of *The Book of Common Prayer*, "an instruction to bee learned of every childe, before he be brought to be confirmed of the bushop." Although catechisms existed in the medieval church, they were used so advantageously by the Reformation that the Council of Trent declared great "mischief" to have been done "especially by those writings called catechisms."

15. Luther's *Lesser Catechism* began with the Decalogue and Apostle's Creed, then moved on to the Lord's Prayer, true and false sacraments, Christian liberty, church government and discipline.

personhood. Funnily enough, the quest to "personalize" our faith usually ends in its depersonalization, because we begin to focus inordinately
on ourselves. Calvin chides, "it is not very sound theology to confine a
man's thoughts so much to himself . . . for we are born first of all for God,
and not for ourselves."[16] Framing our whole existence around the personalness of God—as Father, Son, and Holy Spirit—is what ensures that
our "spirituality" (or "piety") remains *personal*. And it is in this personal,
relational manner that we are led "in" to the *Institutes*.

## BEING SPIRITUALLY FORMED BY UNION WITH CHRIST

Calvin sets the stage for the *Institutes* with a trinitarian shape to reality,
and an understanding of God and his "personalness"—his life of communion—that sets the agenda. But for Calvin, there is only one entrance
to the spiritual life, and that is Jesus. He is our entry-point. All contact
with God, all gifts from God, all prayer, all peace, all ministry, all holiness
comes to us through and in the person of Jesus. Why? Because Calvin
believes this has always been the "nature" of things. This is the trinitarian
way God works. God doesn't do things at a distance. He is personal, and
all aspects of our Christian faith are—at their core—encounter with him.
This is no less the case for us as it was for Adam and Eve who enjoyed
all the benefits of God because, even there in the garden, Christ was the
"mediator" or the "midpoint" between God and themselves.[17] He is the
one in whom we are given all the things of God and—most centrally to
Calvin's thought—God himself.

A big task of being spiritually formed is to begin to recognize this
possibility for Christ-encounter all around us. Spiritual formation in
the *Institutes* does not revolve around set spiritual practices. Nor does
it begin with an understanding of grace and the gifts that God longs
to give us. These gifts have a face—Jesus. This world we have entered
is a Christ-saturated world. All "spirituality" we have is encounter with
Christ. Calvin wouldn't have us become sentimental about this. Instead,
he simply would have us honour the nearness of Christ in and around
us. He would have us recognize that everything we do, as a consequence,
is worship. (Calvin is infamous for his iconoclastic leanings, but it is
imperative that we understand that Calvin was not against statues and

16. Calvin, *A Reformation Debate*, 58.
17. See Canlis, *Calvin's Ladder*, ch. 2.

physical representations of God in and of themselves. No, he hated the fact that they *compromised God's nearness*. He hated the fact that people, believing God to be far off, felt that they could approach the saints and their images with better luck than a distant God.) Calvin desired that people understand the Jesus-saturated elements of our reality[18] and how every aspect of our lived life is God's hand outstretched to us in communion.

If Book I of the *Institutes* is concerned with Christ as the "midpoint" or "mediator" of all creation, Book II is concerned to show how, after the Fall, Jesus becomes the mediator in a new way. Calvin's writings can be seen as one great lament for what humanity could have been, but it is a mistake to ever pull Calvin's virulent language about sin away from what he believed was its true context—the fact that our sin has been provided for in the cross. (For this reason, Calvin refuses to talk about the effects of the Fall under Book I of the *Institutes* on "Creation," but waits until Book II and the story of redemption.) Calvin is convinced that there is so much that God desires to give to humanity, but now what God wants to give will take on a Christ-shape. It will take on the characteristics of Jesus himself: his humanity, his obedience, and—above all—his relationship with the Father.[19] It is this that God desires to give fallen humanity. And it is for this that Christ walks the earth—breaking the power of sin, disease, and destruction—so that it can become ours. "Christ has [no] thing, which may not be applied to our benefit."[20] Every event in Jesus's life was lived with the self-conscious intent that humanity be able to draw from it and be made new by it.[21]

So how do we get in on these hard-won benefits? How do we experience Jesus's salvation, in all its fullness and with all its gifts? Calvin's solution is simple: we get Jesus himself. We get Jesus "adorned" with all his gifts.[22] Book III is devoted entirely to this question:

18. Calvin sees Christ everywhere, not only in our present lives but through all of history, particularly the Old Testament. God's presence in the garden? It was Christ. The insight of the prophets? They were speaking the words of Christ. The cloud in the desert? It was Christ.

19. "The Son of God became man in such a manner, that God was his God as well as ours" (Calvin, *Comm., Ephesians* 1.17).

20. Ibid., *Comm.,* Hebrews 7:25.

21. Ibid., *Comm.,* John 17:19–21.

22. Calvin sees Jesus as a walking treasure-chest, "adorned" with gifts ("not those gifts which he had in the Father's presence from the beginning") but those gifts of his own holy and obedient life, which he desires to give to us. Calvin, *Inst.,* 4.17.9.

> We must now examine this question: How do we receive those
> benefits which the Father bestowed on his only-begotten Son—
> not for Christ's own private use, but that he might enrich poor
> and needy men? First, we must understand that as long as Christ
> remains outside of us, and we are separated from him, all that
> he has suffered and done for the salvation of the human race re-
> mains useless and of no value for us. Therefore, to share with us
> what he has received from the Father, he had to become ours and
> to dwell within us. For this reason, he is called "our Head." . . . We
> also, in turn, are said to be "engrafted into him" . . . for, as I have
> said, all that he possesses is nothing to us until we grow into one
> body with him.[23]

Calvin is anything but vague. We are not to imitate Jesus. We are not to
consent intellectually to Jesus. We are not to receive the gifts of Jesus, as
if they could in some way be "imputed" to us apart from him.[24] We are
to "grow into one body" with him. We are to undergo, what Calvin terms
a few chapters later, "that joining together of Head and members, that
indwelling of Christ in our hearts—in short, that mystical union."[25]

This is Calvin's vision for the spiritual life and all that it includes:
"mystical union" with Christ. Calvin makes clear that the death and resurrection of Christ are not simply things that happened to Christ in the
past. Nor can we imitate them now. We, through the Spirit, participate in
*his* death and *his* resurrection (2.16.8).[26] All of the blessings of salvation
are only offered to us via communion. God has structured our salvation
such that everything of which we have need can only be had *in union
with Christ*. God does not partition his gifts to us piecemeal—justifica-

23. Ibid., 3.1.1.

24. "We do not, therefore, contemplate him outside ourselves from afar in order
that his righteousness may be imputed to us but because we put on Christ and are
engrafted into his body—in short, because he deigns to make us one with him. For this
reason, we glory that we have fellowship of righteousness with him." Ibid., 4.17.9.

25. Ibid., 3.1.10.

26. From these events in the life of Christ, we receive the "double grace" of justification and sanctification. Ibid., 3.11.1. "For in [his flesh] was accomplished the redemption of man, in it a sacrifice was offered to atone for sins, and an obedience yielded
to God, to reconcile him to us; it was also filled with the sanctification of the Spirit
. . ." Calvin, *Comm.,* John 6:51. The classic Protestant emphases on justification and
sanctification here find their proper place, as subsets of a primary union with the person of Christ. Justification, for all its forensic and legal overtones of guilt and pardon,
centres on our being counted righteous *in Christ*. God not only releases us from guilt,
but receives us into his family.

tion, sanctification, peace, wisdom—but they come only as we are in communion with the one who is their source: Jesus. Union with Christ provides a clever defense against the gifts becoming separated from the giver, the work of Christ from the person of Christ, lest we become like those of whom Calvin scornfully says, "they sought in Christ something else than Christ himself."[27] So take note: whenever any aspect of Calvin's theology becomes separated from Christ, we risk misunderstanding all of his theology. Calvin's theology is better seen as radiating out from a centre (a *person*, no less!) than as a linear progression of events (or—worse—as an horticultural mnemonic . . . in the genus *tulipa*) that threaten to break Calvin's emphasis on the intimate, the personal, the relational.[28]

## BEING SPIRITUALLY FORMED BY OUR ADOPTION

What makes Calvin's theology of union unusual is that for all its "mystical" aspect (mystical being Calvin's own term), it is completely anchored in the humanity of Jesus. It is not union with an undifferentiated God, some inarticulate joining of human and divine. Union with God takes the shape of Christ: we are joined, by the Spirit, to Jesus who in turn *opens up to us his earthly relationship to his Father.*[29] For Calvin, God becoming our Father is perhaps the best summary of the gospel: "[Paul] proves that our salvation consists in having God as our Father. It is for children that inheritance is appointed . . . we shall partake of it in common with the only-begotten Son of God."[30] In "union with Christ," Jesus's Father becomes our Father, we become children and we enter the family

27. Ibid., *Comm.*, John 6:26.

28. This is no less true for an overemphasis on justification as the "means" by which we are saved, than for "union with Christ." The recent deluge of articles in the Reformed world on "union with Christ" only underscores the delicious irony of how easy it is to miss the point. For many of these new champions of union with Christ (against the "older" and more outdated proponents of justification), union has become the new mechanism by which we are saved! Once again, we lose the personal for the functional, turning even *unio cum christo* into a way to get our problems solved.

29. Mystical union, in Calvin, has a wonderful upward momentum, because Calvin reminds us that Christ is in heaven, seated at the right hand of the Father. (Heaven is often termed "the heavenly *father*land." Calvin, *Inst.*, 3.9.5). For us to be "in union" with Christ signifies that we are, in some way, taken into this fellowship with the Father. The *christus pro nobis* (Christ for us) in the incarnation and crucifixion is also the *christus pro nobis* in the resurrection and ascension.

30. Calvin, *Comm.*, Romans 8:17.

dynamic. We move from being orphans to suddenly sitting around a table, eating the family food, being included in the Father's legacy, and getting in on everything in this family economy.

Calvin, like other Reformers, revelled in the christological, but I believe his theology is better known as *filial*. In nearly every possible way, and at every critical theological juncture, Calvin paints the Christian life in familial terms, as children with their loving Father. Through the years, Calvin's soteriology has sometimes been understood in a limited way, solely having to do with justification and the event of Christ on the cross.[31] My suspicion is that Calvin's scuttle with Osiander is largely to blame for our Reformed emphasis on justification to the exclusion (or downgrading) of adoption. Osiander was a flamboyant and controversial contemporary of Calvin, who locked horns with Calvin over what it meant to be in union with Christ. Fearing Osiander's focus on union unaccompanied by an appropriate role for the cross, Reformed theology has often compensated by limiting union to the cross—the method by which we are saved.

With this move, however, we are no longer asking the questions that Calvin was asking; instead we are left with questions about how we are saved, from what we are saved, and what we should do now that we have received this salvation. They tend to be the questions that quench rather than nourish spiritual formation because they are stunted. Calvin's questions always centred around God (not ourselves, or even our salvation) and the glory of God. His questions are not stunted because they open up to a reality much larger than themselves, which cannot be accessed with a (frankly consumerist) how-can-I-get-salvation mentality or a (primarily functional) what-should-I-do-now mentality. Instead, Calvin's questions took their cues from God's inexplicable desire to bring us into his trinitarian fullness, by way of Jesus's truly human life.[32]

31. For many years, adoption was relegated to a sequential position in the *ordo salutis* (order of salvation), which caused its importance as a comprehensive category to be overlooked. While adoption is also linked to justification in Calvin—the massive change from darkness to light, the pure gift of God to us in Christ—this is only one of its nuances. Calvin's doctrine of adoption is connected to justification (Calvin, *Inst.*, 1.10.1), sanctification (ibid., 3.6.3; Calvin, *Comm.* Romans 8:14), election (Calvin, *Inst.*, 3.25.4), the *imago dei*—image of God (ibid., 3.11.6; 3.11.8), and the *historia salutis*—history of salvation (ibid., 2.7.1–2; 2.10). For more on the loss of adoption as a category in Reformed theology, see Trumper, "The Theological History of Adoption," 4–28; 177–202.

32. Although Alister McGrath notes that "Calvin is actually concerned not so much

Calvin does not shy away from "mystical union" because Osiander had so twisted it. Instead, he reappropriated it, grounded it in the Trinity, and handed it back to us as the concrete movement of adoption: by the Spirit, in the Son, to the Father. In distancing himself from Osiander, Calvin was not necessarily less radical than Osiander in his description of union with God; he was just relentlessly trinitarian.[33]

When we look at how Calvin uses adoption, we find that he communicates not only the miracle of our justification but that for which we have been saved . . . the miracle of our having become children of God. Calvin is quite explicit that we have been saved not only *from* sin, but *for* a life of trust, joy, intimacy, and holiness as God's own children. Adoption is Calvin's answer both to Osiander's non-trinitarian union and to the sometimes-limited "union" that the Reformed tradition has embraced throughout various stages of its history. The remarkable thing is that Calvin sees Jesus's earthly experience as the Son—his life of obedience and intimacy with his Father—as being offered *to us* through the Spirit. This is no family metaphor . . . "no matter of figures," Calvin argues.[34] Instead, it is the reality into which we, unsuspectingly, have been inserted.

It is in Calvin's analysis of Christ's baptism narrative that this comes across with striking force. When God rends the sky and thunders his blessing over Jesus—calling him *beloved*—Calvin reminds us that this is not a private and personal emotion God felt for his only-begotten Son. This was God's declaration *of our belovedness as well.* "It was rather the design of Christ to lay, as it were, in our bosom, a sure pledge of God's love toward us."[35] The declaration of belovedness at the baptism was a declaration *for us*, who are in Christ. It is the "pledge of our adoption,"

---

with justification, as with incorporation into Christ," it seems as if Reformed theology traded this full-bodied trinitarianism for a narrower (though vital) christocentrism. See McGrath, *Iustitia Dei*, 225.

33. "Although I admit this to be true, yet I say that it has been perversely twisted by Osiander; for he ought to have considered the manner of the indwelling—namely, that the Father and Spirit are in Christ, and even as the fullness of deity dwells in him, so in him we possess the whole of deity. . . . For the fact that it comes about through the power of the Holy Spirit that we grow together with Christ, and he becomes our Head and we his members, he reckons of almost no importance" (Calvin, *Inst.*, 3.11.5).

34. "For here it is not a matter of figures, such as when atonement was set forth in the blood of beasts. Rather, they could not actually be sons of God unless their adoption was founded upon the Head" (ibid., 2.14.5).

35. Calvin, *Comm.*, John 15:9.

whereby we may "boldly call God himself our Father."[36] Christ received this tender title "beloved" not for himself alone but for all of us who would be engrafted into him. Calvin exegetes the passage "this is my beloved Son" thus: "from him [the Father's love] then pours itself upon us, just as Paul teaches: 'We receive grace in the beloved.'"[37] In all this, Calvin's point is not that the Father reluctantly loves us only because we are hidden behind Jesus. The point is that God has a trinitarian, *personal* way of doing things. He refuses to give us gifts in which he himself is not personally involved. "Such is the determination of God," writes Calvin, "not to communicate himself, or his gifts to men, otherwise than by his Son."[38] We really *are* loved, because of the one, saving will of the Triune God—the Father effecting, the Son ordering, and the Spirit empowering.[39] God's Fatherhood is made available to us *in Christ*, the Son.

The Spirit's work is to make God's Fatherhood concrete. There is nothing more concrete than the Sonship of Jesus, so it is to this that the Spirit unites us and makes a living reality within us.[40] Without the Spirit, God is no more than a kindly, fatherly figure. With and by the Spirit, we are engrafted into the Son *who shares his Father with us*. To be sure, Calvin notes, only Christ has the right to the title of "Son," yet "he communicates this honor to us by adoption, when we are engrafted into his body."[41] This is the concrete foundation of our adoption.

> Therefore God both calls himself our Father and would have us
> so address him. By the great sweetness of this name he frees us
> from all distrust, since no greater feeling of love can be found

36. Ibid., Matthew 3:17.

37. Calvin, *Inst.*, 3.2.32.

38. Calvin, *Comm.*, Colossians 1:19.

39. Calvin, *Inst.*, 1.13.18.

40. "But because [Osiander] does not observe the bond of this unity, he deceives himself. Now it is easy for us to resolve all his difficulties. For we hold ourselves to be united with Christ by the secret power of his Spirit" (ibid., 3.11.5). The Spirit, though, is not a "bridge" to Christ and his benefits, but the one who fulfills them within us. Calvin does not use the word "bridge"—as if the Spirit leads us to something somewhere *else*—but uses the word "bond" to connote the Spirit's presence to make these realities within us.

41. Calvin, *Comm.*, John 3.16. Also from Calvin, *Inst.* 2.14.6: "We admit Christ is indeed called 'son' in human flesh; not as believers are sons, by adoption and grace only, but the true and natural, and therefore only, Son in order that by this mark he may be distinguished from all others. For God honors us who have been reborn into new life with the name 'sons,' but bestows the name 'true and only-begotten' upon Christ alone."

elsewhere than in the Father. Therefore he could not attest his own boundless love toward us with any surer proof than the fact that we are called "children of God."[42]

Spiritual formation, as radiating from the *Institutes*, is the ongoing task of uncovering the reality of our adoption. Calvin challenges us to situate ourselves squarely in the love of God—the concrete love of Father, Son, and Spirit—and to allow that to transform all our notions about ourselves. It is the radical orientation of our interior lives to the love of God and forcing ourselves to stay there until we really, truly believe it. God's love can only be understood when we realize that his love is not an abstract force (or sentimental platitude!) but is located in the rich life shared between Father, Son, and Spirit. It is *this* life of divine communion that defines "love" and is the very life into which we have been adopted.

Calvin knew that believing this reality about God and his fatherly love was the hardest task of a child. Why is this? Because the effect of Adam's sin, Calvin summarizes, is that "no one now experiences God as Father."[43] Our assumption that God wants something from us, rather than to be with us, is a mark that our emotions have not yet come under the transformation from slaves to children. Given Calvin's own acquaintance with anxiety, it should come as no surprise that his interpretation of the Fall involves a fall *into fear*. The tragedy of Adam, at least in Calvin's estimation, was that in place of love, now was terror.[44] God comes to us as a father, but we now misinterpret those very things "by which he would draw us to himself." Instead, "regarding him as adverse to us, we, in our turn, flee from his presence."[45] One of Calvin's main grievances against Rome was the fact that priests used fear as a weapon, with "long sermons about the fear of God," making the people "flee from him and terribly afraid before his face."[46] For Calvin, this amounted to nothing other than a living hell, "since there is no more terrifying agony than to tremble from fear and uncertainty."[47] If our sinful predisposition is fear of God, marked by servile obedience that attempts to pacify him

42. Calvin, *Inst.*, 3.20.37.

43. Ibid., 1.2.1.

44. Ibid., 2.12.1.

45. Calvin, *Comm.*, Genesis 28:12.

46. Selderhuis, "Pilgrim," 61.

47. Ibid., 37.

(rather than love him, trust him, and enjoy fellowship with him), faith is its opposite: "a firm and certain knowledge of God's benevolence toward us."[48] Faith, though, finds its strength not in our zeal, but in the fact that it joins us to Christ the Son.[49]

Calvin was no stranger to fear. He knew the fragility of abandonment. He knew how difficult it is to trust and "dare call upon him as Father."[50] And so he understood that the Spirit's most difficult work in our lives is to persuade us to act like children, to trust and pray like children, to delight in God's Fatherhood, and to receive this good news in the depths of our being.

> But the narrowness of our hearts cannot comprehend God's boundless favor, nor only is Christ the pledge and guarantee of our adoption, but he gives the Spirit as witness to us of the same adoption, through whom with free and full voice we may cry, *Abba, Father.*[51]

Our identity as children of God is not something of which we can convince ourselves. It is the jurisdiction of the Holy Spirit, "without whom," says Calvin, "we cannot taste either the fatherly favor of God or the beneficence of Christ."[52] In fact, Calvin notes that we are so slow to believe, that the Spirit must place the very words that the Son prayed into our fearful mouths: *Abba*, as a child to its father. Calvin knew that this was such a supernatural revelation, that it could only happen through the Spirit over and over again.

Before the Spirit ever empowers our *doing*, he first confirms our *being*. Calvin reminds us that of all the titles in the New Testament, he is "*first*"[53] called the Spirit of adoption who "alone can witness to our spirit that we are children of God."[54] This is the Spirit's ministry to us. It is an identity-forming ministry, calling us to trust in God's fatherly goodness and allowing us to cease from perfectionism and performance.

48. Calvin, *Inst.,* 3.2.7.

49. Faith is *in* the person of Christ, but its power comes not from us but from the fact that it joins us *to* Christ, for "how can there be saving faith except in so far as it engrafts us in the body of Christ?" (ibid., 3.2.30).

50. Ibid., 3.20.14.

51. Ibid., 3.20.37.

52. Ibid., 3.1.2.

53. Ibid., 3.1.3.

54. Ibid., 3.2.39.

Our confidence is in our status as *children*, not in our perfection or even in the intensity (or lack) of our emotions. Christian freedom thus comes as not as a command, but as a benefit of sonship; it is a "spiritual thing. Its whole force consists in quieting frightened consciences before God."[55]

Calvin's first and foremost emphasis is on the work of the Spirit to open our hearts and minds to look *away* from what we are in ourselves, to who we are in Jesus the Son, as *sons and daughters*. His primary role is spiritual formation—Spirit-ually forming us to live as children of God. Only then does Calvin speak of the Holy Spirit's second work of bearing fruit in our lives, and even so, this is subsumed under sonship, as its evidence. Traditional disciplines in the Christian life are the fruit of participating in this Father-child relationship and, as such, we have tremendous freedom. "To sum up," writes Calvin,

> Those bound by the yoke of the law are like servants assigned certain tasks for each day by their masters. These servants think they have accomplished nothing, and dare not appear before their masters unless they have fulfilled the exact measure of their tasks. But sons, who are more generously and candidly treated by their fathers, do not hesitate to offer them incomplete and half-done and even defective works, trusting that their obedience and readiness of mind will be accepted by their fathers, even though they have not quite achieved what their fathers intended. Such children ought we to be, firmly trusting that our services will be approved by our most merciful Father, however small, rude, and imperfect these may be. . . . And we need this assurance in no slight degree, for without it we attempt everything in vain. For God considers that he is revered by no work of ours unless we truly do it in reverence toward him. But how can this be done amidst all this dread, where one doubts whether God is offended or honored by our works?[56]

The Holy Spirit ushers us into adoption, not workaholism; the Spirit tells us not so much what to do, but *who we are*. In an era where we are inclined to limit the Spirit to a power, enabling our tasks, we need to allow Calvin to re-form our notions of our Christian identity. And when it is time for work (as Calvin has room aplenty for such minor tasks as changing society[57]), it is not as those who are under the "rigor of the law"

55. Ibid., 3.19.9

56. Ibid., 3.19.5.

57. See the excellent defence of the rightful place of human activity in Calvin in Billings, *Calvin, Participation, and the Gift*.

but as those who "hear themselves called with fatherly gentleness" who can "cheerfully and with great eagerness answer."[58]

Our adoption in Christ cannot be reduced to a mere "legal status" with God. Calvin opens up for us its rich and astoundingly fruitful implications as a new set of relations into which we have entered. This is not for the faint of heart. In an era of "doing"—of activism, of busyness, of measurable ministry—"being" can be one's personal hell. It is the hard task of laying tasks aside in order to contemplate and receive the words, "This is my beloved Son, in whom I am well pleased" (Matt 3:17). Only when we hear that word can our tasks have any meaning at all. Spiritual formation is all about entering this Father-Son relationship, about living out the truth of our adoption. It is *formation as relation*.

## BEING SPIRITUALLY FORMED BY THE CHURCH

Book IV of the *Institutes* articulates what it is to be a family, with God as our Father and "the Church as our Mother." Just as union with Christ is anchored in Christ's humanity, so Calvin anchors our spiritual growth in concrete, human things.[59] Far from being an add-on to the spiritual life, the church is the nurturer, the maternal environment where we are brought into fellowship and, therefore, maturity.[60] Although Zwingli's individualistic ideas have seeped into contemporary Reformed thinking, it is imperative to understand that, for Calvin, the church was essential. The singular Christian is the immature Christian. The isolated Christian is the apostate Christian. For the church is the very one "into whose bosom God is pleased to gather his sons." Calvin shocks us by likening the Christian who only accepts God as Father, but not the church as Mother, to one whose parents have been divorced. This person has "put asunder what God hath joined together."[61] So while the lonely individual has no place in Calvin's spirituality, neither—and this is more to the point—does the pious "child of God" who contemplates her Father in isolation. The Christian no longer has an identity in isolation. She simply doesn't exist.

---

58. Calvin, Inst., 3.19.5.

59. For a deeper discussion, see Canlis, "Downloading our Spirituality," 2–12.

60. Calvin, *Inst.*, 4.1.1.

61. Ibid. Echoing Mark 10:9.

One can discern a great many things from the prepositions that Calvin uses, especially how he employs the little Pauline phrase "in Christ." Paul often tosses it into a sentence where one would least expect it, or where a "normal" reading would leave it out. Every time Calvin came across one of Paul's phrases such as "in Christ," he knew he was standing on holy ground . . . particularly as many of his contemporaries could read the sentence without even realizing that that little phrase altered everything.[62] For Calvin, that phrase signals an altered identity.[63] Not a religious platitude, this phrase required a new self-understanding in which Paul no longer considered himself as individual. He could no longer separate his identity from his being "in Christ" or, indeed, from those who join together forming Christ's body. Calvin picks up on this and declares that "our very being is nothing but subsistence in the one God" (1.1.1), thereby insisting that the self can only be understood in its *relation* to God.[64] Calvin presses this further and (particularly in his commentaries) fights for prepositions that maintain the Christian's position as participating *in Christ*, rather than accomplishing things "for" Christ or "on behalf of" Christ or even "by" Christ.[65] Once again, we find Calvin waging war on using Christ for our own ends—whether it be using Christ for the purpose of "my salvation" or for "my ministry" or, indeed, for "my spiritual identity."

Our identity is ultimately found in union with Christ, and is realized by becoming part of his corporate body. In a sense, the frantic quest to "discover" one's self is over. Instead, we are put in a posture of receiving our selves. To seize one's "unique" identity, particularly one's *Christian* identity, is death to our identity: it is found only in the reality—mystical and corporate—of our being "in Christ." This indeed is

62. "But I prefer to retain the words of Paul, *in Christ Jesus*, rather than to translate with Erasmus, [*alive to God*] *through Jesus Christ*; for thus the grafting, which makes us one with Christ, is better expressed." Calvin, *Comm.*, Romans 6:11.

63. See Calvin's discussion of "and the two shall be one flesh" in ibid., Ephesians 5:30–31.

64. Calvin's famous "negative anthropology" is a reflection on the sinful human condition which is "not our nature, but its derangement" (*Inst.*, 2.1.10).

65. "The phrase *in ipso* (*in him*) I have preferred to retain, rather than render it *per ipsum* (*by him*), because it has in my opinion more expressiveness and force. For we are *enriched in Christ*, inasmuch as we are members of his body, and are engrafted into him: nay more, being made one with him, he makes us share with him in everything that he has received from the Father" (Calvin, *Comm.*, 1 Corinthians 1:4; see also 2 Corinthians 5:21).

confusing for those of us in the twenty-first century who experience "increasing difficulty . . . in translating Paul's imagery of incorporation into another person"[66] into language meaningful within our individualistic notions of the self. Our identity is discovered only as it is relinquished, and as it is sought in its proper place—which is the Spirit's domain. Our uniqueness is not achieved by "staying true" to ourselves, but as we acknowledge that there is one who is better than we are at guarding our uniqueness. The more we discover our identity as being "in Christ," the more our uniqueness is secured. And this, of course, is the Spirit's work—maintaining our identity as persons-in-Christ, ministering to us as the "Spirit of adoption" who works this identity deeper and deeper into the church's consciousness.

Spiritual formation requires a cultivated awareness of our being "in Christ." Like breathing, it is the almost unconscious environment in which we live; it requires attentiveness lest we forget the source of our life and health. Our being "in Christ" is a new relation that requires our participation: "Surely this is so: We ought not to separate Christ from ourselves or ourselves from him. Rather we ought to hold fast bravely with both hands to that fellowship by which he has bound himself to us."[67] Being in "union with Christ" does not mean that we will necessarily live out the truth of this corporate identity (as the primal sin of individualism still holds sway over many of our lives). It is an ongoing task to remain attentive and not forget who we are *in him* and in his church. We need, as Calvin says, to not only "hold fast bravely" to his commitment to us, but also prayerfully to ask him to teach us more of what this means. "It remains for us to seek in him, and in prayers to ask of him, what we have learned to be in him."[68] We need to become what we already are! This is the journey of a lifetime. "But what? It is only an entrance! We must march further in it. . . . So, then, it is not all to have entered, but we must follow further, until we are fully united to Jesus Christ."[69]

66. Dunn, *The Theology of Paul the Apostle*, 393.

67. Calvin, *Inst.*, 3.2.24.

68. Ibid., 3.20.1

69. Calvin, *Sermon*, Acts 1:1–4, found in Calvin, "Sermons on the Deity of Christ," 202.

## LOOKING LIKE CHILDREN OF GOD: BEING SPIRITUALLY FORMED BY SUFFERING

Just as Calvin's understanding of justification is best understood when placed in the larger frame of adoption, so is our sanctification. Calvin's understanding of sanctification is that *children of God look like the Son of God*. This is no magical transformation, no plastic surgery. It happens in the same way that we were justified: participation in Christ, and *in his sufferings*.

Calvin is clear that, through adoption, believers are drawn into Christ's own life and relationship with his Father. But this relationship with his Father was worked out, for us, in a historical way—in the slog and determination and suffering of life on earth (John 16:33). Suffering, therefore, is as much our context as it was for Christ. Being united to Christ does not short-cut suffering. It leads us straight into the heart of it.[70] Christ's path is our own. "The afflictions of the faithful are nothing else than the manner by which they are conformed to the image of Christ."[71] Calvin specifically links adoption and cross-bearing, in order that adoption doesn't usher us into a feel-good realm or into unreality itself. Salvation comes through a cross-shaped life.

Calvin's approach to suffering is not cavalier—one that sees God rewriting people's life-scripts to make it hard and unpleasant. No, suffering is part and parcel of life on earth, which itself can be hard and unpleasant. Calvin gives the naked reality of suffering a purpose: you have been adopted. Now take these circumstances to grow into the family likeness. Using Romans, Calvin sketches out his spirituality of suffering: we are predestined to glory, but the highway to glory is via our ordinary lives. The route to glory begins at the "YOU ARE HERE" signpost under our feet, which means our everyday, fallen life-on-earth including loss, injustice, thwarted dreams. We are predestined to be conformed to the image of Christ (Romans 8:29), but God doesn't need to engineer difficult circumstances for this. Life on fallen earth provides them aplenty.

Suffering is *not* predestined by God, according to Calvin. But the transformational character of suffering is. "Afflictions conform us to Christ"[72] because we are people who have been united to the one who

70. For a thorough study of Calvin and Romans 8, see Garcia, "Christ and the Spirit," 424–42.

71. Calvin, *Comm.*, Romans 8:29.

72. Ibid.

suffered and has overcome the world. For this reason, because of Christ's redemption of suffering, suffering itself can be said to be "appointed by God"[73] for a work far beyond face value. Calvin calls upon Paul for his defense: "[Paul] now draws this conclusion from what had been said, that so far are the troubles of this life from hindering our salvation, that, on the contrary, they are helps to it."[74] Once again, God has taken our context—life on a broken and suffering planet—and creatively worked good from it. It can break us or minister salvation to us. It is *ordinary*. It is not to be analyzed for a deeper spiritual meaning. (After all, the root of suffering and evil is beyond our comprehension.) But it is to be entered into with confidence, as children of God receiving their inheritance: "but Christ came to [his inheritance] by the cross; then we must come to it in the same manner."[75]

If suffering is neither God's intent, nor an orchestrated test, then what is it? Calvin focuses on the vulnerability of suffering . . . how suffering is vulnerable to the transforming sovereignty of God. Suffering is, in Christ, subject to the recapitulating love of the Father who, through the Spirit, draws near to his children—first to comfort, and one day finally to heal. In between that first and final embrace, our transformation occurs, for

> God had so determined that all whom he has adopted should bear the image of Christ. . . . Gratuitous adoption, in which our salvation consists determines that we are to bear the cross; for no one can be an heir of heaven without being confirmed to the image of the only-begotten Son of God. . . . We ought to refuse nothing which he has been pleased to undergo.[76]

This is the life of Christ into which we are being drawn, deeper and deeper, day by day. We are being lured away from the siren-song of the self-contained person, and into a family who together witness to the true human identity. We have been freely adopted and are growing up into our family as we "hold fast" to that fellowship by which the firstborn Son first bound himself to us. But this Son still bears the marks of suffering

---

73. Ibid., Romans 8:28.

74. Ibid.

75. Ibid., Romans 8:17.

76. Ibid., Romans 8:29.

and humiliation, of death and resurrection, in his body. We are joined to these marks as much as we are joined to him.

## CONCLUSION

For Calvin, the gospel is a new set of relations into which we have entered. Spiritual formation begins when we wake up to these relations. Calvin's *Institutes* is a marvelous work opening our eyes to the trinitarian context in which we almost unconsciously live and move and have our being. But Calvin wants more than an awareness of our context. He desires that we be *spiritually formed* by it.

For Calvin, everything hinges on the fact that our salvation moves us from "terror"[77] at the sight of God to knowing God as Father. (Faith, incidentally, is moving away from the belief that God is "out to get us" and instead into the understanding that he is "out to give to us," or to use Calvin's words, that he is "benevolent"[78]). This is not so much a mental adjustment, as it is a *relational adjustment*, occurring when the "Spirit of adoption" engrafts us into the beloved Son, who shares the love and blessing of the Father with us. This, however, is no easy realization. It is a miraculous insight—a special ministry of the Spirit—who persuades us over and over that we truly are God's children.

This same Spirit who places us "in Christ" also places us into Christ's family—the church—challenging us to put our orphan ways behind us, and to start living and acting like family. As family, we are welcomed into the family inheritance, but also included in the "chore chart." These family chores (or commonly called "good works") demonstrate that we are part of the family, and reflect our status as children resembling their Father, in the image of the Son. The Father loves us and "shows favor to the image of his Son which he recognizes in us,"[79] which grows within us day by day, particularly as we face suffering head-on, as our Saviour did.

77. Calvin, *Inst.*, 2.12.1.

78. Ibid., 3.2.7.

79. Calvin, *Comm.*, Romans 2:1.

# BIBLIOGRAPHY

Billings, J. Todd. *Calvin, Participation, and the Gift.* Oxford: Oxford University Press, 2007.

Bouwsma, William. *John Calvin: A Sixteenth-Century Portrait.* New York: Oxford University Press, 1988.

Calvin, John. *Institutes of the Christian Religion.* 2 vols. Library of Christian Classics 20–21. Edited by John T. McNeil. Translated by Ford Lewis Battles. Philadelphia: Westminster, 1960.

———. *Sermons on the Deity of Christ.* Translated by Leroy Nixon. The Comprehensive John Calvin Collection 2.0: Old Paths Publications, 1997. Reprint, Ages Digital Library, 2002.

———. *A Reformation Debate.* Edited by John C. Olin. New York: Harper & Row, 1966.

———. "True Method of Obtaining Concord." In *Tracts and Treatises in Defense of the Reformed Faith III,* 240–343. Edited by Henry Beveridge. Grand Rapids: Eerdmans, 1958.

———. *Calvin's Commentaries.* 1844–56. Reprinted in 22 vols. Grand Rapids: Baker, 2003.

Canlis, Julie. *Calvin's Ladder: A Spiritual Theology of Ascent and Ascension.* Grand Rapids: Eerdmans, 2010.

———. "Downloading our Spirituality: Why Going to Church Doesn't Seem to Matter in this Virtual Age." *Crux* 45 (2009) 2–12.

Dunn, James. *The Theology of Paul the Apostle.* Grand Rapids: Eerdmans, 1998.

Garcia, Mark. "Christ and the Spirit: The Meaning and Promise of a Reformed Idea." In *Resurrection and Eschatology,* edited by Lane Tipton and Jeffrey Waddington, 424–42. Phillipsburg: Presbyterian and Reformed, 2008.

McGrath, Alister. *Iustitia Dei: A History of the Christian Doctrine of Justification.* Cambridge: Cambridge University Press, 1998.

Selderhuis, Herman J. "Pilgrim." In *John Calvin,* 34–58. Nottingham: InterVarsity, 2009.

Trumper, Tim "The Theological History of Adoption." *Scottish Bulletin of Evangelical Theology* 20 (2002) 4–28; 177–202.

# 13

## Idolaters at Providential Prayer

*Calvin's Praying Through the Divine Governance*

JOHN C. McDOWELL

## PREFACE

OVER THE PAST FEW decades in particular, there has been an increasing tendency among theologians to ask after what may be called "the religious significance of atheism." Does atheism have more to say to theology than simply demanding and displaying its utter dissolution? For Paul Ricoeur, among others, "atheism does not exhaust itself in the negation and destruction of religion." Indeed, he continues, "atheism clears the ground for a new faith, a faith for a postreligious age."[1] What is meant by such a claim? The notion of ground clearing could imply that there is a necessary movement that begins *prior* to theological reflection. Such a move would, of course, raise all kinds of difficult questions about natural theology. Yet there is way of reading Ricoeur's assertion here which is more theologically interesting than this. Herein Marx's notion that religion is the opium of the masses, for instance, would become utilisable by theologians themselves concerned to critique "religion." Atheism's protest against suffering, and against the silence of the quiet (quietism) gives a voice to those oppressed by, or at least not-liberated through, religion. This critique would function to hear the silence of the

1. Paul Ricoeur, "On Consolation," 59.

religiously engaged before the evil against them, and the silence of their "god" that fails to provide them with their flourishing.

What this procedure suggests is that there is an intellectually respectable tendency to *theologically* criticize what is often taken to be the "classical" notion of God—the God whose liberating possibilities for women, blacks, poor, Jews, and so on, has been curtailed by some sort of idolatrous co-opting. "God-talk" becomes a way of securing the identity and status, in one way or another, of a certain regionalizing of the human.[2] Identifying the source(s) of the idolatry is a complex business and more complex again is determining where the "productive" and "fruitful" imaginings of "God" begin. According to Kathryn Tanner, "a suspicion that Christian beliefs with abhorrent consequences are essentially bound up with all the rest is probably behind a sense that a fundamental reworking of Christian theology is required to avoid them."[3]

It is in this vein that Thomas Forsyth Torrance's talk of "Evangelical Calvinism" might be broadly located.[4] To take the terms "Evangelical" and "Calvinism" together in such a fashion may be project-determining, and this very book arises out of just such a vision on the part of the editors. But what kind of work is the phrase doing? To ascertain the type of project-determination it involves depends upon how both terms are framed and how they function to qualify and redirect each other. This, of course, can open the phrase to a plurality of understandings, since there is no consensus on what either term means, never mind how their combination operates. For instance, they can function together as a marker, a group-identifying slogan. My own contribution, in contrast, approaches the intellectual conditioning provided by such a broad description in terms of a mood. "Calvinism" has a particular, historically traceable connection to the theological work of the Reformer John Calvin. How far those successors can trace their intellectual lineage back

2. The link between this type of theism and the assumptions of many philosophers of religion would lead us to echo D. Z. Phillips' complaint that "Greater damage is often done to religion by those who think of themselves as its philosophical friends, than by those who present themselves as religion's detractors and despisers" (Phillips, *The Problem of Evil and the Problem of God*, xi). Similarly, see Funkenstein, *Theology and the Scientific Imagination*, 8.

3. Tanner, *The Politics of God*, 5.

4. T. F. Torrance, *Scottish Theology*, 59–60, 65, 224. Torrance sees himself in line with J. Calvin, J. Knox, and many of the early Scottish theologians, as opposed to Calvinists such as T. Beza, W. Perkins, J. Owen, and J. Edwards.

to Calvin is a matter of dispute, and Torrance himself tends to envisage successive generations of the Reformed traditions as diverging from Calvin in key areas, areas of God, grace, and Gospel.[5] Both Thomas Torrance, and his brother James, write in ways that suggest they are attempting to retrieve Calvin from the Calvinists, especially those of the Scottish Federal traditions. Just how far such a project is sustainable is itself a matter of controversy among the work of theological historians such as Richard Muller.[6] Here the best work of an intellectual historian can provide crucial vigilance that restrains the wildest imaginings of the theologians who frequently display impatience with detail and context. Nonetheless, there is something theologically important going on, and it may well be signaled by Torrance's use of the term "Evangelical." His theological approach is not that of many who appear to do little more than carry around the bones of the Reformer, attempting to breathe new life into them for each new generation, as if it is only, or at best primarily, through his work that the *Gospel* is heard (perhaps this could at least partially be described through a term like "Calvinist Evangelicalism").[7] At worst, the term "Evangelical" functions to reveal a particular way of enclosing the range of theological conversation, and thereby deny certain levels of difficulty and complexity.[8] In this garb, it works to secure a parochial and philistine narrowness of vision. This would entail the reduction of "God" to, in Rowan Williams' terms, a "tribal fetish".[9] At best, on the other hand, it can here enable an effort to address "Calvinism" in a way that asks where and how the Gospel might be heard through John Calvin. This project would mean admitting that Calvin was not unsuccessful in fulfilling his dogmatic aim with the *Institutes*, the aim announced in his prefatory address to King Francis I: "My purpose was to transmit certain rudiments by which those who are touched with

5. Cf. J. B. Torrance, "The Incarnation and 'Limited Atonement'," 83–94.

6. See for example Muller, *Christ and the Decree*.

7. Muller has a point when he suggests that it is better to speak of the "Reformed," with its sense of diversity, rather than "Calvinist" tradition (Muller, "John Calvin and Later Calvinism," 130).

8. Sung Wook Chung's rather lightweight collection of essays on Karl Barth largely plays rather singularly and confidently with the term "Evangelical," failing to be attentive to the wide range of uses and appeals to it in the English-speaking world alone. See Chung, *Karl Barth and Evangelical Theology*.

9. Williams, "God and Risk," 19.

any zeal for religion might be shaped to true godliness."[10] This approach
would implicitly make a judgment on any theological conversations that
promote decatholicization by calling them into question as improper
limitations on the theological activity of listening to the plenitudinous
responses to the "all-embracing magnitude in Christ."[11]

According to Torrance, when looked at from within a particular
light "the Orthodox, Roman Catholic and Evangelical Churches are seen
to differ, not in their essential relation to Christ, but in the measure in
which they have expressed their faith and life in divergent cultural traditions during formative periods in the past have taken up into themselves
and sacralised transient forms of life and practice which have come to
be regarded as if they belonged to the enduring form of the Church as
the Body of Christ in history."[12] The suggestion here is that no feature of
the Christian tradition is safe from interrogation, whether that be the
Orthodox, Roman Catholic or even (I say "even" since it was Torrance's
own) *Evangelical*, and within that *Reformed*, tradition.[13] Of course, such
an asketical attempt is fraught with peril, and Torrance recognizes that
there is a real and affecting difficulty: "There are of course psychological difficulties to be overcome, notably the power upon us of habits in
understanding and interpretation slanted by an ecclesiastico-cultural
tradition which can prevent us from appreciating another or a fresh
formulation of doctrine and can thus hinder reconciliation."[14] To put
this another way, there are dangers of failing to identify the very contexts that shape one's very response to any theological work; and thus of
imposing a theological framework upon a particular theologian in such
a way that his/her voice is denied its particularity; and, finally, of being loose and free with the very contexts that are constitutive of a good
understanding of the theologian's work. The point that Torrance would
make, though, is that such an interrogatory process is necessary. It is so
for the critical re-examination of "the connections between historical

10. Calvin, *Inst.*, 9.

11. T.F. Torrance, *Theology in Reconciliation*, 15.

12. Ibid., 8.

13. For a critique of the Church of Scotland as succumbing to the power of tradition
over against scripture, see T. F. Torrance, *Theology in Reconstruction*, 164–65. "There
is scarcely a Church that claims to be *ecclesia reformata* that can truthfully claim to be
*semper reformanda*" (ibid., 165).

14. Torrance, *Theology in Reconciliation*, 9.

theology and the cultural environment of the Church, in order to lay bare the core of basic beliefs and doctrines at the centre of the Church's faith and distinguish it from the body of secondary concepts and relations which may well have served an important purpose in the past at some critical juncture in the history of the Church but which in the last analysis have only a peripheral significance so far as the substance of the faith is concerned."[15] While this use of positioning language ("core," "basic," "centre," "substance," "secondary," "peripheral," "substance') may itself look intellectually quaint and constraining to any contemporary post-foundationalist theological imagination weaned on the mood of philosophical "instability" and fluid forms of doctrinal interrelations, the broad point is well taken. Theology in every context engages in an attempt to hear and follow the Gospel, while hoping to properly identify the ways in which the proclamation of that Gospel unwittingly serve to distort it. The work of theology "will enable us to discern how far what we thought to be sacrosanct patterns of formulation were determined by obsolete notions of philosophy and science; this would have the effect of liberating us from their control, and it would help us also to reformulate our understanding of the faith in a more open dialogue with the advance of human culture in which current forms of thought and speech may be adapted to the service of the Gospel without the Gospel being tied down to what may prove once again to be of only transient significance."[16] This might be well articulated in terms that permit the radicality of Torrance's claim to be rhetorically foremost: good critical theological work would help liberate us from patterns of distortion that call themselves "Christian" (what Torrance refers to with the unhappy phrase "transient significance'), and would redirect us to the healing and reconciling work of God that constitutes the ground of human flourishing (what Torrance refers to with the equally unhappy concept of permanent Gospel substance).

Charles Wood laments "the damage that unexamined doctrine can do", and he highlights "the urgent need for doctrine that has been tested and refashioned . . . to furnish adequate guidance to and for Christian life."[17] Such a mood directs this chapter's contribution to the book collection. The broad theological concern that it emerges from has to do with

15. Ibid., 8–9.

16. Ibid., 10–11.

17. Wood, *The Question of Providence*, 20.

the nature and substance of prayer in Christian life and practice. But to even begin to attempt to make such theological observations some substantive dogmatic work needs to be done, and Calvin's doctrine of providence is selected as the chapter's primary focus.[18]

## PRAYER AND DIVINE AGENCY: BELIEF IN, AND PRACTICES OF, THE GOD AND THE GODS

The relation between critical reflection on prayer and the intellectual work of Christian dogmatics may not be entirely clear in an ecclesiastical environment that has come to bifurcate intellectual work and practical performance, thought and practice. Beliefs have become, claims L. Gregory Jones, largely "disembodied convictions."[19] Before moving on to the dogmatic issue it is worth spending a little time reflecting on what it is that is being done here.

Terry Eagleton has claimed that the study of "ideology" is made difficult by virtue of the fact that ideologies are often associated with what *others* have and do.[20] What Eagleton claims about "ideology" is appropriate for critical theological considerations of what in theological terms is known as "idolatry." Idolatry tends to be a concept used to judge what *others* do, and thus it commonly functions as a rhetorically loaded insult in theological polemics in much the same way as "heresy" does. The way that Jean Cauvin, or John Calvin, has construed the crucial issue of idolatry and iconoclasm in the 1559 edition of *The Institutes of Christian Religion* could conceivably lend itself to such a perspective. While many may find reasonably innocuous the notion that idolatry involves the

---

18. Scholarly attention has generally been paid to Calvin's account of predestination, but as Paul Helm rightly observes, "for Calvin predestination is one aspect of providence, that aspect of God's governance of all things that concerns the destiny of the elect and of the reprobate" (Helm, *John Calvin's Ideas*, 96). That means, among other things, that concerns over Calvin's account of predestination can be directed well into his discussion of providence as the soteriological end of his account of God's sovereign agency over and for the creature. Cf. Muller, *Christ and the Decree*, 19. It can also shed light on "why Calvin placed his discussion of providence in book i and his discussion of predestination in book iii in the final edition of the *Institutes*" (Helm, *John Calvin's Ideas*, 97–98). In editions of the *Institutes* earlier than 1559 both providence and predestination were bound together architecturally. On the other hand Muller claims that when Calvin spoke of the two together, providence serves predestination. Muller, *Christ and the Decree*, 23.

19. Jones, "Beliefs, Practices and the Ends of Theological Education," 194.

20. Eagleton, *Ideology: An Introduction*, 184.

inappropriate materialization of God, and thus a denial God's glorious difference from creatures, Calvin more controversially conceives of this primarily in terms of the liturgical and doxological practices of the Roman Catholic Church.[21] And yet his account of sin pulls somewhat in the opposite direction. He claims to be writing his *Institutes* to provide a manual of instruction to the Reformed churches that, on the grounds of their supposed hearing the Gospel, oppose Roman Catholicism as failing to bear the marks of Christ's Church. In this context one might well expect a perspective characterized by a "righteous-us" against an "unrighteous-them." But Calvin does not offer this for either the Reformed churches or for himself as a teacher within them, or at least he does not at this point in his work.[22] Instead, and somewhat surprisingly, he offers an account of the post-lapsarian condition as necessarily and universally involving sin as labyrinthine,[23] a blindness, and the mind as a veritable "factory of idols."[24] No distinction is made here between sinners *qua* sinners, and consequently, at least in theory, Calvin is bound by a sensibility marked by the fragility and provisionality of theological performance. In other words, he is not here allowing for a Donatist-style evasion of the appeal to sinfulness, even blindness, for Christian churches.[25] In this context, then, theology becomes training in constancy of vigilance, a perennial iconoclastic watchfulness. In other words, theology involves doctrinal therapy or training in how not to speak nonsense. Calvin certainly senses considerable theological nonsense around about him. To Cardinal Sadoleto he complains in a manner not unlike certain forms of Northern European Humanism, "Among the people themselves, the highest veneration paid to thy Word was to revere it at a distance, as a thing inaccessible, and abstain from all inves-

21. See Calvin, *Inst.*, 1.11; Eire, "True Piety Begets True Confession," 248; Leith, "John Calvin's Polemic Against Idolatry," 111–24.

22. Just how far Calvin was successful in this regard is itself contested. Roland Boer's book, for instance, regards Calvin as one whose "radical possibilities" were constrained by his "innate conservatism" (Boer, *Political Grace* xv).

23. Calvin, *Inst.*, 1.5.12.

24. Ibid., 1.11.9.

25. Of course, to speak of Calvin's position as one involving the post-lapsarian condition as one of "total depravity" is somewhat misleading, especially when that is understood in terms of being an anthropological pessimism. See Calvin, *Inst.*, 2.2.16; T. F. Torrance, *Calvin's Doctrine of Man*, 84; Charry, *By the Renewing of Your Minds*, 207; Hart, "Humankind in Christ and Christ in Humankind," 73.

tigation of it. During this supine state of the pastors, and this stupidity of the people, every place was filled with pernicious errors, falsehoods and superstition."[26] Sounding much like Gregory the Theologian, Calvin announces that "nothing is more contrary to reverence for God than the levity that marks an excess of frivolity utterly devoid of awe."[27] This talk is inappropriate, misdirected, distorting, in a word idolatrous because it is not conducted with the due reverence to God's givingness that God-talk requires. The Reformer continues to Sadoleto, "the rudiments in which I had been instructed were of a kind which could neither properly train me for legitimate worship of the Deity, nor train me aright for the duties of the Christian life."[28] After all, as Calvin famously argues in the 1559 edition of the *Institutes*, the knowledge of God and knowledge of human being are bound up together,[29] thus suggesting that idolatry is something that involves a fundamental distortion at the very level of be-ing "human." To his mind the formative ecclesial contexts of the time are not offering pedagogies in discipleship at all, but formations in idolatries instead. His conscious task is to help make contexts and communities in which the asketic dissolves the grip on the imagination of the false gods, and he intends to offer schools for discipleship in hearing God, through learning to read the Scriptures well, through reasoning through them together, and through perceiving the divine glory throughout the world. Geneva was to provide the best model that was practically possible of this learning-to-unlearn-in-order-to-learn (and here Calvin's occa-sional reticence to make grand claims about the success is a noteworthy tempering of any enthusiastic hyperbole over what is achieved by the Genevan Church efforts in this regard).[30]

This prolonged introductory material might seem like an odd way to move into a chapter broadly interested in prayer. However, the con-nection between prayer, theology, and idolatry (or even ideology) is a key one. Prayer is claimed by its practitioners (at least if we are speak-ing of prayer in the so-called "Abrahamic traditions") to be prayer to

26. Calvin, "Reply to Sadoleto," Olin (ed.), 76.

27. Cf. Calvin, *Inst.*, 3.20.5.

28. Calvin, "Reply to Sadoleto," Hillerbrand (ed.), 170.

29. Calvin, *Inst.*, 1.1.1.

30. Although to Sadoleto Calvin is highly positive about the piety of the Reformed Church (Calvin, "Reply to Sadoleto," Hillerbrand (ed.), 167). See Zachman, *John Calvin as Teacher, Pastor and Theologian*, 12.

*God.* Even if one takes seriously Ludwig's Feuerbach's critical reading that prayer is really offered "to" what one most values,[31] and thus to an (unhealthy) expression of the alienated self, the proximity between that and Luther's description of a "god" is sufficient to maintain that there are *theological* reasons for critical reflection on practices of prayer: "A God is that to which we look for all good and where we report for help in every time of need. To have a God is simply to trust and believe in one with our whole heart. . . . The confidence and faith of the heart alone make both God and an idol. . . . Whatever your heart clings to and confides in, that is really your God."[32] That is not to say that other disciplines do not have an important role to play—after all, prayer is an act of persons with histories, of persons who pray in ways that express their desires and self-understandings. The help that non-theological accounts can provide become less helpful when they simply take the place of theological description, reducing prayer always and everywhere to practices of auto-suggestion, therapy for the soul, healing for the self, and so on. The direction of this communicative activity, as was common to early psychologists of religion, is simply an incurved one. The question of what prayer appropriately is has to do with the nature of the One prayed to, and this constitutes it as a theological question. If prayer is offered to an idol then the engagement in prayer itself will be distorted—either in the sense that it is "prayer" misdirected to that which is not "God" or that it is the character and desires of the pray-er that are deformed. And this set of theological interrogations is made all the more pressing by virtue of the fact that prayer involves a set of practices over which there is little consensus or consistency. Theological reflection becomes a critical moment in the regular operation of Christian practices, uncovering and interrogating the commitments that ground these and that educate our desires.

## GOD'S GRIEVING OVER CALVIN'S PRAYER

In recent years Calvin's account of prayer has been subjected to the kind of intense criticism that suggests that the Gospel is insufficiently sounded through it. One such set of criticisms has emerged from the work of those who are collectively referred to as "Open Theists," and from those

31. See Feuerbach, *The Essence of Christianity*, ch. XII.
32. Luther, *Large Catechism*, 44.

who are broadly sympathetic with its theological mood. The following section does not claim that the critical readings of Calvin, by most notably John Sanders, are eminently intellectually sophisticated, particularly well-argued, or sufficiently detailed. Nor does it suggest that readings of Calvin as a "causal determinist" are new with Sanders. Rather, the use of Sanders does at least two broad jobs: it indicates that serious worries about Calvin's theological sensibility continue unabated, and it reflects a critique that expresses an intense area of controversy in contemporary Evangelicalism.

Nevertheless, it is not terribly theologically interesting to consider the near hysteria that Open Theism has provoked among many Evangelicals, especially in North America, with unhelpfully wild and loose accusations of "heresy" in tow.[33] Even so, this may say much for, firstly, the condition that much Evangelicalism finds itself in—it is frequently unable to expend appropriate time and energy on nourishingly listening to the concerns of others in their theological critiques. Secondly, it can indicate that certain prominent forms of Evangelicalism are more concerned with intra-Evangelical disputes (given that Open Theism tends to provoke little attention from non-Evangelical theologies) than with broader theological consideration and conversation. What is interesting, however, theologically speaking, is the concept of "Classical Theism" that the Openness theologians set their faces against, as if the entirety of theological history could be flattened and homogenized in such a fashion. The worry of these thinkers is that theology has demonstrated itself to be insufficiently shaped by the biblical witness to God as its generative and determinative witness. Instead, they attempt, rather heavy-handedly it must be admitted, to identify the problems of Western theological culture (e.g., atheism)[34] with the metaphysical intrusion of Greek philosophical sensibilities and categories of thought.[35] Open Theism involves, among other things, an iconoclastic reorienta-

33. For instance, see Geisler, *Creating God in the Image of Man?*

34. See Pinnock, *Most Moved Mover*, 2.

35. See Sanders, "Historical Consideration," 59–98; Pinnock, *Most Moved Mover*, ch. 2. There is plenty of precedent for such an approach, from the Protestant Reformers who went behind what they considered as the intrusion of idolatries in the development of the Roman Catholic Church to a "pure" apostolic faith; to the nineteenth century liberal theologians, whose project attempted to purge perceived Hellenism that has distorted the Christian message by uncovering the essence that is the Jesus of history.

tion of the question of the divine's world-involvement in order to redirect Christian living into healthier forms.[36]

Sanders is convinced that the depiction of God in Jesus Christ
is central to the most coherent and truthful account of perception of
providence and the life of prayer that can be offered. So Sanders argues
that the doctrine of providence "refers to the way God has chosen to
relate to us and provide for our well-being."[37] That reference to God's
action provides the ground for appropriate reflection on the shape of
the reconciled life or of the formation appropriate to the making of persons as Christians. So, he declares, "The stance we take regarding divine
providence has profound implications for what we believe about evil,
salvation, worship, prayer, following God's will, caring for the environment and helping the poor."[38]

Accordingly, Sanders attempts to demonstrate what that depiction
provides for understanding the specific kinds of activities that are appropriate and necessary for the formation of practices of prayer and of
the perception of the effects of prayer in the world. Those all involve for
him an account of God's relation to the world that entails talk of divine
"risk." "Risk" has to do with the following for Sanders: a sovereignly
freely decided Self-disposing or restraining of the exercise of "meticulous control" or "exhaustive divine control",[39] a consequent "openness"
"to what creatures do", the affect creatures have upon God and the contingent direction of God's governance in and through that genuine and
dynamic interactivity with creaturely agency,[40] and a risk or self-chosen
vulnerability in creating indeterminately free creatures who may sinfully
refuse to co-operate appropriately with the reciprocal relations of God's

36. Arguably, Open Theism is as much a reaction to what is perceived to be
"Classical Theism" as it is a fusion of theological metaphysics with a Hegelian "game
engine," producing a "panentheistic" engagement with divine-creaturely relations. See
McCormack, "The Actuality of God," 190, 199. Cf. Pinnock: "Let us seek a way to revise
classical theism in a dynamic direction without falling into process theology" (Pinnock,
"Systematic Theology," 107).

37. Sanders, *The God Who Risks*, 12. Language of "choice" here needs to be used
with caution. It functions to indicate the contingency of the forms of media of God's
Self-presencing, but it must be careful not to loosen the *trinitarian* nature and shape
of the act of revelation, as if God's act *through the Logos* was itself contingent, freely
"chosen." See T. F. Torrance, *Reality and Evangelical Theology*, 23.

38. Sanders, *The God Who Risks*, 12.

39. Ibid., 14, 43. Even so, does it not remain a matter of divine control if providence
is more "general" than "meticulous"?

40. Ibid., 14.

purposes of love.[41] In this scheme, prayer becomes a dialogical or collaborative event in which pray-ers can act (an asking) and God can react (a responding).

It is not my purpose to spend much time theologically critiquing this perspective, or at least not directly. Yet it is worth noting that the accusation that the tradition has been susceptible to a distorting intrusion of alien thinking (Hellenistic in this context) can potentially be turned around on its head. It can be asked whether the Open Theists themselves been susceptible to a distorting intrusion of alien thinking (post-Hegelian process philosophies). It is a considerable intellectual job to assess such a question, but no swift and careless use of historically light work can sustain the need for deep reflection and conversation between these various theological traditions. Moreover, the appeal to biblical texts by the various "positions" has the tendency to undermine the exercise of deep reasoning and fruitful forms of conversation. Finally, it is arguable that the appeal to divine affectivity and dependence as a response to "classical" divine apathy may not only misread how *apatheia* functions within the traditions but simultaneously demonstrates that it itself is determined by modern cultural connecting of selfhood with affectivity.[42]

My concern, instead, is with Calvin, and in Sanders' assessment Calvin's theological work fairs badly. The sixteenth century Reformer's thinking is supposedly irretrievably blighted by the distinctly problematic theological context in which it is constituted, shaped and which it consequently expresses. However, if Sanders' criticisms are misplaced recognizing this may well indicate some concerning features of his own theological proposals: among other things, at the very least it could indicate a careless handling of texts of "Classical Theism," something which demonstrates that his theology is not taking place in and through the best and most attentive kinds of theological conversation; and it may well even indicate crucial points of vulnerability with his theological work that could potentially open up certain avenues for critique of Sanders' project. On the other hand, if Sanders' concerns are even broadly well-placed then there arises the demand for reflecting again

41. Ibid., 39.

42. Is it obviously the case that "love" *qua* love involves vulnerability, dependency, and affectivity? If love is gratuity then in God's case pure gratuity involves the giving for the sake of the well-being of another, and concepts of divine dependency and reciprocity become considerably more complicated.

on what provides, in John Webster's words, an appropriate "conceptual schema for identifying the identity of God of the Christian confession."[43]

Sanders' critical reading of Calvin takes several forms. The first is biblical, although, in fact, arguably it is evident in practice that Sanders materially privileges Old Testament texts. For Calvin, the references to God experiencing emotions (like grief), or changing God's mind are to be understood as the divine *attemperatio* (accommodation) to our understanding, anthropomorphisms that tell us something about, for instance, God's attitude to sin.[44] According to Sanders, any claim in this regard requires a hermeneutic that enables the reader to perceive anthropomorphism because it has criteria developed from other texts. "Unfortunately, Calvin does not disclose how he decides which biblical tests go into which category."[45] At this point, Sanders urges caution "so that we do not allow our preconceived notions of divinity to run roughshod over biblical teaching." His appeal is instead "to take the anthropomorphic language of Scripture seriously."[46] This, however, is a misleading rhetorical claim since figurative and metaphorical readings of texts are precisely themselves attempts to take equally *particular* texts seriously. More significant is the claim that Calvin uses "philosophical reasoning to argue that it is not "proper" for a deity to change his mind. . . . Calvin's hermeneutic presupposes that sovereignty means domination, and so biblical texts that go against this understanding are read differently."[47] Again, it could be asked whether Sanders' approach is not doing something similar: locating the "strong" or "control" texts in and from a modern account of relations predicated in terms of reciprocity, and love in terms of vulnerability.[48] "My principle argument against exhaustive sovereignty is that it rules out certain experiences, decisions and actions that the Bible and many theists attribute to God. For instance, the biblical portrait depicts God as being grieved (Gen 6:6), changing

43. Webster, "Life in and of Himself," 107.

44. See Calvin, *Commentaries on the First Book of Moses*, 1.248-249; Calvin, *Inst.*, 1.17.12–14. According to Calvin, it is inappropriate to describe God as changing God's mind or grieving since that would suggest "either that he is ignorant of what is going to happen, or cannot escape it, or hastily and rashly rushes into a decision" (ibid., 1.17.12).

45. Sanders, *The God Who Risks*, 30.

46. Ibid., 30.

47. Ibid., 73–74, 157–58.

48. Ibid., 179: "love is *vulnerable*, since lovers grant the beloved a power over themselves." Cf. Sanders, "Divine Providence and the Openness of God," 198.

his mind (Ex 32:14), resorting to alternate plans (Ex 4:14), being open and responsive to what the creatures do (Jer 18:6–10), being surprised at what people have done (Jer 3:7; 32:35). God sometimes makes himself dependent on our prayers (Jas 4:2)."[49]

The second main criticism Sanders levels at Calvin traces a connection between the latter's supposed philosophical presuppositions and his distortion of the Scriptures. This criticism has to do with perceived constraints on the nature of human freedom in an account of divine sovereignty that understands providence as control, meticulous or "exhaustive control over absolutely everything."[50] "[L]ike Augustine and Aquinas, he understood God's knowledge and will to be absolutely independent of the creation. God does not look ahead and see what is going to happen, for that would make God dependent on what the creatures decide. God does not decide what he will do in response to anything the creatures do. All that God knows and wills is not in relation to the creation but simply in relation to his own will. This effectively denies any sort of mutual relationship between God and his creatures."[51] What makes this a theological loss as far as Sanders is concerned? "From the perspective of a free will theist", and by this Sanders means one committed to a strong indeterminist or "libertarian"[52] view of creaturely freedom, "the "conversation" an omnidetermining deity has with humans is more like that between a ventriloquist and a dummy or a programmer and a robot."[53] This, he maintains, is not the freedom granted "as a necessary component to make relations of love possible."[54]

The third criticism involves a dogmatic worry about the relation of the providential divine determination and human sinning. "If God

49. Sanders, *The God Who Risks*, 224-5.

50. Ibid., 157.

51. Ibid., 156.

52. Ibid., 236.

53. Ibid., 227.

54. Ibid., 236. Pinnock reveals the dualistic thinking prevalent among Open Theists: "God does not *monopolize* the power. This means that God is a superior power who does not cling to his right to dominate and control but who voluntarily gives creatures room to flourish. By inviting them to have dominion over the world [for example], God willingly surrenders power and makes possible a partnership with the creature" (Sanders, "Systematic Theology," 113). Sanders' talk of divine "openness" is defined by the wrong kind of theological emphasis: "God is open to what creatures do" [14] should be theologically reordered at least to read "God is open to the *giving* of the divine communal embrace, as manifest in creating, reconciling and redeeming."

always gets precisely what he desires in each and every situation, then it is incoherent to speak of God's being grieved about or responding to the human situation. . . . God's will is never thwarted in any respect."[55] This generates a problem for understanding sin—it cannot but be caused by God, and thus be a matter of God's will. "If God grieves, then there is at least one respect in which God intends the world to be different than it is. To affirm that God grieves is to deny meticulous providence. Either the world is exactly the way God intends or it is not. If God grieves because it is not as he intends, then God is not determining all events."[56] In this regard, Sanders tackles various attempts to resist this conclusion from the "meticulous providence" perspective, for instance the notion that God is the "remote cause" and we are the "proximate cause", thereby denying God as the author of sin.[57] Appeal is sometimes made in this context to the notion of divine "permission," and yet Calvin critically adjudged just such an appeal as improperly rendering God something of a passive spectator.[58] However, both this and Calvin's argument concerning double causality are identified as being insufficient since, Sanders continues, "According to specific sovereignty, everything that occurs is precisely what God meticulously controls to occur."[59] So Calvin admits that God wills the Fall of Adam, the reason for which lies hidden in God's eternal counsel but through which "from man's Fall he might gather occasion for his own glory."[60]

Sanders criticizes the glib notion that wickedness is the occasion for human spiritual development and growth, or belongs to the "best of all possible worlds," by claiming several concerns, three of which are worth articulating here. Firstly, "many people do not experience such growth. They become embittered or overwhelmed, thus casting doubt on God's ability to teach."[61] Secondly, "the inequitable distribution of suffering is disproportionate to the needs of the learners." Thirdly, the defense that appeals to divine inscrutability is turned on its head: "it leads to a vacuous understanding of morality, since we no longer know

55. Sanders, *The God Who Risks*, 225.

56. Ibid., 235.

57. Calvin, *Concerning the Eternal Predestination of God*, 179–81.

58. Calvin, *Inst.*, 1.18.1.

59. Sanders, *The God Who Risks*, 265.

60. Calvin, *Inst.*, 1.15.8.

61. Sanders, *The God Who Risks*, 262.

what divine morality is. God becomes inscrutable, which leads to a resignation and a denial of evil."

The fourth criticism of Calvin has to do with what happens to
prayer. "The God of meticulous providence does not and *cannot respond
to prayers.*"[62] Any talk of God's "answering" prayer can only, he advises,
be understood in the following manner: "God, who ordained the specific request by that particular petitioner, ordained that the "answer"
to the prayer would follow the ordained prayer. . . . If God determines
everything, including our prayers, then God could only "respond" to his
own ordained decisions."[63] This option is, of course, fundamentally denied by Sanders' dialogical understanding in which "Our prayers make
a difference *to God* because of the personal relationship God enters into
with us."[64] Nonetheless, intriguingly Sanders detects a different voice in
Calvin, one that pulls in what the Open Theists consider to be a more
satisfactory direction: "when he discusses the nature and value of prayer
he speaks . . . as though God does, in fact, respond to our prayers, is
receptive and enters into reciprocal relationships with his creatures."[65] A
good example of this is when Calvin claims that God "is ready to hear
our prayers; and above all that he is spontaneously ready to come to our
help."[66]

## DEMYSTIFYING THE "SECRET" THE PROVIDENCE OF GOD INVOLVES FOR PRAY-ERS?

Calvin's account of prayer in his manual for reading Scripture, the 1559
edition of the *Institutes*, is located in his discussion of theological education, or the provision of God for our beneficial receipt of the grace of
God. Thus it belongs to the point at which, T.H.L. Parker claims, "the
*Institutio* reaches its climax",[67] and its title impresses the importance of
the lengthy discussion: "Prayer, Which is the Chief Exercise of Faith,

62. Ibid., 278.

63. Ibid., 278f.

64. Ibid., 280. The scholarship of Terrence Freitheim and Samuel E. Balentine
are utilized substantially to aid Sanders in his reading of this in the Old Testament.
Freitheim, "Prayer in the Old Testament;" Balentine, *Prayer in the Hebrew Bible.*

65. Sanders, *The God Who Risks,* 158. See Calvin, *Inst.,* 3.20.11–16. Cf. Ellis,
*Answering God,* 66–75; Wallace, *Calvin's Doctrine of the Christian Life,* 290.

66. Calvin, *Calvin Commentaries,* 285.

67. Parker, *Calvin: An Introduction to His Thought,* 107.

by Which We Daily Receive God's Benefits." This designation sounds potentially like it offers the sort of reciprocity that Sanders desires and occasionally finds lurking in Calvin's work, especially in his preaching and commentaries.[68] But Calvin's account is more like a kind of God-given spiritual therapy for piety, a reorienting of the pray-er's desires. Prayer is given for our sake and not for God's. It adds nothing to God, does not affect God's redemptive will and the righteousness of God's judgments, and does not change the divine constancy or faithfulness to the engracing of the creature. In a section explaining why this does not make prayer superfluous Calvin says that it has been ordained "not so much for his [viz., God's] own sake as for ours".[69] However, does language of "not so much for his own sake" not suggest a theological pattern in which God is considered to gain *something* from it? This is the kind of text that Sanders would conceive of as revealing a tension in Calvin's work on prayer, with his own un-Calvin-like reorientation of the tension in the direction of reciprocal relationality. Has Calvin not opened the way for an account in which prayer does *affect God*, even if that is only its secondary purpose?[70] Certainly for Calvin, all God's acts are with a view to the *glorification of God*, and this claim sounds like "all for God's sake and not for ours." What does this mean, though, other than that God acts in order to display God's saving mercy and justice and that those are for the sake of the creature? That, then, in one sense would turn the claim into "not at all for God's sake (since God does not *gain* anything) but for ours," and in another "not so much for God's sake (since God gains nothing other than to act graciously *ad extra*) as for

---

68. A similar claim is made by Selderhuis, *Calvin's Theology of the Psalms*, 224–26; and Ware, "The Role of Prayer and the Word in the Christian Life According to John Calvin," 90, cited in Calhoun, "Prayer: 'The Chief Exercise of Faith,'" 352. See, for instance, Calvin's comment on Deuteronomy 9:13–14: God "does so bind himself to our praying and supplications, that they be as it were restraints of his wrath: so that whereas diverse times he would destroy all, he is as it were changed, if we come and humble ourselves before him" (Calvin, *Sermons on Deuteronomy*, 394).

69. Calvin, *Inst.*, 3.20.3, my emphasis.

70. According to David Crump, "any apparently impetratory effects are merely illusory misinterpretations of providence" (Crump, *Knocking on Heaven's Door*, 297). David B. Calhoun, in contrast, claims that "Neither in the *Institutes* nor elsewhere in his writings does Calvin assert that prayer is not at all for God's own sake, but only for ours" (Calhoun, "Prayer," 350). And he cites Selderhuis who claims that "prayer is *not so much* about moving God to a responsive action as it is given to bring a believer to greater confidence" (ibid., 226).

ours (for whom God acts graciously)." This is clear from the discussion in the section on "Objection: Is Prayer Not Superfluous? Six Reasons for It." So Calvin elucidates, "Now he wills—as is right—that his due be rendered to him, in the recognition that everything men desire and account conducive to their own profit comes from him, and in the attestation of this by prayers." That sounds like the claim that "God glorifies" God's Self in and through all things; and significantly it does not have to do with the kind of affective notion of reciprocity that Sanders hopes to claim from Calvin at his perceived best. The glorifying Self-expression of the Creator through the creature, as a reflection of the divine creativity, is quite different in scope and nature from the claim that God is *affected* and *moved* from without. The former is God's own act, while the latter makes God passive at a crucial point (even if that passivity is *chosen* by God, as Sanders maintains).[71]

Calvin speaks in a way that reorients the sense of divine Self-glorification: "But the profit of this sacrifice also, by which he is worshiped, returns to us." In this context, the concept of "sacrifice" carries with it a sense of prayer as a form of self-giving, even a giving up or giving away (carefully constrained, however, lest the creature lose the integrity of its existence). The crucial part, however, is the claim that the "sacrificial" work of prayer in response to God's having profited the creature "returns to us," or profits us further. "[T]hrough it [viz. prayer] our hearts are trained to call upon God's name."[72] Calvin's account is firmly wedded to a particular asymmetrical understanding of divine action. His is an account of providence in which God is provider and creatures (calling on God) are dependent. In prayer, or in what is properly called "prayer," "we give ourselves over to his care, and entrust ourselves to his providence."[73] That is how prayer for God's will to be done is best understood. It is less an admission that God's will is not being done (although, as we will see later, there is a real sense in which Calvin can speak of God's *disapproval* and of sin as an attack on God's will) than a moment of commitment to the doing of God's will. Illuminatingly, Calvin follows the statement "not so much for his [viz., God's] own sake as for ours" with six reasons for prayer, none of which provide the kind of panentheistic reciprocity of divine-human relations that Sanders desires: to make

---

71. See Calvin, *Calvin Commentaries*, 260, commenting on *Psalm* 23:1–4.

72. Calvin, *Inst.*, 3.20.1.

73. Ibid., 3.20.44.

us zealous in love; purification of our desires from sinfulness; to prepare to receive God's benefits; to meditate on God's kindness; to delight more in God's provision; and, finally, to trust in God's providence.[74]

This is all relatively familiar and hardly, at least with this description, offers a reading that responds either to Sanders' critique or theological apprehension over so-called "classical theism." Moreover, it has not yet dealt with what Calvin is doing with a claim such as God "sometimes even helps us unasked," implying that more often than not God helps us *when asked*.[75] Yet three crucial factors that considerably complicate Sanders' reading of Calvin need to be recognized. These importantly free the reader of Calvin up for deeper theological wrestling with his material.

The first thing has to do with how the doctrine of providence is handled in an appreciably modest manner in Calvin, and what makes this observation theologically interesting is the fact that it appears to pull in a different direction from the strongly determinist reading of Calvin. As Williams argues, "there is an aspect of dogmatic utterance that has to do with making it *harder* to speak of God."[76] The matter pivots on the issue of what the doctrine of providence is trying to do. For Calvin it is not an attempt to answer any question of *how* God is present, but rather delineates the nature of the gratuitousness *constancy* of divine care, or God's *faithfulness* with the product of God's "hands" in order to shape the faith of Christian communities or, to adapt Wood's terms, to form a pedagogical instrument "for the cultivation of wisdom".[77] Calvin's theological "instruction manual," *Institutes of the Christian Religion*, is written for communities of Reformed Christians who are being persecuted by particular political and ecclesial authorities that, he believes, no longer perceptibly display the marks of the Church under God's grace. These Reformed congregations are not only suffering but they are urged to *resist* the temptations of falsehood and idolatry, in order to better reflect the truth of the Gospel. Calvin, in other words, is aware of the precarious and utterly contingent character of human life, and in this regard his approach is not that of Job's friends who perceived an equitable order whereby justice is seen to punish the wicked and prosper the

74. Ibid., 3.20.3.

75. Ibid.

76. Williams, *On Christian Theology*, 84.

77. Wood, *The Question of Providence*, 4.

good.[78] In contrast to them, the Reformer maintains, in an exposition of *Psalm* 73:20, that "in this world the wicked abound in riches and power and this confusion, which is, as it were, a dark night, will continue until God shall raise the dead."[79] The Fall is identified with disorder, Adam's rebellion being "the subversion of all equity and well-constituted order."[80] Thus, as Timothy George argues, "Calvin's doctrine of providence did not reflect the pious optimism of "God's in his heaven, all's right with the world." It arose from an utterly realistic assessment of the vicissitudes of life and of the anxiety they produce."[81] Calvin, therefore, observes that "Innumerable are the evils that beset human life; innumerable too the deaths that threaten it. We need not go beyond ourselves since our body is the receptacle of a thousand diseases."[82]

The doctrine of providence can not, then, be an empirically grounded affair, whether (to draw in later theological debates) grounded in the supposed patterns of nature or progressions of history or the affectations of pious experience. Rather, it is a statement of faith in the God who is constant and faithful to creation. In fact, according to Wilhelm Niesel, for Calvin "only believers have eyes to trace the workings of divine providence."[83]

In the context of a persecuted church, the doctrine, properly articulated, functions as something of an encouragement to believe *counterfactually*, or believe *against appearances*. Believers are exhorted to *cling to God's promises*. It is this that drives Calvin's insistence on God's care for *every event*. Not only is he attempting to articulate a specific doctrine of God as sovereign, but he is doing so in a way that refuses to cut any aspect of God's works and their agencies off from the divine care. Given

---

78. Susan Schreiner provides a good description of Calvin's reflections on, and struggles with, the book of *Job* in Schreiner, "Calvin as an Interpreter of Job," 53–84. She notes that Job's friends develop theologically some of Calvin's favored themes in his account of providence, and simultaneously that Calvin was not particularly fond of Job himself.

79. Cited in Schreiner, *The Theater of His Glory*, 33.

80. Calvin, *Commentary on Genesis* 3:1, cited in Schreiner, *The Theater of His Glory*, 28.

81. George, *The Theology of the Reformers*, 205.

82. Calvin, *Inst.*, 1.17.10.

83. Niesel, *The Theology of John Calvin*, 72. Niesel warns against interpreting this statement in a way that sets up and glorifies "the religious certitudes of the pious Christians."

that, so the argument goes, believers suffering under the affliction that wickedness brings can continue to trust in God in the faith that wickedness will not prevail against them. Moreover, Calvin's approach offers a warning against any and all attempts to depend upon readings of *our experiences* or *perceptions*. Prayer does not see in the larger patterns of events (or histories) how God acts, or what fulfils God's will, or "answers" our prayers. There might be clues, and patterns that provide certain kind of signs, but the pressure of Calvin's perspective is to deny any stabilizing or systematizing reading of these necessarily ambiguous appearances.[84] "God's providence," Calvin maintains, "does not always meet us in its naked form, but God in a sense, clothes it with the means employed."[85] Consequently Schreiner argues, "Calvin believed that although history *can* reflect the providence of God, he also knew that the disorders in history often cast a 'cloud' between human perception and God's providential rule. Believers can now only 'see through a mirror dimly' and 'only in part,' because they cannot perceive God's providence at work or comprehend the rational governance and the forces of societal chaos. No wonder, Calvin maintains, there exists an almost universal belief that all things are governed by chance and that the world is aimlessly tossed about by the blind impulse of fortune."[86] After all, "In this world Christ was rejected."[87] The task for Calvin is to learn to see well, to see beyond apparent "chance" and contingency the hidden directing of God. So, commenting on *Psalm* 23 Calvin declares that "the psalmist praises the watchfulness of God so that we may learn God's invisible providence with the eyes of faith."[88]

In this context it is worth reflecting for a moment on Calvin's relationship to Stoicism, that cluster of philosophical sensibilities that is frequently presented as displaying a pronouncedly fate-full (or deterministic/fatalistic) undercurrent. It is well-known that the young Humanist

---

84. A parallel consideration is that of Calvin's account of the assurance of salvation. According to Wilhelm Niesel, considerations of signs of election apart from the sign of Jesus Christ as our election departs from the notion of *sola gratia* (ibid., 178–79). Muller, on the other hand, claims that while "Calvin does point to an assurance that comes not directly from Christ and the Gospel", the *syllogismus practicus*, he warns "against its misuse and misinterpretation" (Muller, *Christ and the Decree*, 25).

85. Calvin, *Inst.*, 1.17.4.

86. Schreiner, *The Theater of His Glory*, 32. See Calvin, *Inst.*, 1.16.2.

87. Schmemann, *The World as Sacrament*, 25.

88. Calvin, *Calvin's Commentaries*, 263.

Calvin published a commentary on Seneca's *De Clementia* (1532) in which he praised the Stoic notion of the superintendence (*procuratio-nem*) of human affairs by the gods that left nothing to mere chance (*for-tunae*). At the very least, François Wendel maintains very generally, "it is quite possible that the importance he afterwards attributed to this notion of providence was at least partly of Stoic origin."[89] On the other hand, P.H. Reardon argues that the "earliest of the Reformer's works shows no great preoccupation with the Stoic doctrine of providence."[90] In the *Institutes* of 1539 Calvin disassociates himself from Stoic fatalism on the grounds that theology does not promote any identification of God with natural processes and thus any *necessitas* in experience that flows from a constant connection of causes (*ex perpetuo causarum nexu*). Instead, among other things, theology affirms the necessary transcendence of the Governor.[91] God, he would say in 1554, is "bound by the necessity of fate" in Stoicism.[92]

Whatever the potential theological difficulties that Calvin's account of the twofold knowledge of God (*duplex cognitio dei*) as Creator *and* as Redeemer (the controversy coming over how to understand this "and") may have, in relation to the doctrine of providence the discussion of sin as blinding, perverting, and misdirecting is instructive. In the post-lapsarian condition, any and all creaturely perceptions are themselves disordered or polluted by sin.[93] So commenting on *Psalm* 23, echoing his reflections in the *Institutes* on sin, Calvin says that "For although the evidences of his care are continually before our eyes, the greater part of mankind is blind, and invent a blind chance to match their blindness."[94]

Given that this is the case, it becomes considerably more difficult to tie Calvin's account of providence to the types of "natural orders" that justified and sustained, for instance, apartheid under the largely Dutch Reformed regime, appeals to Manifest Destiny, the Nazi ap-peal to German culture and the inexorable history/logic of providence

89. Wendel, *Calvin*, 29.

90. Reardon, "Calvin on Providence," 523.

91. See Calvin, *Inst.*, 1.16.8; Calvin, *The Secret Providence of God*, 62; Wendel, *Calvin*, 151; Kirby, "Stoic *and* Epicurean?" 309–22.

92. Cited in Reardon, "Calvin on Providence," 526.

93. See Torrance, *Calvin's Doctrine of Man*, ch. 9.

94. Calvin, *Calvin's Commentaries*, 263.

(*Vorsehung*) or destiny (*Schicksal*), and so on.[95] In effect, then, what is claimed of providence should not be dislocated from its moorings in the Gospel, both in terms of it as a formal claim (that we can only know God as governing agent insofar as our perception is reoriented in the saving encounter), and in terms of its material shape (that providence is ordered towards the well-being of the God of Jesus Christ). As G. C. Berkouwer exclaims, "History illustrates the results of a confession of Providence without Christ, whether in the form of a religiously clothed national socialism or in the conclusions of a consistent natural theology. Phantoms of gods and idols and deified creatures appear on the stage of human existence."[96] For Berkouwer, the events of the 1930s, especially in the capitulations of central Europe to, among other things, a particular appeal to providence by Hitler, is theologically revealing: "The 'German Christians' opened the eyes of many of us to the dangers of reading God's purpose from historical facts."[97] The contextualities of such appeals to history and experiences tell Berkouwer much: "Was it not possible for the Soviet Church to give a similar interpretation of history? . . . In fact, cannot everyone according to his own prejudice and subjective whim canonize a certain event or national rise as a special act of God in which He reveals and demonstrates His favour?"[98] Later, however, we will need to ask the question to what extent this crucial set of theological connections features in Calvin's discussion of providence.

On saying all this, however, one cannot leave uncriticized at this point a considerably less modest feature of Calvin's work. Frequently a Pauline-like sense of the deep connection of his own voice with that of God is on display, and consequently an inattentiveness to the problems of ideology and self-deception (which at the very least would require more hesitancy and modesty in Calvin's self-presentation/understanding). This form of discourse functions in certain political ways, and with distinctly sinister consequences. In his 1558 text *The Secret Providence*

95. The political implications of the doctrine of providence are *critical*. To cite G. C. Berkouwer, "With this concept of [divine] sustenance the confession [of the [Heidelberg Catechism] at once opposes every claimant to absoluteness in this world—gods and idols, and any who would autonomously and sovereignly pretend to a self-existent existence" (Berkouwer, *The Providence of God*, 50).

96. Ibid., 45–46.

97. Ibid., 164.

98. Berkouwer discusses the difference in interpretation between the "Constantinian" theologian Lactantius and the markedly dissimilar Augustine of Hippo (ibid., 164–66).

*of God* Calvin announces against his detractors: "Insofar as you abruptly call this the doctrine of the Devil, you certainly regard yourself as a judge of great authority."[99] His critique here is of the ability of his critics to hubristically overstretch themselves and claim knowledge that one might call "absolute." And yet he clearly associates his work with the work of God, and does so in a manner that prevents criticism of him (since that would entail criticism of God): "You proceed to invent monsters so that by defeating them you might celebrate a triumph over an inoffensive servant of God."[100] Likewise, he deals with his critics in vicious terms, and while not uncommon for the age he certainly nevertheless often dubiously tends to rely on insult as much as, if not more than, argument. His critics' work is unquestionably equated with that of Satan while Calvin excuses his own passionate polemic against them: "No man will ever bear the insults of the Devil with calm moderation unless he turns his thoughts from them and toward God alone. May God restrain you, Satan."[101]

The second broad consideration follows directly from these reflections, and concerns the nature of the *gap* between creaturely events and divine action. Calvin wants both to affirm that "nothing which men undertake is accomplished unless God wills it" and simultaneously to deny that God is the author of sin. Crucially he does the latter not by denying the evilness of evil which would be the normal recourse of a "determinism" in which all things are effectively caused by God solely.[102] In this he

99. Calvin, *The Secret Providence of God*, 75.

100. Ibid., 105. Cf. Ibid., 59, 60.

101. Ibid., 122. Sever critics suggest that T. F. Torrance too verges on an appeal to a privileged knowledge unsullied by cultural contamination. See, for example, Hardy, "T. F. Torrance," 88; Patterson, *Realist Christian Theology*, 17. Firstly, there is his tendency to discount any role for constructing reality in our knowing of it, albeit Torrance's is a "soft" rather than a "hard" realism. Secondly, he underplays the formative role in the epistemic process of historical and cultural conditioning. Thirdly, Torrance spends little time reflecting on the types of particularities that would issue in a less "unreal" or abstract feel in his theological anthropology. Is this a flaw at the level of pneumatology? Whether it is or is not, there is something naïve in Gary W. Deddo's claim that "strong opposition to Torrance's pneumatology will mostly come about at the level of profoundly different presuppositions regarding the Holy Spirit rather than over secondary matters," Deddo, "The Holy Spirit in T. F. Torrance's Theology," 104. As Ray S. Anderson more substantially puts it, "Torrance's firm grounding in the reformed tradition tends toward an epistemology of the Holy Spirit rather than a praxis of the Holy Spirit" (Anderson, "Reading T. F. Torrance as a Practical Theologian," 177).

102. Calvin, *Calvin's Commentaries*, 273.

claims he is following the "clear witness of Scripture".[103] Of course, this form of defense is itself open to suspicion–for instance, over whether Calvin's hermeneutic is sufficiently sophisticated to enable his move from Scriptural witness to theological proposal, and whether he fails to consider attendant difficulties with conceiving of Scripture as a theological *handbook* or *manual* so that theological assertions taken from the diverse set of Scriptural materials can sit uncomfortably alongside each other in a fashion that could legitimately be criticized as inconsistency. For many critics Calvin's holding together of creaturely responsibility for wickedness and the divine sovereignty over all events is an example of just one such inconsistency, and thus better theological assessment needs to be made of Calvin's proposals than one that would stop short at his assertion that he is merely following the example of Scripture.

With regard to the issue of wickedness, Calvin's comments on Acts 2:23 are instructive. He admits that the apostle "Peter seems to suggest that the wicked did God's will."[104] Calvin judges two lines of reading this to be "absurdities": "either that God does evil, or that whatever wickedness men may perpetrate, they do not sin." The latter absurdity is rejected on the grounds "that even though the wicked carry out what God himself has ordained, obeying God is the last thing they do. For obedience comes from a willing disposition, and we know that the purpose of the wicked is inspired by something far different. Besides, nobody but one who knows God's will obeys him. . . . But God has revealed his will to us in the law. Therefore, they only obey God whose deeds fulfill the demands of the rule of the law, who, therefore, submit themselves willingly to its authority." This does not let Calvin off Sanders' hook, but seemingly implicates him in some conceptual nonsense—how can the wicked be held responsible if God has effectively willed their wicked acts? It does, however, at least indicate that Calvin is struggling to resist the notion that God is the author of evil; and that whatever he means by God's will, and the effective carrying out of God's will, it is not the willing of wickedness since God's will is revealed in the Law that unmasks wickedness. Calvin subsequently tackles the first of the two absurdities by denying "that God does evil."[105] His reason is "because it suggests that God is disposed to wickedness." The defense is constructed in terms of

103. Ibid.
104. Ibid., 268.
105. Ibid.

character or disposition, with the sinful creature "bound" to sin by her sinful nature, something that is nonsense when applied to God. "God, who makes use of men's wickedness, must not be put in the same class as them."[106] The reason for this is that God "never deviates from his nature, which is perfect rectitude." This argument suggests two lines of reasoning. The first is the straightforward idea that all of God's acts, no matter what they are, are good. Here, of course, can come the complaint that then God can do anything and it would be accounted good, one horn of the dilemma in Plato's *Euthyphro*. More specifically theologically, God's just nature is reflected in the Law, and Calvin speaks of sin as itself against the Law and thus "The will of God is attacked."[107] The second is the notion that God uses the wicked deeds of sinful creatures in order to bring good out of evil, and this allows Calvin to instrumentalize wickedness without justifying it (or denying its sheer evilness). As he warns, "One must not imagine that God works through an iniquitous man in the same way that he works through a stone or a tree trunk. Rather, according to the quality of nature he has given them, God makes use of them as rational creatures."[108] It is this that permits Calvin to distinguish between God's working in and through wickedness in order to do and produce good, and the creature's misused agential responsibility: "While God accomplishes through the wicked what he has decreed by his secret judgment, they are not excusable, as if they obeyed his precept which out of their own lust they deliberately break."[109]

This line of reasoning is promising for indicating that Calvin's account of divine providence, as the effective directiveness of God's caring will, is not intended to involve divine omnicausality. Yet if the motif of the "secrecy" of divine providence is overplayed it can encourage a dislocation of the will of God from the revealing of that will, even if we only know that will partially. In other words, "secrecy" has to be located as a quantitative term (that God in Self-revealing is too rich for our understanding, thus always entailing a "to be-ness" or a "yet-to-comeness") rather than a qualitative one (that God's "secret" will is materially dif-

106. Ibid., 269.

107. Ibid., 278.

108. Calvin, *Against the Libertines*, 7:188; cited in Schreiner, *The Theater of His Glory*, 18.

109. Calvin, *Inst.*, 1.18.4. God can and does "use evil instruments to do good" (ibid., 1.17.5).

ferent from God's "revealed" will). Otherwise, the concept functions to overdetermine the divine will's hiddenness in a way that separates it from the intensiveness of divine will's revealedness and thus opens up the danger of either the scholastic notion of the two wills of God, or the hiddenness of the single will in a sense that qualitatively distinguishes (rather than quantitatively) the revelation of God and the divine being in and of itself.[110] However, Calvin here can at least be seen as attempting to demystify the notion of the "secret providence of God" lest believers excuse God for tyranny by being "God," and he maintains instead that "God's secret will" does not create "in order to destroy what is good" but "invites all men to repentance" even if we do not yet understand (what is entailed by the "secret") just how it is that God's good creature destroys itself "by his [viz., the creature's] own guilt."[111]

Importantly Calvin cautions of the *inability to understand* God's will.[112] In and of itself this is a potentially ambiguous appeal. At its best, it protects the claim to the imperceptibility of divine providence in the messiness of creaturely life, and sustains the theologically important sense of divine transcendence, and thus uncontrollability from the side of the creature. Calvin feels that the believer is given sufficient reason to continue to trust in and life under the providence of God. So much so that the following confession is both necessary and affirmed with boldness: "Nothing is decreed that is not just and wise. . . . [Consequently,] nothing is decreed by him without the best reason. If today we are unaware of that reason it will be made known in the last day."[113] But on the other, it can function to displace any challenge to Calvin's account. In this latter respect the rhetoric is too closely bound up with issues of power and control, *Calvin's* power and control, as the reflections on the "voice" of Calvin earlier suggests.

What about the question of the "permissive will" of God? Calvin generally rejects the notion. For instance, he claims that "Adam fell not

110. J. G. Riddell: "The fatal separation between the God who wills—in eternal decrees, and the God who acts—in redemptive purpose—has its counterpart in the traditional tension between the justice of God and His mercy" (Riddel, "God's Eternal Decrees," 359).

111. Calvin, *The Secret Providence of God*, 71, see also 76. Calvin declares that God's will is one and simple, even though it may appear to us that there is some discrepancy between God's "secret counsel and what he requires of us" (ibid., 93).

112. E.g., Calvin, *Inst.*, 1.17.1–2; 1.18.3.

113. Calvin, *The Secret Providence of God*, 64. Cf. Calvin, *Inst.*, 1.17.2.

only by the permission of God but by his secret counsel."[114] According to Schreiner, "For Calvin, divine power maintains order, restrains the waters, and curbs or bridles both the savage beasts and the wicked will. To posit a permissive will in God was, in Calvin's view, to cast doubt on this powerful control that God exercised over creation."[115] It is a frightening prospect for Calvin that "if anything is left to fortune, the world is aimlessly whirled about."[116] This is to reduce the providentially active God to something of an idle spectator, and that is the worst indignity that can be paid to God's creative care—it is, in a word, idolatry. So on *Psalm 33* he declares: "heaven is not a palace for idle pleasures, as the Epicureans imagine, but a king's seat of government from which God exercises his empire in all the realms of the world. But if God has set his seat in the sanctuary of the heavens in order to rule the universe, it follows that he by no means ignores earthly affairs, but controls them with the highest reason and wisdom."[117]

Significantly, however, it is actually not a "permissive will" that Calvin worries most about, but rather a *bare* "permission" (which then becomes largely passive) that is separated from God's "will" (which is largely active). In this regard he complains about those "Good men who fear to expose the justice of God to the slanders of the impious [and who consequently] take refuge in the distinction that God *wills* some things to be done and only *permits* others. As if, without his will, any freedom of action would be possible for men!"[118] The question remains, how does this "protection" of the righteousness of God's will that is revealed in the Law relate to the making of the sinner responsible for her sinful work when Calvin insists that all things are the will of God? The key is to make some important conceptual distinctions, and for Calvin one distinction is between "will" and "precept," thus requiring "God's will" not to be understood as a universal term but rather as one which carries multiple meaning. Likewise he declares that while nothing is done except by God's will "it is an intolerable blasphemy to pretend that therefore nothing happens except by his *approval*."[119] In other words, while he can say that

114. Ibid., 65.

115. Schreiner, *The Theater of His Glory*, 34. See Calvin, *Inst.*, 1.16.8, 1.18.1–2.

116. Calvin, *Inst.*, 1.16.8.

117. Calvin, *Calvin's Commentaries*, 263.

118. Ibid., 273.

119. Ibid., 279, my emphasis. Cf. Calvin, *Inst.*, 1.16.8.

wickedness falls somehow under the category of God's willing *it is not approved of by God.* "[N]othing pleases him," Calvin continues, "except righteousness," and thus "we cannot judge our own deeds rightly except by the law of God, which testifies without deception to what pleases and displeases him."[120] Calvin even claims to deny that sinners "are serving God's will," although "we [do] serve his just ordinance by doing evil."[121]

The pressure of this discourse is accordingly towards something like a *properly articulated and defined* understanding of a form of the divine "permission" of wickedness. So Calvin exhorts: "Let them recall that the devil and the whole cohort of the wicked are completely restrained by God's hand as by a bridle, so that they are unable either to hatch any plot against us or, having hatched it, to make preparations or, if they have fully planned it, to stir a finger toward carrying it out, except so far as he has permitted, indeed commanded."[122] Similarly, when writing on Acts 2:23, he declares that "when Christ was delivered by the hands of wicked men, and crucified, it was done by the consent and decree of God."[123] Notice that Calvin does not say that it was done "by the will" of God. While he is concerned to emphasize God's power or control over the creature, he is so in a way that requires an attempt to reorient notions of divine "power" away from suspicions of tyrannical forms of control. Consequently, he rejects the Scotist distinction between the *potentia absoluta* and the *potentia ordinata,* God's "infinite" (and not "absolute") power and justice.[124] By claiming that somehow all deeds are done "by the will of God" and yet being resistant to claiming that sin is done "by God's will" Calvin sounds a broadly Augustinian note–evil is, then, not a "doing," as such, an active expression of the nature of the creature *qua* creature but instead an "undoing," or an expression of the nature of the creature *qua* sinner that perverts and destroys (or at least attempts to destroy) the proper nature of creatureliness. As Wood explains, "God concurs in creaturely doings, but not in what we might call creaturely

---

120. Calvin, *Calvin's Commentaries,* 279.

121. Calvin, *Inst.,* 1.17.5.

122. Ibid., 1.17.11.

123. Calvin, *Calvin's Commentaries,* 268.

124. "I not only repudiate but detest the schoolmen talking nonsense about absolute power, because they separate his justice from his supreme authority" (Calvin, *The Secret Providence of God,* 64).

'undoings.'"[125] If this is indeed the case then, at the very least, Calvin requires a more careful spelling out of his logic at crucial points in his doctrine of providence. Moreover, the conceptuality can enable Calvin to continue to emphasize divine sovereignty or providential care over all things (and indeed *patience* with all things),[126] refusing to make any acts independent of God (those that attempt to be acts of independence are named "sin"), and consequently articulating God's ability to bring good out of wickedness.

Calvin frequently speaks of the instrumentality of sinners, albeit importantly not in the manner of Huldrych Zwingli's omnicausal scheme but rather in terms of God's bringing good out of evil. The Frenchman tends, as a result, to speak of the afflictions experienced by God's people in terms of testing or chastising. Such talk is developed in order to encourage vigilance among his readers and to direct them back to the ground and source of their being. In that respect, as he declares regarding the Assyrians as "the rod of God's anger" in Isaiah 10:5, the announcement of coming punishment functions in a twofold manner: "to terrify the wicked by letting them know that God's threats to destroy them are not empty words," and to "mitigate the sorrow of the faithful with some word of comfort" that the sufferings will not be the fruit of chaotic purposelessness.[127] And yet Calvin is equally determined to dissociate suffering and simple confessions of the guilt of the afflicted, as can be seen in his comments on *John* 9:2, for instance.[128] Of course, an important hermeneutical question arises at this point: how are we to read the situation, to attempt to understand what those reasons are, and thus how we are to respond? Niesel is correct to observe that in Calvin "The question of God and evil cannot be solved."[129] And yet there remains too little sense, at least in his discussion of providence, of the *surd* quality of wickedness, the sheer and irreducible evilness of evil that can make no sense within a theological "system." Sufferings under fallen conditions, and the very existence of those conditions are not absurd in Calvin's rhetoric. Moreover, they are not destructive since Calvin wants

125. Wood, "How Does God Act?" 148.

126. See Calvin, *The Secret Providence of God*, 114.

127. Calvin, *Calvin's Commentaries*, 271, 270.

128. Ibid., 282.

129. Niesel, *The Theology of John Calvin*, 77.

to continually stress that wickedness is bridled or restrained by God.[130] In fact, he claims, God "will not suffer anything to happen but what may turn out to its good and salvation."[131] The pastoral situation is important to understanding how this language functions, and as Schreiner argues, "Calvin's world was simply too dangerous a place to leave it to the realm of secondary causation. It needed God."[132] Of course, Calvin is hesitant to determine where and how God's hand can be seen in events, but offers providence as the "comfort" of believing that nothing happens outwith God's sovereign purposiveness. Nonetheless, as a result there is something of an unreal feel about Calvin's work at this juncture, and the danger is that he relies on an overly glib rhetoric. Moreover, there are political implications. Sufferers are impressed to "patience and peaceful moderation of mind" (despite his exhortations to *prudentia*), which is not the message of radical resistance and righteous protest to ameliorable conditions for the sake of the Gospel of healing but of something closer to quiescence.[133] With such an emphasis on divine determination in world governance there is naturally little place for *lament* in Calvin's treatment of providence in the *Institutes*, and it is unsurprising, therefore, that Calvin finds himself little in sympathy with the complaining Job (he has more empathy with Elihu). Summarizing the attitude of those who have made no little progress in their meditation on divine providence he writes, "The Lord willed it, it must therefore be borne; not only because it is unlawful to strive with him, but because he wills nothing that is not just and befitting."[134]

The third main thing to observe is the way in which Calvin seeks to protect the transcendent sovereignty of God and the integrity and responsibility of creaturely agency through the claim that "God's action

130. See, e.g., Calvin, *Calvin's Commentaries*, 272.

131. Calvin, *Inst.*, 1.17.6.

132. Schreiner, *The Theater of His Glory*, 32. Cf. Calvin, *Calvin's Commentaries*, 272.

133. Citation from Calvin, *Inst.*, 1.17.8. Calvin's rhetorical verging on ethical quietism is for a quite different theological reason than those quietisms that operate by way of dualistically spiritualizing the theological act and thus leaving behind deep ethical commitments to materiality. Wood maintains that "It is no accident . . . that the emphasis in the doctrine [of providence] is on preservation, stability, order, and harmony, and that the virtues it inculcates are mainly passive. Our duty under God's providence is to adjust to the way things are, to accept the order of things, and to receive with all humility and gratitude what God sends us" (Wood, *Providence*, 72).

134. Calvin, *Inst.*, 1.17.8.

is distinct from man's, so that his providence is free from all iniquity, and his decrees have no affinity with the wrongdoings of men."[135] Here Calvin uses to some effect the Thomistic imagery of *causa prima* and *causae secundae*. The Swiss Reformer of Zurich, Zwingli, had so emphasized the immediacy of God to the creature, the one true cause, that secondary causes became largely redundant in his theology of providence. According to Schreiner, "Calvin [himself] was ambivalent about the role of secondary causes."[136] The main reason for this is, Schreiner continues, his fear of slipping into affirming "blind instinct" which imprisons God in a chain of secondary causes. In this sense Calvin continues to stress the instrumentality of creaturely causes in relation to divine agency. Nevertheless, Schreiner's reading would suggest that there is an important question as to be asked: what goes on between the writing of Calvin's treatise against the Libertines, in which there is a strong rebuttal of determinism and a vigorous defense of the integrity of secondary causes, and the 1559 *Institutes* in which this ethos appears less well developed? "Calvin's inclination to mitigate secondary causes resulted from his understanding of nature and of history. Order and harmony are not, in his view, "natural/ to creation. After the fall, disorder further upset a previously beautiful but precarious harmony. And history is always awash in blood. Calvin's world was simply too dangerous a place to leave it to the realm of secondary causation. It needed God."[137] According to R.S. Wallace, commenting on the doctrine of predestination, "He believed that the only way in which he could adequately meet the pastoral care needs of many anxious people around him was to dwell on the theme of God's grace in our predestination."[138] But Schreiner's claim reveals a theological problem. The conceptuality of primary and secondary causes does *not* separate out divine and creaturely in any simple sense, and thus not "*leave*" the world free of a God it actually needs.

Moreover, it is certainly the case that the 1559 text is less emphatic on secondary causality than earlier texts, and the heat of controversy must take the blame for at least some of that shift in ethos, but arguably the theological sensibility has not been destroyed. So Calvin significantly declares, that while "the Christian heart . . . will ever look to him

135. Calvin, *Calvin's Commentaries*, 274.

136. Schreiner, *The Theater of His Glory*, 30.

137. Ibid., 32.

138. Wallace, *Calvin's Doctrine of the Christian Life*, 71.

as the principal cause of things, yet will give attention to the secondary causes in their proper place."[139] It is this conceptuality that allows claims about the existence of sin and wickedness, as evil that is not authored by God, to theologically function beyond being simple rhetorical assertion or conceptual nonsense. Wicked acts are to be assigned to creaturely agencies which, although subordinate to the divine action, carry the sole responsibility for wrongdoing.[140] So Muller declares that "Here also is Calvin's defense against the charges of Bolsec that he had followed Lorenzo Valla in the development of an utterly deterministic system: this is not a thoroughgoing necessitarianism insofar as it respects contingency and real possibility at the level of secondary causes. Calvin could state categorically that God had not 'necessitated the sin of men.'"[141]

It is this perspective that enables Calvin to maintain the integrity of "secondary causes" and therein counsel against rash (because "God-protected') behavior in favor of proper prudence.[142] Thus for Calvin, providence does not negate human endeavor or practical wisdom, but, we could add, *grounds* it while not making any acts, even sinfully distorted ones, theologically insignificant (so that 1. they do not take God by surprise, 2. they are in some way broadly "willed" by God, although "will" here requires the requisite distinctions to be made, and 3. God can still mitigate their destructive potential and direct them to generate more profitable consequences).[143] All the same, it can be somewhat misleading, and under a more hardened monocausally "deterministic" providential scheme than Calvin's this talk directs agency onto paths that can be much less prudentially wise and more quiescent.

It is little wonder, then, that Calvin opposes what looks like a proto-deism, with its connecting of providence with foreknowledge. The references in *Institutes* 1.16.4 seem to be to late-medieval Aristotelian Averroists with their appeal to the First Cause, and to a resurgent Epicureanism,[144] and according to Calvin at least, they claim that God

139. Calvin, *Inst.*, 1.17.6.

140. The example that Calvin provides is that of the rays of the sun which may cause the corpse to putrefy, yet the stink is to be attributed to the corpse and not to the sun (Calvin, *Inst.*, 1.17.5).

141. Muller, *Christ and the Decrees*, 24, citing Calvin's Reply to Bolsec.

142. Cf. Calvin, *Inst.*, 1.17.4.

143. See Calvin, *Calvin's Commentaries*, 274; *Inst.*, 1.17.4.

144. See Schreiner, *The Theater of His Glory*, 20.

"foresaw" events and therefore did not intervene in their unfolding. Yet, in contrast, providence "pertains no less to his hands than to his eyes."[145] Divine foreknowledge is itself a function of the divine will which is a necessary and sufficient condition for what comes to pass. It is crucial for Calvin that God attends to the regulation of all events. All events proceed from God's set plan, thus "nothing takes place by chance." God "in accordance with his wisdom has from the farthest limit of eternity decreed what he was going to do, and now by his might carries out what he has decreed."[146]

It is certainly the case that "causal" conceptuality is limited in its aims and role, but nonetheless if developed appropriately this form of thinking would enable Calvin to maintain both his strong sense of divine sovereignty (that all things are caused by God) and an *equally* strong sense of creaturely integrity, without the kinds of modern compatibalist scrambling since we are not speaking of two *comparable* types of causality, that all things have simultaneously creaturely causes.[147] As Wood maintains, "Ascribing an occurrence to God is not a substitute for a "natural" explanation for it, or vice versa. The two do different sorts of work in different contexts."[148] That is what Sanders fails to appreciate about the *concursus*, and consequently he slips into a conflictual account so that no event can be both a divine and a creaturely free action. His account of prayer, then, operates with a "relay-race" type structure with the pray-er calling upon God, and God *then* reacting by answering the

145. Calvin, *Inst.*, 1.16.4.

146. Ibid., 1.16.8.

147. Terry J. Wright incorrectly claims that "causal" language in the doctrine of providence's sense of *concursus* "risks reducing creaturely activity to the effect of the divine cause" (Wright, "Reconsidering *Concursus*," 207). Indicating that he misunderstands the *function* of "causal" talk he responds, "The biblical witness portrays God not as *causing* creaturely actions but *calling* creatures to act . . . and towards a response rather than to a reaction" (207–8). He claims that "'Cause,' then, has an unnecessary mechanical feel to it" (208). That, however, is because of what modernity has done to causality, reducing the fourfoldness of the Aristotelian distinction. It is that which then forces Wright to misread Calvin (214). As Berkouwer observes, the theme of *concursus* "was not intended to involve God in a system of causality to which He would then be subject and in which He, like man, was just another cause, though the *prima causa*. On the contrary, the purpose of the distinction was to avoid the pantheistic notion which might identify the two, making God a part of the causal system of nature" (Berkouwer, *The Providence of God*, 154). Cf. Torrance, *The Mediation of Christ*, xii.

148. Wood, "How Does God Act?" 144.

prayer in some shape and form.[149] Admittedly Calvin tends not to press his insights sufficiently far here, particularly failing to clearly make and substantively sustain the necessary distinctions between forms of causality, between forms of "patient waiting," and between the willing of God.[150] This means that he makes it more difficult for himself to sufficiently distinguish between those events that God wills and those that are opposed to the divine intention. He needs more of the kind of qualification involved in a claim like "God relates in different ways to different creaturely goings-on."[151] Moreover, it is odd and potentially limiting to prudence or practical reason that, when speaking of providence, Calvin tends to seriously underplay biblical notions of divine and human resistance to wickedness and struggle of the threat to the divine rule.[152]

While the theological tools are arguably present in his work, he regularly depends too much on both an over-determined or distinction flattening and unsubtle rhetoric, and the frequent unqualified assertiveness of simple polemic. It is these, more than his slightly better nuanced *theological arguments*, that have the effect of pulling in a different direction. Thus, in spite of all his hesitancies and claims to nescience it has been difficult to shake off the worry for many readers that he tips over into causal determinism. So Leith argues that Calvin's horror of "deism" leads him to the brink of pantheism, a position he only avoids by repeated stress on divine transcendence.[153] The difficulty is that there is something of a wedge opening up between the reality of God's divinity

---

149. This is accentuated by Sanders' postulation of a "libertarian freedom" for human beings. (Sanders, *The God Who Risks*, 14).

150. Colin E. Gunton regards "the unqualified assertion of divine willing is not adequate to escape a tendency to necessitarianism" (Gunton, *The Triune Creator*, 151). Gunton pushes Calvin in a pneumatological direction in order to solve many of the problems in his account (179–80). While Calvin may have been, not altogether inaccurately, described as "the theologian of the Holy Spirit" by B. B. Warfield, pneumatology is conspicuously absent from his remarks on providence. A fuller doctrine of the Spirit, however, according to Gunton, may enable one to speak of creation as a project or a site under construction, rather than as a perfect expression of a divine scheme. In moving the world to its *telos*, the Spirit is active not in ways that are deterministic, yet as decisively shaping the final outcomes.

151. Wood, "How Does God Act?" 149.

152. Where these are present, they describe at most epistemological limitation. Behind what appears uncertain and confused, there lies the steady and immutable will of God.

153. Leith, *John Calvin's Doctrine of the Christian Life*, 112.

*and* humanity in a way that subverts the integrity of the latter, and the integrity of the form of union (without division or separation) that supports the integrity of both the divine and the human (without confusion or change). Questions about Calvin's ability to sustain the hypostatic union, for example, have been frequent asked when the logic of christological aspects of his work have been pressed.[154] When this tension hardens into a theo-logical system the effect is that God is shut out of the world—the God-given union of divine and human as summed up in the incarnate event will accordingly not sufficiently regulate the matter or mood of the theology. It is this that undermines the more careful theo-logic of the notion of "double agency," replacing it instead with either the kinds of conflictual terms for the relations that give birth to modern theism, deism, and atheism, predicated as they are largely on commitments to creaturely indeterminacy, or an account of the world in which it becomes conceptually difficult for theology to imagine and understand *contingency* in intramundane causality. At the very least, to draw on a more general statement of Berkouwer's, it is crucial to admit that "Only a clear perception of the radical difference between the Providence doctrine and determinism will guard against much confusion . . . Since we have to do with the Providence of *God*, everything else, including planning, determining, and acting, is different."[155]

Context, of course, is crucial to providing a good reading, and the aretological function of Calvin's work is important to remember. Even so, it is of little use arguing, in Leith's words, that "Calvin wrote his theology to persuade, to transform human life."[156] While this claim is indeed a good one insofar as it describes one of Calvin's main objectives, it generates certain problems with regard to the doctrine of providence. For Calvin a statement such as all things come to pass by the divine dispensation is a word of beautiful solitude: "The Lord gave, and the Lord has taken away: blessed be the name of the Lord" (Job 1:21).[157] This elicits an attitude of trust that nothing can happen by fortune or chance, affords comfort, and promotes constancy throughout the Christian life. Or does it? Is it a comfort those suffering unbearably to believe in a God who "wills" (if that term is understood without proper qualification) their suf-

154. See, for example, McCormack, "For Us and Our Salvation," 286, 288.

155. Berkouwer, *The Providence of God*, 142, 151.

156. Leith, *John Calvin's Doctrine of the Christian Life*, 17.

157. Calvin, *Inst.*, 1.17.8.

fering? Does not the question of divine tyranny not again raise its head uncomfortably? Moreover, in the face of life's fragility, what does this do to resist the suppression of proper complaint or questioning, of an interrogation of holy protest that refuses to be silenced in face of injustice by either the powerful or the politically quiescent appealing to the inscrutability of God's ways or asserting the faithfulness of their voices to that of God? One of Karl Barth's worries with later Protestant versions of providence is that Christian obedience comes to be construed in terms more reminiscent of Stoic resignation.[158] In the light of the troubles of history Calvin's urge to acceptance "with humble and docile hearts of all (without exception) that is put before us in Holy Scripture," especially when Calvin's voice functions as something of an oracle for the understanding of those Scriptures, begins to look distinctly sinister.[159]

Of course, this is manifestly a Christological problem since it is in christology that God is Self-identified as the One who is the "power" to give, and give even unto the loss of death on a cross; and that God's ways with creatures in Christ do not *deny* but rather confirm and reform creaturely agencies for the flourishing of all of God's creation. It is in Jesus Christ that the dynamic Reality of God's Being-in-act is intensively, or more precisely incarnately, enacted in creature reality. For this reason, Torrance explains, "everything we actually think and say of God must be constrained and controlled within the bounds of the revelation of the Father in and through the incarnate Son."[160] Unpacking the theology of divine agency with an intensified focus on the narrated performance of Jesus of Nazareth would, therefore, provide a quite different feel. So, Torrance continues, considerations of divine "almightiness" (which inform the concept of divine sovereignty and thus governance) are reconstituted, moving away from "the idea of limitless arbitrary power" in order to ask "what God *has done and continues to do* in Jesus Christ."[161]

Calvin himself has frequently been criticized for underplaying the constitutive significance of christology in his theology, most notably at

---

158. Barth, *Church Dogmatics* III/3, 116.

159. Calvin, *Inst.*, 1.18.4 as cited in Niesel.

160. Torrance, *The Trinitarian Faith*, 82. Cf. Wood, "How Does God Act?" 150.

161. Ibid, 82. Cf. Torrance, *The Mediation of Christ*, 70; Wood, "How Does God Act?" 150. Mackintosh, *The Originality of the Christian Message*, 70: "The same Father who saves the world at the cost of Jesus is he who omnipotently guides the world, and the single lives within the world to a blessed end. Providence is correlative to the cross."

the point of his controversial doctrine of predestination.[162] Barth, for instance, argues that "All the dubious features of Calvin's doctrine result from the basic failing that in the last analysis he separates God and Jesus Christ."[163] Equally, it is noticeable that in his discussions of providence christology appears to play little role, at least explicitly. (It is important to add this last subclause in order to provide a critical hesitation in the logic of the critique being developed here—a lack of explicit discussion is not *necessarily* an indication of a lack at the level of implicit constitution, grounding and regulation.) Barth regards this as a problem with the Reformed tradition in general, complaining of "the astonishing fact" of its "almost total failure even to ask concerning the Christian meaning and character of the doctrine of providence, let alone to assert it."[164] Accordingly, despite all else it says, it offers an "empty shell" as "the object of the Christian belief in providence."[165] McCormack, consequently, damningly proclaims that "Calvin's concept of God was finally that of a being complete in itself before it ever thinks, wills and acts. It was an abstract concept of divine being, fleshed through a process of philosophical reflection without reference to the concrete acts of God."[166]

Nonetheless, with regard to Calvin all is not lost according to many of his critics. So when J.C. McLelland claims that "the normative doctrine of Reformed theology . . . is not so much the doctrine of predestination as the doctrine of *union with Christ*" he indicates one important line of theological repair that theologians like Torrance develop.[167] In this regard, urging that the doctrine of providence requires closer attention to the relevance of such themes as "union with Christ" would precisely appear to offer an *internal critique*.

There is at least one reading, however, that pulls away from the model of straightforward internal repair, and that is the reading of Niesel and Muller which might suggest that there is little need for just such a critique. Calvin, Muller argues, consistently enables christology to play

---

162. So Reid, "The Office of Christ in Predestination," 5–19, 166–83.

163. Barth, *Church Dogmatics* II/2, 111.

164. Barth, *Church Dogmatics* III/3, 30.

165. Barth, *Church Dogmatics* III/3, 31.

166. McCormack, "For Us and Our Salvation," 309.

167. McLelland, "The Reformed Doctrine of Predestination According to Peter Martyr," 255. Cf. J. Todd Billings, *Calvin, Participation, and the Gift*, 26; Garcia, *Life in Christ*.

several roles in his work—not merely in terms of soteriological effectiveness but also in terms of constitutiveness, even in his doctrine of predestination in which "Christ elects in common with the Father and may be considered as the 'author' of the decree."[168] It is for this reason that Christ is depicted as the mediator of the divine predestinating decree, and its "mirror," and election can be claimed to be "in Christ."[169] According to Reardon, "This Christocentricity of God's Providence in Calvin's thinking is not to be overlooked. He can call Christ a "mirror" [*speculum*] of Providence precisely because the counsel of God is to bring his faithful ones to salvation in Christ."[170]

Even so, it would take something of a Herculean effort to defend Calvin against the charge that his account of providence has been Christologically underdetermined, relying too heavily instead on unpacking the Scriptures regarding features like the divine will, suffering, divine hiddenness and chastisement of sinners. Christ is construed in predominantly noetic terms in these passages from Calvin as a teacher of providence,[171] and consequently all too neatly as but one of several media for the exercise and effecting of divine governance.[172]

---

168. Muller, *Christ and the Decree*, 18, 25. Cf. Niesel, 164. Wendel regards Christocentrism as the very hallmark of Calvin's theology (Wendel, *Calvin*, 215–25).

169. A very clear distinguishing of the function of christology in Calvin's and Barth's accounts of election is provided by Gibson: "The identification of Christ with God's Self-revelation in Barth's theology functions in such a way as to cause Christology to operate within a range of other doctrinal *loci* in a way that is markedly different from the function of Christology in Calvin" (*Reading the Decree*, 9–10). A little untidily, but not altogether unhelpfully, Gibson claims that Barth and Calvin have "principal and soteriological christocentrisms" respectively (10).

170. Reardon, *Calvin on Providence*, 531.

171. Calvin, *Inst.,* 1.16.2.

172. See Wyatt, *Jesus Christ and Creation in the Theology of John Calvin*, 72. This is not helped by the way Calvin separates out the knowledge of God the Creator from the knowledge of God the Redeemer, placing providence in the context of the former. Certainly he mitigates the scholastic notion of the "two books," and he does so by denying any knowledge of God that is not *pietas* (Calvin, *Inst.,* 1.2.1). If developed well (dogmatically, and not as the epistemic "foundationalism" of the *preambula fidei* [cf. ibid., 1.6.1]) the dialectic denies that there is a world independent of the significance of knowing God (cf. Parker, "Calvin's Concept of Revelation," 32). But Calvin requires more fluid and dynamic ways of integrating (even within distinction) them so as to prevent Christology from being displaced from the treatments of the theological material of the "first form" of knowing.

## INCONCLUSIVELY PRAYING

Despite its lengthiness, this chapter is radically incomplete. It can offer little more than a modest service to some substantial issues for theological reflection, focusing on a cluster of issues arising from the work of John Calvin, and moving to make connections between theology and practice, the formation and transformation of judgment, and of persons in prayerful correspondence to the God of providential *concursus*, in various ways.

Reviewing Calvin's discussion has yielded some surprising results, especially its theological modesty, its pedagogical purpose, and consequently he has proven to be somewhat less unhelpful than at least Open Theists suggest. Sanders' simple deterministic reading of Calvin requires significantly more careful articulation and considerably less simplistic evaluation. Yet that is far from the end of the story, since a number of critical issues have indeed arisen concerning Calvin's inability or unwillingness to explicate with appropriate clarity and frequency significant governing concepts. In this regard Torrance's frequent governing assumption that it was "Protestant Orthodoxy" that soon "lapsed back into rather static patterns of thought" looks somewhat naïve.[173] As Alasdair Heron argues instead, while "Calvin is certainly not responsible for everything that went wrong in the subsequent Reformed theology, . . . it is hard to let him entirely off the hook at this point."[174]

Certainly he is not a "systematic theologian," at least in the modern sense.[175] Yet this fact cannot be utilized as an excuse if it serves to

173. T. F. Torrance, *Reformed Tradition*, cited in Heron, "T. F. Torrance in Relation to Reformed Theology," 41.

174. Heron, "T.F. Torrance in Relation to Reformed Theology," 41.

175. In making this claim, however, one needs to be careful and not rush headlong into an area of controversy without proper hesitancy and informed judgment. According to William J. Bouwsma, Calvin was a humanist who used rhetoric "to stimulate human beings to appropriate action. . . . The central motif of Calvin's life was not to set forth a true theology for the ages but to remedy the particular evils of his own age. He aimed not so much to state truths—he rarely made truth claims—as to galvanize other human beings to appropriate action, to induce activity, to obtain results" (Bouwsma, *John Calvin*, 35). Calvin, in Bouwsma's reading, becomes an anxious figure in an "age of anxiety," thus suggesting two Calvins—Calvin the schoolman, and Calvin the rhetorician (cf. Bouwsma, "Anxiety and the Formation of Early Modern Culture," 215–46). The rhetorical task was to "induce love, action, obedience, and service" (Bouwsma, *John Calvin*, 38). Richard A. Muller, on the other hand, has a quite different perspective: "Calvin's *Institutes* is a theological system—to the extent the term

mask difficulties with his claims about God's providence.[176] "According to Paul Helm, "Calvin has a great regard for consistency in theology."[177] So in his 1558 defense of *The Secret Providence of God*, for instance, Calvin impresses his sensitivity to the possibility of self-contradiction in his thought. Arguably, he goes insufficiently far in demonstrating his theological consistency, and is too content to operate from "the principle that if two propositions are taught as true in the word of God they cannot be inconsistent." Thus while he explains that *providentia* does not involve the (for Calvin, pastorally terrible) notion of divine idleness but rather the act of God's "especial care", and indeed constancy in care, of creatures,[178] we must ask whether Calvin himself took sufficient "care" in his work on providence at some crucial points. Had he done so, or at least in the sense that this paper hopes he would have, he would have been in a better position to resist the deterministic readings that have blighted the receptions of both Protestant scholastics and anti-Calvinist critics. To operate on the basis of largely unpacking God's provident sovereignty through categories such as "control"[179] (and for Sanders, its opposite, the Self-dispossession of control) and "power" (and, similarly for Sanders, the sharing Self-relinquishing of power) may not be the most fruitful, and an account of providence will subsequently scramble to account for the relations between divine and creaturely agencies in ways that do not dissolve one into the other.[180]

So considerably more is at stake than simple understanding, or even recasting, of Calvin's terms of affirmation, insult, and argument. As Sanders recognizes, the very understanding of "God" is involved,

---

can be applied to the forms used to frame and present Christian doctrine between the twelfth and the seventeenth centuries" (Muller, *The Unaccommodated Calvin*, 101). He compares it with Peter Lombard's *Sentences*, and the seventeenth century "systems of theology." Cf. Wendel, *Calvin*, 146–47; Steinmetz, "The Theology of John Calvin," 118.

176. Bouwsma, *John Calvin*.

177. Helm, *John Calvin's Ideas*, 119.

178. Calvin, *Inst.*, 1.16.4.

179. Ibid., 1.16.4.

180. See Berkouwer, *The Providence of God*, 42. Opposition to "control" may not take us to "risk," or at least not immediately. Sanders' options of "risk" and "no-risk" accounts of providence makes "risk," his preferred option, a negative category that (whatever its other flaws) misses the point of providence—the creative giving of God in faithfulness to sustain the life of God's creatures for the sake of the covenantal *telos*. "Risk" is a category of *lack*, of absence rather than of plenitude, which is what a healthy doctrine of providence demands.

and thus theology here involves substantial considerations of icono-clasm. And this is for the good of divine and creaturely relations which function to nourish creaturely life or flourishing. As Wood claims, "A Christian who lacks a significant doctrine . . . is therefore not simply *uninformed* about the point of Christian teaching. She or he is, in a way, *unformed* as a Christian, lacking in a range of conceptual abilities ger-mane to Christian existence and practice."[181]

To underdetermine, whatever the reason (the extremes of polemic in controversy, overdetermined rhetoric of "control," "comfort" as the pre-eminent spiritual effect of designing the doctrine, and so on), creaturely agencies is to negate the public interrogative dynamic of the Gospel, generating a quiescent "Yes" (or at least a "so be it") before the sins that theo-ethical prudence can act to properly proclaim a "No" to in protest and resistance. "To ask how God is related to what goes on," Wood asserts, "is also to ask how we are to relate ourselves to it, and, through it, to God."[182] This is no minor matter, and the danger is that some of the ways Calvin depicts providence weakens our "setting our faces against" wickedness. At crucial points, then, the doctrine of provi-dence appears malnourished in Calvin's rather clipped discussion when a substantively thicker description is required.

Recasting Calvin's account in this fashion does not open his theolo-gy of prayer up to Sanders' panentheistic reciprocity, but rather sharpens the sense of prayer's place as means of God's gift of grace in several ways. The broad lines that emerge from the previous discussion for shaping a theology of prayer can be briefly summarized in six points.

First, pre-eminently prayer is a gift of God's sovereign graciousness which means that it does not involve a fundamental grasping after God, but rather a following of God's richly gratuitous and hospitality mak-ing communicative way. Prayer is not, in this sense, to be understood as "efficacious" in its own right, but can only be spoken of in terms of efficacy metonymously. It does involve a divine responsiveness, only not in the manner envisaged by Openness Theology—it is instead primarily expressive of God's response of grace to the creature God freely creates, a response that is grounding in pure donation.

Second, prayer involves a second form of responsiveness, but again the difference between this claim and Sanders' has to do with *whose re-*

181. Wood, *Providence*, 4.
182. Ibid., 57.

sponse it is—for Calvin, it is the pray-ers" response to God, whereas for Sanders, the rhetoric of prayer emphasizes God's response to the pray-ers (presumably, this would be couched at some point within a scheme of divine prevenience). Prayer responds to the God on whom the pray-er depends for grace—for her very existence; for the gift of prayer itself; for the gift whereby God makes persons in Christian virtue (or faithful "obedience'); and it follows the movement of *this* God whose ways are and beneficent in being free to create and redemptively recreate all things. Prayer, then, sets the conditions for the proper ordering of human responsiveness. It is for this reason that prayer for certain types of things is *dis*honoring to God *and* disruptive of creaturely well-being, reflecting an ignorance of the divine will, or, to put another way, indicating a fundamental idolatry at the heart of the calling.[183]

The ordering of human being-as-responsive in prayer refuses, moreover, the denials of the integrity of creaturely agency. In the divine giving one receives the truth of who one is, and that giving is *not a loss*, or essentially *sacrifice*. Thus there is an interrogation of economic construals of relations in utilitarian terms, of impositions of the identities of persons as those to sacrifice-themselves-for-others, or even worse for in more depersonalized systems wherein the "greater good" can thus speak of persons in terms of "collateral damage." These deny the subjectivity of praying persons before God, and impose an absoluteness of dependence which is both inappropriate for the relations of creatures to one another, and is a distortion of the absolute dependence creatures have in God – a dependency which absolutely draws us in as *active subjects* into the sharing of the relations that are the divine life.

Equally, because the dependency of receiving our responsive identity is formative of who we are, identities are not formed in self-aggrandizing forms of domination (God's rule is not of that kind of *dominare*). That raises significant questions about calling those forms of communication that reach into the control of the divine, seeking an absolute form of manipulating, "prayer." Even the act of praying itself cannot be understood appropriately when conceived in talk of successful techniques, since these belong to forms of "praying" as possession and control.

183. Yet even here Calvin says that "prayers which do not reach heaven by faith still are not without effect" (Calvin, *Inst.*, 3.20.15).

Third, prayer is particular in the sense that both God as the Giver of prayer and the Pray-er who prays are identified in the person of the *Mediator*, Jesus of Nazareth. Considerations of prayer thus bring before us the image of God and the human—the *imago dei* as christically constitutive and performed because of its ontological shape in Christ, the life of the divinely creative agency in and through the eternal Logos as incarnate, the *Deus manifestus in carne*. Prayer's "constitutive reality [is] in Christ himself, . . . [in] the saving mystery which he is in the unity of his person and work and word as the one Mediator between God and man."[184]

This demands the need to resist all banal and homogenizing attempts to locate the way to the divine in what we generally call "prayer." It equally means that prayer takes its place in and through Jesus, as it is shaped and reshaped to call upon the Name of God in and by participation in Christ's intercessory offering of his humanity-as-prayer to God, as is well exemplified in the Lord's Prayer.[185]

Fourth, as prayer has its theological context in the giving of God *and* creature in Jesus Christ, its ongoing focus is on the flourishing of *all creatures* which are confessed to be the gifts of the divine creative and re-creative hand. Jesus' prayer is not a conversation with himself—not a simple practice of auto-suggestion—but of communication with his Father, which is the context of his very life, and it is so in a way that does not leave the world out. Rather, it is "world-making" (that is the heart of the hallowing of God's name—the social dynamics of feeding, being delivered from evil, of forgiving, and so on, are implications of the hallowing of God's name and it is for the sake of those that God has a name that can be called upon by the creature). Prayer, in one way or another, potentially brings to God the *whole world* precisely because the expansiveness of attention to creation is the irreducible context of the givingness of God in which we have our being and truth. This means that prayer has a social dynamic, taking place in the "Church" (the assemblies of God's people who are drawn into the intercessory prayer of Christ) for the sake of the well-being of "the world" (the complete range

---

184. Torrance, *Theology in Reconciliation*, 108.

185. See Jones, *Transforming Judgment*, 121. This does not involve a mere "imitation" or performative "copying" of Jesus' prayer, but instead it involves a learning to "read" Jesus' ministry in the light of the Lord's Prayer, so that his whole person and work is understood *as* prayer, as the calling upon God's Name in enacting the hallowing of that Name in the theatre of God's world.

of God's creative giving). Prayer directs pray-ers to a form of commonality, enacting a shared common identity precisely because it involves the disposing of all to interdependency on those whom the Reality of the creatively reconciling One makes real.[186]

As a result, prayer cannot be practiced well as a sacred practice in contradistinction from the other practices of the human. The invocation is not for "an "other" world, different from the one god has created and given to us. It is the same world, *already* perfected in Christ, but *not yet* in us. It is our same world redeemed and restored in which Christ "fills all things with Himself."[187] Prayer involves the *public* act of the Christian communities" witness together to the grace of God for all things, and only then the Church as it informs the praying of (non-isolated) individuals.

Fifth, the "theatre of God's glory" in Self-giving for the sake of creaturely flourishing is, in prayer, brought in Christ to God for its *healing.* Pray-ers in Christ are invited into honesty, self-reflection, insight into the truth of the world and the *darkest* and *most shadowy* forms of its experienceable performance, their lamenting the sufferings under the conditions of sin. It is for this reason that at heart of prayer's invocation of the Name of God is confession—that pray-ers recognize the distortions of self, placed under judgment, and thus refuse to close off creaturely living to the need for the *renewal* of relations of interdependency *yet to be given* in the coming of God.[188] Consequently, the Church, as the locus

186. Another way of putting this, crucially, is to inextricably locate the mission-dynamic that necessarily emerges from the Church-at-prayer being performed through the healing pedagogy of the formative practices of baptism, Eucharist, ministry, forgiveness-reconciliation, and the reading of the Scriptures together. In this way prayer is grounded in the generative narrative of the acts of *God* as liturgically performed in the context of the church's celebration of the Lord's Supper, and so on.

187. Schmemann, *The World as Sacrament*, 51.

188. It is precisely in this sense of brokenness that the "imperceptibility" of God's governance has its place, bringing a perceptual hesitancy to claims about the "success" of prayer, or of perceiving God's "answering" of prayer. Prayer requires not merely formation but transformation in perceptive judgment, theological wisdom, and the nature of human living. Sanders would admit the same, but his account of God may well be too untransformed itself, with its affective moments, and specifically its construal of divine agency as an agency among agencies (even if the first). As Gregory Baum argues, "if we say that the I-Thou relationship is the model to be used in theology, then we seem to set up God as the divine subject facing man, the human subject, and again conceptualize God as a fully constituted subject independent from and superior to human subjects" (Baum, "Divine Transcendence," 127). There is a recognition in Sanders

of the making-of/learning-to-be God's people, is irreducibly summoned
to engage in practices that are distinctly counteractive against other
sorts of distorting description (functional reduction of persons to works
of consumption, and place in the production of consumptive system).
Prayer, as Rowan Williams argues with regard to sacramental signification, "then requires us to set aside this damaged or needy condition this
flawed identity, so that in dispossessing ourselves of it we are able to become possessed of a different identity, given the rite, not constructed by
negotiation and co-operation like other kinds of social identity."[189] Other
forms of praying are unmasked to be without integrity, attempting to
hide their "worldly" assumption about the way of power with pious language of the God who wills. Prayer, then, involves the *penitential* testing
of the nature of its own workings.

Sixth, as taking place within a theological context informed by
the understanding of divine and creaturely *concursus* (as the particular
covenantal *telos* of the *conservatio* and *gubernatio*), prayer becomes a
means of grace. It is an instrument of God for the healthy ordering of all
things in and through *communio* with God in Christ. Prayer is a means
of the gracious action of the mystery of the eternally rich God, the action
through which we are transformed. It is not an effort to achieve "things,"
but a calling for the hallowing of God's Name by which creatures trans-
formatively live in the communion with God by the Spirit through the
mediation of Christ. Prayer as pedagogy in the life of *communio* in
Christ, therefore, resists the notion of human development in simple
therapeutic or essentially "private" terms.[190] Prayer is an act of God's giv-

---

that christology involves a relocation of practices of prayer within the providence of
God, although it is not altogether clear just how christology transforms the reading of
the Old Testament in particular, and how far Jesus is *constitutive* of Christian accounts
of prayer. Likewise, within Calvin's scheme there remain questions about how far he
too has reoriented his approach christologically, or, more appropriately, trinitarianly. At
least Calvin's account of prayer emerges from a context of which providence demands a
proper hesitancy in claiming perception.

189. Williams, *On Christian Theology*, 209.

190. It must be asked whether there is even any such thing as a *purely private*
therapy, and thus whether the Open Theist complaint about "therapeutic forms" of
prayer itself involves something of a lazy logic. If I spend time relaxing in the morning
(whether it be to music, through silent meditation, even just having a relaxing bath)
then that affects my mood. But it does more than that–affecting my mood may play
a crucial role in affecting how I treat my children (I may be more patient and relaxed
with them), my wife, other road users (I may be a less aggressive driver), and so on. And

ing and of human response that affects and effects the shape of human formation and re-formation.

If these claims are in any way demonstrably theologically appropriate, then to hear the *euangelion* in and through, but also beyond, Calvin may require the following recognition: *prayer is a gift of God's sovereign graciousness for the pedagogical ordering of worldly life in Christ, a gift for the making of sociality that requires the witness of responsibility for justice and charity for all those whom God loves in the creativity of the Gift of the Word. Prayer is not, then, the self-enacted therapy of the self, or the coming of the divine into involvement with the creature, but rather involves the reordering of the very way we think and experience human life. Engaging in prayer informs the struggle (when under the conditions of being healed from sinfulness) of learning to live in relation to God as paradigmatic of, and generative for, our living with and for others. Personhood requires learning to be in relation, and consequently it is important to specify how ecclesial friendships-in-prayer are the contexts in which such pedagogy takes place are related. It is here that human beings are called forth into the embrace of a life of transformative discipleship or "union with Christ" as the "foretaste" of the flourishing of all things.*

---

this "personal" affectivity itself may prove to be affecting—so by treating people in one way and not another it may affect their mood and possibly equally the way they relate to others that day, as well as their disposition towards me, and so on. Now I am not equating prayer with what we call therapy here, but merely observing that the subjectivist interpretations of therapy do not go far enough in their articulation of its "public" effects. Thus, while what Baelz claims about prayer is not untrue but is misleading by not going far enough into the world when he claims that "we expect prayer to make a difference to the man who prays . . . In communion with God a man comes to a new knowledge of himself and a new apprehension of the world around him" (Baelz, *Prayer and Providence*, 111). In this context, it is very odd to hear Robert Ellis describe prayer that makes no difference to God as "distinctly passive" (Ellis, *Answering God*, xi). In fact, passivity is more of a problem for interventionist and panentheistically patterned accounts—prayer as human activity, and the efficacy of prayer as divine activity with concomitant pray-er's passivity.

# BIBLIOGRAPHY

Anderson Ray S. "Reading T. F. Torrance as a Practical Theologian." In *The Promise of Trinitarian Theology: Theologians in Dialogue with T. F. Torrance,* edited by Elmer M. Colyer, 161–83. Lanham: Rowman and Littlefield, 2001.

Baelz, Peter R. *Prayer and Providence: A Background Study.* London: SCM, 1968.

Balentine, Samuel E. *Prayer in the Hebrew Bible: The Drama of Divine-Human Dialogue.* Minneapolis: Fortress, 1993.

Barth, Karl. *Church Dogmatics.* 4 vols. Edited by G. W. Bromiley and T. F. Torrance. Translated by G.W. Bromiley, et al. Edinburgh: T. & T. Clark, 1956–1975.

Baum, Gregory. "Divine Transcendence." In *The God Experience: Essays in Hope,* edited by Joseph P. Whelan, 120–36. New York: Newman, 1971.

Berkouwer, G. C. *The Providence of God.* Grand Rapids: Eerdmans, 1952.

Billings, J. Todd. *Calvin, Participation, and the Gift: The Activity of Believers in Union with Christ.* Oxford: Oxford University Press, 2007.

Boer, Roland. *Political Grace: The Revolutionary Theology of John Calvin.* Louisville: Westminster John Knox, 2009.

Bouwsma, William J. "Anxiety and the Formation of Early Modern Culture." In *After the Reformation: Essays in Honor of J.H. Hexter,* edited by Barbara C. Malament, 215–46. Philadelphia: University of Pennsylvania Press, 1980.

———. *John Calvin: A Sixteenth Century Portrait.* New York: Oxford University Press, 1988,

———. *The Unaccommodated Calvin: Studies in the Foundation of a Theological Tradition.* Oxford and New York: Oxford University Press, 2000.

Calhoun, David B. "Prayer: 'The Chief Exercise of Faith.'" In *A Theological Guide to Calvin's Institutes: Essays and Analysis,* edited by David W. Hall and Peter A. Lillback, 347–67. Phillipsburg: Presbyterian and Reformed, 2008.

Calvin, John. *Calvin Commentaries.* Translated by Joseph Haroutunian. Louisville: Westminster, 1958.

———. *Commentaries on the First Book of Moses.* 2 Vols. Translated by John King. Grand Rapids: Eerdmans, 1948.

———. *Concerning the Eternal Predestination of God.* Translated by J. K. S. Reid. London: James Clarke, 1961.

———. *The Institutes of the Christian Religion.* Edited by J. T. McNeill. Translated by F. L. Battles. Philadelphia: Westminster, 1960.

———. "Reply to Sadoleto." In *A Reformation Debate: John Calvin and Jacopo Sadoleto,* edited by John C. Olin, translated by Henry Beveridge, 43–88. New York: Harper & Row, 1966.

———. "Reply to Sadoleto." In *The Protestant Reformation,* 153–72. Edited by Hans J. Hillerbrand. New York: Harper & Row, 1968.

———. *Sermons on Deuteronomy.* Edinburgh: Banner of Truth Trust, 1987.

Charry, Ellen T. *By the Renewing of Your Minds: The Pastoral Function of Christian Doctrine.* Oxford: Oxford University Press, 1997.

Chung, Sung Wook. *Karl Barth and Evangelical Theology: Convergences and Divergences.* Milton Keynes: Paternoster, 2006.

Crump, David. *Knocking on Heaven's Door: A New Testament Theology of Petitionary Prayer.* Grand Rapids: Baker, 2006.

Deddo Gary W. "The Holy Spirit in T. F. Torrance's Theology." In *The Promise of Trinitarian Theology: Theologians in Dialogue with T. F. Torrance,* edited by Elmer M. Colyer, 81–114. Lanham: Rowman and Littlefield, 2001.

Eagleton, Terry. *Ideology: An Introduction.* New York and London: Verso, 1991.

Eire, Carlos M. N. "'True Piety Begets True Confession': Calvin's Attack on Idolatry." In *John Calvin and the Church: A Prism of Reform,* edited by Timothy George, 247–76. Louisville: Westminster John Knox, 1990.

Ellis, Robert. *Answering God: Towards a Theology of Intercession.* Milton Keynes: Paternoster, 2005.

Feuerbach, Ludwig. *The Essence of Christianity.* Translated by George Eliot. New York: Harper & Row, 1957.

Freitheim, Terrence. "Prayer in the Old Testament: Creating Space in the World for God." In *A Primer on Prayer,* edited by Paul R. Sponheim, 51–62. Philadelphia: Fortress, 1988.

Funkenstein, Amos. *Theology and the Scientific Imagination: From the Middle Ages to the Seventeenth Century.* Princeton: Princeton University Press, 1986.

Garcia, Mark A. *Life in Christ: Union with Christ and Twofold Grace in Calvin's Theology.* Carlisle: Paternoster, 2008.

Geisler, Norman L. *Creating God in the Image of Man?* Minneapolis: Bethany, 1997.

George, Timothy. *The Theology of the Reformers.* Leicester: Apollos, 1988.

Gibson, David. *Reading the Decree: Exegesis, Election and Christology in Calvin and Barth.* London: T. & T. Clark, 2009.

Gunton, Colin E. *The Triune Creator.* Edinburgh: Edinburgh University Press, 1998.

Hardy, Daniel W. "T. F. Torrance." In *The Modern Theologians: An Introduction to Christian Theology in the Twentieth Century,* edited by David Ford, 1:71–91. Oxford: Basil Blackwell, 1989.

Hart, Trevor A. "Humankind in Christ and Christ in Humankind: Salvation as Participation in our Substitute in the Theology of John Calvin." *Scottish Journal of Theology* 42 (1989) 67–84.

Helm, Paul. *John Calvin's Ideas.* Oxford: Oxford University Press, 2004.

Heron, Alasdair. "T. F. Torrance in Relation to Reformed Theology." In *The Promise of Trinitarian Theology: Theologians in Dialogue with T. F. Torrance,* edited by Elmer Colyer, 31–49. Lanham: Rowman and Littlefield, 2001.

Jones, L. Gregory. "Beliefs, Practices and the Ends of Theological Education." In *Practicing Theology: Beliefs and Practices in Christian Life,* edited by Miroslav Volf and Dorothy C. Bass, 185–205. Grand Rapids: Eerdmans, 2002.

———. *Transforming Judgment: Toward a Trinitarian Account of the Moral Life.* Eugene, OR: Wipf & Stock, 1990.

Kirby, W. J. Torrance. "Stoic *and* Epicurean? Calvin's Dialectical Account of Providence." *International Journal of Systematic Theology* 5 (2003) 309–22.

Leith, John. *John Calvin's Doctrine of the Christian Life.* Louisville: Westminster John Knox, 1989.

———. "John Calvin's Polemic Against Idolatry." In *Soli Deo Gloria: New Testament Studies in Honor of William Childs Robinson,* edited by J. McDowell Richards, 111–24. Richmond: John Knox, 1968.

Luther, Martin. *Large Catechism.* Translated by John Nicholas Lenker. Philadelphia: Augsburg, 1935.

Mackintosh, H. R. *The Originality of the Christian Message.* New York: Charles Scriber's Sons, 1920.

McCormack, Bruce L. "The Actuality of God: Karl Barth in Conversation with Open Theism." In *Engaging the Doctrine of God: Contemporary Protestant Perspectives*, edited by Bruce L. McCormack, 185–42. Grand Rapids: Baker, 2008.

———. "For Us and Our Salvation: Incarnation and Atonement in the Reformed Tradition." *The Greek Orthodox Theological Review* 43 (1998) 281–316.

McLelland, J.C. "The Reformed Doctrine of Predestination According to Peter Martyr." *Scottish Journal of Theology* 8 (1955) 255–71.

Muller, Richard A. *Christ and the Decree: Christology and Predestination in Reformed Theology from Calvin to Perkins*. 1986. Reprint, Grand Rapids: Baker, 2008.

———. "John Calvin and Later Calvinism: The Identity of the Reformed Tradition." In *The Cambridge Companion to Reformation Theology*, edited by David Bagchi and David C. Steinmetz, 130–49. Cambridge: Cambridge University Press, 2004.

Niesel, Wilhelm. *The Theology of John Calvin*. Translated by H. Knight. London: Lutterworth, 1956.

Parker, T. H. L. *Calvin: An Introduction to His Thought*. Louisville: Westminster John Knox, 1995.

———. "Calvin's Concept of Revelation." *Scottish Journal of Theology* 2 (1949) 29–47, 337–51.

Patterson, Sue. *Realist Christian Theology: Realist Christian Theology in a Postmodern Age*. Cambridge: Cambridge University Press, 1999.

Phillips, D. Z. *The Problem of Evil and the Problem of God*. London: SCM, 2004.

Pinnock, Clark H. *Most Moved Mover: A Theology of God's Openness*. Grand Rapids: Baker Academic, 2001.

———. "Systematic Theology." In *The Openness of God*, edited by Clark H. Pinnock, Richard Rice, John Sanders, and William Hasker, 101–25. Downers Grove, IL: InterVarsity, 1994.

Reardon, P. R. "Calvin on Providence: The Development of an Insight." *Scottish Journal of Theology* 28 (1975) 517–33.

Reid, J. K. S. "The Office of Christ in Predestination." *Scottish Journal of Theology* 1 (1948) 5–19.

Ricoeur, Paul. "On Consolation." In *The Religious Significance of Atheism*, by Alasdair MacIntyre and Paul Ricoeur, 81–98. New York: Columbia University Press, 1969.

Riddell, J. G. "God's Eternal Decrees." *Scottish Journal of Theology* 2 (1949) 352–63.

Sanders, John. "Divine Providence and the Openness of God." In *Perspectives on the Doctrine of God: Four Views*, edited by Bruce A. Ware, 196–240. Nashville: Broadman & Holman, 2008.

———. *The God Who Risks: A Theology of Divine Providence*. Revised Edition. Downers Grove, IL: InterVarsity, 2007.

———. "Historical Consideration." *The Openness of God: A Biblical Challenge to the Traditional Understanding of God*, edited by Clark H. Pinnock, Richard Rice, John Sanders, and William Hasker, 59–98. Downers Grove, IL: InterVarsity, 1994.

Schmemann, Alexander. *The World as Sacrament*. London: Darton, Longman & Todd, 1966.

Schreiner, Susan. "Calvin as an Interpreter of Job." In *Calvin and the Bible*, edited by Donald K. McKim, 53–84. Cambridge: Cambridge University Press, 2006.

———. *The Theater of His Glory: Nature and the Natural Order in the Thought of John Calvin*. Grand Rapids: Baker Academic, 1991.

Selderhuis, H.J. *Calvin's Theology of the Psalms*. Grand Rapids: Baker, 2007.

Steinmetz, David C. "The Theology of John Calvin." In *The Cambridge Companion to Reformation Theology,* edited by David Bagchi and David C. Steinmetz, 113–29. Cambridge: Cambridge University Press, 2004.

Tanner, Kathryn. *The Politics of God: Christian Theologies and Social Justice.* Minneapolis: Fortress, 1992.

Torrance, James B. "The Incarnation and 'Limited Atonement.'" *Evangelical Quarterly* 55 (1983) 83–94.

Torrance, Thomas F. *Calvin's Doctrine of Man.* Westport: Greenwood, 1977.

———. *Reality and Evangelical Theology.* Philadelphia: Westminster, 1982.

———. *Scottish Theology: From John Knox to John McLeod Campbell.* Edinburgh: T. & T. Clark, 1996.

———. *Theology in Reconciliation: Essays Towards Evangelical and Catholic Unity in East and West.* London: Geoffrey Chapman, 1975.

———. *Theology in Reconstruction.* Edinburgh: T. & T. Clark, 1965.

———. *The Trinitarian Faith: The Evangelical Theology of the Ancient Catholic Church.* Edinburgh: T. & T. Clark, 1988.

Wallace, R. S. *Calvin's Doctrine of the Christian Life.* Grand Rapids: Eerdmans, 1959.

Ware, Bruce A. "The Role of Prayer and the Word in the Christian Life According to John Calvin." *Studia Biblica et Theologica* 12 (1982) 73–91.

Webster, John. "Life in and of Himself: Reflections on God's Aseity." In *Engaging the Doctrine of God: Contemporary Protestant Perspectives,* edited by Bruce L. McCormack, 107–24. Grand Rapids: Baker, 2008.

Wendel, François. *Calvin: The Origins and Development of His Religious Thought.* Translated by Philip Mairet. London: Collins, 1963.

Williams, Rowan. "God and Risk." In *The Divine Risk,* Edited by Richard Holloway, 11–23. London: Darton, Longman & Todd, 1990.

———. *On Christian Theology.* Oxford: Blackwell, 2000.

Wright, Terry J. "Reconsidering *Concursus.*" *International Journal of Theology* 4 (2002) 205–15.

Wood, Charles M. "How Does God Act?" *International Journal of Theology* 1 (1999) 138–52.

———. *The Question of Providence.* Louisville: Westminster John Knox, 2008.

Wyatt, Peter. *Jesus Christ and Creation in the Theology of John Calvin.* Allison Park: Pickwick, 1996.

Zachman, Randall. *John Calvin as Teacher, Pastor and Theologian: The Shape of His Writings and Thought.* Grand Rapids: Baker, 2006.

# 14

## Worshiping like a Calvinist

### *Cruciform Existence*

SCOTT KIRKLAND

"If God had looked into our minds he would not have been able to see there whom we were speaking of."[1]

## INTRODUCTION

WE MIGHT CONSIDER MARTIN Luther's wisdom: "living, dying and being condemned: it is this that makes a theologian." What concerned Luther was the *embodied* nature of the life of the theologian, but also, the life of the Christian. It is this embodiedness which is the foundation for thinking about forms of doxological living, and this is what we will consider in this essay.

George Steiner, in his famous essay "Absolute Tragedy,"[2] describes the situation of Jews in the eyes of the Nazi regime. The guilt of the Jews was not in any one particular sin or transgression, in any recognisable, external differentiation from the rest of humanity; rather, they had committed the "crime of being." That is, their existence itself was not to be tolerated. While I am cautious of making the situation of humanity before God analogous to that of

1. Wittgenstein, *Philosophical Investigations*, 217.
2. Steiner, "Absolute Tragedy," in *No Passion Spent: Essays 1978–1996*, 129–41.

404

early twentieth century Germanic-Jewish folk, there is something larger at play here whether Steiner deals with it or not. The justification of anyone's existence is dependent upon the relation which one has to the eternal. That is, existence itself is before God, but, in being before God it is existence in guilt-consciousness. This means that there is a direct relationship between theological existence and human existence as such. So, in formulating a conception of worship we are not merely dealing with a set of privatised religious practices, but with the justification of our existence before God, that is, as creatures in his image.

This leads us to consider the problematic of the problem of all human relations to God. The basic problem of God-talk is that God is not a thing amongst other things to be known. That is, God is not any-thing in particular. God is not to be known in the same way as things in creation are known. There is a fundamental creator-creature distinction which provides the basic problem of all theological language.[3] God is other to creation and so all human attempts at description fall well short. The problem of the otherness of God (in kind, not degree of difference) can be expressed more existentially. In a creation in need of redemption there must be some way in which God's activity becomes manifest to creation. However, the difference that God makes to creation cannot be a particular difference, for God is not a particular thing; rather, God must make a universal difference. God's action in creation, as Creator, creates a universal difference which reconfigures existence itself.[4] That is, the Logos becomes incarnate, thus providing the ground a grammar for all God-talk and all existence-talk. It is this we are concerned with in this essay, just what does it mean to be re-oriented back to God so as to *exist* "in Christ" in *worship*. So, with Ju[Set tremla over u]ngel we maintain:

> . . . in Evangelical speech God comes close to men, he carries out his divinity's own humanity, in order to make concrete the difference between his divinity's own humanity and the humanity of man. The difference between God and man, which is constitutive of the essence of the Christian faith, is thus not the difference of a still greater dissimilarity, but rather, conversely, the difference

---

3. This has been expressed in recent times by theologians the likes of Nicholas Lash, Denys Turner, Herbert McCabe, and Rowan Williams.

4. Ticciati, "The Castration of Signs," 161.

of a still greater dissimilarity between God and man in the midst
of a great similarity.[5]

God is, for Jüngel, always "greater than." Proximity is no ground
for speakability. The closer we draw to God the more and more we are
drawn into the mystery and so all speech is but a stutter-step and an
echoing of this incomprehensibility.

## IDEALISM AND REALISM IN THEOLOGICAL DISCOURSE

### Between Idealism and Realism

In more ways than one the legacy of Idealism remains present and active in modern theological discourse. The seeming disconnect between
thought and reality; idea and actuality; abstraction and presence is an
ever present danger in modern discourse, particularly when we come
to discuss the supposedly more "practical" matter of Christian worship.
This essay seeks to re-cast worship around the concept of "theological-
existence." The rationale for this manoeuvre in terminology will become
clear as the essay progresses, however, we might consider it to be an
effort to relocate worship in the domain of the "real" and concrete historical realities in which we have our existence.

Kierkegaard's railing against Hegelianism in Christian theology is
fundamentally a railing against idolatry. Kierkegaard sees the abstraction of Hegelianism(s) as a projection of the human onto the divine.
His whole Socratic endeavour, therefore, could be seen as an attempt
to direct attention to "this" God, the true God who became human, not
the "no-god" of world-historical processes. In this sense Kierkegaard's
entire philosophical/theological edifice is an exercise in doxology, that
is, an ordering of right worship of God. How might this inform the way
we then think of the role of the theologian in explicating patterns for
the worship of God? We might understand our task as one of looking
for idols. The quest of the theologian is then doxological insofar as she
attempts to rid her thinking of all false presumptions and pretences. To
what end? To the end of proper worship of God. So, worship and theology must, and do, go together.

Modern Reformed Christianity is torn between the legacy of pietism on the one hand and of fundamentalism on the other both finding their roots in post-reformation theology. The subjectivist, feeling

5. Jüngel, *God as the Mystery of the World*, 288.

oriented doxologies of modern Protestantism, finding their roots in Schleiermacher's pietism are contrasted with the rigid, programmatic, prescriptive worship of the Reformed tradition finding its roots in Protestant Scholasticism.[6] The danger for the pietist is always the projection of the experience of the divine onto the divine itself, so that the idol is the experience. Conversely, the danger for the Reformed tradition is an overly prescriptive pattern of worship which restricts the *humanness* of worship as existence and so is idolatrous insofar as God is locked within prescribed patterns of offering worship. The task of this essay is to navigate these two extremes to find something of a third way for understanding the relation of the human to the divine in the act of worship—between prescription and feeling—that is, a doxology of *theological-existence.*

### *The Problem of the Enlightenment and Post-Enlightenment Idealism for Doxology More Specifically*

The enlightenment radically altered the way in which humanness was thought of at its very core. The Cartesian revolution—"*Cogito, ergo sum*"—fundamentally altered the way in which we related intellect to action, that is, the ideal to the real. Suddenly the human being was not a whole existing subject but, rather the human being existed insofar as she thought her existence. That is, existence was predicated of idea, not sensory reality. Sensory experience could no longer be trusted, but, *de omnibus dubidantum est,* only in thinking and doubting I exist. Torrance's famous "*The Mediation of Christ*" opens with a broad historical discussion of the epistemic and ontic disconnect between "the sensible appearances of things" and the "intelligible base in which they were grounded." The dualism of thought and existence drove a deep wedge in the Christian (and Western, more broadly) imagination between God's self-revelation and God's act. Thus, Kant's consideration of religion relegates its significance to the realm of the ethical (practical reason) alone.

As Charles Taylor has noted Hegel's system is not only a development in Kantian Idealism and post-Kantianism but also forms a significant development and critique in itself. Hegel's famous dictum "the outer is the inner and the inner the outer" plays an important part in this

---

6. I remind the reader at this point that this is a broad caricature the reality of which is much more complex, however, the basic descriptions serve to make a point more than necessarily a socio-historical comment.

discussion. Hegel conceived of the universe as being in a process of development through dialectic. That is, negation is the foundation for development and in fact is identified as development as the absolute spirit
realises itself in historical process. The ideal was then conceived not only
subjectively (as in Kant) but also objectively, or absolutely, in Hegel's
conception of absolute spirit (*Geist*). Thus, subjective phenomena and
objective truths are unable to be discriminated between. However, because thinking, by virtue of what it is, immediately cannot comprehend,
or get behind, existence there is a problem in perception itself.

In Luther's terms the mind had turned in on itself (*ratio in se ip-
sam incurva*). In order to understand itself the mind had only itself to
turn to. So, Bonheoffer states that ". . . thinking remains perpetually
self-enclosed. Wherever thinking posits freedom from transcendence,
from reality, precisely there it remains imprisoned within itself."[7] With
no external, transcendent reference point with which to find conflict
or ground existence, the mind is simply in a process of self-realisation
under the auspices of reason abstractly construed. Coming back to
Torrance then, modern theological discourse must be increasingly
careful to retain the connection between the "sensible appearances of
things" and the "intelligible base in which they are grounded." That is,
we must be careful not to fall into dualistic patterns of thought which
tear thinking away from existence into abstraction and vice versa. With
Kierkegaard, the question to be asked is: what does it mean to say "the
way is the truth, that is, that the truth is only in the becoming, in the
process of appropriation." Truth is, for Kierkegaard, subjectivity, that is,
truth exists as it is embodied and therefore, does not exist *in abstracto*
to be grasped, but rather, it is lived in existence (which encompasses the
life of the mind, of course).

The abstraction of the enlightenment and the panentheism of
Hegelian Idealism cannot deal with the intricacies of existence for it
deals not with existence in its rawness but with abstraction. In order
to think worship we must think concretely and existentially (in the
Kierkegaardian sense). We are dealing in existence categories, not ideals.
This shall be the central theme of this paper, and shall form the basis for
our engagement with doxological questions.

---

7. Bonhoeffer, *Act and Being*, 112.

# THEOLOGICAL-EXISTENCE AS EXISTENCE "IN CHRIST"

## *The Ease and the Difficulty of Existence*

In keeping with the above I want to now consider the way that we are now able to begin to think about the relationship between the work of reconciliation and the act of worship. Karl Barth will prove instructive at this point. His conception of the atonement as freedom from self-judgement gives us frames through which we can begin to think about existence itself as being renewed and restored in the humanity of Jesus so as to be participated in, in the act of worship.

Living in grace is at one and the same time the ease and difficulty of existence. "It is easier than one thinks to hate oneself. Grace means forgetting oneself. But if all pride were dead in us, the grace of graces would be to love oneself humbly, as one would any of the suffering members of Jesus Christ."[8] That is, Jesus Christ in his person has freed us from the burden of ourselves and standing under our own judgement. The difficulty is to stop judging ourselves and to "exist" in him and therefore in grace.

Jesus's history is "the most basic history of every man."[9] In that way ". . . God is gracious to man, all the limitations of man are God's limitations, all his weaknesses, and more, all his perversities are His."[10] Jesus then, as the one burdened with the difficulty of our existence stands as one who ". . . is obedient . . . He is a suffering servant who wills this profoundly unsatisfactory being, who cannot will anything other in the obedience in which He shows Himself the Son of God."[11] That is, Jesus Christ's very existence is *on our behalf*. The life, death and resurrection of Jesus Christ have fundamentally and finally altered the way in which we are to think of what it means to be human. To be human now is to exist as one who lives out of his existence and the pattern there displayed.

> *He* is broken and destroyed on God. It cannot be otherwise. It has to be like this. His history must be a history of suffering. For God is in the right against Him. He concedes that the Father is right in the will and action which leads Him to the cross . . . his rejection and condemnation, giving Himself to bear the divinely righteous

---

8. Ricour, *Oneself As Another*, 33 n. 31.

9. Barth, *CD*, IV/1, 157.

10. Ibid., 158.

11. Ibid., 164.

consequences of human sin, not merely affirming the divine sentence on man, but allowing it to be fulfilled on Himself.[12]

This is an undoing of sin in that "All sin has its being and origin in
the fact that man wants to be his own judge . . . The obedience which
He [Jesus] rendered in humility as our Brother, is the divine accusation
against every man and the divine condemnation of every man."[13] God
must act to destroy the sinful man. This is his "no" to man. But in this
"no" is the inherent "yes" to man. God says "yes" to man in that he frees
man from the power of sin over him in the cross and there raises him
to new life. The "no" is not a "no" to human existence *per se* but rather
a "no" to the old way of being human, and so it is an act of grace. The
"no" is in the "yes" and the "yes" is in the "no." So, "Without relaxing or
mitigating the sentence, let alone as a judge who is unjust by reason of
his laxity, He can exercise grace even with His judgement and in execution of it."[14] The physics of being human are then reconstituted by the
cross and resurrection. Jesus is not destroyed to appease the anger of a
God who requires satisfaction; rather, Jesus is a God-human who frees
us from *our own* corrupted and enslaving humanity by destroying it in
the obedience to his Father, an obedience which leads to his death. He
stands not under his own judgement, he will not determine what is right
for himself, but, he will be obedient and have faith in the Father's goodness even to death.

So then Barth can ask, *Cur Deus Homo?* "In order to judge the
world. But in the light of what God has actually done we must add at
once: In order to judge it in the exercise of His kingly freedom to show
His grace in the execution of His judgement, to pronounce us free in
passing sentence, to free us by imprisoning us, to ground our life on
our death, to redeem and save us by our destruction."[15] God's showing grace in the execution of judgement and making us free in passing
judgement are the paradoxes of Barth" doctrine of the atonement. It is
in the particularity of the life, death and resurrection of Jesus that the
universal is found. He "made an end to us as sinners and therefore of
sin itself by going to death as the One who took our place as sinners. In

---

12. Ibid., 175.

13. Ibid., 220.

14. Ibid., 221.

15. Ibid., 222.

His person He has delivered up us sinners and sin itself to destruction."[16] Jesus endures punishment in that he delivers to God the old humanity, the first Adam, for destruction. This is in itself an act of grace. As Barth states, in this instance ". . . His love works itself out as death dealing wrath."[17] It is death dealing wrath in so far as God, in his graciousness towards us, destroys the sin which is in us so that we may live again. "The passion of Jesus Christ is the judgement of God in which the Judge Himself was the Judged."[18] It is paramount for Barth that we understand this passion as, through and through, the divine action. For, it is only as this is a radical divine action that we can then begin to conceive of the way it ". . . attacks and destroys at its very root the primary evil in the world . . ."[19] so as to perform an act of new creation. In Dostoyevsky's "*Crime and Punishment*" it is no coincidence that it should be Sonya, the prostitute from the household destroyed by addiction who raises Raskolinkov (a kind of proto-Nietzchean superman) from the dead of isolation, self-defilement and estrangement in to which he has fallen. She restores his humanity. This must take place as he suffers under the sign of the cross. "Go, immediately, this very moment, go and stand at the crossroads, bow down, kiss the ground that you have desecrated, and then bow to the whole world, to all four points of the compass and tell everyone, out loud: "I have killed!" then God will send you life again . . . You must accept suffering and redeem yourself by it, that's what."[20] Dostoyevsky, like Barth, perceives something particularly theologically rich here. Raskolinkov must front-up to who he *really* is so that he might die to it. There is no path through the paradox of death and resurrection for Dostoyevsky. New creation always arises out of the destruction of the evil in the old. Death cannot be bypassed.

If we remember what was said in my introduction: God's act is not a particular act in creation (in terms of its significance and efficaciousness) because God is not a "thing" in creation, God's act, as Creator is always universal in significance. The incarnation and all that is bound up with that is universal in its significance in that is refigures, recreates existence itself by grounding it in Christ's life. The resurrection of Jesus from

16. Ibid., 253.

17. Ibid.

18. Ibid., 254.

19. Ibid.

20. Dostoyevsky, *Crime and Punishment*, 416.

the dead is the act of new-creation in which we now are given to exist. We are not, however, permitted to avoid the death. We *cannot* rise if we have not first died and it is this that is both the ease and the difficulty of existence "in Christ." To die to self so as to rise to God is the most freeing and beautiful expression of humanness, but it is, because of the way in which we continue to give ourselves to sin, the most difficult and arduous way of being human. The paradox is that worship, as existence, is an expression of freedom; but, it is difficult to be free. Incarnation itself is act. "In the beginning was the Logos... and the Logos *became flesh* and dwelled among us." (John 1:1, 14). God himself has *become* among us. God has acted in the person of Christ and in his life we are given to see the divine act of new-creation. This divine act, however, takes the shape and form of a human life. The humanity and divinity of Christ (united) then form the ground of all doxological discourse. That is, Jesus *acts* and *exists* as the true human, and he *acts* and *exists* as God. We have, in him, the act of God and the act of humanity. In his concrete particularity and in his existence we have seen what it is to be human (the universal)—to exist in self-surrendering worship.

Kierkegaard speaks of the difficulty of existing as elect in this way:

> This separation [of election] gives the Christian a certain likeness to a person who has been given preferential treatment, and if a Christian selfishly perceives it as this, we have the desperate arrogation of predestination. The happy person cannot essentially sympathise with others who do not have or are unable to have preferential treatment . . . Having this eternal happiness based on something historical means that the Christian's good fortune is distinguished by suffering . . . this is so difficult to understand that for anyone else but the elect it must be something to despair over.[21]

Living an existence redefined and reconstituted by the death and resurrection means that the elect for Kierkegaard are those who are constantly giving themselves over to death.[22] Paradoxically this is the only way to life. Election or, living "in Christ" is then an arduous existence consisting in consistently dying to self-reliance and rising to obedience.

21. Kierkegaard, *Concluding Unscientific Postscript*, 582.

22. It should be duly noted that there are distinct differences in the Christian practice of death from that of platonic and later stoic thought. Kierkegaard himself acknowledges these differences in his own work on Socrates. The resurrection makes all the difference here.

## Existence and Obedience

How are we then to think about the relationship of divine command to human freedom? In other words: what do I mean by freedom? Christ's freedom is constituted for Barth in his obedience to the divine command. Barth, using the image of the suffering *servant*, thinks of obedience in essential terms:

> . . . the New Testament describes the Son of God as the servant, indeed as the suffering servant of God. Not accidentally and incidentally. Not merely to prove and show His mind and disposition. Not merely to win through by conflict to a concrete goal. Not merely as a foil to emphasise His glory. But necessarily and, as it were, essentially, and so far as can be seen without meaning or purpose. He is a suffering servant who wills this profoundly unsatisfactory being, who cannot will anything other in the obedience in which He shows Himself the Son of God.[23]

Paradoxically it is in his obedience unto suffering and death that Jesus is revealed as the *free* Son of God. God is free *for* us in this "profoundly unsatisfactory being" because he is the God who is free in his love and loves in freedom. As the incarnate Son of God Jesus is the Revealer of both God and humanity. He provides the pattern in which human beings are to live. He embodies the divine command. It is this that Kierkegaard is hinting at above. If election is election to a favourable position in life, we are speaking about a different God, for, in terms reminiscent of Luther's *theologia crucis,* election is to a profoundly cruciform existence. Any connection made between divine command and human freedom must then be made on the grounds of the incarnate Christ's self-giving.

It is no surprise then that Paul, in Phil 2:5–11 describes Jesus in terms of obedience in suffering. ". . . though he was *in very form God* (ὃς ἐν μορφῇ θεοῦ ὑπάρχων), became nothing, taking on the form of a slave (μορφὴν δούλου λαβών) . . . therefore, God gave him the name above all names (ὄνομα τὸ ὑπὲρ πᾶν ὄνομα) . . ." This is all deeply connected to the life of the Christian in that "your attitude should be like that of Jesus Christ who . . ." Paul, the apostle of the free grace of God, writes to this community that they must give themselves up, *become nothing,* so that God will raise them up. This requires a radical and faith-

---

23. Barth, *CD,* IV/1, 16.

ful existence which lets God *be God* over it. That is, to obey the divine command so as to be given new life.

There is then an ethics of doxology developing here. To obey the divine command is to worship, to exist. To exist is to live in the divine command and so to act in obedience in the world and so it is to do with ethics. Theological ethics are grounded in the command of God and the response of humanity first in Christ, and then by participation in the resurrection of Christ, in us. Worship is ethical existence, and so as we proceed to think about the particular institutional acts of Christian worship practice we must retain this ethical dimension, for to forget this would be to forget the very reality of the incarnation. So, Kierkegaard relates the coming of God to the becoming of humanity in this way:

> This is the consequence of the appearance of the god [*Guden*] in time, which prevents the individual from relating himself back to the eternal, since he now moves forward in order to become eternal in time through relation to the god in time.[24]

## DOXOLOGICAL-EXISTENCE

### *Vicarious Humanity*

All of what is to be said below is grounded in a vision of the vicarious humanity of Christ. The opening section considered the modern dilemma of Idealism and Realism. It is, I propose, the vicarious humanity of Christ which provides the Christian with a way through thinking this dilemma christologically, but also in a philosophically serious way by allowing existence itself to become the middle, unconsidered factor. Again, as has been noted, there is no way of thinking behind existence so as to gain that God's-eye-perspective. It is in the particularity of Jesus Christ that we are given to see the reconstitution of existence so to think is to think "in him" and "after" him. This is not to simply the chorus of existential voices of the late nineteenth to early-mid twentieth century, but to ask the question of the ground of existence in a distinctly christological manner, echoing broadly Kierkegaardian concerns.

On the back of Barth's concern with the freedom of the Christian as grounded in the freedom of the love of God we are then able to conceive of Jesus' very humanity as representative. This does not, as has often been the case in modern treatments of Christology, partition the person

24. Kierkegaard, *Concluding Unscientific Postscript,* 583–84.

of Christ off from his work. There is then an actualism which permeates this treatment. Christ's person is expressed in his work and his work is an expression of his person. God acts in history so as to unveil himself. Revelation and reconciliation, are as T. F. Torrance saw so profoundly, inseparable. This allows us to consider Jesus' representation of us as grounded in his humanity. That is, because I am refusing to partition the person and work of Christ off from one-another, his work is his reconstitution of humanness and therefore the incarnation forms the ground of our humanness and so all our activity as human beings is a participation in the already and complete humanity of Jesus. So, in considering particular acts of worship as we are about to do, we must remember that Christ remains the sole mediator between God and humanity in his very humanness which is like us and at the same time radically other to us.

### Eucharist

Eucharistic controversy has often rested on the mechanisms for construing God's presence in the Eucharist (substance, incarnation, symbol etc.). However, this easily overlooks some of the more important aspects of Eucharistic theology which I hope to explore here, whilst avoiding the complex terrain of particular traditional stances on substance and presence. As John McDowell notes:

> . . . without necessarily denying that the question of presence is important, something that is often missed in debates over the eucharist is the role of Jesus as perpetual divine Giver and primordial celebrant, the eventfulness of God (the dynamic of giving) and the hope-*full* responsibility of human being (the human giftedness and giving back in thankful response).[25]

So, this treatment will focus not so much on the actual mechanisms for thinking presence in the elements as this would perhaps become unnecessarily divisive, but rather, we will explore just how, as John Webster reminds us, we cannot speak as though "at his ascension Jesus Christ as it were resigns his office in favour of human ministers, and that henceforth the church is the real centre of ministerial agency."[26] In other words, we must come to think of the Eucharist christologically. "Who is it that is giving us this gift?" "What does that mean?" Zizoulas notes,

---

25. McDowell, "Theology and the Globalised Present."
26. Webster, "The Self-Organising Power of the Gospel," 199.

citing T. F. Torrance, that "Ministry in the church 'points beyond itself' to the action of another."[27] Conceiving of Jesus as perpetual divine Giver and primordial celebrant allows us to speak of the Eucharist in terms of thanksgiving. That is, *eucharista* is a function of the church's response to divine grace but also a participation in that primordial and perpetual act of Christ. As God gives, and continues to give, we give thanks in humility for the gift given. The essential thankfulness of eucharistic celebration then allows us to think of the Eucharist itself as invitation to participate in divine gift. That is, to have our existence refigured by the resurrected Christ in the act of participating in his death in the bread and wine broken and poured out. Thus, acknowledging that all things are from God and grounded in God's self-giving love. There is an encounter with God, in the words of David Ford, in the "ordinary":

> Whatever the interpretation, the realm of the ordinary has been taken up and involved in the most momentous of events without rejection, contrast or competition between the two. There is no middle ground needed, no mediating of the ordinary to the extraordinary. The God who is implied by the blessing of these elements is at home with matter and its routine usage as well as with the climactic drama of Jesus's life.[28]

We can speak of eucharistic living/existence as that which is borne out of and is sustained by the divine gift—existence in the divine life and continuing ministry of Christ. Worship is active participation in the divine life given and sustained in eucharistic *performance*. We continually are given to die to ourselves and so live in thanksgiving for the divine gift of grace. This is the concrete "ordinary-ness" of the Eucharist. Thus, Ford continues "The main thrust is towards blessing the ordinary, and if ritual (or anything else, such as the categories of narrative, drama or "sacramentality') threatens to function as a middle ground . . . then this critical resource can be activated." This "ordinary-ness" of the elements contributes to the "density and universality" of the occasion.[29]

Because of the universality of this gift, we cannot abstract this from its context within the worshiping community. The worshipping community forms the context in which this new kind of existence, this new way of being is prefigured. So, Webster can state that "What the apos-

27. Zizoulas, *Being as Communion*, 201. Quoting Torrance, *Royal Priesthood*, 97.

28. Ford, *Self and Salvation*, 150.

29. Ibid.

tolic ministry of reconciliation indicated is the existence (not simply the potentiality) of the "*one new man*."[30] This is why, in his first letter to the Corinthians, Paul is so enraged by the social disjunction and exclusionary practices of the community. "Fasting from this type of feasting, from this impoverishment of eucharistic performance, is what Paul calls for."[31] These exclusionary practices undermine the universal and all-inclusive nature of the community.

> That which makes the people *ekklesia*, in Henri de Lubac's famous phrase "the eucharist makes the church", then, encourages a constant suspicion of premature claims to divine presence, representation, and possession, and offers an ek-static reference to the uncontrollable presence of the excessive fullness of transcendent life—the people live in the dispossession of properly ordered dependence.[32]

The Eucharist is universally significant and inclusive and so these practices have no place at the table. In this way the Eucharist provides a radical form of resistance to exclusionary cultural practices by inaugurating the new humanity and providing a taste of what is to come. This is grounded, as McDowell's quote illustrates, in the "uncontrollable presence of the excessive fullness of transcendent life," again reminding us of the radical otherness of Christ even in his intense presence in the community.

So as to not overstate the case one must be reticent at this point and so several qualifications are to be made. As Rahner reminds us the church "is a Church of sinners" and as such we are not to lapse back into some imagined or ideal Christian community so as to be disillusioned by the reality of omnipresence of exclusionary practice(s) and the seeming absence of God.[33] There is an unrealised element to all of this. Christ, in his person, has refigured our existence and recreated us vicariously. However, as Nicholas Lash has noted we remain in Holy Saturday groaning for Sunday, but with the scars of Friday very much aching. "Saturday is all those days through which we live or suffer, strive to make something of ourselves or just hang on, endure, from Friday towards Sunday. Saturday, in other words, is every day in every place, all times and sea-

30. Webster, "Christ, Church and Reconciliation," 223. Emphasis added.
31. McDowell, "Theology and the Globalised Present."
32. Ibid.
33. Rahner, *Theological Investigations*, 6:255.

sons of our human hope and patience."[34] Eucharistic performance takes place in this time of tension, waiting and irresolution. We are beings between death and life.

### Baptism

There have been many a theological treatment of the theology of the Eucharist in recent times with the resurgence of social ecclesiologies and the centrality of eating to these ecclesial constructs. It can at times seem that baptism falls by the wayside in these discussions. This chapter, however, will examine the way in which baptism, as a sign of participation in the death and resurrection of Jesus, forms an important part of any ecclesiology and therefore doxology. As stated, the imagery of baptism is that of death and resurrection. The image here runs deep when we consider the vicarious humanity of Christ. Baptism itself is a participation (albeit non-identically) in the baptism of Jesus Christ which is the symbol of his renewal of human existence. The passing through the waters is both a washing and a death, a cleansing and renewal. Thus, it initiates one into the kind of Eucharistic existence outlined above.

> Baptism is the archetypal Christian sign of personal identity, non-identically repeating Jesus's baptism, his death and resurrection, and the baptism of every other Christian. This is the initiating sacrament and the baptism of blessing: being named and blessed in the name of the Father, Son and Holy Spirit. It signifies the reality and availability of the abundance; it invites and initiates into a eucharistic practice in order to sustain a life of flourishing within the infinite love and joy of God.[35]

Baptism identifies the Christian with the death and resurrection of Christ in the same way as the eucharist does. So that "Baptism is, in this regard, the non-identical repetition of the substitutionary self of Jesus Christ, while the eucharist is its continuation. . . ."[36]

However, there is a sense in which baptism, as a non-repeated event is an initiator into the community as well.[37] In considering obvious

---

34. Lash, "Friday, Saturday, Sunday," 114.

35. Ford, *Self and Salvation*, 162–63.

36. Ibid., 164.

37. Remembering Henri de Lubac's often cited and controversial statement "it is the eucharist which makes the church." The force of which we may wish to pull back on a bit, however, the notion of baptism as the initiator and the Eucharist as the continuation of this process is important and can be highlighted using de Lubac.

Exodus overtones in the symbol we might consider baptism as an act which symbolises election. God's giving of freedom to his people is symbolised by their passing through the waters of judgement which swallow up their oppressors. In the same way, in the New Testament, baptism is a passing through the waters which destroy the oppression of sin (remembering Barth's discussion of judgement above) and into new life, the life of the people of God in Christ.[38] We might consider the structure of the opening of Matthew's Gospel here. Matthew has an unmistakably exodus-shaped account of the baptism of Jesus. Jesus initially is in Egypt (Matt 2), he is then called out of Egypt (ch. 2), baptised by John (ch. 3), tempted in the wilderness (ch. 4) and then ascends a "mountain" to give a new law (chs. 5–7). These events parallel those of the exodus narratives so as to illustrate the nature of Jesus' coming into the world—that of a reconstitution of the people of God. Therefore, as we partake of this same baptism, we acknowledge what has been accomplished already in the humanity of Christ in his election for all.

Both as a "sign of personal identity" and a sign of being a part of the people of God, baptism is an act of worship which is a participation in the worship of Christ which fundamentally alters the orientation and substance of our existence as that which is now located in Christ and has been accomplished once-and-for-all in him.

## CONCLUSION

What I have tried to do in this chapter is broaden the discussion of worship in such a way as to retain the traditional theological foci of doxology while examining the broader concern of doxology as that which frames our ethics and existence. Divine command, and therefore, love as expressed in the person of Christ, is that which reconstitutes what it means to be human. This broader conversation allows doxology a public space. Doxological concerns are not simply to do with a set of privatised religious practices but rather, have public import insofar as we understand them as shaping our very existence in all spheres. In many ways this explains the political interest which reformed theology has always maintained. Public life and private life cannot be partitioned off from one another.

---

38. This chapter does not have time to trace this relationship properly; however, there is a rich biblical tradition to be considered here in relation to the passing through waters and the freedom of the people of God.

Existence itself has been refigured by the humanity of God in such a way that we are now given to be free for one another in worship. As we love, that is, as we obey the divine command, we exist in worship. This is what shapes human being in such a way that it comes to reflect something of the divine, that is we become *imago dei* as we life a doxological existence. This is a very broad discussion of worship in one way. It is inclusive of the logic of participation as expressed in the Eastern traditions and the more Anglo-Catholic concern with sacraments as constitutive of the being of the church and the Kierkegaardian-Lutheran concern with the cross as that which shapes existence. Yet, in another way, through thinking the vicarious humanity of Christ, it is a particularly Reformed treatment of these themes, attempting to be in the spirit of the Scottish Calvinists. This is not a Reformed doxology as such, nor is it pretending to be so. Evangelical Calvinism gives the theologian to draw on a breadth of traditions and statements of faith while remaining anchored in a particular theo-logic. It is this which allows the doxological tradition the depth it has.

## BIBLIOGRAPHY

Barth, Karl. *Church Dogmatics.* 4 vols. Edited by G. W. Bromiley and T. F. Torrance. Translated by G.W. Bromiley, et al. Edinburgh: T. & T. Clark, 1956–1975.

Bonhoffer, Dietrich. *Act and Being.* In *Dietrich Bonhoeffer Works.* Vol 2. Edited by Wayne Whitson Floyd Jr. Mineapolis: Augsburg Fortress, 1996.

Dostoyevsky, Fyodor M. *Crime and Punishment.* Translated by David McDuff. London: Penguin, 2003.

Ford, David *Self and Salvation: Being Transformed.* Cambridge: Cambridge University Press, 1999.

Jüngel, Eberhard. *God as the Mystery of the World.* Grand Rapids: Eerdmanns, 1983.

Kierkegaard, Søren. *Concluding Unscientific Postscript to Philosophical Fragments.* Translated by Howard V. Hong and Edna H. Hong. Princeton: Princeton University Press, 1992.

Lash, Nicholas. "Friday, Saturday, Sunday." *New Blackfriars* 71 (1990) 109–19.

McDowell, John C. "Theology and the Globalised Present: Feastings in God at Midnight." No pages. Paper presented to the MCD Centenary Conference & ANZATS, 7 July 2010.

Rahner, Karl. *Theological Investigations.* 23 vols. London: Darton, Longman and Todd, 1961–1992.

Ricour, Paul *Oneself As Another.* London: University of Chicago Press, 1992.

Steiner, George *No Passion Spent: Essays 1978–1996.* London: Faber and Faber, 1996.

Ticciati, Susannah. "The Castration of Signs: Conversing with Augustine on Creation, Language and Truth." *Modern Theology* 23 (2007) 161–79.

Torrance, T. F. *Royal Priesthood: A Theology of Ordained Ministry.* Revised edition. Edinburgh: T. & T. Clark, 1993.

Webster, John. "Christ, Church and Reconciliation." In *Word and Church,* 211–32. Edinburgh: T. & T. Clark, 2001.

———. "The Self-Organising Power of the Gospel." In *Word and Church,* 191–210. Edinburgh: T. & T. Clark, 2001.

Wittgenstein, Ludwig. *Philosophical Investigations.* Translated by G. E. N. Anscombe. Oxford: Blackwell, 1958.

Zizoulas, John. *Being as Communion.* New York: St. Vladimir's Seminary Press, 1985.

PART FOUR

# Prospect

# 15

## Theses on a Theme

MYK HABETS AND BOBBY GROW[1]

IN CONCEIVING THIS VOLUME the editors had in mind a series of theological and methodological commitments which they thought could form something of an outline of what an Evangelical Calvinism could become if it were to develop into a clearly definable position within the Reformed tradition. What follows are fifteen theses in which the editors of this volume have attempted to broadly define some of the key moments and aspects Evangelical Calvinists might be committed to. On saying that, however, the editors recognize that within this volume the very contributors themselves do not share all of the commitments specified in what follows.

### THESIS ONE

*The Holy Trinity is the absolute ground and grammar of all epistemology, theology, and worship.*

Athanasius was fond of saying that it is better to "signify God from the Son and call him Father, than to name God from his works alone and call him Unoriginate."[2] And he was right. The triune God is known ex-

---

1. The editors wish to thank a number of people for their critical interaction with the theses, especially John McDowell, Julie Canlis, Jason Goroncy, Ivor Davidson, Kevin Vanhoozer, and Thomas Weinandy.

2. Athanasius, *Contra Arianos*, 1.34, cited in Torrance, *The Trinitarian Faith*, 49, and often elsewhere.

clusively through the Son of the Father by the Spirit. In Jesus Christ is revealed very God of very God. God is in his own being what he is as God's revealing Word and saving Act toward us. Through Christ and the Spirit we are given access to God as he is in himself. This access to God is, in part, in the form of knowledge of God as he is in himself, in his internal relations as Father, Son, and Holy Spirit. The epistemological strength of the *homoousios* works here with full force for it represents the consubstantial relation between Jesus Christ, the Word made flesh, and God himself. As *the* image of God, identical with his reality, knowledge of the Incarnate Son through the Holy Spirit has a unique and controlling finality in knowledge of God.

> To know this God, who both condescends to share all that we are and makes us share in all that he is in Jesus Christ, is to be lifted up in his Spirit to share in God's own self-knowing and self-loving until we are enabled to apprehend him in some real measure in himself beyond anything that we are capable of in ourselves. It is to be lifted out of ourselves, as it were, into God, until we know him and love him and enjoy him in his eternal Reality as Father, Son, and Holy Spirit, in such a way that the Trinity enters into the fundamental fabric of our thinking of him and constitutes the basic grammar of our worship and knowledge of the One God.[3]

In order to further explicate such a Trinitarian theology the recent proposal of Thomas Weinandy proves useful. Without denying a biblical sense of the Father's *monarchy*, Weinandy argues that a proper understanding of the Trinity can only be attained if all three Persons, logically and ontologically, spring forth in one *simultaneous*, nonsequential, eternal act in which each person of the Trinity subsistently defines, and equally is subsistently defined, by the other persons.[4] This drives Weinandy to present a thesis that, "may seem subtle, yet [is] one that I believe radically transforms and revolutionizes the Christian understanding of the Trinity."[5] His thesis is simply that:

---

3. Torrance, *The Ground and Grammar of Theology*, 155.

4. Weinandy, *The Father's Spirit of Sonship*, 15. Note the affinities with Calvin's formulation of the doctrine of the Trinity. See Warfield, "Calvin's Doctrine of the Trinity," 187–284; Torrance, "Calvin's Doctrine of the Trinity," 41–76; and Letham, *The Holy Trinity*, 252–68.

5. Weinandy, *The Father's Spirit of Sonship*, 17.

The Father begets the Son in or by the Holy Spirit. The Son is begotten by the Father in the Spirit and thus the Spirit simultaneously proceeds from the Father as the one in whom the Son is begotten. The Son, being begotten in the Spirit, simultaneously loves the Father in the same Spirit by which he himself is begotten (is Loved).[6]

This trinitarian construct highlights the Father's *monarchy* without any subordinationist tendencies. To do this a mutual coinherence or *perichoresis* of action within the Trinity must take place whereby the Persons are who they are because of the action of *all three*. While the Son and the Holy Spirit come forth from the Father this is not some prior ontological action but rather in the coming forth all three persons are who they are, and they are so precisely in reciprocally interacting upon one another, *simultaneously* fashioning one another as themselves.[7]

It is this God whom we seek to speak of. "In and through the presence of the Holy Spirit supervening upon the revealing and saving events of his incarnate Son, God really does impart himself to us and actually makes himself known to us *within the conditions of our creaturely forms of thought and speech*, but without any compromise of his sheer Godness or any diminution of the Mystery of his transcendent Being."[8]

The purpose of life is a transforming relationship with God in which the Spirit calls and enables us to become children of God in and alongside the Son and to join in his self-surrender to the Father. As Clark Pinnock writes, "God has not left us outside the circle of his life. We are invited inside the Trinity as joint heirs together with Christ. By the Spirit we cry 'Abba' together with the Son, as we are drawn into the divine filial relationship and begin to participate in God's life."[9] McLeod Campbell beautifully describes adoption as "orphans who have found their lost father."[10] The logic is that believers participate in Christ, the eternal Son of the Father, and so participate in that filial relationship in the Son (John 8:19). It is the intimate relationship between the Father

---

6. Ibid.

7. See further in Habets, *"Filioque? Nein. A Proposal for Coherent Coinherence,"* 161–202.

8. Torrance, *The Christian Doctrine of God,"* 151.

9. Pinnock, *Flame of Love,* 153. Pinnock's entire chapter on "Spirit and Union" (149–83) shows an obvious but unreferenced reliance upon T. F. Torrance's theology.

10. Cited in Kettler, "The Vicarious Repentance of Christ," 540.

and the Son which is communicated to humanity through the Spirit of the Son (Rom 8:29). It is in this sense that we may define salvation as "sonship."

Worship then must be defined as *epiclesis* and *paraclesis*, the invocation of the *Paraclete* Spirit and his coming to help us. In our worship the Holy Spirit comes from God, uniting us to the response, obedience, faith/fullness, and worship of Jesus Christ (also our *Paraclete*), and returns to God, raising us up in Jesus to participate in the worship of heaven and in the eternal communion of the Holy Trinity.[11] As James Torrance explains:

> When we see that the worship and mission of the church are the gift of participating through the Holy Spirit in the incarnate Son's communion with the Father and the Son's mission from the Father to the world, that the unique center of the Bible is Jesus Christ, "the apostle and high priest whom we confess" (Heb 3:1), then the doctrines of the Trinity, the incarnation, the atonement, the ministry of the Spirit, Church and sacraments, our understanding of the kingdom, our anthropology and eschatology, all unfold from that center.[12]

Such is the trinitarian vision we have for theology generally, and for the contents of this little book specifically.

To echo the sentiments of many before us, in thinking and speaking of the Trinity we cannot but clap our hands upon our mouth and fall down before the Lord God in worship. The Holy Trinity is infinitely more to be adored than expressed, so that appropriate and faithful thought and speech about it cannot but break off in sheer wonder, reverence, thanksgiving, and praise.[13]

## THESIS TWO

*The primacy of God's triune life is grounded in love, for "God is love."*

Hugh Binning (1627–1653), a young Scottish theologian, spoke of the primacy of God's life as the ground of salvation. Speaking of the primacy of God's love as the foundation of salvation he wrote:

11. Torrance, *Theology in Reconstruction*, 250.

12. J. B. Torrance, *Worship, Community and the Triune God of Grace*, 9.

13. Charles Partee and Gannon Murphy develop a number of these themes in their respective essays earlier in this volume.

Our salvation is not the business of Christ alone but the whole
Godhead is interested in it deeply, so deeply, that you cannot say,
who loves it most, or likes it most. The Father is the very fountain
of it, his love is the spring of all—"God so loved the world that he
hath sent his Son." Christ hath not purchased that eternal love to
us, but it is rather the gift of eternal love . . . Whoever thou be that
wouldst flee to God for mercy, do it in confidence. The Father, the
Son, and the Holy Ghost, are ready to welcome thee, all of one
mind to shut out none, to cast out none. But to speak properly, it
is but one love, one will, one council, and purpose in the Father,
the Son, and the Spirit, for these Three are One, and not only
agree in One, they are One, and what one loves and purposes, all
love and purpose.[14]

Echoing a similar sentiment John Duns Scotus once remarked: "The
creation of things proceeds from God not out of any necessity whether
of being or knowledge or of will but out of pure freedom which is not
moved, much less necessitated, by anything outside of itself so as to be
brought into operation."[15]

The fact that God's life of love is supreme over all life, presents
Evangelical Calvinism with the resources to claim that our God is truly
the One who provides "Good News" for all.[16]

In soteriology, for instance, Evangelical Calvinism believes the primacy of Christ is the touchstone from whence all else is centered (see
thesis 8). It is our belief that the primacy of Christ best captures and
articulates the truth of the supremacy of God's life in Christ for us; a
theme made explicit and with compelling force by Karl Barth.[17] While

14. Binning, *The Works of Hugh Binning* (1735 ed.), as cited in Torrance, *Scottish Theology*, 78–79.

15. Duns Scotus, *Quaestiones disputatae*, q. 4, a. 1, n. 3. John Duns Scotus correctly understood the primacy of God's life as Love whereas Thomas Aquinas developed a speculative theology elaborated from sense-experience as the starting point for his Theology Proper. See Scotus, *God and Creatures*. For a support for this position see T. F. Torrance, "Intuitive and Abstractive Knowledge," 291–305; and J. B. Torrance and Walls, *John Duns Scotus*.

16. It would be wrong to infer from this thesis that Evangelical Calvinism arbitrarily ranks the divine attributes and, *a priori*, has "love" at the top. This is the method of Open Theism and not of Evangelical Calvinism. Theological reflection on 1 John 4:8 concerns God as relational and personal-Triune-not as a supreme form of *human* love. See for instance the argument of Bruce McCormack at this point, "The Actuality of God," especially 189–210.

17. The alternative at this point is a Thomistic theology from which Federal

much of the Reformed tradition after Calvin adopted certain central insights of Thomas Aquinas at this point, Calvin by contrast, followed the trajectory of thought laid down by Duns Scotus, mediated through John Major in regards to his doctrine of God. As Richard Muller writes:

> Calvin must depart from a doctrine which examines the predestination of an abstract humanity which does not exist apart from the person of Christ. A similar redefinition of the predestination of Christ is seen in the theology of Bonaventure—who will apply the divine determination neither to the Word, since the divine Word disposes all things, nor to the human nature abstractly, but to the God-man as the foundation of the predestination of mankind to salvation. Calvin, I believe, goes farther still than this, but the underlying theological motivation is similar and the precedent, which places Calvin once again *in continuity with* Franciscan and ultimately Scotist rather than Thomist thought, is significant.[18]

As Karl Barth writes at the beginning of *CD* II/1, "§30 The Perfections of the Divine Loving":

> God is He who in His Son Jesus Christ loves all His children, in His children all men, and in men His whole creation. God's being is His loving. He is all that He is as the One who loves. All His perfections are the perfections of His love. Since our knowledge of God is grounded in His revelation in Jesus Christ and remains bound up with it, we cannot begin elsewhere—if we are now to consider and state in detail and in order who and what God is—than with the consideration of His love.[19]

Without wanting to claim too much, Evangelical Calvinism appeals to the primacy of God's triune life as grounded in love—for "God is love"—and identifies and develops Christian practices from this starting point.[20]

---

Theology proceeds. For a discussion of both approaches in their wider contexts, and representing Roman Catholic and Reformed thought, see the recent collection of essays in White ed., *The Analogy of Being: Invention of the Antichrist or the Wisdom of God?* In these essays the debate between Karl Barth and Erich Przywara is studiously discussed and brought up to date.

18. Muller, *Christ and the Decree*, 37.

19. Barth, *CD* II/1, 351. Thesis 7, no less than Barth's theology, is meant to imply that love can be abstracted from God's freedom, or, we might add, any of his other perfections. Cf. Barth, *CD* II/1, 440.

20. See Canlis, chapter 12 and Kirkland, chapter 14.

## THESIS THREE

*There is one covenant of grace.*

According to Evangelical Calvinism there is one covenant of grace, in contrast to two or more Divine covenants variously propounded by Classical Calvinism. Following Calvin, the *Scots Confession* of 1560 clearly teaches the unity of Scripture based around the idea of one covenant between God and humanity. It is when the covenant idea moved from being an organizing principle of Scripture to a theological principle of a system that what we now know as Federal Theology came into being. Within such a scholastic federal system the one covenant found within Scripture is now amplified to *three* covenants expounded in systematic fashion: the *pactum salutis* or "covenant of redemption," the "covenant of works," and the "covenant of grace."[21]

As I. John Hesselink stated in the *Cambridge Companion to John Calvin*:

> Reformed theology has often been described as covenantal theology, and rightly so. However, it is Heinrich Bullinger, not Calvin, who first emphasized the role of the covenant. Nevertheless, Calvin gave classical form to the doctrine of one covenant of grace, in contrast to the later Reformed notion of the covenant of works and the covenant of grace. The covenant takes several forms . . . but the basic covenant promise is one: "I will be your God and you shall be my people"—and the substance of all the covenants is Jesus Christ.[22]

Evangelical Calvinism thus rejects the theology of two or three separate covenants in Scripture because we believe that it artificially collapses the tension of God's personal work in Christ into a schematized system that does not honor the radical and dynamic *personalist* disclosure of God's redemptive history as mediated penultimately through Israel; and ultimately, in and through Christ. As a corollary, the emphasis on "one divine decree" flows from the fact that God is one; in accord with this, we should expect that God's gracious activity towards us is consonant with who he is as the *One* and only living God (as per thesis 1).[23]

21 For an introductory work on the Reformed understanding of the covenants see Horton, *God of Promise: Introducing Covenant Theology*.

22. Hesselink, "Calvin's Theology," 85–86.

23. See further in chapters 4 and 7 earlier in the volume.

## THESIS FOUR

*God is primarily covenantal and not contractual in his dealings with humanity.*

At the heart of any theology is Theology Proper—an Evangelical Calvinist doctrine of God emphasizes the triune God of grace: the *covenantal* God versus any sort of *contractual* god as may be found in, for instance, certain forms of Roman Catholicism, Federal Calvinism, and classic Arminianism.[24]

God's Covenant with humanity is grounded in the freedom of his Triune life which remains constant despite the twists and turns presented by human proclivities for rebellion. This resists the impulse for creating two or three "covenant's" (per Thesis 3), which would suggest a dualism in the Godhead and thus in his interaction with humanity. It is covenant theology cast in this light that an Evangelical Calvinism adopts and from which it seeks to understand the triune God of grace as being covenantal.

## THESIS FIVE

*Election is christologically conditioned.*

This follows on as a corollary from the thesis above. Christ's work is perfect and requires no supplement, such as the faith of an individual. In forms of Classical Calvinism the subjective elements of salvation have tended to dominate its theology so that an experimental predestination (*syllogismus practicus*) developed and faith was separated from assurance in an unhealthy manner as Christ was separated from his work. The resultant crises of faith and assurance threw believers back onto themselves and their own works for assurance, rather than onto Christ our perfect mediator and redeemer. Christ has been sanctified, and in his sanctification he has sanctified the elect in him. Believers find their subjective sanctification in Christ's objective work, and not the other way round. This reflects the *duplex gratia* Calvin made so much about and yet contemporary Reformed theology has tended to separate—

24. Historical antecedents to such an approach in which a doctrine of God *correctly* shaped their doctrines of Christology and soteriology would include, amongst others, Richard St. Victor and John Duns Scotus. For both, Theology Proper was robustly Trinitarian, thus relational, personal, and pastoral.

through union with Christ flows the twin benefits of justification *and* sanctification.[25]

Thomas F. Torrance is instructive as he comments on Scottish Calvinist, John Craig's approach to articulating what a christologically conditioned doctrine of election looks like; with a carnal and spiritual union providing its orientation:

> Craig regarded election as bound up more with adoption into Christ, with union with him, and with the communion of the Spirit, than with an eternal decree. The union of people with Christ exists only within the communion of the redeemed and in the union they conjointly have with Christ the Head of the Church. . . . Union with Christ and faith are correlative, for it is through faith that we enter into union with Christ, and yet it is upon this corporate union with Christ that faith and our participation in the saving benefits or "graces" of Christ rest. John Craig held that there was a twofold union which he spoke of as a "carnal union" and a "spiritual union." By "carnal union" he referred to Christ's union with us and our union with Christ which took place in his birth of the Spirit and in his human life through which took place in his birth of the Spirit and in his human life through which he sanctifies us. The foundation of our union with Christ, then, is that which Christ has made with us when in his Incarnation he became bone of our bone and flesh of our flesh; but through the mighty power of the Spirit all who have faith in Christ are made flesh of his flesh and bone of his bone. It is only through this union, through ingrafting into Christ by faith and through communion with him in his Body and Blood, that we may share in all Christ's benefits—outside of this union and communion there is no salvation, for Christ himself is the ground of salvation. . . . [26] [27]

Thus election is grounded in a personal union with Christ through his "carnal union" with humanity in the Incarnation, and our "spiritual union" with him through his vicarious faith for us by the Holy Spirit. Christ, in this framework, is known to be the one who elects our humanity for himself; by so doing he takes our reprobation, wherein the "Great Exchange" inheres: "by his poverty we are made rich."

25. See further in Johnson, chapter 9.

26. Torrance, *Scottish Theology*, 52–53.

27. See further in Habets, chapter 7.

## THESIS SIX

*Grace precedes law.*

Evangelical Calvinism and Reformed thought generally, is insistent
on the precedence of grace before law, in contradistinction to classic
Lutheran teaching on law before grace. If grace genuinely precedes law
then the five points of Calvinism are stretched beyond their legitimate
use. That is to say, we have to preach grace before law to all people, we
have to preach forgiveness to all, Christ to all, Gospel to all, and it has
to be objectively universal in scope before it may become subjectively
particular in those who believe. Thus *grace* and not law is primary.

When the indicatives of grace are prior to the imperatives of law,
then all forms of strict Westminster Calvinism are left wanting. As
the Marrow Men so rightly perceived in the Neonomians of their day,
Federal Calvinism suitably distorts the Gospel so that it is no longer
Good News but rather, a new law.[28] They stressed the need for an "evangelical repentance" as opposed to some form of "legal repentance." With
Calvin we affirm that the heart of the Gospel is an evangelical repentance, not "*if* you repent God will forgive you"—such as the medieval
schoolmen gave us—but rather, "God has already forgiven you in the
cross of Christ: now repent."

Thus, beyond a *quid pro quo* situation wherein God's will is shaped
by ratification of meeting the conditions of the law, in order for God's
grace to be realized for the elect; God's life is free and self-determined
to be who he is by his life of gracious love. Contrarily, as Lyle Bierma
comments on Caspar Olevianus' Covenant theology:

> . . . To be sure, this oath or testament [Covenant of Grace] was
> not confirmed until the suffering and death of Christ. Christ
> was still the only way to *Seligkeit*, since it was only through His
> sacrifices that the blessing promised to Abraham could be ap-
> plied to us and the forgiveness and renewal promised through
> Jeremiah made possible. Nevertheless even before ratification it
> was still a covenant—a declaration of God's will awaiting its final
> fulfilment.[29]

28. Bozeman, *The Precisianist Strain,* 1–349.

29. Bierma, *German Calvinism in the Confessional Age,* 65–66.

Evangelical Calvinism refuses to introduce a wedge between grace and law (as Federal Calvinism does), as if God's life of grace is contingent upon the fulfillment of the law. It is this kind of construal that Evangelical Calvinism rejects. Bierma describes for us, once again, how an artificial dualism of grace-law looked in the theology of an early "Covenantalism":

> Olevianus not only identifies the covenant with reconciliation itself but describes it as a mutual agreement (*mutuus assensus*) between the estranged parties. Here God binds Himself not to us "who were yet sinners" but to us "who repent and believe," to us who in turn are bound to Him in faith and worship. This "covenant of grace or union between God and us" is not established at just one point in history; it is ratified personally with each believer. . . . When he discusses the covenant of grace in this broader sense, i.e., as a bilateral commitment between God and us, Olevianus does not hesitate to use the term *condition*. We see already in the establishment of the covenant with Abraham that the covenant of grace has not one but two parts: not merely God's *promissio* to be the God of Abraham and his seed, but that promise on the condition (*qua conditione*) of Abraham's (and our) *repromissio* to walk before Him and be perfect. Simply put, God's covenantal blessings are contingent upon our faith and obedience. It is to those who repent, believe, and are baptized that He reconciles Himself and binds Himself in covenant.[30]

We, thus, move beyond "bilateral commitments" between God and human persons; instead Evangelical Calvinists ground the particular application of law in the universal scope provided by God's life of grace (not *vice versa*). This way we make sure that the particularities of creation and salvation history are not allowed to dictate the shape of the all encompassing scope of God's life for us (*pro nobis*) in Christ; and we avoid creating a competitive situation wherein grace is assumed to be God's "side" of the equation, with "law" on humanity's "side." Instead, it is all of grace because both the "sides" are grounded in the *person* of God's gracious life in Christ. The logic of God's life of grace demands that all of salvation is grace all the way through. As Thomas Torrance

---

30. Ibid., 67–68. To be clear, within this context, as Bierma further describes Olevianus' Covenant theology; he qualifies it by asserting that Olevianus understood that none of the "conditions" of the Covenant could be met on the subjective side of our appropriation without God providing us with created grace whereby we are enabled to cooperate with God through meeting the conditions laid out by the Covenant of works.

was fond of saying, "'all of grace does not mean 'nothing of man,' but precisely the opposite: *all of grace means all of man*, for the fullness of grace creatively includes the fullness and completeness of our human response in the equation."[31][32]

## THESIS SEVEN

*Assurance is of the essence of faith.*

Coordinate with theses 2 and 3, Evangelical Calvinism understands assurance of salvation to be inseparably linked with union with Christ. Salvation is not understood as "our" salvation so that our subjectivity over-rides the objective ground in Christ; instead it is of upmost importance that we see both the objective and subjective sides of salvation rooted in the person of Jesus Christ. The basis for assurance of salvation, then, flows from the faith that is founded in Christ's *vicarious* faith/fulness for us; so the subjective side of Christ's faith becomes ours as we are united to Christ "spiritually" by the Holy Spirit's inveterate movement of gracious action, co-extending from the once for all faith realized in the person of Jesus Christ. Commensurate with this understanding, John Calvin framed "assurance" through similar *foci*; as Charles Partee points out:

> The conviction that salvation is not conditional but certain is an almost forgotten mark of the Protestant Reformation. According to Calvin, doubting the certainty of one's salvation is sinful. We do not understand the goodness of God apart from full assurance (III.2.16). "[F]aith is not content with a doubtful and changeable opinion . . . but requires full and fixed certainty" (III.2.15). If salvation were not certainly known to believers, election "would have been a doctrine not only lacking in warmth, but completely lifeless." In summary, Calvin insists, "Our faith is nothing, unless we are persuaded for certain that Christ is ours, and that the Father is propitious to us in Him. There is, therefore, no more pernicious or destructive conception than the scholastic dogma of the uncertainty of salvation" (Com. Rom. 8:33, 34). . . . Union with Christ is exactly the direction Calvin's theology moves. For Calvin certainty is not to be found in a principle or a book but a person. That is, in union with Jesus Christ. Our task is "to estab-

31. Torrance, *The Mediation of Christ*, xii.

32. See further on this theme in Goroncy, chapter 10.

lish with certainty in our hearts that all those who, by the kindness of God the Father, through the working of the Holy Spirit,
have entered into fellowship with Christ, are set apart as God's
property and personal possession" (IV. 1. 3). . . .[33]

With Calvin and early Reformed thought generally, assurance
teaches us we are elect. Tony Lane clearly shows how Calvin considered
assurance to be of the essence of faith and how this was coordinated
with various other aspects of this theology, notably with the doctrine
of election.[34] Salvation is not salvation if one is unsure of possessing it.
That, at least, was Calvin's argument when he wrote:

> Now we shall possess a right definition of faith if we call it a firm
> and certain knowledge of God's benevolence toward us, founded
> upon the truth of the freely given promise in Christ, both re-
> vealed to our minds and sealed upon our hearts through the
> Holy Spirit.[35]

As it is for Calvin at this point, so it is for the Evangelical Calvinist.
The root of assurance is found in Christ himself, and Christ's faith and
faithfulness is mediated to us through our union with him by the personal work of the Holy Spirit, a work which brings humanity into the
effervescent and indestructible life of God's eternal *Logos*.

## THESIS EIGHT

*Evangelical Calvinism endorses a supralapsarian Christology which
emphasizes the doctrine of the primacy of Christ.*

As a direct result of thesis 5 and its concomitant doctrine of God,
Evangelical Calvinists subscribe to a broadly conceived supralapsarian
Christology along the lines of that famously propounded by John Duns
Scotus. That is to say that, Evangelical Calvinists embrace the idea that
who God is for us in Christ is grounded in the pre-temporal reality of his
choice to be for us apart from and prior to the "Fall" or even the creation
itself. This, theo-logically coheres with the Evangelical Calvinist conception of God's life being shaped by who he is as love, and thus both chron-

---

33. Partee, *The Theology of John Calvin*, 205–6.

34. Lane, "Calvin's Doctrine of Assurance Revisited," *Tributes to John Calvin: A Celebration of His Quincentenary*, 270–313.

35. Calvin, *Inst.*, 3.2.7.

ologically and logically places his love and his self-determining freedom as the primary mode of God's life; and thus the basis from which he acts, even in wrath. As such an Evangelical Calvinist may confidently assert that: "There is no wrath of God that is not first experienced as the love of God for you."[36]

As one of us has argued elsewhere: "The *sine qua non* of the Scotistic thesis is that the predestination of Christ took place in an instant which was logically prior to the prevision of sin as *absolutum futurum*. That is, the existence of Christ was not contingent on the fall as foreseen through the *scientia visionis*."[37] It is through this matrix that Evangelical Calvinists can be said to hold to a "supralapsarian Christology," that is that we believe in God's primacy over all of creation; and thus his choice to be for us is in Christ is not contingent upon sin, but instead it is the result of the overflow of who he is as the God for the other—*God is Love!*

The election of the eternal Son for us that occurs pre-temporally becomes temporally externalized in the Incarnation of Christ, and ultimately finds its resounding crescendo in being actualized through the cross-work of Christ, exemplifying that God's life of over-flowing love is in fact cruciform in shape as it is revealed within the conditions of a post-lapsarian world.

In salvation God accomplishes multiple things but perhaps four may be pointed out here: 1) God's glory is revealed; 2) God's salvation is accomplished, 3) God's judgment is made manifest, and 4) God's damnation of the sinner outside of Christ is realized. All four of these components find their extrinsic *locus* in the person of Christ as the primary exemplar and mediator of God's life for humanity. Each of these—God's glory, salvation, judgment, and damnation—take on significance as Jesus' God-shaped humanity brings God and humans together in himself. The Father is glorified through the Son's loving submission as the scapegoat, sacrifice, and representative for fallen humanity; and through this ultimate act of the obedient love of the Son, the Father brings rec-

---

36. This idea is forcefully presented by Torrance in a sermon "The Trinity of Love," when he defines the love of God according to 2 Corinthians 13:14 as a holy, pure, true, and only love, and as such: "If God in His love gives Himself to me, His love would burn up my self-love; His purity would attack my impurity; His truth would slay my falsehood and hypocrisy. The love of God would be my judgment. God's love is wrath against all self-love. God's love is a consuming fire against all that is unloving and selfish and sinful," Torrance, *When Christ Comes*, 187.

37. Habets, "On Getting First Things First," 349.

onciliation (salvation) to humanity as Christ enters into the wilderness of humanity's sin, bears the weight of that sin in his "being" for us; and thus suffers the tragic damnation that rightfully belonged to sinful humanity. Through this mediation of life for life (substitution), Christ not only pays the penalty for sin; but as a corollary with who he is as love, he reconciles humanity's non-being with his resurrected *being* of life and thus brought God and humanity together in a spiritual union such that reconciled and adopted sinners may now experience the love of the Father of the Lord Jesus Christ as our Abba, our Father, and our worship, by the Holy Spirit, may be acceptable to God.

Supralapsarian Christology, correctly understood, does not reflect an Amyraldian, or a hypothetical universalism; but rather an actualized universal atonement which recreates humanity through Christ's humanity, and provides salvation for all who will believe through Spirit generated, *Christic* formed faith. A purview that genuinely can claim to be "Christ-conditioned."[38]

## THESIS NINE

*Evangelical Calvinism is a form of dialogical/dialectical theology.*

The systematic theology of Evangelical Calvinism is dialogical/dialectical in character rather than strictly philosophical or analytical. It is not content to formulate a system of theology whereby Christianity is reduced to timeless, logical truths about God. The God of biblical revelation presents us with logical problems, seeming paradoxes, surprising features which cannot simply be resolved by discursive reason. "Thus, dialectical theology is a protest against rationalistic religion in whatever form it occurs, whether the natural theology of Thomism, a theological liberalism shaped by idealist philosophy or a conservative orthodoxy that reduces theology to logically systematized propositions."[39] Padgett and Wilkins also point out that dialectical theology has two additional tendencies, "a rejection of any philosophical system as normative for theology and a substructure, either implied or explicit, informed by existentialism."[40]

---

38. See Purves, chapter 5, and Goroncy, chapter 10.

39. Padgett and Steve Wilkins, *Christianity and Western Thought*, 132.

40. Ibid. Evangelical Calvinism utilizes existentialism as a method only and not a metaphysical system. This is most clearly evident in its doctrine of the Word of God as

Those working within an Evangelical Calvinism find no compulsion to allow strictly logico-deductive reasoning to determine the final outcomes of their systematic theology, preferring instead to use the conceptual apparatus of philosophy as a servant of the Word so that a truly theo-logic dominates. Charles Partee provides an important and correct insight on John Calvin in this regard, which resonates with Evangelical Calvinism's approach:

> Calvin's theology is properly concerned for right answers, but his right answers should be understood not as a logically unassailable system of ideas but in terms of their adequacy as a heartfelt confession of faith attempting to protect the mystery of God's revelation. This confessional nature of theology takes precedence over all its rational truth, not even a system rationally explicating revealed truth. Calvin's theology is a systematic offering of faithful witness to the truth revealed by God in Jesus Christ.[41]

Evangelical Calvinists (attempt to) resist the urge to fill in the gaps, and remain satisfied with the dialectical situation that often occurs as a result of studying the living triune God and his Word written.

The canon of Scripture knows of no deterministic logical reasoning; this, we argue, is the product of Aristotelian, Augustinian, Newtonian, and much later, Scholastic "causal connections." The alternative is of course a *created* connection in which God reveals himself (personally and propositionally) in an analogous way by means of his Word and Spirit. When philosophical causal connections are adopted as the totality of ones hermeneutic then all manner of topics in Scripture lapse into absurdity (or at the least, are reduced to rational categories and not historical ones). Here one thinks of such dialectical issues as Divine sovereignty and human free will; or salvation and damnation; or the prohibition against "seeing" God and living and the testimony of Scripture of those people who do "see" God and do live. This is not to deny that free rational agency and compulsion by objective reality go together: they do—but they do so within the created categories given to us by the God who alone is free and who, in his freedom, creates humanity in his image but with a contingent freedom and thus with a *contingent confession*.[42]

---

illustrated in Partee, chapter 2, and Nigh, chapter 3, and in our knowledge of God by his self-revelation, see Grow, chapter 4, and Murphy, Chapter 6.

41. Partee, *The Theology of John Calvin*, 31.

42. We are indebted to Charles Partee for this phrase.

An illustration may prove useful at this point; the example of human free-will. We have to assert, in light of Scripture and the life of the Incarnate Son, that our freedom is limited, because it is contingent, but in this limitation we find it is truly free when assessed, not by causal connections we may make within creation (a closed system of reference), but free *in relation* to God who alone is free. We are thus free *for* something—to do the will of God, and not free in any sense of abstract causality. Thus free-will is defined by the Apostle Paul, in light of the Christ event, as a will enslaved to the will of God: "Paul a bond-servant of Christ Jesus, called as an apostle, set apart for the gospel of God" (Rom 1:1 NASB). Jesus himself defined human free-will in the same way when he taught us to pray to the Father that his will be done on earth as it is in heaven (Matt 6:9-10). Jesus further modeled such free human will when he stated, repeatedly, that he came to do the will of the one who sent him and not his own will: "For I have come down from heaven, not to do my own will, but the will of him who sent me" (John 6:38). Thus we affirm that free-will is God's will made our own and not our self-will: "For whoever does the will of my Father who is in heaven, he is my brother and sister and mother" (Matt 12:50). Self-will is, to the contrary, slavery to sin. Thus causal connections—the hermeneutics of Classical Theism and Classical Calvinism—are logical but not *theo*-logical. Thus Evangelical Calvinism operates with a theo-logical hermeneutic and not simply a philosophical logic that results in determinist and dualist ways of thinking and systems of theology.[43]

## THESIS TEN

*Evangelical Calvinism places an emphasis upon the doctrine of union with/in Christ whereby all the benefits of Christ are ours.*

Whether one wishes to adopt a formal *ordo salutis* or not, there is evident in any work of systematic theology at least a rudimentary *historia salutis* or even a *via salutis*, in the sense that one must distinguish between various aspects of reconciliation and an implicit logical (and chronological) articulation of them. From the foundational event of union with Christ several corollaries follow, and it is these corollaries which we may view as an implicit *ordo salutis* within an Evangelical Calvinism. As such

---

43. See further in Partee, chapter 2, Nigh, chapter 3, and Grow, chapter 4.

union with Christ configures the *ordo salutis*, not some abstract, secret, and hidden Divine decree as propounded by the likes of Theodore Beza and William Perkins, *et al*. It is not that this becomes the central dogma or a philosophical *centrum,* but from union with Christ all the blessings and benefits of Christ flow—such as justification, sanctification, and glorification. In this we follow Calvin when he states:

> Therefore, that joining together of Head and members, that indwelling of Christ in our hearts—in short, that mystical union—are accorded by us the highest degree of importance, so that Christ, having been made ours, makes us sharers with him in the gifts with which he has been endowed. We do not, therefore, contemplate him outside ourselves from afar in order that his righteousness may be imputed to us but because we put on Christ and are engrafted into his body—in short, because he deigns to make us one with him. For this reason, we glory that we have fellowship of righteousness with him.[44]

According to William Evans:

> It is here that a concrete soteriological approach is called for. In contrast to the abstractions of the *ordo salutis* framework, in which justification and sanctification are not "in Christ" but rather occur somehow "on the basis of what Christ did," there is a need to reflect more deeply on the relationship of the person and work of Christ. Once again, the Pauline materials provide food for thought. R. B. Gaffin has argued that for St. Paul, all of the traditional loci of Reformed soteriology—justification, sanctification, adoption, and glorification—are comprehended in the experience of Christ as the resurrected Second Adam. Furthermore, the Pauline perspective here is that the redemptive experience of Christ is not only paradigmatic for the Christian, but also is constitutive of the believer's experience (the believer will not merely be raised *like* Christ, but is crucified and raised *with* and *in* Christ, Rom. 6:4–10; Eph 2:4–7). If these insights are to be utilized in Reformed dogmatics, then all of salvation is in a sense "participatory," that is, a participation in the redemptive experience of Christ. All is to be found, as T. F. Torrance rightly suggests, in the "vicarious humanity of Christ."

Evans continues:

---

44. Calvin, *Institutes*, 3.11.10.

A decisive break with the *ordo salutis* thinking that has vitiated Reformed thought since the early seventeenth century is clearly implied here. This historical record shows that as long as justification is viewed as taking place at a specific point in time (either in eternity or upon the exercise of faith) it is nearly impossible to find a meaningful relationship between justification and the economy of faith (the ongoing life of faith and obedience). Only when the traditional *ordo salutis* is eschewed can a truly forensic and synthetic doctrine of justification that is at the same time relational and dynamic be articulated.[45]

Union with Christ and how that relates to salvation is one of the key pillars upon which Evangelical Calvinism rests. This nuance serves to differentiate Evangelical Calvinism from other approaches. Using Thomas Torrance as something of a guide here we can clearly see how our choice for God (conversion) is first grounded in Jesus' choice for us, and is acted out in his Spirit-constituted-humanity in-our-stead (substitution):

> Based upon the mutual mediation of Son and Spirit, there is both a God-humanward movement and a human-Godward movement and Jesus through the Spirit mediates both. This means . . . "the Spirit not only brings to us the objective effects worked out in the vicarious life of Christ, but also the subjective effects worked out in his humanity. That is, the Spirit enables us to share in Jesus' own faithful response to the Father." Torrance's doctrine of human response as previously analyzed provides a foundation for what is developed here by way of the Holy Spirit. . . . Through the Spirit we share in Christ's response to the Father. The Spirit empowers the believer to cry "Abba, Father," in the same way that comes naturally to the Son of God; for to be "in the Spirit" is to be "in Christ". . . . according to Torrance, "our whole lives in every part are constituted a participation: a dynamic life of union and communion with God." Torrance insists that our holiness or sanctification is realised in Christ by the *Holy* Spirit: our repentance, faith, and obedience are actualised in Christ by the Holy Spirit; every part of our relationship with and response to God is thus achieved in, through, and by the Son and the Spirit. Not only is the Holy Spirit instrumental in justification, but now, also, to sanctification. Critically, however, both are located *in* Christ. Here we have, in effect, the other side of redemption: "the side of the subjectification of revelation and reconciliation in the life and faith of the church. That means the Spirit is creating and calling

---

45. Evans, *Imputation and Impartation*, 264–65.

forth the response of man in faith and understanding, in thanksgiving and worship and prayer. . . ."[46]

Of keynote importance is how all the typical concepts—election,
limited atonement, *sola fide, sola gratia, solus Christus,* etc.—which are
usually placed in the *absolutum decretum*—are reified so that it is all
grounded in God's life in Christ by the Spirit. Humans, in this schema,
do not cooperate with God through grace (as if grace is some*thing* given
to humanity that they can cooperate with Christ through) to appropriate
salvation (which is the way Classic Calvinism construes it); instead the
response is through the "free" response of Jesus Christ to the Father by
the Holy Spirit on our behalf. Humanity is placed into, united to Christ,
by the "person" of the Holy Spirit; it is through this union that humanities' response is first instantiated, first accomplished in Christ's mediation for us. Union with Christ is an integral part of Evangelical Calvinist
theology because it holds that God's life itself is salvation (not meeting
the dictates of some decrees), thus if humanity is going to "be saved"
it must be in union with *this* life. And that is what happens through
Christ's humanity by the Spirit first; then humanity is united to his humanity by the Spirit, and it is out of this recreated humanity that we say
"Yes" to the Father—"thy will be done"!

## THESIS ELEVEN

*Christ lived, died, and rose again for all humanity, thus Evangelical
Calvinism affirms a doctrine of universal atonement.*

Evangelical Calvinism can genuinely preach the Good News to *all* that
Christ has died for them and their salvation and has forgiven their sins.
We affirm a universal atonement and forgiveness of sin through the finished work of Christ. This flows theo-logically from the implications of
the Incarnation of Christ: the humanity he assumed was real ontological
humanity, which included all of humanity.

According to Thomas Torrance:

> We must affirm resolutely that Christ died for all humanity—that
> is a fact that cannot be undone. All men and women were rep-
> resented by Christ in life and death, in his advocacy and sub-
> stitution in their place. That is a finished work and not a mere

46. Habets, *Theosis in the Theology of Thomas Torrance,* 152–53.

possibility. It is an accomplished reality, for in Christ, in the incarnation and in his death on the cross, God has once and for all poured himself out in love for all mankind, has taken the cause of all mankind therefore upon himself. And that love has once and for all been enacted in the substitutionary work on the cross, and has become fact—nothing can undo it. That means that God has taken the great positive decision for man, the decision of love translated into fact. But because the work and the person of Christ are one, that finished work is identical with the self-giving of God to all humanity which he extends to everyone in the living Christ. God does not withhold himself from any one, but he gives himself to all whether they will or not—even if they will not have him, he gives himself to them, for he has once and for all given himself, and therefore the giving of himself in the cross when opposed by the will of man inevitably opposes that will of man and is its judgement. As we saw, it is the positive will of God in loving humanity that becomes humanity's judgement when they refuse it.[47]

If we fail to accept this theo-logic, then we are left with the possibility that Christ could have assumed a particular (elect) humanity that was not truly representative of real sinful humanity which potentially injects Nestorianism into Reformed theology.

Torrance further surmises that there is no

suggestion that this atoning sacrifice was offered only for some people and not for all, for that would imply that he who became incarnate was not God the Creator in whom all men and women live and move and have their being, and that Jesus Christ our Lord and Saviour was not God and man in the one Person, but only an instrument in the hands of the Father for the salvation of a chosen few. In other words, a notion of limited atonement implies a Nestorian heresy in which Jesus Christ is not really God and man united in one Person. It must be added that the perfect response offered by Jesus Christ in life and death to God in our place and on our behalf, contains and is the pledge of our response. Just as the union of God and man in Christ holds good in spite of all the contradiction of our sin under divine judgment, so his vicarious response holds good for us in spite of our unworthiness: "not I but Christ". . . .[48]

47. Torrance, *Atonement*, 188–89.
48. Torrance, *Scottish Theology*, 18–19.

This ties back into thesis 8, and the idea that Christ is primary over all creation; Colossians 1:15 is *apropos*, "He is the image of the invisible God, the firstborn of all creation." The extent of the atonement is an interlocking reflection of the extent of his all encompassing life as the Triune God; no-one can escape the reach of God's life of love and grace.

## THESIS TWELVE

*Universalism is not a corollary of universal redemption and is not constitutive for Evangelical Calvinism.*

This thesis juxtaposes with the previous one. Classically, it is thought that if Christ died for all, then logically-causally all will be saved, following the so called physical theory of redemption. But this is only the case if we follow a logically schematized rendition of a metaphysics that necessitates this outcome. Per thesis 9 and Evangelical Calvinism's commitment to theo-logic, we resist succumbing to the necessitarian constraints that Classical Theism operates from; and prefer to allow the inner-logic of Scripture to determine the interpretive moves it makes within its open *Christ-ward* approach. Robert Walker has said that

> For Torrance, apprehension of the cross involves a conversion of the reason in which we bow our own reason before the reality and *mystery* of Christ and seek to understand it (as far as we may) out of itself without reducing it to logical schemata of our own making which inevitably break it up into separate elements and distort it. We need to hold together what scripture holds together, refusing to categorise it in ways that distort that wholeness. If we cannot understand how scripture holds together certain things which we find difficult (such as the unconditional love and forgiveness of God for all, the finished work of Christ, the gospel imperative to repent and believe, and the fact that some refuse and are judged by the very gospel that offers them life) then it is not open to us to resolve the tension through a man-made logical schema which emphasises some elements as *[sic]* the expense of others. We need to be crucified with Christ in our natural reason and through the transforming of our mind begin to penetrate into 'the interior logic of scripture' so that we may learn to think as scripture thinks and hold together what it holds together in

Christ. Both universalism and limited atonement for Torrance
fail to do that. . . .[49]

Universalism, like double predestination, suffers from imposing upon God a logical necessity that is foreign to his being and act.
Universalism, correctly understood, posits that all humanity, by necessity, must be saved. This, as has been pointed out many times in the
tradition, rejects the freedom of God and reduces grace to a logical
abstraction. Rather, following Calvin, and in harmony with the thesis
already here presented, we have to say that salvation is due to election
and election is due to grace. But grace is the hidden cause (God's "Yes")
and faith is the manifest cause (men's and women's "yes"). For the reprobate, we must also posit grace as the hidden cause (God's "Yes"), given
there is only one will in God, and unbelief as the manifest cause (men's
and women's "no"). Now simply because grace is the basis for both the
elect and the reprobate does not mean universalism. It means a universal atonement but not a universal salvation (universalism). But to make
this argument one must adopt a theo-logical method, not, Classical
Calvinism's logical-causal schema, (the method of an Augustinian-
Newtonianism as Thomas Torrance would say).

If we *logicalize* universal atonement, as does Classical Calvinism, we
end up with a split in the being of God which necessitates two wills and
its consequent double predestination. Why does and how can humanity
reply "no" to God? Evangelical Calvinists, again following Calvin, can
only reply that it occurs *accidentally*—that is *per accidens*. It is, to use a
mathematical phrase, a *surd*, and as such no more can be said about it.

## THESIS THIRTEEN

*There is no legitimate theological concept of double predestination as*
*construed in the tradition of Reformed Scholasticism.*

Following immediately on from the previous thesis we deny any form of
double predestination as traditionally construed by Classical Calvinism;
specifically, that there is a mass of humanity predestined by God from
all time to Hell. Those who are on the "broad way" to destruction have
experienced the love and grace of God for them in Christ only to have

---

49. Torrance, *Atonement*, 188.

rejected such grace, and as such have damned themselves to an eternal separation from God.[50]

In commenting on the Scottish Evangelical Calvinist, James Fraser of Brea, Torrance writes:

> Fraser held that Christ died for all people, the unbelieving as well as the believing, the damned as well as the saved, the reprobate as well as the elected. How, then, did he think that the death of Christ, not least his atoning satisfaction for sin, bears upon those who reject Christ and bring damnation upon themselves? This was one of the basic issues where James Fraser sided with the teaching of John Calvin, rather than with that of those "Protestant Divines" who, he complained, had not followed the old road. The particular point we must take into account here is that according to St. Paul the knowledge of Christ is to some people a "savour of life unto life," but to others it can be a "savour of death unto death." In that light it may be said that while the preaching of the Gospel of Christ crucified for all mankind is meant for their salvation, it can also have the unintended effect of blinding and damning people—it becomes a "savour of death unto death." That is how Fraser regarded what happened to the reprobates in becoming "the vessels of wrath."[51]

With Scripture, Calvin, Fraser, Barth, and Torrance, Evangelical Calvinism holds that Christ is the mirror of election and thus he is the elect "man" for others. It is Christ, therefore, and not some divine decree enacted in a pre-temporal decision, that becomes the center of predestination—Christ is both God's "Yes" and "No" in himself. As Suzanne McDonald has convincingly articulated, election has to do primarily with representation—of God to humanity and humanity to God—and thus Christ is the primary subject and object of such election.[52] The consequence, then, is that both the elect and reprobate find their orientation in Christ. In other words, all of humanity is elect in Christ, and their reprobation becomes a reality *per accidens*[53] as they reject, inscrutably, their

---

50. This thesis is not to deny that double predestination may be construed along radically *dissimilar* lines to that of Federal Calvinism, as for instance in the account of Karl Barth, who gave a radically new Christological reformulation of the Reformed doctrine of double predestination in *CD*, II/2, §32–33, 3–506, wherein he argues for a single election but a double predestination—Jesus is the elect and the reprobate.

51. Torrance, *Scottish Theology*, 199–200.

52. McDonald, *Re-Imaging Election*.

53. John Calvin says in his commentary on 2 Corinthians 2:15: ". . . Thus *Christ came not into the world to condemn the world* (John iii. 17,) for what need was there of

election in Christ. To reiterate an earlier point, an Evangelical Calvinist may confidently assert that: "There is no wrath of God that is not first experienced as the love of God for you."[54]

## THESIS FOURTEEN

*The atonement is multifaceted and must not be reduced to one culturally conditioned atonement theory but, rather, to a theologically unified but multi-faceted atonement model.*

While Evangelical Calvinism upholds what is essential in a penal substitutionary theory of the atonement, it does not limit the atonement to juridical metaphors. Instead it prefers to see the atonement through the multifaceted New Testament perspectives, in addition to the many Old Testament antecedents, and speak of an ontological, personal, relational, and even mystical union, centered in Christ, by which any atonement model inheres.[55]

> The language which the New Testament uses to set this out is drawn from the long history of God's dealings in revelation and reconciliation with his covenant people Israel. That language is used in the sovereign freedom of the New Testament revelation, in the sovereign freedom of the Son of God who, as he comes into the situation prepared for him in Israel, acts both critically and creatively in fulfilment of the Old Testament patterns of understanding and worship provided within the covenant. We must

this, inasmuch as without him we are all condemned? Yet he sends his apostles to *bind*, as well as to *loose*, and to *retain* sins, as well as *remit* them. (Matt. Xviii. 18; John xx. 23.) He is the *light of the world*, (John vii. 12,) but he blinds unbelievers. (John ix. 39.) He is a Rock, for a foundation, but he is also to many a stone of stumbling. (Isaiah viii. 14.) We must always, therefore, distinguish between the proper office of the Gospel, and the accidental one (so to speak) which must be imputed to the depravity of mankind, to which it is owing, that life to them is turned into death." Calvin, *Commentary on the Epistles of Paul the Apostle to the Corinthians*, 161.

54. Cf. Thesis 8. According to Torrance, *When Christ Comes*, 188, "That is why we are afraid of God—because He wants to give Himself to us in love, and His love is our judgment. Because we are afraid, our guilty conscience distorts the face of God for us and makes us afraid to look upon Him. We are trapped in the pit of our own fears, and run away from the very One who really loves and the only One who can forgive us." Torrance proceeds to exposit the "wonderful exchange" wrought by God in Christ whereby Christ takes our judgment and our place that we might be given his place (184).

55. See Torrance, *Atonement*, 99.

seek therefore to examine that language, and through it and by means of it, seek to understand what the New Testament teaches us of the death of Christ. And yet we must pass beyond the Old Testament language to the actual person and work of Christ himself and allow his person and work as mediator to remould in our obedient understanding of him, even the language divinely prepared in the old covenant, for here it is with the new covenant in the blood of Christ that we are concerned.[56]

It is this *embodied* aspect of the atonement in Christ that becomes the *centrum* wherein an Evangelical Calvinist understanding of the atonement takes full shape. The imagery and liturgical activity of atonement found throughout the canon of Scripture is grounded and orientated ontologically in the *cruciform* life of Christ. This means that Evangelical Calvinists believe that penal-substitution is *an* aspect of the atonement, and a fundamental one at that; that both forensic realities are present, but that they find their nexus deeper down as Christ takes on the full weight of sin in his very being.

Torrance beautifully describes the implications of such an atonement model when he writes:

> Jesus did not repudiate the preaching of John the Baptist, the proclamation of judgement: on the contrary he continued it, and as we have seen he searched the soul of man with the fire of divine judgement, but in Jesus that is subsidiary to—and only arises out of—the gospel of grace and vicarious suffering and atonement. In the incarnate life of Jesus, and above all in his death, God does not execute his judgement on evil simply by smiting violently away by a stroke of his hand, but by entering into from within, into the very heart of the blackest evil, and making its sorrow and guilt and suffering his own. And it is because it is God himself who enters in, in order to let the whole of human evil go over him, that his intervention in meekness has violent and explosive force. It is the very power of God. And so the cross with all its indelible meekness and patience and compassion is no deed of passive and beautiful heroism simply, but the most potent and aggressive deed that heaven and earth have ever known: the attack of God's holy love upon the inhumanity of man and the tyranny of evil, upon all the piled up contradiction of sin.[57]

56. Ibid., 1.
57. Torrance, *Incarnation*, 150.

If the forensic/juridical components are *the* primary components of an atonement theory, then the concern is that atonement will not have dealt with the real reach of sin; to use the language of Scripture, the juridical/forensic, alone, does not have the capacity to deal with the "heart." Instead, juridical/forensic themes can only provide "payment" to God for legal crimes committed against him; yet the primary issues— the cause of the symptoms—remains untouched. Evangelical Calvinists advance *the ontological theory of the atonement* that helps correct the imbalance left by the classic understanding.

## THESIS FIFTEEN

*Evangelical Calvinism is in continuity with the Reformed confessional tradition.*

Evangelical Calvinism fits into the Reformed family of faith as a participant with the confession-making of the Protestant Reformed tradition. Confessions and catechisms are timely voices that mature in different spaces, and due to various occasions wherein the situation calls for a decisive statement to be made by a body of Christians who submit to biblical authority (*sola scriptura*). Jack Stotts captures well the Evangelical Calvinist perception of the place that confessions have within the Reformed tradition:

> The Reformed sector of the Protestant Reformation is one that holds to what can be called an "open" rather than a "closed" confessional tradition. A closed tradition holds to a particular statement of beliefs to be adequate for all times and places. An open tradition anticipates that what has been confessed in a formally adopted confession takes its place in a confessional lineup, preceded by statements from the past and expectant of more to come as times and circumstances change. Thus, the Reformed tradition—itself a wide river with many currents—affirms that, for it, developing and adopting confessions is indeed an obligation, not an option. These contemporary confessions are recognized as extraordinarily important for a church's integrity, identity, and faithfulness. But they are also acknowledged to be relative to particular times and places. This "occasional" nature of a Reformed confession is as well a reminder that statements of faith are always subordinate in authority to scripture.[58]

58. Jack Stotts in Rohls, *Reformed Confessions*, xi.

In this vein Evangelical Calvinism is not slavishly committed to the *Canons of Dort* or the *Westminster Standards*. While Evangelical Calvinists respect both of these, for instance, as Reformed confessions, they do not necessarily see either as being the definitive standard. What happened at Dordrecht was an historical response to a localized situation and as such the five points were never meant to define Calvinism or the Reformed faith *in toto*; and Westminster, while of abiding value, is couched in its own very specific English Puritan context and logic which again is specific to that time and place and as such does not necessarily translate well into other contexts. The same would go for the other confessions. Nevertheless, Evangelical Calvinists believe that the Reformed confessions reflect a rich heritage to draw from; and, in fact, Evangelical Calvinists find a special affinity for both the Scot's Confession of the Faith and the Heidelberg Catechism. Both of these convey the Trinitarian *foci*, the Christocentric logic, and the relational warmth of the Gospel, each of which is inimical to Evangelical Calvinism.[59]

## CONCLUSION

The editors offer these theses in the hope of stimulating a robust and lively engagement with Scripture and the Tradition, once more with the aim of resourcing the continuing reformation of the Church.

59. See Grow, chapter 4, and Purves, chapter 5.

# BIBLIOGRAPHY

Barth, Karl. *Church Dogmatics*. 4 vols. Edited by G. W. Bromiley and T. F. Torrance. Translated by G. W. Bromiley. Edinburgh: T. & T. Clark, 1961.

———. *The Theology of the Reformed Confessions*. Translated by Darrell L. Guder and Judith J. Guder. Louisville/London: Westminster John Knox Press, 2002.

Bierma, Lyle D. *German Calvinism in the Confessional Age: The Covenant Theology of Caspar Olevianus*. Grand Rapids: Baker Books, 1996.

Bozeman, Theodore Dwight. *The Precisianist Strain: Disciplinary Religion & Antinomian Backlash In Puritanism To 1638*. Chapel Hill/London: University of North Carolina Press, 2004.

Calvin, John. *Commentary on the Epistles of Paul the Apostle to the Corinthians*. Translated by John Pringle. Grand Rapids: Baker Book House, 1979.

———. *Institutes of the Christian Religion*. Edited by John T. McNeill. Translated by Ford Lewis Battles. Philadelphia: The Westminster Press, 1977.

Evans, William B. *Imputation and Impartation: Union with Christ in American Reformed Theology*. Studies in Christian Thought. Eugene, OR: Wipf & Stock, 2008.

Habets, Myk. "*Filioque? Nein*. A Proposal for Coherent Coinherence," in *Trinitarian Theology After Barth*, 161–202. Edited by Myk Habets and Phillip Tolliday. Eugene: Pickwick Publications, 2011.

———. "On Getting First Things First." *New Blackfriars* 90 (2009) 343–64.

———. *Theosis in the Theology of Thomas Torrance*. Surrey: Ashgate, 2009.

Hesselink, I. John "Calvin's Theology," in *The Cambridge Companion to John Calvin*, 74–92. Edited by Donald K. McKim. Cambridge: Cambridge University Press, 2004.

Horton, Michael. *God of Promise: Introducing Covenant Theology*. Grand Rapids: Baker, 2006.

———. "Reformation Essentials—Five Pillars of the Reformation." *Modern Reformation* (March-April, 1994) no pages. Online: http://www.monergism.com/thethreshold/articles/onsite/essentials.html.

———. "Semper Reformanda," *Tabletalk Magazine* (October 1, 2009) no pages. Online: http://www.ligonier.org/learn/articles/semper-reformanda/.

———. "Who Exactly Are the Evangelicals?" No pages. 9Marks E-Journal. Online: http://www.9marks.org/ejournal/who-exactly-are-evangelicals.

Kettler, Christian D. "The Vicarious Repentance of Christ in the Theology of John McLeod Campbell and R C Moberly." *Scottish Journal of Theology* 38 (1985) 529–43.

Lane, Anthony N.S. "Calvin's Doctrine of Assurance Revisited," in *Tributes to John Calvin: A Celebration of His Quincentenary*, 270–313. The Calvin 500 Series. Edited by David W. Hall. Phillipsburg: P. & R. Publishing, 2010.

Letham, Robert. *The Holy Trinity: In Scripture, History, Theology, and Worship*. Phillipsburg: P. & R. Publishing, 2004.

McCormack, Bruce L. "The Actuality of God: *Karl Barth in Conversation with Open Theism*." In *Engaging the Doctrine of God: Contemporary Protestant Perspectives*, 185–242. Edited by Bruce L. McCormack. Grand Rapids: Baker/Edinburgh: Rutherford House, 2008.

McDonald, Suzanne. *Re-Imaging Election: Divine Election as Representing God to Others and Others to God*. Grand Rapids: Eerdmans, 2010.

Muller, Richard A. *Christ And The Decree: Christology And Predestination In Reformed Theology From Calvin To Perkins*. Durham, North Carolina: The Labyrinth Press, 1986.

————. "How Many Points?" *Calvin Theological Journal* 28 (1993) 425–33.

————. "John Calvin and Later Calvinism: The Identity of the Reformed Tradition." In *The Cambridge Companion to Reformation Theology*, 130–49. Edited by David Bagchi and David C. Steinmetz. Cambridge: Cambridge University Press, 2004.

Padgett, Alan G., and Steve Wilkins. *Christianity and Western Thought: A History of Philosophers, Ideas and Movements*. Volume 3: *Journey to Postmodernity in the 20th Century*. Downers Grove, IL: InterVarsity Academic, 2009.

Partee, Charles. *The Theology of John Calvin*. Louisville/London: Westminster John Knox Press, 2008.

Pinnock, Clark H. *Flame of Love: A Theology of the Holy Spirit*. Downers Grove, IL: InterVarsity, 1996.

Rohls, Jan. *Reformed Confessions: Theology from Zurich to Barmen*. Louisville, Kentucky: Westminster John Knox Press, 1998.

Scotus, John Duns. *God and Creatures: The Quodlibetal Questions*. Edited and Translated by F. Alluntis and A. B. Wolter. Princeton and London: Princeton University Press, 1975.

————. Fernández García, M. *Quaestiones disputatae de rerum principio*. Ad Claras Aquas (Quaracchi) probe Florentiam: ex typographia Collegii s. Bonaventurae, 1910.

Torrance, James B. *Worship, Community and the Triune God of Grace*. Downers Grove, IL: InterVarsity, 1996.

Torrance, James B., and R.C. Walls, *John Duns Scotus: Doctor of the Church*. Edinburgh: Handsel Press, 1992.

Torrance, Thomas F. *Atonement: The Person and Work of Christ*. Edited by Robert T. Walker. Downers Grove, IL: InterVarsity Academic, 2009.

————. "Calvin's Doctrine of the Trinity." In *Trinitarian Perspectives: Toward Doctrinal Agreement*, 41–76. Edinburgh: T. & T. Clark, 1994.

————. *The Christian Doctrine of God: One Being Three Persons*. Edinburgh: T. & T. Clark, 1996.

————. *The Ground and Grammar of Theology: Consonacne Between Theolopgy and Science*. Edinburgh: T. & T. Clark, 2001.

————. *Incarnation: The Person and Life of Christ*. Edited by Robert T. Walker. Downers Grove, IL: InterVarsity Academic, 2008.

————. "Intuitive and Abstractive Knowledge: From Duns Scotus to Calvin," in *De Doctrina Ioannis Duns Scoti. Congressus Scotisticus Internationalis. Studia Scholastico-Scotistica* 5. Edited by C. Balic. 291–305. Rome: Societas Internationalis Scotistica, 1968.

————. *The Mediation Of Christ*. Grand Rapids: Eerdmans, 1983.

————. "Memoranda on Orthodox/Reformed Relations," in *Theological Dialogue between Orthodox and Reformed Churches*, vol. 1, 3–18. Edited by Thomas F. Torrance. Edinburgh: Scottish Academic Press, 1985.

————. *Scottish Theology: From John Knox to John McLeod Campbell*. Edinburgh: T. & T. Clark, 1996.

————. *Theology in Reconstruction*. Grand Rapids: Eerdmans, 1965.

————. *When Christ Comes and Comes Again*. London: Hodder & Stoughton, 1957.

Warfield, Benjamin B. "Calvin's Doctrine of the Trinity." In *Calvin and Augustine*, 187–284. Edited by Samuel G. Crig. Philadelphia: Presbyterian and Reformed, 1974.

Weinandy, Thomas G. *The Father's Spirit of Sonship: Reconceiving the Trinity.* Edinburgh: T. & T. Clark, 1995.

White, Thomas J., editor. *The Analogy of Being: Invention of the Antichrist or the Wisdom of God?* Grand Rapids and Cambridge: Eerdmans, 2011.

# Epilogue

## Post-Reformation Lament[1]

Can a Christian with no convictions,
Be called a Christian at all?
Can she be named amongst the numbers,
Of a Jesus, James, or Paul?

"I revel in my dogmatism"
That was Luther's hand,
"Recant your wicked heresy"
"I can't, so here I stand!"

Give me the time when people knew,
That pure Christian doctrine.
Things like grace, and faith, and works,
And reconciliation.

TULIP is an acronym,
That once was quite in vogue.
But now for one to subscribe to it,
One's labeled an eccentric rogue.

There is so much opinion,
what is correct theology?
We debate, discuss, and dialogue,
From *sola fide* to ecclesiology.

---

1. "Post-Reformation Lament," © Myk Habets (1995).

The proponents in these arguments,
Do come to mind so easily.
There's Augustine, Luther, and George Whitfield,
Pelagius, Pope Leo, and John Wesley.

But what's the point behind it all?
What is all this to me?
Well my friend, it's 'faith and practice'
That's at stake, and all eternity!

Christ is Lord, this is the fact,
He's Prophet, Priest, and King.
This is recorded in His word
As clear as anything.

When asked "What is the duty of man?"
We are left with no decision.
It's stated clearly for all to read,
In the Westminster Shorter Catechism.

Five hundred years have come and gone,
And still we do debate.
I wonder when the Bible too,
Some will want to relegate.

"Once and for all," the Bible says,
"The Good News was delivered."
Five hundred years, or so ago,
Some say it was rediscovered.

Well I don't know about all that,
If all they said were true.
But I do know that they have a lot to teach,
To modern Christians like me and you!

# Index of Names

# Index of Subjects

# Index of Scripture